2001

Summer Jobs for Students

Details on more than **55,000** positions

Where the jobs are and how to get them

PETERSON'S
THOMSON LEARNING™

Australia • Canada • Mexico • Singapore • Spain • United Kingdom • United States

Visit Peterson's Education Center on the Internet (World Wide Web) at www.petersons.com

ISSN 1064-6701
ISBN 0-7689-0443-9

Printed in Canada

10 9 8 7 6 5 4 3 2 1

CONTENTS

HOW TO USE THIS BOOK

What are you going to do to make this summer special? You already have a good start. *Summer Jobs for Students 2001* is an indispensable catalog of interesting and enriching summer work experiences for students or anyone looking for summer employment. You'll find detailed, up-to-date information on more than 55,000 positions offered across the country—from counselors, instructors, and lifeguards to theater stagehands, wilderness guides, and office clerical workers. The list is long, and many of these jobs require little or no previous experience.

SEARCH BY YOUR INTERESTS

There are many different ways you can use *Summer Jobs for Students 2001* to find the right work opportunity:

- If your primary consideration is the geographic location of a job (if, for instance, you'd like to spend the summer working near your hometown or in a particular area of the country), you can turn directly to the **State-By-State Listings**, where employers are listed alphabetically by state.

- The **Canada and Countries Outside North America** section features summer employment opportunities in Canada and elsewhere. This section profiles twenty-two employers offering hundreds of summer jobs to young adults.

- If you're interested in working at a U.S. national park, turn to **Working for the National Park Service** to learn about job opportunities for U.S. citizens at National Park Service sites in regions throughout the country.

Another way you can put *Summer Jobs for Students 2001* to work for you is by looking for jobs according to the services they provide. The opportunities featured in this book are divided into thirteen main areas, which are listed in the **Category Index** at the back of the book. If you know, for instance, that you want to work at an amusement or theme park, the **Category Index** lists all such employers that are featured in the book. Use the following list of categories as your guide:

Accommodations and Food Services
Agriculture, Forestry, Fishing, and Hunting
Amusement and Theme Parks
Business and Professional Organizations
Educational Services
Nature Parks and Environmental Organizations
Performing Arts Companies
Professional, Scientific, and Technical Services
Public Administration
Recreational and Vacation Camps
Recreation Industries
Religious Organizations
Retail Trade

Of course, if you already know the name of the employer you want to contact, you can simply turn to the **Employer Index** for a page reference to the description of that employer's job opportunities.

If you're interested in knowing what kinds of jobs are most readily available, turn to the **Job Types Index**. It lists the most frequently cited job types in the book and the facilities that offer them.

READ THE EMPLOYER PROFILES

Once you have found an employer that interests you, you can read about the opportunities provided. The **General Information** section of each profile provides details about the location, size, focus, and special features of the facility. You can check the **Profile of Summer Employees** to get an idea of who your coworkers might be. **Employment Information** includes descriptions of available jobs as well as important details about when positions are available, salaries, and special requirements. Any **Benefits,** such as meals, laundry facilities, health insurance, or the possibility of college credit, and **Preemployment Training,** such as leadership skills or accident prevention and safety, are also noted. The **Contact** paragraph provides you with information on how the employer wants you to apply for a position and the application deadline.

International applicants for any of the positions found in this guide should pay special attention to valuable information found in the **Employment Information** section. If international students are encouraged to apply for available positions, a sentence stating such will appear at the end of this section, along with any special application procedures required of international applicants, such as referral through an agency designed to handle these applications.

The data in this book were collected in the spring and summer of 1999 from employers eager to fill staff vacancies with high-quality, motivated workers. A representative of each employer completed a questionnaire to describe the job opportunities to be offered specifically for the summer of 2000, but more than likely, in subsequent summers as well. Since the data were collected in 1999, you should check with the employer before applying for or accepting a position to verify that all information in the profiles is still accurate and up-to-date. A phone call to the contact person listed in the profile or a visit to the employer's Web site (address is in the **Contact** section) will provide you with even more information about the employer and the type of employment that is available. Peterson's does not assume responsibility for the hiring policies or actions of these employers.

LEARN HOW TO APPLY

Summer Jobs for Students 2001 features four articles that provide additional help in your search for a summer job. If you are just learning how to apply for a summer job, be sure to read "Looking for a Summer Job?" International job hunters are strongly urged to read "International Applicants for Summer Employment in the U.S." "Working for the National Park Service" gives you all the information you'll need if you're a U.S. citizen considering a summer job at a U.S. National Park Service site; the article tells you about the positions offered, job requirements, participating sites, and application contacts. "Do You Want to Work Temporarily in Canada?" tells you the steps you need to take before you begin a summer job in Canada; the article outlines procedures you and your Canadian employer must follow for you to receive employment authorization.

Remember, all of the employers listed in this book are actively looking for your help—they are waiting for your application! We hope that this book will help make your summer a fun, interesting, and profitable experience.

ABBREVIATION CHART

The following are abbreviations commonly used in this book:

ACA	American Camping Association
AHSE	Association for Horsemanship Safety and Education
ALS	Advanced Life Saving
ARC	American Red Cross
BUNAC	British University North American Club
CAA	Camp Archery Association
CIT	Counselor-in-training
CPR	Cardiopulmonary Resuscitation
EMR	Educationally Mentally Retarded
EMT	Emergency Medical Technician
EOE	Equal Opportunity Employer
HSA	Horsemanship Safety Association
ICCP	International Camp Counselors Program
IDC	Instructor Development Center
LD	Learning Disabled
LPN	Licensed Practical Nurse
NAUI	National Association of Underwater Instructors
NRA	National Rifle Association
PADI	Professional Association of Diving Instructors
RN	Registered Nurse
SASE	Self-addressed, stamped envelope
SCI	Small Craft Instructor
SLS	Senior Life Saving
WSI	Water Safety Instructor

LOOKING FOR A SUMMER JOB?

by Shirley J. Longshore

As an older teenager or young adult concerned about your future, working at a job—for pay or not—is an important, if not mandatory, summer undertaking. If you've never done it, looking for a job may seem intimidating, but it's not. Hundreds of thousands of young people *do* find interesting and rewarding jobs every summer.

Many young adults turn to summer employment not only to pay for college expenses but also to earn spending money or even to help out their families. Competition for these jobs can be stiff, but keep in mind that summer employment can provide the background you'll need to compete aggressively both with other college-bound students when applying to schools *and* with other job seekers when looking for a full-time job. Guidance counselors, admissions officers, and corporate human-resource managers look for college and job applications that display outside activities, work experiences, and additional credentials. A good summer job record is a plus that colleges and employers now routinely expect to see.

"Strong academics are not enough any more," says a college admissions officer at a small university in Georgia. "We're looking very hard at what else students are doing, how they use their time, what other skills they are acquiring. Even the less competitive colleges are becoming much more demanding in evaluating prospective students." If you don't need to earn money, working as a volunteer will also give you a competitive edge.

GET STARTED NOW

Landing the summer job that will add to the bottom line in your bank book and bolster your resume is harder than it used to be. The competition can be tough, but you can overcome the obstacles. To increase your chances for success, you must be willing to work at mounting an organized, targeted job search; the sooner you get started, the better!

"The key is to start early," emphasizes the personnel director of a large state park that employs many young people each summer. "You can't wait until May and then see what's around, because there truly won't be anything left. I see this over and over. We have all of our hiring done, and then we get call after call and letter after letter from panicked, although qualified, students who are just applying much too late." A job seeker fortunate enough to get his or her application in early and who is hired also has the opportunity to ensure a somewhat more secure summer job situation throughout the rest of high school or college; those who prove

---

Shirley J. Longshore is a writer, editor, and communications consultant. Her articles about business, work, and education have appeared in national publications.

themselves valuable will likely have first crack at getting the job back the following summer. To help you with your search, this book lists more than 700 U.S. and Canadian employers who are looking for qualified, hard-working people to fill specific openings on their staffs.

PREPARE YOUR RESUME AND COVER LETTER

Your resume should be limited to one page and must communicate your strong points by detailing relevant experience and describing your background. It should present you in a way that will interest an employer enough to arrange an interview.

"I had a student this year who said he didn't have to be convinced that a summer job was important, but he didn't have a clue how to begin looking for one," says a guidance counselor at a large public high school in Florida. "High school students look at me like I'm from outer space when I tell them that, first, they should write a resume. They say things like: 'What would I put on it? I have no real skills; I've never done much of anything. A resume is for older people looking for real jobs.' But when we look at the clubs they have participated in, after-school activities, volunteer work, and baby-sitting jobs, we can often work up quite a list together. It gives young people an idea of what they have to offer an employer."

Everyone has the makings of a resume in their background—even those just starting out. You simply have to look at your past thoroughly. Don't overlook any activities that could enhance your credentials. Don't forget the computer knowledge you gained in school. Do you teach Sunday school? Have you worked in your town's recreation program? Do you assist in a shelter for the homeless or collect newspapers for recycling? All of these activities require skills that can be translated into proven experience for an employer. At the very least, participating in these kinds of activities will show that you are focused, well-rounded, community-minded, responsible, and trustworthy.

A resume should also list people who will give you good recommendations. (Before listing anyone as a reference, check to make sure he or she is willing to be listed.) To prepare a reference list, create a separate page with your name, address, and phone number followed by the names, addresses, and phone numbers of 2 to 4 people who will verify your skills and testify to the qualities that will convince the employer to hire you.

You may want to tailor your resume to appeal to a particular employer—using a computer makes this easy. Perhaps you are intrigued by a counselor's job at an academic-oriented camp. The resume for that position should contain an item that mentions that you put the skill you show in math to good use tutoring a third-grader after school. Phrase the item: "Demonstrated maturity and responsibility tutoring third-grade student in math in after-school sessions." With this entry on your resume, you are showcasing both a skill at an academic subject and experience working with a younger person. If you're using a computer, this item can easily be deleted from the resume you'll send in application to a job that doesn't involve academics or supervising children.

Your resume should also include items mentioning any athletics training you have had, such as swimming lessons, ballet classes, and team memberships. These activities demand those qualities employers look for—self-discipline, high energy, dedication, and a desire for self-improvement.

A college student from Massachusetts didn't think his experience as head cook for the school's international club's dinners was very important. "I just did it for fun," the student admitted. "But then I saw an opening for an assistant chef at a lodge for the summer between my junior and senior years, and I realized I could parlay that experience into a job. It worked."

The best resume is one that is straightforward and clearly presented. If you're composing one for the first time, you should take advantage of the knowledge of older siblings or friends—talk with them and ask to see their resumes. Remember, it must state relevant information about you and your skills.

This is where a strong cover letter comes into play. A cover letter serves as your introduction to a potential employer and, hopefully, will interest him or her enough to want to read your resume. A cover letter should draw the reader's attention to those experiences that best relate to the qualifications required for a particular job. For example, if a camp is looking for counselors to lead activities, your letter should mention your involvement in school plays (an item on your resume) and suggest that this experience would enable you to confidently instruct campers in drama or in a stage production. Although a cover letter should be brief and to the point, it doesn't hurt to help the resume reader along by flagging pertinent information. Sell yourself!

MY RESUME IS READY—NOW WHAT?

After you've identified your skills and written your resume, you need to consider what you want to get out of your summer job. Ask yourself: What do I enjoy doing? What am I really good at? What would I like to learn more about? What work experience would enhance my chances at future opportunities? Do I love to be outdoors in the summer, or do I really prefer the air-conditioned comfort of an office? Is this the time to go far away from home, or would I rather stay close by? Do I need to make money? Keep in mind that some jobs may be too costly for you. If you need to earn money to cover college expenses, for instance, you may not want your pay to be eaten away by transportation and room-and-board costs.

After answering the questions above, turn to the **Category Index** to zero in on the kinds of opportunities that make sense for you. The listings go beyond what you'll find in your local community through the usual pavement-pounding, want-ad-answering, asking-around methods. The jobs in this guide are located all over North America. Some may be in your geographic area, and others may be hundreds or thousands of miles away. Included are camps, resorts, summer theaters, conservation and environmental programs, lodges, ranches, conference and training centers, national parks, and amusement and theme parks that normally hire many young people for each busy summer season. The possibilities are endless, so you don't have to worry about ending up in a job in which you have little interest.

Keep in mind that many summer employers provide on-site training in the particular skills needed for their jobs, so don't be discouraged if your skills don't match exactly. These people are generally looking for qualities other than direct experience—motivation, interest, and the desire to learn. When you read about a position, *read between the lines* to see what kind of employee is really being sought.

Winning Interviews

Once you have contacted the employers you'd like to work for, think about how you'll present yourself at interviews. An interview may take place over the phone or in a face-to-face meeting. In either case, it's an opportunity for you and the employer to get a better sense of each other.

Remember, an interview goes both ways. It is also an opportunity for you to ask any questions and to decide whether you really want the job. You may want to ask about specific duties, hours, pay, what benefits are provided (such as room and board), and when hiring decisions will be made. Always write a brief, sincere thank-you note to follow up an interview, even if it was very short or conducted by telephone.

It's important to dress appropriately for an in-person interview. Bring with you any credentials that are required (i.e., working papers, birth certificate, school records, or Social Security card). If you don't have a Social Security card, you can, and should, get one right away. You can start the process by calling 800-772-1213, the nationwide toll-free number for Social Security information.

Finding a good summer job opportunity is not an impossible task. There are jobs out there. You have a good shot at landing one if you prepare your resume, start going after the jobs you know about early, and present yourself both on paper and in person in the best possible light

SAMPLE COVER LETTER

ANNE MEREDITH

421 South Street
Apartment 2C
City Line, NJ 07685
821-663-4121

218 Tower Hall
State University
Brighton, PA 62451
580-341-6840

January 4, 2001

Name of person in charge, title
Name of camp or resort
Street address
Town, state, zip code

Dear Mr. or Ms. (last name):

I saw the listing describing your summer program in Summer Jobs for Students 2001. It states that you are hiring a Waterfront Director, a summer position for which I would like to apply.

As you will see from the attached resume, I am qualified for such a position. I taught swimming, was a lifeguard, coached a swim team, and swam on my high school team for four years. I was named to the Junior Varsity Swim Team at State University in both my freshman and sophomore years.

I am experienced at supervising and teaching both adults and children in swimming and waterfront safety. I enjoy working with people and sharing my expertise with them. Your summer program sounds like one in which my skills would be fully utilized.

I would appreciate the opportunity to explore this position with you further. I would be happy to talk with you by telephone or to arrange a personal interview during my winter break, which is until the end of this month.

Thank you for your consideration. I look forward to hearing from you soon. You can reach me at my home number in City Line until January 27th.

Sincerely,

Anne Meredith

SAMPLE RESUME

ANNE MEREDITH

<table>
<tr><td>421 South Street
Apartment 2C
City Line, NJ 07685
821-663-4121</td><td>218 Tower Hall
State University
Brighton, PA 62451
580-341-6840</td></tr>
</table>

EDUCATION: State University, Brighton, PA
Expected date of graduation, 2002
Major: Biology GPA: 3.4 Degree track: B.S.

HONORS: Dean's List, first semester, State University
Science Scholar Award, City Line High School
State Merit Scholarship Winner

EXPERIENCE: <u>Head Lifeguard/Swimming Coach</u>
River Edge Athletic Club, Edgeton, NJ
Summer 1999 and 2000
 Responsibilities included scheduling and overseeing the summer staff of ten lifeguards and serving as one of two coaches for the club's competitive children's swim team (35 members). I also gave private swimming lessons to club members.

<u>Lifeguard</u>
YWCA, City Line, NJ; Winter 1998–99

<u>Swimming Instructor/Lifeguard</u>
River Edge Athletic Club; Summer 1998 and 1997

<u>Assistant Swimming Instructor (3- to 5-year-olds)</u>
YWCA, City Line, NJ; Summer 1996

<u>Day Camp Helper (9- and 10-year-olds)</u>
YWCA, City Line, NJ; Summer 1995

ACTIVITIES: Swim Team, Junior Varsity, State University, 1999–2000
Glee Club, State University, 1999–2000
Swim Team, YWCA, City Line, NJ, 1997–98
 Captain, 1997–98
Junior Senior Chorus, City Line High School, 1996–98
Youth Group, St. John's Church, 1996–99
 President, 1999
Springvale Nursing Home, volunteer visitor, 1998–99

SKILLS: Red Cross Certification, Lifesaving
Fluent in Spanish
Teaching experience with children and adults
Computer skills: Microsoft Word

INTERNATIONAL APPLICANTS FOR SUMMER EMPLOYMENT IN THE U.S.

by Elizabeth Chazottes

Nothing is more exciting and rewarding than an international summer job in the United States. International students have been spending their summers in the U.S. for years to learn American methods of business, to perfect their English skills, and to make international connections that last a lifetime. There are more opportunities today than ever before, but you must be well informed. Take the time to learn about your options and which opportunities will best meet your needs. The better prepared you are, the more successful your experience will be. All international students interested in coming to the U.S. for a summer job should make sure they are clear on what they can and cannot do in the workplace on the type of visa they receive to come to the U.S.

In an effort to provide guidance that is as accurate as possible for students from outside the United States, each employer listed in *Summer Jobs for Students 2001* has been asked if applications will be accepted from international students. Peterson's has also asked if the employer is willing to undertake the necessary steps—either directly with the U.S. Immigration and Naturalization Service (INS) or through an educational exchange organization—to make it possible for the student to secure a proper U.S. visa that will allow him or her to complete the program and legally receive a salary or stipend, if applicable, while in the United States.

There are significant penalties for employers who hire foreign nationals illegally. Foreign nationals can be deported and barred from returning to the United States for violating their visa status. If an employer in the United States offers you a summer job, make certain that both you *and* the employer know and follow the requirements of U.S. law *before* you leave home.

PASSPORTS

In order to get a U.S. visa that permits summer employment, you must have a valid passport from your own country. Your passport must be valid for six months beyond the date on which you expect to leave the United States. A number of countries have special "passport validity" agreements with the United States under which a passport is considered to be valid for six months beyond the expiration date stated in the passport. In order to avoid last-minute problems, you should contact U.S. consular officials as early as possible to determine the exact requirement for your country.

Visas

Unlike many countries, the United States does not issue work permits, residence permits, or require police registration. Instead, what an individual may or may not do while in the United States depends entirely on the specific type of visa granted. As a result, the United States has the world's most complex visa system—there are currently forty-six different kinds of nonimmigrant visas! Please note that although an individual may be a full-time student in his or her own country, a "student" visa for admission to the United States applies only to people attending an American school for full-time study. Therefore, the three kinds of student visas (F-1, J-1, and M) cannot be used by a student coming to the United States uniquely for a summer job experience.

As a general rule, there are only four U.S. visas that are likely to be suitable for students coming to the United States for summer employment:

H-2B "Temporary Worker": U.S. companies may use this visa to temporarily employ skilled or unskilled foreign nationals when they have a temporary need and there are no qualified U.S. workers available. There is a two-step process involved that must be initiated by the U.S. employer. First, the employer must request a "temporary labor" certification from the state employment service office serving the area in which the proposed employment is to be offered. Once the state office processes the temporary labor certification, the request must then be forwarded to the U.S. Department of Labor's regional office so that a final determination can be made. The employer has to demonstrate: (a) that a real job exists (i.e., not a job made up to suit the particular background of the foreign national); (b) that substantial efforts have been made to fill the job with a U.S. citizen; (c) that no qualified U.S. citizens can be found for the job; and (d) that the job to be filled is of a one-time, seasonal, peak-load, or intermittent nature. Once the labor certification is approved, a visa petition must then be filed by the employer with the INS. There are also annual limits on the number of H-2B admissions permitted. Once the limit is attained, no new petitions are accepted by INS until the next fiscal year (October 1). This process can be rather lengthy, so it should be initiated well in advance by the U.S. employer.

H-3 "Trainee": This visa is used by U.S. companies to bring foreign employees to the U.S. to participate in established company training programs. The U.S. employer must submit the H-3 application to the Immigration Service District Office that covers the area in which the person will work. The application must include a detailed training plan to show what the trainee will do in the U.S., including how much time will be spent in "classroom and other instruction" and how much time will be devoted to "on-the-job training." Information on the position the individual will fill when he or she returns to his or her home country is also required. The company must demonstrate that the training is provided with the intent to employ the individual abroad upon completion of training or to provide skills that will increase the value of the individual to a foreign business. Any productive work must be incidental to the training program. The employer must also show that the training program provides knowledge or experience that is unavailable in the individual's own country.

J-1 "Exchange Visitor": J-1 visa programs are managed by approved organizations or sponsors, such as U.S. government agencies, schools and universities, hospitals, companies, and private nonprofit educational exchange organizations. The Bureau of Educational and Cultural Affairs of the U.S. Department of State, formerly the U.S. Information Agency, has authority over these programs. There are fourteen different J-1 categories, each with its own specific rules and regulations. Among these categories are those that permit international high school students, university students, trainees, au pairs, and researchers to participate in programs in the U.S. Each sponsor is granted a "program description" that specifies the activities that are permitted for participants in the sponsor's program.

Of the fourteen J-1 categories, the "trainee" category is suitable for most international students coming to the U.S. for summer jobs. J-1 trainees can come to the U.S. to receive training in their field for periods of up to eighteen months. A detailed training program must be prepared by the U.S. host employer, specifying the objectives and skills to be learned as well as the length of time required to complete the program. A trainee cannot replace a U.S. worker but comes to the U.S. to acquire skills and knowledge in U.S. methodology.

The number of trainee programs has grown over the years. Two of the long-standing trainee exchange organizations for students are the International Association of Students in Economics and Business Management (AIESEC)—for business and economics students—and the International Association for the Exchange of Students for Technical Experience (IAESTE)—for students in technical fields. The Council on International Educational Exchange (CIEE) is the largest of the student trainee programs, followed by the Association for International Practical Training (AIPT), which brings in students and professionals from some eighty countries annually. Other programs are also available that deal primarily with trainees from specific countries or regions of the world or specific industries. Some U.S. universities also run trainee programs.

There are three additional J-1 categories that may also be of interest to students who desire a work experience in the U.S.: Summer Travel/Work, Camp Counselor, and Au Pair.

Several organizations have been granted J-1 authorizations for "summer travel/work" programs. These permit university students to work in any job they may find during the summer months (November to February for students from the Southern Hemisphere). No extensions of visas are permitted, and changes to other J-1 visa categories are not allowed. Pre-placement is required for 50 percent of the participants, and students should check with the U.S. sponsoring organization about specific requirements. The Council on International Educational Exchange (CIEE) is the largest of these programs, but several other programs also operate summer travel/work programs.

The second type of additional J-1 visa is for placements in summer camps for camp counselor experience. Participants must be at least 18 years old. Placements are limited to a maximum of four months and must be for genuine camp counseling assignments in accredited U.S. camps. The YMCA, Camp America, Summer Camp USA, and InterExchange operate several of the better-known camp counselor programs.

The third is the au pair category. Au pair programs allow participants to live with and participate in the home life of an American host family while providing child-care services and attending a U.S. postsecondary educational institution. The au pair participant cannot provide child-care services for more than 45 hours per week. All participants must register and attend classes offered by an accredited U.S. postsecondary institution. Au pairs must be between the ages of 18 and 26, be secondary school graduates or the equivalent, and be proficient in spoken English.

In some cases, an individual coming to the United States on the J-1 visa may be subject to something called the "two-year foreign residence requirement". Some countries have asked the U.S. government to establish a "skills list" for its citizens. If the person's field is included on the skills list for his or her country, that means that this particular skill is greatly needed in the home country, and it will generally be necessary for the individual to return to his or her country after completing their program in the U.S. Someone subject to this residence requirement must return to his or her home country for a minimum of two years before coming back to the United States on most of the nonimmigrant visas or as a "permanent resident." Most European countries do not have skills lists, but many other countries do. If the ability to return to the United States within a two-year period after training is of concern, you should get specific information regarding this from U.S. consular officials. Also, participants that receive funding from the sending foreign government or the U.S. government may also be subject to the two-year residency requirement.

J- PROGRAM SPONSORS

Trainee Exchange Programs

Aiesec/US
135 West 50th Street, 17th Floor
New York, New York 10020
212-757-3774
Fax: 212-757-4062
E-mail: aiesec@us.aiesec.org
www.us.aiesec.org

American-Scandinavian Foundation
15 East 65th Street
New York, New York 10021
212-879-9779
Fax: 212-249-3444
E-mail: training@amscan.org
www.amscan.org

Association for International Practical Training (AIPT) and IAESTE–U.S.
10400 Little Patuxent Parkway, Suite 250
Columbia, Maryland 21044-3510
410-997-2200
410-997-2883
Fax: 410-992-3924
E-mail: exchanges@aipt.org
pinpoint@aipt.org (for placements)
www.aipt.org

CDS International
871 United Nations Plaza, 15th Floor
New York, New York 10017-1814

212-497-3500
Fax: 212-497-3535
E-mail: info@cdsintl.org
www.cdsintl.org

Council on International Educational Exchange, CIEE
205 East 42nd Street
New York, New York 10017
212-822-2600
Fax: 212-822-2699
E-mail: info@councilexchanges.org
www.ciee.org

InterExchange, Inc.
161 Sixth Avenue
New York, New York 10013
212-924-0446
Fax: 212-924-0575
E-mail: info@interexchange.org
www.interexchange.org

YMCA International Program Services
71 West 23rd Street, Suite 1904
New York, New York 10010
212-727-8800
Fax: 212-727-8814
E-mail: ips@ymcanyc.org

Agricultural and Agribusiness Trainee Programs

MAST International
University of Minnesota
1954 Buford Avenue, Room 240
St. Paul, Minnesota 55108-6197
612-624-3740
Fax: 612-625-7031
E-mail: mast@coa1.agoff.umn.edu
www.mast.agri.umn.edu

Ohio International Agricultural and Horticultural Intern Program
700 Ackerman Road, Suite 360
Columbus, Ohio 43202
614-292-7720
Fax: 614-688-8611
E-mail: mchrisma@pop.service.ohio-state.edu

Summer Travel/Work Programs

Council on International Educational Exchange, CIEE
(see address in previous list)

InterExchange, Inc.
(see address in previous list)

Work Experience USA
2330 Marinship Way, Suite 250
Sausalito, California 94965
415-339-2728
Fax: 415-339-2744
E-mail: workexperienceusa@compuserve.com

YMCA International Program Services
(see address in previous list)

Au Pair Programs

Au Pair in America
102 Greenwich Avenue
Greenwich, Connecticut 06830
800-727-2437
203-869-9090
Fax: 203-863-6180
www.aifs.org

EF Au Pair
EF Center Boston
One Memorial Drive
Cambridge, Massachusetts 02142
800-333-6056
Fax: 617-619-1001
www.ef.com

InterExchange Au Pair
(see address for InterExchange, Inc. in previous list)

Camp Counselor Programs

Camp America
9 West Broad Street
Stamford, Connecticut 06902-3788
800-727-2437
Fax: 203-399-5590

InterExchange—Camp USA Program
(see address in previous list)

International Camp Counselor Program—YMCA
(see address in previous list)

Summer Camp USA (formerly BUNAC)
P.O. Box 430
Southbury, Connecticut 06488
800-GO BUNAC
203-264-0901

Q "International Cultural Exchange Visitor": The "Q" visa allows the U.S. employer to apply to INS for permission to hire a person over 18 years of age from another country for a period of not more than fifteen months. The purpose of the program is for the international participant to work or train and to share or demonstrate his or her own culture with Americans. A frequently cited example of a major Q employer is the EPCOT Center at Walt Disney World in Florida. Another example would be a museum or a department of a museum devoted to the art and culture of the student's home country.

The "cultural component" must be an integral part of the employment or training offered. The employer must demonstrate that the individual to be hired is fully able to communicate with Americans about his or her culture as well as being fully qualified for the work aspects of the position. Substantial documentation is required as part of the employer's application.

Visa Procedures

If an employer's applications for an H-2B, H-3, or Q visa are successful, the District Office of the Immigration and Naturalization Service will advise the U.S. Embassy in the student's country. The student can then obtain the visa and travel to the U.S. In the case of the J-1 visa, the sponsoring organization that is arranging the program issues a U.S. government document called an IAP-66 (a Certificate of Eligibility). The IAP-66, which is sent to the student, is used to apply for the J-1 visa in his or her own country.

Upon entering the United States, the admitting Immigration Inspector issues a Form I-94 (Arrival/Departure Record) to H-2B, H-3, and Q visa holders that notes the specific visa granted and the date when the "Permit to Stay" expires. J-1 visa holders are issued a Permit to Stay with the notation "D/S" (for duration of status). This means that J-1 trainees may remain in the U.S. as long as they are engaged in their training program or until the end date of their IAP-66, plus thirty days. The I-94 form (and IAP-66 for the J-1 trainee) is the only documentation needed for the student to proceed to the workplace and take up the assignment.

Employment Eligibility Verification

U.S. law requires employers to examine documentation proving that persons hired are either citizens of the United States or noncitizens legally authorized for employment during their stay in the United States.

Essentially, the law requires that within three business days after a person is hired, the employer must *physically examine* documentation that (a) establishes proof of the new employee's identity and (b) establishes that the person is either a U.S. citizen or is a noncitizen who has the legal right to be employed in the United States. The law requires that a record of the verification process be maintained in the employer's files for a period of three years after the date of hiring. For this purpose, the INS has developed the I-9 form.

Virtually all kinds of employment are covered, from a full-time job with a large employer such as IBM to selling hamburgers part-time at the local McDonald's. Certainly, all of the jobs listed in *Summer Jobs for Students 2001* will require you and your employer to complete the I-9 form. The I-9 form is in two parts. The top half must be filled out by the employee—you. You then present the form, together with your documentation, to your employer, who will complete the bottom half of the form.

Social Security Number

In most cases, you will need to obtain a Social Security number. It is widely used in the United States as a basic identification number—and in most automated payroll systems, in university enrollment systems, and for transactions such as opening a bank account.

Individuals entering the U.S. on the F, J, M, and Q visas are usually exempt from the U.S. Social Security tax, but those entering on other visas (such as H-2B or H-3) can expect to have the tax withheld from their pay. Even if you are exempt from paying Social Security tax, you will still need to obtain a Social Security number.

Social Security regulations require that you apply in person, and it is advised that you do this shortly after arrival. Normally, numbers are issued within a few weeks.

It will be important for you to provide full documentation that clearly shows you have a visa that permits employment. The Social Security official to whom you submit your application will want to see your passport, your I-94 form, visa documents (such as the triplicate copy of the IAP-66), and any documents related to your work placement. If you do not present the proper documentation, a Social Security card marked "Not Valid for Employment" will be issued. If this happens, you will not be able to receive a salary or stipend during the program. If you have any problems getting your Social Security card, you should contact your sponsoring organization for assistance.

INCOME TAX

As a general rule, individuals coming to the United States on any of the visas discussed in this article will be subject to U.S. income tax (and possibly state and local income tax) on the money they earn while in the country. H-2B workers are required to obtain a Certificate of Compliance, or Sailing Permit, before departure from the U.S. The Sailing Permit is evidence that they have paid whatever taxes may be due the U.S. government. H-3, J-1, and Q visa holders are exempt from this requirement. However, they are not exempt from filing an income tax return. Between January 1 and April 15 of the year following your employment, you will have to submit an income tax return (Form 1040EZ or Form 1040) to the IRS. The 1040EZ is used if you have no dependents, earned less than $50,000 of income, and have no travel expense deductions. If you have remained in the country from one year to the next, you also must submit a Form 8843 to verify your nonresident status. Tax regulations and procedures are not simple, and you should seek help from your employer and/or your sponsoring organization if your are participating in a J-1 program. You may also wish to secure a copy of IRS Publication 519, *U.S. Tax Guide for Aliens*, which is available free of charge from the Internal Revenue Service. Forms are available online at www.irs.ustreas.gov/prod/forms_pubs/.

FULL-TIME STUDENTS AT U.S. SCHOOLS

Individuals enrolled at U.S. colleges and universities for full-time academic study are usually admitted on the basis of the F-1 (student), M-1 (student), or student category of the J-1 visa. In each case, summer employment may be possible before graduation, after graduation, or both. When such employment may take place, the length of time allowed, and what the employment is called (practical training, curricular practical training, academic training) depend on the specific visa and circumstances of the individual student. A number of schools in the United States offer academic courses—usually known as cooperative education programs—that combine periods of study with periods of practical training employment. Under certain conditions, students from other countries who are enrolled as regular, full-time students in a cooperative education program are allowed to undertake the practical training assignments (usually paid) in the same manner as American students. For information on enrollment in cooperative education programs and the American colleges and universities that offer these opportunities, contact:

Cooperative Education Association
8640 Guilford Road, Suite 215
Columbia, Maryland 21046
Telephone: 410-290-3666
Fax: 410-290-7084
www.ceainc.org

Whether enrolled in a cooperative education program, whether before or after graduation, and regardless of the type of visa (M-1, F-1, or J-1), the student remains under the legal sponsorship of his or her college, university, or (in the case of some J-1 students) Exchange Visitor Program sponsor. Therefore, students should seek assistance from the international student adviser at the their school.

VISA VIOLATIONS OR OVERSTAYS

In recent years, U.S. immigration laws have become more restrictive. All international visitors, trainees, and temporary work visa holders should make sure that they fully understand their responsibilities under the particular visa they use to enter the U.S. It is extremely important that you know exactly what you are permitted to do on the type of visa you have been granted and how long you are permitted to remain in the United States. If you have any questions about this, please check with your program sponsor, employer, or the INS. If your program ends early, you are not permitted to remain in the United States. You must either return home upon completion of your work program or take the steps necessary to legally remain in the United States. There are severe penalties for foreign nationals who overstay their visas or who violate their status. You could be barred from returning to the U.S. for ten years or longer if you violate your visa status, even unintentionally.

IN CONCLUSION

Most countries of the world have very strict regulations regarding employment for noncitizens in order to protect job opportunities for their own citizens. The United States is no different. What is different, however, is the U.S. system of visas and the rules and regulations that apply to each type (and subtype) of visa. The process of acquiring the proper visa takes a good deal of time (sometimes as long as four to six months) and can often be frustrating and confusing. Therefore, it is important to plan ahead and contact prospective employers as early as possible so that the employer has sufficient time to undertake the paperwork involved. If you have applied to or have been accepted by a "trainee" program, make sure that the employer knows the name of the organization, because each sponsoring organization has its own internal procedures that must be followed. Prepare well in advance, ask lots of questions, and make sure you understand what needs to be done. If you do your research and begin early, you will soon be on your way to a fulfilling work experience in the United States.

WORKING FOR THE NATIONAL PARK SERVICE

Since its inception in 1916, the National Park Service has been dedicated to the preservation and management of this country's outstanding natural, historical, and recreational areas. Today the National Park Service encompasses more than 370 sites across the United States and in Guam, Puerto Rico, and the Virgin Islands. There are parks of great natural beauty and grandeur, such as the Grand Canyon and Yellowstone; parks that preserve the nation's cultural and historical treasures, such as Mesa Verde, the Statue of Liberty, and Gettysburg Battlefield; parks of significant recreational value along seashores, lakeshores, and riverways that provide opportunities for outdoor activities and relaxation, such as Assateague Island and Lake Mead. The National Park Service is a bureau of the U.S. Department of the Interior; it should not be confused with the U.S. Forest Service of the Department of Agriculture.

Every year, millions of people from the United States and abroad visit our national park areas. To protect park resources and to serve the public, the National Park Service employs a permanent workforce and an essential seasonal workforce. Seasonals are hired every year to help permanent staff at many National Park Service parks and offices. The variety of positions available may surprise you: campground rangers, fee collectors, tour guides, naturalists, landscape architects, firefighters, laborers, law enforcement rangers, lifeguards, carpenters, clerks, historians; persons are hired for these seasonal jobs and more. Whatever the job, seasonal employees have the opportunity to learn more about the National Park Service and its mission.

Competition for seasonal jobs is keen. The number of applicants far outnumbers the positions available every year, particularly at larger, well-known parks. Some positions are filled by experienced seasonal employees who have worked previously for the National Park Service. And, Office of Personnel Management regulations require that veterans of the United States Armed Forces may be given preference among applicants. In the summer season, when most seasonal employees are hired, employment opportunities are extremely competitive.

ABOUT SEASONAL JOBS

PAY: Many seasonal positions require irregular hours of work, including weekends, holidays, and evenings. Entry-level grades for National Park Service seasonal positions generally range from the GS-3 to GS-7. GS levels indicate the rate of pay for most federal government positions. For current salary information for these grades, check with any federal agency or the Office of Personnel Management in that geographic area where you desire employment. Prevailing local wages govern certain positions, such as laborer, maintenance, and skilled trades and crafts.

WG levels indicate the rate of pay: the higher the WG number, the higher the wage. WG wages are paid on an hourly basis with a standard work week of 40 hours. Overtime may be required; additional compensation is provided for extra hours worked. GS levels and WG levels are not equivalent.

UNIFORMS: Most seasonal park rangers and maintenance personnel are required to wear the official Park Service uniform; specific requirements and ordering information are contained in the employment package forwarded to successful applicants. For those positions requiring a uniform, an allowance is allotted that *partially* covers its cost.

HOUSING: Address specific questions about housing, area living conditions, and similar matters to the park or office where you desire employment. Seasonal employee housing may or may not be available.

EQUAL EMPLOYMENT OPPORTUNITY: The National Park Service is an Equal Opportunity employer. Selection for positions will be made solely on the basis of merit, fitness, and qualifications, without regard to race, sex, color, creed, age, marital status, national origin, sexual orientation, nondisqualifying handicap conditions, or any other nonmerit factors.

GENERAL INFORMATION ON APPLYING

The NPS has a centralized recruitment program for seasonal hiring. In addition, some parks may choose to hire directly. For information on these and other seasonal job opportunities, visit the Office of Personnel Management's Web page: www.usajobs.opm.gov. Information can also be accessed through the NPS Web page on the Internet (www.nps.gov and go to InfoZone for employment information).

CENTRALIZED SEASONAL RECRUITMENT: For information, including the list of parks hiring through the centralized recruitment program, contact the National Park Service's Seasonal Employment Program office. The address is: Seasonal Employment Program, Human Resources Office, National Park Service, 1849 C Street, NW, Mail Stop 2225, Washington, D.C. 20240; telephone: 1-877-554-4550; Web site: http://www.sep.nps.gov. At this Web site, applicants can also apply on-line. Applicants may also apply using a paper application by first calling the seasonal office or checking the Web site for vacant positions, and then requesting an application by providing the park name(s) and the vacancy announcement number(s) for the position(s) for which they wish to apply.

SEASONAL POSITIONS

PARK RANGER

Grades: GS-3, GS-4, GS-5, GS-7

Duties

Duties vary greatly from position to position and may include providing visitor services; interpreting a park's natural, historic, or archeological features through talks, guided walks, and demonstrations; working at an information desk; planning and implementing resource management programs, including fire control; performing search-and-rescue activities; providing for the public's safety through law enforcement; collecting fees; firefighting; lifeguarding; and radio dispatching.

Qualifications

GS-3: 6 months of general experience and 3 months of specialized experience that demonstrates the knowledge, skills, and abilities necessary to perform the job duties **or** 1 year of college (30 semester hours with 6 semester hours of natural sciences, social sciences, park and recreation management, and other disciplines related to management and protection of park resources, both natural and cultural).

GS-4: 6 months of general experience and 6 months of specialized experience that demonstrates the knowledge, skills, and abilities necessary to perform the job duties **or** 2 years of college (60 semester hours with 12 semester hours of natural sciences, social sciences, park and recreation management, and other disciplines related to management and protection of park resources, both natural and cultural).

GS-5: 1 year of specialized experience equivalent to the GS-4 level **or** 4 years of college leading to a bachelor's degree (120 semester hours with 24 semester hours of natural sciences, social sciences, park and recreation management, and other disciplines related to management and protection of park resources, both natural and cultural).

GS-7: 1 year of specialized experience equivalent to the GS-5 or GS-6 level **or** 1 full academic year of graduate education related to the management and protection of park resources or superior academic achievement.

How to Apply: For centralized recruitment, call the Seasonal Employment Office at 1-877-554-4550 for a listing of current vacancies and an application package, or check their Web site at http://www.sep.nps.gov for current vacancies and apply on-line. For information on other seasonal job opportunities, contact the personnel office in the geographic area in which you want to work, or visit the Office of Personnel Management's Web page (www.usajobs.opm.gov) or NPS Web page (www.nps.gov and go to InfoZone for employment information).

PARK GUIDE

Grades: GS-3 through GS-5

Duties

Provides guided tours, gives formal talks on natural and historic features, answers questions, and provides miscellaneous services to visitors.

Requirements

GS-3. 6 months general experience **or** 1 year of college (30 semester hours with 6 semester hours in American history, science, or public speaking).

GS-4: 6 months of general experience and 6 months of specialized experience **or** 1 year as a Park Guide, GS-3 **or** 2 years of college (60 semester hours with 12 semester hours in American history, science, or public speaking).

GS-5: 1 year of specialized experience **or** 1 year as a Guide, GS-4 **or** 4 years of college leading to a bachelor's degree (120 semester hours with 24 semester hours in American history, science, or public speaking).

How to Apply

For centralized recruitment, call the Seasonal Employment Office at 1-877-554-4550 for a listing of current vacancies and an application package, or check their

Web site at http://www.sep.nps.gov for current vacancies and apply on-line. For information on other seasonal job opportunities: contact the personnel office in the geographic area in which you want to work, or visit the Office of Personnel Management's Web page (www.usajobs.opm.gov) or NPS Web page (www.nps.gov and go to InfoZone for employment information).

VISITOR USE ASSISTANT

Grades: GS-4, GS-5

Duties

Collects and accounts for fees and provides miscellaneous services and information to visitors.

Requirements

GS-4: 1 year of general experience **or** 1 year as a Visitor Use Assistant, GS-3 **or** 2 years of college (60 semester hours).

GS-5: 1 year of specialized experience **or** 1 year as a Visitor Use Assistant, GS-4 **or** 4 years of college (120 semester hours).

How to Apply

For centralized recruitment, call the Seasonal Employment Office at 1-877-554-4550 for a listing of current vacancies and an application package, or check their Web site at http://www.sep.nps.gov for current vacancies and apply on-line. For information on other seasonal job opportunities: contact the personnel office in the geographic area in which you want to work, or visit the Office of Personnel Management's Web page (www.usajobs.opm.gov) or NPS Web page (www.nps.gov and go to InfoZone for employment information).

RECREATIONAL AID/ASSISTANT

Grades: GS-3 through GS-6

Duties

Guards and manages beach and swimming areas and performs lifesaving and rescue work as needed for persons in rivers, lakes, and oceans. Positions are located at national recreation areas, seashores, and lakeshores.

Qualifications

GS-3: 6 months of general experience **or** 1 year of college.

GS-4: 6 months of general experience and 6 months specialized experience **or** 2 years of college (60 semester hours with 12 semester hours of courses related to recreation).

GS-5: 1 year of specialized experience equivalent to the GS-4 level **or** 4 years of college leading to a bachelor's degree (120 semester hours with 24 semester hours or a degree in recreation or physical education).

GS-6: 1 year of specialized experience equivalent to the GS-5 level.

How to Apply

Contact the personnel office in the geographic area in which you want to work, or visit the Office of Personnel Management's Web page (www.usajobs.opm.gov) or NPS Web page (www.nps.gov and go to InfoZone for employment information).

BIOLOGICAL TECHNICIAN

Grades: GS-4, GS-5

Duties

Assists researchers and management staff in collecting and analyzing data on flora and fauna in parks.

Qualifications

GS-4: 6 months of general experience and 6 months specialized experience **or** 2 years of college (60 semester hours with 12 semester hours in biology, chemistry, statistics, entomology, animal husbandry, botany, physics, agriculture, and mathematics with 6 of those directly related to the position to be filled).

GS-5: 1 year of specialized experience equivalent to the GS-4 level **or** 4 years of college leading to a bachelor's degree (120 semester hours with 24 semester hours or a degree in biology, chemistry, statistics, entomology, animal husbandry, botany, physics, agriculture, or mathematics with 6 of those directly related to the position to be filled).

How to Apply

For centralized recruitment, call the Seasonal Employment Office at 1-877-554-4550 for a listing of current vacancies and an application package, or check their Web site at http://www.sep.nps.gov for current vacancies and apply on-line. Contact the personnel office in the geographic area in which you want to work, or visit the Office of Personnel Management's Web page (www.usajobs.opm.gov) or NPS Web page (www.nps.gov and go to InfoZone for employment information).

FORESTRY TECHNICIAN

Grades: GS-4, GS-5

Duties

Assists in fire control, prevention, and suppression work on park lands.

Qualifications

GS-4: 6 months of general experience and 6 months of specialized experience **or** 4 seasons of specialized experience **or** 2 years of college (60 semester hours with 12 semester hours in forestry, agriculture, crop or plant science, range management or conservation, wildlife management, and other related fields).

GS-5: 1 year of specialized experience equivalent to the GS-4 level **or** 4 years of college leading to a bachelor's degree (120 semester hours with 24 semester hours or a degree in forestry, agriculture, crop or plant science, range management or conservation, wildlife management, or other related field).

How to Apply

Contact the personnel office in the geographic area in which you want to work, or visit the Office of Personnel Management's Web page (www.usajobs.opm.gov) or NPS Web page (www.nps.gov and go to InfoZone for employment information).

ARCHITECTURE AND LANDSCAPE ARCHITECTURE

Grades: GS-4 and above

Duties

Produces drawings of structures of historical, architectural, landscape, engineering industrials, and maritime significance; prepares field notes; develops and edits measured drawings.

Qualifications

GS-4: 2 years of study (60 semester hours with 12 semester hours in architecture and landscape architecture).

GS-5: 4 years of study leading to a bachelor's degree, with major study or 24 semester hours in architecture or landscape architecture.

GS-7 and above: currently working toward a master's or doctoral degree in architecture or landscape architecture.

How to Apply

Contact Summer Program Administrator, HABS/HAER, National Park Service, 1849 C Street, NW, Washington, D.C. 20240. Submit a personal qualifications statement (resume, SF-171, or OF-612), letter of recommendation from a faculty member or employer familiar with your work, and samples indicating drafting ability (copies of sketches, lettering, and precision drafting).

HISTORIAN

Grades: GS-5, GS-7, and above

Duties

Conducts research using primary and secondary sources to produce inventories and reports on specific sites, structures, or technical processes.

Qualifications

A graduate degree in architectural history, landscape architecture, history of technology, American civilization, historic preservation, or a related field is preferred; a B.A. is required.

How to Apply

Contact Summer Program Administrator, HABS/HAER, National Park Service, 1849 C Street, NW, Washington, D.C. 20240. Submit a personal qualifications statement (resume, SF-171, or OF-612), letter of recommendation from a faculty member or employer familiar with your work, and (a) a paper demonstrating primary research in architectural history, landscape architecture, or history of technology or (b) a paper focusing on an aspect of the built environment.

CLERICAL

Grades: GS-1 through GS-4

Duties

Performs duties of receptionist, administrative clerk, clerk-typist, and data entry. The number of jobs available is limited.

Qualifications

GS-1: no education or experience required.
GS-2: 3 months of experience **or** high school graduate.
GS-3: 6 months of experience **or** 1 year of college (30 semester hours).
GS-4: 1 year of experience **or** 2 years of college (60 semester hours).
For typing positions, must be able to type 40 words per minute.

How to Apply

Contact the personnel office in the geographic area in which you want to work, or visit the Office of Personnel Management's Web page (www.usajobs.opm.gov) or NPS Web page (www.nps.gov and go to InfoZone for employment information).

LABORER

Grades: WG-2 through WG-4

Duties

Performs manual outdoor work on trails and for forestry programs; other park maintenance activities, such as cleaning campgrounds; and similar work in which physical labor must be performed.

Qualifications

Ability to perform the job duties, including necessary physical requirements.

How to Apply

Contact the personnel office in the geographic area in which you want to work, or visit the Office of Personnel Management's Web page (www.usajobs.opm.gov) or NPS Web page (www.nps.gov and go to InfoZone for employment information).

MAINTENANCE, TRADES, AND CRAFTS

Grades: WG-5 and above

Duties

Performs skilled and semi-skilled trades work: carpenter, mechanic, sawyer (woodsworker), trail maintenance worker, motor vehicle operation, and other similar positions.

Qualifications

Helper- to journeyman-level proficiency usually required.

How to Apply

Contact the personnel office in the geographic area in which you want to work, or visit the Office of Personnel Management's Web page (www.usajobs.opm.gov) or NPS Web page (www.nps.gov and go to InfoZone for employment information).

OTHER EMPLOYMENT OPPORTUNITIES

Other types of positions may be available in National Park Service parks and offices. Contact the park or office where you are interested in working for information. In addition, hotels, lodges, restaurants, stores, transportation services, marinas, and many other visitor facilities in National Parks may have positions available. These facilities are operated by private companies and individuals called park concessioners who recruit and hire their own employees. These are not federal government positions. Concessioners usually pay the minimum wage set by the state in which their operation is located. Although some pay a small bonus at the end of the season, they do not pay or make arrangements for travel to and from the parks. The National Park Service Regional Office for the geographic region in which you want to work, or the park itself, can provide names and addresses of concessioners. Contact the concessioner for applications and information about concession jobs, salaries, and working and living conditions.

NATIONAL PARK SERVICE REGIONAL OFFICES AND SITES

ALASKA REGION

Alagnak Wild River
Aniakchak National Monument and
   Preserve
Bering Land Bridge National Preserve
Cape Krusenstern National Monument
Denali National Park and Preserve
Gates of Arctic National Park and Preserve
Glacier Bay National Park and Preserve
Katmai National Park and Preserve
Kenai Fjords National Park

Klondike Gold Rush National Historical
   Park
Kobuk Valley National Park
Lake Clark National Park and Preserve
Noatak National Preserve
Sitka National Historical Park
Wrangell-St. Elias National Park and
   Preserve
Yukon-Charley Rivers National Preserve

For information about seasonal employment opportunities in this region, contact: National Park Service, 2525 Gambell Street, Anchorage, Alaska 99503; telephone: 907-257-2526.

INTERMOUNTAIN REGION

COLORADO PLATEAU CLUSTER

Arches National Park
Aztec Ruins National Monument
Bryce Canyon National Park
California National Historical Trail (Salt
   Lake City)
Canyon de Chelly National Monument
Canyonlands National Park
Capitol Reef National Park
Cedar Breaks National Monument
Chaco Culture National Historical Park
Colorado National Monument
Dinosaur National Monument

El Malpais National Monument
El Morro National Monument
Fossil Butte National Monument
Glen Canyon National Recreation Area
Golden Spike National Historic Site
Grand Canyon National Park
Grand Staircase-Escalante National
   Monument
Hovenweep National Monument
Hubbell Trading Post National Historic Site
Mesa Verde National Park
Mormon Pioneer National Historical Trail
   (Salt Lake City)

Oregon National Historical Trail (Salt Lake City)
Pony Express National Historical Trail (Salt Lake City)
Natural Bridges National Monument
Navajo National Monument
Petrified Forest National Park
Pipe Spring National Monument
Rainbow Bridge National Monument
Sunset Crater Volcano National Monument
Timpanogos Cave National Monument
Walnut Canyon National Monument
Wupatki National Monument
Yucca House National Monument
Zion National Park

ROCKY MOUNTAIN CLUSTER
Bent's Old Fort National Historic Site
Bighorn Canyon National Recreation Area
Black Canyon of the Gunnison National Monument
Curecanti National Recreation Area
Devils Tower National Monument
Florissant Fossil Beds National Monument
Fort Laramie National Historic Site
Glacier National Park
Grand Teton National Park
Grant-Kohrs Ranch National Historic Site
Great Sand Dunes National Monument
John D. Rockefeller, Jr. Memorial Parkway
Little Bighorn Battlefield National Monument
Rocky Mountain National Park
Yellowstone National Park

SOUTHWEST CLUSTER
Alibates Flint Quarrie National Monument
Amistad National Recreation Area
Bandelier National Monument

Big Bend National Park
Big Thicket National Preserve
Capulin Volcano National Monument
Carlsbad Cavern National Park
Casa Grande Ruins National Monument
Chamizal National Monument
Chickasaw National Recreation Area
Chiricahua National Monument
Coronado National Monument
Fort Bowie National Historic Site
Fort Union National Monument
Fort Davis National Historic Site
Gila Cliff Dwellings National Monument
Glorieta Battlefield
Guadalupe Mountains National Park
Hohokam Pima National Monument
Lake Meredith National Recreation Area
Lyndon B. Johnson National Historical Park
Montezuma Castle National Monument
Organ Pipe Cactus National Monument
Padre Island National Seashore
Palo Alto Battlefield National Historic Site
Pecos National Historical Park
Petroglyph National Monument
Rio Grand Wild and Scenic River
Saguaro National Park
Salinas Pueblo Missions National Monument
San Antonio Missions National Historical Park
Sante Fe National Historical Trail (Santa Fe)
Trail of Tears National Historic Trail (Santa Fe)
Tonto National Monument
Tumacacori National Historical Park
Tuzigoot National Monument
White Sands National Monument

For information about seasonal employment opportunities in this region, contact: National Park Service, P.O. Box 25287, 12795 West Alameda Parkway, Denver, Colorado, 80225-0287; telephone: 303-969-2020.

MIDWEST REGION

GREAT LAKES CLUSTER
Apostle Islands National Lakeshore
Cuyahoga Valley National Recreation Area
Dayton Aviation Heritage National Historical Park
George Rogers Clark National Historical Park
Grand Portage National Monument

Hopewell Culture National Historical Park
Ice Age National Scenic Trail
Indiana Dunes National Lakeshore
Isle Royale National Park
James A. Garfield National Historic Site
Keweenaw National Historical Park
Lewis & Clark National Historical Trail
Lincoln Boyhood National Monument

Lincoln Home National Historic Site
Mississippi National River and Recreation
   Area
North Country National Scenic Trail
Perry's Victory and International Peace
   Memorial
Pictured Rocks National Lakeshore
Sleeping Bear Dunes National Lakeshore
St. Croix/Lower St. Croix National Scenic
   Riverways
Voyageurs National Park
William Howard Taft National Historic Site

GREAT PLAINS CLUSTER
Agate Fossil Beds National Monument
Arkansas Post National Monument
Badlands National Park
Brown vs. Board of Education National
   Historic Site
Buffalo National River
Effigy Mounds National Monument
Fort Larned National Historic Site
Fort Smith National Historic Site
Fort Scott National Historic Site

Fort Union Trading Post National Historic
   Site
George Washington Carver National
   Monument
Harry S Truman National Historic Site
Herbert Hoover National Historic Site
Homestead National Monument of America
Hot Springs National Park
Jewel Cave National Monument
Jefferson National Expansion Memorial
Knife River Indian Villages National
   Historic Site
Missouri National Recreational River
Mount Rushmore National Monument
Niobrara National Scenic Riverway
Ozark National Scenic Riverways
Pea Ridge National Military Park
Pipestone National Monument
Scotts Bluff National Monument
Theodore Roosevelt National Park
Ulysses S. Grant National Historic Site
Wilson's Creek National Battlefield
Wind Cave National Park

For information about seasonal employment opportunities in this region, contact: National Park Service,1709 Jackson Street, Omaha, Nebraska 68102; telephone: 402-221-3456.

NATIONAL CAPITAL REGION

NATIONAL CAPITAL CLUSTER
Antietam National Battlefield
Antietam National Cemetery
Arlington House, The Robert E. Lee
   Memorial
Baltimore-Washington Parkway
Battleground National Cemetery
Catoctin Mountain Park
Chesapeake and Ohio Canal National
   Historical Park
Clara Barton National Historic Site
Clara Barton Parkway
Constitution Gardens
Ford's Theatre National Historic Site
Fort Washington Park
Francis Scott Key Memorial
Franklin Delano Roosevelt Memorial Park
Frederick Douglass National Historic Site
George Washington Memorial Parkway
Greenbelt Park
Harpers Ferry National Historical Park
Kahlil Gibran Memorial Garden
Korean War Veterans Memorial
Lincoln Memorial

Lyndon Baines Johnson Memorial Grove
   on the Potomac
Manassas National Battlefield Park
Mary McLeod Bethune Memorial
Mary McLeod Bethune Council House
   National Historic Site
Monocacy National Battlefield
National Capital Parks
National Mall
National Law Enforcement Officers
   Memorial
Pennsylvania Avenue National Historic Site
Piscataway Park
Potomac Heritage National Scenic Trail
Prince William Forest Park
Rock Creek Park
Rock Creek Parkway
Suitland Parkway
Theodore Roosevelt Island
Thomas Jefferson Memorial
United States Navy Memorial
Vietnam Veterans Memorial
Vietnam Woman's Memorial
Washington Monument

White House

Wolf Trap Farm Park

For information about seasonal employment opportunities in this region, contact: National Park Service,1100 Ohio Drive, SW, Washington, D.C. 20242; telephone: 202-619-7256.

NORTHEAST REGION

ALLEGHENY AND CHESAPEAKE CLUSTER

Allegheny Portage Railroad National Historic Site
Appomattox Court House National Historical Park
Assateague Island National Seashore
Bluestone National Scenic River
Booker T. Washington National Monument
Colonial National Historical Park
Delaware & Lehigh Navigation Canal National Heritage Corridor Commission
Delaware Water Gap National Recreation Area
Edgar Allen Poe National Historic Site
Eisenhower National Historic Site
Fort McHenry National Monument and Historic Shrine
Fort Necessity National Battlefield
Fredericksburg and Spotsylvania County Battlefields Memorial National Military Park
Friendship Hill National Historic Site
Gauley River National Recreation Area
George Washington Birthplace National Monument

Gettysburg National Military Park
Gloria Dei National Historic Site
Great Egg Harbor National Scenic and Recreational River
Hampton National Historic Site
Hopewell Furnace National Historical Park
Independence National Historical Park
Johnstown Flood National Monument
Maggie Walker National Historic Site
New Jersey Coastal Heritage Trail Route
New River Gorge National River
Petersburg National Battlefield
Pinelands National Reserve
Richmond National Battlefield Park
Shenandoah National Park
Southwestern Pennsylvania Heritage Preservation Commission
Steamtown National Historic Site
Thaddeus Kosciuszko National Monument
Thomas Stone National Historic Site
Upper Delaware National Scenic and Recreational River
Valley Forge National Historical Park

For information about seasonal employment opportunities in this cluster of the region, contact: National Park Service, U.S. Custom House, 200 Chestnut Street, Philadelphia, Pennsylvania 19106; telephone: 215-597-4972.

NEW ENGLAND CLUSTER

Acadia National Park
Adams National Historic Site
Blackstone River Valley National Heritage Conservation Corridor
Boston African-American National Historic Site
Boston National Historical Park
Cape Cod National Seashore
Castle Clinton National Monument
Edison National Historic Site
Eleanor Roosevelt National Historic Site
Farmington Wild and Scenic River
Federal Hall National Monument
Fire Island National Seashore

Fort Stanwix National Monument
Frederick Law Olmsted National Historic Site
Gateway National Recreation Area
General Grant National Monument
Hamilton Grange National Monument
Home of Franklin D. Roosevelt National Historic Site
John F. Kennedy National Historic Site
Longfellow National Historic Site
Lowell National Historical Park
Maine Acadian Culture Preservation Commission
Marsh-Billings National Historical Park
Martin Van Buren National Historic Site

Minute Man National Historical Park
Morristown National Historical Park
Quinebaug-Shetucket National Heritage
  Corridor
Roger Williams National Monument
Roosevelt Campobello International Park
Sagamore Hill National Historic Site
Saint Paul's Church National Historic Site
Saint Croix Island International Historic
  Site
Saint-Gaudens National Historic Site
Salem Maritime National Historic Site
Saratoga National Historical Park

Saugus Iron Works National Historic Site
Springfield Armory National Historic Site
Statue of Liberty/Ellis Island National
  Monuments
Theodore Roosevelt Birthplace National
  Historic Site
Theodore Roosevelt Inaugural National
  Historic Site
Touro Synagogue National Historic Site
Vanderbilt Mansion National Historic Site
Weir Farm National Historic Site
Wildcat Brook Wild and Scenic River
Women's Rights National Historical Park

For information about seasonal employment opportunities in this cluster of the region, contact: National Park Service, 15 State Street, Boston, Massachusetts 02109; telephone: 617-223-5101.

PACIFIC WEST REGION

COLUMBIA CASCADES CLUSTER
Big Hole National Battlefield
City of Rocks National Reserve
Coulee Dam National Recreation Area
Crater Lake National Park
Craters of the Moon National Monument
Ebey's Landing National Reserve
Fort Vancouver National Historic Site
Fort Clatsop National Monument
Hagerman Fossil Beds National Monument
John Day Fossil Beds National Monument

Klondike Gold Rush National Historical
  Park
Lake Chelan National Recreation Area
Mount Rainier National Park
Nez Perce National Historical Park
North Cascades National Park
Olympic National Park
Oregon Caves National Monument
Ross Lake National Recreation Area
San Juan Island National Historical Park
Whitman Mission National Historic Site

For information about seasonal employment opportunities in this cluster of the region, contact: National Park Service, 909 First Avenue, Seattle, Washington 98104-1060; telephone: 206-220-4053.

PACIFIC GREAT BASIN CLUSTER
Cabrillo National Monument
Channel Islands National Park
Death Valley National Park
Devils Postpile National Monument
Eugene O'Neill National Historic Site
Fort Point National Historic Site
Golden Gate National Recreation Area
Great Basin National Park
John Muir National Historic Site
Joshua Tree National Park
Juan Bautista De Anza National Heritage
  Trail
Kings Canyon National Park
Lake Mead National Recreation Area
Lassen Volcanic National Park

Lava Beds National Monument
Manzanar National Historic Site
Mojave National Preserve
Muir Woods National Monument
Pinnacles National Monument
Point Reyes National Seashore
Redwood National and State Parks
San Francisco Maritime National Historical
  Park
Santa Monica Mountains National
  Recreation Area
Sequoia National Park
Whiskeytown-Shasta-Trinity National
  Recreation Area
Yosemite National Park

For information about seasonal employment opportunities in this cluster of the region, contact: National Park Service, 600 Harrison Street, Suite 600, San Francisco, California 94107; telephone: 415-427-1300, option 2.

PACIFIC ISLANDS CLUSTER
American Memorial Park
Haleakala National Park
Hawaii Volcanoes National Park
Kalaupapa National Historic Site
Kaloko-Honokohau National Historical
    Park
Pu'uhonua O Honaunau National Historical
    Park
Puukohola Heiau National Historic Site
The National Park of American Samoa
USS Arizona Memorial
War in the Pacific National Historical Park

For information about seasonal employment opportunities in this cluster of the region, contact: National Park Service, 300 Ala Moana Boulevard, Suite 6305, P.O. Box 50165, Honolulu, Hawaii 96850; telephone: 808-541-2693.

SOUTHEAST REGION

APPALACHIAN CLUSTER
Abraham Lincoln Birthplace National
    Historic Site
Andrew Johnson National Historic Site
Big South Fork National River and
    National Recreation Area
Blue Ridge Parkway
Carl Sandburg Home National Historic Site
Chickamauga & Chattanooga National
    Military Park
Cowpens National Battlefield
Cumberland Gap National Historical Park
Fort Donelson National Battlefield
Great Smoky Mountains National Park
Guilford Courthouse National Military Park
Kings Mountain National Military Park
Little River Canyon National Preserve
Mammoth Cave National Park
Ninety Six National Historic Site
Obed Wild and Scenic River
Overmountain Victory National Historic
    Trail
Russell Cave National Monument
Stones River National Battlefield

Congaree Swamp National Monument
Cumberland Island National Seashore
Fort Caroline National Monument
Fort Frederica National Monument
Fort Mantanzas National Monument
Fort Pulaski National Monument
Fort Raleigh National Historic Site
Fort Sumter National Monument
Horseshoe Bend National Military Park
Jimmy Carter National Historic Site
Kennesaw Mountain National Battlefield
    Park
Martin Luther King, Jr. National Historic
    Site
Moores Creek National Battlefield
Ocmulgee National Monument
Timucuan Ecological and Historic Preserve
Tuskegee Institute National Historic Site
Wright Brothers National Monument

GULF COAST CLUSTER
Big Cypress National Preserve
Biscayne National Park
Brices Cross Roads National Battlefield
    Site
Buck Island Reef National Monument
Cane River Creole National Historical Park
    and Heritage Area
Christiansted National Historic Site
DeSoto National Monument
Dry Tortugas National Park
Everglades National Park
Gulf Islands National Seashore
Jean Lafitte National Historical Park and
    Preserve

ATLANTIC COAST CLUSTER
Andersonville National Historic Site
Canaveral National Seashore
Cape Hatteras National Seashore
Cape Lookout National Seashore
Castillo de San Marcos National
    Monument
Charles Pinckney National Historic Site
Chattahoochee River National Recreation
    Area

Natchez National Historical Park
Natchez Trace Parkway
New Orleans Jazz National Historical Park
Poverty Point National Monument
Salt River Bay National Historical Park

San Juan National Historic Site
Shiloh National Military Park
Tupelo National Battlefield
Vicksburg National Military Park
Virgin Islands National Park

For information about seasonal employment opportunities in this field area, contact: National Park Service, Atlanta Federal Center, 1924 Building, 100 Alabama Street, SW, Atlanta, Georgia 30303; telephone: 404-562-3296.

Information in this article is supplied by the National Park Service.

DO YOU WANT TO WORK TEMPORARILY IN CANADA?

WHAT YOU NEED TO KNOW

If you wish to work temporarily in Canada, you will likely be required to have an **employment authorization.** An employment authorization is issued by an immigration officer after a Human Resources Centre approves your job offer.

This article outlines what you and your employer must do *before* you arrive in Canada. For additional advice, contact the Canadian Embassy, High Commission, or Consulate General near you.

Additional procedures may be required if you wish to work in Quebec. For further information, contact the Canadian Embassy abroad.

WHAT YOUR EMPLOYER MUST DO

Your employer must give details of your job offer to a Human Resources Centre. An employment counselor will check to determine if your offer of employment meets the prevailing wages and working conditions for the occupation concerned. A check will also be made to see if the job cannot be filled by a suitably qualified and available Canadian or permanent resident. If these conditions are met, the Human Resources Centre will approve your job offer. They will then issue a confirmation of offer of employment and send this to the Canadian Embassy, High Commission, or Consulate in your country.

The employer will be provided with a copy of the confirmation of offer of employment, to be forwarded to you. Your employer is responsible for arranging your worker's compensation and medical coverage when you arrive in Canada.

Some jobs may be exempt from Human Resources Centre approval, and either the centre or a visa office at a Canadian embassy or consulate can advise you on this.

WHAT YOU MUST DO

The Canadian visa office near you will contact you upon receipt of your confirmation of offer of employment. You may be asked to go to an interview or to send some information by mail. You may also be asked to have a medical checkup, which you will have to pay for yourself. If you qualify and have all the necessary documents, you will receive an employment authorization and will possibly have a separate visitor visa placed in your passport.

The employment authorization will state that you can work at a specific job for a specific period of time for a specific employer. You will need to produce the authorization when you arrive in Canada, as well as your passport, visa (if issued), and airline tickets.

There is a processing fee when you submit an application for an employment authorization. There are no refunds if your application is refused. Please request the brochure on immigration fees by calling Public Enquiries or ask an immigration officer for fee information.

Different procedures exist for citizens or permanent residents of the United States. You should seek clarification from the nearest Canadian embassy or consulate; general procedures are stated later in this article.

An employment authorization will not be issued to you to come to Canada to look for work. *It is valid only for the specific job, the specific amount of time, and the employer stated on the form.*

WHEN YOU ARRIVE IN CANADA

When you arrive at the port of entry to Canada, show your confirmation of offer of employment, your employment authorization, and other papers to an immigration officer. You will be given forms to fill out so that you can get a Social Insurance Number (SIN). These forms and proper identification, such as a birth certificate, should be taken to a counselor at a Human Resources Centre, who can help you if you have trouble filling them out. When you receive your SIN card, you will have to give your number to your employer.

Your employment authorization is not a contract. Your job can be ended by you or your employer at any time. However, if your duties change or the job is to be extended, you must contact immigration right away, before the expiry date of your current authorization. You can do this by calling the Citizenship and Immigration Call Centre at 888-242-2100.

SOME WORKERS CAN APPLY AT A PORT OF ENTRY

Most foreign workers must apply for employment authorization outside of Canada, but if you are a resident of the United States, Greenland, or St. Pierre and Miquelon, you can apply for an employment authorization when you arrive at a port of entry to Canada. To apply this way, you must produce your confirmation of offer of employment and other papers when you arrive at the port of entry. Remember that you must find out what papers you will need *before* arriving in Canada. Check with the Canadian Embassy, High Commission, or Consulate General.

REMEMBER

- There is a nonrefundable fee to process a request for an employment authorization.

- Most foreign workers must get their employment authorizations before arriving in Canada. Visitors *cannot* obtain employment authorization while in Canada.

- You must follow the terms of your employment authorization while in Canada. If you do not, you may be asked to leave the country.

- Human Resources Centre staff in Canada and Canadian government representatives in your home country cannot help you find a job.

- If you want to work temporarily or if you have further questions about working in Canada, contact the nearest Canadian Embassy, High Commission, or Consulate.

- This is not a legal document. For precise, legal information consult the Immigration Act and Regulations.

Produced by Communications Branch, Citizenship and Immigration Canada. Reproduced with the permission of Citizenship and Immigration Canada and Public Works and Government Services Canada, 2000. For more information, please visit http://www.cic.gc.ca.

ALABAMA

ACE COMPUTER CAMP–ALABAMA
See ACE Computer Camp–Washington on page 307 for complete description.

CAMP SKYLINE
4888 ALABAMA HIGHWAY 117
MENTONE, ALABAMA 35984

General Information Residential camp located on top of Lookout Mountain serving 275–315 girls. Campers select a "six-a-day" schedule from more than 15 activities. Established in 1947. 80-acre facility located 50 miles from Chattanooga, Tennessee. Features: river access; three oval riding rings and western trails; hut row cabins and triplex; large gymnasium and arts and crafts building; tennis, volleyball, and basketball courts; spacious dining hall.

Profile of Summer Employees Total number: 115–125; typical ages: 18–24. 5% men; 95% women; 10% high school students; 90% college students; 2% non-U.S. citizens; 5% local applicants. Nonsmokers preferred.

Employment Information Openings are from June 11 to August 8. Jobs available: ▶ *Christian leadership instructors* ▶ *canoeing instructors* ▶ *cheerleading/flag twirling/baton twirling instructors* ▶ *circus staff* ▶ *computer instructors* ▶ *fine and performing arts instructors (music, dance, arts and crafts, and drama)* ▶ *lifeguards and swimming instructors* with WSI certification ▶ *nature specialists* ▶ *riflery instructors* ▶ *ropes course instructors for climbing tower* ▶ *sports instructors* including archery, tennis, swimming, diving, horseback riding, and gymnastics. Applicants must submit a formal organization application, four personal references. An in-person interview is recommended, but a telephone interview is acceptable.

Benefits and Preemployment Training Free housing, free meals, and on-the-job training. Preemployment training is required and includes accident prevention and safety, first aid, CPR, leadership skills.

Contact Sally C. Johnson, Director, Camp Skyline, PO Box 287, Mentone, Alabama 35984. Telephone: 256-634-4001. Fax: 256-634-3018. World Wide Web: http://www.campskyline.com. Application deadline: continuous.

THE SOUTHWESTERN COMPANY, ALABAMA
See The Southwestern Company, Tennessee on page 284 for complete description.

STUDENT CONSERVATION ASSOCIATION (SCA), ALABAMA
See Student Conservation Association (SCA), New Hampshire on page 193 for complete description.

ALASKA

ACE COMPUTER CAMP–ALASKA
See ACE Computer Camp–Washington on page 307 for complete description.

A CHRISTIAN MINISTRY IN THE NATIONAL PARKS– ALASKA

See A Christian Ministry in the National Parks–Massachussetts on page 138 for complete description.

ALASKA STATE PARKS VOLUNTEER PROGRAM
3601 C STREET, SUITE 1200
ANCHORAGE, ALASKA 99503-5921

General Information Program offering volunteer positions in state parks throughout the state of Alaska. Established in 1970. 3,000,000-acre facility. Features: wilderness.

Profile of Summer Employees Total number: 184; typical ages: 18–70. 45% college students; 50% retirees; 5% local applicants.

Employment Information Openings are from June 1 to September 1. Winter break positions also offered. Jobs available: ▶ 15 *natural history interpreters* (minimum age 18) outdoor experience, good people skills, and some education in natural resources at $100–$300 per month ▶ 15 *ranger assistants* (minimum age 18) with outdoor experience, good people skills, good physical condition, and some education in natural resources at $100–$300 per month ▶ 10 *trail crew* (minimum age 18) with outdoor experience, good physical condition, familiar with hand and power tools, and some education in natural resources at $100–$300 per month ▶ 30 *various positions* (minimum age 18) at $100–$300 per month. Applicants must submit a formal organization application, cover letter, resume, personal reference, letter of recommendation. A telephone interview is required.

Benefits and Preemployment Training Free housing, on-the-job training, and expense allowance for food. Preemployment training is required.

Contact Kathryn Reid, Volunteer Coordinator, Alaska State Parks Volunteer Program, 3601 C Street, Suite 1200, Anchorage, Alaska 99503-5921. Telephone: 907-269-8708. Fax: 907-269-8907. E-mail: volunteer@dnr.state.ak.us. World Wide Web: http://www.dnr.state.ak.us/parks/vip. Application deadline: April 1.

AMERICA & PACIFIC TOURS, INC. (A&P)
430 K STREET
ANCHORAGE, ALASKA 99501

General Information Japanese land operator for Japanese tourists providing planned, individualized, and special guided trips of Alaska. Established in 1970.

Profile of Summer Employees Total number: 15. 50% men; 50% women; 90% college students; 50% non-U.S. citizens; 50% local applicants. Nonsmokers preferred.

Employment Information Openings are from June 1 to August 31. Jobs available: ▶ 20 *tour guides and office workers* (minimum age 20) with current driver's license and fluency in Japanese (salary depends upon experience as guide) at $1300–$3000 per month. Applicants must submit a cover letter, resume. A telephone interview is required.

Benefits and Preemployment Training On-the-job training. Preemployment training is optional.

Contact Keizo Sugimoto, President, America & Pacific Tours, Inc. (A&P), PO Box 10-1068, Anchorage, Alaska 99510-1068. Telephone: 907-272-9401. Fax: 907-272-0251. Application deadline: continuous.

BRISTOL BAY LODGE
PO BOX 1509
DILLINGHAM, ALASKA 99576

General Information Wilderness sportfishing lodge catering to 20 anglers per week. Established in 1972. 500-acre facility located 350 miles from Anchorage.

Profile of Summer Employees Total number: 25–30; typical ages: 19–28. 75% men, 25% women; 50% college students. Nonsmokers preferred.

Employment Information Openings are from June 1 to September 21. Jobs available: ▶ 1 *chef* with experience in the field at $2000–$2400 per month ▶ 10 *fishing guides* with CPR and standard first aid certification and experience in the field at $800–$1200 per month ▶ 4 *household* *workers* (minimum age 18) with CPR and standard first aid at $1000 per month ▶ 1 *pilot/ mechanic* with communication, instrumentation, and seaplane ratings (P or A and I) ▶ 2 *pilots* with communication, instrumentation, and seaplane ratings (over 1,500 hours). Applicants must submit a cover letter, resume, photo. International applicants accepted; must obtain own visa.

Benefits and Preemployment Training Free housing, free meals, on-the-job training, and travel reimbursement.

Contact Ron McMillan, President/General Manager, Bristol Bay Lodge, 2422 Hunter Road, Ellensburg, Washington 98926. Telephone: 509-964-2094. Fax: 509-964-2269. E-mail: bblodge@ aol.com. Application deadline: April 1.

CAMP TOGOWOODS
HC 30, BOX 5400
WASILLA, ALASKA 99654

General Information Residential program of traditional camping activities for girls ages 7–15. Established in 1958. 260-acre facility located 50 miles from Anchorage. Features: freshwater lake; wooded setting; low ropes course; hiking trails.

Profile of Summer Employees Total number: 26–28; typical ages: 18–50. 100% women; 24% minorities; 95% college students; 10% non-U.S. citizens; 38% local applicants.

Employment Information Openings are from May 29 to August 6. Jobs available: ▶ 1 *adventure trip leader* (minimum age 21) with experience in hiking, trip planning, biking, and low ropes course at $1900–$2025 per season ▶ 1 *assistant director (program)* (minimum age 21) at $2400–$2850 per season ▶ 1 *assistant director of operations* (minimum age 21) with budget and computer skills at $2750–$2900 per season ▶ 2 *cooks* at $2000–$2100 per season ▶ 10 *counselors* (minimum age 18) at $1800–$1925 per season ▶ 1 *creative arts specialist/counselor* at $1900–$2300 per season ▶ 1 *environmental specialist/counselor* at $1900–$2300 per season ▶ 1 *food service manager* (minimum age 21) at $2900–$3100 per season ▶ 1 *health supervisor* (minimum age 21) with RN license (Alaska) or EMT and current CPR certification at $2900–$3100 per season ▶ 2 *lifeguards* with lifeguard certification (waterfront lifeguarding preferred) at $1900–$2025 per season ▶ 1 *operations manager* (minimum age 21) at $2400–$2850 per season ▶ 1 *site ranger* with maintenance, repairs, carpentry, and mechanical skills at $8.00 per hour; this position includes winter housing (August-May) ▶ 4 *unit leaders* with counselor experience preferred at $1950–$2050 per season ▶ 1 *waterfront director* with WSI certification, lifeguard training, and waterfront lifeguarding at $2500–$2800 per season. Applicants must submit a formal organization application, three personal references. International applicants accepted; must obtain own visa, obtain own working papers. An in-person interview is recommended, but a telephone interview is acceptable.

Benefits and Preemployment Training Free housing, free meals, health insurance, and on-the-job training. Preemployment training is required and includes accident prevention and safety, first aid, CPR, leadership skills, supervision training.

Contact Helen Bartholomy, Camp Director, Girl Scouts Susitna Council, Camp Togowoods, PO Box 870230, Wasilla, Alaska 99687. Telephone: 907-376-3822. Fax: 907-376-0565. E-mail: togowoods@matnet.com. World Wide Web: http://www.girlscouts.ak.org. Application deadline: continuous.

KATMAILAND INC.
4550 AIRCRAFT DRIVE
ANCHORAGE, ALASKA 99502

General Information Katmailand Inc. operates three lodges and a restaurant in Katmail National Park. Established in 1949. 4-acre facility located 30 miles from King Salmon. Features: wooded setting; photography; hiking; kayaking; fishing; scenic mountains.

Profile of Summer Employees Total number: 58; typical ages: 22–38. 70% men; 30% women; 85% college students; 15% local applicants.

Employment Information Openings are from May 20 to September 20. Jobs available: ▶ *administrators/auditors/front desk staff* with extensive bookkeeping experience; responsibilities include: front desk operation, customer service, cash handling, credit cards, and ten key and typing 40 wpm ▶ *assistant chef/head chef* must assist in prep work, baking, stocking, cleaning, and other assigned tasks ▶ *auditor* ▶ *bartender* ▶ *bus drivers* (minimum age 25) must have Commercial Driver's License allowing operation of school bus with multiple passengers, good communication skills, and good physical condition ▶ *dishwasher* ▶ *driver/laborers* (minimum age 25) responsibilities include cleaning of facility, float planes, dumping garbage daily, greeting guests at airport or pier, loading luggage; must have customer service skills and Commercial Driver's License ▶ *head maintenance* must have knowledge of carpentry, plumbing, and welding skills; requires well rounded background ▶ *house supervisor* oversees housekeeping, bartender, and storekeeper ▶ *housekeepers* must clean guest's cabins, do laundry, wait tables during meal hours, bus tables, help in kitchen, and have ability to lift 40 pounds ▶ *inn keeper* must oversee all kitchen operations, including ordering, inventory, quality control, special diet requests; clean guest cabins, wait tables, and bus ▶ *sport fishing guides* with extensive fishing experience, knowledge of fly-fishing, casting, trolling, fly-tying, and spin fishing, boat handling skills and maintenance experience. Must have OUPC six pack license and three years Alaska guiding experience ▶ *storekeeper* responsibilities include: inventory control, pricing, stocking, display, daily reports, balancing cash, and being in charge of rental equipment. Should have knowledge of fishing. Applicants must submit a formal organization application, three personal references, three letters of recommendation. International applicants accepted; must obtain own visa, obtain own working papers. A telephone interview is required.

Benefits and Preemployment Training Free housing, free meals, and airfare from Anchorage to Lodge. Preemployment training is required and includes accident prevention and safety, first aid, CPR.

Contact Michael Cruz, Brooks Lodge Manager, Katmailand Inc., 4550 Aircraft Drive, Anchorage, Alaska 99502. E-mail: jobinfo@katmailand.com. World Wide Web: http://www.katmailand.com. Application deadline: continuous.

LONGACRE EXPEDITIONS, ALASKA
ALASKA

General Information Adventure travel program emphasizing group living skills and physical challenges. Using base camp as a staging area, 2–3 staffers and 10–14 campers participate in advanced expeditions on which they engage in human-powered sports. Established in 1981. near Sitka.

Profile of Summer Employees Total number: 2; typical ages: 21–35. 50% men; 50% women; 10% minorities; 40% college students; 30% local applicants. Nonsmokers required.

Employment Information Openings are from June 15 to August 1. Jobs available: ▶ 8 *assistant trip leaders* (minimum age 21) with good driving record, wildernes first aid, WFR, and CPR at $252–$300 per week ▶ 3 *support and logistics staff members* (minimum age 21) with good driving record, wilderness first aid or WFR, and CPR at $180–$300 per week. Applicants must submit a formal organization application, cover letter, resume, three personal references, letter(s) of recommendation. International applicants accepted; must obtain own visa, obtain own working papers. An in-person interview is recommended, but a telephone interview is acceptable.

Benefits and Preemployment Training Free housing, free meals, on-the-job training, and pro-deal purchase program. Preemployment training is required and includes accident prevention and safety, interpersonal skills, leadership skills.

Contact Meredith Schuler, Director, Longacre Expeditions, Alaska, RD 3, Box 106, Newport, Pennsylvania 17074. Telephone: 717-567-6790. Fax: 717-567-3955. E-mail: longacre@longacreexpeditions.com. World Wide Web: http://www.longacreexpeditions.com. Application deadline: continuous.

STUDENT CONSERVATION ASSOCIATION (SCA), ALASKA
See Student Conservation Association (SCA), New Hampshire on page 193 for complete description.

ARIZONA

ACE COMPUTER CAMP–ARIZONA
See ACE Computer Camp–Washington on page 307 for complete description.

A CHRISTIAN MINISTRY IN THE NATIONAL PARKS–ARIZONA
See A Christian Ministry in the National Parks–Massachussetts on page 138 for complete description.

ARAMARK LEISURE SERVICES
PO BOX 1597
PAGE, ARIZONA 86040

General Information Concessionaire at Glen Canyon Recreation Area operating all guest services at five marina locations on Lake Powell with hotel, restaurant, retail, and marina operations. Established in 1972. 1,000,000-acre facility located 127 miles from Flagstaff, USA. Features: 200-mile long lake; 2,000 miles of shore line; 5 resort locations; Colorado River rafting operation; proximity to Grand Canyon, Zion National Park, Bryce National Park, and Monument Valley.

Profile of Summer Employees Total number: 800; typical age: 18. 50% men; 50% women; 40% minorities; 20% high school students; 30% college students; 20% retirees; 5% non-U.S. citizens; 50% local applicants.

Employment Information Openings are from April 1 to November 1. Year-round positions also offered. Jobs available: ▶ 30 *boat cleaners* (minimum age 18) at $5.70 per hour ▶ 60 *boat rental agents* (minimum age 18) with computer and customer service skills at $6–$6.25 per hour ▶ 40 *cashiers* (minimum age 18-21 depending if alcohol is served) with previous cash handling experience at $5.70 per hour ▶ 20 *deckhands* (minimum age 18) at $5.70 per hour ▶ 20 *front desk staff* (minimum age 18) with computer and customer service skills at $5.75 per hour ▶ 20 *fuel attendants* (minimum age 18) at $5.70 per hour ▶ 30 *kitchen help* (minimum age 18) with previous cooking experience at $5.70–$7 per hour. Applicants must submit formal organization application. International applicants accepted; must obtain own visa, obtain own working papers, apply through a recognized agency. A telephone interview is required.

Benefits and Preemployment Training Housing at a cost, meals at a cost, possible full-time employment, on-the-job training, and houseboat vacation if complete employment agreement, retail discounts, free boat tours, free float trips on Colorado River, and discounts on boat rentals and fuel. Preemployment training is required and includes accident prevention and safety, first aid, CPR, interpersonal skills, leadership skills, customer service.

Contact Inta Bingham, Staffing and Placement Specialist, ARAMARK Leisure Services, PO Box 1597, Page, Arizona 86040. Telephone: 520-645-1081. Fax: 520-645-1016. E-mail: bingham-inta@aramark.com. World Wide Web: http://www.coolworks.com/showme//kpowell/. Application deadline: continuous.

GRAND CANYON NATIONAL PARK LODGES
PO BOX 699
GRAND CANYON, ARIZONA 86023

General Information National park concessioner providing all hotel, restaurant, retail, and transportation services on the south rim of the Grand Canyon. Established in 1903. 640-acre facility located 90 miles from Flagstaff. Features: Grand Canyon; San Francisco Peaks; Sedona/Red Rock Wilderness Area; Kendrick Mountain Wilderness Area; Lake Powell/NRA; Lake Havasu.

Profile of Summer Employees Total number: 1,220; typical ages: 18–42. 50% men; 50% women; 30% minorities; 20% college students; 20% retirees; 10% non-U.S. citizens; 30% local applicants.

Employment Information Openings are from March 2 to October 20. Year-round positions also offered. Jobs available: ▶ 15–25 *buspersons/lineservers* (minimum age 18) at $5.50 per hour ▶ 15–25 *cashiers* (minimum age 18) with experience cashiering in food service at $5.50 per hour ▶ 10–15 *cooks' helpers* (minimum age 18) with some food service experience at $5.50 per hour ▶ 15–25 *cooks-I,II,III* (minimum age 18) with a minimum of 6 months restaurant and cooking experience at $6–$10 per hour ▶ 50–60 *guest room attendants* (minimum age 18) at $5.50 per hour ▶ 10–15 *guest service agent* (minimum age 18) with hotel front desk or previous customer service experience at $5.68 per hour ▶ 10–12 *hosts/hostesses* (minimum age 15) with a minimum of 6 months restaurant experience at $5.50 per hour ▶ 30–40 *kitchen/utility person- nel* (minimum age 18) at $5.50 per hour ▶ 25–40 *retail clerks* (minimum age 18) with cashier and/or retail sales experience at $5.25 per hour. Applicants must submit formal organization application. International applicants accepted; must apply through a recognized agency. An in-person interview is recommended, but a telephone interview is acceptable.

Benefits and Preemployment Training Housing at a cost, meals at a cost, possible full-time employment, health insurance, names of contacts, on-the-job training, opportunity to attend seminars/workshops, and living in a National Park.

Contact Nick Marcovecchio, Assistant Director Human Resources, Grand Canyon National Park Lodges. Telephone: 520-638-2812. Fax: 520-638-0143. Application deadline: continuous.

ORME SUMMER CAMP
HC 63, BOX 3040
MAYER, ARIZONA 86333

General Information Residential coed camp serving up to 200 campers with a wide variety of indoor and outdoor activities, including mountain biking, horseback riding, and desert survival/ rock climbing. Established in 1929. 40,000-acre facility located 70 miles from Phoenix. Features: swimming pool; complete gymnasium with weight room; riflery range; high desert climate; 40,000 acres for horseback riding; fully equipped boarding school campus.

Profile of Summer Employees Total number: 45; typical ages: 19–24. 50% men; 50% women; 2% minorities; 10% high school students; 80% college students; 1% retirees; 18% non-U.S. citizens; 10% local applicants. Nonsmokers preferred.

Employment Information Openings are from June 1 to August 14. Jobs available: ▶ 5–10 *general counselors* (minimum age 19) with driver's license and some experience at $1000– $1100 per season ▶ 1–2 *horsemanship staff* (minimum age 21) with driver's license and extensive experience with horses and children at $1100–$1400 per season ▶ 1–2 *outdoor adventure/ survival instructors* (minimum age 21) with Outward Bound or NOLS completion or equivalent and driver's license at $1000–$1300 per season ▶ 1–2 *pool assistants* (minimum age 19) with WSI and lifeguard certification at $1000–$1100 per season ▶ 1 *riflery instructor* (minimum age 19) with driver's license and riflery safety courses at $1100–$1200 per season ▶ 1–3 *senior counselors* (minimum age 20) with one year of college completed, driver's license, and experi- ence working with children in camp setting at $1200–$1300 per season. Applicants must submit formal organization application, writing sample, three personal references, three letters of recommendation. International applicants accepted; must obtain own visa, obtain own working papers, apply through a recognized agency. A telephone interview is required.

Benefits and Preemployment Training Free housing, free meals, on-the-job training, and travel reimbursement. Preemployment training is required and includes accident prevention and safety, first aid, CPR, interpersonal skills, leadership skills.

Contact Doug Bartlett, Director, Orme Summer Camp, HC 63, Box 3040, Mayer, Arizona 86333. Telephone: 520-632-7601. Fax: 520-632-7605. E-mail: dbartlett@orme.k12.az.us. World Wide Web: http://www.ormecamp.org. Application deadline: February 15.

THE SOUTHWESTERN COMPANY, ARIZONA
See The Southwestern Company, Tennessee on page 284 for complete description.

STIVERS TEMPORARY PERSONNEL–ARIZONA
See Stivers Temporary Personnel–Illinois on page 103 for complete description.

STUDENT CONSERVATION ASSOCIATION (SCA), ARIZONA
See Student Conservation Association (SCA), New Hampshire on page 193 for complete description.

ARKANSAS

THE SOUTHWESTERN COMPANY, ARKANSAS
See The Southwestern Company, Tennessee on page 284 for complete description.

STUDENT CONSERVATION ASSOCIATION (SCA), ARKANSAS
See Student Conservation Association (SCA), New Hampshire on page 193 for complete description.

CALIFORNIA

ACE COMPUTER CAMP–CALIFORNIA
See ACE Computer Camp–Washington on page 307 for complete description.

A CHRISTIAN MINISTRY IN THE NATIONAL PARKS–CALIFORNIA
See A Christian Ministry in the National Parks–Massachussetts on page 138 for complete description.

ADVATECH PACIFIC, INC.
2015 PARK AVENUE, SUITE 8
REDLANDS, CALIFORNIA 92373
General Information Engineering and development firm specializing in support of aerospace and defense industries. Conducts engineering analysis and develops engineering applications software. Established in 1995. Located 60 miles from Los Angeles.

Profile of Summer Employees Total number: 20; typical ages: 21–24. 50% minorities; 100% college students. Nonsmokers required.

Employment Information Year-round positions also offered. Jobs available: ▶ 2–4 *engineering assistants* with engineering background with structures, design, or fluids at $10–$20 per hour ▶ 1–2 *marketing assistants* with excellent verbal and writing skills; multilingual desirable at $6–$10 per hour; commission is available ▶ 2–4 *programming assistants* with background in CTT, GUI, UNIX, and desire Motif at $10–$20 per hour. Applicants must submit resume. International applicants accepted; must obtain own working papers. An in-person interview is required.

Benefits and Preemployment Training Possible full-time employment and on-the-job training.

Contact Hong Lien, Administrator, Advatech Pacific, Inc., 2015 Park Avenue, Suite 8, Redlands, California 92373. Application deadline: continuous.

ADVENTURE CONNECTION, INC.
986 LOTUS ROAD
LOTUS, CALIFORNIA 95651

General Information River trips for children and adults ages 7 and up. Established in 1983. 25-acre facility located 45 miles from Sacramento. Features: river-side camp; volleyball court; hot tub.

Profile of Summer Employees Total number: 30; typical ages: 20–50. 50% men; 50% women; 20% minorities; 35% college students; 15% retirees; 10% non-U.S. citizens; 50% local applicants.

Employment Information Openings are from April 1 to October 15. Spring break positions also offered. Jobs available: ▶ 1 *food packer/ordering staff* (minimum age 18) with driver's license (noncommercial license acceptable); training provided at $7–$10 per hour ▶ 25 *river guides* (minimum age 18) with experience guiding or completion of guide school; first aid/CPR at $60–$110 per day. Applicants must submit a formal organization application, resume, personal reference, letter(s) of recommendation. International applicants accepted. An in-person interview is recommended, but a telephone interview is acceptable.

Benefits and Preemployment Training Free housing, formal training, on-the-job training, and opportunity to attend seminars/workshops. Preemployment training is required and includes accident prevention and safety, first aid, CPR, interpersonal skills, leadership skills, swiftwater rescue, natural and human history, interpretive training.

Contact Nate Rangel, President, Adventure Connection, Inc., PO Box 475, Coloma, California 95613. Telephone: 800-556-6060. Fax: 530-626-9268. E-mail: getwet@raftcalifornia.com. Application deadline: continuous.

AMERICAN RIVER TOURING ASSOCIATION
24000 CASA LOMA ROAD
GROVELAND, CALIFORNIA 95321

General Information Guided whitewater rafting trips throughout the western United States. Established in 1963. 125 miles from Sacramento. Features: wilderness outings; physically demanding activities; camping.

Profile of Summer Employees Total number: 50; typical ages: 23–28. 70% men; 30% women; 5% minorities; 50% college students; 20% local applicants. Nonsmokers preferred.

Employment Information Openings are from May 15 to September 15. Jobs available: ▶ 10 *river guides* (minimum age 18) with first aid and CPR certification at $420–$700 per week. Applicants must submit a formal organization application, cover letter.

Benefits and Preemployment Training Free housing.

Contact Steve Welch, General Manager, American River Touring Association, 24000 Casa Loma Road, Groveland, California 95321. Telephone: 209-962-7873. Fax: 209-962-4819. E-mail: arta-info@arta.org. World Wide Web: http://www.arta.org. Application deadline: March 15.

ANGELES GIRL SCOUT COUNCIL/CAMP OSITO-RANCHO
5057 WEST ADAMS, PO BOX 78001
LOS ANGELES, CALIFORNIA 90016

General Information Beautiful mountain setting at 7,500 foot elevation; 62nd year of operation; we emphasize the "girl is first" motto; rustic outdoor program with excellent Western horseback riding program. Established in 1937. 200-acre facility located 25 miles from San Bernardino. Features: rustic camp environment; equestrain center; pond/freshwater springs; high and low ropes; gorgeous meadows; heated swimming pool.

Profile of Summer Employees Total number: 50; typical ages: 18–45. 5% men; 95% women; 20% minorities; 12% high school students; 50% college students; 2% retirees; 4% non-U.S. citizens; 12% local applicants.

Employment Information Openings are from December 1 to July 30. Year-round positions also offered. Jobs available: ▶ 1 *archery specialist* (minimum age 18) with experience and knowledge of archery at $29–$36 per day ▶ 1 *assistant camp director* (minimum age 21) with prior experience in camping at $48–$58 per day ▶ 5 *cook* (minimum age 18) with experience in cooking for over 200 people, menu planning, and food ordering at $40–$50 per day ▶ 1 *food* *service director* (minimum age 18) with experience in cooking for over 200 people, menu planning, and food ordering at $50–$60 per day ▶ 1 *health services supervisor* (minimum age 21) with RN license preferred at $80–$98 per day ▶ 5 *lifeguards* (minimum age 18) with ARC certification at $29–$36 per day ▶ 1 *mountain bike specialist* (minimum age 18) with experience and knowledge with mountain biking at $29–$36 per day ▶ *nature specialist* (minimum age 18) with experience and knowledge of nature at $29–$36 per day ▶ 5 *riding assistants* (minimum age 18) with experience and knowledge with horses at $29–$36 per day ▶ 1 *riding director (Western)* (minimum age 21) with horse experience and knowledge at $42–$52 per day ▶ 5 *ropes course assistants* (minimum age 18) with prior experience at $29–$36 per day ▶ 1 *ropes course director* (minimum age 21) with prior experience at $42–$52 per day ▶ 1 *volunteer coordinator* (minimum age 21) with supervisory skills at $48–$50 per day ▶ 1 *waterfront director* (minimum age 21) with ARC lifeguard certification at $29–$36. Applicants must submit formal organization application, writing sample, three personal references. International applicants accepted; must apply through a recognized agency. An in-person interview is recommended, but a telephone interview is acceptable.

Benefits and Preemployment Training Free housing, free meals, formal training, possible full-time employment, names of contacts, on-the-job training, opportunity to attend seminars/workshops, and worker's compensation. Preemployment training is required and includes accident prevention and safety, first aid, CPR, interpersonal skills, leadership skills, risk managment, ACA standards, program areas, and food handling.

Contact Maureen Bond, Director of Outdoor Programs, Angeles Girl Scout Council/Camp Osito-Rancho, 5057 West Adams Boulevard, Box 78001, Los Angeles, California 90016. Telephone: 323-933-4700. Fax: 323-933-3527. E-mail: maureenbond@angeles.org. World Wide Web: http://www.angeles.org. Application deadline: continuous.

BAR 717 RANCH
STAR ROUTE, BOX 150
HAYFORK, CALIFORNIA 96041

General Information Coed ranch offering horsemanship, swimming, hiking, crafts, animal care, ranch work projects, pottery, and the teaching of responsibility. Established in 1930. 450-acre facility located 80 miles from Redding. Features: located on pristine river; surrounded by acres of pristine forest; barn with 25 horses; miles of trails for horseback riding and hikes; extensive crafts facility; large gardens.

Profile of Summer Employees Total number: 50; typical ages: 16–60. 50% men; 50% women; 10% minorities; 5% high school students; 90% college students; 5% retirees; 10% non-U.S. citizens; 10% local applicants. Nonsmokers required.

Employment Information Openings are from June 20 to September 1. Jobs available: ▶ 12 *counselors* (minimum age 18) with 2 years of college completed, lifesaving, and CPR at $190–$250 per week ▶ 8–12 *junior counselors* (minimum age 18) at $175–$185 per week ▶ 4 *kitchen staff members* (minimum age 16) at $175 per week. Applicants must submit formal organization application, two personal references. International applicants accepted; must obtain own visa, obtain own working papers, apply through a recognized agency. An in-person interview is recommended, but a telephone interview is acceptable.

Benefits and Preemployment Training Housing at a cost, meals at a cost, and on-the-job training. Preemployment training is required and includes accident prevention and safety, first aid, CPR, interpersonal skills, leadership skills.

Contact Kent Collard, Director, Bar 717 Ranch, Star Route Box 150, Hayfork, California 96041. Telephone: 530-628-5992. Fax: 530-628-5992. E-mail: bar717@aol.com. World Wide Web: http://camping.org/bar717.htm. Application deadline: May 15.

CALIFORNIA SUMMER LANGUAGE ADVENTURE
NCOE, 1015 KAISER ROAD
NAPA, CALIFORNIA 94558

General Information Summer language camp in Spanish, French, and German for children ages 6-14 in 1- and 2-week overnight sessions. 400-acre facility located 55 miles from Napa.

Features: geysers and hot springs; swimming pool; soccer field; arts and crafts building; cabins with attached bathrooms.

Profile of Summer Employees Total number: 25; typical ages: 18–29. 65% college students; 35% non-U.S. citizens. Nonsmokers required.

Employment Information Openings are from June 15 to August 14. Jobs available: ▶ 15–20 *camp counselors* (minimum age 18) with minimal international language skills at $200–$350 per week. Applicants must submit a formal organization application, two personal references. International applicants accepted; must obtain own visa, obtain own working papers. A telephone interview is required.

Benefits and Preemployment Training Free housing, free meals, and on-the-job training.

Contact Brian Dutcher, Director, California Summer Language Adventure, 281 Monte Vista Avenue, Napa, California 94559. Telephone: 707-259-1302. Fax: 707-259-1302. E-mail: briand@ napanet.net. World Wide Web: http://www.napanet.net/education/ncoe/CSLAcamp/index.html. Application deadline: continuous.

CAMP HARMON
16409 HIGHWAY 9 NORTH
BOULDER CREEK, CALIFORNIA 95006

General Information Residential camp serving physically and developmentally disabled children and adults. Work involves people with a wide range of disabilities, including the severely disabled. Established in 1964. 23-acre facility located 13 miles from Santa Cruz. Features: modern cabins; redwood forest; 1/2 hour from Pacific Ocean; 1½ hours from San Francisco; pool.

Profile of Summer Employees Total number: 55; typical ages: 18–30. 48% men; 52% women; 10% minorities; 2% high school students; 98% college students; 10% non-U.S. citizens; 30% local applicants. Nonsmokers required.

Employment Information Openings are from June 3 to August 23. Jobs available: ▶ *cabin counselors* (minimum age 18) with experience in personal care of individuals preferred at $180 per week. Applicants must submit formal organization application, cover letter, three personal references. International applicants accepted; must apply through a recognized agency. An in-person interview is recommended, but a telephone interview is acceptable.

Benefits and Preemployment Training Free housing, free meals, and on-the-job training. Preemployment training is required and includes accident prevention and safety, first aid, CPR, interpersonal skills, leadership skills, information about disabilities and care needs.

Contact Jane Carr, Camp Director, Camp Harmon, 430 West Grant Street, Healdsburg, California 95448. Telephone: 707-433-3530. E-mail: janecarres@aol.com.

CAMP JCA SHALOM
34342 MULHOLLAND HIGHWAY
MALIBU, CALIFORNIA 90265

General Information Residential Jewish camp offering a warm, supportive atmosphere for campers ages 7–17. Established in 1961. 135-acre facility located 40 miles from Los Angeles. Features: wooded setting in mountains; ropes course; swimming pool; archery range.

Profile of Summer Employees Total number: 60; typical age: 18. 50% men; 50% women; 10% minorities; 20% high school students; 78% college students; 10% non-U.S. citizens; 70% local applicants. Nonsmokers preferred.

Employment Information Openings are from June 16 to August 23. Spring break and winter break positions also offered. Jobs available: ▶ 1 *Jewish education director* (minimum age 21) with knowledge of Jewish traditions, culture, history, and entertainment, as well as the ability to develop and lead camp-wide programs, including all-day Shabbat programs at $1000–$3000 per season ▶ 1–5 *bus drivers* (minimum age 18) with current Class B California driver's license and a clean driving record (knowledge of mountain driving extremely helpful) at $1000–$3000 per season ▶ 40–60 *counselors* (minimum age 18) at $1000–$3000 per season ▶ 1–4 *registered nurses* with RN and ability to run the infirmary, supervise nurse's aide, and interact well with parents at $1000–$3000 per season ▶ 1 *ropes course leader* (minimum age 21) with ability to lead groups through high and low elements at $1000–$3000 per season ▶ 1 *song leader* with ability to lead camp-wide singing of American and Hebrew folk songs, highly spirited nature, and guitar-playing skills at $1000–$3000 per season ▶ 5 *swimming and water safety instructors* with CPR, ALS, and WSI certifications at $1000–$3000 per season ▶ 2 *teen travel leaders* (minimum age 21) with college degree, knowledge of outdoors (experience with children essential), and current first aid and CPR certification at $1000–$3000 per season ▶ 3–4 *unit heads* (minimum age 21) with college degree, three years of camping experience, and good Jewish program skills (graduate training or social work experience helpful) at $1000–$3000 per season. Applicants must submit formal organization application, three personal references, three letters of recommendation. International applicants accepted; must apply through a recognized agency. An in-person interview is recommended, but a telephone interview is acceptable.

Benefits and Preemployment Training Free housing and on-the-job training.

Contact Mr. David Kaplan, Administrative Director, Camp JCA Shalom, 34342 Mulholland Highway, Malibu, California 90265. Telephone: 818-889-5500. Fax: 818-889-5132. World Wide Web: http://www.shalominstitute.com. Application deadline: continuous.

CAMP LA JOLLA
10050 NORTH TORREY PINES ROAD
LA JOLLA, CALIFORNIA 92037

General Information Weight-loss/fitness camp for ages 8 and older serving separate age and gender groups in fitness, sports, nutrition, behavior modification, field trips, beach visits, theater arts and arts and crafts; emphasis on healthy lifestyle. Established in 1979. 50-acre facility located 10 miles from San Diego. Features: beachside location; numerous athletic fields; outdoor swimming pool; 35 million dollar workout facility; university dormitories- suite style; located in La Jolla.

Profile of Summer Employees Total number: 86. 20% men; 80% women; 25% minorities; 5% high school students; 95% college students; 30% local applicants. Nonsmokers required.

Employment Information Openings are from June 13 to August 20. Jobs available: ▶ *aerobics instructors* at $900–$1600 per season ▶ 3 *behavior modification specialists* at $900–$1600 per season ▶ 15 *counselors* at $900–$1600 per season ▶ 10 *exercise specialists* with WSI and lifeguard certification at $900–$1600 per season ▶ 2 *nurses* with RN, EMT, or LPN license at $2000–$2600 per season ▶ 3 *nutritionists* at $900–$1600 per season ▶ 10 *personal trainers* at $900–$1600 per season ▶ *tennis instructors* at $900–$1600 per season. Applicants must submit a formal organization application, personal reference, letter of recommendation. An in-person interview is recommended, but a telephone interview is acceptable.

Benefits and Preemployment Training Free housing, free meals, on-the-job training, and internship opportunities available. Preemployment training is required and includes accident prevention and safety, first aid, interpersonal skills, leadership skills.

Contact Nancy Lenhart, Director, Camp La Jolla, 176 C Avenue, Coronado, California 92118. Telephone: 800-825-8746. Fax: 619-435-8188. E-mail: camplj@aol.com. World Wide Web: http://www.camplajolla.com. Application deadline: June 1.

CAMP SCHERMAN
PO BOX 8-N, TRAILS END
MOUNTAIN CENTER, CALIFORNIA 92561

General Information Residential Girl Scout camp serving more than 2,500 girls per season. 700-acre facility located 50 miles from Palm Springs. Features: 2 small lakes; high desert chaparral; cabins and platform tents; junior Olympic-size pool.

Profile of Summer Employees Total number: 90; typical ages: 18–25. 5% men; 95% women; 13% minorities; 90% college students; 5% non-U.S. citizens; 5% local applicants. Nonsmokers preferred.

Employment Information Openings are from June 14 to August 21. Year-round positions also offered. Jobs available: ▶ 3 *administrative staff* (minimum age 21) with supervisory skills at $3068 per season ▶ 3 *assistant nurses* (minimum age 21) with RN license at $4720 per season ▶ 2 *awareness aide staff members* (minimum age 18) should have experience working with campers with disabilities at $1770 per season ▶ 1 *boating director* (minimum age 18, 21 preferred) with lifeguard training, first aid, and CPR for professional certification waterfront module at $2065 per season ▶ 5 *boating staff members* (minimum age 18) with lifeguard training, first aid, and CPR for professional certification waterfront module at $1829 per season ▶ 1 *counselor-in-training assistant director* (minimum age 18) at $1829 per season ▶ 1 *counselor-in-training director* (minimum age 18, 21 preferred) at $2006 per season ▶ 8 *kitchen staff members* (minimum age 18) at $2714 per season ▶ 1 *pack-out cook* (minimum age 18) at $2832 per season ▶ 4 *program assistants* (minimum age 18) with skills in nature, arts and crafts, archery, and rock climbing at $1770 per season ▶ 4 *program directors* (minimum age 18, 21 preferred) with leadership ability; skills and experience in nature, arts and crafts, or archery at $1947 per season ▶ 5 *riding assistants* (minimum age 18) with experience at $1829 per season ▶ 1 *rock climbing director* (minimum age 21) with experience in rock climbing and teaching rock climbing (certification preferred) at $1947 per season ▶ 8 *staff supervisors* (minimum age 18, 21 preferred) with leadership ability at $1947 per season ▶ 28 *unit staff members* (minimum age 18) at $1770 per season ▶ 1 *waterfront director* (minimum age 18, 21 preferred) with lifeguard training, first aid, and CPR for professional certification waterfront module at $2065 per season ▶ 5 *waterfront staff members* (minimum age 18) with lifeguard training, first aid, and CPR for professional certification waterfront module at $1829 per season. Applicants must submit formal organization application, three personal references. International applicants accepted; must apply through a recognized agency. An in-person interview is recommended, but a telephone interview is acceptable.

Benefits and Preemployment Training Free housing, free meals, formal training, and on-the-job training. Preemployment training is required and includes accident prevention and safety, first aid, CPR, interpersonal skills, leadership skills.

Contact Mimi Askew, Camp Director, Camp Scherman, PO Box 3739, Costa Mesa, California 92628-3739. Telephone: 714-979-7900 Ext. 350. Fax: 714-850-1299. E-mail: gscoc@juno.com. Application deadline: continuous.

CAMP WASEWAGAN
42121 SEVEN OAKS ROAD
ANGELUS OAKS, CALIFORNIA 92305

General Information Residential camp serving weekly 150 campers from southern California. Established in 1936. 8-acre facility located 40 miles from Riverside. Features: wooded setting; numerous rustic buildings; location by river side.

Profile of Summer Employees Total number: 35; typical ages: 18–30. 50% men; 50% women; 45% minorities; 2% high school students; 80% college students; 15% non-U.S. citizens; 75% local applicants. Nonsmokers required.

Employment Information Openings are from June 22 to August 25. Jobs available: ▶ 1–2 *assistant cooks* (minimum age 18) with local food handler's permit at $1050–$1200 per season ▶ 1 *cook* (minimum age 18) with local food handler's permit at $1500 per season ▶ 1 *craft director* (minimum age 18) at $1000–$1200 per season ▶ 10 *general counselors* (minimum age 18) at $1000–$1200 per season ▶ 1 *nurse* (minimum age 21) with RN or LPN at $1500–$2200 per season ▶ 1 *outdoor specialist* (minimum age 18) at $1000–$1300 per season ▶ 4 *unit directors* (minimum age 18) at $950–$1500 per season ▶ 1 *waterfront assistant* (minimum age 18) with senior lifesaving, first aid, and CPR certification at $1000–$1600 per season ▶ 1 *waterfront director* (minimum age 21) with WSI, senior lifesaving, first aid, and CPR certification at $1500–$1600 per season. Applicants must submit formal organization application, three letters of recommendation. International applicants accepted; must apply through a recognized agency. An in-person interview is recommended, but a telephone interview is acceptable.

Benefits and Preemployment Training Free housing, free meals, formal training, and on-the-job training. Preemployment training is required and includes accident prevention and safety, first aid, CPR, interpersonal skills, leadership skills.

Contact Carl Pontius, Camp Manager, Camp Wasewagan, PO Box 418, Angelus Oaks, California 92305. Telephone: 909-794-2910. Fax: 909-794-8453. E-mail: campfire@artsci.net. World Wide Web: http://www.cwire.com/camp.fire/. Application deadline: continuous.

CATALINA ISLAND CAMPS
HOWLANDS LANDING
AVALON, CALIFORNIA 90704

General Information Private summer camp for children ages 7-15. Established in 1926. 27-acre facility located 26 miles from Los Angeles. Features: private ocean cove; Catalina Island; oceanfront property; skin diving; sailing; sea kayaking.

Profile of Summer Employees Total number: 75; typical ages: 20–25. 10% minorities; 10% high school students; 90% college students; 10% non-U.S. citizens; 10% local applicants.

Employment Information Openings are from June 14 to August 23. Year-round positions also offered. Jobs available: ▶ 35–40 *activity specialists* (minimum age 19) with first aid, CPR, and lifeguard (waterfront) certifications at $165–$180 per week ▶ 20 *cabin counselors* (minimum age 19) with first aid and CPR certification at $165–$180 per week. Applicants must submit formal organization application, two personal references, short answer question. International applicants accepted; must obtain own visa, apply through a recognized agency. An in-person interview is recommended, but a telephone interview is acceptable.

Benefits and Preemployment Training Free housing, free meals, formal training, on-the-job training, and opportunity to attend seminars/workshops. Preemployment training is required and includes accident prevention and safety, first aid, CPR, interpersonal skills, leadership skills, lifeguard.

Contact Brendan Gamb, Assistant Director, Catalina Island Camps, PO Box 94146, Pasadena, California 91109. Telephone: 800-696-CAMP. Fax: 626-794-1401. E-mail: jobs@ catalinaislandcamps.com. World Wide Web: http://www.catalinaislandcamps.com. Application deadline: continuous.

CUBIC CORPORATION
9333 BALBOA AVENUE
SAN DIEGO, CALIFORNIA 92123

General Information Cubic Corporation is a world leader in automated revenue collection and defense systems, head-quartered in San Diego. Established in 1951. 50-acre facility. Features: central location; fair salary; fair benefits; interesting work; world travel; fifty year old business.

Profile of Summer Employees Total number: 1,000; typical ages: 20–25. 60% men; 40% women; 35% minorities; 10% college students.

Employment Information Openings are from May 20 to September 1. Year-round positions also offered. Jobs available: ▶ *electrical engineering intern* must be a junior in college at $13–$17 per hour ▶ 1–5 *software engineering interns* must be a junior in college at $13–$17 per hour. Applicants must submit formal organization application, resume, academic transcripts, two personal references. An in-person interview is required.

Benefits and Preemployment Training Health insurance and on-the-job training. Preemployment training is required.

Contact Bob Stamp, Staffing Manager, Cubic Corporation, 9333 Balboa Avenue, San Diego, California 92123. Fax: 619-505-1524. World Wide Web: http://www.cubic.com. Application deadline: continuous.

DOUGLAS RANCH CAMPS
33200 EAST CARMEL VALLEY ROAD
CARMEL VALLEY, CALIFORNIA 93924

General Information Private, traditional, residential summer camp for 120 children ages 7–14. Structured program in horseback riding, swimming, archery, tennis, riflery, and crafts. Focus is on improving social skills, leadership, and confidence in a positive and fun environment. Established in 1925. 120-acre facility located 15 miles from Carmel. Features: large oval pool; central lodge and dining hall; 4 tennis courts; private hiking and riding trails; shady oak trees on hillside; 15 miles to ocean.

Profile of Summer Employees Total number: 45; typical ages: 19–24. 45% men; 55% women; 20% minorities; 85% college students; 5% retirees; 20% non-U.S. citizens; 20% local applicants. Nonsmokers required.

Employment Information Openings are from June 16 to August 28. Jobs available: ▶ 2–5 *archery instructors* (minimum age 18) with camp, school, or archery team experience and at least one year of college completed at $2250–$2550 per season ▶ 2–5 *crafts instructors* (minimum age 18) with experience working with children, teaching and/or experience with arts and crafts, and at least one year of college completed at $2250–$2550 per season ▶ 30–32 *general counselors* (minimum age 18) with experience working with children, general experience in at least 1 activity (riding, swimming, tennis, archery, riflery, crafts, ballsports); at least one year of college completed at $2250–$2550 per season ▶ 2–3 *kitchen assistants* (minimum age 18) with experience in general food preparation and dishwashing, and at least one year of college completed at $2250–$2550 per season ▶ 4–10 *riding instructors* (minimum age 18) with experience giving riding lessons, teaching children, riding, saddling, and/or general horse care; at least one year of college completed at $2250–$2550 per season ▶ 2–5 *riflery instructors* (minimum age 18) with camp, school, or riflery team experience and at least one year of college completed at $2250–$2550 per season ▶ 4–10 *swimming instructors* (minimum age 18) with WSI and/or lifeguard certification; experience on club or team, and at least one year of college completed at $2250–$2550 per season ▶ 2–5 *tennis instructors* (minimum age 18) with experience on tennis team, club, or in teaching and at least one year of college completed at $2250–$2550 per season. Applicants must submit formal organization application, two personal references, 4 telephone references/recommendations. International applicants accepted; must apply through a recognized agency. An in-person interview is recommended, but a telephone interview is acceptable.

Benefits and Preemployment Training Free housing, free meals, formal training, health insurance, on-the-job training, and CPR and first aid certification. Preemployment training is required and includes accident prevention and safety, first aid, CPR, interpersonal skills, leadership skills, child psychology and development, team building.

Contact Mrs. Kristen Smith, Assistant Director, Douglas Ranch Camps, 6114 LaSalle Avenue, Box 539, Piedmont, California 94611. Telephone: 510-339-2706. Fax: 510-339-1932. E-mail: director@douglascamp.com. World Wide Web: http://www.douglascamp.com. Application deadline: continuous.

DRAKESBAD GUEST RANCH
END OF WARNER VALLEY ROAD
CHESTER, CALIFORNIA 96020

General Information Rustic guest ranch in the heart of Lassen Volcanic National Park. Established in 1974. 100-acre facility located 120 miles from Reno, Nevada. Features: National Park setting; hot spring pool; horse stable; no electricity or television; hiking trails; fishing stream.

Profile of Summer Employees Total number: 22; typical ages: 20–26. 15% men; 85% women; 10% minorities; 80% college students; 10% retirees; 40% non-U.S. citizens; 20% local applicants. Nonsmokers preferred.

Employment Information Openings are from June 1 to October 15. Jobs available: ▶ 5–6 *housekeepers/groundskeepers/waitstaff/children's program staff/kitchen maintenance* (minimum age 18) with knowledge of childrens games and crafts at $5–$7 per hour ▶ 1–2 *kitchen help/food staff* (minimum age 18) at $5–$6 per hour ▶ 1 *kitchen maintenance staff* (minimum age 18) at $5–$6 per hour ▶ 1 *maintenance/groundskeeper* (minimum age 18) with technical skills at $6–$7 per hour ▶ 3–4 *waitstaff* (minimum age 18) at $5–$6 per hour ▶ *wrangler* (minimum age 21) with first aid and CPR certification; 5 years horsemanship, 2 years stable hand experience at $6–$7 per hour. Applicants must submit cover letter, resume, photograph, e-mail address, preference for website application. International applicants accepted; must apply through a recognized agency. An in-person interview is recommended, but a telephone interview is acceptable.

Benefits and Preemployment Training Housing at a cost, meals at a cost, and on-the-job training. Preemployment training is required and includes accident prevention and safety, CPR.

Contact Ed Fiebiger, Ranch Host, Drakesbad Guest Ranch, 2150 North Main Street, Red Bluff, California 96080. Telephone: 530-529-9820. Fax: 530-529-4511. E-mail: billie@goldrush.com.

World Wide Web: http://members.xoom.com/drakesbad/employment.htm. Application deadline: April 15.

EMANDAL–A FARM ON A RIVER
16500 HEARST ROAD
WILLITS, CALIFORNIA 95490

General Information Coeducational residential camp for 70 youngsters ages 6–16 for the first half of the summer; a family vacation farm for 45–55 people of all ages for the second half. Established in 1965. 1,000-acre facility located 160 miles from San Francisco. Features: wild river; farm; organic garden; oaks, firs, madrones; home-made bread; rustic cabins.

Profile of Summer Employees Total number: 30; typical ages: 18–30. 50% men; 50% women; 1% minorities; 15% high school students; 50% college students; 1% retirees; 10% non-U.S. citizens; 20% local applicants. Nonsmokers required.

Employment Information Openings are from June 7 to September 7. Jobs available: ▶ 15–22 *camp counselors (June-July)* (minimum age 18) at $1000 per season ▶ 3–6 *environmental education naturalists (March-June)* (minimum age 21) at $190 per week ▶ 8 *family camp workers (July-August)* (minimum age 16) at $190 per week ▶ 2 *farm workers (until Thanksgiving)* (minimum age 20) at $190 per week ▶ *gardener's apprentice (volunteer from April-November)* ▶ 2 *gardeners (entire summer)* (minimum age 22) at $190 per week ▶ 1 *pickle maker (August-October)* (minimum age 20) at $190 per week. Applicants must submit a formal organization application, two personal references. International applicants accepted; must obtain own working papers. A telephone interview is required.

Benefits and Preemployment Training Free housing, free meals, formal training, health insurance, on-the-job training, and opportunity to attend seminars/workshops. Preemployment training is required and includes accident prevention and safety, first aid, CPR, interpersonal skills, leadership skills.

Contact Tamara Adams, Director, Emandal–A Farm on a River, 16500 Hearst Road, Willits, California 95490. Telephone: 707-459-5439. Fax: 707-459-1808. E-mail: emandal@pacific.net. World Wide Web: http://www.emandal.com. Application deadline: April 1.

GOLD ARROW CAMP
HUNTINGTON LAKE, CALIFORNIA 93634

General Information Private residential camp for boys and girls ages 6–14. Established in 1933. 27-acre facility located 65 miles from Fresno. Features: freshwater lake; creek; Sierra National Forest; island outpost camp.

Profile of Summer Employees Total number: 100; typical ages: 19–25. 55% men; 45% women; 10% minorities; 80% college students; 5% retirees; 10% non-U.S. citizens; 15% local applicants. Nonsmokers required.

Employment Information Openings are from June 20 to August 28. Jobs available: ▶ 30–33 *activity counselors* (minimum age 19) with CPR (lifeguard certification for waterfront postitions) at $1658 per season, plus room and board ▶ 30–32 *group counselors* (minimum age 19) with CPR certification at $1658 per season, plus room and board ▶ 2–10 *kitchen staff* (minimum age 19) at $200–$225 per week ▶ 2–5 *maintenance staff/drivers* (minimum age 21) with class B commercial driver's license at $200–$225 per week. Applicants must submit formal organization application, two personal references, two letters of recommendation. International applicants accepted; must apply through a recognized agency. An in-person interview is recommended, but a telephone interview is acceptable.

Benefits and Preemployment Training Free housing, free meals, formal training, opportunity to attend seminars/workshops, and travel reimbursement. Preemployment training is required and includes accident prevention and safety, first aid, interpersonal skills, leadership skills.

Contact Steven Monke, Director, Gold Arrow Camp, 2900 Bristol Street, Suite A-107, Costa Mesa, California 92626. Telephone: 800-554-2267. Fax: 714-424-0844. E-mail: mail@ goldarrowcamp.com. World Wide Web: http://www.goldarrowcamp.com. Application deadline: continuous.

HUNEWILL GUEST RANCH
TWIN LAKES ROAD
BRIDGEPORT, CALIFORNIA 93517

General Information Guest ranch accommodating 45–55 guests weekly. Established in 1931. 4,800-acre facility located 120 miles from Reno, Nevada. Features: lush mountain meadows; surrounding mountains; mountain lakes nearby; 130 horses; 26 rooms; Victorian-style ranch house and dining room.

Profile of Summer Employees Total number: 20; typical ages: 18–25. 25% men; 75% women; 5% high school students; 85% college students; 10% local applicants. Nonsmokers required.

Employment Information Openings are from May 15 to October 1. Jobs available: ▶ 1 *breakfast/pastry chef* with experience baking for groups at $1400 per month ▶ 3 *cabin staff members* (minimum age 18) with ability to work quickly and eye for neatness at $290–$350 per week ▶ 1 *cook* with cooking experience or cooking school certification at $1400–$1700 per month ▶ 1 *gardener* (minimum age 18) with experience with lawn mowers, some landscaping, and an aptitude for gardening at $290–$350 per week ▶ 1 *maintenance person* (minimum age 18) with general plumbing, electrical, and carpentry ability, including fence building and some work with livestock at $290–$350 per week ▶ 4 *waiters/waitresses* (minimum age 18) with experience at $325–$395 per week ▶ 3–6 *wranglers* (minimum age 18) with extensive horse experience and good people skills at $1000–$1300 per month. Applicants must submit resume, three personal references, three letters of recommendation. A telephone interview is required.

Benefits and Preemployment Training Meals at a cost, free housing, and on-the-job training.

Contact Betsy Hunewill Elliott, Assistant Manager, Hunewill Guest Ranch, 205 Hunewill Lane, Wellington, Nevada 89444. Telephone: 702-465-2238. Application deadline: May 15.

THE INSTITUTE FOR THE ACADEMIC ADVANCEMENT OF YOUTH/THE JOHNS HOPKINS UNIVERSITY–LOYOLA MARYMOUNT UNIVERSITY
See The Institute for the Academic Advancement of Youth/ The Johns Hopkins University on page 135 for complete description.

THE INSTITUTE FOR THE ACADEMIC ADVANCEMENT OF YOUTH/THE JOHNS HOPKINS UNIVERSITY–OCEAN CAMP
See The Institute for the Academic Advancement of Youth/ The Johns Hopkins University on page 135 for complete description.

THE INSTITUTE FOR THE ACADEMIC ADVANCEMENT OF YOUTH/THE JOHNS HOPKINS UNIVERSITY–STANFORD UNIVERSITY
See The Institute for the Academic Advancement of Youth/ The Johns Hopkins University on page 135 for complete description.

THE INSTITUTE FOR THE ACADEMIC ADVANCEMENT OF YOUTH/THE JOHNS HOPKINS UNIVERSITY–UNIVERSITY OF CALIFORNIA, SANTA CRUZ
See The Institute for the Academic Advancement of Youth/ The Johns Hopkins University on page 135 for complete description.

JAMESON RANCH CAMP
GLENNVILLE, CALIFORNIA 93226

General Information Jameson Ranch Camp connects children to a self-sufficient ranch lifestyle where campers grow some of the food and help with the farm animals. Established in 1934. 520-acre facility located 40 miles from Bakersfield.

Profile of Summer Employees Total number: 30. 50% men; 50% women; 20% minorities; 90% college students; 5% retirees; 10% non-U.S. citizens; 5% local applicants. Nonsmokers required.

Employment Information Openings are from June 20 to September 5. Jobs available: ▶ 1 *archery instructor* (minimum age 19) with archery experience at $2300 per season ▶ 2 *crafts instructors* (minimum age 19) with crafts or art experience at $2300 per season ▶ 1 *drama instructor* (minimum age 19) with some theater background at $2300 per season ▶ 1 *head cook* (minimum age 21) with experience in the field at $3300 per season ▶ 2 *horse instructors* (minimum age 19) with Western riding and bareback riding experience at $2300 per season ▶ 1 *horse vaulting instructor* (minimum age 19) with some horse vaulting experience at $2300 per season ▶ 2 *kitchen persons* (minimum age 19) with some food service experience at $2300 per season ▶ 4 *lifeguards* (minimum age 19) with ALS certification or equivalent at $2300 per season ▶ 1 *mountain biking instructor* (minimum age 19) with good technique in mountain biking and bike maintenance skills required at $2300 per season ▶ 1 *photography instructor* (minimum age 19) with darkroom and photo composition experience required at $2300 per season ▶ 1 *riflery instructor* (minimum age 19) with riflery and hunter's safety experience at $2300 per season ▶ 1 *rock climbing instructor* (minimum age 19) with technical expertise and extensive climbing experience at $2300 per season ▶ 2 *swimming instructors* (minimum age 19) with WSI certification at $2300 per season. Applicants must submit formal organization application, cover letter, resume, four personal references. International applicants accepted; must obtain own visa, apply through a recognized agency. An in-person interview is recommended, but a telephone interview is acceptable.

Benefits and Preemployment Training Free housing, free meals, formal training, and on-the-job training. Preemployment training is required and includes accident prevention and safety, interpersonal skills, leadership skills.

Contact Ross Jameson, Owner/Director, Jameson Ranch Camp, PO Box 459, Glennville, California 93226. Telephone: 661-536-8888. Fax: 661-536-8896. E-mail: thejamesons@ jamesonranchcamp.com. World Wide Web: http://www.jamesonranchcamp.com. Application deadline: continuous.

LOS ANGELES DESIGNERS' THEATRE
BOX 1883
STUDIO CITY, CALIFORNIA 91614-0883

General Information Summer theater that produces stage productions and teaches theatrical producing, including the legal aspects of production. Established in 1970.

Profile of Summer Employees Total number: 100. 50% men; 50% women; 20% minorities; 15% high school students; 30% college students; 2% retirees; 35% local applicants. Nonsmokers required.

Employment Information Openings are from January 1 to December 31. Jobs available: ▶ *actors and actresses* salary per show negotiable with experience ▶ 1 *box office/house manager* salary per show negotiable ▶ 3–5 *carpenters* salary per show negotiable with experience ▶ 1 *choreographer* salary per show negotiable with experience ▶ 1–6 *costume designers* salary per show/production negotiable with experience ▶ 4–6 *crew members* salary per show negotiable ▶ 2–3 *cutters/drapers (first hands)* salary per show/per costume negotiable with experience ▶ 6 *directors* with experience; salary per show/production negotiable ▶ 2–4 *electricians* salary per show negotiable with experience ▶ 1–6 *lighting designers* salary per show/production negotiable with experience ▶ 1 *musical director* salary per show negotiable with experience ▶ *production assistants* ▶ 1 *program/graphics designer* salary per image negotiable ▶ 1–6 *property designers* with salary per show/production negotiable ▶ 1–6 *set designers* salary per show/production negotiable with experience ▶ *singers and dancers* salary per show negotiable with experience ▶ 1–6 *sound designers* salary per show/production negotiable with experience. Applicants must submit a cover letter, portfolio.

Benefits and Preemployment Training Names of contacts and on-the-job training.

Contact Richard Niederberg, Artistic Director, Los Angeles Designers' Theatre, PO Box 1883, Department P98, Studio City, California 91614-0883. Telephone: 213-650-9600. Fax: 818-985-9200. E-mail: ladesigners@juno.com. Application deadline: continuous.

RESORT AT SQUAW CREEK
PO BOX 3333
OLYMPIC VALLEY, CALIFORNIA 96146

General Information 405 room luxury resort and conference center with 5 restaurants, 33,000 square feet of conference space, and championship 18-hole golf course located on scenic Lake Tahoe. Established in 1990. 400-acre facility located 40 miles from Reno, Nevada. Features: 2 tennis courts; 3 pools and 3 spas; health and fitness center; located in Squaw Valley, home of the 1960 Winter Olympics.

Profile of Summer Employees Total number: 600; typical ages: 22–30. 60% men; 40% women; 30% minorities; 30% college students; 5% retirees; 15% local applicants.

Employment Information Openings are from April 15 to October 15. Winter break and year-round positions also offered. Jobs available: ▶ 3–10 *banquet servers* (minimum age 21) at $5.75 per hour plus gratuities; with 3 years serving experience at $5.75 per hour ▶ 3–5 *bartenders* (minimum age 21) at $6.25 per hour plus gratuities with at least 2 years bartending experience ▶ 3–5 *bike and tennis attendants* (minimum age 18) with knowledge of tennis and bicycles and customer service experience at $7 per hour ▶ 3–10 *bussers* (minimum age 18) at $5.75 per hour plus gratuities; with restaurant experience ▶ 3–5 *deli attendants* (minimum age 21) with food service experience at $7 per hour ▶ 5–15 *food servers* (minimum age 21) with 2 years serving experience at $5.75 ▶ 5–10 *greenskeepers* (minimum age 21) with some English skills and greenskeeping/landscaping experience preferred at $7 per hour ▶ 3–7 *greeters* (minimum age 21) at $6.75 per hour plus gratuities with restaurant experience ▶ 3–5 *landscapers* (minimum age 18) with some English skills and landscaping experience preferred at $7 per hour ▶ 2–5 *lifeguards* (minimum age 18) with lifeguard certification and experience preferred at $7 per hour ▶ 3–8 *line cooks* (minimum age 18) with culinary experience; culinary institute student or graduate preferred at $8 per hour ▶ 2–5 *mountain buddies attendants* (minimum age 18) with clean criminal record and experience with children at $7 per hour ▶ 1–3 *pantry cooks* (minimum age 18) with culinary experience at $7 per hour ▶ 2–4 *retail sales associates* (minimum age 18) with cash handling experience at $7 per hour ▶ 5–10 *room attendants* (minimum age 18) with some English skills and housekeeping experience preferred at $7.75 per hour ▶ 1–2 *security officers* (minimum age 21) with first aid certification and security experience preferred at $8 per hour ▶ 5–10 *shuttle drivers* (minimum age 21) at $7 per hour plus gratuities; with CA driver's license class B at $7 per hour ▶ 1–4 *stewards* (minimum age 18) with some English and willingness to do physical work at $7 per hour ▶ 1–3 *telephone operators* (minimum age 18) with customer service experience and pleasant, professional demeanor at $7 per hour. Applicants must submit formal organization application, three personal references, two professional references. International applicants accepted; must apply through a recognized agency. An in-person interview is required.

Benefits and Preemployment Training Free meals, possible full-time employment, on-the-job training, and extensive discounts (retail, restaurant, golf).

Contact Paula Wickstrom, Human Resources Manager, Resort at Squaw Creek, PO Box 3333, Olympic Valley, California 96146. E-mail: squawcreek@thegrid.net. World Wide Web: http://www.squawcreek.com. Application deadline: continuous.

SANTA CATALINA SCHOOL SUMMER CAMP
1500 MARK THOMAS DRIVE
MONTEREY, CALIFORNIA 93940

General Information Residential and day camp for girls ages 8–14 with an emphasis on performing and fine arts and athletics. Established in 1953. 35-acre facility located 90 miles from San Jose. Features: 6 tennis courts; heated swimming pool; modern dormitories; library; weight room; computer labs.

Profile of Summer Employees Total number: 50; typical ages: 20–35. 10% minorities; 40% college students; 1% retirees; 60% local applicants. Nonsmokers required.

Employment Information Openings are from June 15 to July 26. Jobs available: ▶ 14 *counselors* (minimum age 18) with one year of college completed at $1000–$1300 per season ▶ 6 *head counselors* (minimum age 18) with two years of college completed and experience in the field at

$1100–$1400 per season. Applicants must submit a formal organization application, two letters of recommendation. A telephone interview is required.

Benefits and Preemployment Training Free housing, free meals, and on-the-job training. Preemployment training is required and includes accident prevention and safety, first aid, CPR, interpersonal skills, leadership skills.

Contact Mrs. Stephanie Zalin, Director of Summer Programs, Santa Catalina School Summer Camp, 1500 Mark Thomas Drive, Monterey, California 93940. Telephone: 408-655-9386. Fax: 408-649-3056. E-mail: summercamp@scs.monterey.ca.us. World Wide Web: http://www.santacatalina.org. Application deadline: continuous.

SARATOGA SPRINGS PICNIC, CAMPGROUNDS, AND DAY CAMP
22801 BIG BASIN HIGHWAY
SARATOGA, CALIFORNIA 95070

General Information Full-service corporate picnic facility serving 50-2000 guests daily. Our services include catering, beverages, an entertainment package, and a summer camp serving children ages 7-12. Established in 1972. 14-acre facility located 10 miles from San Jose. Features: wooded setting; 2 year-round streams; fabulous barbequed food; RV and tent campsites; 6 private picnic groves; general store/arcade.

Profile of Summer Employees Total number: 40–50; typical ages: 14–60. 25% minorities; 60% high school students; 15% college students; 5% retirees; 95% local applicants.

Employment Information Openings are from May 31 to October 31. Jobs available: ▶ *barbecue cook* (minimum age 18) at $8–$8.75 per hour ▶ *cook/beverage assistant* (minimum age 16) at $5.75–$6.50 per hour ▶ 1 *day camp director* (minimum age 21) at $375 per week ▶ 8 *day camp leaders* (minimum age 16) at $250 per week ▶ 1 *day camp program manager* (minimum age 18) at $325 per week ▶ 1 *lifeguard supervisor* (minimum age 18) with supervisory experience; 2 years lifeguarding experience; certifications at $9.50–$11 per hour ▶ 4–8 *lifeguards* (minimum age 16) with lifeguard certification at $7.50–$9 per hour ▶ 5–10 *maintenance/parking attendant* (minimum age 16) at $5.75–$6.50 per hour ▶ 10–15 *recreation leaders* (minimum age 14) at $5.75–$7 per hour ▶ 2–4 *recreation supervisors* (minimum age 16) at $8–$9.50 per hour ▶ 2–4 *store clerks* (minimum age 18) at $6.50–$8 per hour. Applicants must submit a formal organization application. An in-person interview is required.

Benefits and Preemployment Training Free meals and formal training. Preemployment training is required and includes first aid, CPR, training is only available for certain positions.

Contact Kindy Benson, Recreation Director, Saratoga Springs Picnic, Campgrounds, and Day Camp. Telephone: 408-867-3016. Fax: 408-867-0766. E-mail: daycamp@saratoga-springs.com. World Wide Web: http://www.saratoga-springs.com. Application deadline: continuous.

SIERRA SERVICE PROJECT
5856 COLLEGE AVENUE, SUITE 147
OAKLAND, CALIFORNIA 94618

General Information United Methodist-related service organization offering a Christian service learning program to church youth groups and home repair work to Native American communities. Established in 1975. Features: school or church locations; rural; some desert locations; some lake-side locations.

Profile of Summer Employees Total number: 28; typical ages: 19–55. 50% men; 50% women; 7% minorities; 75% college students. Nonsmokers required.

Employment Information Openings are from June 19 to August 18. Jobs available: ▶ *chefs* (minimum age 19) at $1400–$1600 per season ▶ 4–8 *construction supervisors* (minimum age 19) with youth ministry experience and ability to teach at $2000–$2600 per season ▶ 4 *program directors/spiritual life directors* (minimum age 19) with youth ministry experience and program creation experience at $2000–$2200 per season ▶ 8 *supply coordinators* (minimum age 19) at $1400–$1600 per season. Applicants must submit a formal organization application, three personal references. A telephone interview is required.

Benefits and Preemployment Training Free housing, free meals, formal training, and on-the-job training. Preemployment training is required and includes accident prevention and safety, first aid, CPR, interpersonal skills, leadership skills.

Contact Executive Director, Sierra Service Project, 5856 College Avenue, Suite 147, Oakland, California 94618. Telephone: 510-531-1325. Fax: 510-531-1985. E-mail: staffinfo@ sierraserviceproject.org. World Wide Web: http://www.sierraserviceproject.org. Application deadline: March 1.

THE SOUTHWESTERN COMPANY, CALIFORNIA
See The Southwestern Company, Tennessee on page 284 for complete description.

STIVERS TEMPORARY PERSONNEL–CALIFORNIA
See Stivers Temporary Personnel–Illinois on page 103 for complete description.

STUDENT CONSERVATION ASSOCIATION (SCA), CALIFORNIA
See Student Conservation Association (SCA), New Hampshire on page 193 for complete description.

SUMMER DISCOVERY AT UCLA
UNIVERSITY OF CALIFORNIA, LOS ANGELES
LOS ANGELES, CALIFORNIA 90024

General Information Precollege enrichment program for high school students at University of California, Los Angeles. Established in 1986. Features: sport facilities; beaches; mountains; lakes; major cities nearby; college towns.

Profile of Summer Employees Total number: 50; typical ages: 21–35. 10% minorities; 60% college students. Nonsmokers required.

Employment Information Openings are from June 20 to August 25. Jobs available: ▶ 50 *resident counselors* (minimum age 21) with experience working with high school students/children at $150 per week. Applicants must submit a formal organization application, resume, three personal references. International applicants accepted; must obtain own visa, obtain own working papers. An in-person interview is required.

Benefits and Preemployment Training Free housing, free meals, possible full-time employment, on-the-job training, and travel reimbursement. Preemployment training is required and includes accident prevention and safety, CPR, leadership skills.

Contact Jason Walley, Admissions Director, Summer Discovery at UCLA, 1326 Old Northern Boulevard, Roslyn, New York 11576. Telephone: 516-621-3939. Fax: 516-625-3438. E-mail: staff@summerfun.com. World Wide Web: http://www.summerfun.com. Application deadline: continuous.

SUMMER DISCOVERY AT UC SAN DIEGO
UNIVERSITY OF CALIFORNIA, SAN DIEGO
SAN DIEGO, CALIFORNIA 92092

General Information Precollege enrichment program for high school students at the University of California, San Diego. Established in 1998. Features: sport facilities; beaches; mountains; lakes; major cities nearby; college towns.

Profile of Summer Employees Typical ages: 21–35. 60% college students. Nonsmokers required.

Employment Information Openings are from June 20 to August 25. Jobs available: ▶ 20 *resident counselors* (minimum age 21) with experience working with high school students and children at $150–$400 per week. Applicants must submit a formal organization application, resume, three personal references. International applicants accepted; must obtain own visa, obtain own working papers. An in-person interview is required.

Benefits and Preemployment Training Free housing, free meals, possible full-time employment, and travel reimbursement. Preemployment training is required and includes accident prevention and safety, CPR, leadership skills.

Contact Jason Walley, Admissions Director, Summer Discovery at UC San Diego, 1326 Old

Northern Boulevard, Roslyn, New York 11576. Telephone: 516-621-3939. Fax: 516-625-3438. E-mail: staff@summerfun.com. World Wide Web: http://www.summerfun.com. Application deadline: continuous.

SUPERCAMP–CLAREMONT COLLEGES
CLAREMONT COLLEGES
CLAREMONT, CALIFORNIA 91711

General Information Residential program for teens that includes life skills and academic courses designed to build self-confidence and lifelong learning skills. Established in 1981. 60 miles from Los Angeles. Features: university dormitories; outdoor ropes course.

Profile of Summer Employees Total number: 60–80; typical ages: 18–25. 50% men; 50% women; 80% college students. Nonsmokers required.

Employment Information Openings are from June to August. Jobs available: ▶ 10 *counselors* with college degree plus PPS credential or master's degree in counseling or MFCC license at $900–$1500 per season ▶ 4–10 *facilitators* with presentation skills, college degree, and teaching credentials preferred at $1300–$2350 per season ▶ 1 *logistics manager* with excellent organizational skills and high school diploma at $600–$1100 per season ▶ 2 *nurses* with RN license at $600–$1300 per season ▶ 1 *office manager* with high school diploma and prior office experience at $450–$700 per season ▶ 2 *paramedics* with national or state registration at $600–$1300 per season ▶ 50–75 *team leaders (peer counselors)* with high school diploma and prior experience with teens at $250–$600 per season. Applicants must submit a formal organization application, resume, two letters of recommendation, in-person interview recommended (videotape interview acceptable). International applicants accepted; must obtain own visa, obtain own working papers.

Benefits and Preemployment Training Free housing, free meals, and on-the-job training. Preemployment training is required and includes interpersonal skills, leadership skills.

Contact Recruiter, SuperCamp–Claremont Colleges, 1725 South Coast Highway, Oceanside, California 92054-5319. Telephone: 800-285-3276 Ext. 180. Fax: 760-722-3507. E-mail: info@ learningforum.com. World Wide Web: http://www.supercamp.com. Application deadline: continuous.

SUPERCAMP–STANFORD UNIVERSITY
STANFORD UNIVERSITY
PALO ALTO, CALIFORNIA 94305

General Information Residential program for teens designed to build self-confidence and lifelong learning skills through accelerated learning techniques. Established in 1981. 8,200-acre facility located 45 miles from San Francisco. Features: university dormitories; outdoor ropes course.

Profile of Summer Employees Total number: 30–40; typical ages: 18–25. 50% men; 50% women; 80% college students. Nonsmokers required.

Employment Information Openings are from June to August. Jobs available: ▶ 1 *EMT/ wellness person* with national or state registration at $600–$1300 per season ▶ 10 *counselors* with college degree and PPS credential, MFCC license, or master's degree in counseling at $900–$1500 per season ▶ 4–10 *facilitators* with presentation skills and college degree; teaching credential preferred at $1300–$2350 per season ▶ 1 *logistics manager* with excellent organizational skills and high school diploma at $600–$1100 per season ▶ 1 *nurse/paramedic* with national or state registration at $600–$1300 per season ▶ 1 *office manager* with high school diploma and prior office experience at $450–$700 per season ▶ 20–25 *team leaders* with high school diploma and prior experience with teens at $250–$600 per season. Applicants must submit a formal organization application, resume, two letters of recommendation, in-person interview recommended (videotape interview acceptable). International applicants accepted; must obtain own visa, obtain own working papers.

Benefits and Preemployment Training Free housing, free meals, and on-the-job training. Preemployment training is required and includes interpersonal skills, leadership skills.

Contact Recruiter, SuperCamp–Stanford University, 1725 South Coast Highway, Oceanside, California 92054-5319. Telephone: 800-285-3276 Ext. 180. Fax: 760-722-3507. E-mail: info@

learningforum.com. World Wide Web: http://www.supercamp.com. Application deadline: continuous.

TUMBLEWEED DAY CAMP
1024 HANLEY AVENUE
BRENTWOOD, CALIFORNIA 90049

General Information Traditional day camp serving approximately 400 children per day in Los Angeles; helps children learn new activities, meet new people, and develop self-confidence. Established in 1954. 100-acre facility located 5 miles from Los Angeles. Features: 100 rustic acres; wooded canyon setting; 2 outdoor pools; large grassy fields; high ropes course; 2 nature centers.

Profile of Summer Employees Total number: 150; typical ages: 19–30. 40% men; 60% women; 20% minorities; 25% high school students; 65% college students; 5% non-U.S. citizens; 90% local applicants. Nonsmokers required.

Employment Information Openings are from June 21 to August 27. Winter break positions also offered. Jobs available: ▶ 5 *counselors* (minimum age 19) with 1 year of college or more and experience with children at $205–$235 per week ▶ 6 *counselors/bus drivers* (minimum age 21) with good driving record, 1 year of college or more, and experience with children at $250–$280 per week ▶ 30 *counselors/van drivers* (minimum age 19) with good driving record, 1 year of college or more, and experience with children at $235–$265 per week ▶ 4 *horseback riding instructors* (minimum age 19) with 2 years horseback riding experience and experience with children at $230–$275 per week ▶ 2 *office assistants* (minimum age 19) with 1 year college, experience working with children, and Red Cross first aid/CPR certification at $220–$250 per month ▶ 2 *ropes course instructors* (minimum age 19) with 1 year college, experience working with children, and ropes course experience at $220–$250 per week ▶ 8 *specialists* (minimum age 19) with 1 year of college or more, experience with children, and experience in arts and crafts, creative play/video, gymnastics, or nature/science at $220–$250 per week ▶ 4 *swim instructors/ lifeguards* (minimum age 19) with LGT and WSI certification, Red Cross first aid, and CPR for the professional rescuer; and experience teaching swimming at $265–$295 per week. Applicants must submit formal organization application, three personal references, two letters of recommendation. International applicants accepted; must obtain own visa, obtain own working papers, apply through a recognized agency. An in-person interview is required.

Benefits and Preemployment Training Formal training and on-the-job training. Preemployment training is required and includes accident prevention and safety, first aid, CPR, interpersonal skills, leadership skills.

Contact Ms. Teri Naftulin, Executive Director, Tumbleweed Day Camp, PO Box 49291, Los Angeles, California 90049. Telephone: 310-472-7474. Fax: 310-476-7788. E-mail: tnaftulin@ tumbleweed4ever.com. World Wide Web: http://www.tumbleweed4ever.com. Application deadline: June 1.

UNIVERSAL STUDIOS
100 UNIVERSAL CITY PLAZA, EMPLOYMENT OFFICE SC79-3
UNIVERSAL CITY, CALIFORNIA 91608

General Information Theme/amusement park with film- and entertainment- based attractions. Unique rides, stage shows, movie magic, and restaurants. An amphitheatre that hosts musical performances and award shows is also in the park. Established in 1964. Located 1 mile from Burbank. Features: Back to the Future; ET Adventure; T23D; animal actors stage; Universal amphitheatre; Jurrasic Park.

Profile of Summer Employees Total number: 5,500; typical ages: 16–90.

Employment Information Openings are from April to September. Spring break, winter break, and year-round positions also offered. Jobs available: ▶ *Sparky's sales associate* (minimum age 18) with prior cash handling and retail experience at $6 per hour ▶ *Sparky's store lead* with cash handling and retail experience; prior management or supervisory experience; salary is based upon experience ▶ *T23D attraction attendants* (minimum age 18) with ability to demonstrate patience in handling difficult guest situations at $5.75 per hour ▶ *cook-theme park* (minimum age 18) with prior line and/or prep cook experience. Prior experience in a high-volume restaurant environment at $5.75-$7.00 per hour based upon experience and written cook's test ▶ *food service associate* (minimum age 16) with prior cash handling experience at $5.75 per hour ▶ *merchandise sales associate* (minimum age 16) with ability to hande cash accurately and efficiently at $5.75 per hour ▶ *park attendant* (minimum age 16) with ability to lift 40 pounds at $5.75 per hour ▶ *parkit lot attendant* with prior cash handling experience; excellent self-management skills at $5.75 per hour ▶ *ride operator* (minimum age 18) must have a clear speaking voice at $5.75 per hour ▶ *runner* (minimum age 18) with ability to lift 50 pounds; prior food service experience at $5.75 per hour ▶ *ticket seller/admission host* (minimum age 16) with ability to lift 20 pounds; must have a clear speaking voice at $5.75 per hour ▶ *tram tour driver* (minimum age 18) must possess Class A driver's license, passenger endorsement, medical certificate, and present DMV report at $14.56 per hour ▶ *valet parking attendant* (minimum age 18) with clean DMV report; must be able to drive automatic and manual transmission vehicles at $5.75 per hour plus tips ▶ *wardrobe attendant* with ability to work at a fast pace with a variety of people at $5.75 per hour. Applicants must submit a formal organization application, three personal references, departmental interview may be required. International applicants accepted; must obtain own visa, obtain own working papers. An in-person interview is required.

Benefits and Preemployment Training Formal training, possible full-time employment, on-the-job training, and free meals for food service workers.

Contact Employment Office, Universal Studios. Telephone: 818-622-JOBS. Fax: 818-622-0483. World Wide Web: http://www.universalstudios.com. Application deadline: continuous.

WHITEWATER EXPEDITIONS AND TOURS (W.E.T.)
PO BOX 160024
SACRAMENTO, CALIFORNIA 95816

General Information Whitewater rafting on Class III to Class V rivers throughout the western United States with majority in California, Oregon, and Arizona. Program emphasizes adventure sports.

Profile of Summer Employees Typical ages: 20–40. 90% men; 10% women; 5% minorities; 1% high school students; 99% college students; 80% local applicants.

Employment Information Openings are from March to September. Jobs available: ▶ *bus drivers* with driver's license, DMV records class B, medical release, and auto mechanic experience at $300–$2000 per month ▶ *whitewater guides* with CPR, first aid, EMT, and mountain medicine certification at $300–$2000 per month.

Benefits and Preemployment Training On-the-job training. Preemployment training is required and includes accident prevention and safety, whitewater rescue.

Contact Betty Lopez, Promotional Director, Whitewater Expeditions and Tours (W.E.T.), PO Box 160024, Sacramento, California 95816. Telephone: 916-451-3241. Fax: 916-455-8620. World Wide Web: http://www.raftwet.com. Application deadline: February 15.

YMCA CAMP OAKES RANGERS
PO BOX 452
BIG BEAR CITY, CALIFORNIA 92314

General Information Residential summer camp serving children from around the world in a traditional camp program. Established in 1958. 230-acre facility located 120 miles from Los Angeles. Features: lake for boating; pool; observatory with 17-inch telescope.

Profile of Summer Employees Total number: 45; typical ages: 18–25. 50% men; 50% women; 10% minorities; 5% high school students; 95% college students; 10% non-U.S. citizens; 80% local applicants. Nonsmokers preferred.

Employment Information Openings are from June 14 to September 8. Jobs available: ▶ 8 *cabin counselors* with one year of college completed and equivalent of 3 years camping experience at $150–$170 per week ▶ 4 *cooks* with experience at $120–$225 per week ▶ 1 *health care coordinator* with RN or EMT training at $175–$250 per week ▶ 8 *junior counselors* (minimum age 16) with work permit at $110–$130 per week ▶ 4 *lifeguards* with certification at $150–$170 per week ▶ 3 *program directors* with three years of experience at $190–$250 per week ▶ 9 *program specialists* with experience in riflery, crafts, wrangling, nature, archery, ropes-challenge course, astronomy, mountain biking, or rock climbing at $150–$170 per week. Applicants must submit formal organization application, writing sample, three personal references. International applicants accepted; must apply through a recognized agency. An in-person interview is recommended, but a telephone interview is acceptable.

Benefits and Preemployment Training Free housing, free meals, formal training, health insurance, and on-the-job training. Preemployment training is required and includes accident prevention and safety, CPR, interpersonal skills, leadership skills.

Contact Troy Lacy, Program Director, YMCA Camp Oakes Rangers, PO Box 90995, Long Beach, California 90809-0995. Telephone: 909-585-2020. Fax: 909-585-8338. E-mail: lbymca@ juno.com. World Wide Web: http://www.lbymca.org. Application deadline: May 1.

YMCA CAMP SURF
106 CARNATION AVENUE
IMPERIAL BEACH, CALIFORNIA 91932

General Information Residential oceanside camp serving groups and individuals for summer camp, outdoor education, teen leadership, youth retreats, mission projects to Mexico, and beach tent camping. Established in 1969. 40-acre facility located 2 miles from San Diego. Features: beach camping; guarded waterfront; salt marsh reserve; 13 wooden cabins; outdoor dining deck; nearby town pier.

Profile of Summer Employees Total number: 60; typical ages: 19–28. 25% minorities; 15% high school students; 84% college students; 1% retirees; 30% non-U.S. citizens; 40% local applicants. Nonsmokers required.

Employment Information Openings are from June 25 to September 1. Year-round positions also offered. Jobs available: ► *camp counselors* (minimum age 18) with first aid and CPR certification at $150–$165 per week ► 5 *coordinators* (minimum age 21) with leadership experience, Class B license, and lifeguard training at $240–$300 per week ► 1 *health services coordinator* (minimum age 21) with first aid, CPR, BLS, and EMT certification at $150–$250 per week ► *ocean lifeguard* (minimum age 18) with lifeguarding and Basic Life Support certification at $150–$200 per week. Applicants must submit formal organization application, personal reference, three letters of recommendation. International applicants accepted; must apply through a recognized agency. An in-person interview is recommended, but a telephone interview is acceptable.

Benefits and Preemployment Training Free housing, free meals, on-the-job training, and opportunity to attend seminars/workshops. Preemployment training is required and includes accident prevention and safety, first aid, CPR, interpersonal skills, leadership skills, lifeguard training.

Contact Mark Thompson, Camp Director, YMCA Camp Surf, 106 Carnation Avenue, Imperial Beach, California 91932. Telephone: 619-423-5850. Fax: 619-423-4141. E-mail: campsurf@ymca. org. World Wide Web: http://www.ymca.org/camp. Application deadline: continuous.

YOSEMITE CONCESSION SERVICES CORPORATION
PO BOX 578
YOSEMITE NATIONAL PARK, CALIFORNIA 95389

General Information Main concessionaire for Yosemite National Park, providing all aspects of guest services. 100 miles from Fresno. Features: wooded setting; high sierra lakes; steep granite walls; waterfalls; meadows.

Profile of Summer Employees Total number: 1,800; typical ages: 18–25. 50% men; 50% women; 19% minorities; 45% college students; 55% local applicants.

Employment Information Openings are from April 1 to September 30. Year-round positions also offered. Jobs available: ► 20 *buspeople* with restaurant experience at $5.81 per hour ► 25 *cooks* with experience in the field at $8–$9 per hour ► 25 *custodians* at $5.87 per hour ► 150 *food service utility person* at $5.87 per hour ► 25 *front desk personnel* with cash handling and computer experience at $6.70 ► 20 *hosts/hostesses* with restaurant experience at $6 per hour ► 50–75 *kitchen utility person* at $6 per hour ► 14 *lifeguards* (minimum age 15) with CPR for Professional Rescuer, BFA, lifeguard certification, and Title 22 at $7.07 per hour ► 250 *roomkeepers* at $5.87 per hour ▶ 100 *sales clerks* with cash handling experience at $5.87 per hour ▶ 20 *waitresses/waiters* with restaurant experience at $5.75 per hour. Applicants must submit a formal organization application. International applicants accepted; must obtain own visa, obtain own working papers.

Benefits and Preemployment Training Housing at a cost, meals at a cost, possible full-time employment, health insurance, on-the-job training, and opportunity to attend seminars/workshops.

Contact Human Resources, Yosemite Concession Services Corporation, PO Box 578, Yosemite National Park, California 95389. Telephone: 209-372-1236. Fax: 209-372-1050. World Wide Web: http://www.yosemitepark.com. Application deadline: continuous.

COLORADO

ACE COMPUTER CAMP–COLORADO
See ACE Computer Camp–Washington on page 307 for complete description.

A CHRISTIAN MINISTRY IN THE NATIONAL PARKS–COLORADO
See A Christian Ministry in the National Parks–Massachussetts on page 138 for complete description.

ANDERSON WESTERN COLORADO CAMPS, LTD.
7177 COLORADO RIVER ROAD
GYPSUM, COLORADO 81637

General Information Residential coed camp serving 125 campers per session. Children are given daily choices of noncompetitive activities. Our Wilderness Pioneer Camp for 14-17 year olds participates in out-of-camp trips 80 percent of the time. Established in 1962. 200-acre facility located 140 miles from Denver. Features: Colorado River; climbing wall; ropes course; cliffs for rappelling; creek; pond.

Profile of Summer Employees Total number: 40; typical ages: 19–22. 50% men; 50% women; 25% minorities; 3% high school students; 60% college students; 5% retirees; 15% non-U.S. citizens; 20% local applicants. Nonsmokers required.

Employment Information Openings are from May 12 to August 20. Year-round positions also offered. Jobs available: ▶ 20 *camp counselors* with two years of college preferred at $975–$1200 per season ▶ 2 *cooks* at $2500–$7000 per season ▶ 4 *lodge/grounds staff members* (minimum age 16) at $975–$1200 per season ▶ *nurse* with RN at $200–$400 per week ▶ 1 *rafting director* (minimum age 21) with rafting ability, organizational skills, and teaching skills ▶ 1 *riding instructor* (minimum age 21) at $1200–$1500 per season ▶ 3 *wranglers* with knowledge of horses at $975–$1200 per season. Applicants must submit a formal organization application, writing sample, three personal references. International applicants accepted; must obtain own visa, obtain own working papers. An in-person interview is recommended, but a telephone interview is acceptable.

Benefits and Preemployment Training Free housing, free meals, formal training, possible full-time employment, names of contacts, on-the-job training, and travel reimbursement. Preemployment training is required and includes accident prevention and safety, first aid, CPR, interpersonal skills, leadership skills.

Contact Christopher Porter, Director, Anderson Western Colorado Camps, Ltd., 7177 Colorado River Road, Gypsum, Colorado 81637. Telephone: 970-524-7766. Fax: 970-524-7107. E-mail: andecamp@rof.net. World Wide Web: http://www.andersoncamps.com. Application deadline: continuous.

THE ASPEN LODGE AND RESORT
6120 HIGHWAY 7
ESTES PARK, COLORADO 80517

General Information Resort, conference center, and ranch providing lodging, entertainment, and meals. 85-acre facility located 80 miles from Denver.

Profile of Summer Employees 50% men; 50% women.

Employment Information Openings are from January to December. Jobs available: ▶ *children's counselors* at $5 per hour ▶ *livery staff* ▶ *recreation staff* ▶ *various positions* ▶ *waitstaff.*

Benefits and Preemployment Training Housing at a cost, meals at a cost, formal training, health insurance, on-the-job training, and travel reimbursement.

Contact Human Resources, The Aspen Lodge and Resort, 6120 Highway 7, Estes Park, Colorado 80517. Telephone: 970-586-8133. Fax: 970-586-8133. E-mail: aspen@aspenlodge.com. World Wide Web: http://www.aspenlodge.com. Application deadline: continuous.

BAR LAZY J GUEST RANCH
447 COUNTY ROAD 3, BOX N
PARSHALL, COLORADO 80468

General Information Guest ranch with capacity for 40 people. Established in 1912. 70-acre facility located 110 miles from Denver. Features: 60 horses; 2/3 mile of Colorado River; pool; hot tub; 12 cabins; mountain bikes.

Profile of Summer Employees Total number: 18; typical age: 18. 50% men; 50% women; 82% college students; 18% retirees.

Employment Information Openings are from May 1 to September 30. Jobs available: ▶ 1 *assistant cook* at $550 per month ▶ 2 *counselors* with experience working with children at $450 per month ▶ 1 *head cook* with experience running a kitchen and serving 60 people at $1000 per month ▶ 1 *head wrangler* with experience in the field at $800 per month ▶ 2 *housekeepers* at $450 per month ▶ 1 *kitchen helper* at $450 per month ▶ 2 *waitresses/waiters* at $450 per month ▶ 5 *wranglers* with experience in the field at $500 per month. Applicants must submit a formal organization application, resume, writing sample, three personal references. A telephone interview is required.

Benefits and Preemployment Training Free housing, free meals, formal training, and on-the-job training. Preemployment training is required and includes first aid, CPR, required for wranglers and children's counselors.

Contact Cheri Amos Helmicki, Owners, Bar Lazy J Guest Ranch, Box N, Parshall, Colorado 80468. Telephone: 970-725-3437. Fax: 970-725-0121. E-mail: barlazyj@rkymtnhi.com. World Wide Web: http://www.dude-ranch.com or www.guestranches.com/barlazyj. Application deadline: April 15.

BAR NI RANCH
6614 HIGHWAY 12, STONEWALL GAP
WESTON, COLORADO 81091

General Information Private guest ranch with 15–35 guests per week, gentle, resistance-free horse training and riding; quarter horse breeding; ranch style, health conscious and gourmet meals; hiking; fishing; ninety percent repeat guests; conservation easement; and a fabulous staff. Established in 1946. 36,000-acre facility located 35 miles from Trinidad. Features: Sangre de Cristo Mountain range; 13,000 and 14,000-foot mountain peaks; 36,000 acres of forests, meadows, and alpine basins; environmentally protected setting; 7 streams and 5 ponds; abundant wildlife: elk, deer, wild turkey, bear, eagles.

Profile of Summer Employees Total number: 12–14; typical ages: 18–50. 50% men; 50% women; 10% minorities; 10% high school students; 30% college students; 40% local applicants. Nonsmokers preferred.

Employment Information Openings are from April 15 to November 1. Year-round positions also offered. Jobs available: ▶ 1 *baker* (minimum age 18) with some experience and a love for baking at $900 per month ▶ 1 *chef* with cooking school certification preferred at $1200 per month ▶ 2–4 *cook's helpers/waitstaff/child care/lawn care* at $800 per month ▶ 2 *housekeepers* at $800 per month ▶ 2 *mechanics/general ranch help* with large and small engine mechanical skills at $800 per month ▶ 2 *wranglers/general ranch help* with CPR and first aid certification preferred and experience at $800 per month. Applicants must submit a formal organization application, resume, personal reference. A telephone interview is required.

Benefits and Preemployment Training Free housing, free meals, possible full-time employment, and on-the-job training.

Contact Tom and Linda Perry, Ranch Managers, Bar NI Ranch, 6614 Highway 12, Weston, Colorado 81091. Fax: 719-868-2708. E-mail: barniranch@aol.com. Application deadline: continuous.

BLAZING ADVENTURES
BOX 5068
SNOWMASS VILLAGE, COLORADO 81615

General Information Organization providing outdoor adventure tours. Established in 1979. near Aspen. Features: mountains; rivers; national forest; summer resort.

Profile of Summer Employees Total number: 100; typical ages: 22–40. 55% men; 45% women; 15% college students; 80% local applicants.

Employment Information Openings are from May 1 to September. Jobs available: ▶ *adventure guides* (minimum age 21) at $9–$11 per hour ▶ 3 *group coordinators* (minimum age 20) at $9–$12 per hour ▶ 10 *office staff* (minimum age 20) at $9–$11 per hour ▶ 10 *sales and marketing coordination reservation interns* (minimum age 20) at $9–$11 per hour. Applicants must submit 3-4 letters of recommendations, 3-4 personal references. International applicants accepted; must obtain own visa, obtain own working papers, apply through a recognized agency.

Benefits and Preemployment Training Formal training, possible full-time employment, and on-the-job training. Preemployment training is required.

Contact Laurie Harris, General Manager, Blazing Adventures, Box 5068, Snowmass Village, Colorado 81615. Telephone: 970-923-4544. Fax: 970-923-4994. E-mail: blazing@rof.net. World Wide Web: http://www.blazingadventures.com. Application deadline: continuous.

CHELEY COLORADO CAMPS
ESTES PARK, COLORADO 80517

General Information Residential camp serving 475 campers ages 9–17 for four-week sessions in a rigorous outdoor western adventure program. Owned by Don and Carole Cheley. Established in 1921. 1,600-acre facility located 75 miles from Denver. Features: wooded setting; mountain streams; 14,000-foot peak; 5 western riding rings; historic log lodges; freshwater lake.

Profile of Summer Employees Total number: 195; typical ages: 19–65. 50% men; 50% women; 1% minorities; 90% college students; 15% retirees; 5% non-U.S. citizens; 20% local applicants. Nonsmokers required.

Employment Information Openings are from June 1 to August 20. Jobs available: ▶ 40 *cooks* (minimum age 19) with experience at $1600–$2200 per season ▶ 100 *counselors* (minimum age 19) with CPR/first aid certification at $1200–$1300 per season ▶ 10–12 *drivers* (minimum age 21) with CDL and clean driving record at $1300–$1400 per season ▶ 6 *nurses* (minimum age 24) with Colorado RN license at $2100 per season ▶ 4–6 *office staff members* (minimum age 19) with office experience at $1200–$1300 per season. Applicants must submit formal organization application, resume, two personal references, two letters of recommendation. International applicants accepted; must apply through a recognized agency. An in-person interview is recommended, but a telephone interview is acceptable.

Benefits and Preemployment Training Free housing, free meals, formal training, health insurance, on-the-job training, opportunity to attend seminars/workshops, and travel reimbursement. Preemployment training is required and includes accident prevention and safety, first aid, CPR, interpersonal skills, leadership skills.

Contact Don and Carole Cheley, Directors, Cheley Colorado Camps, PO Box 6525, Denver, Colorado 80206. Telephone: 303-377-3616. Fax: 303-377-3605. E-mail: cheley@ix.netcom.com. World Wide Web: http://www.cheley.com. Application deadline: continuous.

CHEROKEE PARK RANCH
436 CHEROKEE HILLS DRIVE
LIVERMORE, COLORADO 80536

General Information Summer guest ranch providing fun outdoor activities for the entire family and specializing in Western hospitality. 300-acre facility located 180 miles from Denver. Features: heated swimming pool; hot tub; horseback riding; lake and river; Rocky Mountain location.

Profile of Summer Employees Total number: 22; typical ages: 20–24. 42% men; 58% women; 11% minorities; 90% college students; 12% local applicants. Nonsmokers preferred.

Employment Information Openings are from May 10 to September 30. Jobs available: ▶ 2 *children's counselors* (minimum age 19) with CPR/first aid and lifesaving certification; experience working with children preferred at $425 per month ▶ 1 *cook* (minimum age 19) with experience cooking for large groups preferred at $550 per month ▶ 5 *housekeepers/waitresses/waiters* (minimum age 19) at $425 per month ▶ 1 *prep cook/dishwasher* (minimum age 19) with kitchen experience preferred at $425–$450 per month ▶ 1 *secretary* (minimum age 19) with office/clerical experience preferred at $450 per month ▶ 6 *wranglers* (minimum age 19) with CPR certification (preferred); experience with horses and tack and Western riding at $450 per month. Applicants must submit a formal organization application, three personal references, photograph. International applicants accepted; must obtain own visa, obtain own working papers. A telephone interview is required.

Benefits and Preemployment Training Free housing, free meals, on-the-job training, and gratuity pool.

Contact Christine Prince, Owner, Cherokee Park Ranch, 436 Cherokee Hills Drive, Livermore, Colorado 80536. Telephone: 800-628-0949. Fax: 970-493-5802. E-mail: cpranch@gateway.net. World Wide Web: http://www.ranchweb.com/cherokeepark. Application deadline: January 15.

THE COLORADO MOUNTAIN RANCH
10063 GOLD HILL ROAD
BOULDER, COLORADO 80302

General Information Day camp serving approximately 100 boys and girls ages 6–16 and enjoyed by other clientele as a mountain retreat. Established in 1947. 200-acre facility located 10 miles from Boulder. Features: pine and aspen forests and wildflower meadows; snowy peak vistas; lodge and cabins; heated swimming pool; horse and foot trails; dirt basketball and volleyball.

Profile of Summer Employees Total number: 35; typical ages: 19–25. 40% men; 60% women; 5% minorities; 90% college students; 5% non-U.S. citizens. Nonsmokers preferred.

Employment Information Openings are from June 5 to August 15. Jobs available: ▶ 1 *Indian lore instructor* (minimum age 18) at $1300 per season ▶ 1 *archery instructor* (minimum age 18) with experience in the field at $1300 per season ▶ 1 *arts and crafts instructor* (minimum age 18) at $1300 per season ▶ 3 *bus drivers* (minimum age 18) with commercial driver's license; training and certification given at $1650 per season ▶ 10 *day-camp counselors* (minimum age 18) at $1300 per season ▶ 1 *drama/creative writing/newspaper instructor* (minimum age 18) at $1300 per season ▶ 2 *gymnastics instructors* (minimum age 18) at $1300 per season ▶ 1 *head cook/kitchen manager* (minimum age 21) with experience in menu planning, food ordering, and staff management at $2575 per season ▶ 2 *kitchen workers* (minimum age 18) at $1650 per season ▶ 2 *maintenance staff* (minimum age 18) at $1650 per season ▶ 1 *nanny* (minimum age 18) at $1300 per season ▶ 1 *office staff* (minimum age 18) at $1300 per season ▶ 2 *outcamp/hiking/backpacking/outdoor living/nature instructors* (minimum age 21) at $1300 per season ▶ 1 *riflery instructor* (minimum age 18) with experience in the field at $1300 per season ▶ 1 *ropes course instructor* (minimum age 18) at $1300 per season ▶ 2 *swimming instructors* (minimum age 18) with one required to have WSI certification and both required to have LGT certification at $1350 per season ▶ 1 *tutor* (minimum age 18) at $1300 per season ▶ 8 *wranglers* (minimum age 18) at $1300 per season. Applicants must submit a formal organization application, 3 personal references and/or letters of recommendation. International applicants accepted; must obtain own visa, obtain own working papers. A telephone interview is required.

Benefits and Preemployment Training Free housing, free meals, on-the-job training, and opportunity to attend seminars/workshops. Preemployment training is required and includes accident prevention and safety, first aid, CPR, interpersonal skills, leadership skills.

Contact Lynn Walker, Director, The Colorado Mountain Ranch, 10063 Gold Hill Road, Boulder, Colorado 80302. Telephone: 800-267-9573. E-mail: office@coloradomountainranch.com. World Wide Web: http://www.coloradomountainranch.com. Application deadline: May 15.

COLORADO TRAILS RANCH
12161 C.R. 240
DURANGO, COLORADO 81301

General Information Full service, family-oriented guest ranch offering cabin accommodations, meals, and a full activity program including horseback riding, fishing, marksmanship, sports and more. Established in 1960. 500-acre facility located 12 miles from Durango. Features: mountain location; heated pool; beautiful lodge; excellent children's program; excellent riding program; excellent fishing program.

Profile of Summer Employees Total number: 40; typical ages: 19–22. 40% men; 60% women; 95% college students; 5% non-U.S. citizens; 5% local applicants. Nonsmokers preferred.

Employment Information Openings are from May 20 to August 31. Jobs available: ▶ 3–4 *counselors* (minimum age 18) with horse experience required; experience with children and teens preferred at $5.15 per hour ▶ 4 *general staff (floaters)* (minimum age 18) with flexible attitude and willingness to help where needed at $5.15 per hour ▶ 4 *housekeepers* (minimum age 18) at $5.15 per hour ▶ 4 *kitchen staff* (minimum age 18) with kitchen experience preferred at $5.15 per hour ▶ 3 *maintenance staff* (minimum age 18) with general maintenance experience preferred at $5.15 per hour ▶ 7 *waitstaff* (minimum age 18) with serving experience preferred at $5.15 per hour ▶ 7–8 *wranglers* (minimum age 18) with extensive horse experience at $5.15 per hour. Applicants must submit formal organization application, three personal references, three letters of recommendation, riding video for wranglers and counselors. International applicants accepted; must obtain own visa, obtain own working papers, apply through a recognized agency. An in-person interview is recommended, but a telephone interview is acceptable.

Benefits and Preemployment Training Free housing, free meals, on-the-job training, and able to participate in ranch activities. Preemployment training is required and includes accident prevention and safety, first aid, CPR, job specific skills.

Contact Robin Williams, General Manager, Colorado Trails Ranch, 12161 C.R. 240, Durango, Colorado 81301. Telephone: 970-247-5055. Fax: 970-385-7372. E-mail: cotranch@aol.com. World Wide Web: http://www.colotrails.com. Application deadline: continuous.

COLVIG SILVER CAMPS
9665 FLORIDA ROAD
DURANGO, COLORADO 81301

General Information Outdoor adventure camp located in natural surroundings; mix of traditional summer camp activities and wilderness adventure. Established in 1969. 600-acre facility located 250 miles from Albuquerque, New Mexico. Features: rustic setting; creek running through site; Ponderosa Forest; 3 ponds; National Forest access; proximity to high alpine and desert areas.

Profile of Summer Employees Total number: 45–55; typical ages: 18–25. 50% men; 50% women; 90% college students; 5% local applicants. Nonsmokers required.

Employment Information Openings are from June 4 to August 10. Jobs available: ▶ 1 *arts and crafts director* (minimum age 21) with first aid and CPR certification, supervisory experience and experience with all types of arts and crafts at $800–$900 per season ▶ 7 *assistant counselors* (minimum age 18) with first aid and CPR certification; additional consideration for lifeguarding and wilderness first aid; should have experience with children and wilderness skills at $700–$900 per season ▶ 1 *assistant wrangler* (minimum age 18) with CPR/first aid certification; experience with horses and riding instruction at $750–$900 per season ▶ 20 *counselors* (minimum age 21) with first aid and CPR certification; additional consideration for lifeguarding and wilderness first aid; should have experience with children and wilderness skills at $750–$1000 per season ▶ 1 *head wrangler* (minimum age 21) with first aid and CPR certification; experience with horses and riding instruction at $750–$900 per season ▶ 1 *nurse* (minimum age 21) with

RN license, CPR certification, and pediatric/summer camp experience at $2500–$3000 per season ▶ 6 *program coordinators* (minimum age 21) with first aid and CPR certification; supervisory and program planning experience; experience with children at $850–$1000 per season ▶ 1 *rock climbing specialist* (minimum age 21) with first aid, CPR, and ropes course/rock climbing certification; experience teaching rock climbing, anchor building, and top rope set-up at $1000–$1200 per season. Applicants must submit a formal organization application, three personal references. A telephone interview is required.

Benefits and Preemployment Training Free housing, free meals, formal training, health insurance, on-the-job training, and laundry; workmen's compensation insurance. Preemployment training is required and includes accident prevention and safety, first aid, interpersonal skills, leadership skills, individual program area and wilderness training.

Contact Scott Kelley, Program Director, Colvig Silver Camps, 9665 Florida Road, Durango, Colorado 81301. Telephone: 970-247-2564. Fax: 970-247-2547. E-mail: 76601.2705@compuserve.com. World Wide Web: http://www.colvigsilver.com. Application deadline: continuous.

CROSS BAR X YOUTH RANCH
2111 COUNTY ROAD 222
DURANGO, COLORADO 81301

General Information Christian camp for low income and inner city youth. Established in 1977. 35-acre facility located 12 miles from Durango.

Profile of Summer Employees Typical ages: 18–22. 50% men; 50% women; 90% college students. Nonsmokers required.

Employment Information Openings are from May 27 to August 11. Jobs available: ▶ *activities coordinator* with experience in backpacking, mountain biking, and leadership at $50–$100 per week ▶ 1 *cook* ▶ 8 *counselors* (minimum age 18) with general understanding of the Bible at $50–$100 per week. Applicants must submit a formal organization application.

Benefits and Preemployment Training Free housing, free meals, and on-the-job training. Preemployment training is required and includes accident prevention and safety, first aid, CPR, interpersonal skills, leadership skills.

Contact Nick Brothers, Director, Cross Bar X Youth Ranch, 2111 County Road 222, Durango, Colorado 81301. Telephone: 970-259-2716. Fax: 970-259-8006. E-mail: crossbar@frontier.net. World Wide Web: http://www.crossbarxcamp.org. Application deadline: May 15.

DROWSY WATER RANCH
PO BOX 147 J
GRANBY, COLORADO 80446

General Information Mountain dude ranch serving 60 guests weekly. Established in 1977. 600-acre facility located 110 miles from Denver. Features: mountains; horses; entertainment; Colorado River.

Profile of Summer Employees Total number: 27; typical ages: 18–50. 48% men; 52% women; 15% high school students; 75% college students; 5% local applicants. Nonsmokers required.

Employment Information Openings are from May 1 to September 30. Jobs available: ▶ 3 *assistant cooks* with experience in the field at $1350 per month ▶ 2 *counselors* with first aid certification and experience in the field at $1350 per month ▶ 2 *dishwashers* at $1350 per month ▶ 1 *head chef* with experience in the field at $1700 per month ▶ 8 *horse wranglers/trail guides* with first aid certification and experience in the field at $1400 per month ▶ 6 *housekeeping staff members/wait persons* at $1350 per month ▶ 3 *maintenance staff members* at $1350 per month ▶ 1 *office person* with experience in the field at $1350 per month. Applicants must submit formal organization application, cover letter, resume, personal reference. International applicants accepted; must obtain own visa, obtain own working papers, apply through a recognized agency. A telephone interview is required.

Benefits and Preemployment Training Free housing, free meals, possible full-time employment, and on-the-job training. Preemployment training is optional and includes accident prevention and safety, first aid, CPR, leadership skills.

Contact Randy Sue Fosha, Owner, Drowsy Water Ranch, PO Box 147 J, Granby, Colorado

80446. Telephone: 970-725-3456. Fax: 970-725-3611. E-mail: dwrken@aol.com. World Wide Web: http://www.drowsywater.com. Application deadline: continuous.

DVORAK'S KAYAKING AND RAFTING EXPEDITIONS
17921 HIGHWAY 285
NATHROP, COLORADO 81236

General Information Outfitters offering whitewater rafting and kayaking expeditions on 10 rivers and in 29 canyons in 5 states of the Southwest. Established in 1984. 10-acre facility located 130 miles from Denver.

Profile of Summer Employees Total number: 40; typical ages: 20–60. 60% men; 40% women; 60% college students; 10% non-U.S. citizens; 30% local applicants. Nonsmokers required.

Employment Information Openings are from April 15 to September 15. Jobs available: ▶ 3 *instructors (multi-day, kayaking, rafting)* with instruction skills and guide experience at $575–$2000 per month ▶ 1 *logistics manager* with computer skills and ordering and packing experience at $1200 per month ▶ 2 *reservations/office staff members* with computer and telephone skills and outdoor background for sales and customer service at $650–$1200 per month ▶ 35 *river guides (multi-day)* with advanced first aid/CPR valid to season-end at $575–$2000 per month ▶ 1 *transportation manager/mechanic* with CDL license/driver and mechanic skills on buses/vans/trucks at $900–$1200 per month. Applicants must submit a formal organization application, resume, three personal references, three letters of recommendation, if hired there is a 14-day training course; the fee is $600 which includes all food and equipment. International applicants accepted; must obtain own visa. An in-person interview is recommended, but a telephone interview is acceptable.

Benefits and Preemployment Training Free housing, free meals, on-the-job training, and travel reimbursement. Preemployment training is required and includes accident prevention and safety, interpersonal skills, leadership skills.

Contact Bill or Jaci Dvorak, President, Dvorak's Kayaking and Rafting Expeditions, 17921 Highway 285, Nathrop, Colorado 81236. Telephone: 719-539-6851. Fax: 719-539-3378. E-mail: dvorakex@amigo.net. World Wide Web: http://www.dvorakexpeditions.com. Application deadline: April 15.

ROCKY MOUNTAIN VILLAGE
2644 ALVARADO ROAD, PO BOX 115
EMPIRE, COLORADO 80438

General Information Nonprofit organization which provides services for children and adults with physical and/or mental disabilities. Established in 1951. 140-acre facility located 45 miles from Denver. Features: fishing ponds; outdoor swimming pool; horseback riding/barn yard; ropes/adventure course; zip line; accessible trails/facilities.

Profile of Summer Employees Total number: 50; typical ages: 18–30. 45% men; 55% women; 2% minorities; 15% high school students; 75% college students; 8% non-U.S. citizens. Nonsmokers preferred.

Employment Information Openings are from May 28 to August 13. Jobs available: ▶ 1 *arts and crafts instructor* (minimum age 18) at $1300–$1400 per season ▶ 1 *assistant cook* (minimum age 19) at $2000–$2100 per season ▶ 1 *athletics specialist* (minimum age 18) at $1300–$1400 per season ▶ 14 *boys counselors* (minimum age 18) at $1200 per season ▶ 1 *computer specialist* (minimum age 18) with knowledge of MAC and IBM; assistive technology experience preferred at $1300–$1400 per season ▶ 14 *girls counselors* (minimum age 18) at $125 per week ▶ 1 *horseback specialist* (minimum age 21) with therapeutic riding experience at $1300–$1400 per season ▶ 3 *kitchen helpers* (minimum age 16) at $125 per week ▶ 3 *maintenance helpers* (minimum age 16) at $125 per week ▶ 1 *pool specialist* (minimum age 21) with WSI/advanced lifesaving certification at $1300–$1400 per season ▶ 1 *public relations specialist* (minimum age 18) with PR/journalism experience at $1300–$1400 per season ▶ 2 *registered nurses* (minimum age 21) at $5000 per season ▶ 1 *trip specialist* (minimum age 21) with outdoor camping experience and first aid/CPR certification at $1300–$1500 per season. Applicants must submit personal reference, one writing sample is required for the public relations specialist position.

International applicants accepted; must apply through a recognized agency. An in-person interview is recommended, but a telephone interview is acceptable.

Benefits and Preemployment Training Free housing, free meals, formal training, and on-the-job training. Preemployment training is required and includes accident prevention and safety, first aid, CPR, interpersonal skills, leadership skills, providing personal care for people who have disabilities.

Contact Ms. Christine Newell, Director, Rocky Mountain Village, PO Box 115, Empire, Colorado 80438. Telephone: 303-569-2333. Fax: 303-569-3857. E-mail: campinfo@cess.org. World Wide Web: http://www.eastersealsco.org. Application deadline: continuous.

ECHO CANYON RIVER EXPEDITIONS
45000 U.S. HIGHWAY 50 WEST
CAÑON CITY, COLORADO 81212

General Information Professional white-water river outfitter offering guided river trips ranging from mild to wild to more than 20,000 guests per year. Established in 1978. 4-acre facility located 8 miles from Canon City.

Profile of Summer Employees Total number: 75; typical age: 24. 60% men; 40% women; 10% minorities; 2% high school students; 65% college students; 4% retirees; 20% local applicants.

Employment Information Openings are from April to September. Jobs available: ► 10 *bus drivers* with CDL license for Colorado, pre-employment drug/alcohol test, and physical at $200–$400 per week ► 10 *customer service representatives* with guest service experience (preferred) at $200–$400 per week ► 2 *equipment maintenance staff* experienced in raft and boating equipment repair at $200–$600 per week ► 40 *river guides* with standard first aid and CPR certification and river guide experience or completion of our training program (fee charged) at $200–$800 per week ► 2 *vehicle mechanics* with CDL (preferred) at $300–$500 per week. Applicants must submit resume, three personal references, letter(s) of recommendation. An in-person interview is recommended, but a telephone interview is acceptable.

Benefits and Preemployment Training Free housing, free meals, and on-the-job training. Preemployment training is required and includes accident prevention and safety, first aid, CPR, interpersonal skills, leadership skills.

Contact David and Kim Burch, Owners, Echo Canyon River Expeditions, PO Box 1002, Colorado Springs, Colorado 80901. Telephone: 719-576-1234. E-mail: echocanyon@worldnet.att.net. World Wide Web: http://www.echocanyonrafting.com.

ELK MOUNTAIN RANCH
13300 COUNTY ROAD 185B
BUENA VISTA, COLORADO 81211

General Information Guest ranch serving 35 guests. A true western vacation experience offering weekly packages from June through the end of September. Established in 1981. 5-acre facility located 90 miles from Colorado Springs. Features: highest elevation in Colorado (9,500 feet); family-oriented; very remote setting; horseback through unspoiled wilderness; white-water rafting; hot tub.

Profile of Summer Employees Total number: 14; typical ages: 19–27. 50% men; 50% women; 100% college students. Nonsmokers required.

Employment Information Openings are from May 15 to September 30. Jobs available: ► 1 *assistant cook* with service-and quality-oriented personality at $650 per month plus gratuities ► 1 *children's counselor* with experience, love of children 4-7, familiarity with horses, and first aid/CPR preferred at $550 per month plus gratuities ► 1 *cook* with high-quality service and love of great food at $800 per month plus gratuities ► 1 *general maintenance person* with knowledge of minor repairs, groundskeeping, and vehicle maintenance at $550 per month plus gratuities ► 5 *waitstaff/housekeeping personnel/dishwashers* with service- and quality-oriented personality at $550 per month plus gratuities ► 6 *wranglers* with experience riding and/or instructing horsemanship and basic knowledge of horses (care, feeding, and grooming) and good people skills; first aid/CPR preferred at $550 per month plus gratuities. Applicants must submit a formal organization application, three personal references. A telephone interview is required.

Benefits and Preemployment Training Free housing, free meals, on-the-job training, and gratuities. Preemployment training is required and includes first aid, CPR.

Contact Sue Murphy, Manager, Elk Mountain Ranch, PO Box 910, Buena Vista, Colorado 81211. Telephone: 800-432-8812. Fax: 719-539-4430. E-mail: murphs1@sni.net. World Wide Web: http://www.elkmtn.com.

FLYING G RANCH
400 SOUTH BROADWAY
DENVER, COLORADO 80209

General Information Residential camp serving approximately 1,500 girls ages 6–17 throughout the summer. Established in 1946. 365-acre facility located 65 miles from Denver. Features: Rocky Mountain setting; surrounded by National Forest; rustic housing-tents; dry-cool climate.

Profile of Summer Employees Total number: 40; typical ages: 19–23. 1% men; 99% women; 15% minorities; 1% high school students; 90% college students; 1% retirees; 17% non-U.S. citizens; 50% local applicants.

Employment Information Openings are from May 22 to August 8. Jobs available: ▶ 1 *administrative assistant* (minimum age 18) with skill in several program areas, business experience, and summer camp experience at $120–$160 per week ▶ 1 *arts and crafts specialist* (minimum age 18) with ability to teach craft activities to a variety of age levels at $120–$160 per week ▶ 1 *assistant camp director/program director* (minimum age 21) with first responder/ EMT certification (can obtain after hire); successful administrative/supervisory experience (preferably in a camp); skill in several program specialties at $165–$250 per week ▶ 18 *assistant unit leaders* (minimum age 18) with experience working with children and/or camp experience at $120–$140 per week ▶ 1 *campcraft specialist* (minimum age 18) with knowledge of hiking, backpacking, compass use, and cooking at $120–$160 per week ▶ 2 *challenge course instructors* (minimum age 18) with training and employment in different levels of challenge courses and first aid and CPR certifications at $130–$170 per week ▶ 1 *health supervisor* (minimum age 21) with RN or LPN license; recent first aid training; school/camp work with children preferred at $300–$400 per week ▶ 8 *horseback riding counselors* (minimum age 18) with training in Western riding, at least 2 years riding experience, and first aid and CPR certifications at $135– $170 per week ▶ 1 *horseback riding director* (minimum age 21) with ability to teach, train, and supervise campers and staff in horsemanship; should have Western riding background and at least 5 years experience in horsemanship training, preferably with children; first aid and CPR certifications at $200–$275 per week ▶ 1 *nature specialist* (minimum age 18) with experience working with children in nature awareness and outdoor appreciation activities at $120–$160 per week ▶ 6 *unit leaders* (minimum age 21) with supervisory skills, experience working with children including camp counseling or leadership techniques, and first aid and CPR certifications at $145–$180 per week. Applicants must submit formal organization application, three personal references. International applicants accepted; must obtain own visa, apply through a recognized agency. An in-person interview is recommended, but a telephone interview is acceptable.

Benefits and Preemployment Training Free housing, free meals, health insurance, on-the-job training, opportunity to attend seminars/workshops, and health/accident insurance. Preemployment training is required and includes accident prevention and safety, interpersonal skills, leadership skills, legal issues dealing with children.

Contact Julie Martinek, Camp Administrator, Flying G Ranch, PO Box 9407, Denver, Colorado 80209-0407. Telephone: 303-778-8774. Fax: 303-733-6345. E-mail: juliecm@gsmhc.org. Application deadline: continuous.

HARMEL'S RANCH RESORT
6748 COUNTY ROAD 742
ALMONT, COLORADO 81210

General Information Family-oriented guest ranch with 38 units, stables, dining room, lounge, heated pool, and store situated at the confluence of 3 river canyons, surrounded by the National Forest. Established in 1958. 300-acre facility located 150 miles from Colorado Springs. Features:

gold medal fishing; horseback riding; white-water rafting; fine dining; guided wilderness pack trips; nightly entertainment.

Profile of Summer Employees Total number: 72; typical ages: 18–27. 50% men; 50% women; 80% college students; 10% non-U.S. citizens; 10% local applicants. Nonsmokers preferred.

Employment Information Openings are from May 1 to November 7. Jobs available: ▶ 25 *housekeepers/waitpersons* (minimum age 18) at $750 to $1200 per month plus room and board ▶ *kitchen workers* (minimum age 18) at $750 to $1200 per month plus room and board ▶ 5 *ranch hands* (minimum age 18) at $750 to $1200 per month plus room and board ▶ 5 *store and office personnel* (minimum age 18) at $750 to $1200 per month plus room and board ▶ 12 *wranglers* (minimum age 18) at $750 to $1200 per month plus room and board. Applicants must submit formal organization application, cover letter, resume, two personal references, two letters of recommendation. International applicants accepted; must apply through a recognized agency. An in-person interview is recommended, but a telephone interview is acceptable.

Benefits and Preemployment Training Free housing, free meals, formal training, possible full-time employment, on-the-job training, and opportunity to attend seminars/workshops.

Contact Brad Roberts, Manager, Harmel's Ranch Resort, PO Box 399, Almont, Colorado 81210. Telephone: 970-641-1740. Fax: 970-641-1944. E-mail: stay@harmels.com. World Wide Web: http://www.harmels.com. Application deadline: continuous.

LONGACRE EXPEDITIONS, COLORADO
TAYLOR PARK, COLORADO

General Information Adventure travel program emphasizing group living skills and physical challenges. Using base camp as a staging area, 2–3 staffers and 10–16 campers participate in various expeditions in which they engage in human-powered sports. Established in 1981. 60-acre facility located 20 miles from Crested Butte. Features: old lodge in Colorado.

Profile of Summer Employees Total number: 20; typical ages: 21–30. 50% men; 50% women; 10% minorities; 40% college students; 30% local applicants. Nonsmokers required.

Employment Information Openings are from June 15 to August 15. Jobs available: ▶ 8 *assistant trip leaders* (minimum age 21) with advanced first aid or advanced wilderness first aid, CPR, and good driving record at $252–$300 per week ▶ 1 *mountaineering instructor* (minimum age 21) with good driving record, WFR, and CPR at $300–$400 per week ▶ 1 *rock climbing instructor* (minimum age 21) with good driving record, WFR, and CPR at $300–$400 per week ▶ 3 *support and logistics staff members* (minimum age 21) with good driving recored, CPR, and WFR at $180–$240 per week. Applicants must submit a formal organization application, three personal references. International applicants accepted; must obtain own visa, obtain own working papers. An in-person interview is recommended, but a telephone interview is acceptable.

Benefits and Preemployment Training Free housing, free meals, on-the-job training, and pro-deal purchase program. Preemployment training is required and includes accident prevention and safety, interpersonal skills, leadership skills.

Contact Meredith Schuler, Directors, Longacre Expeditions, Colorado, RD 3, Box 106, Newport, Pennsylvania 17074. Telephone: 717-567-6790. Fax: 717-567-3955. E-mail: longacre@ longacreexpeditions.com. World Wide Web: http://www.longacreexpeditions.com. Application deadline: continuous.

NATIONAL PARK SERVICE BLACK CANYON OF THE GUNNISON NATIONAL MONUMENT AND CURECANTI NATIONAL RECREATION AREA
102 ELK CREEK
GUNNISON, COLORADO 81230

General Information Preserves resources, provides for public enjoyment, and offers educational programs on natural and historic aspects of area. Established in 1916. 75,000-acre facility located 10 miles from Gunnison. Features: river; reservoir; canyon; mesas; mountains; vistas.

Profile of Summer Employees Total number: 100; typical ages: 18–70. 50% men; 50% women; 2% minorities; 50% college students; 25% retirees; 2% local applicants. Nonsmokers preferred.

Employment Information Jobs available: ▶ 1–3 *interpretation interns* (minimum age 18) with education, life sciences, or history background at $50 per week ▶ 1–5 *outreach environmental education interns* (minimum age 18) with education, life sciences, or history background at $50 per week. Applicants must submit formal organization application, academic transcripts, three personal references, three letters of recommendation. International applicants accepted; must obtain own visa. A telephone interview is required.

Benefits and Preemployment Training Free housing, formal training, on-the-job training, opportunity to attend seminars/workshops, and food stipend. Preemployment training is required and includes accident prevention and safety, leadership skills.

Contact Wm. C. Johnson, PhD, Education Specialist, National Park Service Black Canyon of the Gunnison National Monument and Curecanti National Recreation Area, 102 Elk Creek, Gunnison, Colorado 81230. Telephone: 970-641-2337 Ext. 204. Fax: 970-641-3127. E-mail: bj_johnson@nps.gov. World Wide Web: http://www.nps.gov/blca. Application deadline: continuous.

THE NAVIGATORS EAGLE LAKE CAMP–COLORADO
3820 NORTH 30TH STREET
COLORADO SPRINGS, COLORADO 80904

General Information 5 camps including wilderness adventure, horsemanship, mountain and road biking, resident experiences, and karate. Serves more than 2000 campers ages 8-18 each summer. Something for every kid so every kid succeeds. Established in 1957. 320-acre facility located 9 miles from Colorado Springs. Features: located in Pikes National Forest; 10-acre freshwater lake; zipline; covered basketball courts; cabins and teepees; waterslide.

Profile of Summer Employees Total number: 110; typical ages: 19–28. 45% men; 55% women; 10% minorities; 90% college students; 10% local applicants. Nonsmokers required.

Employment Information Openings are from May 20 to August 15. Jobs available: ▶ 65 *counselors* with one year of college and CPR/SFA certification at $1000 per season ▶ 2 *emergency medical technicians* with EMT basic training at $1000 per season ▶ 2 *food service staff members* at $1000 per season ▶ 5 *maintenance staff members* with experience at $1000 per season ▶ 2 *office administration staff members* at $1000 per season ▶ 2 *registered nurses* at $1000–$1400 per season ▶ 1 *transportation director* (minimum age 22) with first aid/CPR certifications at $1000 per season ▶ 1 *videographer* with experience in the field at $1000 per season. Applicants must submit a formal organization application, two personal references. International applicants accepted; must obtain own visa, obtain own working papers. A telephone interview is required.

Benefits and Preemployment Training Free housing, free meals, health insurance, and on-the-job training. Preemployment training is required and includes accident prevention and safety, interpersonal skills, leadership skills.

Contact Craig Dunham, Associate Director, The Navigators Eagle Lake Camp–Colorado, PO Box 6000, Colorado Springs, Colorado 80934. Telephone: 719-472-1260. Fax: 719-472-1208. E-mail: craigd@navyouth.org. World Wide Web: http://www.eaglelake.org. Application deadline: continuous.

NORTH FORK GUEST RANCH
55395 HIGHWAY 285, PO BOX B
SHAWNEE, COLORADO 80475

General Information Small ranch offering a weekly family-oriented vacation. All-inclusive package (meals, activities, and lodging) with lots of personal attention and western fun. Established in 1985. 520-acre facility located 50 miles from Denver. Features: horseback riding; fly fishing; swimming pool; fishing pond and river; mountain setting.

Profile of Summer Employees Total number: 22; typical ages: 19–29. 40% men; 60% women; 90% college students; 10% local applicants. Nonsmokers required.

Employment Information Openings are from April 1 to November 1. Jobs available: ▶ 3 *activity personnel/maintenance/drivers* (minimum age 19) with good driving record at $500–$600 per month ▶ 3 *cooks* (minimum age 19) must enjoy cooking at $450–$550 per month ▶ *editors* ▶ 3 *kids' counselors* (minimum age 19) with WSI/lifeguard certification; CPR and first aid training preferred at $500–$600 per month ▶ 6 *waitresses/waiters and cabin staff members* (minimum age 19) with food service experience preferred at $500–$600 per month ▶ 8 *wranglers* (minimum age 19) with CPR/first aid training and experience with horses at $500–$600 per month. Applicants must submit a formal organization application, letter of recommendation. International applicants accepted; must obtain own visa, obtain own working papers. A telephone interview is required.

Benefits and Preemployment Training Free housing, free meals, possible full-time employment, and on-the-job training.

Contact Dean and Karen May, Owners/Managers, North Fork Guest Ranch, PO Box B, Shawnee, Colorado 80475. Telephone: 800-843-7895. Fax: 303-838-1549. E-mail: northforkranch@ worldnet.att.net. World Wide Web: http://www.northforkranch.com. Application deadline: continuous.

PEACEFUL VALLEY LODGE AND GUEST RANCH
475 PEACEFUL VALLEY ROAD
LYONS, COLORADO 80540

General Information Dude ranch serving 80–130 people in weeklong programs that include horseback lessons and rides, 4-wheel drive trips, fishing, hiking, swimming, a children's program, entertainment, 3 meals per day, cabins, and rooms. Established in 1953. 320-acre facility located 60 miles from Denver. Features: 800,000-acre National Forest; 8,400-foot elevation; on the St. Vrain River; location near Continental Divide; indoor/outdoor riding arenas; indoor pool.

Profile of Summer Employees Total number: 45; typical ages: 18–25. 50% men; 50% women; 5% minorities; 75% college students; 5% retirees; 5% non-U.S. citizens; 5% local applicants. Nonsmokers preferred.

Employment Information Openings are from May 1 to October 15. Year-round positions also offered. Jobs available: ▶ 4 *assistant cooks* (minimum age 18) at $5.35 per hour ▶ 4 *counselors* (minimum age 18) with first aid and water safety certification at $5.35 per hour ▶ 3 *dishwashers* (minimum age 18) at $5.35 per hour ▶ 2 *drivers/mechanical personnel* (minimum age 18) with a copy of driver's license and record; first aid certification at $5.35 per hour ▶ 2 *gardeners/ grounds crew* (minimum age 18) at $5.35 per hour ▶ 7 *housekeepers* (minimum age 18) at $5.35 per hour ▶ 1 *office person* (minimum age 18) with typing ability at $5.35 per hour ▶ 4 *skilled maintenance staff members* (minimum age 18) with mechanical aptitude at $5.35 per hour ▶ 8 *waiters/waitresses* (minimum age 18) at $5 per hour ▶ 12 *wranglers* (minimum age 18) with first aid certification at $5.35 per hour. Applicants must submit a formal organization application, three personal references, three letters of recommendation. International applicants accepted; must obtain own visa. An in-person interview is recommended, but a telephone interview is acceptable.

Benefits and Preemployment Training Housing at a cost, meals at a cost, and on-the-job training.

Contact Rick Kagen, General Manager, Peaceful Valley Lodge and Guest Ranch, 475 Peaceful Valley Road, Lyons, Colorado 80540. Telephone: 303-747-2881. Fax: 303-747-2167. E-mail: howdy@peacefulvalley.com. Application deadline: continuous.

THE PEAKS AT TELLURIDE RESORT
PO BOX 2702
TELLURIDE, COLORADO 81435

General Information Luxury resort and spa located in the southwest section of Colorado in Telluride Mountain Village and surrounded by 14,000-foot peaks of the San Juan Mountain Range. 6-acre facility located 65 miles from Montrose. Features: largest spa in North America; hiking; biking; horseback riding; largest concentration of 14,000-foot peaks; pristine mountain setting.

Profile of Summer Employees Total number: 400; typical ages: 18–25. 50% men; 50% women; 30% minorities; 70% college students; 10% non-U.S. citizens; 35% local applicants.

Employment Information Openings are from May 21 to September 7. Winter break and year-round positions also offered. Jobs available: ▶ 1–3 *bell staff* (minimum age 18) with valid driver's license and good driving record, neat appearance and pleasant demeanor; must take prescreen drug test at $3.85 to $4.25 per hour plus gratuities ▶ 10–20 *food/beverage staff* (minimum age 18) (minimum age 21 for servers, 18 for others) with neat appearance and pleasant demeanor at $3.85 to $4.25 per hour plus gratuities ▶ 10–15 *housekeeping staff* (minimum age 18) with neat appearance and pleasant demeanor at $6.75–$7.50 per hour ▶ 1–3 *kids spa counselors* (minimum age 18) with first aid, CPR, or lifeguard certification, childcare experience; neat appearance and pleasant demeanor at $6.75–$7.75 per hour ▶ 5–8 *kitchen staff* (minimum age 18) with culinary school certification and neat appearance and pleasant demeanor at $7–$9.50 per hour ▶ 3–6 *spa staff* (minimum age 18) with computer skills, guest service experience, neat appearance and pleasant demeanor at $6.75–$8.25 per hour. Applicants must submit formal organization application, resume. International applicants accepted; must apply through a recognized agency. An in-person interview is recommended, but a telephone interview is acceptable.

Benefits and Preemployment Training Free meals, possible full-time employment, health insurance, on-the-job training, and opportunity to attend seminars/workshops. Preemployment training is required and includes accident prevention and safety, first aid, CPR.

Contact Brenda Colwell, Assistant Human Resources Director, The Peaks at Telluride Resort, PO Box 2702, Telluride, Colorado 81435. Telephone: 800-766-5627. Fax: 970-728-4765. E-mail: peakshire@telluridecolorado.net. World Wide Web: http://www.grandbay.com. Application deadline: continuous.

POULTER COLORADO CAMPS
STEAMBOAT SPRINGS, COLORADO 80477

General Information Residential camp and adventure programs serving 80 campers (ages 8–18) per session with group dynamics and outdoor education emphasis. There are frequent wilderness excursions. Established in 1966. 180-acre facility located 160 miles from Denver. Features: riding arena and trails; athletic fields; picturesque wooded setting; climbing wall; natural hot springs.

Profile of Summer Employees Total number: 40; typical ages: 19–26. 43% men; 57% women; 10% minorities; 15% high school students; 71% college students; 5% non-U.S. citizens. Nonsmokers required.

Employment Information Openings are from June 4 to August 20. Jobs available: ▶ 1 *arts and crafts counselor* (minimum age 18) with first aid/CPR; strong arts/crafts skills and teaching experience at $900–$1200 per season ▶ 6–8 *assistant counselors* (minimum age 18) with first aid/CPR required; wilderness first aid preferred at $700–$1000 per season ▶ 3 *cooks* (minimum age 17) with first aid/CPR and experience cooking for large groups at $1000–$3000 per season ▶ 1 *nurse* (minimum age 21) with RN license, first aid, and CPR required (wilderness first aid preferred); camp experience or work with youth preferred at $2000–$3000 per season ▶ 1 *office manager* with strong organizational and leadership skills (camp experience preferred) and administrative/secretarial experience at $1800–$2000 per season ▶ 13 *senior counselors* (minimum age 21) with wilderness first aid/CPR required; lifeguard training (preferred); and experience working with youth at $1000–$1200 per season ▶ 4–8 *wilderness instructors* (minimum age 21) with Wilderness First Responder/EMT and CPR; technical skills and teaching experience at $1100–$2000 per season ▶ 3 *wranglers* (minimum age 18) with first aid/CPR; strong horsemanship and teaching skills; and experience leading Western riding at $1000–$1500 per season. Applicants must submit a formal organization application, three personal references, three letters of recommendation. International applicants accepted; must obtain own visa. An in-person interview is recommended, but a telephone interview is acceptable.

Benefits and Preemployment Training Free housing, free meals, formal training, and on-the-job training. Preemployment training is required and includes accident prevention and safety, first aid, interpersonal skills, leadership skills, wilderness skills, team building.

Contact Jay B. Poulter, Director, Poulter Colorado Camps, PO Box 772947-P, Steamboat Springs, Colorado 80477. Telephone: 888-879-4816. Fax: 970-879-1307. E-mail: poulter@poultercamps.com. World Wide Web: http://www.poultercamps.com. Application deadline: continuous.

ROCKY MOUNTAIN OUTDOOR CENTER
10281 HIGHWAY 50
HOWARD, COLORADO 81233

General Information White-water rafting, kayaking, and canoeing instruction on the Arkansas and Dolores Rivers. Established in 1983. 4-acre facility located 75 miles from Colorado Springs. Features: river; mountains; trails; biking; paddling.

Profile of Summer Employees Total number: 30; typical ages: 20–40. 50% men; 50% women; 5% high school students; 50% college students; 5% local applicants. Nonsmokers required.

Employment Information Openings are from May 1 to September 1. Jobs available: ▶ 2–4 *dishwashers* (minimum age 18) must be ready for hard work; at minimum wage ▶ 1–2 *food preparation staff* (minimum age 18) with some experience at $6–$7 per hour ▶ 5–6 *kayak and canoe instructors* (minimum age 21) with two seasons teaching experience, formal training, and ACA instructor certification at $50–$75 per day ▶ 5 *raft guides* (minimum age 21) with one season experience, formal training and ability to satisfy Colorado requirements at $50–$75 per day. Applicants must submit a cover letter, resume, three personal references, three letters of recommendation. International applicants accepted; must obtain own visa, obtain own working papers. An in-person interview is recommended, but a telephone interview is acceptable.

Benefits and Preemployment Training Housing at a cost, meals at a cost, formal training, on-the-job training, and opportunity to attend seminars/workshops. Preemployment training is required and includes accident prevention and safety, first aid, CPR.

Contact Andy Waldbart, President, Rocky Mountain Outdoor Center, 10281 Highway 50, Howard, Colorado 81233. Telephone: 719-942-3214. Fax: 719-942-3215. E-mail: 73354.2030@ compuserv.com. World Wide Web: http://www.rmoc.com. Application deadline: January 31.

ROYAL GORGE COMPANY OF COLORADO
4218 FREMONT COUNTY ROAD 3-A
CAÑON CITY, COLORADO 81212

General Information Scenic attraction with world's highest suspension bridge located 1,053 feet above the Arkansas River offers rides, picnic areas, gift shops and food concessions. Established in 1947. 5,120-acre facility located 65 miles from Colorado Springs. Features: Silverrock Railway; incline railway; aerial tramway; multimedia theater; carousel; picnic areas.

Profile of Summer Employees Total number: 180–200; typical ages: 16–21. 50% men; 50% women; 10% minorities; 50% high school students; 20% college students; 30% retirees; 99% local applicants.

Employment Information Openings are from May 1 to October 31. Spring break and year-round positions also offered. Jobs available: ▶ 6–10 *admission cashiers* (minimum age 14) with cash handling and customer service experience preferred at $5.15–$6 per hour ▶ 6–10 *admission rangres* (minimum age 14) with customer service skills at $5.15–$6 per hour ▶ 4–6 *costume characters* (minimum age 14) at $5.15–$5.50 per hour ▶ 50–55 *food service associates* (minimum age 16, 18 to serve alcohol) at $6–$6.50 per hour ▶ 1–3 *group sales associates* (minimum age 14) at $5.15–$5.50 per hour ▶ 2–4 *information booth workers* (minimum age 16) with customer service skills and friendly personality at $5.15–$5.50 per hour ▶ 2–3 *landscapers* (minimum age 16) at $5.15–$6 per hour ▶ 1–2 *maintenance staff* (minimum age 18) at $6–$6.50 per hour ▶ 6–8 *multimedia theater personnel* (minimum age 16) at $5.15–$6 per hour ▶ 6–8 *park services (janitorial)* (minimum age 16) at $5.15–$6 per hour ▶ 2–4 *park tour guides* (minimum age 16) with good oral communication skills at $7–$7.50 per hour ▶ 2–4 *playport supervisors* (minimum age 16) at $5.15–$6 per hour ▶ 20–25 *retail associates* (minimum age 14) at $5.15–$6 per hour ▶ 8–10 *ride operators* (minimum age 18) at $5.15–$6 per hour ▶ 1–2 *various clerical positions* (minimum age 14) at $5.15–$5.75 per hour. Applicants must submit formal organization application, three personal references. International applicants accepted; must obtain own visa, obtain own working papers, apply through a recognized agency. An in-person interview is required.

Benefits and Preemployment Training Meals at a cost, formal training, possible full-time employment, names of contacts, on-the-job training, opportunity to attend seminars/workshops, and travel reimbursement. Preemployment training is required and includes accident prevention and safety, first aid, CPR, interpersonal skills, leadership skills.

Contact Christine Blazer, Director of Accounting and Personnel, Royal Gorge Company of Colorado, PO Box 549, Cañon City, Colorado 81215. Telephone: 719-275-7507. Fax: 719-269-3501. E-mail: rgb@ris.net. World Wide Web: http://www.rgberis.net. Application deadline: continuous.

SANBORN WESTERN CAMPS
PO BOX 167
FLORISSANT, COLORADO 80816

General Information Boys and girls camps serving ages 7–17 in 2 five-week sessions. Established in 1948. 6,000-acre facility located 35 miles from Colorado Springs. Features: 2 riding stables; science interpretive center; 3 lakes; 17½-inch telescope; 2 heated and filtered pools; 4 tennis courts.

Profile of Summer Employees Total number: 120; typical ages: 20–23. 50% men; 50% women; 20% minorities; 100% college students; 5% non-U.S. citizens. Nonsmokers preferred.

Employment Information Openings are from June 1 to August 19. Jobs available: ▶ 8 *arts and crafts instructors* (minimum age 20) with experience in the field at $1300 per season ▶ 20 *backpacking instructors* (minimum age 20) with experience in the field at $1300 per season ▶ 8 *campcraft instructors* (minimum age 20) with experience in the field at $1300 per season ▶ 8 *canoeing instructors* (minimum age 20) with experience in the field at $1300 per season ▶ 8 *caving instructors* (minimum age 20) with experience in the field at $1300 per season ▶ 4–6 *cooks* (minimum age 18) with experience in the field at $1800–$2000 per season ▶ 4 *drama instructors* (minimum age 20) with experience in the field at $1300 per season ▶ 10 *ecology instructors* (minimum age 20) with experience in the field at $1300 per season ▶ 60 *general counselors* (minimum age 20) with interest and experience in working with children at $1300 per season ▶ 4 *geology instructors* (minimum age 20) with experience in the field at $1300 per season ▶ 10 *mountaineering instructors* (minimum age 20) with experience in the field at $1300 per season ▶ 4 *nurses* (minimum age 22) with RN license and experience at $2500–$3000 per season ▶ 8 *riding instructors* (minimum age 20) with experience in the field at $1300 per season ▶ 8 *rock climbing instructors* (minimum age 20) with experience in the field at $1300 per season ▶ 8 *sports instructors* (minimum age 20) with experience in the field at $1300 per season ▶ 8 *swimming instructors* (minimum age 20) with lifeguard training and experience in the field at $1300 per season ▶ 8 *tennis instructors* (minimum age 20) with experience in the field at $1300 per season. Applicants must submit a formal organization application, cover letter, resume, four letters of recommendation. International applicants accepted; must obtain own visa. An in-person interview is recommended, but a telephone interview is acceptable.

Benefits and Preemployment Training Free housing, free meals, formal training, health insurance, and on-the-job training. Preemployment training is required and includes accident prevention and safety, interpersonal skills, leadership skills.

Contact Rick and Jane Sanborn, Directors, Sanborn Western Camps, 2000 Old Stage Road, PO Box 167, Florissant, Colorado 80816. Telephone: 719-748-3341. Fax: 719-748-3259. E-mail: interbarn@aol.com. World Wide Web: http://www.iex.net/sanborn/sanborn.htm. Application deadline: continuous.

THE SOUTHWESTERN COMPANY, COLORADO
See The Southwestern Company, Tennessee on page 284 for complete description.

STIVERS TEMPORARY PERSONNEL–COLORADO
See Stivers Temporary Personnel–Illinois on page 103 for complete description.

STUDENT CONSERVATION ASSOCIATION (SCA), COLORADO
See Student Conservation Association (SCA), New Hampshire on page 193 for complete description.

SUPERCAMP–COLORADO COLLEGE
COLORADO COLLEGE
COLORADO SPRINGS, COLORADO 80903

General Information Residential program for teens designed to build self-confidence and lifelong learning skills through accelerated learning techniques. Established in 1981. 1,227-acre facility. Features: university dormitories; outdoor ropes course.

Profile of Summer Employees Total number: 30–40; typical ages: 18–22. 50% men; 50% women; 80% college students. Nonsmokers required.

Employment Information Openings are from June to August. Jobs available: ▶ 1 *EMT* with national or state registration at $700–$2800 per season ▶ 10 *counselors* with college degree and PPS credentials, MFCC license, or master's degree in counseling at $1000–$4000 per season ▶ 4–10 *facilitators* with presentation skills and college degree; teaching credentials preferred at $1500–$6000 per week ▶ 1 *nurse/paramedic* with national or state registration at $1000–$4000 per season ▶ 1 *office manager* with high school diploma at $1000–$2000 per season ▶ 15 *team leaders* with high school diploma at $500–$1000 per season. Applicants must submit a formal organization application, two letters of recommendation, in-person interview recommended (videotape interview acceptable). International applicants accepted; must obtain own visa, obtain own working papers.

Benefits and Preemployment Training Free housing, free meals, possible full-time employment, and on-the-job training. Preemployment training is required.

Contact Programs Department, SuperCamp–Colorado College, 1725 South Coast Highway, Oceanside, California 92054-5309. Telephone: 800-285-3276. Fax: 760-722-3507. E-mail: supercamp@aol.com. World Wide Web: http://www.supercamp.com. Application deadline: continuous.

TOMAHAWK RANCH
DENVER, COLORADO 80209

General Information Residential camp serving approximatley 1,500 girls ages 6-17 throughout the summer. Established in 1953. 480-acre facility located 45 miles from Denver. Features: Rocky Mountain setting; surrounded by National Forrest; cabins and tents.

Profile of Summer Employees Total number: 40; typical ages: 19–23. 1% men; 99% women; 15% minorities; 1% high school students; 90% college students; 1% retirees; 17% non-U.S. citizens; 50% local applicants.

Employment Information Openings are from June 4 to August 8. Jobs available: ▶ 1 *administrative assistant* (minimum age 18) with skill in several program areas, and summer camp experience at $120–$155 per week ▶ 1 *arts and crafts specialist* (minimum age 18) with ability to teach craft activities to a variety of age levels at $120–$160 per week ▶ 1 *arts/drama specialist* (minimum age 18) with ability to teach music, dance, puppetry, or theater to groups of children at $120–$160 per week ▶ 1 *assistant camp director/program director* (minimum age 21) with first responder/EMT certification (can obtain after hire); successful administrative/supervisory experience (preferably in a camp); skill in several program specialties at $150–$250 per week ▶ 18 *assistant unit leaders* (minimum age 18) with experience working with children and/or camp experience at $120–$140 per week ▶ 1 *campcraft specialist* (minimum age 18) with knowledge of hiking, backpacking, compass use, and cooking at $120–$160 per week ▶ 1 *farm specialist* (minimum age 18) with ability to care for small farm animals and teach programs at $120–$160 per week ▶ 1 *health supervisor* (minimum age 21) with RN or LPN license; recent first aid training; school/camp work with children preferred at $300–$400 per week ▶ 1 *nature specialist* (minimum age 18) with experience working with children in nature awareness and outdoor appreciation activities at $120–$160 per week ▶ 1 *sports/archery instructor* (minimum age 18) with certification in archery instruction or proven teaching experience with children and ability to teach games and non-competitive sports at $120–$160 per week ▶ 6 *unit leaders* (minimum age 21) with supervisory skills, experience working with children including camp counseling or leadership techniques, and first aid and CPR certifications at $145–$180 per week. Applicants must submit formal organization application, three personal references. International applicants accepted; must obtain own visa, apply through a recognized agency. An in-person interview is recommended, but a telephone interview is acceptable.

Benefits and Preemployment Training Free housing, free meals, health insurance, on-the-job training, opportunity to attend seminars/workshops, and health/accident insurance. Preemployment training is required and includes accident prevention and safety, interpersonal skills, leadership skills, legal issues dealing with children.

Contact Julie Martinek, Camp Administrator, Tomahawk Ranch, PO Box 9407, Denver, Colorado 80209-0407. Telephone: 303-778-8774. Fax: 303-733-6345. E-mail: juliecm@gsmhc.org. Application deadline: continuous.

TUMBLING RIVER RANCH
PO BOX 30
GRANT, COLORADO 80448

General Information Guest ranch serving families. Established in 1940. 200-acre facility located 62 miles from Denver. Features: wilderness area; 9,200-12,000-foot mountains; remote area; rustic and very comfortable; family-oriented.

Profile of Summer Employees Total number: 30; typical ages: 19–40. 50% men; 50% women; 75% college students. Nonsmokers preferred.

Employment Information Openings are from May 1 to October 1. Year-round positions also offered. Jobs available: ▶ 2 *assistant cooks* (minimum age 19) ▶ 8–12 *cabin staff/ waitstaff* (minimum age 19) with willingness to alternate jobs weekly ▶ 3 *children's counselors* (minimum age 19) first aid certification ▶ 2 *cooks* (minimum age 19) ▶ 3 *general maintenance personnel* (minimum age 19) ▶ *mechanics* ▶ 1 *secretary* (minimum age 19) ▶ 7 *wranglers* (minimum age 19) with first aid/CPR certification. Applicants must submit a formal organization application, cover letter, resume, writing sample, two personal references, 3-4 work references.

Benefits and Preemployment Training Free housing, free meals, formal training, and on-the-job training.

Contact Mary Dale Gordon / Megan Gordon-Dugan, Owner/Hiring Manager, Tumbling River Ranch, PO Box 30, Grant, Colorado 80448. Telephone: 303-838-5981. Fax: 303-838-5133. E-mail: info@tumblingriver.com. World Wide Web: http://www.tumblingriver.com. Application deadline: continuous.

VAIL RESORTS
PO BOX 7
VAIL, COLORADO 81658

General Information Owners and operators of Vail, Beaver Creek, Keystone, and Breckenridge ski resorts. 100 miles from Denver. Features: Rocky Mountains of Colorado.

Profile of Summer Employees Total number: 2,500; typical ages: 21–25. 50% men; 50% women.

Employment Information Openings are from January 1 to December 31. Spring break, winter break, and year-round positions also offered. Jobs available: ▶ *childcare staff members* at $8 per hour ▶ *day camp attendants* at $8 per hour ▶ *food service personnel* at $8 per hour ▶ *golf course staff members* at $6–$8 per hour ▶ *grounds/maintenance persons* at $8 per hour ▶ *hospitality positions* at $8 per hour ▶ *lift-operations personnel* at $8–$8 per hour ▶ *wranglers* at $8 per hour. Applicants must submit a formal organization application. International applicants accepted; must obtain own visa. An in-person interview is required.

Benefits and Preemployment Training Housing at a cost, formal training, possible full-time employment, health insurance, and on-the-job training.

Contact Human Resources, Vail Resorts, PO Box 7, Vail, Colorado 81658. Telephone: 970-845-2460. Fax: 970-845-2465. World Wide Web: http://www.snow.com. Application deadline: continuous.

VILLAGE AT BRECKENRIDGE RESORT
655 PARK STREET, PO BOX 8329
BRECKENRIDGE, COLORADO 80424

General Information Mountain resort hosting individuals, families, groups, and conventions in 6 hotel/lodge buildings with over 350 condos and rooms. 20-acre facility located 80 miles from

Denver. Features: Breckenridge Ski Resort; Colorado/Green River; Lake Dillon; weekly live concerts (summer); mountain/wooded setting; central to town.

Profile of Summer Employees Total number: 300. 50% men; 50% women; 10% minorities; 40% college students; 5% non-U.S. citizens; 45% local applicants.

Employment Information Openings are from January to December. Jobs available: ▶ *PBX operators* with excellent phone skills at $7.50 per hour ▶ 2 *activities rangers* with ability to plan and lead activities at $7.50 per hour ▶ *buspersons* with pleasant, service-oriented attitude at $4 to $6 per hour plus gratuities ▶ *cashiers/hosts/hostesses* with pleasant and detail-oriented personality and experience at $7 per hour ▶ *cooks (all types)* with knife, cooking, prep skills, and experience in the field at $8–$10 per hour ▶ *dishwasher* at $7.50–$8.50 per hour ▶ *front desk clerks* with congenial personality and computer skills at $8.25–$9.25 per hour ▶ *grounds staff members* at $8 per hour ▶ *health club attendants* with friendly personality at $7 per hour ▶ *kitchen stewards* at $7.25–$8.50 per hour ▶ *laundry personnel* at $7 per hour ▶ *reservationists* with excellent phone, computer, and selling skills at $7.75-$8.25 per hour plus commission ▶ *room attendants* with friendly, thorough, and efficient work habits at $8–$12 per hour ▶ *waitstaff members* with pleasant, service-oriented attitude at $2.13 per hour plus gratuities. Applicants must submit a formal organization application. International applicants accepted; must obtain own visa, obtain own working papers. An in-person interview is required.

Benefits and Preemployment Training Housing at a cost, possible full-time employment, health insurance, and on-the-job training. Preemployment training is required and includes accident prevention and safety, interpersonal skills, leadership skills, hotel/resort knowledge.

Contact Sarah Ziesmer, Human Resources Recruiter, Village at Breckenridge Resort, PO Box 8329, Breckenridge, Colorado 80424. Telephone: 303-453-3120. Fax: 303-453-3127. World Wide Web: http://www.breckresort.com. Application deadline: continuous.

VISTA VERDE RANCH
PO BOX 465
STEAMBOAT SPRINGS, COLORADO 80477

General Information Upscale dude ranch with a wide variety of activities and adventures in both summer and winter. Established in 1975. 500-acre facility located 25 miles from Steamboat Springs. Features: secluded setting; surrounded by forest; adjacent to continental divide; elegantly furnished accommodations; on-property streams and ponds; wonderful vistas.

Profile of Summer Employees Total number: 35; typical ages: 20–25. 50% men; 50% women; 95% college students; 5% non-U.S. citizens. Nonsmokers preferred.

Employment Information Openings are from May 1 to October 31. Winter break positions also offered. Jobs available: ▶ 2–4 *fishing/hiking guides* with knowledge of flyfishing and biology at $400 per month plus tips ▶ 2–4 *housekeepers/ranch hands* at $400 per month plus tips. Applicants must submit formal organization application, cover letter, resume, five personal references, photo. International applicants accepted; must obtain own visa, obtain own working papers, apply through a recognized agency. A telephone interview is required.

Benefits and Preemployment Training Free housing, free meals, possible full-time employment, and on-the-job training. Preemployment training is required and includes accident prevention and safety, first aid, CPR, interpersonal skills.

Contact Konrad Vallard, Operations Manager, Vista Verde Ranch, PO Box 465, Steamboat Springs, Colorado 80477. Telephone: 800-526-7433. Fax: 970-879-1413. E-mail: vistaverde@compuserve.com. World Wide Web: http://www.vistaverde.com. Application deadline: January 1.

WILDERNESS EDUCATION INSTITUTE–TEEN ADVENTURE COLORADO
COLORADO

General Information Nonprofit environmental education organization that runs camping and backpacking programs for ages 9-18 during the sumer. Established in 1996. Located 100 miles from Denver. Features: very scenic; high ropes course; access to national parks; hiking trails; rustic setting.

Profile of Summer Employees Total number: 20; typical ages: 19–30. 50% men; 50% women;

80% college students; 2% non-U.S. citizens; 10% local applicants. Nonsmokers preferred.

Employment Information Openings are from June 20 to August 20. Jobs available: ▶ 8–12 *backpacking instructors* (minimum age 21) with first aid and CPR certifications, backpacking and teaching experience at $1600 per season ▶ 6–8 *teaching counselors/instructors* (minimum age 19) with first aid and CPR certifications, teaching, and camp experience at $1600 per season. Applicants must submit formal organization application, resume, academic transcripts, three personal references, three letters of recommendation. International applicants accepted; must obtain own visa, obtain own working papers. A telephone interview is required.

Benefits and Preemployment Training Free housing, free meals, formal training, health insurance, names of contacts, and on-the-job training. Preemployment training is required and includes accident prevention and safety, interpersonal skills, leadership skills, backpacking, "leave no trace" camping, and basic mountaineering.

Contact Anne Dubinsky, Co-Director, Wilderness Education Institute–Teen Adventure Colorado, PO Box 660652, Sacramento, California 95866. Telephone: 877-628-9692. Fax: 877-628-9692. E-mail: dubinsky@alumni.stanford.org. World Wide Web: http://www.pages.prodigy.net/wilderness/wei. Application deadline: March 15.

WILDERNESS TRAILS RANCH
23486 COUNTY ROAD 501
BAYFIELD, COLORADO 81122

General Information American plan ranch located in secluded mountain valley accommodating 48 guests weekly offering children's and teen programs, nightly entertainment, and a variety of activities. Established in 1950. 160-acre facility located 220 miles from Albuquerque, New Mexico. Features: exceptional setting; adjacent to wilderness; well-trained horses and riding program; heated 72-foot pool and hot tub; water skiing; horse-drawn hay rides.

Profile of Summer Employees Total number: 30; typical ages: 18–25. 50% men; 50% women; 87% college students; 7% non-U.S. citizens; 7% local applicants. Nonsmokers required.

Employment Information Openings are from May 15 to October 3. Jobs available: ▶ 8 *cabin/kitchen staff members* (minimum age 18) with food service/housekeeping experience preferred (training available) at $850 per month ▶ 1–2 *chefs/assistant chefs* (minimum age 22) should be culinary school graduate or have several years cooking experience at $1200–$2000 per month ▶ 3 *children's counselors* (minimum age 18) with CPR/first aid certification, love of children, and extensive experience working with children at $850–$900 per month ▶ 1 *grounds/maintenance person* (minimum age 18) with electrical, woodworking, and pool/grounds maintenance experience at $850–$1000 per month ▶ 1 *kitchen aide* (minimum age 18) with organizational skills, cooking, and prep work experience at $850 per month ▶ 2 *office/clerical persons* (minimum age 18) with clerical and computer experience and excellent telephone skills at $850 per month ▶ 10 *wranglers* (minimum age 18) with CPR/first aid certification; advanced riding skills, and experience teaching riding at $850–$1200 per month. Applicants must submit formal organization application, resume, three personal references, three letters of recommendation. International applicants accepted; must obtain own visa, obtain own working papers, apply through a recognized agency. A telephone interview is required.

Benefits and Preemployment Training Free housing, free meals, and on-the-job training. Preemployment training is required and includes accident prevention and safety, ranch procedures, guest relations.

Contact Jan Roberts, Owner, Wilderness Trails Ranch, 1766 County Road 302, Durango, Colorado 81301. Telephone: 970-247-0722. Fax: 970-247-1006. E-mail: jobs@wildernesstrails.com. World Wide Web: http://www.wildernesstrails.com/jobs. Application deadline: continuous.

WINTER PARK RESORT
PO BOX 36
WINTER PARK, COLORADO 80482

General Information Mountain resort offering a variety of mountain bike and hiking trails, an alpine slide, an indoor and outdoor climbing wall, and an 18-hole mini golf course. Established in 1940. 1,413-acre facility located 67 miles from Denver. Features: mountain setting; mountain biking; hiking; music festivals; rodeos; outdoor activities.

Profile of Summer Employees Total number: 100; typical ages: 18–25. 60% men; 40% women; 30% college students; 70% local applicants.

Employment Information Openings are from June 1 to September 5. Spring break, winter break, and year-round positions also offered. Jobs available: ▶ 10 *mountain bike rental and repair shop staff* (minimum age 18) with high school diploma or GED at $6.65 per hour ▶ 25 *summer program attendants* (minimum age 18) with high school diploma or GED at $6.65 per hour. Applicants must submit a formal organization application. International applicants accepted; must obtain own visa. An in-person interview is recommended, but a telephone interview is acceptable.

Benefits and Preemployment Training Housing at a cost, possible full-time employment, health insurance, and on-the-job training. Preemployment training is required and includes accident prevention and safety, first aid, CPR, interpersonal skills.

Contact Kristen Busch, Recruitment Coordinator, Winter Park Resort, Box 36, Winter Park, Colorado 80482. Telephone: 970-726-1536. Fax: 303-892-5823. E-mail: wpjobs@mail. skiwinterpark.com. World Wide Web: http://www.skiwinterpark.com.

YMCA CAMP SHADY BROOK
8716 SOUTH Y-CAMP ROAD
SEDALIA, COLORADO 80135

General Information Residential facility serving campers ages 7–18 in 1- or 2-week sessions. Camp houses 182 campers and about 50 staff members. Activities include horsemanship, environmental arts and crafts, wilderness trips, canoeing, kayaking, nature trips, archery, riflery, and drama. 150-acre facility located 43 miles from Colorado Springs.

Profile of Summer Employees 45% men; 55% women; 5% minorities; 5% high school students; 85% college students; 2% non-U.S. citizens; 60% local applicants.

Employment Information Openings are from May to August. Jobs available: ▶ 1 *archery instructor* (minimum age 18) with first aid, CPR certification, and experience and/or education in archery at $120–$135 per week ▶ 1 *arts and crafts instructor* (minimum age 18) with first aid, CPR certification, and experience and/or education in art-related field or area at $120–$135 per week ▶ 1 *assistant trips coordinator* (minimum age 18) with first aid, CPR certification, and wilderness camping experience at $125–$135 per week ▶ 1 *assistant wrangler* (minimum age 18) with first aid, CPR certification, and experience riding and working with horses at $100–$115 per week ▶ 1 *canoe/kayak instructor* (minimum age 18) with first aid, CPR certification, and experience in canoeing, kayaking, and boat maintenance at $120–$135 per week ▶ 20 *counselors* (minimum age 18) with first aid, CPR certification, lifeguarding and wilderness camping experience (preferred) at $115–$135 per week ▶ 1 *drama instructor* (minimum age 18) with first aid, CPR, and ability to direct plays at $120–$135 per week ▶ 1 *head wrangler* (minimum age 18) with Camp Horsemanship Association, first aid, and CPR certification at $130–$145 per week ▶ 2 *kitchen assistants* (minimum age 16) with first aid and CPR certification at $100–$115 per week ▶ 1 *lifeguard* (minimum age 18) with first aid, CPR, and lifeguarding certification at $115–$120 per week ▶ 1 *naturalist* (minimum age 18) with first aid, CPR certification, and experience and/or education in natural sciences at $120–$135 per week ▶ 1 *office assistant/store manager* (minimum age 18) with first aid, CPR certification, and general clerical skills at $130–$140 per week ▶ 1 *recreation/ropes course instructor* (minimum age 18) with first aid, CPR, and low challenge course facilitator certification at $120–$135 per week ▶ *registered nurse* with current license ▶ 1 *riflery instructor* (minimum age 18) with first aid, CPR certification, and experience and/or education in riflery at $120–$135 per week ▶ 4 *sectional leaders* (minimum age 18) with first aid, CPR certification, and counseling experience at $145–$160 per week ▶ 10 *tripping assistants* (minimum age 18) with first aid, CPR certification, and lifeguarding at $100–$115 per week ▶ 1 *trips apprentice* (minimum age 18) with first aid and CPR certification at $75–$100 per week ▶ 1 *trips coordinator* (minimum age 18) with first aid, CPR certification, wilderness camping experience, and management skills at $140–$160 per week ▶ 1 *waterfront assistant* (minimum age 18) with lifeguard, first aid, and CPR certification at $115–$125 per week ▶ 1 *waterfront supervisor* (minimum age 18) with WSI, first aid, lifeguarding, and CPR certification at $125–$135 per week ▶ 1 *wrangler* (minimum age 18) with first aid, CPR certification, and desire to learn more about riding and instruction at $75–$100 per week.

Benefits and Preemployment Training Free housing, free meals, formal training, and on-the-job training. Preemployment training is required and includes accident prevention and safety, first aid, CPR, interpersonal skills, leadership skills.

Contact Chris Pierce, Program Coordinator YMCA Camp Shady Brook, Department P98, YMCA Camp Shady Brook, 2380 Montebello Drive West, Colorado Springs, Colorado 80918. Telephone: 303-647-2313. Fax: 303-647-0513. Application deadline: continuous.

YMCA OF THE ROCKIES–CAMP CHIEF OURAY
PO BOX 648
GRANBY, COLORADO 80446-0648

General Information Residential camp dedicated to helping children grow in spirit, mind, and body. Programs for teens include backpacking, leadership training, rafting, and mountain biking. Established in 1907. 4,950-acre facility located 80 miles from Denver. Features: challenge course; reservoir; wooded setting; frisbee golf course; biathalon range; teepee village.

Profile of Summer Employees Total number: 75; typical ages: 19–30. 50% men; 50% women; 1% minorities; 1% high school students; 98% college students; 1% retirees; 1% non-U.S. citizens. Nonsmokers required.

Employment Information Openings are from May 19 to August 21. Jobs available: ▶ 46 *cabin counselors* (minimum age 18) with CPR and first aid certification at $120–$135 per week ▶ 4 *dishwashers* (minimum age 16) with CPR and FA at $110–$120 per week ▶ 2 *nurses* (minimum age 21) with RN preferred at $400–$600 per week ▶ 5 *riding staff members* (minimum age 19) with CPR and FA; experience with horses and teens at $125–$200 per week ▶ 10 *support staff members* (minimum age 21) with CPR and FA at $125–$175 per week ▶ 15 *wilderness adventure staff* (minimum age 20) with CPR and FA; backpacking, rafting, mountain biking, and experience working with teens at $135–$200 per week. Applicants must submit formal organization application, three personal references. International applicants accepted; must obtain own visa, obtain own working papers, apply through a recognized agency. A telephone interview is required.

Benefits and Preemployment Training Free housing, free meals, health insurance, and on-the-job training. Preemployment training is required and includes accident prevention and safety, first aid, CPR, interpersonal skills, leadership skills.

Contact Trueman Hoffmeister, Camp Director, YMCA of the Rockies–Camp Chief Ouray, PO Box 648, Granby, Colorado 80446-0648. Telephone: 970-887-2152 Ext. 4174. Fax: 303-449-6781. E-mail: chiefouray@aol.com. Application deadline: continuous.

YMCA OF THE ROCKIES ESTES PARK CENTER
2515 TUNNEL ROAD
ESTES PARK, COLORADO 80511-2550

General Information Large Christian-oriented family resort and conference center offering a day camp and serving an average of 3,500 family and conference guests daily during the summer months. Established in 1907. 850-acre facility located 60 miles from Denver. Features: located next to Rocky Mountain National Park; property surrounded by majestic mountains; variety of recreational activities.

Profile of Summer Employees Total number: 500; typical ages: 18–75. 40% men; 60% women; 8% minorities; 10% high school students; 45% college students; 25% retirees; 14% non-U.S. citizens; 10% local applicants.

Employment Information Openings are from January 1 to December 31. Jobs available: ▶ 12 *craft shop staff members* (minimum age 18) with artistic talent and/or experience with arts and crafts at $145 per week ▶ 60 *day camp/adventure camp counselors* (minimum age 21) with first aid/CPR and training and/or practical experience in education/day camp work/childcare at $145 per week ▶ *environmental education counselor* (minimum age 18) with CPR/first aid, background in environmental sciences, and experience in the field at $145 per week ▶ 8 *family programmers* (minimum age 18) should enjoy working with families planning activities; first aid/CPR preferred at $145 per week ▶ 105 *food service personnel* (minimum age 18) at $145 per week ▶ 12 *front desk clerks* (minimum age 18) with computer and public relations skills at $145 per week ▶ 80 *housekeeping staff members* (minimum age 18) at $145 per week ▶ 12 *maintenance workers* (minimum age 18) with good driving record at $145 per week ▶ 2 *miniature golf and roller skating rink attendants* (minimum age 18) at $145 per week ▶ 11 *pool guards* with lifeguard certification (Red Cross or YMCA), first aid, and CPR at $145 per week ▶ 3 *resident assistants* (minimum age 21) with good driving record and at least one year experience as a college resident assistant at $195 per week ▶ 2 *telephone operators* with computer and public relations skills at $145 per week. Applicants must submit formal organization application, three personal references, telephone interview in some positions. International applicants accepted; must apply through a recognized agency.

Benefits and Preemployment Training Free housing, free meals, possible full-time employment, health insurance, and on-the-job training. Preemployment training is required and includes accident prevention and safety, interpersonal skills, leadership skills.

Contact Patrice A. Flauné, Human Resource Director, YMCA of the Rockies Estes Park Center, 2515 Tunnel Road, Estes Park, Colorado 80511-2550. Telephone: 970-586-3341 Ext. 1031. Fax: 970-586-6078. E-mail: pflaune@epcenter.org.

YMCA OF THE ROCKIES, SNOW MOUNTAIN RANCH
PO BOX 169
WINTER PARK, COLORADO 80482

General Information A year-round YMCA conference center and family resort accommodating up to 2,100 guests per day. Owned by YMCA of the Rockies. Established in 1907. 5,150-acre facility located 90 miles from Denver. Features: located in beautiful Rocky Mountains; indoor swimming pool; tennis; trail system for hiking and mountain biking; basketball courts; climbing wall.

Profile of Summer Employees Total number: 200; typical ages: 19–22. 40% men; 60% women; 15% minorities; 1% high school students; 62% college students; 10% retirees; 25% non-U.S. citizens; 2% local applicants. Nonsmokers preferred.

Employment Information Openings are from May 26 to August 22. Spring break, winter break, and year-round positions also offered. Jobs available: ▶ 1 *chaplain's assistant* (minimum age 18) with valid driver's license issued by a US state's Department of Motor Vehicles at $145 per week ▶ 1–2 *conference associates* (minimum age 18) with office and/or guest relations experience preferred at $145 per week ▶ 7 *conference services staff members* (minimum age 18) with valid driver's license issued by a US state's Department of Motor Vehicles at $145 per week ▶ 7 *crafts shop instructors* (minimum age 18) at $145 per week ▶ 2 *family programs assistants* (minimum age 18) with first aid and CPR certification at $145 per week ▶ 47 *food service personnel* (minimum age 18) at $145 per week ▶ 13 *front desk clerks* (minimum age 18) at $145 per week ▶ 65 *housekeeping personnel* (minimum age 18) at $145 per week ▶ 1 *human resources associate* (minimum age 18) with valid driver's license issued by a US state's Department of Motor Vehicles; interest in human resources as a career preferred at $145 per week ▶ 5 6 *janitorial crew* (minimum age 18) at $145 per week ▶ 15 *lifeguards* (minimum age 18) with American Red Cross lifeguard, first aid, and CPR certification or equivalent at $155 per week ▶ 10 *maintenance personnel* (minimum age 18) with valid driver's license issued by a US state's Department of Motor Vehicles at $145 per week ▶ 2 *recreation attendants* (minimum age 18) with first aid and CPR certification at $145 per week ▶ 4 *retail sales personnel* (minimum age 18) at $145 per week ▶ 11 *youth program and early childhood counselors* (minimum age 18) with CPR and first aid certification at $145 per week. Applicants must submit a formal organization application, three letters of recommendation. International applicants accepted; must obtain own visa, obtain own working papers.

Benefits and Preemployment Training Free housing, free meals, formal training, possible full-time employment, on-the-job training, and extensive seasonal staff activities. Preemployment training is required and includes accident prevention and safety, customer service.

Contact Julie Watkins, Human Resources Director, YMCA of the Rockies, Snow Mountain

Ranch, PO Box 169, Winter Park, Colorado 80482. Telephone: 970-887-2152. Fax: 303-449-6781. E-mail: jfuqua@snowmtnranch.org. World Wide Web: http://www.ymcarockies.org. Application deadline: continuous.

CONNECTICUT

ACE COMPUTER CAMP–CONNECTICUT
See ACE Computer Camp–Washington on page 307 for complete description.

AWOSTING AND CHINQUEKA CAMPS
BANTAM, CONNECTICUT 06750
General Information Residential camps serving 140 boys and 125 girls in programs of two to eight weeks. There are two separate campuses 4 miles apart that have daily coed programs as well as coed evening activities. Established in 1900. 200-acre facility located 10 miles from Torrington. Features: large 3½-mile long lake; cabins with facilities; wooded setting; 1,000-foot elevations with great weather; more than 100 watercraft; go-kart and minibike tracks.

Profile of Summer Employees Total number: 85; typical ages: 19–26. 50% men; 50% women; 10% minorities; 80% college students; 5% retirees; 30% non-U.S. citizens; 5% local applicants. Nonsmokers required.

Employment Information Openings are from June 22 to August 22. Jobs available: ▶ 2 *archery instructors* (minimum age 19) with NAA certification (clinic available) at $1200–$1600 per season ▶ 3 *arts and crafts instructors* (minimum age 19) with experience teaching or assisting instruction at $1200–$1600 per season ▶ 4 *black-and-white photography/video/filming instructors* (minimum age 19) with knowledge of equipment at $1200–$1600 per season ▶ 2 *ceramics/clay instructors* (minimum age 19) with pottery wheel and kiln firing knowledge at $1200–$1600 per season ▶ 4 *computers and journalism staff members* (minimum age 19) with ability to operate Apple and IBM computers and experience in the field at $1200–$1600 per season ▶ 3 *dance/theater/music instructors* (minimum age 19) with some stage and music background at $1200–$1600 per season ▶ 2 *fencing instructors* (minimum age 19) with some coaching background at $1200–$1600 per season ▶ 2 *go-cart/minibike personnel* (minimum age 20) with knowledge of equipment and racing at $1200–$1600 per season ▶ 2 *golf instructors* (minimum age 19) with experience at $1200–$1600 per season ▶ 3 *gymnastics instructors* (minimum age 19) with coach certification and experience in the field at $1200–$1600 per season ▶ 6 *kitchen aides* (minimum age 20) with food service experience at $1500–$1900 per season ▶ 2 *laundry workers* with some laundry experience at $1400–$1600 per season ▶ 2 *maintenance personnel* (minimum age 21) with background in painting, carpentry, and grounds maintenance at $1400–$1800 per season ▶ 2 *mountain biking instructors* (minimum age 19) with off-road biking experience at $1200–$1600 per season ▶ 2 *nurses or first aid persons* (minimum age 21) with RN, LPN, EMT, or standard first aid and CPR certification at $1600–$2200 per season ▶ 2 *outdoor camping and hiking staff members* (minimum age 21) with first aid/CPR and experience in Outward Bound/scouting at $1200–$1600 per season ▶ 2 *ropes instructors* (minimum age 20) with certification in ACCT, prior experience with rapelling and zipline (training and certification clinic is available) at $1200–$1700 per season ▶ 6 *small craft instructors* (minimum age 19) with certification in one or more of the following: canoeing, sailing, kayaking, or boating (clinic available) at $1200–$1600 per season ▶ 6 *sports instructors* (minimum age 19) with background in one or more of the following: softball, soccer, tennis, or golf (varsity level or coaching) at $1200–$1600 per season ▶ 6 *swimming instructors* (minimum age 19) with WSI, LGT, or LGTI certification (clinic available) at $1200–$1700 per season ▶ 3 *waterskiing instructors* (minimum age 19) with LGT and CPR certification and teaching experience at $1200–$1600 per season

▶ 2 *woodworking instructors* (minimum age 20) with teaching or assisting woodworking experience; background in woodworking as a hobby; and ability with wood, tools, and machines at $1200–$1600 per season. Applicants must submit formal organization application, personal reference, two letters of recommendation, any certificates of certification (copies). International applicants accepted; must apply through a recognized agency. An in-person interview is recommended, but a telephone interview is acceptable.

Benefits and Preemployment Training Free housing, free meals, on-the-job training, opportunity to attend seminars/workshops, and travel reimbursement. Preemployment training is required and includes accident prevention and safety, first aid, CPR, interpersonal skills, leadership skills.

Contact Oscar Ebner, Director, Awosting and Chinqueka Camps, 4 Breezy Hill, Harwinton, Connecticut 06791. Telephone: 860-485-9566. Fax: 860-485-1681. E-mail: camps@netrax.net. World Wide Web: http://www.awosting.com or www.chinqueka.com. Application deadline: continuous.

BUCK'S ROCK CAMP
59 BUCK'S ROCK ROAD
NEW MILFORD, CONNECTICUT 06776

General Information Creative arts camp primarily devoted to the development of talents and the potential of boys and girls ages 11–16. Established in 1943. 165-acre facility located 75 miles from New York, New York. Features: wooded setting; Olympic-size pool; more than 30 art studios of the highest standard; glass blowing facility; 75 miles from New York City; 5 performance sites.

Profile of Summer Employees Total number: 230; typical ages: 21–39. 50% men; 50% women; 10% minorities; 66% college students; 20% non-U.S. citizens; 5% local applicants. Nonsmokers preferred.

Employment Information Openings are from June 25 to August 24. Jobs available: ▶ 2–3 *batik instructor* (minimum age 21) at $1300–$1750 per season ▶ 4–8 *ceramics instructors* (minimum age 21) at $1350–$1750 per season ▶ *clowning instructors* (minimum age 21) at $1300–$1800 per season ▶ 2–4 *computer science instructors* (minimum age 21) with HTML and programing skills at $1350–$1750 per season ▶ *creative writing instructor* (minimum age 21) at $1350–$1750 per season ▶ 4–6 *dining room staff members* (minimum age 18) at $1250–$1600 per season ▶ 2–4 *farming instructors* (minimum age 21) at $1250–$1600 per season ▶ 6–8 *fine arts instructors* (minimum age 21) at $1300–$1750 per season ▶ 7–8 *graphic artists* (minimum age 21) at $1350–$1650 per season ▶ 16–26 *guidance counselors* (minimum age 21) at $1250–$1700 per season ▶ 8–15 *kitchen staff members* (minimum age 19) at $1250–$1700 per season ▶ 6–10 *maintenance staff members* (minimum age 19) at $1250–$1600 per season ▶ 8–16 *music instructors* (minimum age 21) at $1250–$1750 per season ▶ 2–4 *office assistants* (minimum age 21) at $1300–$1800 per season ▶ 5–7 *photography instructors* (minimum age 21) at $1350–$1750 per season ▶ 2–4 *printing instructors* (minimum age 21) at $1350–$1600 per season ▶ 2–3 *registered nurses* (minimum age 25) with RN or LPN license at $1500–$2500 per season ▶ 2–4 *sculpture instructors* (minimum age 21) at $1300–$1750 per season ▶ 4–8 *sewing instructors* (minimum age 21) at $1300–$1650 per season ▶ 4–8 *silversmithing instructors* (minimum age 21) at $1350–$1750 per season ▶ 1–2 *sports instructors* (minimum age 21) at $1350–$1650 per season ▶ 4–7 *stage design and construction personnel* (minimum age 21) at $1350–$1700 per season ▶ 2–3 *swimming instructors* (minimum age 21) with WSI certification or ARC at $800–$1000 per month ▶ 2–4 *videotaping instructors* (minimum age 21) at $1350–$1750 per season ▶ 2–4 *waterfront staff members* (minimum age 21) with WSI and ARC certifications at $1350–$1850 per season ▶ 3–5 *weaving instructors* (minimum age 21) at $1250–$1650 per season ▶ 5–9 *woodworking instructors* (minimum age 21) at $1300–$1750 per season. Applicants must submit formal organization application, resume, portfolio, three personal references, slides of art work in a s.a.s.e. International applicants accepted; must apply through a recognized agency. An in-person interview is recommended, but a telephone interview is acceptable.

Benefits and Preemployment Training Free housing, free meals, formal training, health insurance, on-the-job training, and laundry service. Preemployment training is required and includes first aid, general orientation to the program.

Contact Laura Morris, Directors, Buck's Rock Camp. Telephone: 860-354-5030. Fax: 860-354-1355. E-mail: buckrock@ix.netcom.com. World Wide Web: http://bucksrock.olm.net. Application deadline: continuous.

CAMP JEWELL YMCA
PROCK HILL ROAD
COLEBROOK, CONNECTICUT 06021

General Information Full-featured coeducational residential camp with teen adventure trips, year-round environmental education, and team building. Established in 1901. 540-acre facility located 35 miles from Hartford. Features: located in the Berkshire Mountains; 55 acrea private lake; unique and innovated; indoor boulding room; giant slide; rope swing.

Profile of Summer Employees Total number: 155; typical ages: 16–65. 50% men; 50% women; 10% minorities; 5% high school students; 85% college students; 1% retirees; 10% non-U.S. citizens; 25% local applicants. Nonsmokers required.

Employment Information Openings are from June 15 to August 22. Year-round positions also offered. Jobs available: ▶ 4 *aquatic program specialists* at $1600–$2300 per season ▶ 30 *cabin counselors* with one year of college completed at $1600–$1700 per season ▶ 3 *crafts program specialists* at $1600–$2500 per season ▶ 1 *drama program specialist* at $1600–$2200 per season ▶ 1 *leader-in-training director* at $1800–$2500 per season ▶ 4 *leader-in-training staff* at $1800–$2000 per season ▶ 2 *naturalists* at $1600–$2500 per season ▶ 2 *ropes course directors* with experience in the field at $1750–$2500 per season ▶ 2 *sailing program specialists* at $1600–$2300 per season ▶ 15 *teen trip leaders* at $1700–$2400 per season ▶ 2 *tennis program specialists* at $1600–$2200 per season ▶ 6 *village directors* with experience in the field at $1800–$2500 per season ▶ 1 *waterfront director* with lifeguard/WSI certification and experience in the field at $1700–$3500 per season. Applicants must submit a formal organization application, three personal references, drug screening provided by camp. An in-person interview is recommended, but a telephone interview is acceptable.

Benefits and Preemployment Training Free housing, free meals, and health insurance. Preemployment training is required and includes accident prevention and safety, first aid, CPR, interpersonal skills, leadership skills.

Contact Paul Kamin, Camp Director, Camp Jewell YMCA, Prock Hill Road, Colebrook, Connecticut 06021. Telephone: 860-379-2782. Fax: 860-397-8715. E-mail: ymca.met.hfd@snet.net. World Wide Web: http://www.ghymca.org. Application deadline: continuous.

CAMP SLOANE YMCA, INC.
124 INDIAN MOUNTAIN ROAD
LAKEVILLE, CONNECTICUT 06039-1950

General Information Non for profit, independent YMCA camp in Northwest Connecticut Berkshire Mountains. Established in 1928. 250-acre facility located near New York City. Features: lake; pool; high/low ropes; climbing wall; indoor/outdoor stage at Performing Arts Building; tent living.

Profile of Summer Employees Total number: 155; typical ages: 17–25. 45% men; 55% women; 20% minorities; 10% high school students; 85% college students; 30% non-U.S. citizens; 5% local applicants.

Employment Information Openings are from June 21 to August 21. Jobs available: ▶ 80 *counselors* (minimum age 18) at $950–$1400 per season ▶ 35 *supervisors* (minimum age 21) at $1500–$2000 per season. Applicants must submit formal organization application, writing sample, two personal references. International applicants accepted; must apply through a recognized agency. A telephone interview is required.

Benefits and Preemployment Training Free housing and free meals. Preemployment training is required and includes accident prevention and safety, CPR, interpersonal skills, leadership skills.

Contact Sharon Brown, Director of Camping Services, Camp Sloane YMCA, Inc., PO Box

1950, Lakeville, Connecticut 06039. Telephone: 860-435-2557. Fax: 860-435-2599. E-mail: info@camp-sloane.org. World Wide Web: http://www.camp-sloane.org. Application deadline: continuous.

CAMP WASHINGTON
190 KENYON ROAD
LAKESIDE, CONNECTICUT 06758

General Information Episcopal, coeducational summer resident and day camp serving a diverse population of campers from Connecticut. Traditional and specialty programs available: tripping program with backpacking, canoeing/kayaking, mountain biking; theater week; choir camp; inner-city day camp; family camps. Established in 1917. 300-acre facility located 25 miles from Waterbury. Features: private pond for swimming; 300 private woodland acres; Adirondack shelter on property for primitive camp set up; 8 dormitory-style cabins (heated with indoor plumbing); easy train access to New York City; located in foothills of Berkshire Mountains in historic Litchfield County.

Profile of Summer Employees Total number: 50–60; typical ages: 18–28. 50% men; 50% women; 15% minorities; 20% high school students; 80% college students; 10% non-U.S. citizens; 90% local applicants. Nonsmokers required.

Employment Information Openings are from June to August. Jobs available: ▶ 1 *counselor-in-training coordinator* (minimum age 21) with experience facilitating young people (ages 16-17) in leadership positions, prior camp work or school equivalent at $1500–$2000 per season ▶ 16–18 *general counselors* (minimum age 18) with experience working with children at $1300–$1500 per season ▶ 2 *head counselors* (minimum age 21) with ability to work with staff, campers, and community in a conflict and behavior management position; ability to conduct staff meetings at $1500–$2000 per season ▶ 1 *nurse* (minimum age 21) with RN or LPN license (valid in Connecticut) at $3000 per season ▶ 5–6 *program coordinators* (minimum age 19) with ability to teach a specific activity, facilitate program area, supervise staff, program inventory and order, and evaluate program at $1500–$1800 per season ▶ 7 *waterfront staff* (minimum age 18) with WSI certification and lifeguard training at $1300–$1500 per season ▶ 6–7 *wilderness trip staff* (minimum age 21) with ability to lead 10-14 day primitive camping trips in the areas of backpacking, canoeing, kayaking, and mountain biking, Good communication skills are a must at $1800–$2000 per season. Applicants must submit formal organization application, three personal references, criminal record background check. International applicants accepted; must apply through a recognized agency. An in-person interview is recommended, but a telephone interview is acceptable.

Benefits and Preemployment Training Free housing, free meals, formal training, possible full-time employment, on-the-job training, opportunity to attend seminars/workshops, and travel reimbursement. Preemployment training is required and includes accident prevention and safety, interpersonal skills, leadership skills, multiculturalism, team-building, behavior management, conflict-resolution.

Contact Elia Vecchitto, Camp Director, Camp Washington, 190 Kenyon Road, Lakeside, Connecticut 06758. Telephone: 860-567-9623. Fax: 860-567-3037. E-mail: elia_v@hotmail.com. Application deadline: continuous.

CHANNEL 3 COUNTRY CAMP
73 TIMES FARM ROAD
ANDOVER, CONNECTICUT 06232

General Information Camp for underprivileged children. Established in 1910. 365-acre facility located 18 miles from Hartford. Features: woods; cabins; river; garden; trails; campsites.

Profile of Summer Employees Total number: 50; typical ages: 18–30. 50% men; 50% women; 35% minorities; 75% college students; 15% non-U.S. citizens; 60% local applicants.

Employment Information Openings are from June 20 to August 23. Jobs available: ▶ 1 *archery instructor* with archery safety course certification at $2000–$2800 per season ▶ 2 *athletics instructors* (minimum age 18) should be good with children at $1500–$2500 per season ▶ 8 *counselors* with two years of organizational camp experience and college junior or senior status at $1500–$2000 per season ▶ 1 *creative crafts instructor* (minimum age 18) with child-handicraft experience and college junior or senior status at $2000–$2800 per season ▶ 1 *environmental education instructor* (minimum age 18) with interest and experience in nature, and college junior or senior status at $2000–$2800 per season ▶ 1 *health care director* with American Red Cross first aid, BLS, and CPR certification at $2800–$3300 per season ▶ 1 *swimming director* with lifeguard training and WSI, American Red Cross BLS, and CPR certification at $2700–$2900 per season ▶ 2 *swimming instructors* (minimum age 18) with LG/CPR; WSI and American Red Cross ALS certification (preferred) *at $2000–$2500 per season. Applicants must submit formal organization application, three personal references. International applicants accepted; must obtain own visa, apply through a recognized agency. An in-person interview is recommended, but a telephone interview is acceptable.*

Benefits and Preemployment Training Free housing, free meals, health insurance, and on-the-job training. Preemployment training is required and includes accident prevention and safety, first aid, CPR, interpersonal skills, leadership skills.

Contact Bob Lilienthal, Executive Director, Channel 3 Country Camp, 73 Times Farm Road, Andover, Connecticut 06232. Telephone: 860-742-2267. Fax: 860-742-3298. E-mail: ch3cc@aol. com. Application deadline: continuous.

LAUREL GIRL SCOUT RESIDENT CAMP
LEBANON, CONNECTICUT 06247

General Information Residential camp with an informal outdoor educational program serving 700 girls ages 6-17. Owned by Girl Scouts Connecticut Trails Council. Established in 1956. 350-acre facility located 16 miles from Hartford. Features: horseback riding trails; 2 lighted riding rings; live-in cabins and tents; large private lake with extensive aquatic programs; farm animals and garden; high/low ropes course.

Profile of Summer Employees Total number: 70; typical ages: 16–35. 5% men; 95% women; 10% minorities; 2% high school students; 50% college students; 10% non-U.S. citizens; 20% local applicants. Nonsmokers required.

Employment Information Openings are from June 20 to August 18. Jobs available: ▶ 1 *archery director* (minimum age 20) with experience in the field at $1200–$1600 per season ▶ 1 *arts and crafts director* (minimum age 18) with experience in the field at $1200–$1600 per season ▶ 1 *assistant camp director* (minimum age 21) with driver's license and experience in the field at $2800–$3200 per season ▶ 2 *assistant cooks* (minimum age 18) with experience in the field at $1600–$1900 per season ▶ 2 *boating instructors* (minimum age 16) with experience in the field at $1000–$1300 per season ▶ 1 *business manager* (minimum age 18) with business training and driver's license at $1200–$1500 per season ▶ 1 *farm life director* with experience in the field at $1200–$1600 per season ▶ 1 *food supervisor* (minimum age 21) with experience in the field at $2500–$2800 per season ▶ 2 *health directors* (minimum age 21) with nurse, LPN, or EMT license; CPR professional certification, and driver's license at $2000–$2800 per season ▶ 1 *horseback riding director* (minimum age 21) with ability to develop and supervise equestrian programs at $1500–$2000 per season ▶ 5 *horseback riding staff members* (minimum age 18) with experience in the field at $750–$1600 per season ▶ 4 *kitchen assistants* (minimum age 16) at $750–$900 per season ▶ 2 *maintenance assistants* (minimum age 16) with ability to lift and to work outdoors at $800–$1200 per season ▶ 1 *naturalist* with experience in the field at $1200–$1600 per season ▶ 2 *program directors* (minimum age 21) with driver's license and experience in the field at $2200–$2800 per season ▶ 1 *ropes course director* (minimum age 18) with experience in the field at $1200–$1600 per season ▶ 1 *trip leader* (minimum age 21) with experience in the field at $1200–$1600 per season ▶ 24 *unit assistants* (minimum age 18) with experience camping and working with children at $1000–$1200 per season ▶ 8 *unit leaders* (minimum age 21) with experience supervising children at $1300–$1600 per season ▶ 6 *waterfront assistants* (minimum age 18) with lifeguard, CPR, FA, or WSI certification at $1200–$1500 per season ▶ 2 *waterfront directors* (minimum age 20) with lifeguard, CPR, and FA certification at $1500–$1900 per season. Applicants must submit formal organization application, personal reference, three letters of recommendation, copies of certifications. International applicants accepted; must apply through a recognized agency. An in-person interview is recommended, but a telephone interview is acceptable.

Benefits and Preemployment Training Free housing, free meals, formal training, health insurance, names of contacts, on-the-job training, opportunity to attend seminars/workshops, and travel reimbursement. Preemployment training is required and includes accident prevention and safety, first aid, CPR, interpersonal skills, leadership skills.

Contact Jan Bruch, Outdoor Program Manager, Laurel Girl Scout Resident Camp, Girls Scouts Connecticut Trails Council, 20 Washington Avenue, North Haven, Connecticut 06473. Telephone: 203-239-2922. Fax: 203-239-7220. E-mail: jan@cttrails.com. Application deadline: continuous.

SJ RANCH, INC.
130 SANDY BEACH ROAD
ELLINGTON, CONNECTICUT 06029

General Information Residential camp offering extensive riding and horse care programs for 48 girls ages 7–15. Established in 1956. 100-acre facility located 20 miles from Hartford. Features: 3 riding rings; cross-country course; lake; tennis and basketball courts; rustic cedar cabins; dining hall and recreation hall.

Profile of Summer Employees Total number: 12; typical ages: 18–35. 1% men; 99% women; 10% high school students; 90% college students; 5% non-U.S. citizens; 10% local applicants. Nonsmokers required.

Employment Information Openings are from June 21 to August 21. Jobs available: ▶ *crafts, kitchen, general, and sports staff members* (minimum age 18) at $1100–$1300 per season ▶ *kitchen and general counselors* (minimum age 18) at $1300–$1500 per season ▶ 4–5 *riding counselors* (minimum age 18) with one year of college completed; should be experienced riders; teaching experience helpful; at $1100–$1600 per season ▶ *swimming counselor* (minimum age 20) with lifeguard training and FPR/CPR certification at $1300–$1500 per season ▶ 2 *swimming instructors* (minimum age 18) with WSI certification at $1100–$1300 per season. Applicants must submit formal organization application, three personal references. International applicants accepted; must obtain own visa, obtain own working papers, apply through a recognized agency. An in-person interview is recommended, but a telephone interview is acceptable.

Benefits and Preemployment Training Free housing, free meals, formal training, on-the-job training, and riding instructors may attend seminars/workshops. Preemployment training is required and includes accident prevention and safety, interpersonal skills, leadership skills, working with children, teaching skills.

Contact Pat Haines, Director, SJ Ranch, Inc., 130 Sandy Beach Road, Ellington, Connecticut 06029. Telephone: 860-872-4742. Fax: 860-870-4914. E-mail: sjranch@erols.com. Application deadline: continuous.

THE SOUTHWESTERN COMPANY, CONNECTICUT
See The Southwestern Company, Tennessee on page 284 for complete description.

STUDENT CONSERVATION ASSOCIATION (SCA), CONNECTICUT
See Student Conservation Association (SCA), New Hampshire on page 193 for complete description.

SUNRISE RESORT
ROUTE 151, PO BOX 415
MOODUS, CONNECTICUT 06469

General Information Summer resort catering to families, day outing groups, music festivals, and weddings. Established in 1916. 140-acre facility located 20 miles from Hartford. Features: 50 x 100-foot pool; Salmon River; mountain biking; horseback riding; rural setting.

Profile of Summer Employees Total number: 125; typical ages: 17–24. 40% men; 60% women; 5% minorities; 40% high school students; 40% college students; 5% retirees; 8% non-U.S. citizens; 75% local applicants.

Employment Information Openings are from May 15 to September 15. Jobs available: ▶ 3–5 *housekeeping staff* (minimum age 19) at $3500–$4500 per season ▶ 2–3 *kitchen help* (minimum age 19) at $3500–$4500 per season ▶ 2–3 *lifeguards* (minimum age 19) with lifesaving and CPR; WSI certification preferred at $3500–$4500 per season ▶ 1–3 *office personnel* (minimum age 19) with typing ability at $3500–$4500 per season ▶ 1 *tennis instructor* (minimum age 19) at $3500–$4500 per season ▶ 10–12 *waiters/waitresses* (minimum age 19) at $3500–$4500 per season. Applicants must submit a formal organization application. International applicants accepted; must obtain own visa. A telephone interview is required.

Benefits and Preemployment Training Possible full-time employment, on-the-job training, and room and board at $40 per week. Preemployment training is optional.

Contact Jim Johnson, Director, Sunrise Resort, PO Box 415, Moodus, Connecticut 06469. Telephone: 860-873-8681. Fax: 860-873-8681. E-mail: suntimes@connix.com. World Wide Web: http://www.sunriseresort.com. Application deadline: April 15.

TENNIS: EUROPE
73 ROCKRIDGE LANE
STAMFORD, CONNECTICUT 06903

General Information TENNIS: EUROPE takes teams of junior players to USTA and international tennis tournaments, allowing them to gain valuable experience in match play and providing them with intercultural educational experiences. There is one team in North America and eight in Europe. Established in 1973.

Profile of Summer Employees Typical ages: 21–45. 50% men; 50% women; 5% minorities; 33% college students; 5% non-U.S. citizens. Nonsmokers required.

Employment Information Openings are from June 22 to August 14. Jobs available: ▶ 22 *tennis coaches/chaperones* (minimum age 21) with ability to coach tennis at high school varsity level or ranked players' and must serve as chaperone to students during travel; all positions require extensive travel and no positions are in Connecticut; 2 positions for California/Hawaii itinerary and 20 positions for Europe; at $400 to $550 per trip. Applicants must submit a formal organization application, cover letter, resume, four personal references. International applicants accepted; must obtain own visa.

Benefits and Preemployment Training Free housing, free meals, possible full-time employment, names of contacts, on-the-job training, and travel reimbursement ($100). Preemployment training is required and includes accident prevention and safety, interpersonal skills, leadership skills.

Contact Dr. Martin Vinokur, Director, TENNIS: EUROPE, 73 Rockridge Lane, Stamford, Connecticut 06903. Telephone: 203-322-9803. Fax: 203-322-0089. E-mail: tenniseuro@aol.com. World Wide Web: http://www.tenniseurope.com.

UNITED CEREBRAL PALSY ASSOCIATION OF GREATER HARTFORD
301 GREAT NECK ROAD
WATERFORD, CONNECTICUT 06385

General Information Residential camping program serving the physically disabled, ages 8–adult, during an eight-week summer program. 5 miles from New London. Features: beachfront facility; fully accessible; basketball courts; heated, fully equipped cabins; horseback riding; acres of fields.

Profile of Summer Employees Total number: 23; typical ages: 19–35. 30% men; 70% women; 20% minorities; 1% high school students; 60% college students; 1% non-U.S. citizens; 50% local applicants. Nonsmokers preferred.

Employment Information Openings are from June 14 to August 15. Jobs available: ▶ 3 *activity leaders* (minimum age 21) with experience in skill area preferred and ability to work with others at $2000–$2500 per season ▶ 1 *assistant director* (minimum age 21) with camp experience preferred at $3000–$5000 per season ▶ 14 *general counselors* (minimum age 18) with dedication and maturity, willingness to learn, and experience working with disabled persons (preferred) at $1875–$2200 per season ▶ 2 *head counselors* (minimum age 21) with experience in personal care and working in a camp or residential setting; returning staff with one year experience at $2300–$2700 per season ▶ 1 *nurse* (minimum age 21) with RN certification and experience caring for individuals with disabilities preferred at $4000–$5000 per season. Applicants must submit formal organization application, two personal references, two letters of recommendation, physical, background check, drug test. International applicants accepted; must apply through a recognized agency. An in-person interview is recommended, but a telephone interview is acceptable.

Benefits and Preemployment Training Free housing, free meals, formal training, names of contacts, and on-the-job training. Preemployment training is required and includes accident prevention and safety, first aid, CPR, interpersonal skills, leadership skills, bloodborne pathogens, abuse and neglect prevention.

Contact Paige McCullough-Casciano, Camp Services Consultant, United Cerebral Palsy Association of Greater Hartford, 80 Whitney Street, Hartford, Connecticut 06105. Telephone: 860-236-6201. Fax: 860-236-6205. Application deadline: continuous.

WESTPORT COUNTRY PLAYHOUSE
25 POWERS COURT
WESTPORT, CONNECTICUT 06880

General Information Professional summer theater producing six plays each year. Established in 1931. 3-acre facility located 42 miles from New York, New York. Features: red barn.

Profile of Summer Employees Total number: 50; typical ages: 18–45. 50% men; 50% women; 10% high school students; 40% college students; 50% local applicants. Nonsmokers preferred.

Employment Information Openings are from May 24 to September 12. Jobs available: ▶ 2 *administrative/press interns* (minimum age 18) at $200–$250 per week ▶ 6 *box office staff members* (minimum age 16) at $240–$250 per week ▶ 1 *carpenter* (minimum age 18) with prior theatre shop experience at $250–$300 per week ▶ 3–7 *production staff members* (minimum age 18) at $200–$400 per week ▶ 1 *properties master* (minimum age 18) with prior theatre props experience at $250–$350 per week ▶ 1 *scenic artist* (minimum age 18) with prior theatre scenic experience and course work at $250–$300 per week ▶ 10 *technical interns* (minimum age 17) at $100 per week ▶ 1 *wardrobe supervisor* (minimum age 18) with prior theatre wardrobe experience at $200–$250 per week. Applicants must submit portfolio, writing sample, personal reference, letter of recommendation, application requirements depend upon position. International applicants accepted; must obtain own visa, obtain own working papers.

Benefits and Preemployment Training Housing at a cost, free housing, on-the-job training, and opportunity to attend seminars/workshops.

Contact Julie Monahan, General Manager, Westport Country Playhouse, PO Box 629, Westport, Connecticut 06881. Telephone: 203-227-5137. Fax: 203-221-7482. E-mail: westportplay@mindspring.com. World Wide Web: http://www.westportplayhouse.org. Application deadline: continuous.

CHILDREN'S BEACH HOUSE, INC.
1800 BAY AVENUE
LEWES, DELAWARE 19958

General Information Private nonprofit residential camp for Delaware children, ages 6–12, with speech, hearing, and/or mild orthopedic disabilities. 23 children attend each 4-week session (2 sessions per summer). Established in 1936. 6-acre facility located 5 miles from Rehoboth Beach.

Features: beach front on Deleware Bay; in-ground pool; semi-private rooms for staff with bathroom; near state park; near resort town.

Profile of Summer Employees Total number: 25; typical ages: 18–25. 50% men; 50% women; 10% high school students; 70% college students; 10% local applicants.

Employment Information Openings are from June to August. Jobs available: ▶ 1–2 *camp health managers* (minimum age 25) with Deleware nursing license, first aid/CPR certification; and camp/pediatric experience at $4700 to $4900 per season (paid bi-weekly) ▶ 2 *program counselors (arts and crafts)* (minimum age 18) with experience working with special needs children; should be flexible, creative, energetic and multi-task oriented from base pay of $2500 per season (paid bi-weekly); increases with responsibility ▶ 2 *program counselors (nature crafts)* (minimum age 18) with background in environmental studies and experience working with special needs children; should be flexible, creative, energetic, and multi-task oriented from base pay of $2500 per season (paid bi-weekly); increases with responsibility ▶ 2 *program counselors (waterfront)* (minimum age 18) with lifeguarding/WSI certification and experience working with special needs children; should be flexible, creative, energetic, and multi-task oriented from base pay of $2500 per season (paid bi-weekly); increases with responsibility. Applicants must submit a formal organization application, three personal references, biographical sketch. An in-person interview is recommended, but a telephone interview is acceptable.

Benefits and Preemployment Training Free housing, free meals, and on-the-job training. Preemployment training is required and includes accident prevention and safety, first aid, CPR, interpersonal skills, leadership skills, behavior management program.

Contact Diane O'Hara, Program Director, Children's Beach House, Inc., 1800 Bay Avenue, lewes, Delaware 19958. Fax: 302-645-9467. E-mail: childrens.beach.house@dol.net. Application deadline: continuous.

FUNLAND
6 DELAWARE AVENUE
REHOBOTH BEACH, DELAWARE 19971

General Information Amusement park providing family entertainment. Established in 1962. 2-acre facility located 30 miles from Dover. Features: rides for children and adults; games; arcade.

Profile of Summer Employees Total number: 80; typical ages: 16–22. 50% men; 50% women; 5% minorities; 40% high school students; 60% college students; 5% non-U.S. citizens; 50% local applicants. Nonsmokers preferred.

Employment Information Openings are from May 9 to September 13. Jobs available: ▶ 80 *ride and game attendants* (minimum age 16) st $6.25 per hour plus performance bonus ($1.00 per hour potential); wages increase during last 3 weeks of season. Applicants must submit a formal organization application, cover letter, resume, letter of recommendation. International applicants accepted; must obtain own visa. An in-person interview is recommended, but a telephone interview is acceptable.

Benefits and Preemployment Training Housing at a cost, free housing, free meals, formal training, and on-the-job training. Preemployment training is required and includes accident prevention and safety.

Contact Steve Hendricks, Vice President/Personnel Manager, Funland, 6 Delaware Avenue, Rehoboth Beach, Delaware 19971. Telephone: 302-227-2785. Fax: 302-227-8276. E-mail: srhfunland@compuserve.com. Application deadline: continuous.

THE SOUTHWESTERN COMPANY, DELAWARE
See The Southwestern Company, Tennessee on page 284 for complete description.

STUDENT CONSERVATION ASSOCIATION (SCA), DELAWARE
See Student Conservation Association (SCA), New Hampshire on page 193 for complete description.

VIKING GOLF THEME & WATERPARK
CORNER OF ROUTE 1 AND ROUTE 54
FENWICK ISLAND, DELAWARE 19944

General Information Amusement/theme park with mini-golf, go-kart track, waterslide, bumper boats, and food shops. Established in 1984. 2-acre facility located 120 miles from Washington, DC. Features: one block from beach; bayside; located on 10-mile island.

Profile of Summer Employees Total number: 40–50; typical ages: 15–29. 50% men; 50% women; 30% high school students; 40% college students; 30% local applicants. Nonsmokers preferred.

Employment Information Openings are from May 14 to September 30. Jobs available: ▶ 10 *amusement ride attendants* (minimum age 15) at $5.75–$7 per hour ▶ 15–25 *food shop attendants* (minimum age 15) with short order cooking skills (a plus but not required for all shops) at $5.65–$7 per hour ▶ 20–30 *waterpark lifeguards* (minimum age 15) with CPR and lifeguard certification preferred at $5.75–$7.25 per hour. Applicants must submit a formal organization application. International applicants accepted; must obtain own working papers. An in-person interview is required.

Benefits and Preemployment Training Names of contacts and on-the-job training.

Contact Jon Andersen, Vice President, Viking Golf Theme & Waterpark, 6910 Hall Drive, Berlin, Maryland 21811. Telephone: 302-539-1644. Fax: 302-537-1909. Application deadline: continuous.

DISTRICT OF COLUMBIA

ACE COMPUTER CAMP–DISTRICT OF COLUMBIA
See ACE Computer Camp–Washington on page 307 for complete description.

THE SOUTHWESTERN COMPANY, DISTRICT OF COLUMBIA
See The Southwestern Company, Tennessee on page 284 for complete description.

STUDENT CONSERVATION ASSOCIATION (SCA), DISTRICT OF COLUMBIA
See Student Conservation Association (SCA), New Hampshire on page 193 for complete description.

SUMMER DISCOVERY AT GEORGETOWN
GEORGETOWN UNIVERSITY
WASHINGTON, DISTRICT OF COLUMBIA 20057

General Information Precollege enrichment program for high school students at Georgetown University. Established in 1994. Features: sport facilities; beaches; mountains; lakes; major cities nearby; college towns.

Profile of Summer Employees Total number: 20; typical ages: 21–35. 10% minorities; 40% college students. Nonsmokers required.

Employment Information Openings are from June 20 to August 25. Jobs available: ▶ 20 *resident counselors* (minimum age 21) with experience working with high school students/children at $125–$400 per week. Applicants must submit a formal organization application, resume, personal reference. An in-person interview is required.

Benefits and Preemployment Training Free housing and on-the-job training. Preemployment training is required and includes accident prevention and safety, CPR, leadership skills.

Contact Jason Walley, Admissions Director, Summer Discovery at Georgetown, 1326 Old Northern Boulevard, Roslyn, New York 11576. Telephone: 516-621-3939. Fax: 516-625-3438.

E-mail: staff@summerfun.com. World Wide Web: http://www.summerfun.com. Application deadline: continuous.

FLORIDA

ACE COMPUTER CAMP–FLORIDA
See ACE Computer Camp–Washington on page 307 for complete description.

A CHRISTIAN MINISTRY IN THE NATIONAL PARKS–FLORIDA
See A Christian Ministry in the National Parks–Massachussetts on page 138 for complete description.

ACTIONQUEST PROGRAMS
PO BOX 5517
SARASOTA, FLORIDA 34277
General Information Live-aboard sailing and diving certification voyages for 13-19 year olds. Waterskiing, windsurfing, and marine biology available. No experience necessary. Established in 1986. Features: locations in British Virgin Islands, Mediterranean, Leeward Islands, Galapagos, Australia, and South Pacific; 12 50-foot sailing yachts.

Profile of Summer Employees Total number: 30; typical age: 28. 60% men; 40% women; 50% college students; 10% non-U.S. citizens. Nonsmokers required.

Employment Information Openings are from June 10 to August 20. Jobs available: ▶ 12 *diving instructors* with PADI instructor-level certification and/or USCG license at $2200 per season ▶ *marine science instructors* with PADI scuba instructor-level certification at $2200 per season ▶ 12 *sailing instructors* should be United States Coast Guard licensed or British Yachtmasters at $3000 per season ▶ *windsurfing instructors* with certification in field at $1000 per season. Applicants must submit a formal organization application, cover letter, resume. International applicants accepted. A telephone interview is required.

Benefits and Preemployment Training Free housing, free meals, and travel reimbursement. Preemployment training is required and includes accident prevention and safety, first aid, CPR, interpersonal skills, leadership skills.

Contact James Stoll, Director, Actionquest Programs, PO Box 5517, Sarasota, Florida 34277. Telephone: 941-924-2115. Fax: 941-924-6075. E-mail: actionquest@msn.com. World Wide Web: http://www.actionquest.com. Application deadline: continuous.

CAMP BLUE RIDGE
BOX 2888
MIAMI, FLORIDA 33140
General Information Residential camp with an average of 200 campers providing athletics, waterfront, roller hockey, paintball, arts and crafts, rappelling, horseback riding, and waterskiing activities. Established in 1969. 212-acre facility. Features: freshwater lake and pool; roller hockey rink; rapelling tower; recreation hall and game room; go-cart track; tennis courts.

Profile of Summer Employees Total number: 85; typical ages: 19–40. 50% men; 50% women; 5% high school students; 80% college students; 50% non-U.S. citizens; 50% local applicants. Nonsmokers required.

Employment Information Openings are from June 15 to August 15. Jobs available: ▶ 4 *arts and crafts instructors* at $1000–$1200 per season ▶ 10 *athletics instructors* at $1000–$1200 per season ▶ 6 *dance and drama instructors* at $1000–$1200 per season ▶ 1 *martial arts instructor* at $1000–$1200 per season ▶ 3 *rappelling instructors* at $1000–$1500 per season ▶ 12 *swim-*

ming, boating, all-waterfront, and skiing instructors at $1000–$1500 per season. Applicants must submit formal organization application, personal reference. International applicants accepted; must apply through a recognized agency. A telephone interview is required.

Benefits and Preemployment Training Free housing and free meals. Preemployment training is required and includes accident prevention and safety, first aid, CPR, leadership skills.

Contact Joey or Lori Waldman, Directors, Camp Blue Ridge, PO Box 2888, Miami Beach, Florida 33140. Telephone: 305-538-3434. Fax: 305-532-3152. E-mail: campcbr@aol.com. Application deadline: continuous.

CAMP JCC
18900 NORTHEAST 25TH AVENUE
NORTH MIAMI BEACH, FLORIDA 33180

General Information Full-service day camp on 17 acres of green in the heart of the city. Established in 1970. 17-acre facility. Features: 12 tennis courts; 2 olympic size pools; 2 baseball fields; indoor gymnasium; full-scale gymnastics facility; dance studio and state of the art fitness center.

Profile of Summer Employees Total number: 150; typical ages: 16–40. 40% men; 60% women; 15% high school students; 40% college students; 10% non-U.S. citizens; 90% local applicants. Nonsmokers required.

Employment Information Openings are from June 21 to August 13. Year-round positions also offered. Jobs available: ▶ *senior counselors* (minimum age 23) with preference for teachers or coaches at $1200–$2000 per season. Applicants must submit a formal organization application, personal reference. International applicants accepted; must obtain own visa, obtain own working papers. An in-person interview is required.

Benefits and Preemployment Training Free meals, formal training, possible full-time employment, and on-the-job training. Preemployment training is required and includes accident prevention and safety, first aid, interpersonal skills, leadership skills.

Contact Karen Meister Hodson, Camp JCC, 18900 Northeast 25th Avenue, North Miami Beach, Florida 33180. Telephone: 305-932-4200. Fax: 305-937-1829. E-mail: campdirctr@aol.com. Application deadline: continuous.

CAMP THUNDERBIRD
909 EAST WELCH ROAD
APOPKA, FLORIDA 32712

General Information Residential camp designed exclusively to benefit children and adults who have a developmental disability. Campers participate in traditional camping activities which help increase the camper's level of independence and self-esteem. 20-acre facility located 15 miles from Orlando. Features: freshwater lake; wooded setting; air-conditioned dorms; ropes challenge course; private staff recreation room; close to local attractions and beaches.

Profile of Summer Employees Total number: 70; typical ages: 18–40. 25% men; 75% women; 17% minorities; 60% college students; 50% non-U.S. citizens; 35% local applicants.

Employment Information Openings are from June 14 to August 14. Jobs available: ▶ 6 *activity leaders* with experience leading a specific activity at $1300–$1800 per season ▶ 30 *cabin counselors* with experience working with the mentally retarded at $1100–$1800 per season ▶ 2–3 *camp nurses* with Florida nursing license (1 RN, 2 LPN) at $650–$800 per week ▶ 6 *head counselors* (minimum age 21) with experience working at summer camps; supervisory experience preferred at $1300–$1800 per season ▶ 3 *kitchen staff members* with experience at $4–$6 per hour ▶ 2 *staff managers* (minimum age 21) with experience in a camp setting and supervisory experience at $1500–$2000 per season ▶ 5 *swimming pool staff members* with WSI and lifeguard certification at $1400–$1600 per season. Applicants must submit formal organization application, three personal references, three letters of recommendation. International applicants accepted; must obtain own visa, obtain own working papers, apply through a recognized agency. An in-person interview is recommended, but a telephone interview is acceptable.

Benefits and Preemployment Training Free housing, free meals, on-the-job training, travel reimbursement, and possible free admission to local attractions: Disney, Universal Studios, Sea

World, and more. Preemployment training is required and includes accident prevention and safety, first aid, CPR, interpersonal skills, leadership skills.

Contact Christi Padgett, Assistant Director, Camp Thunderbird, 909 East Welch Road, Apopka, Florida 32712. Telephone: 407-889-8088. Fax: 407-889-8072. E-mail: campthun@aol.com. World Wide Web: http://www.questinc.org. Application deadline: continuous.

KAMPUS KAMPERS
3601 NORTH MILITARY TRAIL
BOCA RATON, FLORIDA 33431

General Information Residential camp serving 200 campers from the end of June to mid-August in three-week sessions. Camp provides computer, performing arts, circus, sports, and traditional programs. Established in 1992. 123-acre facility located 5 miles from Boca Raton. Features: air-conditioned university dormitories; 6 lakes; wooded area; gymnasium; sports field and tennis courts; pool.

Profile of Summer Employees Total number: 55; typical ages: 19–26. 50% men; 50% women; 10% minorities; 80% college students; 30% non-U.S. citizens; 40% local applicants. Nonsmokers preferred.

Employment Information Openings are from June 8 to August 14. Jobs available: ▶ 1–2 *activity coordinators* (minimum age 25) with college degree and experience in the field at $265–$340 per week ▶ 1 *assistant activities coordinator* (minimum age 25) with experience in organizing and implementing activities at $340 per week ▶ 10–20 *counselors* (minimum age 19) with at least one year of college completed at $285 per week ▶ *floor supervisor* (minimum age 22) with college degree and camp leadership experience at $325 per week ▶ 1 *unit director* with experience as a teacher or in a camp leadership position at $425 per week. Applicants must submit formal organization application, cover letter, two personal references, two letters of recommendation. International applicants accepted; must apply through a recognized agency. An in-person interview is recommended, but a telephone interview is acceptable.

Benefits and Preemployment Training Free housing, free meals, formal training, and on-the-job training. Preemployment training is required and includes accident prevention and safety, first aid, CPR, interpersonal skills, leadership skills.

Contact Mrs. Sue Merrill, Kampus Kampers, 3601 North Military Trail, Boca Raton, Florida 33431. Telephone: 561-994-2267. Fax: 561-994-6662. Application deadline: March 15.

PINE TREE CAMPS AT LYNN UNIVERSITY
3601 NORTH MILITARY TRAIL
BOCA RATON, FLORIDA 33431

General Information Day camp serving campers ages 3–15. Established in 1978. 123-acre facility located 15 miles from West Palm Beach. Features: 6 small lakes; 6 tennis courts; 2 pools; soccer and baseball fields; library; fitness center.

Profile of Summer Employees Total number: 200; typical ages: 18–50. 40% men; 60% women; 10% minorities; 20% high school students; 59% college students; 1% retirees; 15% non-U.S. citizens; 100% local applicants. Nonsmokers preferred.

Employment Information Openings are from June 10 to August 15. Jobs available: ▶ 1–3 *computer instructors* (minimum age 22) with experience working with children and computers with educational software at $250–$300 per week ▶ 10–20 *general counselors* (minimum age 18) with experience working with children at $180–$210 per week ▶ 2–5 *pre-school teachers* (minimum age 22) with Health and Rehabilitative Services clearance and education certification at $180–$225 per week ▶ 5–10 *swim instructors* (minimum age 18) with lifeguard training and WSI certification preferred at $180–$250 per week ▶ 1–2 *tennis instructors* (minimum age 18) with experience teaching ages 4-13 at $250–$300 per week. Applicants must submit formal organization application, resume, two personal references, two letters of recommendation. International applicants accepted; must apply through a recognized agency. An in-person interview is recommended, but a telephone interview is acceptable.

Benefits and Preemployment Training On-the-job training. Preemployment training is required and includes accident prevention and safety, first aid, CPR, interpersonal skills, leadership skills.

Contact Diane DiCerbo, Director, Pine Tree Camps at Lynn University, 3601 North Military Terrace, Boca Raton, Florida 33431. Telephone: 561-237-7310. Fax: 561-237-7962. E-mail: ddicerbo@lynn.edu. Application deadline: continuous.

SABIN-MULLOY-GARRISON TENNIS CAMP
11550 LASTCHANCE ROAD
CLERMONT, FLORIDA 34711

General Information Residential camp for boys and girls who have an interest in competitive tennis. Established in 1961. 5-acre facility located 30 miles from Orlando. Features: freshwater lake; 5 tennis courts; wooded setting; trips to Orlando area attractions; sanctioned tennis tournaments; waterskiing.

Profile of Summer Employees Total number: 3; typical ages: 19–23. 50% men; 50% women; 25% minorities; 75% college students; 25% non-U.S. citizens; 25% local applicants. Nonsmokers required.

Employment Information Openings are from July to August. Jobs available: ▶ *cook* (minimum age 19) at $700–$800 per season ▶ 2–3 *tennis instructors* (minimum age 19) at $700–$800 per season. Applicants must submit resume, two personal references, two letters of recommendation. International applicants accepted; must obtain own visa, obtain own working papers.

Benefits and Preemployment Training Free housing and free meals.

Contact Dickey W. Garrison, Owner, Sabin-Mulloy-Garrison Tennis Camp, 11550 Lastchance Road, Clermont, Florida 34711. Telephone: 352-394-3543. Fax: 352-394-3543. E-mail: smgtennis@yahoo.com. Application deadline: continuous.

THE SOUTHWESTERN COMPANY, FLORIDA
See The Southwestern Company, Tennessee on page 284 for complete description.

STUDENT CONSERVATION ASSOCIATION (SCA), FLORIDA
See Student Conservation Association (SCA), New Hampshire on page 193 for complete description.

ACE COMPUTER CAMP–GEORGIA
See ACE Computer Camp–Washington on page 307 for complete description.

CAMP BARNEY MEDINTZ
4165 HIGHWAY 129 NORTH
CLEVELAND, GEORGIA 30528-2309

General Information Residential camp serving 900 campers ages 8–16 during two 4-week sessions.Camp also offers Wonder Weeks, serving second and third graders during four 2-week sessions, and Chalutzim, serving children ages 9–16 with special needs during a four-week session. Established in 1963. 500-acre facility located 75 miles from Atlanta. Features: 2 lakes; 30 stall equestrian center; climbing wall; swimming pool; high ropes course; tennis courts.

Profile of Summer Employees Total number: 200; typical ages: 18–24. 50% men; 50% women; 5% minorities; 28% high school students; 66% college students; 20% non-U.S. citizens; 65% local applicants.

Employment Information Openings are from June 12 to August 15. Jobs available: ▶ 50 *counselors* (minimum age 18) at $750–$1500 per season ▶ 9 *horseback staff members* with first aid certificate at $750–$2000 per season ▶ 14 *nature crafts staff members* (minimum age 18) with CPR and first aid certification at $750–$2200 per season ▶ 2 *song leaders* at $1200–$2500 per season ▶ 10 *special-needs staff members* at $800–$1800 ▶ 2 *theater directors* at $1200–$2300 per season ▶ 15 *waterfront staff members* (minimum age 18) with LGT, WSI, CPR, and first aid certification at $750–$2200 per season. Applicants must submit formal organization application, three letters of recommendation. International applicants accepted; must apply through a recognized agency. An in-person interview is recommended, but a telephone interview is acceptable.

Benefits and Preemployment Training Free housing, free meals, formal training, and on-the-job training. Preemployment training is required and includes accident prevention and safety, first aid, CPR, interpersonal skills, leadership skills.

Contact Mark Balser, Associate Director, Camp Barney Medintz, 5342 Tilly Mill Road, Atlanta, Georgia 30338-4499. Telephone: 770-396-3250. Fax: 770-481-0101. E-mail: summer@ campbarney.org. World Wide Web: http://www.campbarney.org. Application deadline: continuous.

CAMP WOODMONT FOR BOYS AND GIRLS ON LOOKOUT MOUNTAIN
1339 YANKEE ROAD
CLOUDLAND, GEORGIA 30731

General Information Residential summer camp serving up to 80 boys and girls ages 6–14 for one- to two-week sessions; wholesome, fun activities emphasizing nature. Established in 1981. 170-acre facility located 28 miles from Chattanooga, Tennessee. Features: small lake; swimming pool; challenge trail; recreation/dining hall; cabins with central bathhouses; pavillion.

Profile of Summer Employees Total number: 10–20; typical ages: 18–35. 50% men; 50% women; 2% high school students; 98% college students; 2% non-U.S. citizens; 98% local applicants. Nonsmokers required.

Employment Information Openings are from June 7 to August 15. Jobs available: ▶ 10 *counselors* (minimum age 18) with CPR/FA certification required; LGT and experience preferred at $950–$2000 per season ▶ 2 *swimming instructors* (minimum age 18) with LGT/WSI certification at $950–$2000 per month. Applicants must submit a formal organization application, resume, two writing samples, three personal references. International applicants accepted; must obtain own visa, obtain own working papers. An in-person interview is recommended, but a telephone interview is acceptable.

Benefits and Preemployment Training Free housing, free meals, and on-the-job training. Preemployment training is required and includes accident prevention and safety, interpersonal skills, leadership skills.

Contact Jane and Jim Bennett, Camp Directors, Camp Woodmont for Boys and Girls on Lookout Mountain, 2339 Welton Place, Dunwoody, Georgia 30338. Telephone: 770-457-0862. E-mail: campdirector@campwoodmont.com. World Wide Web: http://www.campwoodmont.com. Application deadline: continuous.

CLUB CARE: LIFEGUARDS INC.
270 AZALEA DRIVE
ROSWELL, GEORGIA 30075

General Information Supplying lifeguards to neighborhood pools in the Fulton, Gwinett, and Forsyth county areas. Established in 1997. Located 20 miles from Atlanta. Features: outdoors; pool side environment; flexible schedule; great hours; networking opportunities.

Profile of Summer Employees Total number: 40; typical ages: 16–23. 50% men; 50% women; 35% high school students; 65% college students. Nonsmokers preferred.

Employment Information Openings are from May 15 to September 30. Spring break, winter break, and year-round positions also offered. Jobs available: ▶ 15–25 *lifeguards* at $6.25–$7.25 per hour. An in-person interview is recommended, but a telephone interview is acceptable.

Benefits and Preemployment Training Preemployment training is required and includes first aid, CPR, lifeguarding (Red Cross or YMCA).

Contact Chris Orsey, CEO, Club Care: Lifeguards Inc., 270 Azalea Drive, Roswell, Georgia 30025. Telephone: 770-587-1389. Fax: 770-998-8841. E-mail: orseylooo@aol.com. Application deadline: continuous.

THE SOUTHWESTERN COMPANY, GEORGIA
See The Southwestern Company, Tennessee on page 284 for complete description.

STUDENT CONSERVATION ASSOCIATION (SCA), GEORGIA
See Student Conservation Association (SCA), New Hampshire on page 193 for complete description.

HAWAII

ACE COMPUTER CAMP–HAWAII
See ACE Computer Camp–Washington on page 307 for complete description.

LONGACRE EXPEDITIONS, HAWAII
HAWAII

General Information Adventure travel program in Hawaii for teenagers, emphasizing group living skills and physical challenges. Established in 1981.

Profile of Summer Employees Total number: 5; typical ages: 23–30. 50% men; 50% women; 100% college students. Nonsmokers required.

Employment Information Openings are from June 30 to July 30. Jobs available: ▶ 2 *assistant leaders* (minimum age 21) with scuba certification, first aid or WFR, CPR, and lifeguard training at $252–$300 per week. Applicants must submit a formal organization application, three personal references. International applicants accepted; must obtain own visa, obtain own working papers. An in-person interview is recommended, but a telephone interview is acceptable.

Benefits and Preemployment Training Free housing, free meals, on-the-job training, and pro-deal purchase program. Preemployment training is required and includes accident prevention and safety, interpersonal skills, leadership skills.

Contact Meredith Schuler, Director, Longacre Expeditions, Hawaii, RD 3, Box 106, Newport, Pennsylvania 17074. Telephone: 717-567-6790. Fax: 717-567-3955. E-mail: longacre@ longacreexpeditions.com. World Wide Web: http://www.longacreexpeditions.com. Application deadline: continuous.

STUDENT CONSERVATION ASSOCIATION (SCA), HAWAII
See Student Conservation Association (SCA), New Hampshire on page 193 for complete description.

IDAHO

ACE COMPUTER CAMP–IDAHO
See ACE Computer Camp–Washington on page 307 for complete description.

EPLEY'S WHITEWATER ADVENTURES
BOX 987
MCCALL, IDAHO 83638

General Information River rafting on Salmon River offering adventures to groups of up to 100 people on short trips. Also offers overnight trips for 2–24 people. Established in 1962. 1-acre facility located 150 miles from Boise. Features: River of No Return; free flowing river with no dams; wildlife; very deep canyon; large sandy beaches; Class III river run.

Profile of Summer Employees Total number: 18; typical ages: 18–28. 80% men; 20% women; 75% college students; 25% local applicants. Nonsmokers required.

Employment Information Openings are from May 1 to September 15. Jobs available: ► 4 *food service, laundry and office staff, and shuttle drivers* (minimum age 18) with Red Cross, first aid, and CPR (training provided); experience preferred at $700–$1000 per month ► 12–15 *river guides* (minimum age 18) with Red Cross, first aid, and CPR; training provided for license at $700–$1200 per month ► 2 *summer horse guides* (minimum age 18) with license (training provided) at $700–$1200 per month. Applicants must submit a formal organization application, cover letter, resume, portfolio, three personal references, letter of recommendation. An in-person interview is recommended, but a telephone interview is acceptable.

Benefits and Preemployment Training Free housing, free meals, formal training, on-the-job training, and laundry service.

Contact Ted or Karen Epley, Owners, Epley's Whitewater Adventures, Box 987, McCall, Idaho 83638. Telephone: 208-634-5173. Fax: 208-634-5270.

HIDDEN CREEK RANCH
7600 EAST BLUE LAKE ROAD
HARRISON, IDAHO 83833

General Information Guest ranch conducting six-day programs with daily scheduled activities including horseback riding, rodeo, mountain biking, pond fishing, trap shooting, archery, hiking, boat tours, Native American activities, and activities for fitness, mind, body, and spirit well-being. Established in 1992. 570-acre facility located 35 miles from Coeur d'Alene. Features: 100 horses, 40 mountain bikes, abundant wildlife; spring-fed pond and hot tubs in a private mountain valley; ropes challenge course; 7,000-square foot lodge and 6 guest cabins; tipi village and 2 sweat lodges; trails overlook Coeur d'Alene chain of lakes.

Profile of Summer Employees Total number: 22; typical ages: 18–51. 50% men; 50% women; 1% minorities; 10% college students; 1% non-U.S. citizens; 1% local applicants.

Employment Information Openings are from April 1 to October 31. Jobs available: ► 1 *assistant cook* (minimum age 18) with standard first aid/CPR certification and kitchen experience at $500 per month plus room and board; $500 per month bonus payable at end of contract ► 1 *baker* (minimum age 18) with standard first aid/CPR certification and kitchen and baking experience at $500 per month plus room and board; $500 per month bonus payable at end of contract ► 3 *children's counselors* (minimum age 18) with standard first aid/CPR certification and child care or camp experience at $500 per month plus room and board; $500 per month bonus payable at end of contract ► 2 *children's wranglers* (minimum age 18) with standard first aid/CPR certification, child care or camp experience, and horse background mat $500 per month plus room and board; $500 per month bonus payable at end of contract ► 6 *housekeeping/waitstaff members* (minimum age 18) with standard first aid/CPR certification at $500 per month plus room and board; $500 per month bonus payable at end of contract ► 1 *kitchen assistant/prep/dishwasher* (minimum age 18) with standard first aid/CPR certification and kitchen experience at $500 per month plus room and board; $500 per month bonus payable at end of contract ► 4 *maintenance staff* (minimum age 18) with standard first aid/CPR certification; grounds maintenance, construction, and mechanical background at $500 per month plus room and board; $500 per month bonus payable at end of contract ► *office/waitstaff* (minimum age 18) with standard first aid/CPR certification and office experience at $500 per month plus room and board; $500 per month bonus payable at end of contract ► 7 *wranglers* (minimum age 18) with standard first aid/CPR certification and horse background at $500 per month plus room and board; $500 per month bonus payable at end of contract. Applicants must submit a formal organization application, video detaining horsemanship skills for manager applicants. International applicants accepted; must obtain own visa, obtain own working papers. A telephone interview is required.

Benefits and Preemployment Training Free housing, free meals, on-the-job training, and participation in guest activities on days off and time off; housing is not available for couples or families. Preemployment training is required and includes accident prevention and safety, interpersonal skills.

Contact Cindy Loe, Head of Human Resources, Hidden Creek Ranch. Telephone: 208-689-3209. Fax: 208-689-9115. E-mail: hiddencreek@hiddencreek.com. World Wide Web: http://www. hiddencreek.com.

MYSTIC SADDLE RANCH
STATE HIGHWAY 75
STANLEY, IDAHO 83278

General Information Program offering pack trips, trail rides, and fall hunting trips. 130 miles from Boise.

Profile of Summer Employees Total number: 17. 80% men; 20% women; 60% college students.

Employment Information Openings are from June 1 to November 15. Jobs available: ▶ *cook/ house help* (minimum age 18) at $1100–$1800 per month ▶ *corral manager* (minimum age 18) with no Fish and Game violations at $1100–$1800 per month ▶ *fall hunting guides* (minimum age 18) with no Fish and Game violations at $1100–$1800 per month ▶ *horse packers* (minimum age 18) with no Fish and Game violations at $1100–$1800 per month ▶ *trail ride guides* with no Fish and Game violations at $1100–$1800 per month.

Benefits and Preemployment Training Housing at a cost, meals at a cost, on-the-job training, and workmen's compensation insurance. Preemployment training is required and includes accident prevention and safety.

Contact Deb Bitton, Owner, Mystic Saddle Ranch, Mystic Saddle Ranch, Stanley, Idaho 83278. Telephone: 208-774-3591. Fax: 208-774-3455. E-mail: packid@cyberhighway.net. World Wide Web: http://www.mysticsaddleranch.com. Application deadline: continuous.

THE SOUTHWESTERN COMPANY, IDAHO
See The Southwestern Company, Tennessee on page 284 for complete description.

STUDENT CONSERVATION ASSOCIATION (SCA), IDAHO
See Student Conservation Association (SCA), New Hampshire on page 193 for complete description.

ILLINOIS

ACE COMPUTER CAMP–ILLINOIS
See ACE Computer Camp–Washington on page 307 for complete description.

CAMP HENRY HORNER
PO BOX 297
INGLESIDE, ILLINOIS 60041

General Information Nonprofit social service agency looking to make a positive impact on the youth of our community. Established in 1907. 180-acre facility located 45 miles from Chicago. Features: lake; pool; 5 tennis courts; 45 buildings; 3 basketball courts/hockey rink; several open fields.

Profile of Summer Employees Total number: 100. 10% minorities; 15% high school students; 65% college students; 2% retirees; 20% non-U.S. citizens; 25% local applicants. Nonsmokers required.

Employment Information Openings are from June 1 to August 15. Year-round positions also offered. Jobs available: ▶ 50 *general counselors* (minimum age 19) with previous experience working with children at $1000–$2000 per season ▶ 10 *unit heads/specialists* (minimum age

21) with previous experience with specialty at $1500–$2500 per season. Applicants must submit formal organization application, cover letter, resume, three personal references. International applicants accepted; must apply through a recognized agency. An in-person interview is recommended, but a telephone interview is acceptable.

Benefits and Preemployment Training Free housing, free meals, formal training, possible full-time employment, on-the-job training, opportunity to attend seminars/workshops, travel reimbursement, and membership to health club and community transportation. Preemployment training is required and includes accident prevention and safety, first aid, CPR, interpersonal skills, leadership skills, conference seminars.

Contact "H" Rothenberg, Director of Camp and Conference Services, Camp Henry Horner. Telephone: 847-740-5010. Fax: 847-740-5014. E-mail: rothenberg@theramp.net. World Wide Web: http://www.jcys.com. Application deadline: continuous.

CAMP LITTLE GIANT AT TOUCH OF NATURE ENVIRONMENTAL CENTER
MAILCODE 6888, SOUTHERN ILLINOIS UNIVERSITY
CARBONDALE, ILLINOIS 62901-6888

General Information Residential camping program for persons of varying ability levels and medical conditions with a focus on success-building therapeutic recreation activities. Established in 1951. 3,200-acre facility. Features: freshwater lake; rich, wooded grouds; high and low ropes courses; swimming area; dining lodge; epontoon and other watercraft.

Profile of Summer Employees Total number: 45; typical ages: 18–35. 40% men; 60% women; 25% minorities; 2% high school students; 90% college students; 2% non-U.S. citizens; 6% local applicants. Nonsmokers preferred.

Employment Information Openings are from May 30 to July 31. Jobs available: ▶ 1–2 *activity coordinators* (minimum age 21) with 2 years of leadership experience with special populations; CPR/first aid certifications at $805 per month ▶ 1 *adventure/outdoor living specialist* with 2 years of experience in camping/adventure programs; lifeguard and CPR/first aid certifications at $587 per month ▶ 1 *aquatics assistant* with lifeguard, CPR/first aid, and WSI training; 1 or 2 years of experience at $493 per month ▶ 1 *aquatics specialist* with lifeguarding, CPR/first aid, and WSI training; 2 years experience with special populations at $587 per month ▶ 1 *arts and crafts specialist* with 2 years of camp experience; art background; first aid/CPR certifications at $587 per month ▶ 1 *boating specialist* with lifeguarding, CPR/first aid, and small craft certifications at $587 per month ▶ 1 *camp nurse* with RN or LPN license and CPR/first aid certifications at $1957 per month ▶ 2–4 *camp nurse assistants* with RN, LPN, or EMT license; CPR/first aid certifications at $805–$1537 per month ▶ 1–3 *communication specialists* with sign language proficiency at $500 per month ▶ 10–15 *general counselors* (minimum age 16) with experience or interest in working with special populations; CPR/first aid certifications at $493–$544 per month ▶ *head counselor* (minimum age 21) with 1 or 2 years of leadership, counseling, and group process experience; CPR/first aid certifications at $805 per month ▶ 1–4 *interns* with experiece or interest in working with people with disabilities at $326 per month ▶ *music/drama specialist* with 1 or 2 years of experience in camping; knowledge of drama, music, and dance; CPR/first aid certifications at $587 per month ▶ 1 *naturalist* with 2 years of camping experience; training in nature lore/outdoor education; CPR/first aid cerifications at $587 per month ▶ 1 *recreation specialist* with 2 years leadership experience in new games/sports and adapting at $587 per month. Applicants must submit formal organization application, two personal references, background check. International applicants accepted; must obtain own visa, obtain own working papers, apply through a recognized agency. An in-person interview is recommended, but a telephone interview is acceptable.

Benefits and Preemployment Training Free housing, free meals, formal training, on-the-job training, and opportunity to attend seminars/workshops. Preemployment training is required and includes accident prevention and safety, first aid, CPR, interpersonal skills, leadership skills, information on disabilities and related issues.

Contact Pamela Schadt, Director, Camp Little Giant at Touch of Nature Environmental Center.

Telephone: 618-453-1121. Fax: 618-453-1188. E-mail: pschadt@siu.edu. World Wide Web: http://www.pso.siu.edu/tonec.

CAMP TAPAWINGO
ROUTE 5, BOX 15
METAMORA, ILLINOIS 61548

General Information Residential camp serving 120 Girl Scouts and non–Girl Scouts per week. Established in 1951. 640-acre facility located 15 miles from Peoria. Features: pool; lake; wooded setting.

Profile of Summer Employees Typical ages: 18–22. 100% women; 1% minorities; 98% college students; 15% local applicants. Nonsmokers preferred.

Employment Information Openings are from June 1 to August 15. Jobs available: ▶ 1 *business manager* (minimum age 21) at $184–$204 per week ▶ 1 *health supervisor* (minimum age 21) with RN, LPN, or EMT license at $200–$220 per week ▶ 1 *lakefront director* (minimum age 21) with lifeguard certification and canoeing background at $184–$204 per week ▶ 1 *teams course/ campcraft instructor* (minimum age 21) at $184–$204 per week ▶ 12–15 *unit assistants* (minimum age 18) at $154–$174 per week ▶ 5 *unit leaders* (minimum age 21) at $165–$185 per week ▶ 3 *waterfront assistants* (minimum age 18) with lifeguard certification at $159–$175 per week ▶ 1 *waterfront director* (minimum age 21) with WSI certification at $184–$204 per week. Applicants must submit formal organization application, 2-3 personal references, 2-3 letters of recommendation. International applicants accepted; must apply through a recognized agency. An in-person interview is recommended, but a telephone interview is acceptable.

Benefits and Preemployment Training Free housing, free meals, health insurance, and on-the-job training. Preemployment training is required and includes accident prevention and safety, first aid, CPR, leadership skills.

Contact Beth Stalker or Keelie Lawson, Director of Program and Properties, Camp Tapawingo, 1103 West Lake, Peoria, Illinois 61614. Telephone: 309-688-8671. Fax: 309-688-7358. E-mail: kcgs@mtco.com. Application deadline: continuous.

CATERING BY MICHAEL'S
6203 PARK AVENUE
MORTON GROVE, ILLINOIS 60053

General Information Off-premises catering. From summer picnic/April parties to very elegant and sophisticated "black tie" parties. Catering events for 10 to 10,000 people; fun, outdoor work. Much of it is on weekends. Established in 1983. Located 7 miles from Chicago.

Profile of Summer Employees Total number: 125–150; typical ages: 15–30. 65% men; 35% women; 10% minorities; 15% high school students; 20% college students; 10% non-U.S. citizens; 55% local applicants. Nonsmokers preferred.

Employment Information Spring break, winter break, and year round positions also offered. Jobs available: ▶ 10–20 *part-time waiters* (minimum age 18) with good manners, pleasant disposition, and good appearance at $10–$13 per hour ▶ 40–50 *summer picnic staff* (minimum age 15) with good manners, pleasant disposition, and good appearance at $7.50 per hour. Applicants must submit a formal organization application, 2-3 personal references. International applicants accepted; must obtain own visa, obtain own working papers. An in-person interview is required.

Benefits and Preemployment Training Free meals, possible full-time employment, and on-the-job training. Preemployment training is required and includes general meeting with hand-outs and discussions as well as demonstrations.

Contact Brendan Kennedy, Supervisor, Catering by Michael's, 6203 Park Avenue, Morton Grove, Illinois 60053. Telephone: 847-966-8950. Fax: 847-966-6626. World Wide Web: http://www. cateringbymichaels.com. Application deadline: continuous.

PEACOCK CAMP
38685 NORTH DEEP LAKE ROAD
LAKE VILLA, ILLINOIS 60046

General Information Residential camp offered every two weeks for 36 children ages 7–17 with physical disabilities. Established in 1935. 22-acre facility located 50 miles from Chicago. Features: heated pool; exercise course; private beach; wooded setting; accessible lodge.

Profile of Summer Employees Total number: 35; typical ages: 18–30. 40% men; 60% women; 40% minorities; 5% high school students; 70% college students; 15% retirees; 5% non-U.S. citizens; 5% local applicants. Nonsmokers preferred.

Employment Information Openings are from June 5 to August 15. Spring break positions also offered. Jobs available: ▶ 2 *cooks* (minimum age 18) with food service experience at $2000 per season ▶ 1 *counselor/aquatics team leader* (minimum age 19) with CPR, first aid, WSI certification, and lifeguard training at $1600–$1850 per season ▶ 1 *counselor/arts and crafts team leader* (minimum age 19) with CPR/first aid certification at $1600–$1850 per season ▶ 1 *counselor/recreation team leader* (minimum age 19) with CPR/first aid certification at $1600–$1850 per season ▶ 5 *counselors/aquatics instructors* with CPR/first aid/lifeguard certification; lifeguard experience preferred at $1425–$1650 per season ▶ 5 *counselors/arts and crafts instructors* (minimum age 18) with CPR/first aid certification at $1425–$1650 per season ▶ 5 *counselors/recreation personnel* (minimum age 18) with CPR and first aid certification at $1425–$1650 per season ▶ 1 *head counselor* (minimum age 19) with first aid/CPR, program administration, and supervisory experience; experience in therapeutic recreation, adaptive physical education, or special education preferred at $1900–$2500 per season ▶ 1–2 *junior counselors* (minimum age 16) at $1200–$1400 per season ▶ 1–2 *maintenance staff* (minimum age 18) at $1500–$1850 per season ▶ 1–2 *night attendants* (minimum age 19) with CPR and first aid; must be willing to work 11 pm to 7 am, CNA prefered at $2000 per season ▶ 1 *nurse* with RN license (Illinois), first aid, and CPR at $4800 per season ▶ 1 *program director* (minimum age 21) with BS in related field at $325–$425 per week. Applicants must submit formal organization application, three letters of recommendation. International applicants accepted; must obtain own visa, obtain own working papers, apply through a recognized agency. An in-person interview is recommended, but a telephone interview is acceptable.

Benefits and Preemployment Training Free housing, free meals, formal training, possible full-time employment, on-the-job training, and opportunity to attend seminars/workshops. Preemployment training is required and includes accident prevention and safety, first aid, CPR, interpersonal skills, leadership skills, lifeguard certification.

Contact Lance Johnson, Camp Director, Peacock Camp, 38685 North Deep Lake Road, Lake Villa, Illinois 60046. Telephone: 847-356-5201. Fax: 847-356-7206. E-mail: peacockcmp@aol.com. Application deadline: continuous.

RGIS INVENTORY SPECIALISTS
2604 EAST DEMPSTER, SUITE 309-B
DES PLAINES, ILLINOIS 60016

General Information Inventory service that goes to different retail locations and counts inventory using a hand held computer similar to a calculator. Established in 1959. Located 10 miles from Chicago.

Profile of Summer Employees Total number: 175–200; typical ages: 18–70. 50% men; 50% women; 20% minorities; 20% college students; 5% retirees; 10% non-U.S. citizens; 45% local applicants.

Employment Information Year-round positions also offered. Jobs available: ▶ 30 *inventory counters* (minimum age 18) at $9 per hour. International applicants accepted; must obtain own visa, obtain own working papers. An in-person interview is required.

Benefits and Preemployment Training Possible full-time employment and on-the-job training. Preemployment training is required and includes introduction to our system and equipment.

Contact Pat Kasza, District Manager, RGIS Inventory Specialists. Telephone: 847-296-3031. Fax: 847-296-3226. Application deadline: continuous.

THE ROAD LESS TRAVELED
2053 NORTH MAGNOLIA AVENUE
CHICAGO, ILLINOIS 60614

General Information Worldwide adventure activities, wilderness exploration, and cultural exposure. Two 3-week programs for campers ages 13–14 and three 4-week and one 6-week program that features hiking, rafting, rock climbing, mountaineering, kayaking, backpacking, and leadership programs. Established in 1990. 120-acre facility.

Profile of Summer Employees Total number: 40; typical ages: 21–32. 50% men; 50% women. Nonsmokers required.

Employment Information Openings are from June 10 to August 28. Jobs available: ▶ 28–38 *general staff members* (minimum age 21) with Wilderness First Responder, WEMT or EMT, and lifeguard training; experience working with teens and in wilderness at $30–$40 per day ▶ 10–20 *trip leaders* (minimum age 21) with WEMT or EMT and lifeguard training; experience working with teens and in leading wilderness trips and advanced certification in Wilderness First Responder at $40–$80 per day. Applicants must submit a formal organization application, resume, two personal references, 2 professional references. International applicants accepted; must obtain own visa, obtain own working papers. An in-person interview is required.

Benefits and Preemployment Training Free housing, free meals, possible full-time employment, on-the-job training, opportunity to attend seminars/workshops, and workmen's compensation insurance. Preemployment training is required and includes accident prevention and safety, interpersonal skills, leadership skills.

Contact Sarah Midgley, Associate Director, The Road Less Traveled, 2053 North Magnolia Avenue, Chicago, Illinois 60614. Telephone: 773-348-4100. Fax: 773-348-4399. E-mail: rlt1road@ aol.com. World Wide Web: http://www.theroadlesstraveled.com. Application deadline: continuous.

THE SOUTHWESTERN COMPANY, ILLINOIS
See The Southwestern Company, Tennessee on page 284 for complete description.

STIVERS TEMPORARY PERSONNEL–ILLINOIS
ILLINOIS

General Information National temporary help company that places people in office support positions throughout the United States. Locations include: Arizona (Phoenix, Scottsdale, Temple); Colorado (Aurora, Denver, Lakewood); Indiana (Indianapolis); Kansas (Overland Park); Missouri (Grandview, Kansas City, St. Ann, St. Louis, St. Peters); Wisconsin (Milwaukee); California (Encino, Irvine, Los Angeles, Pasadena, San Diego, San Francisco); Illinois (Aurora, Chicago, Deerfield, Des Plaines, Evanston, Oak Brook, Schaumburg); New York (White Plain); Pennsylvania (Philadelphia, Pittsburgh, Wayne); Canada (Toronto). Established in 1945. Features: office settings; professional environments.

Profile of Summer Employees Total number: 2,000. 5% high school students; 60% college students; 10% retirees; 20% local applicants.

Employment Information Openings are from January to December. Year-round positions also offered. Jobs available: ▶ *clerk/typist* with six months office experience at $7–$10 per hour ▶ *receptionist* with six months office experience at $7–$10 per hour. Applicants must submit a formal organization application, testing. International applicants accepted; must obtain own visa, obtain own working papers. An in-person interview is required.

Benefits and Preemployment Training Possible full-time employment, health insurance, and on-the-job training.

Contact Chris Goodfarb, Internet Specialist, Stivers Temporary Personnel–Illinois, 1717 West Northern, #117, Phoenix, Arizona 85021. Telephone: 602-264-4580. Fax: 602-678-5649. E-mail: chrisg@stivers.com. World Wide Web: http://www.stivers.com. Application deadline: continuous.

STUDENT CONSERVATION ASSOCIATION (SCA), ILLINOIS
See Student Conservation Association (SCA), New Hampshire on page 193 for complete description.

INDIANA

ACE COMPUTER CAMP–INDIANA
See ACE Computer Camp–Washington on page 307 for complete description.

CULVER SUMMER CAMPS
1300 ACADEMY ROAD, #138
CULVER, INDIANA 46511

General Information Six-week all-activity program followed by a two-week session of ten specialty camps. Established in 1902. 1,800-acre facility located 50 miles from South Bend. Features: Indiana's 2nd largest natural lake; 120 sail and power boats; hockey and ice skating facilities; 6 Piper Cherokee "140" aircraft; more than 100 horses; ropes/initiatives challenge courses.

Profile of Summer Employees Total number: 300; typical ages: 19–25. 60% men; 40% women; 5% minorities; 20% college students; 5% retirees; 1% non-U.S. citizens; 10% local applicants. Nonsmokers required.

Employment Information Openings are from June 20 to August 23. Jobs available: ▶ *CEPSOL-Culvers English Program for Speakers of Other Languages instructor* with proficiency in Spanish and English and teaching experience with children; competitive salary ▶ *English instructor* with at least one year of experience and must be a certified English teacher; competitive salary ▶ *Indian lore instructor* with adequate knowledge in Indian lore, background, and dancing; competitive salary ▶ *administrattive assistants* with good typing, computer, phone, and organizational skills; competitive salary ▶ *aerobics instructor* with knowledge and experience in area; ability to work with children; competitive salary ▶ *art instructor* with knowledge and teaching experience in the area; competitive salary ▶ *assistant couselors* with one year of college, responsible, mature, and experience working with children; competitive salary ▶ *athletic instructor* with knowledge and experience in the field and one year of teaching experience; competitive salary ▶ *aviation flight instructor* with certification by FAA to give flying instruction and experience teaching children; competitive salary ▶ *computer instructor* with knowledge and experience teaching children in related area; competitive salary ▶ 35 *counselors* with at least one year of college and experience working with children; competitive salary ▶ *dance instructor* with knowledge and teaching experience required; competitive salary ▶ *dining hall assistant* with one year of college experience, responsible, mature young adult; competitive salary ▶ *drivers training experience instructor* with certification and at least one year teaching experience; competitive salary ▶ *equitation instructor* with knowledge and experience teaching children equitation skills, basic care for animals; competitve salary ▶ *fenching instuctor* with teaching experience and skills in epee, foil, and saber; competitive salary ▶ *golf instructor* with knowledge and teaching experience with children a plus; competitive salary ▶ *hockey instructor* with adequate knowledge and teaching experience in the field competitive salary ▶ *ice skating instructor* with adequate knowledge and teaching experience in the area; competitive salary ▶ *math instructor* with al least one year experience and must be a certified math teacher; competitive salary ▶ *music instructors* with music/band teaching experience preferred; competitive slary ▶ *nature director* with degree in related field and teaching experience desired; very competitive salary ▶ *nurse assistant* with one year of college, responsible, mature young adult; competitive salary ▶ *photography instructor* with adequate knowledge, skills, and teaching experience in area; competitive salary ▶ *reading instructor* with teacher certification in related field and at least one year of experience; competitive salary ▶ *rifle instructor* with adequate knowledge and teaching experience in the field; competitive salary ▶ *sailing instructors* with knowledge and experience teaching sailing in a variety of craft; competitive salary ▶ *scouting instructor* with knowledge and experience in scouting; competitive salary ▶ *scuba instructor* with certification in scuba and experience teaching skills and techniques to children; competitive salary ▶ *soccer instructors* with knowledge and experience in coaching; competitive salary ▶ 4 *swimming instructors* with lifeguard and WSI certification; competitive salary ▶ *tennis instructors* with knowledge and coaching experience in tennis; competitive salary ▶ *theater instructor* with adequate knowledge, skills, and teaching experience; competitive salary ▶ *waterski instructor* with proficiency in teaching waterskiing and dealing with children; competitive salary. Applicants must submit formal organization application, three personal references. International applicants accepted; must obtain own working papers, apply through a recognized agency. An in-person interview is recommended, but a telephone interview is acceptable.

Benefits and Preemployment Training Free housing, free meals, and on-the-job training. Preemployment training is required and includes accident prevention and safety, first aid, CPR, interpersonal skills, leadership skills.

Contact Mr. Anthony T. Mayfield, Director, Culver Summer Camps, Box 138 CEF, Culver, Indiana 46511. Telephone: 800-221-2020. Fax: 219-842-8462. E-mail: mayfiea@culver.org. World Wide Web: http://www.culver.org. Application deadline: continuous.

GIRL SCOUTS OF LIMBERLOST COUNCIL SUMMER CAMPS
2135 SPY RUN AVENUE
FORT WAYNE, INDIANA 46805

General Information Residential camp serving 60 girls ages 7–17 weekly. Established in 1958. 200-acre facility located 50 miles from Fort Wayne. Features: freshwater lake; wooded setting; rustic dining lodge; natural wetland area; wetland observation platform; tent-cabin units.

Profile of Summer Employees Total number: 25; typical ages: 18–22. 5% men; 95% women; 5% minorities; 10% high school students; 75% college students; 15% non-U.S. citizens; 50% local applicants. Nonsmokers preferred.

Employment Information Openings are from June 6 to August 8. Jobs available: ▶ 1 *assistant director* with three years experience in camp setting, one year administration experience, and strong organizational, supervisory, and communication skills at $2100 per season ▶ 1 *business manager* (minimum age 21) with excellent orgnizational and communicatin skills. Experience in bookkeeping or accounting at $1800 per season ▶ 1 *environmental education director* (minimum age 21) with leadership, organization, and communication skills, teaching experience, and environmental education/nature study knowledge at $1900 per season ▶ 2–4 *food service staff* with food service experience and excellent organizational skills at $1250–$1800 per season ▶ 1 *health manager* (minimum age 21) with CPR and advanced first aid certifications, LPN/RN/ EMT, and strong organizational and people skills at $1700 per season ▶ 1–2 *program directors* (minimum age 21) with first aid/CPR certifications, three years experience in camp setting or programming. Strong organizatinal and communication skills. Certification or experience in ropes course, teambuilding, primitive camping, tripping, environmental education, arts and crafts or other specialty area at $1900 per season ▶ 3–4 *riding assistants* (minimum age 18) with ability to work as part of a team. Knowledge of horse care and western horseback riding. Experience with children or teaching at $1360 per season ▶ 1 *riding director* (minimum age 21) with CHA/AAHS certification or extensive background in western horseback riding. Strong organizational and supervisory skills at $1800 per season ▶ 7–12 *unit assistants* (minimum age 18) with ability to work as part of a team. Experience or background with children, camping, or Girl Scouting at $1260 per season ▶ 3–6 *unit coordinators* (minimum age 21) with strong organizational and communication skills. Background in leadership and supervision. Experience in teaching and working with children. Camping and Girl Scout experience preferred at $1650 per season ▶ 3–4 *waterfront assistants* with lifeguard training and CPR/first aid certification and experience with children or teaching at $1360 per season ▶ 1 *waterfront director* (minimum age 21) with CPR/first aid/lifeguard training/WSI certifications. Aquatic facility or program management experience. Teaching and supervisory experience. Certification or experience in canoeing, sailing, kayaking, rowing, or other boating activities at $1800 per season. Applicants must submit formal organization application, three personal references, copies of certifications. International applicants accepted; must apply through a recognized agency. An in-person interview is recommended, but a telephone interview is acceptable.

Benefits and Preemployment Training Free housing, free meals, formal training, health insurance, and on-the-job training. Preemployment training is required and includes accident prevention and safety, first aid, CPR, interpersonal skills, leadership skills, child development and program skills.

Contact Brigitta Modglin, Director, Camp Logan, Girl Scouts of Limberlost Council Summer Camps, 203 EMS Lane D14, Syracuse, Indiana 46567. Telephone: 219-457-2841. Fax: 219-457-3021. E-mail: camplogan@hotmail.com. Application deadline: continuous.

HAPPY HOLLOW CHILDREN'S CAMP, INC.
3049 HAPPY HOLLOW ROAD
NASHVILLE, INDIANA 47448

General Information Residential camp with separate programs for diabetic, asthmatic, and inner-city children; serving 110 youths per week. Established in 1951. 776-acre facility located 60 miles from Indianapolis. Features: 776 forested acres; 16-acre freshwater lake; horseback riding; newly constructed living quarters; team challenge course; mountain biking trails.

Profile of Summer Employees Total number: 48; typical ages: 18–26. 50% men; 50% women; 20% minorities; 10% high school students; 90% college students; 2% non-U.S. citizens; 20% local applicants. Nonsmokers required.

Employment Information Openings are from June 1 to August 15. Jobs available: ▶ 20 *general counselors* (minimum age 18) at $190–$210 per week ▶ 10 *program instructors* (minimum age 18) with certification in the field of horseback riding, farm, arts and crafts, nature, mountain biking, challenge course, or canoeing at $190–$210 per week ▶ *registered nurse* (minimum age 21) with RN license at $300–$450 per week ▶ 8 *support staff* (minimum age 17) at $190–$210 per week ▶ *swimming instructors* (minimum age 18) with lifeguard, CPR, first aid, and WSI certification; lake experience preferred at $190–$210 per week. Applicants must submit formal organization application, two letters of recommendation. International applicants accepted; must apply through a recognized agency. An in-person interview is recommended, but a telephone interview is acceptable.

Benefits and Preemployment Training Free housing, free meals, health insurance, and on-the-job training. Preemployment training is required and includes accident prevention and safety, first aid, CPR, interpersonal skills, leadership skills, lifeguard and small crafts training.

Contact Bernie Schrader, Director, Happy Hollow Children's Camp, Inc., 3049 Happy Hollow Road, Nashville, Indiana 47448. Telephone: 812-988-4900. Fax: 812-988-7505. E-mail: hhcdir@aol.com. Application deadline: May 1.

HOWE MILITARY SCHOOL SUMMER CAMP
PO BOX 191
HOWE, INDIANA 46746

General Information A residential camp serving boys ages 8–16, in a modified military setting, emphasizing leadership, sports and academics. Established in 1932. 50-acre facility located 30 miles from South Bend. Features: freshwater lake; wooded setting; cabins; basketball courts and baseball fields; full waterfront; tennis courts.

Profile of Summer Employees Total number: 30; typical ages: 18–55. 80% men; 20% women; 20% minorities; 50% high school students; 30% college students; 20% local applicants. Nonsmokers preferred.

Employment Information Openings are from June 23 to August 6. Jobs available: ▶ 2 *English instructors* (minimum age 19) with a major in teaching at $1600–$1800 per season ▶ 6 *cabin counselors* (minimum age 19) with one year of college completed at $1500–$1800 per season ▶ 2 *math instructors* (minimum age 19) with a major in teaching at $1600–$1800 per season ▶ 3 *waterfront staff members* (minimum age 18) with WSI or lifeguard certifications at $1400–$1800 per season. Applicants must submit formal organization application, three personal references, three letters of recommendation. International applicants accepted; must apply through a recognized agency. An in-person interview is required.

Benefits and Preemployment Training Free housing, free meals, formal training, possible full-time employment, and on-the-job training. Preemployment training is required and includes

accident prevention and safety, first aid, CPR, interpersonal skills, leadership skills.
Contact Duane Van Orden, Camp Director, Howe Military School Summer Camp, Howe Military School, Howe, Indiana 46746. Telephone: 219-562-2131. Fax: 219-562-3678. E-mail: howemil@ aol.com. Application deadline: May 15.

THE SOUTHWESTERN COMPANY, INDIANA
See The Southwestern Company, Tennessee on page 284 for complete description.

STIVERS TEMPORARY PERSONNEL–INDIANA
See Stivers Temporary Personnel–Illinois on page 103 for complete description.

STUDENT CONSERVATION ASSOCIATION (SCA), INDIANA
See Student Conservation Association (SCA), New Hampshire on page 193 for complete description.

SUPERCAMP–ST. MARY'S COLLEGE
ST. MARY'S COLLEGE
NOTRE DAME, INDIANA 46556

General Information Residential program for teens designed to build self-confidence and lifelong learning skills through accelerated learning techniques. Established in 1981. Features: university dormitories; outdoor ropes course.

Profile of Summer Employees Typical ages: 18–25. 80% college students. Nonsmokers required.

Employment Information Openings are from June to August. Jobs available: ▶ 1 *EMT/ wellness person* with national or state registration at $600–$1300 per season ▶ 10 *counselors* with college degree and PPS credential, MFCC license, or master's degree in counseling at $900–$1500 per season ▶ 4–10 *facilitators* with presentation skills and college degree; teaching credential preferred at $1300–$2350 per season ▶ 1 *logistics manager* with excellent organizational skills and high school diploma at $600–$1100 per season ▶ 1 *nurse/paramedic* with national or state registration at $600–$1300 per season ▶ 1 *office manager* with high school diploma and prior office experience at $450–$700 per season ▶ 20–25 *team leaders* with high school diploma and prior experience with teens at $250–$600 per season. Applicants must submit a formal organization application, resume, two letters of recommendation, in-person interview recommended (videotape interview acceptable). International applicants accepted; must obtain own visa, obtain own working papers.

Benefits and Preemployment Training Free housing, free meals, and on-the-job training. Preemployment training is required and includes interpersonal skills, leadership skills.

Contact Recruiter, SuperCamp–St. Mary's College, 1725 South Coast Highway, Oceanside, California 92054. Telephone: 800-285-3276 Ext. 180. Fax: 760-722-3507. E-mail: info@ learningforum.com. World Wide Web: http://www.supercamp.com. Application deadline: continuous.

CAMP COURAGEOUS OF IOWA
12007 190TH STREET, PO BOX 418
MONTICELLO, IOWA 52310-0418

General Information Year-round camp for children and adults with disabilities. Traditional camp activities such as swimming, canoeing, nature activities, and crafts are offered. Also adventure activities such as rock climbing, high ropes, and caving are available. Established in 1972. 70-acre facility located 35 miles from Cedar Rapids. Features: wooded setting; indoor pool; nature center; caves; bluffs to rock climb and rappel; staff dormitory.

Profile of Summer Employees Total number: 30; typical ages: 18–30. 30% men; 70% women; 3% minorities; 70% college students; 1% retirees; 10% non-U.S. citizens; 5% local applicants. Nonsmokers required.

Employment Information Openings are from May 21 to August 18. Year-round positions also offered. Jobs available: ► 1 *adventure specialist* (minimum age 18) with belaying training and experience leading rock climbing, rapelling, and high/low ropes; training can be provided at $600–$1000 per month ► 15–20 *camp counselors* (minimum age 18) with a sincere desire to work with people with disabilities at $600–$1000 per month ► 1 *canoeing specialist* with current lifeguard training certification and experience leading canoeing at $600–$1000 per month ► 1 *crafts specialist* (minimum age 18) with experience with projects for people with disabilities at $600–$1000 per month ► 1 *nature specialist* (minimum age 18) with experience leading nature activities and working with small farm animals at $600–$1000 per month ► 1 *outdoor living skills specialist* (minimum age 18) with experience teaching outdoor living skills for people with disabilities at $600–$1000 per month ► 1 *recreation specialist* (minimum age 18) with experience with recreational activities for people with disabilities at $600–$1000 per month ► 1 *swimming specialist* (minimum age 18) with current lifeguard training certification at $600–$1000 per month. International applicants accepted; must obtain own visa, obtain own working papers, apply through a recognized agency.

Benefits and Preemployment Training Free housing, free meals, formal training, possible full-time employment, health insurance, on-the-job training, and first aid/CPR training. Preemployment training is required and includes accident prevention and safety, first aid, CPR, interpersonal skills, leadership skills, behavior management.

Contact Jeanne Muellerleile, Camp Director, Camp Courageous of Iowa, 12007 190th Street, PO Box 418, Monticello, Iowa 52310-0418. Telephone: 319-465-5916 Ext. 206. Fax: 319-465-5919. E-mail: jeanne_muellerleile@campcourageous.org. World Wide Web: http://www.camp@campcourageous.org. Application deadline: continuous.

CAMP HANTESA
1450 ORIOLE ROAD
BOONE, IOWA 50036

General Information Residential and day camp serving boys and girls ages 5–18 with small group activities in noncompetitive atmosphere. Established in 1919. 144-acre facility located 3 miles from Boone. Features: hills; woods; hiking trails; lodges and cabins.

Profile of Summer Employees Total number: 40; typical ages: 18–22. 30% men; 70% women; 1% minorities; 99% college students; 80% local applicants. Nonsmokers preferred.

Employment Information Openings are from June 1 to August 15. Jobs available: ► 1 *arts and crafts instructor* (minimum age 18) at $1300 per season ► 5 *cooks* (minimum age 18) at $1300 per season ► 20 *general counselors* (minimum age 18) with interest in children at $1300 per season ► 3 *riding instructors* (minimum age 18) with riding skills (English or Western style); AAHS (clinic provided) at $1300 per season ► 1 *swimming guard* (minimum age 18) with ARC lifeguard certification at $1300 per season ► 1 *swimming instructor* (minimum age 18) with Red Cross WSI certification at $1300 per season ► 6 *unit directors* (minimum age 20) with management skills at $1300 per season. Applicants must submit formal organization application, three personal references. International applicants accepted; must apply through a recognized agency. An in-person interview is recommended, but a telephone interview is acceptable.

Benefits and Preemployment Training Free housing, free meals, health insurance, and on-the-job training. Preemployment training is required and includes accident prevention and safety, first aid, CPR, interpersonal skills, leadership skills.

Contact Suz Welch, Director, Camp Hantesa, 1450 Oriole Road, Boone, Iowa 50036. Telephone: 515-432-1417. Fax: 515-432-1294. E-mail: hantesa@opencominc.com. Application deadline: continuous.

CAMP HITAGA
5551 HITAGA ROAD
WALKER, IOWA 52352

General Information Day camp serving boys and girls from kindergarten through fifth grade. Residential camp serving boys and girls from first to ninth grade. Conference center serving community groups. Established in 1930. 240-acre facility located 20 miles from Cedar Rapids.

Profile of Summer Employees 25% men; 75% women; 100% college students; 25% local applicants.

Employment Information Openings are from June 6 to August 7. Jobs available: ▶ *assistant director* at $1200–$1500 per season ▶ *general counselors* at $900–$1300 per season ▶ *riding, aquatic, arts and crafts, and nature staff heads* at $1000–$1250 per season.

Benefits and Preemployment Training Free housing, free meals, and on-the-job training. Preemployment training is required and includes accident prevention and safety, first aid, CPR, interpersonal skills, leadership skills.

Contact Naomi Corridon, Camp Director, Camp Hitaga, 226 29th Street Drive SE, Suite E-2, Cedar Rapids, Iowa 52403. Telephone: 319-362-8268. Fax: 319-362-7963.

GIRL SCOUT CAMP TANGLEFOOT
14948 DOGWOOD AVENUE
CLEAR LAKE, IOWA 50428

General Information Residential summer camp serving 116 Girl Scouts weekly. Established in 1947. 50-acre facility located 5 miles from Clear Lake. Features: freshwater lake; cabins and platform tents; prairie and wooded site; new showerhouses; waterfront building and dock complex; new staff/program building.

Profile of Summer Employees Total number: 31; typical ages: 17–28. 5% men; 95% women; 1% minorities; 25% high school students; 70% college students; 1% non-U.S. citizens; 90% local applicants. Nonsmokers preferred.

Employment Information Openings are from June 1 to August 15. Jobs available: ▶ 1 *arts director* (minimum age 18) with driver's license at $1200–$1400 per season ▶ 1 *business manager* (minimum age 20) with computer (Win95) skills, some bookkeeping experience, and driver's license at $1200–$1300 per season ▶ 3 *food service staff members* (minimum age 18) at $1400–$1600 per season ▶ *health and wellness supervisor* (minimum age 20) with first aid, CPR (will train), driver's license, and health education and record keeping experience at $1300–$1500 per season ▶ 15 *program counselors* (minimum age 17) with LG, first aid, CPR (will offer additional training); driver's license preferred at $1100–$1300 per season ▶ 1 *program director* (minimum age 21) with organizational and supervisory skills, and driver's license at $1500–$1600 per season ▶ 1 *waterfront director* (minimum age 17) with Red Cross LG (LGI preferred), WSI, CPR, first aid, small craft safety, and driver's license at $1400–$1500 per season ▶ 5 *waterfront staff members* (minimum age 17) with Red Cross lifeguard training, WSI certification, and driver's license at $1200–$1400 per season. Applicants must submit formal organization application, three personal references, background check. International applicants accepted; must apply through a recognized agency. An in-person interview is recommended, but a telephone interview is acceptable.

Benefits and Preemployment Training Free housing, free meals, health insurance, on-the-job training, opportunity to attend seminars/workshops, and certification training. Preemployment training is required and includes accident prevention and safety, first aid, CPR, interpersonal skills, leadership skills, waterfront/small craft certification.

Contact C. L. Findley, Camp Director, Girl Scout Camp Tanglefoot, 14948 Dogwood Avenue, Clear Lake, Iowa 50428. Telephone: 515-357-2481. Fax: 515-357-7735. E-mail: cindy@niowagirlscouts.org. World Wide Web: http://www.niowagirlscouts.org. Application deadline: continuous.

THE SOUTHWESTERN COMPANY, IOWA
See The Southwestern Company, Tennessee on page 284 for complete description.

STUDENT CONSERVATION ASSOCIATION (SCA), IOWA
See Student Conservation Association (SCA), New Hampshire on page 193 for complete description.

KANSAS

MITCHELL HARVESTING
2298 NORTH ROAD I
ULYSSES, KANSAS 67880

General Information We harvest grain, wheat, barley, oats, and milo. We start in Texas May 15 and work our way north to Montana then back to Colorado and Texas for fall harvest ending in November. Established in 1992. Located 200 miles from Amarillo. Features: beautiful, vast wheat fields; historical sites; mountains; rolling hills; working outdoors; rural city setting.

Profile of Summer Employees Total number: 1; typical ages: 25–30. 90% men; 10% women; 20% high school students; 30% retirees; 50% local applicants. Nonsmokers preferred.

Employment Information Openings are from May 1 to November 1. Year-round positions also offered. Jobs available: ▶ 1 *combine operator* (minimum age 18) with farm background at $1000-$1400 per month plus bonus for full season ▶ 1–2 *truck drivers* (minimum age 18) with CDL or willing to obtain it at $1000-$1400 per month plus bonus for full season. International applicants accepted; must obtain own working papers. An in-person interview is recommended, but a telephone interview is acceptable.

Benefits and Preemployment Training Free housing, free meals, possible full-time employment, names of contacts, on-the-job training, opportunity to attend seminars/workshops, and travel reimbursement. Preemployment training is optional and includes accident prevention and safety, leadership skills.

Contact Bryan or Tammi Mitchell, Owners, Mitchell Harvesting, 2298 North Road I, Ulysses, Kansas 67880. Telephone: 316-424-1771. Fax: 316-424-1778. E-mail: mitchelt@pld.com. Application deadline: continuous.

THE SOUTHWESTERN COMPANY, KANSAS
See The Southwestern Company, Tennessee on page 284 for complete description.

STIVERS TEMPORARY PERSONNEL–KANSAS
See Stivers Temporary Personnel–Illinois on page 103 for complete description.

STUDENT CONSERVATION ASSOCIATION (SCA), KANSAS
See Student Conservation Association (SCA), New Hampshire on page 193 for complete description.

KENTUCKY

A CHRISTIAN MINISTRY IN THE NATIONAL PARKS–KENTUCKY
See A Christian Ministry in the National Parks–Massachussetts on page 138 for complete description.

CAMP WOODMEN OF THE WORLD
93 SCHWARTZ ROAD
MURRAY, KENTUCKY 42071

General Information Residential camp serving Woodmen of the World members ages 8–15; also a senior program serving adults ages 60 and over with a general camp program that provides transportation Monday and Friday. Established in 1984. 14-acre facility located 3 miles from Murray. Features: junior olympic swimming pool; 45' rapelling tower; 24' pool slide; 2 tennis courts; 6 cabins.

Profile of Summer Employees Total number: 25–30; typical ages: 18–25. 50% men; 50% women; 2% minorities; 30% high school students; 70% college students; 2% non-U.S. citizens; 40% local applicants.

Employment Information Openings are from June 1 to August 7. Jobs available: ▶ *archery instructor* (minimum age 18) with certification in field at $700–$1100 per season ▶ *arts and crafts instructor* (minimum age 18) with experience in the field at $100–$110 per week ▶ *general counselors* (minimum age 18) with experience in the field at $90–$100 per week ▶ *rifle instructor* (minimum age 21) with experience or NRA certification at $100–$105 per week ▶ *water safety instructor/pool manager* (minimum age 21) with WSI certification at $100–$110 per week. Applicants must submit formal organization application, three personal references. International applicants accepted; must apply through a recognized agency. An in-person interview is recommended, but a telephone interview is acceptable.

Benefits and Preemployment Training Free housing, free meals, health insurance, names of contacts, and on-the-job training. Preemployment training is required and includes accident prevention and safety, first aid, CPR, leadership skills, lifeguard certification.

Contact Colleen Anderson, Camp Director, Camp Woodmen of the World, 401-A Maple Street, Murray, Kentucky 42071. Telephone: 502-753-4382. Fax: 502-753-4396. E-mail: campwow@idd.net. Application deadline: April 1.

LIFE ADVENTURE CAMP
1122 OAK HILL DRIVE
LEXINGTON, KENTUCKY 40505

General Information Primitive wilderness camp with weekly programs that serve 32–40 campers per session (ages 9–18) who are either emotionally or behaviorally challenged, or who are in need of enhanced self-esteem, cooperation, and team-building skills. Established in 1977. 500-acre facility located 65 miles from Lexington. Features: wooded setting; 6 caves on site; large creek; tent camping.

Profile of Summer Employees Total number: 15; typical ages: 19–23. 31% men; 69% women; 6% high school students; 94% college students; 50% local applicants. Nonsmokers required.

Employment Information Openings are from May 28 to July 30. Year-round positions also offered. Jobs available: ▶ 12 *counselors* (minimum age 19) with first aid/CPR certification, one year of college or related work experience, some camping or outdoor experience, ability to live and work comfortably in a primitive outdoor setting, and some experience in a leadership role with children, preferably with children who have emotional and/or behavioral problems at $1200–$1300 per season ▶ 1 *food director* (minimum age 18) with experience with food management and valid driver's license at $900–$1000 per season ▶ 1 *health supervisor* (minimum age 19) with first aid/CPR certification and valid driver's license at $1200–$1400 per season. Applicants must submit a formal organization application, three personal references, background check. An in-person interview is recommended, but a telephone interview is acceptable.

Benefits and Preemployment Training Free housing, free meals, formal training, and on-the-job training. Preemployment training is required and includes first aid, CPR, interpersonal skills, leadership skills.

Contact Lynda LeVan, Executive Director, Life Adventure Camp, 1122 Oak Hill Drive, Lexington, Kentucky 40505. Telephone: 606-252-4733. Fax: 606-225-5115. Application deadline: April 30.

THE SOUTHWESTERN COMPANY, KENTUCKY
See The Southwestern Company, Tennessee on page 284 for complete description.

STUDENT CONSERVATION ASSOCIATION (SCA), KENTUCKY
See Student Conservation Association (SCA), New Hampshire on page 193 for complete description.

LOUISIANA

ACE COMPUTER CAMP–LOUISIANA
See ACE Computer Camp–Washington on page 307 for complete description.

CAMP FIRE CAMP WI-TA-WENTIN
2126 OAK PARK BOULEVARD
LAKE CHARLES, LOUISIANA 70601
General Information Three-week day camp and two-week resident camp. Established in 1950. 96-acre facility located 13 miles from Lake Charles. Features: freshwater bay; wooded setting; rustic cabins; nature trails.
Profile of Summer Employees Total number: 24; typical ages: 18–25. 50% men; 50% women; 5% minorities; 20% high school students; 80% college students; 85% local applicants. Nonsmokers required.
Employment Information Openings are from June 7 to July 16. Jobs available: ▶ *canoeing instructor* at $450 per season ▶ *general counselors* at $450–$550 per season ▶ *lifeguards* at $450–$550 per season ▶ *program director* at $600 per season ▶ 1 *water safety instructor* at $600 per season. Applicants must submit a formal organization application, three personal references, two letters of recommendation. An in-person interview is recommended, but a telephone interview is acceptable.
Benefits and Preemployment Training Free housing, free meals, formal training, and on-the-job training. Preemployment training is required and includes accident prevention and safety, first aid, CPR.
Contact Joe Hill, Director, Camp Fire Camp Wi-Ta-Wentin, 2126 Oak Park Boulevard, Lake Charles, Louisiana 70601. Telephone: 318-478-6550. Fax: 318-478-6551. E-mail: jdhill@iamerica. net. World Wide Web: http://www.cfsowela.org. Application deadline: June 1.

MARYDALE RESIDENT CAMP
10317 MARYDALE ROAD
ST. FRANCISVILLE, LOUISIANA 70775
General Information Residential camp serving girls ages 7 –17 with a general outdoor program and specialty programs in horseback riding and swimming. Established in 1948. 400-acre facility located 40 miles from Baton Rouge. Features: lake; 2 outdoor horse arenas; pool; challenge course; several hiking trails; new multi-purpose facility.
Profile of Summer Employees Total number: 40; typical age: 20. 1% men; 99% women; 25% minorities; 5% high school students; 95% college students; 90% local applicants.
Employment Information Openings are from June 1 to July 31. Jobs available: ▶ 1 *arts and crafts director* (minimum age 18) at $125–$200 per week ▶ 1 *business manager* (minimum age 21) with some type of accounting or bookkeeping experience at $200–$250 per week ▶ 16–20 *counselors* (minimum age 18) with leadership experience at $125–$200 per week ▶ 2 *health supervisors* (minimum age 21) with RN, LPN, or physician's license at $225–$275 per week ▶ 4 *lifeguards* (minimum age 18) with American Red Cross certification and swimming experience; will train at $125–$175 per week ▶ 1 *naturalist* (minimum age 18) with experience in wildlife education at $125–$175 per week ▶ 1 *program director/assistant director* (minimum age 21) with camp experience, preferably in Girl Scout programming, documented experience in leadership and activity organization, and recreation background at $225–$275 per week ▶ 1

riding director (minimum age 21) with CHA certification or documented experience (possible nine-week contract) at $150–$225 per week ▶ 4 *riding instructors* (minimum age 18) with Camp Horsemanship Association certification or documented experience at $125–$175 per week ▶ 5 *unit leaders* (minimum age 21) with camp and documented leadership experience at $150–$200 per week ▶ 1 *waterfront director* (minimum age 21) with lifeguard, CPR, first aid, and WSI certification recommended (possible nine-week contract and weekend employment) at $150–$225 per week. Applicants must submit a formal organization application, two personal references. An in-person interview is recommended, but a telephone interview is acceptable.

Benefits and Preemployment Training Free housing, free meals, formal training, and on-the-job training. Preemployment training is required and includes accident prevention and safety, first aid, CPR, interpersonal skills, leadership skills, child abuse prevention, conflict resolution, outdoor living skills.

Contact Ms. Leigh Bonfanti, Program Specialist, Marydale Resident Camp, 545 Colonial Drive, Baton Rouge, Louisiana 70806-6520. Telephone: 800-852-8421. Fax: 225-927-8402. E-mail: agscouncil@aol.com. Application deadline: continuous.

THE SOUTHWESTERN COMPANY, LOUISIANA
See The Southwestern Company, Tennessee on page 284 for complete description.

STUDENT CONSERVATION ASSOCIATION (SCA), LOUISIANA
See Student Conservation Association (SCA), New Hampshire on page 193 for complete description.

ACADIA CORPORATION
85 MAIN STREET, BOX 24
BAR HARBOR, MAINE 04609

General Information National park concessioner operating a restaurant and three gift shops in Acadia National Park and several shops in the town of Bar Harbor. Established in 1932. 18 miles from Ellsworth. Features: national park setting; near Atlantic Ocean; hiking, biking, and sailing activities available; busy resort community; tea and popovers on the lawn.

Profile of Summer Employees Total number: 150; typical ages: 18–70. 44% men; 56% women; 4% minorities; 1% high school students; 89% college students; 10% retirees; 2% non-U.S. citizens; 20% local applicants.

Employment Information Openings are from May 15 to October 26. Jobs available: ▶ 2 *bartenders* (minimum age 18) with ability to operate service bar and cash register per hour at $6.00 per hour plus tips ▶ 1 *building and grounds personnel* (minimum age 18) with ability to perform a variety of tasks (indoors and outdoors) and to interact well with park visitors at $7 per hour ▶ 5 *buspersons* (minimum age 18) with ability to lift and carry more than 25 pounds up to 100 times per day at $6.00 per hour plus tips ▶ 2 *cashiers* (minimum age 18) with ability to operate cash register, count money, and prepare bank accounts (must have valid driver's license) at $6.00 per hour plus tips ▶ 6 *hosts* (minimum age 18) with pleasant personality and calm demeanor to greet and seat customers and take reservations at $6.00 per hour plus tips ▶ 1–2 *housekeepers* (minimum age 18) with willingness to clean housing, offices, and restrooms at $8 per hour ▶ 15 *kitchen workers* (minimum age 18) with ability to run cold food line and bakery and to perform food prep work, dishwashing, cleaning and lifting and carrying more that 25 pounds up to 100 times per day at $7.25 per hour ▶ 3 *lead cooks* (minimum age 18) with strong creative cooking skills, including saute and sauces, and two years of supervisory experience or equivalent at $8.75 per hour ▶ 3 *office clerks* (minimum age 18) with ability to perform work accurately, pay attention to detail, and type (must have valid driver's license) at $7 per hour ▶ 32 *shop clerks* (minimum age 18) with ability to perform various duties, including operating cash register, assisting with purchases, stocking and ordering merchandise, and orienting park visitors at $7 per hour ▶ 36 *waiters/waitresses* (minimum age 18) at $2.58 per hour plus gratuities with pleasant personality, and calm demeanor and ability to lift and carry more than 25 pounds up to 100 times per day ▶ 4 *warehouse clerks* (minimum age 18) with ability to maintain accurate records and pay attention to detail, clean driving record, valid driver's license; ability to frequently lift and carry up to 50 pounds at $7 per hour. Applicants must submit formal organization application, two personal references, letter of recommendation. International applicants accepted; must obtain own visa, obtain own working papers, apply through a recognized agency. A telephone interview is required.

Benefits and Preemployment Training Housing at a cost, meals at a cost, and on-the-job training. Preemployment training is required and includes accident prevention and safety, interpersonal skills, information about camping policies and information about Acadia National Park and surrounding area.

Contact Rebecca Ghelli, Personnel, Acadia Corporation, PO Box 24, Bar Harbor, Maine 04609. Telephone: 207-288-5592. Fax: 207-288-2420. E-mail: acadia@acadia.net. Application deadline: continuous.

ACE COMPUTER CAMP–MAINE

See ACE Computer Camp–Washington on page 307 for complete description.

A CHRISTIAN MINISTRY IN THE NATIONAL PARKS–MAINE

See A Christian Ministry in the National Parks–Massachussetts on page 138 for complete description.

ALFORD LAKE CAMP
258 ALFORD LAKE ROAD
HOPE, MAINE 04847

General Information Residential camp for girls offering a multiactivity program for 175 girls ages 8–15. Extensive trip programs for girls and/or boys on the Appalachian Trail and in Great Britain offered, as well as exchange programs in Mexico, Japan, and Nova Scotia. Established in 1907. 416-acre facility located 10 miles from Camden. Features: freshwater lake; wooded setting; 4 tennis courts; library; stables and riding rings.

Profile of Summer Employees Total number: 90; typical ages: 17–25. 2% men; 98% women; 60% college students; 6% non-U.S. citizens. Nonsmokers required.

Employment Information Openings are from June 12 to August 17. Jobs available: ▶ 1 *campcraft instructor* (minimum age 18) with Maine trip-leading certification at $900–$1200 per season ▶ 1 *canoeing instructor* (minimum age 18) with Red Cross canoeing (or equivalent) and ALS certification (minimum) at $900–$1200 per season ▶ *drama instructor* (minimum age 18) with teaching and production experience at $900–$1200 per season ▶ 1 *gymnastics instructor* (minimum age 18) with teaching experience and certification or documentation at $900–$1200 per season ▶ *nature counselor* (minimum age 18) with background in nature, environmental studies, and related fields at $900–$1200 per season ▶ 2 *office personnel* with knowledge of computers and attention to detail at $1000–$1800 per season ▶ 5 *riding instructors* (minimum age 18) with British Horse Society, Pony Club certification, or equivalent at $900–$1200 per season ▶ *sailboarding instructor* (minimum age 18) with sailboarding experience documentation and ALS certification (minimum) at $900–$1200 per season ▶ 3 *sailing instructors* (minimum age 18) with Red Cross lifeguard training and sailing experience at $900–$1200 per season ▶ 5 *swimming instructors* (minimum age 18) with WSI and American Red Cross lifeguard certification at $900–$1500 per season ▶ 4 *tennis counselors* (minimum age 18) with teaching experience at $900–$1200 per season ▶ 4 *trip leaders* (minimum age 21) with LGT, CPR, first aid, and experience leading 2-to 3-day trips at $1500–$1800 per season. Applicants must submit formal organization application, three personal references. International applicants accepted; must apply through a recognized agency. A telephone interview is required.

Benefits and Preemployment Training Free housing, free meals, formal training, and on-the-job training. Preemployment training is required and includes accident prevention and safety, interpersonal skills, leadership skills.

Contact Ms. Betsy Souter, Director, Alford Lake Camp, 17 Pilot Point Road, Cape Elizabeth, Maine 04107. Telephone: 207-799-3005. Fax: 207-799-5044. E-mail: alc@alfordlake.com. Application deadline: continuous.

CAMP AGAWAM
CRESCENT LAKE, 54 AGAWAM ROAD
RAYMOND, MAINE 04071

General Information Residential camp serving 125 boys ages 8–15 in a single 7-week session. There is also a 1-week session for 85 disadvantaged boys. Established in 1919. 115-acre facility located 35 miles from Portland. Features: freshwater lake; wooded setting; renovated screened cabins and bathrooms; new dining hall and main lodge; 4 tennis courts; well-maintained facility.

Profile of Summer Employees Total number: 65; typical ages: 18–70. 90% men; 10% women; 5% minorities; 20% high school students; 80% college students; 10% non-U.S. citizens; 10% local applicants. Nonsmokers required.

Employment Information Openings are from June 10 to August 15. Jobs available: ► 1 *counselor/crafts instructor* (minimum age 18) with experience preferred at $1150–$1500 per season ► 1 *counselor/dramatics instructor* (minimum age 18) with acting classes, directing, and performing experience at $1150–$1500 per season ► 1 *counselor/woodworking instructor* (minimum age 19) at $1150–$2000 per season ► 2 *counselors/archery and riflery instructors* (minimum age 19) with NAA or NRA certification or equivalent at $1150–$1750 per season ► 4 *counselors/campcraft and trip leaders* with LGT, CPR/first aid, and Maine Trip Leader certification at $1150–$1500 per season ► 15 *counselors/sports instructors/coaches* with experience, including attending clinics at $1150–$1500 per season ► 4 *counselors/water sports instructors* (minimum age 18) with CPR, first aid, and WSI or LGT certification at $1150–$1750 per season ► *ropes course facilitator* (minimum age 19) with ropes course facilitator certification at $1150–$1750 per season ► *watercraft counselor (sailboards, sailboats, canoes, rowboats)* (minimum age 18) at $1150–$1500 per season. Applicants must submit formal organization application, three personal references. International applicants accepted; must apply through a recognized agency. An in-person interview is recommended, but a telephone interview is acceptable.

Benefits and Preemployment Training Free housing, free meals, and on-the-job training. Preemployment training is required and includes accident prevention and safety, first aid, CPR, interpersonal skills, leadership skills, child development.

Contact Scott Malm, Program Director, Camp Agawam, 30 Fieldstone Lane, Hanover, Massachusetts 02339. Telephone: 781-826-5913. Fax: 781-829-0208. E-mail: bowman@campagawam. org. World Wide Web: http://www.campagawam.org. Application deadline: continuous.

CAMP ANDROSCOGGIN
WAYNE, MAINE 04284

General Information Private residential camp serving 250 boys from the United States and abroad in one 8-week session. Established in 1907. 125-acre facility located 40 miles from Portland. Features: freshwater lake; wooded setting; 12 tennis courts; 4 sports fields; 30 watercraft; indoor gymnasium.

Profile of Summer Employees Total number: 90; typical ages: 19–25. 90% men; 10% women; 80% college students; 10% non-U.S. citizens; 10% local applicants. Nonsmokers preferred.

Employment Information Openings are from June 20 to August 22. Jobs available: ► 1 *animation/video instructor* at $1000–$1500 per season ► 1 *archery instructor* at $1000–$1250 per season ► 4 *baseball instructors* at $1000–$1250 per season ► 4 *basketball instructors* at $1000–$1250 per season ► 1 *bicycling instructor* at $1000–$1250 per season ► 1 *campcraft* *instructor* at $1000–$1250 per season ▶ 2 *canoeing instructors* at $1000–$1250 per season ▶ 1 *ceramics instructor* at $1000–$1250 per season ▶ 1 *crafts instructor* at $1000–$1250 per season ▶ 2 *drama instructors* at $1000–$1250 per season ▶ 1 *kayaking instructor* at $1000–$1250 per season ▶ 2 *lacrosse instructors* at $1000–$1250 per season ▶ 2 *nurses* at $2500–$3500 per season ▶ 1 *photography instructor* at $1000–$1250 per season ▶ 1 *radio broadcasting instructor* at $1000–$1250 per season ▶ 1 *riflery instructor* at $1000–$1250 per season ▶ 4 *ropes course instructors* at $1000–$1500 per season ▶ 3 *sailing instructors* at $1000–$1250 per season ▶ 2 *secretaries* at $1750–$2250 per season ▶ 4 *soccer instructors* at $1000–$1250 per season ▶ 10 *swimming instructors* with WSI certification or lifeguard training at $1000–$1250 per season ▶ 10 *tennis instructors* at $1000–$1500 per season ▶ 4 *waterskiing instructors* at $1000–$1250 per season ▶ 1 *windsurfing instructor* at $1000–$1250 per season ▶ 1 *woodworking instructor* at $1000–$1250 per season. Applicants must submit formal organization application, cover letter, three personal references, two letters of recommendation. International applicants accepted; must apply through a recognized agency. An in-person interview is recommended, but a telephone interview is acceptable.

Benefits and Preemployment Training Free housing, free meals, on-the-job training, and travel reimbursement. Preemployment training is required and includes accident prevention and safety, first aid, CPR, interpersonal skills, leadership skills.

Contact Peter Hirsch, Director, Camp Androscoggin, 601 West Street, Harrison, New York 10528. Telephone: 914-835-5800. Fax: 914-777-2718. E-mail: staff@campandro.com. World Wide Web: http://www.campandro.com. Application deadline: continuous.

CAMP ARCADIA
ROUTE 121
CASCO, MAINE 04015

General Information Residential camp for girls serving 160 campers for part of the season or seven full weeks concentrating on individual camper growth and development in a warm, family atmosphere. Established in 1916. 365-acre facility located 35 miles from Portland. Features: extensive freshwater lake frontage; 2 natural sandy beaches; sunny fields and pine woods; tennis courts; riding ring and stables.

Profile of Summer Employees Total number: 80; typical ages: 19–23. 10% men; 90% women; 5% minorities; 75% college students; 10% non-U.S. citizens. Nonsmokers preferred.

Employment Information Openings are from June 15 to August 10. Jobs available: ▶ 1 *archery instructor* at $1100–$1300 per season ▶ 2 *arts and crafts instructors* with silk-screening, block-printing, batik, drawing, and painting experience at $1000–$1500 per season ▶ 4 *canoeing instructors* with lifeguard training certification at $1000–$1500 per season ▶ 1 *ceramics instructor* with electric kiln and potter's wheel experience at $1000–$1200 per season ▶ *chef/baker* with negotiable salary ▶ 2 *drama instructors* with experience in children's drama, directing, lighting, and sets at $1000–$1500 per season with driver's license ▶ 1 *environmental (nature) instructor* at $1000–$1500 per season ▶ 1 *gymnastics instructor* with rhythmic, floor, and low beam gymnastics experience at $1000–$1300 per season ▶ 1 *music instructor* with piano playing and camp song leadership ability at $1000–$1400 per season ▶ 2 *nurses* with RN license; salary negotiable ▶ 2 *office workers* with 50 wpm typing and knowledge of computers at $1000–$1500 per season ▶ 1 *photography instructor* with black-and-white darkroom experience at $1000–$1200 per season ▶ 2 *riding instructors* with English balance seat-riding and stable management ability at $1000–$1400 per season ▶ 4 *sailing instructors* with lifeguard training and knowledge of racing at $1000–$1500 per season ▶ *swimming instructors* with WSI and lifeguard training certification at $1200–$1600 per season ▶ 4 *tennis instructors* with tennis team background at $1000–$1500 per season ▶ 3 *trip instructors* (minimum age 21) with driver's license at $1000–$1500 per season ▶ 2 *weaving instructors* with knowledge of floor, table, and hand looms at $1000–$1200 per season. Applicants must submit formal organization application, personal reference, letter of recommendation. International applicants accepted; must obtain own visa, obtain own working papers, apply through a recognized agency. An in-person interview is recommended, but a telephone interview is acceptable.

Benefits and Preemployment Training Free housing, free meals, formal training, health insurance, on-the-job training, travel reimbursement, and free uniforms. Preemployment training is required and includes accident prevention and safety, first aid, CPR, leadership skills.

Contact Anne Henderson Fritts, Director, Camp Arcadia, Pleasantville Road, New Vernon, New Jersey 07976. Telephone: 973-538-5409. Fax: 973-540-1555. Application deadline: continuous.

CAMP CEDAR
PO BOX 240
CASCO, MAINE 04015-0240

General Information Residential private camp for 250 boys offering one 8-week session including land sports, water sports, adventure activities and creative arts in a warm, nurturing environment. Established in 1954. 150-acre facility located 30 miles from Portland. Features: freshwater spring-fed lake; wooded setting; great facilities; close to mountains and ocean; modern cabins; great food.

Profile of Summer Employees Total number: 110; typical ages: 19–26. 75% men; 25% women; 10% minorities; 5% high school students; 80% college students; 10% non-U.S. citizens; 5% local applicants. Nonsmokers preferred.

Employment Information Openings are from June 20 to August 20. Jobs available: ▶ 75 *counselors* with ability to teach an activity at $1000–$1500 per season ▶ 5 *rock climbers* with experience in technical rock climbing, top roping, and belaying at $1000–$1500 per season ▶ 10 *swimming instructors* with WSI and/or lifeguard certification at $1000–$1500 per season ▶ 10 *tennis instructors* with high school or college varsity experience at $1000–$1500 per season. Applicants must submit formal organization application, three personal references, three letters of recommendation. International applicants accepted; must apply through a recognized agency. An in-person interview is recommended, but a telephone interview is acceptable.

Benefits and Preemployment Training Free housing, free meals, formal training, health insurance, on-the-job training, and travel reimbursement. Preemployment training is required and includes accident prevention and safety, first aid, CPR, interpersonal skills, leadership skills.

Contact Jeff Hacker, Director, Camp Cedar, 1758 Beacon Street, Brookline, Massachusetts 02445. Telephone: 617-277-8080. Fax: 617-277-1488. E-mail: campcedar@aol.com. World Wide Web: http://www.campcedar.com/cedar. Application deadline: continuous.

CAMP COBBOSSEE
RFD 1, ROUTE 135
WINTHROP, MAINE 04364

General Information Residential competitive and instructionally-oriented sports camp serving 200 boys. Established in 1902. 150-acre facility located 15 miles from Augusta. Features: climbing wall and zip line; location on 11-mile lake; extensive waterfront area; ball fields and courts; clay and all-weather tennis courts.

Profile of Summer Employees Total number: 100; typical ages: 19–25. 90% men; 10% women; 15% minorities; 85% college students; 10% non-U.S. citizens. Nonsmokers required.

Employment Information Openings are from June 19 to August 23. Jobs available: ▶ *activity heads* (minimum age 19) with teaching and/or coaching experience (preference for high school or college coaches or teachers) at $1500–$4500 per season ▶ *chef* with cooking experience with salary negotiable ▶ *hiking/camping/rock climbing staff members* (minimum age 19) with experience in working with children and rock climbing/ropes certification (training available) at $1250–$3000 per season ▶ *nurses* with RN license with salary negotiable ▶ *swimming instructors* (minimum age 19) with LGT and WSI certification (training available) at $1250–$3000 per season ▶ *team sports staff members* (minimum age 19) with experience in coaching or working with children and ability to instruct one or more of the following: baseball, basketball, soccer, lacrosse, street hockey, ice hockey, or team handball at $1250–$3000 per season ▶ *tennis staff members* (minimum age 19) with high school and/or college varsity or tournament competition experience preferred at $1250–$3000 per season ▶ *waterfront staff members* (minimum age 19) with sailing, waterskiing, or scuba experience; WSI and lifeguard certification (training available) at $1250–$3000 per season. Applicants must submit formal organization application, cover letter, resume, two personal references. International applicants accepted; must obtain own visa, obtain own working papers, apply through a recognized agency. An in-person interview is recommended, but a telephone interview is acceptable.

Benefits and Preemployment Training Free housing, free meals, on-the-job training, travel reimbursement, and laundry service. Preemployment training is required and includes accident prevention and safety, first aid, CPR, interpersonal skills, leadership skills, lifeguard training, ropes/climbing certification, WSI.

Contact Steven Rubin, Owner, Camp Cobbossee, 10 Silvermine Drive, South Salem, New York 10590. Telephone: 914-533-6104. Fax: 914-533-6069. E-mail: cobbachief@aol.com. Application deadline: continuous.

CAMP ENCORE-CODA FOR A GREAT SUMMER OF MUSIC, SPORTS, AND FRIENDS
STEARNS POND
SWEDEN, MAINE 04040

General Information Encore/Coda is a residential coed music and sports camp. Ensembles and private instruction in the areas of classical, jazz, and rock music as well as musical theater are featured. Established in 1950. 80-acre facility located 40 miles from Portland. Features: freshwater lake; wooded setting; 2 tennis courts; cabins; 28 pianos.

Profile of Summer Employees Total number: 75; typical ages: 17–50. 50% men; 50% women; 5% minorities; 10% high school students; 50% college students; 5% non-U.S. citizens; 5% local applicants. Nonsmokers required.

Employment Information Openings are from June 21 to August 19. Jobs available: ▶ 1 *arts and crafts counselor* (minimum age 19) at $1000–$1500 per season ▶ *assistant head counselor* with camp leadership experience, good organizational skills, and a college degree at $1500–$2000 per season ▶ *boating counselor* (minimum age 19) with LGT certification (ARC, Boy Scouts, Y, Ellis all acceptable) at $1000–$1500 per season ▶ *head counselor* with camp leadership experience, good organizational skills, and a college degree at $2300–$3000 per season ▶ 4 *land sports counselors* with CPR and first aid at $1000–$1500 per season ▶ 10 *music counselors* (minimum age 21) with solid performing skills on your instrument or voice. Ability to teach these skills to students aged 7-17. Prior teaching experience desired at $1200–$1600 per season ▶ 3 *piano accompanists* (minimum age 19) with excellent sight reading skills at $1000–$1600 per season ▶ 1–2 *sailing counselors* (minimum age 19) with LGT certification (ARC, Boy Scouts, Y, Ellis all acceptable) at $1000–$1500 per season ▶ 7 *swimming instructors* (minimum age 19) with LGT certification at $1100–$1600 per season ▶ 2 *tennis counselors* (minimum age 19) with CPR and first aid at $1100–$1500 per season ▶ 1 *waterfront director* (minimum age 21) with LGT/WSI certification; CPR, first aid; LGI preferred at $2000–$2500 per season. Applicants must submit formal organization application, three personal references. International applicants accepted; must apply through a recognized agency. An in-person interview is recommended, but a telephone interview is acceptable.

Benefits and Preemployment Training Free housing, free meals, and on-the-job training. Preemployment training is required and includes accident prevention and safety, interpersonal skills, leadership skills.

Contact Ellen Donohue-Saltman, Director, Camp Encore-Coda for a Great Summer of Music, Sports, and Friends, 32 Grassmere Road, Brookline, Massachusetts 02467. Telephone: 617-325-1541. Fax: 617-325-7278. E-mail: ellen@encore-coda.com. World Wide Web: http://www.encore-coda.com. Application deadline: continuous.

CAMP HAWTHORNE
PLUMMER ROAD, PANTHER POND
RAYMOND, MAINE 04071

General Information Coed residential camp with visual and performing arts programs and noncompetitive sports. Established in 1919. 140-acre facility located 20 miles from Portland. Features: 2½ miles of shorefront; pristine lake; professional staff for theatre, art, and movie making; great sailing instruction.

Profile of Summer Employees Total number: 45; typical ages: 19–26. 50% men; 50% women;

15% minorities; 5% high school students; 80% college students; 5% non-U.S. citizens. Nonsmokers preferred.

Employment Information Openings are from June 23 to August 17. Jobs available: ▶ 2 *archery/riflery instructors* (minimum age 18) ▶ 2 *canoeing/boating instructors* ▶ 4 *creative arts teachers* (minimum age 18) ▶ 2 *drama instructors* (minimum age 18) ▶ 6 *sailing instructors* (minimum age 18) ▶ 6 *sports instructors* at $1200–$1500 per season ▶ 5 *swimming instructors* with lifeguard training or WSI certification at $1000–$1400 per season. Applicants must submit a formal organization application, cover letter, resume. International applicants accepted; must obtain own visa.

Benefits and Preemployment Training Free housing, free meals, on-the-job training, travel reimbursement, and leadership skills, accident prevention and safety, first aid, and CPR training available.

Contact Ronald Furst, Owner, Camp Hawthorne, 10 Scotland Bridge Road, York, Maine 03909. Telephone: 207-363-1773. Fax: 207-363-1773. Application deadline: May 30.

CAMP LAUREL SOUTH
48 LAUREL ROAD
CASCO, MAINE 04015

General Information Laurel South is a family-oriented, coed, residential camp in Maine. We operate two 4-week sessions offering a variety of land and water sports, theater, arts, adventure, riding, and much more. Established in 1921. 120-acre facility located 24 miles from Portland. Features: freshwater, sandy-bottom lake; 8 hardcourt tennis courts; extensive staff lounge/cafe; wooded setting; top-notch program facilities; family atmosphere.

Profile of Summer Employees Total number: 135; typical ages: 19–50. 50% men; 50% women; 2% high school students; 85% college students; 8% non-U.S. citizens; 5% local applicants. Nonsmokers preferred.

Employment Information Openings are from June 20 to August 20. Jobs available: ▶ *adventure/ropes course instructors* at $1225 and up per season ▶ *aerobics instructor* at $1225 and up per season ▶ *archery instructors* at $1225 and up per season ▶ *arts and crafts instructors* at $1225 and up per season ▶ *baseball instructors* at $1225 and up per season ▶ *basketball instructors* at $1225 and up per season ▶ *campus leaders* at $2500 and up per season ▶ *ceramics instructors* at $1225 and up per season ▶ *dance instructors* at $1225 and up per season ▶ *field hockey instructor* at $1225 and up per season ▶ *fishing instructor* at $1225 and up per season ▶ *fitness intructors* at $1225 and up per season ▶ *football instructors* at $1225 and up per season ▶ *golf instructor* at $1225 and up per season ▶ *gymnastics instructors* at $1225 and up per season ▶ *horseback riding (English) instructors* at $1225 and up per season ▶ *lacrosse instructor* at $1225 and up per season ▶ *maintenance staff* at $1225 and up per season ▶ *nature counselor* at $1225 and up per season ▶ *nurses* at $3000 and up per season ▶ *office staff* at $1225 and up per season ▶ *photography instructors* at $1225 and up per season ▶ *piano player* at $1225 and up per season ▶ *program heads* at $2000 and up per season ▶ *riflery instructor* at $1225 and up per season ▶ *rocketry instructor* at $1225 and up per season ▶ *sailing instructors* at $1225 and up per season ▶ *soccer instructors* at $1225 and up per season ▶ *special programs coordinator* at $2000 and up per season ▶ *street/roller hockey instructors* at $1225 and up per season ▶ *swimming instructors* at $1225 and up per season ▶ *tennis instructors* at $1225 and up per season ▶ *theater staff* at $1225 and up per season ▶ *volleyball instructor* at $1225 and up per season ▶ *waterski instructors* at $1225 and up per season ▶ *windsurfing instructors* at $1225 and up per season. Applicants must submit formal organization application, three personal references. International applicants accepted; must apply through a recognized agency. An in-person interview is recommended, but a telephone interview is acceptable.

Benefits and Preemployment Training Free housing, free meals, formal training, on-the-job training, travel reimbursement, and laundry service. Preemployment training is required and includes accident prevention and safety, interpersonal skills, leadership skills, teamwork training.

Contact Roger Christian, Director, Camp Laurel South, PO Box 14130, Gainesville, Florida

32604. Telephone: 888-528-7357. Fax: 352-336-1026. E-mail: fun@camplaurelsouth.com. World Wide Web: http://www.camplaurelsouth.com.

CAMP MATOAKA FOR GIRLS
1 GREAT PLACE, RR 1
SMITHFIELD, MAINE 04978-1288

General Information Residential camp serving 225 girls with a variety of activities. Established in 1951. 150-acre facility located 9 miles from Waterville. Features: 1½ miles of shore frontage; large gymnasium; heated 25-meter swimming pool; 3 waterslides 200' each; professional waterski program; full bathrooms in cabins.

Profile of Summer Employees Total number: 110; typical ages: 20–24. 20% men; 80% women; 3% minorities; 10% high school students; 45% college students; 2% retirees; 30% non-U.S. citizens; 10% local applicants. Nonsmokers required.

Employment Information Openings are from June 14 to August 20. Jobs available: ▶ 3 *English equitation instructors* (minimum age 19) with high skill level and horsemanship certification at $1100–$2000 per season ▶ 6 *arts and crafts instructors* (minimum age 19) with a major in fine arts at $1000–$1200 per season ▶ 2 *dance instructors* (minimum age 19) with a major in dance/movement and aerobics instructor experience at $1100–$1200 per season ▶ 3 *drama/ music instructors* (minimum age 19) with a major in theater/drama at $1100–$1300 per season ▶ 3 *gymnastics instructors* (minimum age 19) with previous coaching/instructing and college team experience at $1200–$1400 per season ▶ 4 *land sports instructors* (minimum age 19) with a major in physical education or health/recreation at $1000–$1300 per season ▶ 2 *photographers* (minimum age 19) with major in photography at $1100–$1300 per season ▶ 1 *pianist/accompanist* (minimum age 19) with ability to sight read at $1100–$1600 per season ▶ 2 *ropes course instructors* (minimum age 23) with Project Adventure or Outward Bound certification at $1500 per season ▶ 2 *sewing instructors* (minimum age 19) with a major in home economics at $1200 per season ▶ 6 *ski instructors* (minimum age 19) with high skill level at $1100–$1500 per season ▶ 6 *small craft instructors* (minimum age 19) with Red Cross, CPR, and lifeguard certification at $1200–$1400 per season ▶ 6 *swimming instructors* (minimum age 19) with WSI certification at $1100–$1300 per season ▶ 6 *tennis instructors* (minimum age 19) with teaching and college team experience at $1000–$1400 per season ▶ 4 *trip instructors* (minimum age 19) with valid driver's license and experience in the field at $1200–$1400 per season ▶ 7 *video/ radio personnel* (minimum age 19) with major in video/radio/communication at $1150–$1400 per season. Applicants must submit formal organization application, resume. International applicants accepted; must apply through a recognized agency.

Benefits and Preemployment Training Free housing, free meals, possible full-time employment, and travel reimbursement. Preemployment training is required and includes accident prevention and safety, first aid, CPR, interpersonal skills, leadership skills.

Contact Mr. Michael Nathanson, Director/Owner, Camp Matoaka for Girls, 8751 Horseshoe Lane, Boca Raton, Florida 33496. Telephone: 800-MATOAKA. Fax: 561-488-6386. E-mail: matoaka@matoaka.com. World Wide Web: http://www.matoaka.com. Application deadline: continuous.

CAMP MODIN
RR 2, BOX 3445
BELGRADE, MAINE 04917

General Information Privately owned Jewish camp in New England serving 300 international campers. Established in 1922. 50-acre facility located near Boston, Massachusetts. Features: 13,000-square foot indoor recreation center; roller blading; climbing tower and zip line; state-of-the art waterfront; overnight camping trips; specialized program for teens.

Profile of Summer Employees Total number: 130; typical age: 21. 50% men; 50% women; 100% college students; 20% non-U.S. citizens. Nonsmokers required.

Employment Information Openings are from June 18 to August 21. Jobs available: ▶ 2–3 *arts and crafts instructors* with teaching experience in numerous areas at $1500–$2500 per season with teaching experience in numerous areas ▶ 5–10 *athletics instructors* with experience in field at $1250–$2000 per season ▶ 40–50 *general counselors* with experience at $1100–$2000 per season ▶ 3–4 *music, theater, and dance instructors* with experience in the field at $1500–$2500 per season ▶ 1 *photography instructor* with experience in the field at $1500–$2500 per season ▶ 4 *registered nurses* with RN or LPN and experience in the field at $3000–$4000 per season ▶ 2–3 *riflery/archery instructors* with experience and/or certification at $1500–$2500 per season ▶ 4–5 *swimming instructors* with WSI certification (minimum) and experience in the field at $1500–$2500 per season ▶ 3–4 *tennis instructors* with coaching experience at $1500–$2500 per season ▶ 5–10 *tripping/ropes/outdoor pursuits instructors* with certification and/or experience at $1500–$2500 per season ▶ 4 *waterskiing/sailing instructors* with experience in the field at $1250–$2500 per season. Applicants must submit formal organization application, three letters of recommendation. International applicants accepted; must apply through a recognized agency. A telephone interview is required.

Benefits and Preemployment Training Free housing, free meals, formal training, on-the-job training, and travel reimbursement. Preemployment training is required and includes accident prevention and safety, interpersonal skills, leadership skills.

Contact Howard Salzberg, Director, Camp Modin, 401 East 80th Street, Suite 31B, New York, New York 10021. Telephone: 212-570-1600. Fax: 212-570-1677. E-mail: modin@modin.com. World Wide Web: http://www.modin.com. Application deadline: continuous.

CAMP NASHOBA NORTH
198 RAYMOND HILL ROAD
RAYMOND, MAINE 04071

General Information International camp community of 180 boys and girls offering high-quality instruction in horsemanship, arts, sports, aquatics, theater, hiking, and dance. Established in 1933. 70-acre facility located 20 miles from Portland. Features: beautiful lake; regulation soccer field; large golf facility; modern cabins; large modern stable; beautiful dining hall.

Profile of Summer Employees Typical ages: 20–55. 40% men; 60% women; 10% minorities; 90% college students; 30% non-U.S. citizens. Nonsmokers required.

Employment Information Openings are from June 20 to August 21. Jobs available: ▶ 1 *boat driver/waterskiing instructor* (minimum age 19) with LGT certification at $1100–$1800 per season ▶ 1 *canoeing instructor* (minimum age 19) with LGT certification at $1100–$1800 per season ▶ 1 *chef* (minimum age 22) at $3000–$4000 per season ▶ 4 *kitchen helpers* at $1000–$1700 per season ▶ 1 *nurse* (minimum age 25) with RN license at $4000 per season ▶ 1 *photography instructor* (minimum age 19) at $1100–$1800 per season ▶ 4 *riding instructors* (minimum age 19) with Pony Club, eventing, or showing experience at $1100–$1800 per season ▶ *rock climbing instructor* (minimum age 20) at $1200–$1800 per season ▶ 2 *sailing instructors* (minimum age 19) with LGT certification at $1100–$1900 per season ▶ 3 *swimming instructors* (minimum age 19) with LGT and WSI certifications at $1100–$1900 per season ▶ 2 *tennis instructors* (minimum age 19) with experience at $1100–$1800 per season ▶ 2 *theater instructors* (minimum age 20) at $1200–$1800 per season ▶ 2 *trip instructors* (minimum age 20) with first aid/CPR certification at $1200–$1800 per season ▶ 2 *windsurfing instructors* (minimum age 19) with LGT certification at $1100–$1800 per season. Applicants must submit formal organization application, resume, three personal references. International applicants accepted; must apply through a recognized agency. An in-person interview is recommended, but a telephone interview is acceptable.

Benefits and Preemployment Training Free housing, free meals, formal training, health insurance, and on-the-job training. Preemployment training is required and includes accident prevention and safety, first aid, CPR, leadership skills.

Contact Sarah Seaward, Director, Camp Nashoba North, 140 Nashoba Road, Littleton, Massachusetts 01460. Telephone: 978-486-8236. Fax: 978-952-2442. E-mail: sseaward@ma.ultranet.com. World Wide Web: http://www.campnashoba.com. Application deadline: June 15.

CAMP PINECLIFFE
HARRISON, MAINE 04040

General Information Traditional residential camp offering high-quality instruction at all levels. Established in 1917. 75-acre facility located 40 miles from Portland.

Profile of Summer Employees Total number: 80. 25% men; 75% women; 10% minorities; 60% college students; 25% non-U.S. citizens; 15% local applicants. Nonsmokers preferred.

Employment Information Openings are from June 18 to August 21. Jobs available: ▶ 1 *archery instructor* at $1200–$2000 per season ▶ *boating/sailing instructors* with Red Cross lifesaving certification or equivalent at $1200–$2000 per season ▶ *ceramics instructors* at $1200–$2000 per season ▶ 1 *dance instructor* at $1200–$2000 per season ▶ 1 *drama instructor* with experience in the field at $1200–$2000 per season ▶ *highly skilled arts and crafts instructors* at $1200–$2000 per season ▶ 1 *highly skilled gymnastics instructor* at $1200–$2000 per season ▶ *highly skilled waterskiing instructors* with lifesaving certification at $1200–$2000 per season ▶ *land sports instructors* at $1200–$2000 per season ▶ 1 *music instructor* with ability to play piano by ear at $1200–$2000 per season ▶ 4 *nurses* with RN license; salary negotiable ▶ *riding instructor* with Pony Club experience at $1200–$2000 per season ▶ 1 *silversmithing instructor* at $1200–$2000 per season ▶ *swimming instructors* with WSI/lifeguard certification at $1200–$2000 per season ▶ *tennis instructors* with high school or college team experience at $1200–$2000 per season ▶ *trip leaders* at $1200–$2000 per season. Applicants must submit formal organization application, resume, three personal references, three letters of recommendation. International applicants accepted; must apply through a recognized agency. An in-person interview is recommended, but a telephone interview is acceptable.

Benefits and Preemployment Training Free housing, free meals, formal training, on-the-job training, and travel reimbursement. Preemployment training is required and includes accident prevention and safety, first aid, CPR, interpersonal skills, leadership skills.

Contact Susan R. Lifter, Director, Camp Pinecliffe, 277 South Cassingham Road, Columbus, Ohio 43209. Telephone: 614-236-5698. Fax: 614-235-2267. E-mail: pinecliff@mfn.com. World Wide Web: http://www.pinecliffe.com. Application deadline: continuous.

CAMP PONDICHERRY
RR 2, BOX 588
BRIDGTON, MAINE 04009

General Information Residential camp serving 144 girls ages 7–17 per session; season includes three 2-week sessions and one week of pre-camp. Established in 1971. 700-acre facility located 45 miles from Portland. Features: freshwater lake; platform tents; wooded setting; view of White Mountains; food service; program center.

Profile of Summer Employees Total number: 40; typical ages: 18–42. 1% men; 99% women; 5% minorities; 1% high school students; 90% college students; 30% non-U.S. citizens; 50% local applicants. Nonsmokers preferred.

Employment Information Openings are from June 20 to August 16. Jobs available: ▶ 1 *assistant camp director* (minimum age 21) with degree and administrative experience; valid driver's license at $2450 per season ▶ 6 *assistant unit leaders* (minimum age 18) with experience working with children at $1470 per season ▶ 1 *business manager* (minimum age 21) with skills in money management and valid driver's license at $1570 per season ▶ 1 *camp director* (minimum age 25) with administrative and supervisory skills; ability to work with adults and children at $3500–$5000 per season ▶ 1 *counselor-in-training director* (minimum age 21) with experience working with older girls at $1680 per season ▶ 1 *handy person* (minimum age 18) with valid driver's license at $1120 per season ▶ 1 *health supervisor* (minimum age 21) with RN, LPN, or EMT license at $2520 per season ▶ 3 *kitchen helpers* (minimum age 16) at $1120 per season ▶ *kitchen steward* (minimum age 21) with ability to supervise kitchen helpers and packout at $1540 per season ▶ 1 *pack-out person* (minimum age 16) with organizational skills and detail oriented at $1225 per season ▶ 3 *program consultants* (minimum age 21) with experience in designated field (dance, arts and crafts, sports, and games) at $1840 per season ▶ 6 *unit leaders* (minimum age 21) with leadership ability and experience working with children at $1680 per season ▶ 6 *waterfront assistants* (minimum age 18) with current lifeguard, first aid, and CPR certification at $1570 per season ▶ 1 *waterfront director* (minimum age 21) with certification in first aid, CPR, lifeguard training, and waterfront administration experience at $2420 per season. Applicants must submit formal organization application, three personal references. International applicants accepted; must apply through a recognized agency. An in-person interview is recommended, but a telephone interview is acceptable.

Benefits and Preemployment Training Free housing, free meals, formal training, health insurance, on-the-job training, and travel reimbursement. Preemployment training is required and includes accident prevention and safety, first aid, CPR, interpersonal skills, leadership skills.

Contact Jean M. Schroeder, Program Manager Kennebec Girl Scout Council, Inc., Camp Pondicherry, PO Box 9421, South Portland, Maine 04116-9421. Telephone: 207-772-1177. Fax: 207-874-2646. Application deadline: continuous.

CAMP RUNOIA FOR GIRLS
PO BOX 450
BELGRADE LAKES, MAINE 04918

General Information Residential camp for girls ages 7–17. Traditional program offering waterfront, riding, outdoor living skills, and more. Established in 1907. 88-acre facility located 12 miles from Augusta. Features: location at the end of a rural road; 128-square mile freshwater lake; clear lake water; mixture of woods and fields; clay tennis courts; stables.

Profile of Summer Employees Total number: 35; typical ages: 20–28. 5% men; 95% women; 5% minorities; 65% college students; 5% retirees; 15% non-U.S. citizens; 25% local applicants. Nonsmokers required.

Employment Information Openings are from June 15 to August 15. Jobs available: ▶ 1 *arts and crafts teacher* (minimum age 19) with documented experience at $1000–$1400 per season ▶ 1 *canoeing instructor* (minimum age 19) with lifeguard (or equivalent), first aid, CPR, and/or small watercraft certification at $1000–$1400 per season ▶ 1 *director of waterfront* (minimum age 21) with WSI certification, lifeguard, first aid, and CPR training at $1200–$1500 per season ▶ 2 *riding instructors* (minimum age 21) with documented experience at $1100–$1500 per season ▶ 2 *sailing instructors* (minimum age 19) with lifeguard (or equivalent), first aid, CPR, and/or small watercraft certification at $1000–$1400 per season ▶ 2 *target sports* (archery and riflery) *instructors* (minimum age 19) with American Archery Association and National Riflery Association certification (or equivalent) at $1000–$1400 per season ▶ 1 *tennis instructor* (minimum age 19) with documented experience at $1000–$1400 per season. Applicants must submit formal organization application, three personal references. International applicants accepted; must apply through a recognized agency. An in-person interview is recommended, but a telephone interview is acceptable.

Benefits and Preemployment Training Free housing, free meals, formal training, names of contacts, on-the-job training, opportunity to attend seminars/workshops, and travel allowance. Preemployment training is required and includes accident prevention and safety, first aid, CPR, interpersonal skills, leadership skills.

Contact Pamela N. Cobb, Director, Camp Runoia for Girls, 56 Jackson Street, Cambridge, Massachusetts 02140. Telephone: 617-547-4676. Fax: 617-661-1964. E-mail: runoia@citysource. com. World Wide Web: http://www.runoia.com. Application deadline: continuous.

CAMP SKYLEMAR
RR 1, BOX 508
NAPLES, MAINE 04055

General Information Sports-oriented seven-week program for boys ages 8–16. Established in 1948. 200-acre facility located 30 miles from Portland. Features: freshwater lake; location in the White Mountains; 8 tennis courts; golf course; wooded setting; numerous athletic fields.

Profile of Summer Employees Total number: 70; typical ages: 18–30. 5% women; 90% college students; 5% non-U.S. citizens; 5% local applicants. Nonsmokers required.

Employment Information Openings are from June 22 to August 15. Jobs available: ▶ 2 *arts and crafts instructors* (minimum age 18) with experience in the field at $1300–$2000 per season ▶ 2 *basketball instructors* (minimum age 18) with experience in the field at $1300–$1500 per season ▶ 2 *boating and skiing instructors* (minimum age 18) with small craft certification at $1300–$2000 per season ▶ 15 *general sports counselors* (minimum age 18) with experience in the field at $1300–$2000 per season ▶ 2 *golf instructors* (minimum age 18) with experience in the field at $1300–$1500 per season ▶ 3 *lifeguards* with certification at $1500–$2000 per season ▶ 1 *riflery instructor* (minimum age 18) with NRA instructor certification at $1300–$1400 per season ▶ 4 *ropes course leaders* (minimum age 18) with experience in the field at $1500–$2000 per season ▶ 4 *swimming instructors* (minimum age 18) with Red Cross lifeguard and WSI certification at $1500–$1800 per season ▶ 4 *tennis counselors* (minimum age 18) with experience in the field at $1300–$2000 per season ▶ 2 *trip counselors* (minimum age 18) with experience in the field at $1300–$2000 per season. Applicants must submit formal organization application, five personal references. International applicants accepted; must apply through a recognized agency. An in-person interview is recommended, but a telephone interview is acceptable.

Benefits and Preemployment Training Free housing, free meals, formal training, on-the-job training, opportunity to attend seminars/workshops, and travel reimbursement. Preemployment training is required and includes accident prevention and safety, interpersonal skills, leadership skills.

Contact Lee Horowitz, Director, Camp Skylemar, 7900 Stevenson Road, Baltimore, Maryland 21208. Telephone: 410-653-2480. Fax: 410-653-1271. E-mail: skylemar99@aol.com. World Wide Web: http://www.skylemar.com. Application deadline: continuous.

CAMP TAPAWINGO
ROUTE 93
SWEDEN, MAINE 04040

General Information Residential private girls camp offering an eight-week program to 170 campers with a focus on developing self-confidence and independence in a caring environment. Established in 1919. 200-acre facility located 50 miles from Portland. Features: private lake; foothills of the White Mountains; 6 tennis courts; sports fields and courts; bunks with running water and electricity; main lodge and dining room.

Profile of Summer Employees Total number: 60; typical ages: 19–22. 10% men; 90% women; 1% minorities; 80% college students; 8% non-U.S. citizens; 1% local applicants. Nonsmokers preferred.

Employment Information Openings are from June 15 to August 19. Jobs available: ▶ 2 *art instructors* at $1500–$1600 per season ▶ 2 *canoeing instructors* with lifeguard certification and instructor rating at $1500–$1900 per season ▶ *ceramics instructor* at $1500–$1600 per season ▶ 2 *dramatics instructors* (minimum age 19) at $1500–$1700 per season ▶ 2 *gymnastics instructors* (minimum age 19) with experience in the field at $1500–$1900 per season ▶ 2 *nurses* (minimum age 19) with RN or LPN license at $2500–$2800 per season ▶ 1 *photography instructor* with knowledge of black-and-white photography and developing at $1500–$1600 per season ▶ 1 *piano accompanist* with sight-reading and transposing ability at $1500–$1600 per season ▶ 2 *ropes instructors* (minimum age 19) with first aid, CPR, and instructor certification at $1500–$1800 per season ▶ 2 *sailboard/sailing instructors* with lifeguard certification and instructor rating at $1500–$1600 per season ▶ 1 *stained glass instructor* at $1500–$1600 per season ▶ 8 *swimming instructors* (minimum age 19) with WSI and lifeguard certification at $1500–$1800 per season ▶ 5 *tennis instructors* at $1500–$1800 per season ▶ 6 *trip leaders* (minimum age 21) with lifeguard, first aid, and CPR certification at $1500–$1800 per season ▶ 4 *waterskiing instructors* with lifeguard certification and instructor rating at $1500–$1800 per season. Applicants must submit formal organization application, three personal references. International applicants accepted; must apply through a recognized agency. A telephone interview is required.

Benefits and Preemployment Training Free housing, free meals, on-the-job training, and laundry service. Preemployment training is required and includes accident prevention and safety, CPR, interpersonal skills, leadership skills, child development.

Contact Jane Lichtman, Director, Camp Tapawingo, PO Box 248, Maplewood, New Jersey 07040. Telephone: 973-275-1139. Application deadline: continuous.

CAMP WAWENOCK
33 CAMP WAWENOCK ROAD
RAYMOND, MAINE 04071-6824

General Information Residential camp serving 110 campers ages 8–16, all of whom attend for the full 7-week season. Features traditional camp experience with emphasis on human relationships and personal development. Established in 1910. 100-acre facility located 26 miles from Portland. Features: natural sand beach; freshwater lake; cabins; stables and paddocks; 4 tennis courts; wooded setting.

Profile of Summer Employees Total number: 50; typical ages: 18–21. 5% men; 95% women; 3% minorities; 5% high school students; 95% college students; 1% retirees; 10% non-U.S. citizens; 3% local applicants. Nonsmokers required.

Employment Information Openings are from June 15 to August 15. Jobs available: ▶ 1 *riding instructor* (minimum age 19) with certification or documented experience at $1000–$1400 per season ▶ 1 *riflery instructor* (minimum age 19) with instructor certification at $1000–$1400 per season ▶ 2 *swimming instructors* (minimum age 19) with WSI certification at $900–$1300 per season. Applicants must submit formal organization application, resume, three personal references. International applicants accepted; must apply through a recognized agency. An in-person interview is recommended, but a telephone interview is acceptable.

Benefits and Preemployment Training Free housing, free meals, on-the-job training, opportunity to attend seminars/workshops, travel reimbursement, and laundry service. Preemployment training is required and includes accident prevention and safety, first aid, CPR, interpersonal skills, leadership skills.

Contact June W. Gray, Director/Owner, Camp Wawenock, 33 Camp Wawenock Road, Raymond, Maine 04071-6824. Telephone: 207-655-4657. Application deadline: May 15.

CAMP WAZIYATAH
RR 2, BOX 465
WATERFORD, MAINE 04088

General Information Traditional residential camp serving 220 campers in two-, three-, four-, and eight-week sessions featuring junior and teen programs. Established in 1922. 150-acre facility located 51 miles from Portland. Features: sparkling lake; on-site stables; beautiful barn theater; 10 tennis courts; 50-foot climbing tower; charming rustic cabins.

Profile of Summer Employees Total number: 100; typical ages: 19–62. 55% men; 45% women; 2% minorities; 70% college students; 3% retirees; 45% non-U.S. citizens; 2% local applicants. Nonsmokers required.

Employment Information Openings are from June 1 to September 1. Jobs available: ▶ 3–6 *English riding instructors* (minimum age 21) with certification in field at $1400–$1800 per season ▶ 1 *archery instructor* (minimum age 21) with certification in field at $1400–$2000 per season ▶ 3 *arts and crafts instructors* (minimum age 19) with experience in the field at $1400–$1800 per season ▶ 1 *baseball/softball instructor* (minimum age 19) with experience in the field at $1400–$1800 per season ▶ 1 *canoe instructor* (minimum age 19) with certification in field at $1400–$1800 per season ▶ 1 *photo instructor* (minimum age 21) with professional training and experience at $1400–$1800 per season ▶ 1 *pianist/accompanist* (minimum age 21) with facile Broadway style at $1400–$2000 per season ▶ 2 *rifle instructors* (minimum age 21) with certification in field at $1400–$1800 per season ▶ 1 *sailing instructor* (minimum age 19) with Red Cross sailing certification at $1400–$2000 per season ▶ *song leader* (minimum age 21) with experience in the field at $1400–$1800 per season ▶ 1 *special events coordinator* (minimum age 21) with 2-10 years camp experience at $1500–$2000 per season ▶ 6–10 *swimming instructors* (minimum age 19) with LGT/WSI certification at $1400–$2000 per season ▶ 6 *tennis instructors* (minimum age 19) at $1400–$1800 per season ▶ 2 *theater personnel* (minimum age 19) with experience in the field at $1400–$2500 per season ▶ 2 *trip leaders* (minimum age 21) with CPR, first aid, lifeguard, WFR, Maine Guide, EMT certification, and experience at $1400–$2500 per season ▶ 1 *video instructor* (minimum age 21) with professional training and experience at $1400–$1800 per season ▶ 4–6 *waterskiing instructors* (minimum age 21) with LGT and experience as a boat driver/ski instructor at $1400–$1800 per season ▶ 1 *windsurfing* *instructor* (minimum age 19) with Red Cross sailing, small craft, and LGT certification at $1400–$2000 per season. Applicants must submit formal organization application, resume, two personal references, two letters of recommendation. International applicants accepted; must obtain own visa, apply through a recognized agency. An in-person interview is recommended, but a telephone interview is acceptable.

Benefits and Preemployment Training Free housing, free meals, on-the-job training, and travel reimbursement. Preemployment training is required and includes accident prevention and safety, first aid, CPR, interpersonal skills, leadership skills.

Contact Penny and Peter Kerns, Directors, Camp Waziyatah, 19 Vose Lane, East Walpole, Massachusetts 02032. Telephone: 800-732-0223. Fax: 508-668-2665. E-mail: waziotters@aol. com. World Wide Web: http://www.wazi.com. Application deadline: continuous.

CAMP WEKEELA
RFD 1, BOX 275, ROUTE 219
CANTON, MAINE 04221

General Information Residential traditional coeducational camp serving 270 campers with an emphasis on sports, water sports, and arts. Established in 1922. 150-acre facility located 20 miles from Lewiston. Features: freshwater lake; wooded setting; 10 tennis courts; multiple athletic fields; gymnasium; extensive waterfront.

Profile of Summer Employees Total number: 120; typical ages: 20–65. 50% men; 50% women; 84% college students; 1% retirees; 10% non-U.S. citizens; 5% local applicants. Nonsmokers required.

Employment Information Openings are from June 19 to August 22. Jobs available: ▶ *ceramics staff members* (minimum age 19) at $1200–$1600 per season ▶ *creative arts staff members* (minimum age 19) at $1200–$1600 per season ▶ 1 *department program head* (minimum age 24) with management skills as well as knowledge of program area at $2300–$3000 per season ▶ 3 *group leaders* (minimum age 23) with college degree; must oversee counselors and campers at $2000–$2500 per season ▶ *guitar instructors* (minimum age 19) at $1200–$1600 per season ▶ *gymnastics staff members* (minimum age 19) at $1200–$1600 per season ▶ *land sports staff members (tennis)* (minimum age 19) at $1200–$1600 per season ▶ *piano/music staff members* (minimum age 19) at $1200–$1600 per season ▶ *pioneering staff members* (minimum age 19) at $1200–$1600 per season ▶ *radio staff members* (minimum age 19) at $1200–$1500 per season ▶ *ropes instructors* (minimum age 19) at $1200–$1600 per season ▶ *tennis staff members* (minimum age 19) at $1200–$1600 per season ▶ *theatrical arts staff members* (minimum age 19) at $1200–$1500 per season ▶ *video/photo staff members* (minimum age 19) at $1200–$1500 per season ▶ *waterfront staff members* (minimum age 19) at $1200–$1600 per season ▶ *waterskiing staff members* (minimum age 19) at $1200–$1800 per season ▶ *woodworking staff members* (minimum age 19) at $1200–$1600 per season. Applicants must submit formal organization application, resume, portfolio, three personal references, three letters of recommendation. International applicants accepted; must apply through a recognized agency. An in-person interview is recommended, but a telephone interview is acceptable.

Benefits and Preemployment Training Free housing, free meals, formal training, on-the-job training, and travel reimbursement. Preemployment training is required and includes accident prevention and safety, first aid, CPR, interpersonal skills, leadership skills.

Contact Eric Scoblionko, Director, Camp Wekeela, 2807 C Delmar Drive, Columbus, Ohio 43209. Telephone: 614-253-3177. Fax: 614-253-3661. E-mail: wekeela1@aol.com. World Wide Web: http://www.campwekeela.com. Application deadline: continuous.

CAMP WINNEBAGO
RR 2, BOX 1400
KENTS HILL, MAINE 04349

General Information Residential camp serving 140 boys for four- and eight-week sessions. Established in 1919. 350-acre facility located 17 miles from Augusta. Features: 3½-mile freshwater lake; wooded setting; 7 tennis courts; extensive waterfront program; campers from 13 countries and 20 states.

Profile of Summer Employees Total number: 75; typical age: 24. 90% men; 10% women; 10% minorities; 60% college students; 15% non-U.S. citizens; 15% local applicants. Nonsmokers required.

Employment Information Openings are from June 20 to August 19. Jobs available: ▶ 2 *archery instructors* with certification in field; experience instructing archery preferred at $1100–$2500 per season ▶ 2 *arts and crafts instructors* (minimum age 19) with experience in clay, woodwork, weaving, or other crafts; teaching experience preferred at $1100–$2500 per season ▶ 4 *athletics instructors* (minimum age 19) with coaching experience preferred; competitive experience acceptable at $1100–$2500 per season ▶ 3 *camping skills instructors* (minimum age 19) with outdoor camping skills at $1100–$2500 per season ▶ 1 *nature instructor* (minimum age 19) with ability to relate the natural environment to children at $1100–$2500 per season ▶ 1 *newspaper instructor* (minimum age 19) with college or high school newspaper experience preferred at $1100–$2500 per season ▶ 2 *photography instructors* (minimum age 19) with experience in photography or teaching at $1100–$2500 per season ▶ 1 *piano accompanist* (minimum age 19) with knowledge of show music at $1100–$2500 per season ▶ 2 *riflery instructors* with certification in field; experience instructing riflery preferred at $1100–$2500 per season ▶ 4 *swimming instructors* (minimum age 19) with WSI or lifeguard certification at $1100–$2500 per season ▶ 4 *tennis instructors* (minimum age 19) with coaching experience preferred; competitive playing experience acceptable at $1100–$2500 per season ▶ 2 *theater instructors* (minimum age 19) with theater experience; experience directing children preferred at $1100–$2500 per season ▶ 1 *videography instructor* (minimum age 19) with facility in use of video camera and ability to script shows at $1100–$2500 per season ▶ 2 *waterskiing instructors* (minimum age 19) with waterskiing and boat driving experience; teaching experience preferred at $1100–$2500 per season. Applicants must submit formal organization application, two personal references, two letters of recommendation. International applicants accepted; must apply through a recognized agency. An in-person interview is recommended, but a telephone interview is acceptable.

Benefits and Preemployment Training Free housing, travel reimbursement, and health insurance at cost. Preemployment training is required and includes accident prevention and safety, first aid, interpersonal skills, leadership skills.

Contact Phil Lilienthal, Director, Camp Winnebago, 1606 Washington Plaza, Box P, Reston, Virginia 20190. Telephone: 703-437-0808. Fax: 703-437-8620. E-mail: philcwhv@aol.com. World Wide Web: http://www.campwinnebago.com. Application deadline: continuous.

FOREST ACRES CAMP FOR GIRLS
RR 1, BOX 48
FRYEBURG, MAINE 04037

General Information Residential camp for 125 girls ages 6 to 16 for seven weeks. Established in 1927. 100-acre facility located 150 miles from Boston, Massachusetts. Features: heated Olympic-size pool; 6 tennis courts; indoor gym; lake area; White Mountains; many fields.

Profile of Summer Employees Total number: 60; typical age: 25. 2% men; 98% women; 50% college students; 2% retirees; 10% non-U.S. citizens; 10% local applicants. Nonsmokers preferred.

Employment Information Openings are from June 1 to August 16. Jobs available: ▶ 3 *arts and crafts instructors* (minimum age 19) at $1000–$1800 per season ▶ 3 *gymnastics instructors* (minimum age 19) at $1000–$1800 per season ▶ 3–5 *sailing and waterskiing instructors* at $1000–$1800 per season ▶ 3–5 *swimming instructors* with certification in field at $1000–$1800 per season ▶ 4 *tennis instructors* at $1000–$1800 per season ▶ 4 *unit leaders/administrators* (minimum age 22) at $1500–$2000 per season. Applicants must submit formal organization application, resume, three personal references. International applicants accepted; must apply through a recognized agency. An in-person interview is recommended, but a telephone interview is acceptable.

Benefits and Preemployment Training Free housing, free meals, formal training, on-the-job training, and opportunity to attend seminars/workshops. Preemployment training is required and includes accident prevention and safety, interpersonal skills, leadership skills.

Contact Lisa and Geoffrey Newman, Directors, Forest Acres Camp for Girls, 2914 Medinah, Weston, Florida 33332. Telephone: 904-385-3545. E-mail: campdad@gate.net. World Wide Web:

http://www.forestacres.com. Application deadline: continuous.

HIDDEN VALLEY CAMP
HIDDEN VALLEY CAMP ROAD
FREEDOM, MAINE 04941

General Information Residential, international, noncompetitive camp offering two 4-week sessions to 270 campers. Established in 1948. 350-acre facility located 80 miles from Portland. Features: spring-fed private lake; miles of wooded trails; modern, fully equipped art studios; adventure ropes course; heated pool.

Profile of Summer Employees Total number: 90; typical age: 23. 40% men; 60% women; 10% minorities; 5% high school students; 40% college students; 3% retirees; 20% non-U.S. citizens; 10% local applicants. Nonsmokers required.

Employment Information Openings are from June 1 to August 25. Jobs available: ▶ 10 *English riding instructors* with experience in the field at $1000–$1400 per season ▶ 4 *animal care personnel* with experience in the field at $1000–$1400 per season ▶ 5 *dance instructors* with experience in the field at $1000–$1400 per season ▶ 3 *guitar/music staff* at $1000–$1400 per season ▶ 2 *gymnastics instructors* at $1000–$1400 per season ▶ 2 *outdoor living staff* with experience in the field at $1000–$1500 per season ▶ 2 *outdoor travel leaders* with experience in the field at $1000–$1500 per season ▶ 2 *pottery instructors* at $1000–$1400 per season ▶ 6 *ropes instructors* with experience in the field at $1000–$1400 per season ▶ 2 *soccer instructors* at $1000–$1400 per season ▶ 3 *stained glass instructors* at $1000–$1400 per season ▶ 10 *swimming instructors* with WSI/lifeguard certification at $1000–$1400 per season. Applicants must submit formal organization application, cover letter, resume, three personal references, letter of recommendation. International applicants accepted; must apply through a recognized agency. An in-person interview is recommended, but a telephone interview is acceptable.

Benefits and Preemployment Training Free housing, free meals, formal training, and on-the-job training. Preemployment training is required.

Contact Peter and Meg Kassen, Directors/Owners, Hidden Valley Camp, RR 1, Box 2360, Freedom, Maine 04941. Telephone: 207-342-5177. Fax: 207-342-5685. E-mail: summer@hiddenvalleycamp.com. World Wide Web: http://www.hiddenvalleycamp.com. Application deadline: continuous.

INDIAN ACRES CAMP FOR BOYS
RR 1, BOX 48
FRYEBURG, MAINE 04037

General Information Residential camp for 125 boys ages 6–16. Established in 1924. 100-acre facility located 150 miles from Boston, Massachusetts. Features: heated Olympic-size pool; 6 tennis courts; indoor gym; lake area; location in the White Mountains; many fields for soccer and baseball.

Profile of Summer Employees Total number: 60; typical ages: 24–26. 98% men; 2% women; 50% college students; 2% retirees; 10% non-U.S. citizens; 10% local applicants. Nonsmokers preferred.

Employment Information Openings are from June 1 to August 16. Jobs available: ▶ 4 *archery and riflery instructors* (minimum age 19) at $1000–$1800 per season ▶ *basketball, baseball, hockey, and soccer instructors* (minimum age 19) at $1000–$1800 per season ▶ 3–5 *sailing and skiing instructors and lifeguards* (minimum age 19) at $1000–$1800 per season ▶ 3–5 *swimming instructors* (minimum age 19) with certification at $1000–$1800 per season ▶ *tennis instructors* (minimum age 19) at $1000–$1800 per season ▶ 4 *unit leaders, administrators, and teachers* (minimum age 22) at $1500–$2000 per season. Applicants must submit formal organization application, resume, three personal references. International applicants accepted; must apply through a recognized agency. An in-person interview is recommended, but a telephone interview is acceptable.

Benefits and Preemployment Training Free housing, free meals, formal training, on-the-job training, and opportunity to attend seminars/workshops. Preemployment training is required and includes accident prevention and safety, interpersonal skills, leadership skills.

Contact Lisa and Geoffrey Newman, Directors, Indian Acres Camp for Boys, 2914 Medinah, Weston, Florida 33332. Telephone: 954-385-3545. E-mail: campdad@gate.net. World Wide Web: http://www.indianacres.com. Application deadline: continuous.

KAMP KOHUT
151 KOHUT ROAD
OXFORD, MAINE 04270

General Information Residential camp serving 75 girls and 75 boys with traditional activities in 2 four-week sessions. Focuses on single-gender classes at one campus facility. Established in 1907. 115-acre facility located 38 miles from Portland. Features: large freshwater lake; beautiful wooded setting; top-notch facilities; excellent waterfront program; large adventure and tripping program; 1 hour from Maine coast and White Mountains.

Profile of Summer Employees Total number: 50; typical ages: 21–22. 50% men; 50% women; 1% minorities; 73% college students; 2% retirees; 25% non-U.S. citizens; 5% local applicants. Nonsmokers required.

Employment Information Openings are from June 18 to August 22. Jobs available: ▶ 50 *activity specialists* (minimum age 19) with enthusiasm, friendliness, energy, and reliability at $900–$3000 per season. Applicants must submit formal organization application, three personal references. International applicants accepted; must apply through a recognized agency. A telephone interview is required.

Benefits and Preemployment Training Free housing, free meals, formal training, health insurance, on-the-job training, opportunity to attend seminars/workshops, and travel reimbursement. Preemployment training is required and includes accident prevention and safety, interpersonal skills, leadership skills.

Contact Lisa Tripler, Director, Kamp Kohut, Two Tall Pine Road, Cape Elizabeth, Maine 04107. Telephone: 207-767-2406. Fax: 207-767-0604. E-mail: kampkohut@aol.com. World Wide Web: http://www.kampkohut.com. Application deadline: continuous.

LONGACRE EXPEDITIONS
UNITY, MAINE 04988

General Information Adventure travel program emphasizing group living skills and physical challenges. Using base camp as a staging area 2–3 staffers and 10–16 campers participate in expeditions in which they engage in human-powered sports. Established in 1981. Located 20 miles from Waterville.

Profile of Summer Employees Total number: 30; typical ages: 21–32. 50% men; 50% women; 10% minorities; 40% college students; 10% local applicants. Nonsmokers required.

Employment Information Openings are from June 15 to August 15. Jobs available: ▶ 20 *assistant trip leaders* (minimum age 21) with wilderness first aid, CPR, and good driving record at $150–$175 per week ▶ 1 *rock climbing instructor* (minimum age 21) with good driving record, wilderness first aid or WFR training, and CPR certification at $300–$450 per week ▶ 4 *support and logistics staff members* (minimum age 21) with good driving record and wilderness first aid and CPR certifications at $180–$240 per week. Applicants must submit a formal organization application, cover letter, resume, three personal references. International applicants accepted; must obtain own visa, obtain own working papers. An in-person interview is recommended, but a telephone interview is acceptable.

Benefits and Preemployment Training Free housing, free meals, on-the-job training, and pro-deal purchase program. Preemployment training is required and includes accident prevention and safety, interpersonal skills, leadership skills.

Contact Meredith Schuler, Directors, Longacre Expeditions, RD 3, Box 106, Newport, Pennsylvania 17074. Telephone: 717-567-6790. Fax: 717-567-3955. E-mail: longacre@longacreexpeditions.com. World Wide Web: http://www.longacreexpeditions.com. Application deadline: continuous.

MAINE TEEN CAMP
481 BROWNFIELD ROAD
PORTER, MAINE 04068

General Information Residential coed camp for teenagers offering two sessions with 250 campers participating in each session. Established in 1985. 50-acre facility located 45 miles from Portland. Features: freshwater lake; wooded setting; 5 tennis courts; cabins; large main lodge; large ropes course.

Profile of Summer Employees Total number: 75; typical ages: 21–40. 47% men; 53% women; 10% minorities; 50% college students; 2% retirees; 30% non-U.S. citizens; 2% local applicants.

Employment Information Openings are from June 18 to August 21. Jobs available: ▶ 1 *ESL/academics head coordinator* (minimum age 21) with teacher certification and an ESL course ▶ 1 *MIDI instructor* (minimum age 21) with experience and/or certification at $1300 per season ▶ 1–3 *arts instructors* (minimum age 21) with experience and/or certification at $1300 per season ▶ 2 *dance instructors* (minimum age 21) with experience and/or certification at $1300 per season ▶ 1 *drum instructor* (minimum age 21) with experience and/or certification at $1300 per season ▶ 1 *jewelry-crafting instructor* (minimum age 21) with experience and/or certification at $1300 per season ▶ 1 *keyboard instructor* (minimum age 21) with experience and/or certification at $1300 per season ▶ 1–5 *land sports instructors* (minimum age 21) with experience and/or certification and ability to teach one or more of the following: soccer, basketball, baseball, field hockey, lacrosse, golf, volleyball, badminton at $1300 per season ▶ 2–3 *mountain biking instructors* (minimum age 21) with experience and/or certification at $1300 per season ▶ 2 *nurses* (minimum age 21) with RN or LPN preferred at $1300 per season ▶ 1 *photography head* (minimum age 21) with specific training and high level experience ▶ 4–10 *ropes instructors* (minimum age 21) with experience and/or certification at $1300 per season ▶ 2 *sailing/windsurfing instructors* (minimum age 21) with experience and/or certification at $1300 per season ▶ 1 *voice instructor* (minimum age 21) with experience and/or certification at $1300 per season ▶ 1 *waterfront director* (minimum age 22) with experience and/or certification; EMT preferred; WSI at $1800–$2200 per season ▶ 2 *waterskiing instructors* (minimum age 21) with experience and/or certification at $1300 per season. Applicants must submit formal organization application, 2-3 personal references or letters of recommendation. International applicants accepted; must apply through a recognized agency. A telephone interview is required.

Benefits and Preemployment Training Free housing, free meals, formal training, and on-the-job training. Preemployment training is required and includes accident prevention and safety, first aid, CPR, interpersonal skills, leadership skills, lifeguard training, ropes course training.

Contact Bob Briskin and Monique Rafuse, Director/Assistant Director, Maine Teen Camp, 180 Upper Gulph Road, Radnor, Pennsylvania 19087. Telephone: 610-527-6759. Fax: 610-520-0182. E-mail: teencamp@ix.netcom.com. World Wide Web: http://www.teencamp.com. Application deadline: continuous.

NEW ENGLAND CAMPING ADVENTURES
PANTHER POND, PO BOX 160
RAYMOND, MAINE 04071

General Information Coed wilderness rafting and sailing programs for 120 campers that include backpacking, white-water canoe trips, rock climbing, ocean kayaking, mountain biking, ocean sailing, and wilderness adventure trips. 140-acre facility located 25 miles from Portland. Features: 2½ miles of shoreline; freshwater lake; acres of pine woods; small camp with family atmosphere.

Profile of Summer Employees Total number: 40. 50% men; 50% women; 15% minorities; 5% high school students; 80% college students; 5% non-U.S. citizens; 20% local applicants. Nonsmokers preferred.

Employment Information Openings are from June 23 to August 17. Jobs available: ▶ 4 *backpacking leaders* at $1100–$1400 per season ▶ 15–20 *camp counselors (crafts, sports, waterfront)* (minimum age 18) at $1000–$1450 per season ▶ 5 *canoe trip leaders* at $1100–$1600 per season ▶ 2 *rock climbing leaders* at $1100–$1400 per season ▶ 6 *sailing instructors* (minimum age 18) with ability to sail a 14-foot boat with 2 sails (FJ's) at $1100–$1400 per season. Applicants must submit a formal organization application, resume. International applicants accepted.

Benefits and Preemployment Training Free housing, free meals, formal training, on-the-job training, and travel reimbursement.

Contact Ronald Furst, Director, New England Camping Adventures, 10 Scotland Bridge Road, York, Maine 03909. Telephone: 207-363-1773. Fax: 207-363-1773. E-mail: camphaw@nh.ultranet. com. Application deadline: May 10.

OAKLAND HOUSE
HERRICK ROAD
BROOKSVILLE, MAINE 04617

General Information Rural low-key family vacation resort and adults-only inn accommodating a combined total of approximately 75 guests. Established in 1889. 50-acre facility located 50 miles from Bangor. Features: 1/2-mile of ocean front; freshwater lake; rowboats; hiking trails; 1 hour from Acadia National Park; recreation hall.

Profile of Summer Employees Total number: 23; typical ages: 18–50. 48% men; 52% women; 5% minorities; 52% college students; 22% non-U.S. citizens; 35% local applicants. Nonsmokers preferred.

Employment Information Openings are from June 14 to September 7. Jobs available: ▶ 1 *cabin service staff member* at $209–$300 per week ▶ 1 *gardener* with gardening experience at $209–$264 per week ▶ 1 *host/hostess* at $3000–$5000 per season ▶ 4 *housekeepers* at $170–$400 per week ▶ 4 *kitchen staff members* at $209–$249 per week ▶ 2 *maintenance and grounds staff members* at $209–$264 per week ▶ 1 *office receptionist* at $209–$249 per week ▶ 6 *waiters/waitresses* (minimum age 18) at $190–$425 per week. Applicants must submit formal organization application, cover letter, resume, three personal references. International applicants accepted; must apply through a recognized agency. A telephone interview is required.

Benefits and Preemployment Training Housing at a cost, meals at a cost, and on-the-job training. Preemployment training is required and includes first aid, hospitality training.

Contact James Littlefield, Owner, Oakland House, RR 1, Box 400, Brooksville, Maine 04617. Telephone: 207-359-8521. E-mail: jim@oaklandhouse.com. World Wide Web: http://www. oaklandhouse.com. Application deadline: continuous.

QUISISANA RESORT
CENTER LOVELL, MAINE 04016

General Information Summer resort for families, couples, and individuals. Established in 1947. 55-acre facility located 50 miles from Portland. Features: freshwater lake and beaches; wooded setting; 3 tennis courts; nightly entertainment; water boats and waterskiing; full American plan.

Profile of Summer Employees Total number: 70–80; typical ages: 20–30. 50% men; 50% women; 90% college students. Nonsmokers required.

Employment Information Openings are from June 3 to August 30. Jobs available: ▶ 1–2 *beach staff members* ▶ 3–6 *chamber staff members* ▶ 3–10 *kitchen staff members* ▶ 3–6 *maintenance persons* ▶ 1–2 *office staff members*. Applicants must submit a formal organization application, resume, business references. An in-person interview is recommended, but a telephone interview is acceptable.

Benefits and Preemployment Training Free housing, free meals, and on-the-job training.

Contact Jane Orans, Owner, Quisisana Resort, PO Box 142, Larchmont, New York 10538. Telephone: 914-833-0293. E-mail: quisisanar@aol.com. Application deadline: May 1.

THE SOUTHWESTERN COMPANY, MAINE
See The Southwestern Company, Tennessee on page 284 for complete description.

STUDENT CONSERVATION ASSOCIATION (SCA), MAINE
See Student Conservation Association (SCA), New Hampshire on page 193 for complete description.

WOHELO-LUTHER GULICK CAMPS
PO BOX 39
SOUTH CASCO, MAINE 04077

General Information Residential camp for girls on Sebago Lake emphasizing lifelong activities and personal growth. Established in 1907. 250-acre facility located 25 miles from Portland. Features: large lake; 27 sailboats; rustic cabins; beautiful sunsets; friendly people.

Profile of Summer Employees Total number: 65; typical ages: 18–25. 5% men; 95% women; 5% high school students; 75% college students; 2% retirees; 15% non-U.S. citizens; 3% local applicants. Nonsmokers preferred.

Employment Information Openings are from June 18 to August 30. Jobs available: ▶ *canoeing instructor* at $1100–$1400 per season ▶ 2 *dramatics instructors* at $1100–$1400 per season ▶ 2 *nature/ecology instructors* at $1100–$1400 per season ▶ 1 *pianist* at $1100–$1400 per season ▶ 1 *pottery instructor* at $1100–$1400 per season ▶ *sailing instructor* at $1100–$1400 per season ▶ 2 *swimming instructors* with WSI or LG certification at $950–$1350 per season ▶ *tennis instructor* at $1100–$1400 per season. Applicants must submit formal organization application, resume, three letters of recommendation. International applicants accepted; must apply through a recognized agency. An in-person interview is recommended, but a telephone interview is acceptable.

Benefits and Preemployment Training Free housing, free meals, and on-the-job training. Preemployment training is required and includes accident prevention and safety, interpersonal skills, leadership skills.

Contact W. Davis Van Winkle, Director, Wohelo-Luther Gulick Camps, PO Box 39, South Casco, Maine 04077. Telephone: 207-655-4739. Fax: 207-655-2292. E-mail: staff@wohelo. com. World Wide Web: http://www.wohelo.com. Application deadline: continuous.

MARYLAND

ACE COMPUTER CAMP–MARYLAND
See ACE Computer Camp–Washington on page 307 for complete description.

CAMP AIRY FOR BOYS
14938 OLD CAMP AIRY ROAD
THURMONT, MARYLAND 21788

General Information Nonprofit residential camp serving 400 boys in each of four 2-week sessions or two 4-week sessions. Established in 1924. 450-acre facility located 50 miles from Washington, DC. Features: numerous ball fields; several craft facilities; outdoor living area with high and low element ropes courses; tennis courts and gym; theaters; comfortable bunk with counselor rooms.

Profile of Summer Employees Total number: 150; typical ages: 18–23. 95% men; 5% women; 2% minorities; 95% college students; 3% retirees; 20% non-U.S. citizens; 10% local applicants. Nonsmokers preferred.

Employment Information Openings are from June 13 to August 13. Jobs available: ▶ 2–4 *archery instructors (counselors)* (minimum age 18) with formal training and at least one year of college completed; NAA instructor certification preferred (we will locate classes and provide $400 bonus for successful completion) at $850 to $1000 per season with annual increments for returning staff ▶ 3–6 *arts and crafts instructors(counselors)* (minimum age 18) with formal training and at least one year of college completed; teaching experience preferred at $850 to $1000 per season with annual increments for returning staff ▶ 30 *athletics instructors (counselors)* (minimum age 18) with at least one year of college completed at $850 to $1000 per season with annual increments for returning staff ▶ 3–6 *ceramics instructors (counselors)* (minimum age 18) with formal training and at least one year of college completed; teaching experience preferred at $850 to $1000 per season with annual increments for returning staff ▶ 4 *drama instructors (counselors)* (minimum age 18) with at least one year of college completed at $850 to $1000 per season with annual increments for returning staff ▶ 1–2 *fencing instructors (counselors)* (minimum age 18) with formal training and at least one year of college completed; teaching experience preferred at $850 to $1000 per season with annual increments for returning staff ▶ 30 *general counselors* (minimum age 18) with at least one year of college completed at $850 to $1000 per season with annual increments for returning staff ▶ 2 *karate instructors (counselors)* (minimum age 18) with formal training and at least one year of college completed; teaching experience preferred at $850 to $1000 per season with annual increments for returning staff ▶ 5 *music instructors (counselors)* (minimum age 18) with one year of college completed and ability to teach one or more instruments (all types) at $850 to $1000 per season with annual increments for returning staff ▶ 2 *nature instructors (counselors)* (minimum age 18) with formal training and at least one year of college completed; teaching experience preferred at $850 to $1000 per season with annual increments for returning staff ▶ 12–15 *nurses* (minimum age 18) with RN (Maryland); flexible committment of one of eight weeks at $250 per week or generous tuition discount for staff with children ▶ 10 *outdoor living instructors (counselors)* (minimum age 18) with one year of college completed and ability to teach rock climbing, rapelling, caving, survival training, and backpacking at $1000 to $1600 per season plus annual increments for returning staff ▶ 3–6 *photography instructors (counselors)* (minimum age 18) with formal training and at least one year of college completed; teaching experience preferred at $850 to $1000 per season with annual increments for returning staff ▶ 2–4 *riflery instructors (counselors)* (minimum age 18) with NRA instructor certification preferred and at least one year of college completed; (salary increases $400 for NRA instructor certification, $200 for NRA associate instructor) at $850 to $1000 per season with annual increments for returning staff ▶ 15 *swimming instructors (counselors)* (minimum age 18) with lifeguard training and one year of college completed; $400 bonus for WSI or LGI certification at $850 to $1000 per season with annual increments for returning staff. Applicants must submit formal organization application, two personal references, fingerprinting/background check to complete hiring process; international applicants apply through BUNAC. International applicants accepted; must apply through a recognized agency. An in-person interview is recommended, but a telephone interview is acceptable.

Benefits and Preemployment Training Free housing, free meals, formal training, on-the-job training, travel reimbursement, and worker's compensation. Preemployment training is required and includes accident prevention and safety, interpersonal skills, leadership skills.

Contact Mike Schneider, Executive Director, Camp Airy for Boys, 5750 Park Heights Avenue, Baltimore, Maryland 21215. Telephone: 410-466-9010. Fax: 410-466-0560. E-mail: airlou@ airylouise.org. World Wide Web: http://airylouise.org.

CAMP LOUISE
24959 PEN MAR ROAD
CASCADE, MARYLAND 21719

General Information Nonprofit residential camp serving 400 girls in each of four 2-week sessions or two 4-week sessions. Established in 1922. 400-acre facility located 50 miles from Washington, DC. Features: athletic fields; arts and crafts facilities; ropes course; tennis courts; theater/dance studio; comfortable bunk with counselor rooms.

Profile of Summer Employees Total number: 150; typical ages: 18–23. 100% women; 2% minorities; 95% college students; 3% retirees; 20% non-U.S. citizens; 10% local applicants. Nonsmokers preferred.

Employment Information Openings are from June 13 to August 13. Jobs available: ▶ 2–4 *archery instructors* (minimum age 18) with formal training and at least one year of college completed; NAA instructor certification preferred (we will locate classes and provide $400 bonus for successful completion) at $850 to $1000 per season with annual increments for returning staff ▶ 3–6 *arts and crafts instructors (counselors)* (minimum age 18) with relevant experience and at least one year of college completed; teaching experience preferred at $850 to

$1000 per season with annual increments for returning staff ▶ 30 *athletics instructors* (minimum age 18) with at least one year of college completed; relevant experience in team and individual sports at $850 to $1000 per season with annual increments for returning staff ▶ 3–6 *ceramics instructors (counselors)* (minimum age 18) with experience and at least one year of college completed; teaching experience preferred at $850 to $1000 per season with annual increments for returning staff ▶ 6–10 *dance instructors (counselors)* (minimum age 18) with formal training and at least one year of college completed; teaching experience preferred at $850 to $1000 per season with annual increments for returning staff ▶ 4 *drama instructors (counselors)* (minimum age 18) with at least one year of college completed and relevant experience at $850 to $1000 per season plus annual increments for returning staff ▶ 1–2 *fencing instructors (counselors)* (minimum age 18) with formal training and at least one year of college completed; teaching experience preferred at $850 to $1000 per season with annual increments for returning staff ▶ 30 *general counselors* (minimum age 18) with at least one year of college completed at $850 to $1000 per season with annual increments for returning staff ▶ 2 *karate instructors (counselors)* (minimum age 18) with formal training and at least one year of college completed; teaching experience preferred at $850 to $1000 per season with annual increments for returning staff ▶ 5 *music instructors (counselors)* (minimum age 18) with one year of college completed and ability to teach one or more instruments (all types) at $850 to $1000 per season plus annual increments for returning staff ▶ 2 *nature instructors (counselors)* (minimum age 18) with relevant experience and at least one year of college completed; teaching experience preferred at $850 to $1000 per season with annual increments for returning staff ▶ 12–15 *nurses* (minimum age 18) with RN (Maryland); flexible committment of one to eight weeks at $250 per week or generous tuition discount for staff with children ▶ 10 *outdoor living instructors (counselors)* (minimum age 18) with one year of college completed and ability to teach rock climbing, rapelling, caving, survival training, backpacking at $1000 to $1600 per season plus annual increments for returning staff ▶ 3–6 *photography instructors (counselors)* (minimum age 18) with relevant experience and at least one year of college; teaching experience preferred at $850 to $1000 per season with annual increments for returning staff ▶ 15 *swimming instructors (counselors)* (minimum age 18) with lifeguard training and one year of college completed; $400 bonus for WSI or LGI certification at $850 to $1000 per season with annual increments for returning staff. Applicants must submit formal organization application, two personal references, fingerprinting/background check to complete the hiring process; international applicants apply through BUNAC. International applicants accepted; must apply through a recognized agency. An in-person interview is recommended, but a telephone interview is acceptable.

Benefits and Preemployment Training Free housing, free meals, formal training, on-the-job training, travel reimbursement, and worker's compensation. Preemployment training is required and includes accident prevention and safety, interpersonal skills, leadership skills.

Contact Roberta Miller, Associate Director, Camp Louise, 5750 Park Heights Avenue, Baltimore, Maryland 21215. Telephone: 410-466-9010. Fax: 410-466-0560. E-mail: airlou@airylouise.org. World Wide Web: http://airylouise.org.

CAMP SONSHINE
16819 NEW HAMPSHIRE AVENUE
SILVER SPRING, MARYLAND 20905

General Information Nonprofit Christian day camp for kids 3-16 years old. Activities include go-karts, paddleboats, crafts, nature, drama, swimming, and much more. Established in 1981. 60-acre facility located 10 miles from Washington D.C. Features: pond; woods; go-karts; paddleboats.

Profile of Summer Employees Total number: 160; typical ages: 18–34. 80% college students; 13% non-U.S. citizens; 7% local applicants. Nonsmokers required.

Employment Information Openings are from June 12 to August 16. Jobs available: ▶ 40 *activity counselors (lifeguards, archery, drama, crafts, and go-karts)* (minimum age 18) at $1120 per season ▶ 50–100 *group counselors* (minimum age 18) at $1120 per season. Applicants must submit formal organization application, three personal references. International applicants accepted; must apply through a recognized agency. A telephone interview is required.

Benefits and Preemployment Training Free housing and free meals. Preemployment training is required and includes accident prevention and safety, interpersonal skills, leadership skills.
Contact Nathan Haas, Director, Camp Sonshine. Telephone: 888-883-2285. Fax: 301-989-1640. E-mail: staff@campsonshine.org. World Wide Web: http://www.campsonshine.org. Application deadline: continuous.

ECHO HILL CAMP
13655 BLOOMINGNECK ROAD
WORTON, MARYLAND 21678

General Information Coeducational residential camp serving 140 campers per session in two-, four-, and eight-week sessions along with one-week postcamp sail and ski and fishing and crabbing camps. Established in 1915. 350-acre facility located 90 miles from Washington, DC. Features: Chesapeake Bay location.
Profile of Summer Employees Total number: 50; typical ages: 17–24. 55% men; 45% women; 2% minorities; 10% high school students; 70% college students; 10% non-U.S. citizens; 2% local applicants.
Employment Information Openings are from June 10 to August 30. Jobs available: ▶ *counselors* (minimum age 18) ▶ 2 *swimming instructors* with WSI and American Red Cross lifeguard certification at $600 per month. Applicants must submit formal organization application. International applicants accepted; must apply through a recognized agency.
Benefits and Preemployment Training Free housing, free meals, formal training, possible full-time employment, on-the-job training, and opportunity to attend seminars/workshops. Preemployment training is required and includes accident prevention and safety, first aid, CPR, interpersonal skills, leadership skills.
Contact Peter Rice, Director, Echo Hill Camp. Telephone: 410-348-5303. Fax: 410-348-2010. World Wide Web: http://www.echohillcamp.com. Application deadline: continuous.

THE INSTITUTE FOR THE ACADEMIC ADVANCEMENT OF YOUTH/ THE JOHNS HOPKINS UNIVERSITY
3400 NORTH CHARLES STREET
BALTIMORE, MARYLAND 21218

General Information Residential and commuter camps for academically talented youth serving second through sixth graders and seventh graders through 16½-year-olds. Concentration on accelerated academic courses and recreational activities. Marine ecology camps take place on a ship. Established in 1980. Features: university dormitories; libraries; athletic facilities; playing fields; small, quiet campuses.
Profile of Summer Employees Total number: 1,555; typical ages: 18–50. 50% men; 50% women; 10% minorities; 60% college students; 2% non-U.S. citizens; 10% local applicants.
Employment Information Openings are from June 24 to August 7. Jobs available: ▶ 1 *academic counselor* with graduate training in counseling with 2 years counseling experience, familiarity with Attention Deficit Disorder, and experience in a boarding school or residential camp environment at $4000–$5000 per season ▶ 1 *academic dean* with graduate training in an academic discipline and teaching experience at $4000–$5000 per season ▶ 1 *dean of residential life* with master's degree preferred, 2 years residential administrative experience in a school or college, and counseling experience at $4600–$5000 per season ▶ 1 *health assistant* should be junior or senior in college or medical student; interested in medicine and health issues; CPR and first aid certified at $1800 per season ▶ 30–40 *instructors* with BA or BS (master's degree preferred), experience with students in this age group, and leadership skills at $1700–$2400 per season ▶ 1 *office manager* with excellent office skills, bookkeeping experience, at least junior status in college; GPA 3.2 or higher at $3200 per season ▶ 2 *office/general assistants* with office experience, at least one year of college, and 3.2 GPA at $1800 per season ▶ 20–30 *resident assistants* with experience as a college RA or as a camp counselor, GPA of 3.2 or higher, and experience in events planning at $1800 per season ▶ 1 *site director* with master's degree preferred, teaching and administrative background, and leadership in an educational environment at $5000–$7000 per season ▶ 30–40 *teaching/laboratory assistants* with GPA of 3.2 or higher, strong interest in

teaching, and experience with young people at $1600–$1800 per season. Applicants must submit formal organization application, cover letter, resume, academic transcripts, three letters of recommendation. International applicants accepted. A telephone interview is required.

Benefits and Preemployment Training Free housing, free meals, and on-the-job training. Preemployment training is required and includes accident prevention and safety, first aid, CPR, interpersonal skills.

Contact Kimberley Theobald, Coordinator for Academic Programs, The Institute for the Academic Advancement of Youth/ The Johns Hopkins University, 3400 North Charles Street, The Johns Hopkins University/IAAY, Baltimore, Maryland 21218. Telephone: 410-516-0053. Fax: 410-516-0093. E-mail: academic@jhunix.hcf.jhu.edu. World Wide Web: http://www.jhu.edu/~gifted/acadprog/jobs.html.

THE INSTITUTE FOR THE ACADEMIC ADVANCEMENT OF YOUTH/THE JOHNS HOPKINS UNIVERSITY–GARRISON FOREST SCHOOL

See The Institute for the Academic Advancement of Youth/ The Johns Hopkins University on page 135 for complete description.

THE INSTITUTE FOR THE ACADEMIC ADVANCEMENT OF YOUTH/THE JOHNS HOPKINS UNIVERSITY–HOOD COLLEGE

See The Institute for the Academic Advancement of Youth/ The Johns Hopkins University on page 135 for complete description.

THE INSTITUTE FOR THE ACADEMIC ADVANCEMENT OF YOUTH/THE JOHNS HOPKINS UNIVERSITY–MARINE ECOLOGY

See The Institute for the Academic Advancement of Youth/ The Johns Hopkins University on page 135 for complete description.

THE INSTITUTE FOR THE ACADEMIC ADVANCEMENT OF YOUTH/THE JOHNS HOPKINS UNIVERSITY–SANDY SPRING FRIENDS SCHOOL

See The Institute for the Academic Advancement of Youth/ The Johns Hopkins University on page 135 for complete description.

THE INSTITUTE FOR THE ACADEMIC ADVANCEMENT OF YOUTH/THE JOHNS HOPKINS UNIVERSITY–WASHINGTON COLLEGE

See The Institute for the Academic Advancement of Youth/ The Johns Hopkins University on page 135 for complete description.

MANIDOKAN OUTDOOR MINISTRY CENTER
1620 HARPERS FERRY ROAD
KNOXVILLE, MARYLAND 21758

General Information Residential camp with a variety of accommodations and programs for all ages. Established in 1949. 426-acre facility located 70 miles from Washington, DC. Features: ropes and iniatives course; on the Potomac River; historic sites close by Harper's Ferry and Antietam Battlefield; 10 miles of hiking trails; climbing wall.

Profile of Summer Employees Total number: 20. 50% men; 50% women; 7% minorities; 7% high school students; 73% college students; 20% retirees; 35% local applicants. Nonsmokers preferred.

Employment Information Openings are from June 6 to August 25. Year-round positions also offered. Jobs available: ▶ 1 *canoe instructor* with Red Cross canoe instructor certification at $175–$225 per week ▶ 2 *cooks* at $200–$300 per week ▶ 3 *kitchen aides* at $150 per week ▶ 1 *lifeguard* with WSI certification (preferred) at $150–$200 per week ▶ 1 *maintenance person* at $130–$150 per week ▶ 1 *nurse* at $250–$350 per week ▶ 4 *program resource personnel* with lifeguard training (preferred) at $150–$200 per week. Applicants must submit three personal references, letter of recommendation. International applicants accepted; must apply through a recognized agency. An in-person interview is required.

Benefits and Preemployment Training Free housing, free meals, and on-the-job training. Preemployment training is required and includes accident prevention and safety, first aid, CPR, interpersonal skills, leadership skills.

Contact Carl Zenkert, Manager, Manidokan Outdoor Ministry Center, 1620 Harpers Ferry Road, Knoxville, Maryland 21758. Telephone: 301-834-7244. Fax: 301-834-7244. World Wide Web: http://www.bwconf.org/camping.

THE SOUTHWESTERN COMPANY, MARYLAND
See The Southwestern Company, Tennessee on page 284 for complete description.

STUDENT CONSERVATION ASSOCIATION (SCA), MARYLAND
See Student Conservation Association (SCA), New Hampshire on page 193 for complete description.

WEST RIVER UNITED METHODIST CENTER
5100 CHALK POINT ROAD, PO BOX 429
CHURCHTON, MARYLAND 20733

General Information Residential camp on a mile-long waterfront near the Chesapeake Bay. Established in 1951. 45-acre facility located 15 miles from Annapolis. Features: diverse program; wooded setting; sailing and boating; lodges; one mile of waterfront; near Chesapeake Bay.

Profile of Summer Employees Total number: 25; typical ages: 17–24. 40% men; 60% women; 18% minorities; 12% high school students; 62% college students; 37% local applicants. Nonsmokers preferred.

Employment Information Openings are from June 8 to August 15. Jobs available: ▶ 2 *cooks* at $300–$400 per week ▶ 1 *head lifeguard* (minimum age 18) with WSI certification at $200–$250 per week ▶ 4 *kitchen aides* (minimum age 18) at $175–$200 per week ▶ 3 *lifeguards* (minimum age 18) with Red Cross lifeguard training at $175–$200 per week ▶ 2 *maintenance personnel* (minimum age 18) at $175–$200 per week ▶ 1 *nurse* (minimum age 20) with state RN license at $300–$400 per week ▶ 2–5 *program resource persons* (minimum age 18) with lifesaving training (preferred) at $200–$250 per week ▶ 1 *sailing instructor* (minimum age 18) with US Coast Guard or Red Cross sailing instructor certification or equivalent at $200–$250 per week. Applicants must submit formal organization application, cover letter, resume, three personal references, criminal background check. International applicants accepted; must apply through a recognized agency. An in-person interview is recommended, but a telephone interview is acceptable.

Benefits and Preemployment Training Free housing, free meals, and on-the-job training. Preemployment training is required and includes accident prevention and safety, interpersonal skills, leadership skills.

Contact Andrew Thornton, Manager, West River United Methodist Center, PO Box 429, Churchton, Maryland 20733. Telephone: 410-867-0991. Fax: 410-867-3741. E-mail: westrivercenter@juno.com. World Wide Web: http://www.bwconf.org/camping. Application deadline: continuous.

MASSACHUSETTS

ACE COMPUTER CAMP–MASSACHUSETTS
See ACE Computer Camp–Washington on page 307 for complete description.

A CHRISTIAN MINISTRY IN THE NATIONAL PARKS–MASSACHUSSETTS
MASSACHUSETTS

General Information Nonprofit interdenominational Christian ministry that places individuals in the national parks to work, witness, and conduct worship services and activities. Established in 1952.

Profile of Summer Employees Typical ages: 19–25. 10% minorities; 80% college students; 5% retirees.

Employment Information Openings are from January 1 to December 31. Year-round positions also offered. Jobs available: ▶ *ministry staff leaders* with abilities in leading worship, preaching, providing pastoral care, teaching, administration, and music at $1200–$2000 per three months ▶ *ministry staff members* with abilities in leading bible studies, Christian education, drama, music, leading discussion groups, and offering recreation ideas at $1200–$2000 per three months ▶ *ministry staff musicians* to provide music for weekly services of worship, lead choirs, and organize special musical events at $1200–$2000 per three months. Applicants must submit a formal organization application, three letters of recommendation. International applicants accepted; must obtain own visa, obtain own working papers.

Benefits and Preemployment Training Housing at a cost and meals at a cost.

Contact Rev. Richard P. Camp, Jr., Director, A Christian Ministry in the National Parks–Massachussetts, A Christian Ministry in the Parks, 45 School Street, 4th Floor, Boston, Massachusetts 02108. Telephone: 617-720-5655. Fax: 617-720-7899. E-mail: acmnp@juno.com. World Wide Web: http://http://www.coolworks.com/showme/acmnp/. Application deadline: continuous.

ASPEN OUTDOOR ADVENTURE PROGRAM
PO BOX 95007
NEWTON, MASSACHUSETTS 02495

General Information Campus- and travel-based outdoor adventure program for boys and girls ages 12-15. Established in 1995. 35-acre facility located 10 miles from Boston. Features: high ropes; low ropes; swimming pool; day trips; overnight trips.

Profile of Summer Employees Total number: 6; typical ages: 18–25. 40% men; 60% women; 100% college students; 100% local applicants. Nonsmokers required.

Employment Information Openings are from June 25 to August 20. Jobs available: ▶ 2–6 *adventure counselors* (minimum age 18) with first aid/CPR cerifications and wilderness/camping experience at $300–$500 per week. Applicants must submit a formal organization application, resume. An in-person interview is recommended, but a telephone interview is acceptable.

Benefits and Preemployment Training On-the-job training. Preemployment training is required and includes accident prevention and safety, interpersonal skills, leadership skills.

Contact Martha Hull, Aspen Outdoor Adventure Program, PO Box 95007, Newton, Massachusetts 02495. Telephone: 617-527-4445. World Wide Web: http://www.aspencamp.com. Application deadline: continuous.

BELVOIR TERRACE
LENOX, MASSACHUSETTS 01240

General Information Residential camp serving 180 girls with a focus on fine and performing arts. The program provides specific services for the academically talented and the gifted. Established in 1954. 48-acre facility located 4 miles from Pittsfield. Features: mansion; 2 pools; 6 tennis courts; 5 modern dorms; 4 theaters; 4 dance studios; 16 art studios.

Profile of Summer Employees Total number: 90; typical ages: 25–40. 10% men; 90% women; 5% minorities; 10% college students; 5% non-U.S. citizens. Nonsmokers required.

Employment Information Openings are from June 16 to August 24. Jobs available: ▶ 2 *gymnastics staff* (minimum age 20) with first aid certification and coaching license; team and coaching experience at $1600–$2400 per season ▶ *musicians (graduate students only)* with expertise in an instrument or in voice at $1600–$2400 per season ▶ 1 *riding instructor* (minimum age 21) with driver's license and experience teaching riding at $1600–$2400 per season ▶ 2 *swimming counselors* (minimum age 20) who are upperclassmen and graduate students only; with Red Cross lifeguard training and WSI certification; team and teaching experience preferred at $1600–$2400 per season ▶ 2 *tennis counselors (graduate students only)* (minimum age 20) with tennis team playing ability and teaching experience at $1600–$2400 per season ▶ *theater teacher/director* (minimum age 22) with a graduate degree in theater and directing experience at $2400 per season. Applicants must submit formal organization application, cover letter, resume, portfolio, three personal references, letter of recommendation. International applicants accepted; must apply through a recognized agency. An in-person interview is recommended, but a telephone interview is acceptable.

Benefits and Preemployment Training Free housing, free meals, on-the-job training, opportunity to attend seminars/workshops, and travel reimbursement. Preemployment training is required and includes accident prevention and safety, first aid, CPR, interpersonal skills, leadership skills.

Contact Nancy S. Goldberg, Director, Belvoir Terrace, 101 West 79th Street, New York, New York 10024. Fax: 212-579-7282. E-mail: belvoirt@aol.com. World Wide Web: http://www. belvoirterrace.com. Application deadline: continuous.

BONNIE CASTLE RIDING CAMP
574 BERNARDSTON ROAD
GREENFIELD, MASSACHUSETTS 01301

General Information Residential camp for girls ages 10–16 with two 3-week sessions, plus one 2-week session for advanced riders. Established in 1982. 100-acre facility located 50 miles from Hartford, Connecticut. Features: swimming pool; 5 tennis courts; boarding school facilities; gymnasium; dance studio; ceramics studio.

Profile of Summer Employees Total number: 12; typical ages: 18–30. 100% women; 10% minorities; 10% high school students; 90% college students; 60% local applicants. Nonsmokers preferred.

Employment Information Openings are from June 25 to August 19. Jobs available: ▶ 2 *arts/ photography instructors* (minimum age 20) with specific art media experience at $1100–$1800 per season ▶ 1 *camp nurse* with RN license and current CPR certification at $2700 per season ▶ 1 *dance instructor* (minimum age 20) at $1100–$1800 per season ▶ 1 *drama instructor* (minimum age 20) with theater/drama experience at $1100–$1800 per season ▶ 1–3 *riding instructors* (minimum age 20) with extensive Hunt Seat riding and showing experience at $1100–$1800 per season ▶ 1 *swimming instructor* (minimum age 20) with WSI and CPR certification at $1100–$1800 per season. Applicants must submit a formal organization application, cover letter, resume, three personal references. International applicants accepted. An in-person interview is required.

Benefits and Preemployment Training Free housing and free meals. Preemployment training is required and includes accident prevention and safety, leadership skills.

Contact Lisa Bailey, Director, Bonnie Castle Riding Camp, 574 Bernardston Road, Greenfield, Massachusetts 01301. Telephone: 413-774-2711. Fax: 413-772-2602. E-mail: lbailey@sbschool. org. World Wide Web: http://www.sbschool.org. Application deadline: May 15.

CAMP EMERSON
212 LONGVIEW AVENUE
HINSDALE, MASSACHUSETTS 01235

General Information Residential camp serving 220 boys and girls ages 7–15½. 150-acre facility located 5 miles from Pittsfield. Features: heated pool; 2 lakes; 6 tennis courst (2 clay); large level playing fields; roller rink and ropes course; large art studio.

Profile of Summer Employees Total number: 110; typical age: 24. 50% men; 50% women; 50% college students. Nonsmokers required.

Employment Information Openings are from June 19 to August 19. Jobs available: ▶ 4 *administrative program assistants* with word processing and additional computer skills (such as desktop publishing) ▶ 3 *chefs/cooks* (minimum age 20) with experience in quantity cooking ▶ 12 *creative arts instructors* with experience in fine arts/drawing and painting, ceramics, sculpting, batik, leather, jewelry, model rocketry, woodworking, photography, yearbook, newspaper/creative writing, and cartooning ▶ 10 *key staff members* with supervisory experience in directing waterfront, aquatics, theater, sports, tennis, art, programming, and wilderness programs ▶ 20 *land sports instructors* with experience in archery, basketball, fencing, golf, gynmnastics, hockey, judo, karate, soccer, softball, tennis, track, volleyball, fitness, baseball, and lacrosse ▶ 1–6 *nurses* with RN license (half and full season positions available) ▶ 10 *performing arts instructors* with experience in dramatics/directing, stagecraft, costuming/sewing, skits and stunts, storytelling, music (all instruments), piano (play by ear and/or play for shows and transpose), dance (jazz/aerobic/ballet/modern), choreograhpy, radio, guitar (play, sing, teach), and puppetry ▶ 15 *water sports instructors* with experience in sailing, canoeing, kayaking, water polo, windsurfing, waterskiing, motorboat driving, lifeguarding, competitive swimming (WSI certification), and water aerobics ▶ 3 *wilderness instructor* with experience in campcraft, fire building, outdoor cooking, overnight trips, forestry, nature, hiking, fishing, and ropes. Applicants must submit formal organization application, resume, three personal references. International applicants accepted; must apply through a recognized agency. A telephone interview is required.

Benefits and Preemployment Training Free housing, free meals, formal training, on-the-job training, and internship opportunities available. Preemployment training is required and includes accident prevention and safety, first aid, CPR, interpersonal skills, leadership skills, lifeguard training.

Contact Sue Lein, Camp Director, Camp Emerson, 91 Minuteman Road, Ridgefield, Connecticut 06877. Telephone: 800-782-3395. Fax: 203-894-9673. E-mail: cmpemerson@aol.com. World Wide Web: http://www.campemerson.com. Application deadline: continuous.

CAMP GOOD NEWS
ROUTE 130
FORESTDALE, MASSACHUSETTS 02644

General Information Coeducational residential and day camp serving 220 children ages 6–16. Established in 1935. 214-acre facility located 10 miles from Hyannis. Features: freshwater lake with sandy beach; wooded setting; 6 miles from ocean; 3 new tennis courts; tutoring center.

Profile of Summer Employees Total number: 80; typical ages: 18–45. 45% men; 55% women; 3% minorities; 1% high school students; 58% college students; 1% retirees; 2% non-U.S. citizens; 5% local applicants. Nonsmokers required.

Employment Information Openings are from June 15 to August 15. Jobs available: ▶ 2 *arts and crafts instructors* (minimum age 25) with experience in the field at $1200 per season ▶ 35 *counselors* (minimum age 18) should be college student at $1400–$1500 per season ▶ 10 *kitchen staff members* (minimum age 18) at $1200 per season ▶ 2 *nurses* (minimum age 25) at $1500 per season ▶ *sports experts* with boating certification at $1000–$1200 per season ▶ 1 *store manager* at $1000–$1200 per season. Applicants must submit a formal organization application, three personal references. International applicants accepted; must obtain own visa, obtain own working papers. An in-person interview is recommended, but a telephone interview is acceptable.

Benefits and Preemployment Training Free housing, free meals, on-the-job training, and tuition assistance. Preemployment training is required and includes first aid, CPR, LGT, WSI.

Contact Faith Willard, Director, Camp Good News, PO Box 95, Forestdale, Massachusetts 02644. Telephone: 508-477-9731. Fax: 508-477-8016. E-mail: goodnews@capecod.net. Application deadline: continuous.

CAMP TACONIC
770 NEW WINDSOR ROAD
HINSDALE, MASSACHUSETTS 01235

General Information Residential 8-week coed camp for 280 children offering top instruction in a wide range of program areas. Established in 1931. 250-acre facility located 10 miles from Pittsfield. Features: beautiful Berkshire Mountains; 2 heated swimming pools; 10 tennis courts; golf driving range; freshwater lake; ball fields and courts.

Profile of Summer Employees Total number: 140; typical ages: 19–25. 50% men; 50% women; 85% college students. Nonsmokers required.

Employment Information Openings are from June 18 to August 18. Jobs available: ▶ 16 *aquatics staff members (swimming, sailing, waterskiing, and boating)* with WSI certification for swimming at $1200–$2000 per season ▶ 10 *arts and crafts staff members (fine arts, ceramics, crafts, and silver jewelry)* at $1200–$4000 per season ▶ 14 *athletics staff members (team and individual sports)* at $1200–$2000 per season ▶ 2 *cooking instructors* with ability to teach cooking to campers at $1200–$2000 per season ▶ 12 *general counselors for 7-10 year olds* must be a college sophomore at $1200–$2000 per season ▶ 6 *media arts staff members (newspaper, photography, and video)* at $1200–$2000 per season ▶ 5 *outdoor adventure staff members (pioneering, climbing wall, and ropes course)* at $1200–$2000 per season ▶ 12 *tennis staff members* at $1200–$2000 per season ▶ 12 *theater arts staff members (dance, costume making, musical theater, and stagecraft)* at $1200–$2000 per season. Applicants must submit formal organization application. International applicants accepted; must apply through a recognized agency. A telephone interview is required.

Benefits and Preemployment Training Free housing, free meals, formal training, on-the-job training, and travel reimbursement. Preemployment training is required and includes accident prevention and safety, interpersonal skills, leadership skills.

Contact Bob and Barbara Ezrol, Directors, Camp Taconic, 66 Chestnut Hill Lane, Briarcliff Manor, New York 10510. Telephone: 914-762-2820. Fax: 914-762-4437. E-mail: ctaconic@aol. com. Application deadline: continuous.

CAMP WATITOH
CENTER LAKE
BECKET, MASSACHUSETTS 01223

General Information Residential summer camp serving 200 children with a wide variety of land and water sports activities, including drama, nature, and trips to all Berkshire area attractions. Established in 1937. 85-acre facility located 130 miles from Boston. Features: mountain-top setting; attractive lakefront; noted cultural arts region; cabins with bathrooms; wide variety of athletic facilities.

Profile of Summer Employees Total number: 75; typical ages: 19–28. 50% men; 50% women; 85% college students; 10% non-U.S. citizens. Nonsmokers preferred.

Employment Information Openings are from June 25 to August 21. Jobs available: ▶ 3 *arts and crafts instructors* (minimum age 20) with experience preferred at $1500–$2500 per season ▶ *general sports instructor* (minimum age 18) must be completing first year of college and have some experience with sports at $1100–$1600 per season ▶ 2 *sailing instructors* (minimum age 20) with experience in open water sailing; competitive experience is helpful at $1200–$1600 per season ▶ 6 *swimming instructors* (minimum age 20) with WSI or LGT certification at $1200–$1600 per season ▶ 2 *waterskiing instructors* (minimum age 21) with teaching experience; able to slalom and trick ski at $1200–$1600 per season. Applicants must submit formal organization application, two letters of recommendation. International applicants accepted; must apply through a recognized agency.

Benefits and Preemployment Training Free housing, free meals, on-the-job training, and travel reimbursement. Preemployment training is required and includes accident prevention and safety, interpersonal skills, leadership skills.

Contact William Hoch, Director, Camp Watitoh, 28 Sammis Lane, White Plains, New York 10605. Telephone: 914-428-1894. Fax: 914-428-1648. E-mail: bihoc@aol.com. World Wide Web: http://www.campwatitoh.com. Application deadline: continuous.

CAPE COD SEA CAMPS
PO BOX 1880
BREWSTER, MASSACHUSETTS 02631

General Information Residential camp serving 350 campers for 3½ or 7 weeks and a daycamp serving 240 campers weekly. Established in 1922. 125-acre facility located 90 miles from Boston. Features: Cape Cod Bay; site on Cape's largest lake; 9 tennis courts; more than 40 sailboats; outdoor theater; photography lab.

Profile of Summer Employees Total number: 200; typical age: 20. 50% men; 50% women; 5% minorities; 80% college students; 5% non-U.S. citizens; 10% local applicants. Nonsmokers preferred.

Employment Information Openings are from June 20 to August 17. Jobs available: ▶ 3–6 *activity department heads* (minimum age 21) with CPR, first aid, and teaching certification at $2000–$3000 per season ▶ 10–40 *general counselors* (minimum age 19) with documented experience in camp activities; CPR, first aid certification at $1200–$1800 per season ▶ 2–5 *photography counselors* (minimum age 19) with CPR, first aid; should have taken photography courses and have experience developing pictures at $1400–$2000 per season ▶ 5–16 *sailing staff members* (minimum age 19) with instruction and racing experience; CPR, first aid, small boat sailing, and small craft safety certification at $1400–$2200 per season ▶ 4–10 *swimming instructors* (minimum age 19) with WSI, LG certification at $1400–$1800 per season. Applicants must submit formal organization application, either 3 personal references or 3 letters of recommendation. International applicants accepted; must apply through a recognized agency. An in-person interview is recommended, but a telephone interview is acceptable.

Benefits and Preemployment Training Free housing, free meals, and on-the-job training. Preemployment training is required and includes accident prevention and safety, first aid, CPR, interpersonal skills, leadership skills, certification courses: small boat sailing, lifeguard training, small craft water safety, archery and riflery instructor training, kayak clinic.

Contact Sherry Mernick, Associate Director, Cape Cod Sea Camps, PO Box 1880, Brewster, Massachusetts 02631. Telephone: 508-896-3451. Fax: 508-896-8272. E-mail: capecodsea@ capecod.net. World Wide Web: http://www.kidscamps.com/traditional/capecodsea. Application deadline: continuous.

CHAPPAQUIDDICK BEACH CLUB, INC.
37 CHAPPAQUIDDICK ROAD
EDGARTOWN, MASSACHUSETTS 02539

General Information Nonprofit private beach club is a family-oriented facility with an oceanfront location offering children's programs. Established in 1963. 4-acre facility located 86 miles from Boston. Features: location on Martha's Vineyard; kayaks and sailboats; oceanfront property; employee housing at club.

Profile of Summer Employees Total number: 14; typical ages: 18–22. 50% men; 50% women; 11% minorities; 100% college students; 11% non-U.S. citizens. Nonsmokers preferred.

Employment Information Openings are from May 9 to September 9. Jobs available: ▶ 1 *floater* (minimum age 18) with maintenance/carpentry experience preferred; must be able to work through September 6; at $275 per week with bonus of $1200-$2000 ▶ 1–4 *lifeguards* (minimum age 18) with Red Cross lifeguard training, first aid, CPR, and driver's license; experience preferred; must be able to work through September 6; at $275 per week with bonus of $1200-$2000 ▶ 1 *receptionist* (minimum age 18) with driver's license and superior interpersonal and organizational skills; must be able to work through September 6; at $275 per week with bonus of $1200-$2000 ▶ 1 *swim instructor* (minimum age 18) with Red Cross/YMCA certification and experience; able to conduct swim meets; July 2-August 26 at $325–$350 per week ▶ 1 *van* *driver* (minimum age 18) with driver's license and clean driving record; easy going personality; must be able to work through September 6; at $275 per week with bonus of $1200-$2000. Applicants must submit a formal organization application, 3 professional/work references. International applicants accepted; must obtain own visa, obtain own working papers. An in-person interview is required.

Benefits and Preemployment Training Meals at a cost, free housing, on-the-job training, and cooking facilities included with housing.

Contact Peter MacRae, Manager, Chappaquiddick Beach Club, Inc., Star Route #9, Edgartown, Massachusetts 02539. Telephone: 508-627-8221. Fax: 508-627-8221. E-mail: pmacrae@gis.net. Application deadline: continuous.

CHIMNEY CORNERS CAMP FOR GIRLS
748 HAMILTON ROAD
BECKET, MASSACHUSETTS 01223

General Information Residential YMCA camp serving 250 girls in each four-week session. Camp is international, and it promotes character development and personal growth. Established in 1931. 1,200-acre facility located 150 miles from Boston. Features: Berkshire Mountains; near cultural/historic points of interest; wooded setting; private, freshwater lake; tennis courts; horseback riding.

Profile of Summer Employees Total number: 125; typical ages: 16–30. 10% men; 90% women; 5% minorities; 25% high school students; 75% college students; 20% non-U.S. citizens; 1% local applicants. Nonsmokers preferred.

Employment Information Openings are from June 13 to August 22. Year-round positions also offered. Jobs available: ▶ 1 *carpenter* with construction experience preferred; salary negotiable ▶ 10–15 *counselors* (minimum age 18) at $1400–$1800 per season ▶ 3–6 *food service assistants* (minimum age 18) at $1600–$1800 per season ▶ *horseback riding instructors* at $1400–$2000 per season ▶ *lifeguards/swimming instructors* at $1400–$2500 per season ▶ 3 *nurses* with RN (preferred) or LPN license at $2000–$4000 per season ▶ *performing and creative arts staff* at $1400–$2200 per season ▶ 1 *riding director* (minimum age 21) with experience teaching English Hunt Seat; stable managment skills and/or experience at $2000–$2500 per season ▶ 2–6 *sports instructors* (minimum age 18) at $1500–$1800 per season ▶ 1–3 *tennis coaches* (minimum age 18) with tennis skills and teaching experience at $1400–$2000 per season ▶ 2 *waterfront directors* (minimum age 21) with certification in WSI and lifeguard training or equivalent; will certify right candidate at $2000–$2500 per season ▶ 1–2 *woodworking instructors* (minimum age 18) at $1800–$2000 per season. Applicants must submit formal organization application, two personal references. International applicants accepted; must apply through a recognized agency. An in-person interview is recommended, but a telephone interview is acceptable.

Benefits and Preemployment Training Free housing, free meals, formal training, possible full-time employment, names of contacts, on-the-job training, and opportunity to attend seminars/workshops. Preemployment training is required and includes accident prevention and safety, first aid, CPR, interpersonal skills, leadership skills.

Contact Shannon Donovan-Monti, Chimney Corners Camp Director, Chimney Corners Camp for Girls, 748 Hamilton Road, Becket, Massachusetts 01223. Telephone: 413-623-8991. Fax: 413-623-5890. E-mail: bccymca@bcn.net. World Wide Web: http://www.bccymca.org. Application deadline: continuous.

COLLEGE LIGHT OPERA COMPANY
HIGHFIELD THEATRE, PO DRAWER 906
FALMOUTH, MASSACHUSETTS 02541

General Information Residential summer-stock music theater for training undergraduate and graduate students. Established in 1969. 6-acre facility located 70 miles from Boston. Features: wooded setting on salt water; 100 yards from salt water beach

Profile of Summer Employees Total number: 80; typical ages: 17–23. 50% men; 50% women; 5% minorities; 2% high school students; 80% college students; 2% local applicants.

Employment Information Openings are from June 5 to August 30. Jobs available: ▶ 1 *assistant*

business manager with word processing skills, driver's license, and experience in the field at $1200 per season ▶ 2 *box office treasurers* with outgoing, friendly personality and driver's license at $1200 per season ▶ 1 *choreographer* with experience in the field at $1600 per season ▶ 2 *chorus masters* with piano experience at $1200 per season ▶ 1 *co-op work director* with driver's license and experience in the field at $2500–$3000 per season ▶ 1 *cook* with driver's license and experience in the field at $3500–$4000 per season ▶ 5 *costume crew* with experience in the field at $1000 per season ▶ 1 *costume designer* with driver's license and experience in the field at $2500–$3000 per season ▶ 18 *orchestra staff* with experience in the field at $500 per season ▶ 2 *piano accompanists* with experience in the field at $1000 per season ▶ 1 *publicity director* with driver's license and car, word processing skills, and experience in the field at $1200 per season ▶ 1 *set designer/technical director* with driver's license and experience in the field at $2500–$3000 per season ▶ 6 *stage crew* with experience in the field at $1000 per season ▶ 32 *vocalists* salary is room and board with experience in the field. Applicants must submit mandatory audio tape audition for vocal and orchestra candidates. International applicants accepted; must obtain own visa, obtain own working papers.

Benefits and Preemployment Training Free housing, free meals, and on-the-job training.

Contact Ursula P. Haslun, Producer, College Light Opera Company, 162 South Cedar Street, Oberlin, Ohio 44074. Telephone: 440-774-8485. Fax: 440-775-8642. E-mail: ursula.haslun@ oberlin.edu. World Wide Web: http://www.capecod.net/cloc.

CRANE LAKE CAMP
STATE LINE ROAD
WEST STOCKBRIDGE, MASSACHUSETTS 01266

General Information Reform Jewish coeducational camp serving children ages 6–15 with traditional sports and a full cultural program. 120-acre facility located 15 miles from Pittsfield. Features: Springfield Lake; all water sports; all land sports; in the Berkshires.

Profile of Summer Employees Total number: 130; typical ages: 18–24. 50% men; 50% women; 75% college students; 5% retirees; 25% non-U.S. citizens; 5% local applicants. Nonsmokers preferred.

Employment Information Openings are from June 15 to August 28. Jobs available: ▶ 2 *arts and crafts instructors* at $1200–$1600 per season ▶ 10 *athletics counselors* (minimum age 18) with a major in physical education or varsity athletics experience at $1200–$1600 per season ▶ 3–5 *dance staff* (minimum age 18) with teaching experience at $1200–$1600 per season ▶ 4 *doctors* must be a physician ▶ 2–4 *guitar instructors* (minimum age 18) at $1200–$1600 per season ▶ 4 *gymnastics instructors* with experience in the field at $1200–$1600 per season ▶ 1 *horseback riding instructor* (minimum age 18) at $1200–$1600 per season ▶ 2–4 *nature instructors* (minimum age 18) åt $1200–$1600 per season ▶ 3 *nurses* with RN license at $3000 per season ▶ 1–2 *painting/sketching instructors* (minimum age 18) at $1200–$1600 per season ▶ 1 *piano player* (minimum age 18) with ability to play by ear at $1200–$1600 per season ▶ 2–3 *pioneering/hiking instructor* (minimum age 18) at $1200–$1600 per season ▶ 6–9 *tennis instructor* (minimum age 18) with teaching experience at $1200–$1600 per season ▶ 6 *waterfront instructors* (minimum age 18) with small crafts certification and waterskiing, sailing, or canoeing experience at $1200–$1600 per season. Applicants must submit formal organization application, three personal references. International applicants accepted; must apply through a recognized agency. An in-person interview is recommended, but a telephone interview is acceptable.

Benefits and Preemployment Training Free housing, free meals, formal training, health insurance, on-the-job training, travel reimbursement, and tuition assistance. Preemployment training is required and includes accident prevention and safety, first aid, CPR, leadership skills.

Contact Brad Gerstle, Director, Crane Lake Camp, 633 3rd Avenue, New York, New York 10017. Telephone: 212-650-4208. Fax: 212-650-4139. E-mail: iluvcamp@aol.com. World Wide Web: http://www.cranelakecamp.com. Application deadline: continuous.

4-H FARLEY OUTDOOR EDUCATION CENTER
615 ROUTE 130
MASHPEE, MASSACHUSETTS 02649

General Information Camp emphasizing overnight and day programs for boys and girls ages 4-14. There is limited mainstreaming of special needs children. Activities include nature, agriculture, outdoor living skills, arts, canoeing, kayaking, horseback riding, archery, swimming, snorkeling, and a ropes course. Established in 1934. 32-acre facility located 80 miles from Boston. Features: large freshwater lake; wooded setting; location on Cape Cod; close to ocean beaches; nearby historic sites; nearby entertainment options.

Profile of Summer Employees Total number: 50; typical ages: 18–26. 10% minorities; 80% college students; 20% non-U.S. citizens; 10% local applicants. Nonsmokers preferred.

Employment Information Openings are from June 25 to August 25. Spring break positions also offered. Jobs available: ▶ *archery instructors* with documented experience or certification at $220–$250 per week ▶ 1 *child care coordinator* with background in youth development at $300–$350 per week ▶ 30 *counselors* with specialized program skills and camping experience at $180–$230 per week ▶ 1 *health-care provider* with EMT, RN, or LPN license or special training in first aid at $400–$450 per week ▶ *kayaking and canoeing instructors* with documented experience or certification at $230–$250 per week ▶ 3 *kitchen staff members* at $240–$300 per week ▶ 8 *lifeguards* with LGT certification or equivalent and first aid/CPR at $200–$230 per week ▶ *ropes instructor* with documented experience or certification at $250–$275 per week ▶ 3 *waterfront directors* with WSI certification and 6 weeks prior experience in a supervisory position at $300–$350 per week. Applicants must submit a formal organization application, three personal references, authorization for criminal background check. International applicants accepted. An in-person interview is required.

Benefits and Preemployment Training Free housing, free meals, formal training, health insurance, on-the-job training, and opportunity to attend seminars/workshops. Preemployment training is required and includes accident prevention and safety, first aid, CPR, interpersonal skills, leadership skills, teaching skills and curricula.

Contact Mr. Michael Campbell, Executive Director, 4-H Farley Outdoor Education Center, 615 Route 130, Mashpee, Massachusetts 02649. Fax: 508-539-0080. E-mail: 4hfarley@cape.com. World Wide Web: http://www.umass.edu/umext/camps/c-farley.htm. Application deadline: continuous.

HORIZONS FOR YOUTH
121 LAKEVIEW STREET
SHARON, MASSACHUSETTS 02067

General Information Residential environmental education center that works with children from low-income families. Established in 1938. Located 25 miles from Boston. Features: freshwater lake; basketball court; 13 cabins; tennis court; baseball field.

Profile of Summer Employees Total number: 65; typical ages: 20–28. 50% men; 50% women; 20% minorities; 85% college students; 1% retirees; 20% non-U.S. citizens; 20% local applicants. Nonsmokers preferred.

Employment Information Openings are from June 7 to August 19. Jobs available: ▶ 1 *CIT director* (minimum age 21) with significant experience in working with disadvantaged teens; first aid/CPR certification preferred at $1350 per season ▶ 4 *activity specialists* (minimum age 21) with experience with disadvantaged children and in activity area; supervisory experience and first aid/CPR certification preferred at $1350 per season ▶ 1 *assistant cook* (minimum age 21 preferred) with cooking experience (quantity cooking experience preferred) at $200 per week ▶ 1 *cook* (minimum age 21 preferred) with supervisory and cooking experience; quantity cooking experience preferred at $300 per week ▶ 36 *counselors* (minimum age 18) with experience working with disadvantaged children; first aid/CPR certification preferred, American Red Cross certification required for lifeguards at $1100 per season ▶ 1 *driver* (minimum age 21) with valid driver's license and clean driving record; CPR/first aid certification preferred; experience with disadvantaged youth helpful at $1350 per season ▶ 4 *kitchen staff* (minimum age 20 preferred) with experience preferred in general kitchen skills; first aid/CPR certification preferred at $1100 per season ▶ 3 *maintenance staff members* (minimum age 20 preferred) with general skills including carpentry, painting, and landscaping; first aid/CPR certification preferred at $1100 per season ▶ 2 *nurses* (minimum age 21 preferred) with RN or LPN license, current first aid/CPR certification, and relevant experience; salary negotiable ▶ 4 *unit leaders* (minimum age 21) with supervisory and extensive experience with disadvantaged children; first aid/CPR certification preferred at $1800 per season ▶ 2 *waterfront directors* (minimum age 21) with American Red Cross CPR, LGT, WSI, and first aid certification, experience with disadvantaged children and supervisory experience at $1350 per season. Applicants must submit formal organization application, two personal references, three letters of recommendation, 3 references. International applicants accepted; must apply through a recognized agency.

Benefits and Preemployment Training Free housing, free meals, formal training, on-the-job training, and opportunity to attend seminars/workshops. Preemployment training is required and includes accident prevention and safety, interpersonal skills, leadership skills.

Contact Julie Wiggins, Summer Program Director, Horizons for Youth, 121 Lakeview Street, Sharon, Massachusetts 02067. Telephone: 781-828-7550. Fax: 781-784-1287. E-mail: camp@ horizons.tiac.net. World Wide Web: http://www.hfy.org. Application deadline: continuous.

THE INSTITUTE FOR THE ACADEMIC ADVANCEMENT OF YOUTH/THE JOHNS HOPKINS UNIVERSITY–MOUNT HOLYOKE COLLEGE

See The Institute for the Academic Advancement of Youth/ The Johns Hopkins University on page 135 for complete description.

LIGHTHOUSE INN, INC.
1 LIGHTHOUSE INN ROAD, PO BOX 128
WEST DENNIS, MASSACHUSETTS 02670

General Information Seasonal, oceanfront resort specializing in banquets, weddings, and group conferences in May, June, September, and October. July and August cater to social guests vactioning. Established in 1938. 9-acre facility located 80 miles from Boston. Features: oceanfront; swiming pool; tennis court; restaurant; private beach; children's program.

Profile of Summer Employees Total number: 100; typical ages: 19–28. 50% men; 50% women; 1% high school students; 15% college students; 10% local applicants.

Employment Information Openings are from May 15 to October 20. Jobs available: ▶ 5–10 *dining room staff* (minimum age 18) at $2.63 per hour plus tips. Applicants must submit a formal organization application, resume, three personal references, two letters of recommendation, photograph. International applicants accepted; must obtain own visa, obtain own working papers. An in-person interview is recommended, but a telephone interview is acceptable.

Benefits and Preemployment Training Meals at a cost.

Contact Bill Sherman, Food and Beverage Manager, Lighthouse Inn, Inc. Telephone: 508-398-2244. Fax: 508-398-5658. E-mail: shoe@lighthouseinn.com. World Wide Web: http://www. lighthouseinn.com. Application deadline: continuous.

NORTH AMERICAN TRAILS
PO BOX 594
CARLISLE, MASSACHUSETTS 01741

General Information Cross country camping trips for teenagers, throughout North America, which focus on group dynamics in an outdoor setting. Predominately camping in full service campgrounds, with some nights on college campuses. Established in 1981. Features: national parks; whitewater rafting; day hikes; mountain biking; explore cities; camping.

Profile of Summer Employees Total number: 20; typical ages: 21–30. 50% men; 50% women; 40% college students; 60% local applicants. Nonsmokers required.

Employment Information Openings are from June 26 to August 15. Jobs available: ▶ 10–15 *counselors* (minimum age 21) with CPR/first aid certifications, drivers license, and previous experience with adolescents at $650–$950 per season ▶ 1 *food manager* (minimum age 21) with CPR/first aid certifications, drivers license, food preparation skills, and previous experience with adolescents at $1400 per season. Applicants must submit a formal organization application, cover letter, resume, three personal references. An in-person interview is required.

Benefits and Preemployment Training Free housing, free meals, formal training, names of contacts, and on-the-job training. Preemployment training is required and includes accident prevention and safety, interpersonal skills, leadership skills, procedures/logistics.

Contact Lori Pritchard, Director, North American Trails. Telephone: 978-371-2566. Fax: 978-287-0742. E-mail: lori@natrails.com. World Wide Web: http://www.natrails.com. Application deadline: continuous.

NORTH SHORE MUSIC THEATRE
DUNHAM ROAD, PO BOX 62
BEVERLY, MASSACHUSETTS 01915-0062

General Information Musical theater with a six-show season of Broadway musicals as well as children's shows, concerts, and special events. Professional theater dedicated to the American musical and programs for young audiences, serving more than 300,000 patrons from April through December. Established in 1955. Located 20 miles from Boston. Features: 1800-seat arena theatre; celebrity concert series; on-site shop facilities; half hour north of Boston.

Profile of Summer Employees Total number: 100; typical ages: 18–25. 40% men; 60% women; 10% minorities; 10% high school students; 70% college students; 75% local applicants.

Employment Information Openings are from April to December 21. Jobs available: ▶ 20 *technical theater interns* (minimum age 18) with experience in the field at $150–$200 per week ▶ 20 *technical theater staff members* with experience in the field at $275–$425 per week. International applicants accepted; must obtain own visa.

Benefits and Preemployment Training Possible full-time employment, on-the-job training, and opportunity to attend seminars/workshops.

Contact Ali Sheehan Mignone, Assistant Production Manager, North Shore Music Theatre, PO Box 62, Beverly, Massachusetts 01915-0062. Fax: 978-922-0768. World Wide Web: http://www. nsmt.org. Application deadline: continuous.

OFFENSE-DEFENSE GOLF CAMP, MASSACHUSETTS
THE WINCHENDON SCHOOL AND GOLF FACILITY
WINCHENDON, MASSACHUSETTS 01475

General Information Residential and day camp teaching golf to boys and girls ages 10–18. Established in 1992. 1,000-acre facility located 28 miles from Boston. Features: prep school dorms and cafeteria; putting green; 18-hole regulation golf course; golf range; 4 tennis courts; outdoor swimming pool and gymnasium.

Profile of Summer Employees Total number: 40; typical ages: 19–50. 80% men; 20% women; 10% minorities; 80% college students. Nonsmokers preferred.

Employment Information Openings are from July 1 to July 30. Jobs available: ▶ 1 *bus driver* (minimum age 21) with license to drive yellow school bus and CDL at $200–$350 per week ▶ 10 *general (non-golf) counselors* (minimum age 19) must like working with children at $175–$225 per week ▶ 10 *golf instructors* with college varsity, college coaching, PGA Pro (very low handicap players) status, or USGTA certification at $250–$350 per week ▶ *swimming counselors* (minimum age 19) with WSI certification at $200–$250 per week. International applicants accepted; must obtain own visa. A telephone interview is required.

Benefits and Preemployment Training Free housing, free meals, formal training, and on-the-job training. Preemployment training is required and includes accident prevention and safety, first aid, CPR, interpersonal skills, leadership skills

Contact Mike Meshken, President, Offense-Defense Golf Camp, Massachusetts, PO Box 6, Easton, Connecticut 06612. Telephone: 800-824-7336. Fax: 203-255-5666. World Wide Web: http://www.offensedefensegolf.com. Application deadline: May 10.

SOUTH SHORE YMCA CAMPS
75 STOWE ROAD
SANDWICH, MASSACHUSETTS 02563

General Information Brother/sister residential camp on Cape Cod. It is a non-profit, YMCA traditional camp. Established in 1928. 400-acre facility located 65 miles from Boston. Features: freshwater lake; wooded setting; high/low ropes; horseback riding; tennis courts; basketball courts.

Profile of Summer Employees Total number: 165; typical ages: 18–28. 40% men; 60% women; 2% minorities; 10% high school students; 90% college students; 40% non-U.S. citizens; 5% local applicants.

Employment Information Openings are from June 14 to August 29. Jobs available: ▶ 74 *cabin counselors* (minimum age 18) with one year of college completed at $130–$150 per week ▶ 2 *cooks* (minimum age 21) at $300–$400 per week ▶ 3 *nurses* (minimum age 21) with RN and experience in the field at $300–$400 per week ▶ 3 *office staff* (minimum age 18) at $130–$150 per week ▶ 14 *specialists* (minimum age 21) with any appropriate specialized skills and WSI, CPR, and first aid certification at $140–$160 per week ▶ *support staff (in kitchen, maintenance, and bathroom)* (minimum age 18) at $130–$140 per week ▶ 8 *unit leaders* (minimum age 21) with leadership qualities at $150–$160 per week ▶ 2 *van drivers/security staff* (minimum age 21) with driver's license for at least two years; first aid and CPR certification at $130–$160 per week. Applicants must submit a formal organization application, three personal references. International applicants accepted. An in-person interview is recommended, but a telephone interview is acceptable.

Benefits and Preemployment Training Free housing, free meals, formal training, and on-the-job training. Preemployment training is required and includes accident prevention and safety, first aid, interpersonal skills, leadership skills.

Contact Carol Sharman, Camp Director, South Shore YMCA Camps, 75 Stowe Road, Sandwich, Massachusetts 02563. Telephone: 508-428-2571. Fax: 508-420-3545. E-mail: ssymca@capecod. net. World Wide Web: http://www.oncapecod.net/ssymca. Application deadline: continuous.

THE SOUTHWESTERN COMPANY, MASSACHUSETTS
See The Southwestern Company, Tennessee on page 284 for complete description.

STUDENT CONSERVATION ASSOCIATION (SCA), MASSACHUSETTS
See Student Conservation Association (SCA), New Hampshire on page 193 for complete description.

SUMMER THEATER AT MOUNT HOLYOKE COLLEGE
SOUTH HADLEY, MASSACHUSETTS 01075

General Information Professional summer-stock company producing eight mainstage plays and three plays for children in one-week stock. Established in 1970. 20-acre facility located 5 miles from Springfield. Features: 2 lakes; tennis courts; beautiful campus; movie theater within walking distance; restaurants; bookstore.

Profile of Summer Employees Total number: 70; typical ages: 21–45. 50% men; 50% women; 5% minorities; 7% high school students; 30% college students; 2% non-U.S. citizens; 16% local applicants. Nonsmokers preferred.

Employment Information Openings are from June 1 to August 31. Jobs available: ▶ 12 *actors* (non-Equity) at $200 per season ▶ 1 *box office manager* at $750–$1000 per season ▶ 3 *carpenters* at $750–$1000 per season ▶ 1 *costume designer* at $1800 per season ▶ 1 *master electrician* at $1000–$1500 per season ▶ 3 *prop artisans* at $750–$1000 per season ▶ 1 *prop master* at $1000 per season ▶ 3 *stage managers* (non-Equity) at $200–$900 per season ▶ 2 *stitchers* at $750–$1000 per season ▶ 1 *technical director* at $1200–$1800 per season ▶ 1 *wardrobe staff member* at $850–$1000 per season. Applicants must submit a formal organization application, resume, three personal references. International applicants accepted; must obtain own visa, obtain own working papers.

Benefits and Preemployment Training Free housing, formal training, on-the-job training, and travel reimbursement.

Contact Jack Neary, Producing Director, Summer Theater at Mount Holyoke College, South Hadley, Massachusetts 01075. Telephone: 413-538-2632. Fax: 413-538-3036. E-mail: janeary@ aol.com. Application deadline: continuous.

SUPERCAMP–HAMPSHIRE COLLEGE
HAMPSHIRE COLLEGE
AMHERST, MASSACHUSETTS

General Information Residential program for teens designed to build self-confidence and lifelong learning skills through accelerated learning techniques. Established in 1981. Near Hartford, Connecticut. Features: university dormitories; outdoor ropes course.

Profile of Summer Employees Total number: 30–40; typical ages: 18–25. 50% men; 50% women; 80% college students. Nonsmokers required.

Employment Information Openings are from June to August. Jobs available: ▶ 10 *counselors* with college degree and PPS credential, MFCC license, or master's degree in counseling at $900–$1500 per season ▶ 4–10 *facilitators* with presentation skills and college degree; teaching credentials preferred at $1300–$2350 per season ▶ 1 *logistics manager* with excellent organizational skills and a high school diploma at $600–$1100 per season ▶ 1 *nurse* with national or state registration at $600–$1300 per season ▶ 1 *office manager* with high school diploma and prior office experience at $450–$700 per season ▶ 1 *paramedic* with national or state registration at $600–$1300 per season ▶ 20–25 *team leaders* with high school diploma and prior experience with teens at $250–$600 per season. Applicants must submit a formal organization application, resume, two personal references, in-person interview recommended (videotape interview acceptable). International applicants accepted; must obtain own visa, obtain own working papers.

Benefits and Preemployment Training Free housing, free meals, and on-the-job training. Preemployment training is required and includes interpersonal skills, leadership skills.

Contact Recruiter, SuperCamp–Hampshire College, 1725 South Coast Highway, Oceanside, California 92054. Telephone: 800-285-3276 Ext. 180. Fax: 760-722-3507. E-mail: info@ learningforum.com. World Wide Web: http://www.supercamp.com. Application deadline: continuous.

WILDERNESS EXPERIENCES UNLIMITED
499 LOOMIS STREET
WESTFIELD, MASSACHUSETTS 01085

General Information Residential program which ranges from five days to two weeks. It serves approximately 30–40 campers ages 8–17 per week, and it offers general outdoor activities through high adventure. Established in 1981. 75-acre facility located 15 miles from Springfield. Features: wooded setting; ropes course.

Profile of Summer Employees Total number: 18; typical ages: 16–28. 70% men; 30% women; 50% high school students; 50% college students. Nonsmokers required.

Employment Information Openings are from July to September 31. Jobs available: ▶ 2–3 *senior counselors* (minimum age 18) with first aid/CPR certification and LGT; should be outdoor-loving and fun at $150–$200 per week ▶ 2–3 *trip leaders* (minimum age 18) with outdoor and leadership skills, climbing and mountain biking experience, first aid/CPR, kayak instructors certification, and LGT at $150–$200 per week. Applicants must submit a formal organization application, cover letter, resume, photo of applicant on a trip/adventure. International applicants accepted.

Benefits and Preemployment Training Free housing, free meals, possible full-time employment, on-the-job training, and opportunity to attend seminars/workshops. Preemployment training is required and includes accident prevention and safety, first aid, CPR, leadership skills, specific training/certification areas: kayaking, climbing, and others.

Contact T. Scott Cook, Executive Director, Wilderness Experiences Unlimited, 499 Loomis

Street, Westfield, Massachusetts 01085. Fax: 413-569-6445. E-mail: adventures@weu.com. World Wide Web: http://www.weu.com. Application deadline: May 15.

WILLIAMSTOWN THEATER FESTIVAL
1000 MAIN STREET, PO BOX 517
WILLIAMSTOWN, MASSACHUSETTS 01267

General Information Summer theater festival presenting productions of revivals of classics and new works by new and established playwrights. Established in 1953. Located 40 miles from Albany, New York. Features: Williams College campus; culturally rich area; idyllic New England town; 3 hours to New York City and Boston; fully equipped theatre facility; beautiful Berkshires.

Profile of Summer Employees Total number: 60; typical ages: 17–35. 50% men; 50% women; 10% minorities; 1% high school students; 50% college students; 1% retirees; 1% non-U.S. citizens; 5% local applicants.

Employment Information Openings are from June 1 to September 1. Year-round positions also offered. Jobs available: ▶ 60 *Equity actors* with salary as per AEA contract ▶ 60–70 *acting apprentices* (minimum age 17) who pay fee of $2550 for room, board, and tuition (1998 rate); no salary ▶ 50–70 *administrative and technical interns* with some experience in chosen field (no salary) ▶ 12–16 *non-Equity actors* with advanced educational and/or professional acting experience (no salary) ▶ 60–70 *staff members* with advanced educational and/or professional experience at $50–$400 per week. Applicants must submit 2–3 personal references or 2–3 letters of recommendation. International applicants accepted; must obtain own visa, obtain own working papers.

Benefits and Preemployment Training Meals at a cost, names of contacts, on-the-job training, opportunity to attend seminars/workshops, and housing is free for staff, $500 for interns (1999 rate).

Contact Anne Lowrie, Company Manager, Williamstown Theater Festival, 100 East 17th Street, 3rd Floor, New York, New York 10003. Telephone: 212-228-2286. Fax: 212-228-9091. E-mail: alowrie@wtfestival.org. World Wide Web: http://www.wtfestival.org.

YMCA CAMP HI-ROCK
162 EAST STREET
MT. WASHINGTON, MASSACHUSETTS 01258

General Information Year-round YMCA camp and conference center offering residential and day camp, teen adventure trips, leader-in-training program, and experiential and environmental activities for all groups. Established in 1947. 1,000-acre facility located 70 miles from Albany. Features: high ropes course; climbing wall; private lake; 1000 mountain acres; 3 waterskiing boats; year-round facilities and programs.

Profile of Summer Employees Total number: 120; typical ages: 18–27. 45% men; 55% women; 10% minorities; 25% high school students; 70% college students; 33% non-U.S. citizens; 5% local applicants. Nonsmokers preferred.

Employment Information Openings are from June 9 to August 20. Year-round positions also offered. Jobs available: ▶ 4 *adventure leaders* (minimum age 21) with first aid/CPR certifications and lifeguard training at $180 per week ▶ 1 *arts and crafts director* with first aid/CPR certifications, arts and crafts background, and must be at least a college sophomore at $155 per week ▶ 1 *assistant camp director* with first aid/CPR certifications, 2 years administrative experience, and must be a collge graduate at $230 per week ▶ 1 *assistant day camp director* with first aid/CPR certifications, camp experience, and must be a college sophomore at $155 per week ▶ 1 *assistant nurse/medic* (minimum age 21) must be a RN, LPN, or EMT at $270 per week ▶ 6 *assistant unit directors* with first aid/CPR certifications, camp experience, and must be at least a college sophomore at $150 per week ▶ 1 *day camp director* with first aid/CPR certifications, administrative experience, and must be at least a college graduate at $195 per week ▶ 1 *head nurse* (minimum age 21) must be a Massachusetts RN or MD at $360 per week ▶ 1 *intervention specialist* (minimum age 21) with first aid/CPR certifications and experience dealing with troubled youth at $180 per week ▶ 26 *junior counselors* with first aid/CPR certifications and must be at least a high school senior at $80 per week ▶ 3 *program directors* with first aid/CPR certifications, program staff experience, and must be at least a college sophomore at $180 per week ▶ 1 *quartermaster* (minimum age 21) with first aid/CPR certifications and organizational skills at $180 per week ▶ 1 *ropes course director* (minimum age 21) with first aid/CPR certifications and ropes training and experience at $180 per week ▶ 32 *senior counselors* with first aid/CPR certifications and must be at least a high school senior at $140 per week ▶ 14 *support staff-kitchen, maintenance, office* with first aid/CPR certifications and must be a college sophomore at $150 per week ▶ 1 *transportation director* (minimum age 21) with first aid/CPR certifications and a clean driving record at $155 per week ▶ *unit director* with first aid/CPR certificaitons, camp experience, and must be at least a college sophomore at $155 per week ▶ 2 *waterfront directors* (minimum age 21) with lifeguard and WSI certifications and administrative experience at $180 per week ▶ 2 *waterski directors* (minimum age 21) with lifeguard certification and waterski experience at $180 per week ▶ 1 *wrangler* (minimum age 21) with first aid/CPR certifications and horseback riding experience at $155 per week. Applicants must submit formal organization application, three personal references. International applicants accepted; must apply through a recognized agency. A telephone interview is required.

Benefits and Preemployment Training Free housing, free meals, formal training, and on-the-job training. Preemployment training is required and includes accident prevention and safety, first aid, CPR, interpersonal skills, leadership skills.

Contact Greg Huff, Camping Director, YMCA Camp Hi-Rock. Telephone: 413-528-1227 Ext. 14. Fax: 413-528-4234. E-mail: campingdir@aol.com. World Wide Web: http://www.camphirock. com. Application deadline: continuous.

YMCA CAMP LYNDON
117 STOWE ROAD
SANDWICH, MASSACHUSETTS 02563

General Information Day camp serving 400 children. Established in 1969. 80-acre facility located 45 miles from Boston. Features: freshwater lake; ropes course; outdoor school; wooded setting; boating program; diversified program.

Profile of Summer Employees Total number: 75–85; typical ages: 18–45. 40% men; 60% women; 2% minorities; 35% high school students; 55% college students; 10% non-U.S. citizens; 65% local applicants. Nonsmokers preferred.

Employment Information Openings are from June 15 to August 31. Year-round positions also offered. Jobs available: ▶ *age-specific unit directors* with certification or related experience with specific age group at $180–$250 per week ▶ 2 *archery specialists* with leadership experience in an archery program and archery certification at $250–$280 per week ▶ 3 *arts and crafts specialists* with teaching certification and experience in the field at $240–$280 per week ▶ 10 *boating instructors* with small craft or equivalent certification and sailing and canoeing experience at $250–$280 per week ▶ 60 *counselors* with youth experience at $200–$240 per week ▶ *dramatic arts specialist* with formal training and experience in the field at $230–$280 per week ▶ 3 *horseback riding directors* with Massachusetts riding license; must live on property; at $180–$250 per week ▶ *horseback riding instructors* with experience in the field at $150–$170 per week ▶ 3 *nature specialists* with degree in related subject and experience in the field at $250–$280 per week ▶ 2 *ropes/initiative specialists* with completion of course and experience in the field at $280–$340 per week ▶ *special populations director* must be Massachusetts resident familiar with ADA laws at $200–$250 per week ▶ 12 *swimming instructors* with LGT certification (minimum) at $200–$260 per week ▶ 2 *waterfront directors* with WSI and LGT certifications at $300–$320 per week. Applicants must submit formal organization application, three personal references. International applicants accepted; must obtain own visa, obtain own working papers, apply through a recognized agency. An in-person interview is recommended, but a telephone interview is acceptable.

Benefits and Preemployment Training Formal training and on-the-job training. Preemployment training is required and includes accident prevention and safety, interpersonal skills, leadership skills.

Contact Brian Jenney, Youth and Camping Services Director, YMCA Camp Lyndon, PO Box

188, West Barnstable, Massachusetts 02668. Telephone: 508-362-6500. Fax: 508-362-5379. Application deadline: continuous.

YMCA CAPE COD
PO BOX 188
WEST BARNSTABLE, MASSACHUSETTS 02668

General Information Traditional day camp providing one-week program sessions to 70 youth ages 5–12. Established in 1969. 5-acre facility located 45 miles from Boston. Features: two swimming pools; theme days; Friday tripping program; small program with family atmosphere; basketball and tennis courts; wooded area.

Profile of Summer Employees Total number: 11; typical ages: 17–35. 40% men; 60% women; 30% high school students; 40% college students; 30% local applicants. Nonsmokers preferred.

Employment Information Openings are from June 15 to August 31. Year-round positions also offered. Jobs available: ▶ 8–10 *counselors* (minimum age 18) at $200–$240 per week ▶ 1–3 *program specialists (arts and crafts, sports, nature)* (minimum age 20) with experience and appropriate certifications for program specialty at $250–$280 per week. Applicants must submit formal organization application, three personal references. International applicants accepted; must obtain own visa, obtain own working papers, apply through a recognized agency. An in-person interview is recommended, but a telephone interview is acceptable.

Benefits and Preemployment Training Formal training and on-the-job training. Preemployment training is required and includes accident prevention and safety, interpersonal skills, leadership skills.

Contact Brian Jenney, Youth and Camping Services Director, YMCA Cape Cod, PO Box 188, West Barnstable, Massachusetts 02668. Telephone: 508-362-6500. Fax: 508-362-5379. Application deadline: continuous.

MICHIGAN

ACE COMPUTER CAMP–MICHIGAN
See ACE Computer Camp–Washington on page 307 for complete description.

A CHRISTIAN MINISTRY IN THE NATIONAL PARKS– MICHIGAN
See A Christian Ministry in the National Parks–Massachussetts on page 138 for complete description.

AMERICAN YOUTH FOUNDATION–CAMP MINIWANCA FOR BOYS
8845 WEST GARFIELD ROAD
SHELBY, MICHIGAN 49455

General Information Camp focusing on developing the leadership capacities of young people by helping them achieve their personal best, lead balanced lives, and serve others. Established in 1925. 360-acre facility located 80 miles from Grand Rapids. Features: 1 mile of Lake Michigan beach; Stoney Lake; wooded dunes; sand dunes; council circle at base of 2 dunes; open-air cabins and dormitories.

Profile of Summer Employees Total number: 200; typical ages: 18–60. 40% men; 60% women; 3% minorities; 10% high school students; 55% college students; 5% retirees; 8% non-U.S. citizens; 10% local applicants. Nonsmokers preferred.

Employment Information Openings are from May 1 to October 1. Spring break and year-round positions also offered. Jobs available: ▶ 1 *Four Trails program coordinator* (minimum age 21) with WFR, CPR, first aid, and lifeguard certifications, current physical, TB test, and police background check at $2000 per month ▶ 1 *bike mechanic* (minimum age 18) with a current physical, TB test, and police background check at $250 per week ▶ 5 *building/grounds personnel* (minimum age 18) with some skill with tools and power equipment at $300 per week ▶ 6 *camp cleaning personnel* (minimum age 18) should be college student or retired person at $300 per week ▶ 4 *camp store staff members* (minimum age 18) should be college student or retired person at $275 per week ▶ 20 *central summer staff members* (minimum age 18) should be teachers or instructors at $200–$400 per week ▶ 2–4 *craft house staff members* (minimum age 18) should be college student or retired person at $200–$250 per week ▶ 2 *drivers* (minimum age 21) with a current physical, police background check, TB test, and a valid driver's license at $8.10 per hour ▶ *food/equipment manager* (minimum age 18) with CPR and first aid certifications, TB test, current physical, and police background checks at $250 per week ▶ 2–4 *health center staff* with EMT, RN, LPN or 2nd year RN students (BSN) at $275–$400 per week ▶ 6 *interns* (minimum age 20) junior/senior status in college or college degree at $325 per month ▶ 90 *leaders* (minimum age 18) should be college student or teacher at $135–$205 per week ▶ 1 *logistics coordinator* (minimum age 18) with CPR and first aid certifications, TB test, current physical, and police background checks at $350 per week ▶ 1 *logistics specialist category A* (minimum age 21) with first aid and CPR certifications, current physical, TB test, police background check, and a valid driver's license at $270 per week ▶ 1 *logistics specialist category B* (minimum age 21) with CPR and first aid certifications, current physical, TB test, police background check, and a valid driver's license at $270 per week ▶ *logistics specialist category C* (minimum age 21) with CPR and first aid certifications, current physical, TB test, police background check, and a valid driver's license at $270 per week ▶ 2 *office staff members* (minimum age 18) should be college student or retired person at $200–$250 per week ▶ *secretary (Four Trails)* with a current physical, TB test, and police background chek at $250 per week ▶ 2 *security personnel* (minimum age 21) at $300 per week ▶ 2 *trip coordinators categories A and B* (minimum age 21) with first aid and CPR certifications, current physical, TB test, and police background check at $350 per week ▶ 12 *trip leaders category A* (minimum age 18) with first aid and CPR certifications, current physical, TB test, and police background check at $305 per week ▶ 5 *trip leaders category B* (minimum age 18) with first aid and CPR certifications, current physical, TB test, and police background check at $295 per week ▶ 7 *trip leaders category C* (minimum age 18) with a current physical, CPR and first aid certifications, TB test, and police background check at $270 per week ▶ 1 *waterfront management* (minimum age 21) with LS/LGT/WSI and sailing and canoeing experience at $350 per week ▶ 2 *wood shop staff members* (minimum age 18) should be college student or retired person at $200–$300 per week. Applicants must submit formal organization application, cover letter, resume, three personal references, three letters of recommendation. International applicants accepted; must obtain own visa, obtain own working papers, apply through a recognized agency. An in-person interview is recommended, but a telephone interview is acceptable.

Benefits and Preemployment Training Free housing, formal training, on-the-job training, travel reimbursement, and free meals with program; health insurance for interns. Preemployment training is required and includes accident prevention and safety, first aid, CPR, interpersonal skills, leadership skills.

Contact Poppy Potter/David Jones, Director of Programs/Director of Maintenance, American Youth Foundation–Camp Miniwanca for Boys, 8845 West Garfield Road, Shelby, Michigan 49455. Telephone: 616-861-2262. Fax: 616-861-5244. E-mail: wancadave@oceana.net. World Wide Web: http://www.ayf.com. Application deadline: May 31.

BAY CLIFF HEALTH CAMP
BIG BAY, MICHIGAN 49808

General Information Residential therapy camp serving 200 handicapped children ages 3–17 during one 8-week session. Established in 1934. 170-acre facility located 323 miles from Milwaukee, Wisconsin. Features: outdoor setting; pool and beachfront.

Profile of Summer Employees Total number: 147; typical ages: 19–25. 30% men; 70% women;

5% minorities; 10% high school students; 50% college students; 2% retirees; 15% local applicants. Nonsmokers preferred.

Employment Information Openings are from June 13 to September 8. Jobs available: ▶ *arts and crafts aide* at $1200 per season ▶ 1 *arts and crafts instructor* with ability to plan and implement classes for all camp units, experience preferred at $2000 per season ▶ 1 *assistant cook* with experience in the field at $225–$275 per week ▶ 1 *baker* at $2000 per season ▶ 50 *counselors* with one year of college completed (preferably in the study of special education, therapy, nursing, or human services) at $1500 per season ▶ 1 *dental assistant* with license at $1500 per season ▶ 1 *dental hygienist* with license at $2000 per season ▶ 1 *dentist* with license at $3000 per season ▶ 12 *dining room aides* at $1000 per season ▶ 1 *head cook* at $300–$350 per week ▶ 3 *instructors for hearing impaired* at $2900 per season ▶ 2 *instructors for visually impaired* at $2900 per season ▶ 3 *laundry/housekeeping personnel* at $1500 per season ▶ 2 *linen room personnel* at $1200 per season ▶ 4 *maintenance personnel* with experience at $1500 per season ▶ 1 *music therapist* with certification in field at $2600 per season ▶ 1 *nature instructor* with ability to plan and implement classes for all camp units, experience preferred at $2000 per season ▶ 3 *nurses* with RN or LPN license at $3000 per season ▶ 5 *occupational therapists* with certification in field at $3000 per season ▶ 5 *physical therapists* with certification in field at $3000 per season ▶ 1 *recreation instructor* with ability to plan and implement classes for all camp units, experience preferred at $2000 per season ▶ 8 *roving counselors* with one year of college completed (preferably in the study of special education, therapy, nursing, or human services) at $1500 per season ▶ 2 *secretaries* with good clerical skills and a pleasant, enthusiastic personality at $1400 per season ▶ 10 *speech therapists* with certification in field at $2900 per season ▶ 6 *student therapists* with formal school affiliation and ability to work with a supervising therapist at $600 per season ▶ 5 *unit leaders* with teaching experience and special education degree (preferred) at $2300 per season ▶ 4 *waterfront staff members* with WSI or lifeguard certification at $1400–$2000 per season ▶ *waterfront/pool supervisor* at $2000 per season. Applicants must submit a formal organization application, 3-6 personal references. An in-person interview is recommended, but a telephone interview is acceptable.

Benefits and Preemployment Training Free housing, free meals, and travel reimbursement. Preemployment training is required and includes accident prevention and safety, first aid, interpersonal skills.

Contact Tim Bennett, Camp Director, Bay Cliff Health Camp, 310 West Washington Street, Suite 300, Marquette, Michigan 49855. Telephone: 906-228-5770. Fax: 906-228-5769. E-mail: baycliffhc@aol.com. Application deadline: continuous.

BLACK RIVER FARM AND RANCH
5040 SHERIDAN LINE
CROSWELL, MICHIGAN 48422

General Information Residential camp serving 125 girls ages 7–15 in one- and two-week sessions with Western riding and vaulting program. Established in 1962. 150-acre facility located 80 miles from Detroit. Features: heated pool; 2 tennis courts; 65 horses; rural farm setting; 1/2 hour from Canada; 5 miles from Lake Huron and beach.

Profile of Summer Employees Total number: 50; typical ages: 16–24. 100% women; 20% high school students; 40% college students; 20% non-U.S. citizens; 20% local applicants. Nonsmokers required.

Employment Information Openings are from June 12 to August 30. Jobs available: ▶ 4–6 *kitchen staff* (minimum age 18) ▶ 1–3 *lifeguards/cabin counselors* (minimum age 18) with ARC-lifeguard or Bronze Medallion at $2000 per season ▶ 5 *riding instructors/cabin counselors* (minimum age 18) with teaching experience (preferred) at $2000 per season ▶ 1–2 *vaulting instructors/cabin counselors* (minimum age 18) with teaching experience (preferred) at $2000 per season. Applicants must submit formal organization application, resume, a total of 3 references and/or letters of recommendation. International applicants accepted; must apply through a recognized agency. An in-person interview is recommended, but a telephone interview is acceptable.

Benefits and Preemployment Training Free housing, free meals, formal training, and on-the-job training. Preemployment training is required and includes accident prevention and safety, CPR, interpersonal skills, leadership skills.

Contact Meg Graham, Director, Black River Farm and Ranch, 5040 Sheridan Line, Croswell, Michigan 48422. Telephone: 810-679-2505. Fax: 810-679-3188. E-mail: brranch@greatlakes. net. Application deadline: continuous.

BLUE LAKE FINE ARTS CAMP
300 EAST CRYSTAL LAKE ROAD
TWIN LAKE, MICHIGAN 49457

General Information Summer school of the arts serving more than 4,000 junior high and high school students over an eight-week season. Established in 1966. 1,400-acre facility located 45 miles from Grand Rapids. Features: wooded setting; on small lake; music shell seats 5,000; 3 athletic fields and 2 pools; in Manistee National Forest; over 260 cabins, structures, buildings, and facilities.

Profile of Summer Employees Total number: 450; typical ages: 21–45. 45% men; 55% women; 20% minorities; 60% college students; 5% retirees; 5% non-U.S. citizens; 15% local applicants. Nonsmokers preferred.

Employment Information Openings are from June 15 to August 30. Jobs available: ▶ 1 *assistant waterfront director* (minimum age 20) with WSI certification at $1500–$1800 per season ▶ 4 *camp nurses* with RN or LPN license at $650 per 12 day session ▶ 96 *counselors* (minimum age 18) with one year of college and interest and/or experience in the fine arts at $950–$1850 per season ▶ 1 *health lodge director* (minimum age 21) with First Responder or EMT certification; camp and administrative experience at $3000–$4000 per season ▶ 10 *health lodge staff members* (minimum age 19) with Red Cross Response to Emergencies, EMT, or First Responder certification at $1500–$2000 per season ▶ 4 *music library staff members* (minimum age 18) with clerical and/or music library experience at $6 per hour ▶ 1 *waterfront director* (minimum age 21) with WSI certification, managerial, and supervisory experience at $3500–$4300 per season. Applicants must submit a formal organization application, three personal references, audition cassette for musical openings. International applicants accepted; must obtain own visa, obtain own working papers. A telephone interview is required.

Benefits and Preemployment Training Free housing, free meals, formal training, on-the-job training, opportunity to attend seminars/workshops, and opportunities to perform in summer arts festival. Preemployment training is required and includes accident prevention and safety, first aid, CPR, interpersonal skills, leadership skills.

Contact Heidi Stansell, Camp Director, Blue Lake Fine Arts Camp, 300 East Crystal Lake Road, Twin Lake, Michigan 49457. Telephone: 616-894-1966. Fax: 616-893-5120. World Wide Web: http://www.bluelake.org. Application deadline: continuous.

BOYNE U.S.A. RESORTS, INC.
PO BOX 19, 1 BOYNE MOUNTAIN ROAD
BOYNE FALLS, MICHIGAN 49713

General Information Resorts offering an escape from the big city; with over 56 ski runs, a wealth of world class golf courses, and conference and tennis centers. 15,000-acre facility.

Employment Information Openings are from May to September. Spring break, winter break, and year-round positions also offered. Jobs available: ▶ 15 *bus staff* (minimum age 16) at $5–$6 per hour ▶ 20 *dishwashers* (minimum age 16) at $5.80 per hour ▶ 5 *front desk/reservations staff* (minimum age 18) at $6 per hour ▶ 10–20 *golf course maintenance* (minimum age 18) at $5–$6 per hour ▶ 60 *housekeepers* (minimum age 16) at $5.80 per hour ▶ 10 *line cooks* (minimum age 18) at $6–$8 per hour ▶ 15 *maintenance staff* (minimum age 18) at $5.80–$7 per hour ▶ 40 *waitstaff* (minimum age 18) at $3.86 per hour.

Benefits and Preemployment Training Formal training and on-the-job training.

Contact Gretchen Crum, Recruitment/Personnel Administrator, Boyne U.S.A. Resorts, Inc., PO Box 19, Boyne Falls, Michigan 49713. Telephone: 616-549-6048. Fax: 616-549-6896. World Wide Web: http://www.boyne.com. Application deadline: continuous.

CAMP FOWLER AT THE FOWLER CENTER
2315 HARMON LAKE ROAD
MAYVILLE, MICHIGAN 48744-9737

General Information Accessible outdoor recreation camp for children and adults with developmental disabilities promoting personal growth in those with special needs. Established in 1957. 202-acre facility located 90 miles from Detroit. Features: spring-fed lake; organic garden; equestrian stables; wheelchair-accessible nature trails; small animal barn; sports fields.

Profile of Summer Employees Total number: 75; typical ages: 18–30. 45% men; 55% women; 12% minorities; 3% high school students; 85% college students; 5% retirees; 5% non-U.S. citizens; 15% local applicants. Nonsmokers preferred.

Employment Information Openings are from May 15 to October 31. Spring break, winter break, and year-round positions also offered. Jobs available: ▶ 15–20 *counselors* must be highly motivated to work with special needs campers (will train) at $1800–$2300 per season ▶ 1 *creative arts instructor* with experience or desire to work with special needs campers at $1800–$2300 per season ▶ *horseback riding instructors* with NARHA or CHA certification and experience or desire to work with special needs campers at $1800–$2300 per season ▶ 1 *organic garden and barn instructor* with gardening experience and experience or desire to work with special needs campers at $1800–$2300 per season ▶ 1 *outdoor education instructor* with camping experience and desire to work with special needs campers at $1800–$2300 per season ▶ 1 *sports and recreation instructor* with experience or desire to work with special needs campers at $1800–$2300 per season ▶ *waterfront staff members* with lifeguard and WSI certification and experience or desire to work with special needs campers at $1800–$2300 per season. Applicants must submit formal organization application, three letters of recommendation, criminal background check. International applicants accepted; must apply through a recognized agency. An in-person interview is recommended, but a telephone interview is acceptable.

Benefits and Preemployment Training Free housing, free meals, formal training, possible full-time employment, health insurance, on-the-job training, and opportunity to attend seminars/workshops. Preemployment training is required and includes accident prevention and safety, first aid, CPR, interpersonal skills, leadership skills, direct care.

Contact Naomi Kranz, Assistant Camp Director, Camp Fowler at The Fowler Center, 2315 Harmon Lake Road, Mayville, Michigan 48744-9737. Telephone: 517-673-2050. Fax: 517-673-6355. E-mail: camp@thefowlercenter.org. World Wide Web: http://www.thefowlercenter.com. Application deadline: continuous.

CAMP LOOKOUT
4410 LOOKOUT ROAD
FRANKFORT, MICHIGAN 49635

General Information Small, coeducational, loosely-structured residential camp that is noncompetitive and nonsectarian, emphasizing individual growth. Camp Lookout has a 10-acre island. Established in 1995. 10-acre facility located 30 miles from Traverse City. Features: large inland lake; proximity to National Lakeshore; Lake Michigan (sand dunes and a beach accessible only by boat).

Profile of Summer Employees Total number: 45; typical ages: 19–28. 5% minorities; 20% high school students; 65% college students; 5% retirees; 15% non-U.S. citizens; 5% local applicants. Nonsmokers preferred.

Employment Information Openings are from June 12 to August 16. Jobs available: ▶ 1 *art specialist* (minimum age 19) with ability to organize art program (teacher preferred) at $1000–$2000 per season ▶ 1 *assistant director/program director* with ability to conduct programs for small and large groups at $1500–$3000 per season ▶ 2–3 *cooks* with experience at $1200–$3000 per season ▶ 8 *counselors* (minimum age 19) with lifesaving training and art, sailing, trip, and sports skills at $900–$1500 per season ▶ 5 *junior counselors (high school students)* (minimum age 17) at $500–$700 per season ▶ 2 *nurses* with RN, LPN, or EMT license at $1200–$2200 per season ▶ 1 *riding instructor* (minimum age 19) with experience and ability to manage Western-style riding program at $950–$1600 per season ▶ 3 *sailing/windsurfing instructors* (minimum age 19) with lifesaving training and experience in the field at $950–$1600 per season ▶ *sports specialist* with experience in competitive and noncompetitive sports and games at $1000–$1500 per season ▶ 1 *stable helper* (minimum age 19) at $60–$150 per week ▶ 1 *trip coordinator* (minimum age 19) with ability to organize wilderness camping trips, train staff, and maintain bicycles, tents, and camping euipment at $950–$2300 per season ▶ 2 *waterfront directors* with current LGT and WSI certification and experience at $1200–$2700 per season. Applicants must submit formal organization application, resume. International applicants accepted; must apply through a recognized agency. An in-person interview is recommended, but a telephone interview is acceptable.

Benefits and Preemployment Training Free housing, free meals, and formal training. Preemployment training is required and includes accident prevention and safety, first aid, CPR, interpersonal skills, leadership skills.

Contact David B. Reid, Director, Camp Lookout, 2766 South Shore Road East, Frankfort, Michigan 49635. Telephone: 616-352-7589. Fax: 616-352-6609. E-mail: xtalaire@benzie.com. Application deadline: continuous.

CAMP MAAS
4361 PERRYVILLE ROAD
ORTONVILLE, MICHIGAN 48462

General Information Residential camp and outdoor travel program to Alaska and western United States. Established in 1902. 1,500-acre facility located 45 miles from Detroit. Features: wooded setting; lake for all water sports; 6 tennis courts; horseback riding; 2 complete athletic fields and sports facilities; outdoor camping.

Profile of Summer Employees Total number: 400; typical ages: 18–25. 50% men; 50% women; 10% high school students; 80% college students; 40% non-U.S. citizens; 50% local applicants. Nonsmokers preferred.

Employment Information Openings are from June 17 to August 15. Jobs available: ▶ *counselors* at $1000–$1500 per season ▶ *head nurse* at $3000–$5000 per season ▶ *song leader* at $2000–$3000 per season ▶ *specialists in all areas* at $1000–$1500 per season ▶ *supervisors in all areas* at $2000–$3500 per season. Applicants must submit formal organization application, three letters of recommendation. International applicants accepted; must apply through a recognized agency. An in-person interview is recommended, but a telephone interview is acceptable.

Benefits and Preemployment Training Free housing and free meals. Preemployment training is required and includes first aid, CPR, interpersonal skills, leadership skills.

Contact Harvey Finkelberg, Executive Director, Camp Maas, 6600 West Maple Road, Suite 301, West Bloomfield, Michigan 48322. Telephone: 248-661-0600. Fax: 248-661-1725. E-mail: tamarackcamps@ix.netcom.com. World Wide Web: http://www.tamarackcamps.com. Application deadline: continuous.

CAMP MAPLEHURST
12055 WARING ROAD
KEWADIN, MICHIGAN 49648

General Information Residential camp serving 100 campers per session. Wide variety of activities offered. Community spirit and development of decision-making abilities is encouraged among campers. Established in 1955. 400-acre facility located 18 miles from Traverse City. Features: private, freshwater lake; views of 7 lakes; wooded setting with open fields; 3 tennis courts; 2 waterfronts; cabins and main lodge.

Profile of Summer Employees Total number: 40; typical ages: 18–50. 50% men; 50% women; 5% high school students; 70% college students; 5% retirees; 10% non-U.S. citizens. Nonsmokers preferred.

Employment Information Openings are from June 15 to August 18. Jobs available: ▶ 2 *cooks* (minimum age 18) with food handler's card at $150–$350 per week ▶ 1 *nurse* (minimum age 21) with RN; experience with children preferred at $150–$300 per week ▶ 1 *sailing instructor* (minimum age 19) at $900–$1500 per season ▶ 1 *scuba instructor* (minimum age 21) with teaching experience and instructor certification preferred at $1000–$1600 per season ▶ 4 *sports* *instructors* (minimum age 18) at $900–$1500 per season ▶ 2 *swimming instructors* (minimum age 19) with WSI and lifeguard certification at $1000–$1600 per season ▶ 1 *tennis instructor* (minimum age 19) at $900–$1500 per season. Applicants must submit formal organization application, three letters of recommendation. International applicants accepted; must apply through a recognized agency. An in-person interview is recommended, but a telephone interview is acceptable.

Benefits and Preemployment Training Free housing, free meals, formal training, and on-the-job training. Preemployment training is required and includes accident prevention and safety, first aid, CPR, interpersonal skills, leadership skills.

Contact Laurence Cohn, Director, Camp Maplehurst, 1455 Quarton Road, Birmingham, Michigan 48009. Telephone: 248-647-2646. Fax: 248-647-6716. E-mail: campmaple@aol.com. World Wide Web: http://www.campmaplehurst.com. Application deadline: continuous.

CEDAR LODGE
47138 52ND STREET
LAWRENCE, MICHIGAN 49064

General Information Residential coeducational camp serving 60 campers in a relaxed, loosely structured program with a special emphasis on horsemanship from the beginner to the show jumper. 160-acre facility located 105 miles from Chicago, Illinois.

Profile of Summer Employees Typical age: 23. 25% men; 75% women; 95% college students; 5% retirees; 60% non-U.S. citizens; 5% local applicants.

Employment Information Openings are from June to August. Jobs available: ▶ 1 *arts and crafts instructor* at $1000–$1200 per season ▶ 1 *biking/trip instructor* at $1000–$1200 per season ▶ *kitchen assistants* at $1200–$1500 per season ▶ 1 *music/dance/drama instructor* at $1000–$1200 per season ▶ *riding instructors* with English riding experience at $1000–$1500 per season ▶ 1 *sports instructor* at $1000–$1200 per season ▶ *swimming instructors* with swimming experience at $1000–$1500 per season. Applicants must submit a formal organization application.

Benefits and Preemployment Training Free housing, free meals, formal training, and on-the-job training. Preemployment training is required and includes first aid, CPR.

Contact Amy Edwards, Program Director, Cedar Lodge, PO Box 218, Lawrence, Michigan 49064. Telephone: 616-674-8071. Fax: 616-674-3143. E-mail: eddy@cedarlodge.com. Application deadline: continuous.

CIRCLE PINES CENTER SUMMER CAMP
8650 MULLEN ROAD
DELTON, MICHIGAN 49046

General Information A small, coeducational, residential, multicultural camp for children ages 8–17 promoting peace, cooperation, and social justice. Established in 1938. 284-acre facility located 30 miles from Kalamazoo. Features: springfed lake; woodlands; meadows; organic garden; pre-Civil War farmhouse.

Profile of Summer Employees Total number: 24. 45% men; 55% women; 15% minorities; 40% college students; 5% retirees; 5% non-U.S. citizens; 5% local applicants. Nonsmokers preferred.

Employment Information Openings are from June 20 to August 22. Jobs available: ▶ 4 *cooks* with experience working with whole foods, large groups, and children at $700–$800 per season ▶ 14 *counselors* with experience with children, skills in leading activities at $700–$800 per season ▶ 1 *health officer* with RN, LPN, or EMT license at $1000–$1500 per season ▶ 1 *kitchen manager* (minimum age 18) with menu planning, supervisory, inventory and purchasing experience at $900–$1000 per season ▶ 1 *maintenance staff member* must have manintenance skills and ability to work with children at $500–$600 per season ▶ 1 *office manager* with office experience at $500–$600 per season ▶ 1 *waterfront assistant* with CPR certificate plus lifeguard and first aid training at $900–$1000 per season ▶ 1 *waterfront director* with WSI, CPR, and lifeguard training/certification at $1000–$1200 per season. Applicants must submit formal organization application, three personal references. International applicants accepted; must obtain own visa, obtain own working papers, apply through a recognized agency. An in-person interview is recommended, but a telephone interview is acceptable.

Benefits and Preemployment Training Free housing, free meals, and on-the-job training. Preemployment training is required and includes accident prevention and safety, interpersonal skills, leadership skills.

Contact Traci Furman, Camp Director, Circle Pines Center Summer Camp, 8650 Mullen Road, Delton, Michigan 49046. Telephone: 616-623-5555. Fax: 616-623-9054. E-mail: circle@net-link. net. World Wide Web: http://www.circlepinescenter.org. Application deadline: continuous.

CRYSTALAIRE CAMP
2768 SOUTH SHORE ROAD EAST
FRANKFORT, MICHIGAN 49635

General Information Small, coeducational, loosely-structured residential camp that is noncompetitive and nonsectarian, emphasizing individual growth. Established in 1924. 145-acre facility located 30 miles from Traverse City. Features: large inland lake; proximity to National Lakeshore; Lake Michigan (sand dunes and beach accessible only by boat).

Profile of Summer Employees Total number: 45; typical ages: 19–28. 50% men; 50% women; 5% minorities; 20% high school students; 65% college students; 5% retirees; 15% non-U.S. citizens; 5% local applicants. Nonsmokers preferred.

Employment Information Openings are from June 12 to August 16. Jobs available: ▶ 1 *art specialist* (minimum age 19) with ability to organize art program (teacher preferred) at $1000–$2000 per season ▶ 1 *assistant director/program director* with ability to conduct programs for small and large groups at $1500–$3000 per season ▶ 2–3 *cooks* with experience at $1200–$3000 per season ▶ 14 *counselors* (minimum age 19) with lifesaving training; and art, sailing, trip, and sports skills at $900–$1500 per season ▶ 5 *junior counselors (high school students)* (minimum age 17) at $500–$700 per season ▶ 2 *nurses* with RN, LPN, or EMT license at $1200–$2200 per season ▶ 1 *riding instructor* (minimum age 19) with experience and ability to manage Western-style riding program at $950–$1600 per season ▶ 3 *sailing/windsurfing instructors* (minimum age 19) with lifesaving training and experience in the field at $950–$1600 per season ▶ *sports specialist* with experience in competitive and noncompetitive sports and games at $1000–$1500 per season ▶ 1 *stable helper* (minimum age 19) at $60–$150 per week ▶ 1 *trip coordinator* (minimum age 19) with ability to organize wilderness camping trips, train staff, and maintain bicycles, tents, and camping equipment at $950–$2300 per season ▶ 2 *waterfront directors* with current LGT and WSI certification and experience at $1200–$2700 per season. Applicants must submit formal organization application, resume. International applicants accepted; must apply through a recognized agency. An in-person interview is recommended, but a telephone interview is acceptable.

Benefits and Preemployment Training Free housing, free meals, and formal training. Preemployment training is required and includes accident prevention and safety, first aid, CPR, interpersonal skills, leadership skills.

Contact David B. Reid, Director, Crystalaire Camp, 2768 South Shore Road East, Frankfort, Michigan 49635. Telephone: 616-352-7589. Fax: 616-352-6609. E-mail: xtalaire@benzie.com. Application deadline: continuous.

CYO BOYS CAMP
1295 LAKESHORE ROAD
CARSONVILLE, MICHIGAN 48419

General Information CYO summer camps are open to boys ages 7½–16. The Pioneer Program is especially designed to meet the needs of experienced campers ages 14–16. Special programs for developmentally disabled youth are also available. Established in 1946. 70-acre facility located 90 miles from Detroit. Features: climbing wall; ropes course; lakeside setting; acres of woods and nature trails.

Profile of Summer Employees Total number: 40; typical ages: 17–25. 90% men; 10% women; 25% minorities; 45% high school students; 50% college students; 5% retirees.

Employment Information Openings are from June 23 to August 7. Jobs available: ▶ *archery* *director* (minimum age 18) at $800–$1000 per season ▶ *arts and crafts director* (minimum age 18) at $800–$1000 per season ▶ *business manager* (minimum age 20) with bookkeeping skills at $1000–$1200 per season ▶ 10–15 *counselors-in-training* (minimum age 17) at $650 per season ▶ *group counselors/assistants* (minimum age 18) at $800–$1000 per season ▶ *nurse or health officer* (minimum age 21) with RN, LPN, or EMT with CPR training at $1400–$1600 per season ▶ *waterfront director/assistant* (minimum age 18) with WSI certification at $1000–$1200 per season. Applicants must submit formal organization application, three personal references. International applicants accepted; must obtain own visa, obtain own working papers, apply through a recognized agency. An in-person interview is recommended, but a telephone interview is acceptable.

Benefits and Preemployment Training Free housing, free meals, and on-the-job training. Preemployment training is required and includes accident prevention and safety, first aid, CPR, interpersonal skills, leadership skills.

Contact Steve Johnson, Camp Service Director, CYO Boys Camp, 305 Michigan Avenue, 9th Floor, Detroit, Michigan 48266. Telephone: 313-963-9758. Fax: 313-963-7179. E-mail: steve@ cyocamps.org. World Wide Web: http://www.cyocamps.org. Application deadline: continuous.

CYO GIRLS CAMP
1564 LAKESHORE ROAD
PORT SANILAC, MICHIGAN 48469

General Information CYO summer camps are open to girls ages 7½–16. The Pioneer Program is especially designed to meet the needs of experienced campers ages 14–16. Special programs for developmentally disabled youth are also available. Established in 1946. 30-acre facility located 90 miles from Detroit. Features: location on the shore of Lake Huron; with long sandy beaches; acres of woods and nature trails; climbing wall.

Profile of Summer Employees Total number: 40; typical ages: 17–25. 10% men; 90% women; 25% minorities; 40% high school students; 50% college students; 10% local applicants.

Employment Information Openings are from June 23 to August 7. Jobs available: ▶ 1 *archery director* (minimum age 21) at $800–$1000 per season ▶ 1 *arts and crafts director* (minimum age 18) at $800–$900 per season ▶ 1 *business manager* (minimum age 20) with bookkeeping skills at $1000–$1200 per season ▶ 10–15 *counselors-in-training* (minimum age 17) at $650 per season ▶ 10 *group counselors/assistants* (minimum age 18) at $800–$1400 per season ▶ *nurse or health officer* (minimum age 21) with RN, LPN, EMT, or advanced first aid with CPR at $1400–$1600 per season ▶ 2 *waterfront directors/assistants* (minimum age 18) with WSI certification at $1000–$1200 per season. Applicants must submit a formal organization application, three personal references. International applicants accepted; must obtain own visa, obtain own working papers. An in-person interview is recommended, but a telephone interview is acceptable.

Benefits and Preemployment Training Free housing, free meals, health insurance, and on-the-job training. Preemployment training is required and includes accident prevention and safety, first aid, CPR, interpersonal skills, leadership skills.

Contact Steve Johnson, Camp Service Director, CYO Girls Camp, 305 Michigan Avenue, 9th Floor, Detroit, Michigan 48226. Telephone: 313-963-9758. Fax: 313-963-7179. E-mail: steve@ cyocamps.org. World Wide Web: http://www.cyocamps.org. Application deadline: continuous.

DOUBLE JJ RESORT
PO BOX 94
ROTHBURY, MICHIGAN 49452

General Information Full service resort ranch with exclusive programming for adults, families, and children. Established in 1937. 1,000-acre facility located 20 miles from Muskegon. Features: horseback riding; championship 18-hole golf course; year-round activities; pools, spas, water slide; cabins, hotel and condominiums; snow tubing/dogsledding.

Profile of Summer Employees Total number: 250; typical ages: 18–30. 50% men; 50% women; 2% minorities; 5% high school students; 50% college students; 5% retirees; 8% non-U.S. citizens; 30% local applicants.

Employment Information Openings are from January 1 to December 31. Year-round positions also offered. Jobs available: ▶ 15 *children's counselors* (minimum age 18) at $150 per week ▶ 6 *cooks* (minimum age 18) with experience in the field at $200–$350 per week ▶ 10 *day care staff* (minimum age 18) at $150 per week ▶ 3 *dining room managers* (minimum age 18) with waiter/waitressing experience at $150–$220 per week ▶ 1 *disc jockey* (minimum age 18) with experience at $150–$200 per week ▶ 4 *dishwashers* (minimum age 18) at $150 per week ▶ 10 *golf course groundskeepers* (minimum age 18) at $150–$200 per week ▶ 10 *golf course personnel* (minimum age 18) at $150 per week ▶ 15 *housekeepers* (minimum age 18) at $150–$200 per week ▶ 20 *lawn maintenance personnel* (minimum age 18) at $130–$200 per week ▶ 12 *lifeguards* (minimum age 18) with American Red Cross or Ellis lifeguard certification at $150–$200 per week ▶ 15 *office staff members* (minimum age 18) with computer experience and ability to answer phones and make reservations at $150 per week ▶ 10 *prep cooks/bakers* (minimum age 18) with experience at $150–$200 per week ▶ 12 *pro shop/gift shop staff members* (minimum age 18) at $150 per week ▶ 10 *snack bar/bar staff members* (minimum age 18) at $130 per week ▶ 9 *talented entertainers (guitarists, singers, pianists, and musicians)* (minimum age 18) with outgoing personality at $150–$200 per week ▶ 20 *waiters/waitresses* (minimum age 18) at $130 per week ▶ 10 *wranglers* (minimum age 18) with experience at $150–$220 per week. Applicants must submit formal organization application. International applicants accepted; must apply through a recognized agency. An in-person interview is recommended, but a telephone interview is acceptable.

Benefits and Preemployment Training Free housing, free meals, possible full-time employment, on-the-job training, and use of all resort ammenities. Preemployment training is required and includes resort-wide orientation to familiarize employees with facility, procedures, and job description.

Contact Jeanne Robinet, Human Resources, Double JJ Resort, PO Box 94, Rothbury, Michigan 49452. Telephone: 616-894-4444. Fax: 616-893-5355. E-mail: info@doublejj.com. World Wide Web: http://www.doublejj.com. Application deadline: continuous.

EL RANCHO STEVENS
2332 EAST DIXON LAKE ROAD
GAYLORD, MICHIGAN 49735

General Information Family resort serving 80 people weekly, specializing in horses, waterskiing, and children's programs. Established in 1948. 1,000-acre facility located 3 miles from Gaylord. Features: freshwater lake; wooded setting; tennis; archery; trail rides; water sports.

Profile of Summer Employees Total number: 35; typical ages: 18–24. 20% men; 80% women; 10% minorities; 10% high school students; 75% college students; 10% retirees; 50% non-U.S. citizens; 25% local applicants. Nonsmokers preferred.

Employment Information Openings are from June 15 to September 7. Jobs available: ▶ 2 *bartenders/barmaids* at $170–$200 per week ▶ 3 *children's counselors* at $170–$200 per week ▶ 2 *cooks* (minimum age 18) with experience in the field at $200–$250 per week ▶ 3 *housekeepers* at $170–$200 per week ▶ 2 *kitchen helpers* at $170–$200 per week ▶ 2 *office personnel* with good phone, typing, and bookkeeping skills at $170–$200 per week ▶ 1 *recreational director* with ability to work with people of all ages at $170–$200 per week ▶ 2 *riding instructors/trail guides* (minimum age 18) with experience in the field at $170–$200 per week ▶ 5 *waitresses/waiters* at $170–$200 per week ▶ 1 *waterskiing instructor/boat driver* (minimum age 18) with knowledge of water safety rules at $170–$200 per week. Applicants must submit formal organization application, personal reference. International applicants accepted; must apply through a recognized agency. A telephone interview is required.

Benefits and Preemployment Training Free housing, free meals, and on-the-job training. Preemployment training is required and includes accident prevention and safety.

Contact Cyndie Cole, Assistant Manager, El Rancho Stevens, PO Box 495, Gaylord, Michigan 49734. Telephone: 517-732-5090. E-mail: info@elranchostevens. World Wide Web: http://www.elranchostevens.com. Application deadline: continuous.

THE ISLAND HOUSE HOTEL
1 MAIN STREET
MACKINAC ISLAND, MICHIGAN 49757

General Information Seasonal Resort with shops, two restaurants, bar, and sandwich shop. Established in 1852. Located 100 miles from Traverse City. Features: the Great Lakes; historical sites; state park; premier mountain biking; outstanding hiking; dormitory style housing.

Profile of Summer Employees Total number: 115; typical ages: 18–35. 40% men; 60% women; 25% minorities; 1% high school students; 90% college students; 25% non-U.S. citizens; 10% local applicants.

Employment Information Openings are from May 1 to November 1. Jobs available: ▶ 10 *bellstaff* (minimum age 18) at $5 per hour plus gratuities ▶ 10 *front desk/ reservationists* (minimum age 18) at $5.75 per hour ▶ 10 *prep cooks* (minimum age 18) at $5.50 per hour ▶ 20 *sales clerks* (minimum age 18) at $6 per hour ▶ 20 *waitstaff* (minimum age 18) at $2.65 per hour plus gratuities. Applicants must submit formal organization application, resume and cover letter acceptable. International applicants accepted; must obtain own visa, apply through a recognized agency. A telephone interview is required.

Benefits and Preemployment Training Housing at a cost, meals at a cost, on-the-job training, and $.50 per hour bonus for each hour worked payed at end of contract.

Contact Ryan Macy, Human Resources Manager, The Island House Hotel, 31181 Kendall Drive, Fraser, Michigan 48206. Telephone: 810-293-0600. Fax: 810-293-4850. E-mail: ryan@ theislandhouse.com. World Wide Web: http://www.theislandhouse.com. Application deadline: continuous.

LAKE OF THE WOODS CAMP FOR GIRLS AND GREENWOODS CAMP FOR BOYS
47½ STREET
DECATUR, MICHIGAN 49045

General Information Private residential summer camp for children with a program that runs 4 to 8 weeks. Established in 1935. 60-acre facility located 35 miles from Kalamazoo. Features: natural spring-fed lake; wooded setting; modern cabins and facilities; more than 40 land and water activities; tennis courts; driving range.

Profile of Summer Employees Total number: 70; typical age: 21. 50% men; 50% women; 2% minorities; 88% college students; 1% retirees; 10% non-U.S. citizens. Nonsmokers required.

Employment Information Openings are from June 14 to August 15. Jobs available: ▶ *archery instructor* (minimum age 19) at $1400 per season ▶ 2 *arts and crafts instructors* (minimum age 19) at $1400 per season ▶ *ceramics instructor* (minimum age 19) at $1400 per season ▶ 3 *climbing wall instructor* (minimum age 21) at $1400 ▶ 1 *computer instructor* (minimum age 19) with Basic, Logo, and PASCAL experience (preferred) at $1400 per season ▶ 1 *dance/aerobics instructor* (minimum age 19) at $1400 per season ▶ 1 *dramatics instructor* (minimum age 19) at $1400 per season ▶ 1 *golf instructor* (minimum age 19) at $1400 per season ▶ 1 *gymnastics instructor* (minimum age 19) at $1400 per season ▶ *kitchen personnel (cooks and assistants)* (minimum age 19) at $175–$500 per week ▶ *model rocketry instructor* (minimum age 19) at $1400 per season ▶ 3 *nurses* (minimum age 22) with RN license (any state) at $2500 per season ▶ 2 *office persons* (minimum age 19) with experience at $1300 per season ▶ 3 *riding instructors* (minimum age 19) at $1500 per season ▶ *riflery instructor* (minimum age 19) with LGT certification at $1400 per season ▶ *rowing/canoe instructor* (minimum age 19) with LGT certification at $1400 per season ▶ 3 *sailing instructors* (minimum age 19) with LGT certification at $1400 per season ▶ 2 *sports coaches* (minimum age 19) at $1400 per season ▶ 8 *swimming instructors* (minimum age 19) with lifeguard training or WSI certification at $1500 per season ▶ 2 *tennis instructors* (minimum age 19) at $1400 per season ▶ 7 *waterskiing instructors* (minimum age 19) with boat driving experience and LGT certification at $1400 per season ▶ 2 *windsufing instructor* (minimum age 19) at $1400. Applicants must submit formal organization application, three personal references. International applicants accepted; must apply through a recognized agency. A telephone interview is required.

Benefits and Preemployment Training Free housing, free meals, formal training, on-the-job training, and travel reimbursement. Preemployment training is required and includes accident prevention and safety, first aid, CPR, interpersonal skills, leadership skills.

Contact Dayna Hardin, Owner/Director, Lake of the Woods Camp for Girls and Greenwoods Camp for Boys, 22936 North 91st Place, Scottsdale, Arizona 85255. Telephone: 602-502-6014. Fax: 602-515-3698. E-mail: lwcgwc@aol.com. World Wide Web: http://www.campchannel.com/lwcgwc. Application deadline: continuous.

MCGAW YMCA CAMP ECHO AND THE OUTDOOR DISCOVERY CENTER
2000 WEST 32ND STREET
FREMONT, MICHIGAN 49412

General Information Residential coeducational camp serving 250 youngsters in two-week sessions. Emphasis is on building self-esteem through YMCA principles. Outdoor education center operates during nonsummer months for Michigan schools and interest groups. Established in 1896. 460-acre facility located 40 miles from Grand Rapids. Features: freshwater lake; wooded setting; low and high ropes course; numerous water sports; numerous land sports.

Profile of Summer Employees Total number: 100; typical ages: 18–60. 50% men; 50% women; 10% minorities; 25% high school students; 75% college students; 5% non-U.S. citizens; 75% local applicants. Nonsmokers required.

Employment Information Openings are from April 15 to October 15. Jobs available: ▶ 10 *adventure trip leaders* (minimum age 21) with lifeguard, wilderness first aid, and CPR certification at $130–$200 per week ▶ 1 *aquatic director* with first aid, CPR, and Lifeguard Instructor certification, or WSI and LG at $150–$175 per week ▶ 1 *arts and crafts director* with standard first aid and CPR certification at $120–$140 per week ▶ 1 *assistant wrangler* (minimum age 18) with standard first aid and CPR certification at $120–$140 per week ▶ 3 *cooks* (minimum age 18) with CPR certification and experience with large groups at $100–$300 per week ▶ *head trip guide* (minimum age 21) with CPR, wilderness first aid, and LG certification; management experience and experience leading adventure trips at $200–$225 per week ▶ 5 *health officers* (minimum age 21) with MD, RN, EMT or paramedic license, CPR and standard first aid certification at $250–$275 per week ▶ 1 *office manager* with first aid and CPR certification at $130–$150 per week ▶ 18 *outdoor education staff members* (minimum age 18) with CPR/first aid at $120–$150 per week ▶ 1 *riflery area head* (minimum age 21) with CPR and first aid certifications; experience with 22 range at $120–$140 per week ▶ 1 *ropes course director* (minimum age 21) with CPR, first aid, and extensive experience in supervising high and low ropes course at $175–$235 per week ▶ 3 *sailing/canoeing/waterskiing directors* (minimum age 18) with standard first aid, CPR, and lifeguard certification at $120–$140 per week ▶ 18 *senior counselors* with standard first aid, LG, and CPR certification at $115–$125 per week ▶ 1 *social worker* (minimum age 21) with MSW; CPR and first aid certifications at $200 per week ▶ 1 *van driver* (minimum age 21) with standard first aid and CPR certification, US driver's license, and good driving record at $140–$175 per week ▶ 2 *wilderness site leaders* (minimum age 21) with lifeguard, first aid, and CPR certification at $130–$150 per week ▶ 1 *wrangler* (minimum age 21) with first aid and CPR certification at $140–$150 per week. Applicants must submit a formal organization application, three personal references. International applicants accepted; must obtain own visa, obtain own working papers. An in-person interview is recommended, but a telephone interview is acceptable.

Benefits and Preemployment Training Free housing, free meals, on-the-job training, and opportunity to attend seminars/workshops. Preemployment training is required and includes accident prevention and safety, interpersonal skills, leadership skills.

Contact Debbie Guy, Director, McGaw YMCA Camp Echo and the Outdoor Discovery Center, 1000 Grove Street, Evanston, Illinois 60201. Telephone: 847-475-7400. Fax: 847-475-7959. E-mail: dlkguy@juno.com. Application deadline: continuous.

MICHIGAN TECHNOLOGICAL UNIVERSITY SUMMER YOUTH PROGRAM
1400 TOWNSEND DRIVE
HOUGHTON, MICHIGAN 49931

General Information Summer program for students ages 12–18 in 70 explorations designed to introduce students to careers and knowledge (theater, engineering, pottery, and more). Established in 1973. 250 miles from Green Bay. Features: Lake Superior location; waterfalls; old growth forests; biking/hiking paths; Isle Royale; all university facilities.

Profile of Summer Employees Total number: 120; typical ages: 18–28. 50% men; 50% women; 20% minorities; 97% college students; 1% retirees; 10% local applicants. Nonsmokers preferred.

Employment Information Openings are from June 8 to August 31. Jobs available: ▶ *counselors* (minimum age 18) at $230 per week ▶ *teaching assistants* (minimum age 18) at $190 per week. Applicants must submit formal organization application. International applicants accepted; must obtain own visa, obtain own working papers, apply through a recognized agency. An in-person interview is recommended, but a telephone interview is acceptable.

Benefits and Preemployment Training Free housing, free meals, and on-the-job training. Preemployment training is required and includes accident prevention and safety, first aid, interpersonal skills, leadership skills.

Contact Cheryl Gherna, Youth Programs Secretary, Michigan Technological University Summer Youth Program, Michigan Technological University, 1400 Townsend Drive, Houghton, Michigan 49931. Telephone: 906-487-2219. Fax: 906-487-3101. E-mail: yp@mtu.edu. World Wide Web: http://www.yth.mtu.edu/syp.

SILVER MINE
276 MAIN STREET
MACKINAC ISLAND, MICHIGAN 49757

General Information Retail gift shop located on summer resort Mackinac Island, Michigan; open May through October. Established in 1945. near Detroit. Features: no automobiles-transportation by foot, bicycles, or horse and buggy; 85% of Mackinac Island is state park; Victorian summer homes; located between Michigan's 2 peninsulas in the Straits of Mackinac; hiking, biking, rollerblading, and many other outdoor interests.

Profile of Summer Employees Total number: 6; typical ages: 18–25. 100% women; 100% college students. Nonsmokers preferred.

Employment Information Openings are from May 1 to November 1. Jobs available: ▶ 6–8 *sales clerks* (minimum age 18) must be able to work well with the public, knowledge of cash register and making change helpful, light lifting, and able to be on feet for 8-hour shift at $6.50 per hour. Applicants must submit formal organization application, cover letter, resume, three personal references, letter of recommendation. International applicants accepted; must apply through a recognized agency. A telephone interview is required.

Benefits and Preemployment Training Housing at a cost.

Contact C. Arbib, Silver Mine, PO Box 276, Mackinac Island, Michigan 49757. E-mail: thesilvermine@yahoo.com. Application deadline: continuous.

THE SOUTHWESTERN COMPANY, MICHIGAN
See The Southwestern Company, Tennessee on page 284 for complete description.

STUDENT CONSERVATION ASSOCIATION (SCA), MICHIGAN
See Student Conservation Association (SCA), New Hampshire on page 193 for complete description.

SUMMER DISCOVERY AT MICHIGAN
UNIVERSITY OF MICHIGAN
ANN ARBOR, MICHIGAN 48109

General Information Precollege enrichment program for high school students at University of Michigan. Established in 1991. near Detroit. Features: sport facilities; beaches; mountains; lakes; major cities nearby; college towns.

Profile of Summer Employees Total number: 30; typical ages: 21–35. 10% minorities; 60% college students. Nonsmokers required.

Employment Information Openings are from June 20 to August 25. Jobs available: ▶ 30 *resident counselors* (minimum age 21) with experience working with high school students/children at $150–$400 per week. Applicants must submit a formal organization application, resume, three personal references. International applicants accepted; must obtain own visa, obtain own working papers. An in-person interview is required.

Benefits and Preemployment Training Free housing, free meals, possible full-time employment, on-the-job training, and travel reimbursement. Preemployment training is required and includes accident prevention and safety, CPR, leadership skills.

Contact Jason Walley, Admissions Director, Summer Discovery at Michigan, 1326 Old Northern Boulevard, Roslyn, New York 11576. Telephone: 516-621-3939. Fax: 516-625-3438. E-mail: staff@summerfun.com. World Wide Web: http://www.summerfun.com. Application deadline: continuous.

ACE COMPUTER CAMP–MINNESOTA
See ACE Computer Camp–Washington on page 307 for complete description.

AUDUBON CENTER OF THE NORTH WOODS
PO BOX 530
SANDSTONE, MINNESOTA 55072

General Information Environmental education center that stresses the positive relationship between people and nature. Programs combine natural history, outdoor skills, and ethics and serve youth, college, and adult audiences. Established in 1968. 535-acre facility located 100 miles from Minneapolis. Features: freshwater lake; red pine forest; maple forest; high ropes challenge course; beaver pond and stream; raptor center.

Profile of Summer Employees Total number: 14; typical ages: 20–28. 50% men; 50% women; 10% minorities; 90% college students; 20% non-U.S. citizens; 10% local applicants. Nonsmokers preferred.

Employment Information Openings are from June 1 to August 30. Year-round positions also offered. Jobs available: ▶ 1 *administrative staff member* (minimum age 20) at $250 per month ▶ 4 *environmental education staff members* (minimum age 20) with WSI and first aid certification at $250–$500 per month ▶ 1 *land management staff member* (minimum age 20) at $250 per month ▶ 1–2 *raptor rehabilitation/education staff members* (minimum age 20) at $200–$250 per month. Applicants must submit three letters of recommendation. International applicants accepted; must obtain own visa. An in-person interview is recommended, but a telephone interview is acceptable.

Benefits and Preemployment Training Free housing, free meals, and on-the-job training. Preemployment training is required and includes accident prevention and safety, first aid, CPR, interpersonal skills, leadership skills.

Contact Intern Coordinator, Audubon Center of the North Woods, PO Box 530, Sandstone, Minnesota 55072. Telephone: 320-245-2648. Fax: 320-245-5272. E-mail: audubon1@ecenet. com. World Wide Web: http://www.audubon-center.com. Application deadline: continuous.

CAMP BUCKSKIN
PO BOX 389
ELY, MINNESOTA 55731

General Information Residential camp offering two 32-day sessions for youths with academic and/or social skills difficulties (learning disabilities, Attention Deficit Disorder, and related difficulties). Established in 1959. 165-acre facility located 80 miles from Duluth. Features: freshwater lake; wooded setting; library; hiking trails; cabins; dining hall.

Profile of Summer Employees Total number: 70; typical ages: 19–25. 50% men; 50% women; 5% minorities; 10% high school students; 80% college students; 10% non-U.S. citizens; 10% local applicants. Nonsmokers preferred.

Employment Information Openings are from June 1 to August 25. Jobs available: ▶ 3 *counselors/archery instructors* with experience and certification from such organizations as the National Archery Association at $1350–$1850 per season ▶ 6 *counselors/arts and crafts instructors* with creativity and ability to teach at $1350–$1800 per season ▶ 10 *counselors/canoeing instructors* with lifeguard training, standard first aid, and CPR (preferred) at $1350–$1850 per season ▶ 6 *counselors/nature and environment instructors* with experience and certification in programs such as NOLS and Nature Quest (preferred) at $1350–$1850 per season ▶ 3 *counselors/ riflery instructors* with gun and range safety training with the National Rifle Association, military, or similar agency (preferred) at $1350–$1850 per season ▶ 8 *counselors/swimming instructors* (minimum age 19) with WSI certification, lifeguard training, standard first aid, and CPR (preferred) at $1350–$1850 per season ▶ 5 *kitchen assistants* with positive attitude and ability to work with others at $1100–$1350 per season ▶ 2 *nurses* with RN license (preferred), or LPN license ▶ 2 *office assistants* with good typing and phone skills (computer experience a plus) at $1200–$1700 per season ▶ 8 *reading teachers* with license in elementary or secondary education or special education certification (preferred) at $1500–$2000 per season ▶ 8 *trip counselors* with lifeguard, CPR, and standard first aid training at $1350–$1850 per season. Applicants must submit formal organization application, writing sample, three personal references. International applicants accepted; must apply through a recognized agency. An in-person interview is recommended, but a telephone interview is acceptable.

Benefits and Preemployment Training Free housing, free meals, formal training, names of contacts, on-the-job training, opportunity to attend seminars/workshops, and travel reimbursement. Preemployment training is required and includes accident prevention and safety, interpersonal skills, leadership skills, seminars relate to ADHD/learning disabilities, behavior management, teaching methodologies, and social skills goal setting.

Contact Thomas Bauer, Director, Camp Buckskin, 8700 West 36th Street, Suite 6W, St. Louis Park, Minnesota 55426-3936. Telephone: 612-930-3544. Fax: 612-938-6996. E-mail: buckskin@ spacestar.net. World Wide Web: http://www.spacestar.net/users/buckskin. Application deadline: continuous.

CAMP CHIPPEWA
CASS LAKE, MINNESOTA 56633

General Information Residential camp for 60 boys offering land and water activities including extensive Canadian fishing, canoe, and kayak tripping. Established in 1935. 88-acre facility located 250 miles from Minneapolis. Features: isthmus between 2 lakes; one mile of shoreline; island fishing lodge in Ontario; location in Chippewa National Forest; 3 tennis courts.

Profile of Summer Employees Total number: 30; typical ages: 19–45. 95% men; 5% women; 5% minorities; 10% high school students; 60% college students; 10% non-U.S. citizens; 5% local applicants. Nonsmokers required.

Employment Information Openings are from June 12 to August 11. Jobs available: ▶ *NRA rifle instructor* (minimum age 19) with NRA certification at $1200–$1400 per season ▶ *archery instructor* (minimum age 19) at $1200–$1400 per season ▶ *general cabin counselors* (minimum age 19) at $1000–$1200 per season ▶ *swimming instructor* (minimum age 19) with Red Cross WSI certification at $1200–$1500 per season. Applicants must submit formal organization application. International applicants accepted; must apply through a recognized agency.

Benefits and Preemployment Training Free housing, free meals, health insurance, on-the-job training, and travel reimbursement. Preemployment training is required and includes accident prevention and safety, interpersonal skills, leadership skills.

Contact John P. Endres, Director, Camp Chippewa, 11427 North Pinehurst Circle, Mequon, Wisconsin 53092. Telephone: 414-241-5733. Fax: 414-241-3893. World Wide Web: http://www. campchippewa.com. Application deadline: continuous.

CAMP COURAGE
8046 83RD STREET, NW
MAPLE LAKE, MINNESOTA 55358

General Information Programs offered for physically disabled children and adults, including adventure camping for the deaf and speech therapy for speech/language-impaired children. Established in 1955. 300-acre facility located 50 miles from Minneapolis. Features: pool; gymnasium; tennis courts; lake; horses; accessible site.

Profile of Summer Employees Total number: 120; typical ages: 18–50. 50% men; 50% women; 8% minorities; 10% high school students; 80% college students; 1% retirees; 8% non-U.S. citizens; 60% local applicants.

Employment Information Openings are from June to August. Year-round positions also offered. Jobs available: ▶ 6 *cooks* at $9 per hour ▶ 36 *counselors* at $155–$175 per week ▶ 3 *nurses* with RN, LPN, or GN license at $350–$450 per week ▶ 20 *program specialists* with appropriate certification for area at $150–$175 per week ▶ 14 *speech clinicians* with MS in speech pathology/communications disorders (BA acceptable at lower pay rate) at $335–$455 per week ▶ 6 *waterfront personnel* with lifeguard certification at $155–$180 per week. Applicants must submit formal organization application, 2 personal references or 2 letters of recommendation. International applicants accepted; must obtain own visa, obtain own working papers, apply through a recognized agency. An in-person interview is recommended, but a telephone interview is acceptable.

Benefits and Preemployment Training Free housing, free meals, formal training, health insurance, on-the-job training, opportunity to attend seminars/workshops, travel reimbursement, and tuition assistance.

Contact Roger Upcraft, Program Manager, Camp Courage, 8046 83rd Street, NW, Maple Lake, Minnesota 55358. Telephone: 320-963-3121. Fax: 320-963-3698. E-mail: camping@mtn.org. World Wide Web: http://www.lkdllink.net/~ccourage. Application deadline: continuous.

CAMP LINCOLN FOR BOYS/CAMP LAKE HUBERT FOR GIRLS
LAKE HUBERT, MINNESOTA 56459

General Information Separate boys and girls camps offering 30 land and water activities, staff from around the world, one- to four-week sessions for ages 8 to 17. Excellent leadership experience. Established in 1909. 800-acre facility located 140 miles from Minneapolis. Features: 800 acres; boys and girls camps; mile of lakeshore; 30 land water activities; log cabins; 150 fun staff.

Profile of Summer Employees Total number: 155; typical ages: 19–42. 50% men; 50% women; 5% minorities; 80% college students; 2% retirees; 15% non-U.S. citizens; 15% local applicants. Nonsmokers required.

Employment Information Openings are from June 1 to August 29. Jobs available: ▶ 6–10 *activity directors* (minimum age 20) with experience and ability to teach one or more of the following: sports, riflery, archery, campcraft, riding, windsurfing, arts and crafts at $1400–$2100 per season ▶ 2–4 *cooks, bakers* (minimum age 21) with food service experience at $1700–$2700 per season ▶ 10–20 *counselors* (minimum age 19) with some experience working with young people at $1250–$2000 per season ▶ 1–2 *drivers* (minimum age 21) with Class B driver's license, clean driving record, and ability to complete training course at $1400–$2000 per season ▶ 6–10 *general food service staff members* (minimum age 19) at $1300–$2000 per season ▶ *head counselors* (minimum age 21) with leadership experience at $1400–$2000 per season ▶ 2–4 *nurses* (minimum age 21) with LPN, RN, EMT at $1700–$2500 per season ▶ 3–5 *office staff members* with computer experience at $1250–$2000 per season ▶ 2–4 *trip leaders* (minimum age 21) with lifeguard training, CPR, first aid, canoe and pack experience at $1400–$2000 per season. Applicants must submit formal organization application, three personal references. International applicants accepted; must apply through a recognized agency. An in-person interview is recommended, but a telephone interview is acceptable.

Benefits and Preemployment Training Free housing, free meals, formal training, on-the-job training, and travel reimbursement. Preemployment training is required and includes accident prevention and safety, interpersonal skills, leadership skills, lifeguard training.

Contact Sam Cote, Directors, Camp Lincoln for Boys/Camp Lake Hubert for Girls, 5201 Eden Circle, Suite 202, Minneapolis, Minnesota 55436. Telephone: 800-242-1909. Fax: 612-922-7149. E-mail: clclh@uslink.net. World Wide Web: http://www.Lincoln-Lakehubert.com. Application deadline: continuous.

CAMP THUNDERBIRD FOR BOYS
ROUTE 2, BOX 225
BEMIDJI, MINNESOTA 56601

General Information Residential camp serving 200 boys from forty U.S. cities and five other countries. Established in 1946. 700-acre facility located 12 miles from Bemidji. Features: 7½ miles of sand beach shoreline; 700 pristine acres of property; strong waterfront activities; climbing wall; tennis courts; Western riding program.

Profile of Summer Employees Total number: 100; typical ages: 19–60. 55% men; 45% women; 5% minorities; 12% high school students; 60% college students; 1% retirees; 10% non-U.S. citizens; 1% local applicants. Nonsmokers preferred.

Employment Information Openings are from June 1 to August 21. Jobs available: ▶ 1 *arts and crafts specialist* with experience as an art teacher or student status preferred (completion of junior year required); salary negotiable ▶ 40 *cabin counselors* with freshman year of college completed, experience working with children, high-energy, caring attitude, ability to assist or teach in several camp activities, and outdoor orientation; salary negotiable ▶ 2 *horseback specialists* with experience in Western riding, completion of junior year of college; and CHA or HSA certification preferred, but will send to clinic for certification; salary negotiable ▶ 10 *kitchen personnel* (minimum age 19) with ability to assist with kitchen operations, food preparation, dishwashing, and cleanup and one year of college completed; salary negotiable ▶ 2 *nurses* with RN or LPN license at $300 and up per week ▶ 2 *office personnel* (minimum age 19) with bookkeeping and computer knowledge, ability to handle camper/staff cash accounts, sophomore year of college completed, and average or above-average typing skills; salary negotiable ▶ 1 *program director* with experience encompassing staff supervision and direct leadership of children in outdoor recreation/camp activities and college degree; salary negotiable ▶ 1 *riflery instructor* with certification and teaching experience (required); salary negotiable ▶ 1 *sailing instructor* with sailing and lifeguard certification; salary negotiable ▶ 6 *swimming instructors* with WSI, lifeguard, and CPR certification and teaching experience (preferred); salary negotiable ▶ 1 *trip director* with experience in diverse kinds of wilderness trips and equipment use, and college degree; salary negotiable ▶ 4 *unit directors* (minimum age 23) with experience encompassing staff supervision and direct leadership of children in outdoor recreation/camp activities and college degree; salary negotiable ▶ 1 *waterfront director* with WSI first aid, CPR, and lifeguard certification; college degree, and knowledge of various water sports; salary negotiable ▶ 15 *wilderness and trip leaders* (minimum age 21) with certifications in CPR, lifeguard, and advanced first aid (must be comfortable and confident living in the wilderness) at $1200–$1800 per season. Applicants must submit formal organization application, three personal references. International applicants accepted; must apply through a recognized agency. An in-person interview is recommended, but a telephone interview is acceptable.

Benefits and Preemployment Training Free housing, free meals, on-the-job training, and travel reimbursement. Preemployment training is required and includes accident prevention and safety, first aid, CPR, interpersonal skills, leadership skills, with WSI, lifeguard training.

Contact Carol A. Sigoloff, Director, Camp Thunderbird for Boys, 967 Gardenview Office Parkway, St. Louis, Missouri 63141. Telephone: 314-567-3167. Fax: 314-567-7218. E-mail: tbirdcamp@primary.net. Application deadline: continuous.

CAMP THUNDERBIRD FOR GIRLS
ROUTE 8, BOX 532
BEMIDJI, MINNESOTA 56601

General Information Residential camp serving 150 girls from forty U.S. cities and five other countries. Established in 1970. 700-acre facility located 12 miles from Bemidji. Features: 7½ miles of sand beach shoreline; 700 pristine acres of property; extensive waterfront program and equipment; English riding program; gymnastic program; tennis courts.

Profile of Summer Employees Total number: 100; typical ages: 19–60. 10% men; 90% women; 5% minorities; 12% high school students; 60% college students; 1% retirees; 10% non-U.S. citizens; 1% local applicants. Nonsmokers preferred.

Employment Information Openings are from June 1 to August 21. Jobs available: ▶ 1 *arts and crafts specialist* with experience as an art teacher or art student preferred; junior year of college completed; salary negotiable ▶ 2 *horseback specialists* with experience in English Hunt Seat specialty; junior year of college completed; CHA or HSA certification preferred, but will send to clinic for certification; salary negotiable ▶ 10 *kitchen personnel* (minimum age 19) with ability to assist with kitchen operations, food preparation, dishwashing, and cleanup; one year of college completed; salary negotiable ▶ 2 *nurses* with RN or LPN at $300 and up per week ▶ 2 *office personnel* (minimum age 19) with bookkeeping and computer knowledge; ability to handle camper/staff cash accounts; average or above-average typing skills; sophomore year of college completed; salary negotiable ▶ 1 *program director* with experience encompassing staff supervision and direct leadership of children in outdoor recreation/camp activities; college graduate; salary negotiable ▶ 1 *sailing instructor* with sailing and lifeguard certification; salary negotiable ▶ 6 *swimming instructors* with WSI, lifeguard, and CPR certification; teaching experience preferred; salary negotiable ▶ 1 *trip director* with experience in diverse kinds of wilderness trips and equipment use; college graduate; salary negotiable ▶ 3 *unit directors* (minimum age 23) with experience encompassing staff supervision and direct leadership of children in outdoor recreation/camp activities; college graduate; salary negotiable ▶ 1 *waterfront director* with WSI, first aid, lifeguard, and CPR certification; college degree and knowledge of various water sports; salary negotiable ▶ 10 *wilderness and trip leaders* (minimum age 21) with certifications in CPR, lifeguard, and advanced first aid; must be comfortable and confident living in the wilderness at $1200–$1800 per season. Applicants must submit formal organization application, three personal references. International applicants accepted; must apply through a recognized agency. An in-person interview is recommended, but a telephone interview is acceptable.

Benefits and Preemployment Training Free housing, free meals, on-the-job training, and travel reimbursement. Preemployment training is required and includes accident prevention and safety, first aid, CPR, interpersonal skills, leadership skills, WSI, lifeguard training.

Contact Carol A. Sigoloff, Director, Camp Thunderbird for Girls, 967 Gardenview Office Parkway, St. Louis, Missouri 63141. Telephone: 314-567-3167. Fax: 314-567-7218. E-mail: tbirdcamp@ primary.net. Application deadline: continuous.

DEEP PORTAGE CONSERVATION RESERVE
2197 NATURE CENTER DRIVE, NW
HACKENSACK, MINNESOTA 56452

General Information 6000-acre forest and conservation education center that conducts programs in environmental education. Established in 1973. 6,307-acre facility located 50 miles from Brainerd. Features: rolling, wooded glacial hills; 10 lakes; bogs; streams; large modern dormitory.

Profile of Summer Employees Total number: 16. 50% men; 50% women; 10% minorities; 10% high school students; 70% college students; 10% non-U.S. citizens.

Employment Information Openings are from June 5 to August 25. Jobs available: ▶ 12 *instructors/naturalists* with college training in related fields at $150–$165 per week. Applicants must submit a cover letter, resume, three personal references. International applicants accepted; must obtain own visa, obtain own working papers. A telephone interview is required.

Benefits and Preemployment Training Free housing, free meals, formal training, and on-the-job training.

Contact Dale Yerger, Executive Director, Deep Portage Conservation Reserve, 2197 Nature Center Drive, NW, Hackensack, Minnesota 56452. Telephone: 218-682-2325. Fax: 218-682-3121. E-mail: portage@uslink.net. World Wide Web: http://www.deep-portage.org. Application deadline: continuous.

DRIFTWOOD FAMILY RESORT & GOLF
ROUTE 1, BOX 404
PINE RIVER, MINNESOTA 56474

General Information Resort specializing in family vacations with an emphasis on many different types of recreation. Established in 1900. 44-acre facility located 30 miles from Brainerd. Features: freshwater lakes; wooded setting; tennis court; 9-hole golf course; authentic Norwegian smorgasbord; family resort.

Profile of Summer Employees Total number: 25; typical ages: 16–65. 50% men; 50% women; 50% high school students; 50% college students; 10% retirees; 50% non-U.S. citizens; 50% local applicants. Nonsmokers required.

Employment Information Openings are from May 1 to October 1. Jobs available: ▶ 2–4 *cabin maids* (minimum age 16) at $5–$6 per hour ▶ 2 *cooks or cook's helpers* (minimum age 18) at $5–$6 per hour ▶ 1 *dining room host/hostess* (minimum age 20) at $6–$7 per hour ▶ 2 *front desk/office staff members* (minimum age 16) at $5–$6 per hour ▶ 2 *lawn/golf maintenance staff members/gardeners* (minimum age 16) at $5–$6 per hour ▶ 1 *recreation director* (minimum age 18) at $5–$6 per hour ▶ 8 *waiters/waitresses* (minimum age 17) at $800–$1000 per month. Applicants must submit writing sample, two personal references, two letters of recommendation. International applicants accepted; must obtain own visa, obtain own working papers, apply through a recognized agency. An in-person interview is recommended, but a telephone interview is acceptable.

Benefits and Preemployment Training Housing at a cost, meals at a cost, and contract completion bonus.

Contact Tim and Sue Leagjeld, Owners, Driftwood Family Resort & Golf, Route 1, Box 404, Pine River, Minnesota 56474. Telephone: 218-568-4221. Fax: 218-568-4222. E-mail: ponyride@ uslink.net. World Wide Web: http://www.driftwoodresort.com.

FRIENDSHIP VENTURES/CAMP FRIENDSHIP
10509 108TH STREET, NW
ANNANDALE, MINNESOTA 55302

General Information Residential camp serving children and adults with developmental disabilities. Established in 1964. 115-acre facility located 60 miles from Minneapolis. Features: wooded setting; large waterfront; challenege course; cabins.

Profile of Summer Employees Total number: 150; typical ages: 16–25. 25% men; 75% women; 5% minorities; 15% high school students; 85% college students; 10% non-U.S. citizens; 20% local applicants.

Employment Information Openings are from May 29 to September 1. Year-round positions also offered. Jobs available: ▶ 5 *adventure/recreation specialists* with preference for current major in recreation, physical education, or adaptive physical recreation and leadership skills involving group activities at $125–$165 per week ▶ 2 *arts and crafts specialists* with preference for current major in therapeutic recreation, occupational therapy, or art education/therapy or experience planning and implementing arts and crafts activities/projects at $125–$165 per week ▶ 1 *camping specialist* with tent camping and outdoor experience and environmental education knowledge at $125–$165 per week ▶ 1 *canteen/camp store manager* with record-keeping skills at $125–$165 per week ▶ 60 *counselors* at $125–$165 per week ▶ 1 *dietary specialist* with experience in food service area with an emphasis on special diets at $125–$165 per week ▶ 2 *dining hall workers* experience working in food service or dining hall areas; salary is negotiable ▶ 12 *junior counselors* (minimum age 16) with physical and emotional strength, mental alertness, creativity, flexibility, and high school student status (successful volunteer experience may be substituted for the age requirement) at $90–$100 per week ▶ 2 *laundry/housekeeping staff members* salary is negotiable ▶ 2 *music specialists* with preference for current major in music, music therapy, or special education and experience planning and implementing activities at $125–$165 per week ▶ 4 *nurses* with RN, LPN, or GN license or BSN degree; salary is negotiable ▶ 2 *office support staff* with computer, typing, phone, and filing experience at $125–$165 per week ▶ 1 *outdoor specialist* with preference for current major in an environmental, outdoor, or education field at $125–$165 per week ▶ 1 *public relations assistant* with current major in journalism, photography, or related field and experience with a 35mm camera at $125–$165 per week ▶ 1 *waterfront director* with WSI and lifeguard certification at $150–$180 per week ▶ 4 *waterfront lifeguards* with WSI and lifeguard certification (preferred) at $125–$165 per week ▶ 3 *weekend counselors* with physical strength, mental alertness, and at least one year of college completed; at $150 per weekend. Applicants must submit formal organization application, personal reference, letter of recommendation. International applicants accepted; must apply through a recognized agency. An in-person interview is recommended, but a telephone interview is acceptable.

Benefits and Preemployment Training Free housing, free meals, formal training, and on-the-job training. Preemployment training is required and includes accident prevention and safety, first aid, CPR, interpersonal skills, leadership skills.

Contact Joanne Fieldseth, Human Resources Director, Friendship Ventures/Camp Friendship, 10509 108th Street, NW, Annandale, Minnesota 55302. Telephone: 320-274-8376. Fax: 320-274-3238. E-mail: fv@friendshipventures.org. Application deadline: continuous.

FRIENDSHIP VENTURES/EDEN WOOD CAMP
6350 INDIAN CHIEF ROAD
EDEN PRAIRIE, MINNESOTA 55346

General Information Residential and day camp serving children and adults with developmental disabilities. Established in 1958. 12-acre facility located 15 miles from Minneapolis. Features: wooded setting; walking trails; cabins/dormitory; close to lakes area; challenge course.

Profile of Summer Employees Total number: 35; typical ages: 16–25. 25% men; 75% women; 5% minorities; 15% high school students; 85% college students; 10% non-U.S. citizens; 20% local applicants.

Employment Information Openings are from May 29 to September 1. Year-round positions also offered. Jobs available: ▶ 1 *arts and crafts specialist* with preference for current major in therapeutic recreation, occupational therapy, or art education/therapy or experience planning and implementing arts and crafts activities/projects at $125–$165 per week ▶ 30 *counselors* (minimum age 16) at $125–$165 per week ▶ 1 *creative movement/drama specialist* with experience in the performing arts field at $125–$165 per week ▶ 1 *dining hall staff worker* with experience in food service/dining hall area; salary is negotiable ▶ 6 *junior counselors* (minimum age 16) with physical and emotional strength, mental alertness, creativity, flexibility, and high school student status (successful volunteer experience may be substituted for the age requirement) at $90–$100 per week ▶ 2 *laundry/housekeeping staff members* (minimum age 18) at $125–$165 per week ▶ 2 *lifeguards* with WSI and lifeguard certification (preferred) at $125–$165 per week ▶ 1 *music specialist* with preference for major in music, music therapy, or special education and experience planning and implementing activities at $125–$165 per week ▶ 2 *nurses* with RN, LPN, or GN license or BSN degree; salary is negotiable ▶ 1 *office support staff* with computer, typing, phone, and filing experience at $125–$165 per week ▶ 1 *outdoor specialist* with preference for current major in environmental, outdoor, or education field at $125–$165 per week ▶ 1 *recreation specialist* with preference for current major in recreation, physical education, or adaptive physical recreation and leadership skills involving group activities at $125–$165 per week ▶ 6 *travel leaders* (minimum age 21) with leadership skills and valid driver's license at $125–$165 per week ▶ 10 *weekend counselors* with physical strength, mental alertness, and at least one year of college completed at $150 per weekend. Applicants must submit formal organization application, two personal references, letter of recommendation. International applicants accepted; must apply through a recognized agency. An in-person interview is recommended, but a telephone interview is acceptable.

Benefits and Preemployment Training Free housing, free meals, formal training, and on-the-job training. Preemployment training is required and includes accident prevention and safety, first aid, CPR, interpersonal skills, leadership skills.

Contact Joanne Fieldseth, Human Resources Director, Friendship Ventures/Eden Wood Camp, 10509 108th Street NW, Annandale, Minnesota 55302. Telephone: 320-274-8376. Fax: 320-274-3238. E-mail: fv@friendshipventures.org. Application deadline: continuous.

GRAND VIEW LODGE GOLF AND TENNIS CLUB
SOUTH 134 NOKOMIS AVENUE
NISSWA, MINNESOTA 56468

General Information Resort that caters to families and business conventions and operates the most popular public golf courses in Minnesota. Established in 1914. 1,300-acre facility located 150 miles from Minneapolis. Features: tennis courts; golf; beautiful lake for swimming, fishing, and waterskiing; wooded areas; indoor pool.

Profile of Summer Employees Total number: 500; typical ages: 16–25. 45% men; 55% women; 10% minorities; 20% high school students; 50% college students; 10% retirees; 20% non-U.S. citizens; 20% local applicants.

Employment Information Openings are from April 15 to November 1. Jobs available: ▶ 5 *bartenders* with experience in the field at $175–$195 per week ▶ 5 *beach staff members* with knowledge of boats and motors at $190–$220 per week ▶ 3 *children's program instructors* at $190–$220 per week ▶ 25 *dining room personnel* at $190–$220 per week ▶ 10 *golf course maintence staff* with knowledge of equipment at $190–$230 per week ▶ 5 *golf shop staff* with golf background and merchandise skills at $175–$210 per week ▶ 15 *housekeepers* at $195–$220 per week ▶ 3 *skilled desk clerks* at $185–$205 per week. Applicants must submit formal organization application, resume. International applicants accepted; must obtain own visa, apply through a recognized agency. An in-person interview is recommended, but a telephone interview is acceptable.

Benefits and Preemployment Training Housing at a cost, meals at a cost, formal training, and on-the-job training. Preemployment training is required and includes accident prevention and safety, leadership skills.

Contact Paul Welch, Operations Manager, Grand View Lodge Golf and Tennis Club, South 134 Nokomis Avenue, Nisswa, Minnesota 56468. Telephone: 218-963-2234. Fax: 218-963-2269. E-mail: vacation@grandviewlodge.com. Application deadline: continuous.

GUNFLINT LODGE AND OUTFITTERS
143 SOUTH GUNFLINT LAKE
GRAND MARAIS, MINNESOTA 55604

General Information Family and fishing resort offering cabin accommodations with modified or full- American plan packages; guide services, naturalist activities, and access to boundary Waters Canoe Area (B.W.C.A.). Established in 1928. 100-acre facility located 43 miles from Grand Marais. Features: freshwater lake; BWCA wilderness; Superior National Forest; canoeing and hiking; horse stable.

Profile of Summer Employees Total number: 50; typical ages: 20–40. 55% men; 45% women; 1% minorities; 5% high school students; 60% college students; 20% retirees; 8% non-U.S. citizens; 5% local applicants. Nonsmokers preferred.

Employment Information Openings are from May 1 to November 1. Winter break and year-round positions also offered. Jobs available: ▶ 1–2 *activity leaders/naturalists* (minimum age 18) with driver's license and good driving record; training in biology/forestry/geography and experience preferred at $1065 per month ▶ 1 *baker* (minimum age 18) with great desire to learn, experience preferred at $1065–$1300 per month ▶ 1 *breakfast and lunch cook* (minimum age 18) with great desire to learn, experience preferred at $1065–$1400 per month ▶ 6 *busters, haulers, and packers* (minimum age 18) with driver's license, good driving record, and ability to lift and carry 75 pounds at $1065 per month ▶ 3 *dishwashers* (minimum age 17) at $1065 per month ▶ 1 *dock staff* (minimum age 18) with ability to lift and carry 75 pounds, knowledge of outboard motors, driver's license, and good driving record at $1065 per month ▶ 3 *kitchen assistants/bartenders* (minimum age 18) at $1065 per month ▶ 1 *prep cook* (minimum age 18) with great desire to learn, experience preferred at $1065–$1400 per month ▶ 1–2 *stable hands* (minimum age 18) with experience handling horses, riding, and grooming at $1065 per month ▶ 10 *waitresses/housekeepers (combined positions)* (minimum age 18) with experience preferred at $1065 per month. Applicants must submit a formal organization application. International applicants accepted; must obtain own visa, obtain own working papers. A telephone interview is required.

Benefits and Preemployment Training Housing at a cost, possible full-time employment, on-the-job training, and discounted equipment rental rates. Preemployment training is required and includes accident prevention and safety, CPR.

Contact Shari Baker, Assistant Manager, Gunflint Lodge and Outfitters, 143 South Gunflint Lake, Grand Marais, Minnesota 55604. Telephone: 800-328-3325. Fax: 218-388-9429. E-mail: gunflint@gunflint.com. World Wide Web: http://www.gunflint.com. Application deadline: continuous.

LAKE HUBERT TENNIS CAMP
BOX 308
LAKE HUBERT, MINNESOTA 56459

General Information Seven day tennis camps featuring five hours of court time instruction daily for all skill levels; 12 courts for 36 campers. Established in 1973. 750-acre facility located 15 miles from Brainerd. Features: 12 outdoor courts; true camp setting; waterfront.

Profile of Summer Employees Total number: 15; typical ages: 19–35. 50% men; 50% women; 75% college students. Nonsmokers required.

Employment Information Openings are from June 6 to August 28. Jobs available: ▶ 6 *cabin counselors* (minimum age 19) at $140–$200 per week ▶ 10 *tennis instructors* (minimum age 19) with experience in the field at $200–$300 per week ▶ 2 *waterfront staff* (minimum age 21) with lifeguard training at $200–$250 per week. Applicants must submit formal organization application, three personal references. International applicants accepted; must apply through a recognized agency. An in-person interview is recommended, but a telephone interview is acceptable.

Benefits and Preemployment Training Free housing, free meals, formal training, and travel reimbursement.

Contact Sam Cote, Director, Lake Hubert Tennis Camp, 5201 Eden Circle, Minneapolis, Minnesota 55436. Telephone: 800-242-1909. Fax: 612-922-7149. E-mail: clclh@uslink.net. World Wide Web: http://www.lincoln-lakehubert.com. Application deadline: continuous.

MENOGYN–YMCA WILDERNESS ADVENTURES
55 MENOGYN TRAIL
GRAND MARAIS, MINNESOTA 55604

General Information Wilderness camp specializing in canoeing, backpacking, and rock-climbing trips in wilderness areas of North America. Established in 1922. 80-acre facility located 30 miles from Grand Marais. Features: 2,000,000 acres of wilderness; freshwater lakes; mountain hiking; rustic wilderness base camp; rock climbing.

Profile of Summer Employees Total number: 56; typical ages: 20–35. 50% men; 50% women; 5% minorities; 90% college students; 5% non-U.S. citizens; 75% local applicants. Nonsmokers required.

Employment Information Openings are from June to August 30. Jobs available: ▶ 1 *assistant camp director* (minimum age 21) with CPR, first aid, and lifeguard training at $350–$420 per week ▶ 1 *cook* (minimum age 20) with experience in the field and references at $6–$9 per hour ▶ 3–120 *in-camp staff members* with CPR, first aid, and lifeguard training at $140–$203 per week ▶ 1 *nurse* with current license at $1200–$2000 per season ▶ 24–36 *trail counselors* (minimum age 19) with CPR, first aid, and lifeguard training at $140–$189 per week. Applicants must submit formal organization application, three personal references. International applicants accepted; must apply through a recognized agency. An in-person interview is recommended, but a telephone interview is acceptable.

Benefits and Preemployment Training Free housing, free meals, formal training, and on-the-job training. Preemployment training is required and includes accident prevention and safety, first aid, CPR, interpersonal skills, leadership skills.

Contact Nick Schneider, Camp Director, Menogyn–YMCA Wilderness Adventures, 4 West Rustic Lodge Avenue, Minneapolis, Minnesota 55409. Telephone: 612-823-5282. Fax: 612-823-2482. Application deadline: April 30.

NELSON'S RESORT
7632 NELSON ROAD
CRANE LAKE, MINNESOTA 55725

General Information Family resort with conventions in the fall. Established in 1931. 84-acre facility located 70 miles from Virginia. Features: freshwater lake; wooded setting; proximity to Voyageurs National Park; near Boundary Water Canoe Area; Canadian Border Waters.

Profile of Summer Employees Total number: 30; typical ages: 18–40. 44% men; 56% women; 25% college students; 2% retirees; 1% non-U.S. citizens; 6% local applicants.

Employment Information Openings are from May 1 to October 15. Jobs available: ▶ 1–2 *bartenders* at $800–$1000 per month ▶ 1 *bellperson* at $800–$900 per month ▶ 5 *cabin staff members* at $800–$900 per month ▶ 3 *dock attendants* at $800–$900 per month ▶ 3 *kitchen helpers* at $800–$900 per month ▶ 1 *store clerk* at $800–$900 per month ▶ 6 *waiters/waitresses* at $800–$900 per month. Applicants must submit formal organization application. International applicants accepted; must apply through a recognized agency.

Benefits and Preemployment Training Meals at a cost, free housing, and on-the-job training.

Contact Jerry Pohlman, Co-Owner, Nelson's Resort, 7632 Nelson Road, Crane Lake, Minnesota 55725. Telephone: 218-993-2295. Fax: 218-993-2242. E-mail: nelsons@uslink.net. World Wide Web: http://www.nelsonresort.com. Application deadline: continuous.

THE SOUTHWESTERN COMPANY, MINNESOTA
See The Southwestern Company, Tennessee on page 284 for complete description.

STRAW HAT PLAYERS
CENTER FOR THE ARTS–MOORHEAD STATE UNIVERSITY
MOORHEAD, MINNESOTA 56563

General Information Summer stock theater producing four shows in a nine-week season. Established in 1963. 20-acre facility located near Fargo, North Dakota. Features: 900-seat proscenium theater; 350-seat thrust theater; scene shops, costume shops, and dance studio; access to library, pool, athletic center; largest metropolitan area between Minneapolis and Seattle.

Profile of Summer Employees Total number: 60; typical age: 22. 40% men; 60% women; 5% minorities; 10% high school students; 80% college students; 40% local applicants.

Employment Information Openings are from May 26 to July 26. Jobs available: ▶ 40 *acting company members* must be high school junior or senior (minimum) at $100–$180 per week ▶ 3 *costume stitchers* at $100–$250 per week ▶ 1 *musical director* with extensive professional experience at $200–$300 per week ▶ 1 *properties master* at $150–$250 per week ▶ 5 *theater technicians* must be high school junior or senior (minimum) at $100–$300 per week. Applicants must submit formal organization application, cover letter, resume, videotape. International applicants accepted; must obtain own visa, obtain own working papers, apply through a recognized agency. An in-person interview is required.

Benefits and Preemployment Training Meals at a cost, free housing, formal training, on-the-job training, and tuition assistance.

Contact Jim Bartruff, Director of Theater, Straw Hat Players, Moorhead State University, Moorhead, Minnesota 56560. Telephone: 218-236-4613. Fax: 218-236-2168. Application deadline: April 15.

STUDENT CONSERVATION ASSOCIATION (SCA), MINNESOTA
See Student Conservation Association (SCA), New Hampshire on page 193 for complete description.

VALLEYFAIR FAMILY AMUSEMENT PARK
1 VALLEYFAIR DRIVE
SHAKOPEE, MINNESOTA 55379

General Information Family amusement park offering a variety of entertainment attractions. Established in 1976. 90-acre facility located 20 miles from Minneapolis/St. Paul. Features: 5

roller coasters; waterpark; adventure golf and go karts; Berenstain Bear Country; Imax theater; live entertainment.

Profile of Summer Employees Total number: 1,500; typical ages: 16–22. 50% men; 50% women; 10% minorities; 40% high school students; 45% college students; 1% retirees; 10% non-U.S. citizens; 4% local applicants.

Employment Information Openings are from May 1 to September 30. Jobs available: ▶ 30 *accounting clerks/tellers* (minimum age 18) ▶ 40 *admissions cashiers* (minimum age 18) ▶ 270 *food hosts/hostesses* (minimum age 16) ▶ 140 *game attendants* (minimum age 16) ▶ 30 *lifeguards* (minimum age 16) with Ellis and Associates certification (training provided) ▶ 90 *merchandise attendants* (minimum age 16) ▶ 25 *park-service attendants* (minimum age 18) ▶ 280 *ride hosts/hostesses* (minimum age 18) at $2500–$5000 per season ▶ 28 *security officers/EMT's* (minimum age 18) with Emergency Medical Technician certification for some positions ▶ 40 *ticket takers* (minimum age 16). Applicants must submit formal organization application. International applicants accepted; must obtain own visa, obtain own working papers, apply through a recognized agency.

Benefits and Preemployment Training Housing at a cost and on-the-job training. Preemployment training is required and includes accident prevention and safety, first aid, CPR, leadership skills, guest service training.

Contact Human Resources Department, Valleyfair Family Amusement Park, 1 Valleyfair Drive, Shakopee, Minnesota 55379. Telephone: 612-445-7600. Fax: 612-496-5267. World Wide Web: http://www.valleyfair.com.

YMCA CAMP IHDUHAPI
BOX 37
LORETTO, MINNESOTA 55357

General Information Residential camp serving 150 boys and girls 8-13 year olds weekly, offering sailing and horsemanship as well as leadership program for campers ages 13-15. Established in 1930. 200-acre facility located 25 miles from Minneapolis. Features: freshwater lake; wooded setting; rustic cabins and lodge; low and high ropes course; close proximity to metro area; many beautiful overnight camp sites.

Profile of Summer Employees Total number: 65; typical ages: 16–24. 50% men; 50% women; 5% minorities; 30% high school students; 70% college students; 10% non-U.S. citizens; 50% local applicants. Nonsmokers required.

Employment Information Openings are from June 8 to August 30. Year-round positions also offered. Jobs available: ▶ 1 *arts and crafts director* at $1250–$1450 per season ▶ 3 *cooks* at $1400–$1700 per season ▶ 20 *counselors* (minimum age 16) with experience working with children at $1250–$1400 per season ▶ 1 *nature director* at $1300–$1450 per season ▶ 1 *nurse* with RN license/LPN/EMT certification or graduating RN at $1700–$2000 per season ▶ 1 *program director* with past camp experience at $1500–$1800 per season ▶ 1 *riding director* with experience with horses at $1350–$1600 per season ▶ 1 *ropes course director* with experience in the field at $1350–$1600 per season ▶ *summer business manager* at $1300–$1500 per season ▶ 1 *trip director* with organization and trip planning experience, and experience with trip camping gear at $1250–$1500 per season ▶ 2 *unit directors* with past camp experience at $1400–$1700 per season ▶ 1 *waterfront director* with WSI certification at $1400–$1700 per season. Applicants must submit formal organization application, two personal references. International applicants accepted; must obtain own visa, apply through a recognized agency. An in-person interview is recommended, but a telephone interview is acceptable.

Benefits and Preemployment Training Free housing, free meals, formal training, and on-the-job training. Preemployment training is required and includes accident prevention and safety, first aid, CPR, interpersonal skills, leadership skills.

Contact Anna Raske, Summer Program Director, YMCA Camp Ihduhapi, Box 37, Loretto, Minnesota 55357. Telephone: 612-479-1146. Fax: 612-479-1333. E-mail: ymca-ihd@mtn.org. World Wide Web: http://www.mtn.org/~ymca-ihd/serv.htm. Application deadline: May 15.

YMCA CAMP PEPIN
434 MAIN STREET
RED WING, MINNESOTA 55066

General Information Established in 1935. 40-acre facility located 60 miles from Minneapolis. Features: freshwater lake; bluff setting; canoe trips; camping/hiking; rock climbing; ropes course.

Profile of Summer Employees Total number: 30; typical ages: 18–24. 45% men; 55% women; 30% minorities; 10% high school students; 60% college students; 10% non-U.S. citizens; 20% local applicants. Nonsmokers preferred.

Employment Information Openings are from June 12 to August 14. Year-round positions also offered. Jobs available: ▶ *adventure director* (minimum age 21) with Wilderness First Responders certification at $145–$175 per week ▶ 1 *arts and crafts/camp store manager* (minimum age 19) at $145–$185 per week ▶ 1–3 *assistant counselors* (minimum age 16) at $75–$105 per week ▶ 2 *dishwashers/support staff* (minimum age 16) at $75–$105 per week ▶ *health director* (minimum age 21) with RN or EMT license at $195–$245 per week ▶ 1 *program director* (minimum age 21) with previous program experience at $195–$235 per week ▶ 1 *ropes/trips director* (minimum age 21) with previous ropes course work at $155–$175 per week ▶ *sailing director* (minimum age 19) at $145–$175 per week ▶ 1–5 *senior counselors* (minimum age 19) at $135–$170 per week ▶ 1 *teen leadership director/senior counselor* (minimum age 19) with experience in teen programming at $145–$175 per week ▶ 2 *unit leaders/senior counselors* (minimum age 21) at $150–$185 per week ▶ *waterfront director* (minimum age 21) with CPR, LGT, and WSI certifications at $160–$195 per week. Applicants must submit formal organization application, three personal references. International applicants accepted; must apply through a recognized agency. An in-person interview is recommended, but a telephone interview is acceptable.

Benefits and Preemployment Training Free housing, free meals, formal training, on-the-job training, and opportunity to attend seminars/workshops. Preemployment training is required and includes accident prevention and safety, first aid, CPR, interpersonal skills, leadership skills.

Contact Eric Syndell, Director, YMCA Camp Pepin. Telephone: 651-388-4724. Fax: 651-388-5340. E-mail: rwymca@win.bright.net. Application deadline: continuous.

MISSISSIPPI

MARINE LIFE OCEANARIUM
JOSEPH T. JONES PARK, HIGHWAY 90
GULFPORT, MISSISSIPPI 39501

General Information Oceanarium with dolphins, sea lions, sharks, rays, giant sea turtles, exotic birds, and more. Established in 1956. 25-acre facility located 60 miles from New Orleans. Features: location on Gulf Coast; diving; boating; gift shop; snack bar; gravity ship.

Profile of Summer Employees Total number: 50; typical ages: 15–20. 66% men; 33% women; 40% high school students; 10% college students; 50% local applicants.

Employment Information Openings are from May 20 to September 20. Jobs available: ▶ *operations department staff, divers* (minimum age 18) with scuba certification at $150 per week ▶ 2–5 *operations department staff, fish sellers* (minimum age 15) at $150 per week. Applicants must submit a formal organization application, cover letter. An in-person interview is recommended, but a telephone interview is acceptable.

Benefits and Preemployment Training Formal training, possible full-time employment, names of contacts, and on-the-job training.

Contact Jeffrey Siegel, Operations Manager/Education Director, Marine Life Oceanarium, PO Box 4078, Gulfport, Mississippi 39502. Fax: 228-863-3673. E-mail: jefdolfin@aol.com. World

Wide Web: http://www.dolphinsrus.com. Application deadline: continuous.

THE SOUTHWESTERN COMPANY, MISSISSIPPI
See The Southwestern Company, Tennessee on page 284 for complete description.

STUDENT CONSERVATION ASSOCIATION (SCA), MISSISSIPPI
See Student Conservation Association (SCA), New Hampshire on page 193 for complete description.

MISSOURI

ACE COMPUTER CAMP–MISSOURI
See ACE Computer Camp–Washington on page 307 for complete description.

CAMP SABRA
HCR 2, BOX 640
ROCKY MOUNT, MISSOURI 65072
General Information Residential coed summer camping facility of St. Louis Jewish Community Center serving boys, girls, and teens entering grades 3-10 with complete waterfront and land activity program. Established in 1938. 960-acre facility located 10 miles from Eldon. Features: 3½ miles of private shoreline; large fleet of ski and sailboats; 12 miles of horseback riding trails; 3 lighted tennis courts; summer theater; 960 tree-shaded acres.

Profile of Summer Employees Total number: 130; typical ages: 18–22. 50% men; 50% women; 20% high school students; 75% college students; 10% non-U.S. citizens; 5% local applicants. Nonsmokers preferred.

Employment Information Openings are from June 6 to August 8. Jobs available: ▶ 10–20 *counselors* (minimum age 17) with experience preferred at $1000 and up per season ▶ 2 *male unit head programmers* (minimum age 21) with experience with 6th-8th grade children and supervision at $2000 per season (additional salary for experience) ▶ 4–5 *ropes course specialists* (minimum age 17) with experience with climbing tower, low ropes courses, and high ropes courses $1000 and up per season ▶ 20–30 *specialists* (minimum age 17) with LGT for waterfront staff and experience in specialty required at $1000 and up per season. Applicants must submit formal organization application, three personal references. International applicants accepted; must apply through a recognized agency. An in-person interview is recommended, but a telephone interview is acceptable.

Benefits and Preemployment Training Free housing and free meals. Preemployment training is required and includes accident prevention and safety, first aid, CPR, interpersonal skills, leadership skills.

Contact Stephen J. Engel, Director, Camp Sabra, 2 Millstone Campus Drive, St. Louis, Missouri 63146. Telephone: 314-432-5700 Ext. 3125. Fax: 314-432-5825. E-mail: sabral@concentric.net. World Wide Web: http://www.campsabra.com. Application deadline: continuous.

THE SOUTHWESTERN COMPANY, MISSOURI
See The Southwestern Company, Tennessee on page 284 for complete description.

STIVERS TEMPORARY PERSONNEL–MISSOURI
See Stivers Temporary Personnel–Illinois on page 103 for complete description.

STUDENT CONSERVATION ASSOCIATION (SCA), MISSOURI
See Student Conservation Association (SCA), New Hampshire on page 193 for complete description.

WORLDS OF FUN/OCEANS OF FUN
4545 WOF AVENUE
KANSAS CITY, MISSOURI 64161

General Information Amusement park. Established in 1973. 170-acre facility located near Kansas City. Features: Mamba-roller coaster; 3 roller coasters; 2 restaurants; 2 live entertainmnet shows; water rides; rip cord.

Profile of Summer Employees Total number: 2,000. 40% men; 60% women; 70% high school students; 20% college students; 10% retirees.

Employment Information Openings are from February to October 17. Spring break positions also offered. Jobs available: ▶ *food operations staff* (minimum age 15) at $6 to $8 per hour plus bonus ▶ *games staff* (minimum age 15) at $6 to $8 per hour plus bonus ▶ *grounds personnel* (minimum age 15) at $6 to $8 per hour plus bonus ▶ *lifeguards* (minimum age 16) at $6 to $8 per hour plus bonus ▶ *merchandise staff* (minimum age 15) at $6 to $8 per hour plus bonus ▶ *ride operations staff* (minimum age 16) per hour at $6 to $8 per hour plus bonus ▶ *ticket sellers* (minimum age 16) at $6 to $8 per hour plus bonus. Applicants must submit a formal organization application, three personal references, internships require a resume. An in-person interview is required.

Benefits and Preemployment Training On-the-job training and discounted meals. Preemployment training is required and includes accident prevention and safety, first aid, leadership skills.

Contact Brent A. Barr, Employment Manager, Worlds of Fun/Oceans of Fun. Telephone: 816-454-4545. Fax: 816-454-4655. World Wide Web: http://www.worldsoffun.com. Application deadline: continuous.

MONTANA

A CHRISTIAN MINISTRY IN THE NATIONAL PARKS– MONTANA
See A Christian Ministry in the National Parks–Massachussetts on page 138 for complete description.

BEST WESTERN BUCKS T-4 LODGE OF BIG SKY
PO BOX 160279
BIG SKY, MONTANA 59716

General Information 75-unit Best Western Lodge serving skiers, outdoor enthusiasts, and visitors to Yellowstone National Park. Established in 1972. 20-acre facility located 40 miles from Bozeman. Features: Yellowstone National Park; Big Sky Resort; Gallatin River; mountain setting.

Profile of Summer Employees Total number: 60; typical ages: 19–25. 50% men; 50% women; 10% minorities; 5% high school students; 20% college students; 5% retirees; 80% local applicants.

Employment Information Openings are from May 21 to October 1. Year-round positions also offered. Jobs available: ▶ 10 *cooks* at $5–$8 per hour ▶ 8 *dishwashers* at $6 per hour ▶ 5 *front desk staff* with computer and typing skills at $7 per hour ▶ 10 *housekeeping staff* at $6–$7 per hour ▶ 25 *waitstaff* at $5 per hour. Applicants must submit a formal organization application. International applicants accepted; must obtain own visa, obtain own working papers. An in-person interview is recommended, but a telephone interview is acceptable.

Benefits and Preemployment Training Housing at a cost, meals at a cost, possible full-time employment, and on-the-job training.

Contact Deb Dechert, Operations Manager, Best Western Bucks T-4 Lodge of Big Sky, PO Box 160279, Big Sky, Montana 59716. Telephone: 406-995-4111. Fax: 406-995-2191. E-mail: buckst4@mcn.net. World Wide Web: http://www.buckst4.com. Application deadline: continuous.

BIG SKY OF MONTANA SKI AND SUMMER RESORT
PO BOX 160001
BIG SKY, MONTANA 59716

General Information Winter and summer resort attracting both families and conventions. Established in 1976. 10,000-acre facility located 45 miles from Bozeman. Features: full-service resort facilities; Rocky Mountain setting; golf course.

Profile of Summer Employees Total number: 350; typical ages: 19–27. 50% men; 50% women; 5% minorities; 5% high school students; 80% college students; 5% local applicants.

Employment Information Openings are from June 1 to October 4. Winter break and year-round positions also offered. Jobs available: ▶ *accountants* (minimum age 18) with bookkeeping experience preferred ▶ *bartender* (minimum age 18) with previous barteding experience ▶ *bellmen* (minimum age 18) ▶ *bussers* (minimum age 18) ▶ *concierge staff* (minimum age 18) ▶ *conference services personnel* (minimum age 18) ▶ *cooks* (minimum age 18) with cooking experience preferred ▶ *dishwashers* (minimum age 18) ▶ *food and beverage positions* (minimum age 18) ▶ *front desk personnel* (minimum age 18) ▶ *golf course maintenance persons* (minimum age 18) ▶ *golf pro-shop staff* (minimum age 18) ▶ *hosts/hostesses* (minimum age 18) ▶ *housekeepers* (minimum age 18) ▶ 3 *housekeeping dispatchers* ▶ *laundry staff* (minimum age 18) ▶ *public area attendants* (minimum age 18) ▶ *reservations staff* (minimum age 18) ▶ *retail sales personnel* (minimum age 18) ▶ *room inspectors* (minimum age 18) with supervisory skills and an eye for detail ▶ *ticket sales/lift operators (winter season)* (minimum age 18) ▶ *waitstaff* (minimum age 18) with food service experience required. Applicants must submit a formal organization application, two letters of recommendation. International applicants accepted; must obtain own visa, obtain own working papers. A telephone interview is required.

Benefits and Preemployment Training Housing at a cost, meals at a cost, possible full-time employment, on-the-job training, and bonus program, facility activity discounts, lodging discounts for family. Preemployment training is required and includes CPR.

Contact Cindy Olsen, Human Resources Recruiter, Big Sky of Montana Ski and Summer Resort, PO Box 160001 c/o Personnel, Big Sky, Montana 59716. Telephone: 406-995-5812. Fax: 406-995-5001. E-mail: jstice@bigskyresort.com. World Wide Web: http://www.bigskyresort. com. Application deadline: continuous.

HAMILTON STORES, INC.
PO BOX 250
WEST YELLOWSTONE, MONTANA 59758

General Information Fourteen general stores located throughout Yellowstone National Park with general offices and a warehouse in West Yellowstone, Montana. Established in 1915. 2,000,000-acre facility located 90 miles from Bozeman. Features: National Park; thermal features; fishing; hiking; white water rafting; canoeing.

Profile of Summer Employees Total number: 1,000; typical ages: 18–82. 49% men; 51% women; 12% minorities; 30% college students; 70% retirees; 1% non-U.S. citizens; 1% local applicants.

Employment Information Openings are from March 23 to October 20. Jobs available: ▶ 20–25 *auditors* (minimum age 19) with background in 10-key and money handling at $5.40 to $6.25 per hour plus $.40 per hour incentive completion bonus ▶ 5 *clerical personnel* (minimum age 19) with office experience at $5.15 to $6.00 per hour plus $.40 per hour incentive completion bonus ▶ 10–15 *custodians* (minimum age 19) with ability to lift 50 pounds at $5.15 per hour plus $.40 per hour incentive completion bonus ▶ 20–25 *dining room assistants* (minimum age 18) at $5.15 per hour plus $.40 per hour incentive completion bonus ▶ 10 *dishwashers* (minimum age 18) at $5.15 per hour plus $.40 per hour incentive completion bonus ▶ 10–12 *dormitory* *managers* (minimum age 19) with ability to lift 50 pounds; must work May through September at $5.30 per hour plus $.40 per hour incentive completion bonus ▶ 20–30 *employee dining room cooks* (minimum age 19) with experience in large volume food preparation at $5.40 to $7 per hour plus $.40 per hour incentive completion bonus ▶ 40–100 *food service clerks* (minimum age 18) at $3.15-5.15 per hour plus $.40 per hour incentive completion bonus plus gratuities for some jobs ▶ 30–50 *fry cooks* (minimum age 19) (prior experience is helpful but not necessary) at $6.15 per hour plus $.40 per hour incentive completion bonus ▶ 50–100 *grocery clerks* (minimum age 21) at $5.15 per hour plus $.40 per hour incentive completion bonus ▶ 8 *maintenance workers* with general maintenance experience in plumbing, electrical work, etc. at $7 to $10 per hour plus $.40 per hour incentive completion bonus (season is March through November) ▶ 100–200 *sales clerks* (minimum age 18) with cash register experience preferred at $5.15 per hour plus $.40 per hour incentive completion bonus ▶ 50 *warehouse workers* (minimum age 19) must be able to lift 70 pounds at $5.15 to $6.50 per hour plus $.40 per hour incentive completion bonus. Applicants must submit formal organization application, letter of recommendation, personal statement. International applicants accepted; must obtain own visa, obtain own working papers, apply through a recognized agency. A telephone interview is required.

Benefits and Preemployment Training Housing at a cost, meals at a cost, and on-the-job training. Preemployment training is required and includes accident prevention and safety, sales and other job related training.

Contact Charlene Owens, Human Resources Assistant, Hamilton Stores, Inc., 1709 West College Street, Bozeman, Montana 59715. Telephone: 406-587-2208. Fax: 406-587-3105. E-mail: jobs@hamiltonstores.com. World Wide Web: http://www.hamiltonstores.com/employment. Application deadline: August 20.

LAZY K BAR RANCH
PO BOX 550
BIG TIMBER, MONTANA 59011

General Information One-hundred-seventeen-year-old operating cattle and horse ranch that has welcomed selected guests for 76 summers. Established in 1887. 22,000-acre facility located 100 miles from Billings. Features: river; swimming pool; mountains; lakes; timber; seclusion.

Profile of Summer Employees Total number: 15–18; typical ages: 16–25. 40% men; 60% women; 1% minorities; 45% high school students; 40% college students; 5% retirees; 5% non-U.S. citizens; 5% local applicants. Nonsmokers preferred.

Employment Information Openings are from June 10 to September 10. Jobs available: ▶ 1 *children's wrangler (female)* with extensive childcare experience and horse expertise at $550 per month ▶ 1 *chore person* (minimum age 16) with experience with milk cows at $450 per month ▶ 1 *dishwasher* (minimum age 17) at $500 per month ▶ 1 *head cook* (minimum age 20) with ability to cook for 45-50 people and experience in the field at $800–$1200 per month ▶ 3 *housekeepers/laundry workers* (minimum age 16) with housekeeping and laundry experience at $500 per month ▶ 1 *second cook/baker* (minimum age 18) with baking experience at $600 per month ▶ 1 *split-shift worker* (minimum age 20) with experience in cooking, baking, cleaning, waiting tables, and laundry at $535 per month ▶ 1 *storekeeper* (minimum age 18) with attention to detail at $500 per month ▶ 3 *waiters/waitresses* (minimum age 16) with serving experience at $500 per month ▶ 1 *winter caretaker* with desire for solitude and experience with chainsaws and other tools (position available from September 12 to June 12) at $500 per month ▶ 3 *wranglers* (minimum age 17) with extensive experience in the field at $550 per month. Applicants must submit formal organization application, resume, three letters of recommendation. International applicants accepted; must obtain own visa, obtain own working papers, apply through a recognized agency. An in-person interview is recommended, but a telephone interview is acceptable.

Benefits and Preemployment Training Free housing, free meals, and on-the-job training.

Contact Carol Kirby, Partner, Lazy K Bar Ranch, Box 1181, Big Timber, Montana 59011. Telephone: 406-932-4449. Fax: 406-932-4442. E-mail: kirby@mcn.net. World Wide Web: http://www.mcn.net/~kirby/lazykbar.htm. Application deadline: April 1.

NINE QUARTER CIRCLE RANCH
5000 TAYLOR FORK ROAD
GALLATIN GATEWAY, MONTANA 59730

General Information Family-oriented dude ranch hosting 75 guests weekly. 1,000-acre facility located 60 miles from Bozeman.

Profile of Summer Employees 40% men; 60% women; 90% college students; 10% retirees.

Employment Information Openings are from May 15 to September 15. Jobs available: ▶ 2 *baby sitters* with first aid and adult, child, and infant CPR certification at $700–$800 per month ▶ 4 *cabin cleaners/servers* at $700–$800 per month ▶ 2 *kitchen helpers/dishwashers* ▶ 1 *laundry worker* at $750 per month ▶ *maintenance workers* with ability to make minor repairs and knowledge of carpentry at $700–$800 per month ▶ 4 *ranch hands* with first aid and adult, child, and infant CPR certification at $700–$800 per month ▶ 1 *second cook* at $700–$800 per month.

Benefits and Preemployment Training Free housing, free meals, and on-the-job training.

Contact Kelly Kelsey, Owners, Nine Quarter Circle Ranch, 5000 Taylor Fork Road, Gallatin Gateway, Montana 59730. Telephone: 406-995-4276. World Wide Web: http://www.ninequartercircle. com. Application deadline: continuous.

ST. MARY LODGE & RESORT
GLACIER NATIONAL PARK
ST. MARY, MONTANA 59417

General Information One of Montana's noted full-service high country resorts. Established in 1932. 100-acre facility located 90 miles from Kalispell. Features: mountain setting; updated rustic physical setting; small town atmosphere; 900 miles of hiking trails; exceptional staff.

Profile of Summer Employees Total number: 180; typical ages: 19–24. 40% men; 60% women; 2% minorities; 3% high school students; 80% college students; 3% retirees; 2% non U.S. citizens; 10% local applicants. Nonsmokers preferred.

Employment Information Openings are from May 1 to October 15. Jobs available: ▶ 4 *accounting/secretarial staff members* with experience in the field at $910 per month ▶ 6 *bartenders/cocktail servers* with experience at $893 per month ▶ 5 *clerical staff members* at $910 per month ▶ 11 *deli cooks* at $910 per month ▶ 14 *dishwashing/kitchen personnel* at $910 per month ▶ 4 *front desk clerks* at $910 per month ▶ 5 *gas station attendants* at $910 per month ▶ 10 *gift shop clerks* with experience at $910 per month ▶ 6 *hosts/buspersons* at $893 per month ▶ 15 *housekeepers* at $936 per month ▶ 10 *maintenance personnel* at $910 per month ▶ 12 *pantry/fry cooks* with experience at $936–$953 per month ▶ 4 *pizza parlor staff members* at $910–$936 per month ▶ 3 *sporting-goods clerks* at $910 per month ▶ 9 *supermarket staff members* at $910 per month ▶ 26 *waiters/waitresses* with experience at $893 per month. Applicants must submit formal organization application, three personal references. International applicants accepted; must obtain own visa, obtain own working papers, apply through a recognized agency. An in-person interview is recommended, but a telephone interview is acceptable.

Benefits and Preemployment Training Housing at a cost, meals at a cost, and on-the-job training. Preemployment training is required and includes accident prevention and safety, interpersonal skills, leadership skills.

Contact Rocky Black, Resort Manager, St. Mary Lodge & Resort, PO Box 1808, Sun Valley, Idaho 83353. Telephone: 208-726-6279. Fax: 208-726-6282. E-mail: jobs@glcpark.com. World Wide Web: http://www.glcpark.com. Application deadline: continuous.

63 RANCH
PO BOX 979
LIVINGSTON, MONTANA 59047

General Information Working cattle and dude ranch operating from June through September with capacity for 30 guests. Ranch specializes in teaching horseback riding on all levels. Established in 1929. 2,000-acre facility located 50 miles from Bozeman. Features: Gallatin National Forest; Absaroka—BearTooth Wilderness; Yellowstone National Park; Yellowstone River; 5 mountain ranges; where the mountains meet the prairie.

Profile of Summer Employees Total number: 20; typical ages: 18–70. 47% men; 53% women;

5% high school students; 45% college students; 10% retirees; 10% local applicants. Nonsmokers required.

Employment Information Openings are from June 1 to September 15. Jobs available: ▶ 6–8 *cabin cleaners, dishwashers, and dining room servers* (minimum age 18) with first aid and CPR certifications at $800–$1000 per month ▶ 1 *head cook* (minimum age 18) with health certificate, first aid, CPR, and ability to run a kitchen and cook for 50 people at $1700–$2200 per month ▶ 1 *kitchen helper* (minimum age 18) with first aid, CPR, and health certificate at $800 per month ▶ 1 *second cook* (minimum age 18) with first aid, CPR, health certificate, and experience at $1000–$1500 per month. Applicants must submit formal organization application, cover letter, three personal references, three work references with phone numbers. International applicants accepted; must obtain own visa, obtain own working papers, apply through a recognized agency. An in-person interview is recommended, but a telephone interview is acceptable.

Benefits and Preemployment Training Free housing, free meals, on-the-job training, opportunity to attend seminars/workshops, and reimbursement for travel by bus. Preemployment training is required and includes accident prevention and safety, first aid, CPR, job skills.

Contact Sandra C. Cahill, President, 63 Ranch, PO Box 979-P, Livingston, Montana 59047. Telephone: 406-222-0570. Fax: 406-222-9446. E-mail: sixty3ranch@mcn.net. Application deadline: continuous.

THE SOUTHWESTERN COMPANY, MONTANA
See The Southwestern Company, Tennessee on page 284 for complete description.

STUDENT CONSERVATION ASSOCIATION (SCA), MONTANA
See Student Conservation Association (SCA), New Hampshire on page 193 for complete description.

SWEET GRASS RANCH
MELVILLE ROUTE, BOX 161
BIG TIMBER, MONTANA 59011

General Information Working cattle ranch that accepts 20 guests to live ranch life. Established in 1965. 20,000-acre facility located 120 miles from Billings. Features: mountains; stream for fishing; horseback riding; working ranch experience; guests from around the world.

Profile of Summer Employees Total number: 10; typical ages: 20–30. 50% men; 50% women; 100% college students; 25% local applicants. Nonsmokers preferred.

Employment Information Openings are from June 1 to September 10. Jobs available: ▶ 2 *cabin staff members* (minimum age 19) with organizational and interpersonal skills, and attention to cleanliness and detail at $700-$750 per month plus room, board, and tips ▶ 2 *cooks* (minimum age 19) with group cooking experience and love of cooking; experience or training as a baker/cook; attention to detail and ability to work well with others at $800-$1000 per month plus room, board, and tips ▶ 1 *swingshift worker* (minimum age 19) with organizational and interpersonal skills; attention to cleanliness and detail; experience with group cooking; experience or training as a baker/cook; and ability to work well with others at $750-$800 per month, plus room, board, and tips. Applicants must submit a formal organization application, resume, personal reference, two letters of recommendation. International applicants accepted; must obtain own visa, obtain own working papers. A telephone interview is required.

Benefits and Preemployment Training Free housing, free meals, and on-the-job training.

Contact Shelly Carroccia, Owner, Sweet Grass Ranch, HC 87 Box 2161, Big Timber, Montana 59011. Telephone: 406-537-4477. Fax: 406-537-4477. E-mail: sweetgrass@mcn.net. Application deadline: April 30.

NEBRASKA

ACE COMPUTER CAMP–NEBRASKA
See ACE Computer Camp–Washington on page 307 for complete description.

CALVIN CREST CAMP, RETREAT, AND CONFERENCE CENTER
2870 COUNTY ROAD 13
FREMONT, NEBRASKA 68025

General Information Church-affiliated camp and conference/retreat facility serving approximately 800 campers annually. Established in 1958. 255-acre facility located 5 miles from Fremont. Features: swimming pool; low ropes challenge course; tennis court; frisbee golf course.

Profile of Summer Employees Total number: 30; typical ages: 16–21. 50% men; 50% women; 20% high school students; 50% college students; 30% retirees; 80% local applicants. Nonsmokers preferred.

Employment Information Openings are from June 1 to August 15. Jobs available: ▶ 14 *core counselor* (minimum age 19) at $1040 per season ▶ 2–4 *food service staff members* (minimum age 16) at $5.40–$6.25 per hour ▶ 1–2 *housekeeping staff members* (minimum age 16) at $5.40–$6 per hour ▶ 3 *lifeguards* (minimum age 18) with Red Cross lifeguard training at $130–$150 per week ▶ 2 *wranglers* (minimum age 19) with wrangler certification at $900 per season. Applicants must submit three personal references, two letters of recommendation. An in-person interview is recommended, but a telephone interview is acceptable.

Benefits and Preemployment Training Free housing, free meals, and on-the-job training. Preemployment training is required and includes accident prevention and safety, first aid, CPR, interpersonal skills, leadership skills.

Contact Doug Morton, Administrator, Calvin Crest Camp, Retreat, and Conference Center, 2870 County Road 13, Fremont, Nebraska 68025. Telephone: 402-628-6455. Fax: 402-628-8255. E-mail: calvin_crest@navix.net. Application deadline: continuous.

CAMP EASTER SEAL
2470 VAN DORN ROAD
MILFORD, NEBRASKA 68405

General Information Residential camp serving children and adults with physical and developmental disabilities. Established in 1968. 70-acre facility located 5 miles from Lincoln. Features: wooded setting; high and low ropes course; computer center with internet access; modern cabins; surrounded by the Big Blue River; recreational and therapeutic experiences.

Profile of Summer Employees Total number: 35–40; typical ages: 18–25. 33% men; 67% women; 5% minorities; 33% high school students; 50% college students; 25% local applicants.

Employment Information Openings are from June 1 to August 15. Jobs available. ▶ *assistant cook* (minimum age 21) who knows way around the kitchn, is hardworking, and fun at $200–$250 per week ▶ 9 *cabin leaders* (minimum age 18) must have a caring heart, be safety conscious, fun, and energetic at $175–$195 per week ▶ 1 *camp office manager* (minimum age 21) with some clerical experience, knowledge about computers, ambitious, and energetic at $195–$215 per week ▶ 1–10 *head counselors* (minimum age 18) must be willing to learn, be energetic, and have a caring heart at $195–$215 per week ▶ 3 *kitchen assistants* (minimum age 18) must be hard working, ambitious, with some knowledge of food preparation at $150–$160 per week ▶ 1 *lifeguard* (minimum age 20) with WSI certification at $175–$275 per week ▶ 2 *nurses* (minimum age 23) with RN/LPN license (Nebraska) at $350–$450 per week ▶ 1–2 *program directors* (minimum age 20) must be creative, energetic, fun, have experience with some programming, and have a caring heart at $250–$300 per week ▶ 6 *program positions* (minimum age 19) must have a caring heart and be creative, energetic, and fun at $175–$195 per week ▶ 1 *ropes/adventure instructor* (minimum age 21) with some experience, safety conscious, and has current first aid and CPR certifications at $195–$225 per week. Applicants must submit formal organization application, three personal references, three letters of recommendation. International applicants accepted; must obtain own visa, obtain own working papers, apply through a recognized agency. An in-person interview is recommended, but a telephone interview is acceptable.

Benefits and Preemployment Training Free housing, free meals, and formal training. Preemployment training is required and includes accident prevention and safety, first aid, CPR, interpersonal skills, leadership skills.

Contact Brian Stirton, Director of Camping and Recreation, Camp Easter Seal, 2470 Van Dorn Road, Milford, Nebraska 68405. Telephone: 402-761-2875. Fax: 402-761-2282. E-mail: bstirton@ aol.com. Application deadline: May 25.

THE SOUTHWESTERN COMPANY, NEBRASKA
See The Southwestern Company, Tennessee on page 284 for complete description.

STUDENT CONSERVATION ASSOCIATION (SCA), NEBRASKA
See Student Conservation Association (SCA), New Hampshire on page 193 for complete description.

NEVADA

ACE COMPUTER CAMP–NEVADA
See ACE Computer Camp–Washington on page 307 for complete description.

HARVEYS RESORT & CASINO
PO BOX 128
STATELINE, NEVADA 89449

General Information Resort hotel/casino with 740 hotel rooms, 7 restaurants, and 88,000 square miles of casino space. Established in 1944. Located 50 miles from Reno. Features: 740 hotel rooms; 7 restaurants; health club; Lake Tahoe; cabaret theatre; 88,000 square feet casino floor.

Profile of Summer Employees Total number: 2,800; typical ages: 18–30. 50% men; 50% women; 30% minorities; 8% high school students; 40% college students; 2% retirees; 40% non-U.S. citizens; 10% local applicants.

Employment Information Openings are from May 15 to October 1. Winter break and year-round positions also offered. Jobs available: ▶ *various positions* with excellent customer service skills at $5.15–$8 per hour. Applicants must submit formal organization application. International applicants accepted; must obtain own visa, obtain own working papers, apply through a recognized agency. An in-person interview is recommended, but a telephone interview is acceptable.

Benefits and Preemployment Training Free meals, possible full-time employment, and on-the-job training. Preemployment training is required and includes customer service.

Contact Cheryll Pearson, Employment Supervisor, Harveys Resort & Casino. Telephone: 800-553-1022 Ext. 2085. Fax: 775-588-8084. E-mail: work@harveys.com. World Wide Web: http:// http://www.harveys-tahoe.com/employment. Application deadline: continuous.

THE SOUTHWESTERN COMPANY, NEVADA
See The Southwestern Company, Tennessee on page 284 for complete description.

STUDENT CONSERVATION ASSOCIATION (SCA), NEVADA
See Student Conservation Association (SCA), New Hampshire on page 193 for complete description.

WILD ISLAND FAMILY ADVENTURE PARK
250 WILD ISLAND COURT
SPARKS, NEVADA 89434

General Information Amusement park with miniature golf course, go-kart track, indoor arcade, and waterpark. Established in 1988. 11-acre facility located 5 miles from Reno. Features: wave pool; 2 speed slides; 36-hole mini golf course; 3 family slides; interactive water play area; go-kart racetrack.

Profile of Summer Employees Total number: 250; typical ages: 14–20. 60% men; 40% women; 20% minorities; 80% high school students; 10% college students; 3% retirees; 100% local applicants. Nonsmokers preferred.

Employment Information Openings are from May 1 to September 30. Year-round positions also offered. Jobs available: ▶ 12–16 *admissions attendants* (minimum age 14) at $4.50–$5.50 per hour ▶ 4–6 *admissions cashiers* (minimum age 15) at $5–$6 per hour ▶ 4–6 *golf course cashiers* (minimum age 16) at $5–$7 per hour ▶ 6–10 *kitchen cashiers* (minimum age 15) at $4.50–$7 per hour ▶ 20–30 *kitchen runners* (minimum age 14) at $4.50–$5 per hour ▶ 75–90 *lifeguards* (minimum age 15) with Ellis and Associates certification at $4.50–$6.50 per hour ▶ 15–20 *park services attendants* (minimum age 14) at $4.50–$6 per hour ▶ 6–10 *raceway attendants* (minimum age 16) with small engine repair experience preferred; at $5.50–$7 per hour. Applicants must submit a formal organization application. An in-person interview is required.

Benefits and Preemployment Training Meals at a cost, possible full-time employment, names of contacts, and on-the-job training. Preemployment training is required and includes accident prevention and safety, first aid, CPR, interpersonal skills, leadership skills, customer service, job specific.

Contact Erica Millick, Office Manager, Wild Island Family Adventure Park, 250 Wild Island Court, Sparks, Nevada 89434. Telephone: 702-359-2927 Ext. 101. Fax: 702-359-5942. Application deadline: continuous.

NEW HAMPSHIRE

ACE COMPUTER CAMP–NEW HAMPSHIRE
See ACE Computer Camp–Washington on page 307 for complete description.

THE BALSAMS GRAND RESORT HOTEL
ROUTE 26
DIXVILLE NOTCH, NEW HAMPSHIRE 03576-9710

General Information Facility catering to vacationers (July, August, and winter) as well as convention groups (spring and fall). Established in 1866. 15,000-acre facility located 200 miles from Boston, MA. Features: lake; mountains; hiking trails; 2 golf courses; 2 tennis courts; mountain biking trails.

Profile of Summer Employees Total number: 400; typical ages: 18–30. 50% men; 50% women; 11% minorities; 4% high school students; 22% college students; 6% retirees; 6% non-U.S. citizens; 53% local applicants.

Employment Information Openings are from June 15 to October 18. Winter break positions also offered. Jobs available: ▶ 5 *bellpersons* (minimum age 18) at $5.25 per hour ▶ 5 *beverage servers* (minimum age 18) at $200 to $300 per week plus gratuities ▶ 30 *dining room waitstaff members* at $200 to $400 per week plus gratuities ▶ 10 *housekeeping staff members* (minimum age 18) at $200 to $300 per week plus gratuities ▶ 5 *kitchen staff members* (minimum age 18) at $6 per hour ▶ 5 *laundry staff members* (minimum age 18) at $6 per hour ▶ 3 *lifeguards* (minimum age 18) with lifeguard certification at $720–$840 per month. Applicants must submit a formal organization application, resume, writing sample. International applicants accepted; must obtain own visa, obtain own working papers.

Benefits and Preemployment Training Housing at a cost, meals at a cost, formal training, on-the-job training, and free tennis, golf, hiking (winter: skiing, ice skating, snow shoeing).

Contact Suzanne Ingram, Director of Personnel, The BALSAMS Grand Resort Hotel, Route 26, Dixville Notch, New Hampshire 03576. Telephone: 603-255-3400 Ext. 2666. Fax: 603-255-4670. World Wide Web: http://www.thebalsams.com. Application deadline: continuous.

BROOKWOODS FOR BOYS/DEER RUN FOR GIRLS
CHESTNUT COVE ROAD
ALTON, NEW HAMPSHIRE 03809

General Information Residential religious camps serving 250 campers in two-, four-, six-, and eight-week sessions. Established in 1944. 300-acre facility located 100 miles from Boston, Massachusetts. Features: large freshwater lake.

Profile of Summer Employees Total number: 115; typical ages: 18–55. 50% men; 50% women; 10% minorities; 10% high school students; 90% college students; 10% non-U.S. citizens; 20% local applicants. Nonsmokers required.

Employment Information Openings are from June 18 to August 22. Winter break and year-round positions also offered. Jobs available: ▶ 10 *general counselors* with minimum one year of college completed at $2000 per season ▶ 3 *riding instructors* with CHA certification at $1750 per season ▶ 2 *riflery instructors* with NRA certification at $2000 per season ▶ 4 *trip staff members* (minimum age 21) with CPR and first aid certification; must be over 21 to drive 15-passenger van at $2200 per season ▶ 10 *waterfront staff members* with WSI and LGT certification at $2200 per season ▶ 2 *waterskiing instructors* with LGT certification at $2000 per season. Applicants must submit formal organization application, three personal references. International applicants accepted; must apply through a recognized agency. An in-person interview is recommended, but a telephone interview is acceptable.

Benefits and Preemployment Training Free housing, free meals, formal training, on-the-job training, and travel reimbursement. Preemployment training is required and includes accident prevention and safety, first aid, CPR, interpersonal skills, leadership skills.

Contact Bob Strodel, Executive Director, Brookwoods for Boys/Deer Run for Girls, Chestnut Cove Road, Alton, New Hampshire 03809. Telephone: 603-875-3600. Fax: 603-875-4602. E-mail: brook@worldpath.net. Application deadline: continuous.

CAMP DEERWOOD
HOLDERNESS, NEW HAMPSHIRE 03245

General Information Residential camp serving 120 boys for seven weeks. 80-acre facility located 100 miles from Boston, Massachusetts.

Profile of Summer Employees Typical ages: 19–30. 100% men; 60% college students.

Employment Information Openings are from June 20 to August 15. Jobs available: ▶ *general counselors* with WSI/lifeguard certification preferred at $1200–$2500 per season ▶ *swimming instructors* with WSI/lifeguard certification at $1200–$2500 per season.

Benefits and Preemployment Training Free housing, free meals, and on-the-job training. Preemployment training is required and includes accident prevention and safety, first aid, CPR, interpersonal skills, leadership skills.

Contact Tommy Thomsen, Director-Deerwood, Camp Deerwood, Box 188, Holderness, New Hampshire 03245. Telephone: 603-279-4237. Application deadline: February 1.

CAMP MERROWVISTA
147 CANAAN ROAD
OSSIPEE, NEW HAMPSHIRE 03864

General Information Coed residential program for students ages 8–16. The focus is on leadership development and includes general program activities for students ages 8–12 and extended backpacking, canoeing, and cycling for students ages 13–16. Established in 1924. 600-acre facility located 140 miles from Boston, Massachusetts. Features: freshwater lake; beautiful mountains; trails leave right from camp into mountains; rustic, wooded setting.

Profile of Summer Employees Total number: 85; typical ages: 18–56. 50% men; 50% women; 2% minorities; 10% high school students; 60% college students; 3% non-U.S. citizens. Nonsmokers required.

Employment Information Openings are from June 15 to August 23. Winter break and year-round positions also offered. Jobs available: ▶ 1 *arts and crafts coordinator* (minimum age 18, 21 preferred) with crafts knowledge at $1200–$1800 per season ▶ 1 *bike mechanic* (minimum age 18, 21 preferred) with experience repairing and assembling touring bicycles, instruction of touring road safety, and bike maintenance at $1000–$1800 per season ▶ 1–4 *kitchen staff members* (minimum age 18, 21 preferred) with desire to pursue culinary arts as a career at $600–$2000 per season ▶ 1 *naturalist* (minimum 18, 21 preferred) with experience teaching environmental activities; live animal experience preferred at $1200–$1800 per season ▶ 1 *nurse* (minimum age 21) with RN eligibility for New Hampshire license at $275–$350 per week ▶ 1 *office staff member* (minimum age 18, 21 preferred) with computer skills at $1300–$2000 per season ▶ 1 *outcamping equipment coordinator* (minimum age 18, 21 preferred) with ability to perform repair, inventory, check-out/check-in of backpacking and canoeing equipment; some driving of passenger vans required at $1000–$1800 per season ▶ 1 *outcamping food coordinator* (minimum age 18, 21 preferred) with an interest in outdoor education at $1000–$1800 per season ▶ *program directors* (minimum age 21) with supervisory experience at $2000–$3000 per season ▶ 1–3 *sailing instructors* (minimum age 18) with experience sailing Laser I and Laser II boats and lifeguard certification at $1000–$1800 per season ▶ 12 *trip leaders* (minimum age 21) with experience leading trips, WFR, lifeguard, and CPR/first aid training preferred at $170–$270 per week ▶ 20 *village leaders* (minimum age 18) with WSI and lifeguard certification, CPR/first aid training preferred at $135–$240 per week ▶ 2 *waterfront staff members* (minimum age 21) with WSI and lifeguard certification required at $1000–$3000 per season. Applicants must submit formal organization application, three personal references, trip resume outlining outdoor experiences for trip leading. International applicants accepted; must apply through a recognized agency. A telephone interview is required.

Benefits and Preemployment Training Free housing, free meals, formal training, and travel reimbursement. Preemployment training is required and includes accident prevention and safety, first aid, interpersonal skills, leadership skills, Wilderness First Responder.

Contact Heather R. Kiley, Director of Camp Programs, Camp Merrowvista, 147 Canaan Road, Ossipee, New Hampshire 03864. Telephone: 603-539-6607. Fax: 603-539-7504. E-mail: merrowvist@aol.com. World Wide Web: http://www.ayf.com. Application deadline: continuous.

CAMP MOWGLIS
ROUTE 3A, PO BOX 9, NEWFOUND LAKE
HEBRON, NEW HAMPSHIRE 03241

General Information Residential camp for boys ages 7-14 offers traditional camp activities including crafts, archery, riflery, crew program, canoeing, sailing, tennis, and extensive trip program hiking in the mountains of New England. Established in 1903. 57-acre facility located 45 miles from Concord. Features: on Newfound Lake; forest setting; mountains; 2 tennis courts; canoes, sailboats, rowboats, and shells.

Profile of Summer Employees Total number: 35; typical ages: 15–45. 97% men; 3% women; 5% minorities; 10% high school students; 70% college students; 7% non-U.S. citizens; 8% local applicants. Nonsmokers required.

Employment Information Openings are from June 15 to August 20. Jobs available: ▶ 20 *counselors* (minimum age 18) with first aid/CPR preferred and ability to teach one or more of the following: tennis, riflery, archery, arts and crafts, rowing, canoeing, sailing, waterskiing, music, photography, swimming, hiking, nature, campcraft at $1200–$2500 per season ▶ 1 *nurse* with RN or LPN, and current first aid/CPR; salary negotiable ▶ 1 *ropes course facilitator* (minimum age 18) with ropes/challenge course certification and experience preferred at $1200–$2500 per season. Applicants must submit resume, letter of recommendation. International applicants accepted; must obtain own visa, obtain own working papers, apply through a recognized agency. A telephone interview is required.

Benefits and Preemployment Training Free housing and free meals. Preemployment training is required and includes accident prevention and safety, first aid, CPR, interpersonal skills, leadership skills.

Contact Tim Platt, Director, Camp Mowglis, PO Box 449, Moody, Maine 04054. Telephone: 207-646-3911. Fax: 207-646-3920. E-mail: cplattiv@mowglis.org. World Wide Web: http://www. mowglis.org. Application deadline: continuous.

CAMP PEMIGEWASSETT
ROUTE 25A ·
WENTWORTH, NEW HAMPSHIRE 03282

General Information Traditional residential camp for 170 boys ages 8–15. We have a seven–week session and a broad range of activities including sports, hiking, nature study, dramatics, and art. Established in 1908. 600-acre facility located 75 miles from Manchester. Features: private lake; 7 tennis courts; 3 baseball fields; 2 soccer/lacrosse fields; fully equipped woodshop; superb nature facility.

Profile of Summer Employees Total number: 75; typical ages: 17–60. 90% men; 10% women; 5% minorities; 20% high school students; 40% college students; 8% retirees; 8% non-U.S. citizens; 10% local applicants. Nonsmokers required.

Employment Information Openings are from June 21 to August 16. Jobs available: ▶ *assistant counselors* (minimum age 17) with Red Cross CPR certification preferred at $950–$1000 per season ▶ *cabin counselors/instructors* (minimum age 18) with Red Cross first aid and CPR certification preferred; minimum of one year of college completed at $1100–$1400 per season ▶ *cabin counselors/swimming instructors* (minimum age 18) with Red Cross WSI certification; minimum of one year of college completed at $1100–$1500 per season ▶ *kitchen workers* (minimum age 16) at $1000–$1300 per season. Applicants must submit formal organization application, cover letter, three personal references. International applicants accepted; must apply through a recognized agency. An in-person interview is required.

Benefits and Preemployment Training Free housing, free meals, formal training, and on-the-job training. Preemployment training is required and includes accident prevention and safety, interpersonal skills, leadership skills.

Contact Robert Grabill, Director, Camp Pemigewassett, 25 Rayton Road, Hanover, New Hampshire 03755. Telephone: 603-643-8055. Fax: 603-643-9601. E-mail: robert.grabill@valley. net. Application deadline: continuous.

CAMP ROBIN HOOD FOR BOYS AND GIRLS
OSSIPEE LAKE ROAD
FREEDOM, NEW HAMPSHIRE 03836

General Information Residential camp serving 260 boys and girls ages 7–16 for 4- and 8-week sessions. Established in 1927. 210-acre facility located 60 miles from Portland, Maine. Features: freshwater lake; wooded setting; extensive athletic fields; cabins with electricity and bathrooms; beautiful stables and riding facilities; lighted tennis, basketball, and volleyball courts.

Profile of Summer Employees Total number: 120; typical ages: 18–70. 60% men; 40% women; 3% minorities; 15% high school students; 70% college students; 20% non-U.S. citizens. Nonsmokers preferred.

Employment Information Openings are from June 20 to August 20. Jobs available: ▶ 1 *archery instructor* (minimum age 19) with experience in the field at $700–$1400 per season ▶ 1 *ceramics instructor* (minimum age 19) with experience with wheel and kiln at $800–$1200 per season ▶ 2 *crafts instructors* (minimum age 19) with experience in the field at $800–$1200 per season ▶ 1 *dance instructor* (minimum age 19) at $1000–$1200 per season ▶ 10 *general counselors* (minimum age 19) at $600–$800 per season ▶ 1 *gymnastics instructor* (minimum age 19) with experience in the field at $700–$1200 per season ▶ 10 *kitchen/pantry staff* (minimum age 17) at $500–$1200 per season ▶ 2 *maintenance staff* (minimum age 19) with general carpentry skills at $1000–$1500 per season ▶ 2 *nurses* with RN certification at $2000–$3000 per season ▶ 3 *riding instructors* with English riding teaching experience at $800–$1500 per season ▶ 3 *sailing and canoeing instructors* (minimum age 19) with experience in the field at $700–$1200 per season ▶ 2 *secretaries* (minimum age 18) with computer skills at $700–$1200 per season ▶ 8 *sports coaches* (minimum age 19) with experience in the field at $800–$1500 per season ▶ 4 *swimming instructors* (minimum age 19) with WSI certification, lifeguard training, or Bronze Medallion at $800–$1400 per season ▶ 1 *tennis director* (minimum age 20) with teaching and program directing experience at $1800–$3000 per season ▶ 5 *tennis instructors* (minimum age 18) with playing and/or teaching experience at $800–$1500 per season ▶ 3 *waterskiing instructors/boat drivers* (minimum age 19) with experience in the field at $800–$1400 per season. Applicants must submit formal organization application, three personal references. International applicants accepted; must apply through a recognized agency. An in-person interview is recommended, but a telephone interview is acceptable.

Benefits and Preemployment Training Free housing, free meals, formal training, and on-the-job training. Preemployment training is required and includes accident prevention and safety, first aid, CPR, interpersonal skills, leadership skills.

Contact John Klein, Director, Camp Robin Hood for Boys and Girls, 344 Thistle Trail, Mayfield Heights, Ohio 44124. Telephone: 440-646-1911. Fax: 440-646-1972. E-mail: robinhdnh@aol. com. World Wide Web: http://www.camprobinhood.com. Application deadline: continuous.

CAMP TOHKOMEUPOG
HC 63, BOX 90
EAST MADISON, NEW HAMPSHIRE 03849

General Information Residential camp accommodating 120 boys ages 6–16 and featuring sports, mountain and canoe camping trips, and adventure program including ropes course and rock climbing. Established in 1932. 1,000-acre facility located 50 miles from Portland, ME. Features: freshwater lake; 5 tennis courts; near White Mountain National Forest; 1000 acres; climbing wall- ropes course; street hockey rink.

Profile of Summer Employees Total number: 35; typical ages: 17–65. 95% men; 5% women; 5% minorities; 10% high school students; 50% college students; 5% retirees; 10% non-U.S. citizens; 85% local applicants. Nonsmokers preferred.

Employment Information Openings are from June 23 to August 21. Winter break positions also offered. Jobs available: ▶ 1 *archery instructor* (minimum age 20) at $1300–$1800 per season ▶ 4 *cabin counselors* (minimum age 20) with CPR, lifeguard, and first aid training at $700–$1400 per season ▶ *kitchen helper* (minimum age 18) at $2000–$3000 per season. Applicants must submit formal organization application, resume, three personal references, two letters of recommendation. International applicants accepted; must obtain own visa, obtain own working papers, apply through a recognized agency. An in-person interview is recommended, but a telephone interview is acceptable.

Benefits and Preemployment Training Free housing, free meals, formal training, on-the-job training, and opportunity to attend seminars/workshops. Preemployment training is required and includes accident prevention and safety, first aid, CPR, interpersonal skills, leadership skills.

Contact Mr. Ted Hoyt, Director, Camp Tohkomeupog, HC 63, Box 40, East Madison, New Hampshire 03849. Telephone: 603-367-8362. Fax: 603-367-8664. E-mail: tohko@tohko.com. World Wide Web: http://www.tohko.com. Application deadline: continuous.

CAMP WALT WHITMAN
1000 CAPE MOONSHINE ROAD
PIERMONT, NEW HAMPSHIRE 03779

General Information Coeducational residential camp serving 350 campers and offering a strong general program. Established in 1948. 300-acre facility located 110 miles from Boston, Massachusetts. Features: freshwater lake; heated swimming pool; 11 clay tennis courts; multi sports complex; 3 arts studios; wooded, mountain setting.

Profile of Summer Employees Total number: 190; typical ages: 18–30. 50% men; 50% women; 75% college students; 2% retirees; 10% non-U.S. citizens. Nonsmokers required.

Employment Information Openings are from June 18 to August 19. Jobs available: ▶ 3 *art/*

woodshop instructors (minimum age 20) with experience at $1300–$2000 per season ▶ 1 *arts and crafts director* (minimum age 23) with experience at $1500–$3000 per season ▶ 2 *dance/ gymnastics instructors* (minimum age 19) with experience at $1200–$1800 per season ▶ 20 *general counselors* (minimum age 19) with experience at $1000–$1400 per season ▶ 3 *hiking and camping specialists* (minimum age 20) with experience at $1300–$1800 per season ▶ 6 *kitchen and maintenance personnel* (minimum age 20) with experience at $1200–$2500 per season ▶ 1 *radio station manager* (minimum age 19) with experience at $1200–$1500 per season ▶ 3 *sailing, canoeing, and windsurfing instructors* (minimum age 19) with experience at $1300–$2000 per season ▶ 6 *sports coaches* (minimum age 20) with experience in the field at $1200–$2000 per season ▶ 6 *swimming instructors* (minimum age 19) with WSI certification at $1300–$2000 per season ▶ 6 *tennis instructors* (minimum age 19) with experience at $1300– $2000 per season ▶ 2 *water skiing instructors* (minimum age 19) with experience at $1300– $2000 per season. Applicants must submit formal organization application, three personal references. International applicants accepted; must apply through a recognized agency. A telephone interview is required.

Benefits and Preemployment Training Free housing, free meals, formal training, on-the-job training, travel reimbursement, and leadership and management training. Preemployment training is required and includes accident prevention and safety, first aid, CPR, interpersonal skills, leadership skills.

Contact Jancy Dorfman, Director, Camp Walt Whitman, PO Box 938, Bedford, New York 10506. Telephone: 800-657-8282. Fax: 914-234-5487. E-mail: campwalt@aol.com. World Wide Web: http://www.campwalt.com. Application deadline: continuous.

CHENOA
BRIMSTONE CORNER ROAD
ANTRIM, NEW HAMPSHIRE 03440

General Information Girl Scout residential camp serving 125 girls ages 6–16 in one- and two-week sessions, emphasizing girl decision-making and leadership development. Established in 1994. 250-acre facility located 80 miles from Boston, Massachusetts. Features: freshwater lake; wooded area; all new buildings; beaver pond.

Profile of Summer Employees Total number: 40; typical ages: 18–35. 1% men; 99% women; 2% minorities; 50% college students; 15% non-U.S. citizens; 15% local applicants. Nonsmokers preferred.

Employment Information Openings are from June 16 to August 25. Jobs available: ▶ 2 *cooks* (minimum age 18) with experience in quantity cooking at $2400–$3200 per season ▶ 1 *nurse* (minimum age 21) with RN, LPN or EMT at $2000–$4000 per season ▶ 2–3 *program specialists* (minimum age 18) with experience teaching groups of children and ability to lead programs in science, math, diversity, and gender issues at $1400–$3200 per season ▶ 8–12 *unit counselors* (minimum age 18) with high school diploma and experience working with groups of children at $1400–$2400 per season ▶ 2–4 *waterfront assistants* (minimum age 18) with WSI, LGT at $1400–$2400 per season ▶ 1 *waterfront director* (minimum age 21) with WSI, LGT certification at $2400–$3200 per season. Applicants must submit formal organization application, three personal references. International applicants accepted; must apply through a recognized agency. An in-person interview is recommended, but a telephone interview is acceptable.

Benefits and Preemployment Training Free housing, free meals, formal training, health insurance, and on-the-job training. Preemployment training is required and includes accident prevention and safety, first aid, CPR, interpersonal skills, leadership skills, program skills.

Contact Missy Long, Camp Director, Chenoa, SWGSC, 88 Harvey Road, Manchester, New Hampshire 03103. Telephone: 800-654-1270. Fax: 603-627-4169. E-mail: camping@swgirlscouts. org. World Wide Web: http://www.swgirlscouts.org. Application deadline: continuous.

COLD RIVER CAMP, A.M.C.
HCR BOX 221
CENTER CONWAY, NEW HAMPSHIRE 03813

General Information Family camp for hiking and outdoor activities in White Mountain National Forest owned by Appalachian Mountain Club. Established in 1919. 135-acre facility located 65 miles from Portland, ME. Features: mountain setting; rustic setting; individual cabins; excellent meals; organized hikes; mountain streams.

Profile of Summer Employees Total number: 14; typical ages: 18–23. 50% men; 50% women; 20% high school students; 80% college students; 10% retirees; 30% non-U.S. citizens; 10% local applicants. Nonsmokers preferred.

Employment Information Openings are from June 24 to September 2. Jobs available: ▶ 8 *crew* (minimum age 18) at $2100 per season ▶ 2 *kitchen positions* (minimum age 18) with food preparation experience at $2700–$3500 per season. Applicants must submit formal organization application, cover letter, three personal references, three letters of recommendation. International applicants accepted; must apply through a recognized agency. An in-person interview is recommended, but a telephone interview is acceptable.

Benefits and Preemployment Training Free housing and free meals.

Contact Bill Waste, Manager, Cold River Camp, A.M.C., 69 Washburn Hill Road, Lyme, New Hampshire 03768. Telephone: 603-795-4440. Fax: 603-795-4277. E-mail: bill_waste@valley. net. Application deadline: January 31.

GENEVA POINT CENTER
MOULTONBORO, NEW HAMPSHIRE 03254

General Information Ecumenical conference center hosting groups and Elderhostel. Established in 1919. 200-acre facility located 40 miles from Concord. Features: freshwater lake; 200 acres; located in lakes region of New Hampshire; near White Mountains.

Profile of Summer Employees Total number: 30–40; typical ages: 18–24. 50% men; 50% women; 5% minorities; 20% college students; 25% retirees; 45% non-U.S. citizens; 5% local applicants. Nonsmokers required.

Employment Information Openings are from May 13 to October 19. Jobs available: ▶ 4 *dining room staff* at $170–$206 per week ▶ *general kitchen staff* at $170–$206 per week ▶ 3 *housekeepers* at $170–$206 per week ▶ 5 *lifeguards* at $200–$220 per week. Applicants must submit formal organization application, three personal references, three letters of recommendation. International applicants accepted; must apply through a recognized agency. A telephone interview is required.

Benefits and Preemployment Training Housing at a cost, free meals, on-the-job training, and opportunity to attend seminars/workshops. Preemployment training is required and includes accident prevention and safety.

Contact Tom MacKay, Operations Manager, Geneva Point Center, HCR 62, Box 469, Center Harbor, New Hampshire 03226. Telephone: 603-253-4366. Fax: 603-253-4883. E-mail: geneva@ genevapoint.org. Application deadline: continuous.

INTERLOCKEN INTERNATIONAL SUMMER CAMP
RR 2, BOX 165
HILLSBORO, NEW HAMPSHIRE 03244

General Information Creative, noncompetitive international summer camp offering a wide range of activities to 160 campers from the United States and around the world. Established in 1961. 500-acre facility located 100 miles from Boston, Massachusetts. Features: freshwater lake; wooded setting; architect designed buildings; rope swing and lake launch; red pine forest; starry sky.

Profile of Summer Employees Total number: 60; typical ages: 20–28. 50% men; 50% women; 20% minorities; 50% college students; 20% non-U.S. citizens. Nonsmokers required.

Employment Information Openings are from June 15 to August 24. Jobs available: ▶ 4 *applied arts staff members* with experience in the field ▶ 2 *environmental education staff members* with experience in the field ▶ 4 *music staff members* with experience in the field ▶ 4 *performing arts* *staff members* with experience in the field ▶ 4 *sports staff members* with experience in the field ▶ 2 *waterfront instructors* with experience in the field ▶ 6 *wilderness staff members* with experience in the field. Applicants must submit formal organization application, cover letter, resume, three personal references. International applicants accepted; must apply through a recognized agency. An in-person interview is recommended, but a telephone interview is acceptable.

Benefits and Preemployment Training Free housing, free meals, and on-the-job training. Preemployment training is required and includes accident prevention and safety, first aid, CPR, interpersonal skills, leadership skills, lifeguard training.

Contact Judi Wisch, Staffing Director, Interlocken International Summer Camp, RR 2, Box 165, Hillsboro, New Hampshire 03244. Telephone: 603-478-3166. Fax: 603-478-5260. E-mail: judi@ interlocken.org. World Wide Web: http://www.interlocken.org. Application deadline: continuous.

INTERLOCKEN TRAVEL PROGRAMS
RR 2, BOX 165
HILLSBORO, NEW HAMPSHIRE 03244

General Information Experientially-based domestic and international small group travel programs that focus on performing arts, adventure/wilderness, commmunity service, language, leadership training, and environment. Our travel programs are an outgrowth of the Interlocken International Summer Camp. Established in 1967. 500-acre facility located near Boston, Massachusetts.

Profile of Summer Employees Total number: 30; typical ages: 24–35. 50% men; 50% women; 20% minorities; 20% non-U.S. citizens. Nonsmokers required.

Employment Information Openings are from June 12 to August 22. Jobs available: ▶ 12 *adventure/wilderness leaders* (minimum age 24) with WFR certification, and experience leading high school students at $1200–$2000 per season ▶ 8 *cycling leaders* (minimum age 24) with experience working with high school age students as well as expertise in program focus and geographic location at $250 per week ▶ 4 *environmental study leaders* (minimum age 24) with WFR certification, experience with high school students, and experience in the field at $1200–$2000 per season ▶ 2 *leadership training leaders* (minimum age 24) with residential camp background and experience teaching leadership training at $1200–$2000 per season ▶ 6 *performing arts leaders* (minimum age 24) with background in physical theatre and experience teaching teenagers at $1200–$2000 per season ▶ 35 *travel leaders* (minimum age 24) with experience working with high school age students as well as expertise in program focus and geographic location at $250 per week. Applicants must submit formal organization application, cover letter, resume, three letters of recommendation. International applicants accepted; must apply through a recognized agency. An in-person interview is recommended, but a telephone interview is acceptable.

Benefits and Preemployment Training Free housing, free meals, formal training, opportunity to attend seminars/workshops, and travel reimbursement. Preemployment training is required and includes accident prevention and safety, first aid, CPR, interpersonal skills, leadership skills, lifeguard training.

Contact Judi Wisch, Staffing Coordinator, Interlocken Travel Programs, RR 2, Box 165, Hillsboro, New Hampshire 03244. Telephone: 603-478-3166. Fax: 603-478-5260. E-mail: mail@interlocken. org. World Wide Web: http://www.interlocken.org. Application deadline: continuous.

KINYON/JONES TENNIS CAMP AT DARTMOUTH COLLEGE
6083 ALUMNI GYM
HANOVER, NEW HAMPSHIRE 03755-3512

General Information Tennis camp for boys and girls age 10–17. Established in 1988. 120 miles from Boston, Massachusetts. Features: 9 outdoor courts; 4 indoor courts; college dorms; college dining hall.

Profile of Summer Employees Total number: 10; typical ages: 19–40. 50% men; 50% women; 90% college students. Nonsmokers required.

Employment Information Openings are from June 16 to July 18. Jobs available: ▶ 8–10 *tennis instructors* (minimum age 19) with experience in tennis instruction at $235 per week. Applicants

must submit a formal organization application, resume. A telephone interview is required.
Benefits and Preemployment Training Free housing, free meals, and on-the-job training.
Contact David Jones, Co-Director, Kinyon/Jones Tennis Camp at Dartmouth College, 24 College Hill, Hanover, New Hampshire 03755. Telephone: 603-646-3819. Fax: 603-646-3348. E-mail: chuck.kinyon@dartmouth.edu. Application deadline: continuous.

ROCKYWOLD–DEEPHAVEN CAMPS, INC. (RDC)
PINEHURST ROAD, PO BOX B
HOLDERNESS, NEW HAMPSHIRE 03245

General Information Family vacation camp providing guests with a unique family living experience offering rustic simplicity, high-quality services, and a natural setting. Established in 1897. 115-acre facility located 50 miles from Concord. Features: Squam Lake; location on the southern edge of White Mountain National Forest; 8 clay tennis courts; hiking and mountain bike trails leading from the property; old-fashioned ice boxes and fire places in each cottage; ballfield and basketball courts.

Profile of Summer Employees Total number: 90–100; typical ages: 18–25. 50% men; 50% women; 5% minorities; 4% high school students; 70% college students; 1% retirees; 5% non-U.S. citizens; 10% local applicants. Nonsmokers required.

Employment Information Openings are from May 15 to October 7. Jobs available: ▶ 20–25 *food service personnel* (minimum age 18) with a positive and flexible attitude and high work standards at $5.15–$9 per hour ▶ 10–12 *grounds/maintenance personnel* (minimum age 18) with experience in soft-surface tennis court maintenance and carpentry at $5.15–$6.05 per hour ▶ 22–24 *housekeeping personnel* (minimum age 18) with a positive and flexible attitude and high work standards at $5.15–$6.05 per hour ▶ 6–8 *office staff members* (minimum age 18) with word processing and money handling skills and experience working with the public at $5.25–$6.15 per hour ▶ 5–7 *recreation staff members* (minimum age 18) with experience in tennis, water sports, outdoor recreation, crafts, and working with various age groups at $235–$260 per week. Applicants must submit formal organization application, three personal references, three recommendation forms. International applicants accepted; must apply through a recognized agency. An in-person interview is recommended, but a telephone interview is acceptable.

Benefits and Preemployment Training Free housing, free meals, on-the-job training, and opportunity to attend seminars/workshops.

Contact John Jurczynski, General Manager, Rockywold–Deephaven Camps, Inc. (RDC), PO Box B, Holderness, New Hampshire 03245. Telephone: 603-968-3313. Fax: 603-968-3438. E-mail: rdc@lr.net. World Wide Web: http://www.rdcsquam.com. Application deadline: March 15.

THE SOUTHWESTERN COMPANY, NEW HAMPSHIRE
See The Southwestern Company, Tennessee on page 284 for complete description.

STUDENT CONSERVATION ASSOCIATION (SCA), NEW HAMPSHIRE
NEW HAMPSHIRE

General Information Nonprofit organization that places volunteers year-round in expense-paid conservation projects in national parks, forests, and wildlife refuges nationwide. Established in 1957.

Profile of Summer Employees Total number: 75; typical ages: 16–25. 50% men; 50% women; 35% high school students; 65% college students.

Employment Information Openings are from January to December. Year-round positions also offered. Jobs available: ▶ 100–150 *high school crew leaders* (minimum age 19) with experience working with high school students at $800–$2300 per season ▶ 450 *high school trail crew members* (must be 16 to 19 years of age) ▶ 1100 *resource assistants* (minimum age 18) with high school diploma at $50 per week. Applicants must submit a formal organization application, personal reference, three letters of recommendation, additional requirements on searchable database at Web site. International applicants accepted; must obtain own visa. A telephone interview is required.

Benefits and Preemployment Training Free housing, formal training, health insurance, names of contacts, on-the-job training, and travel reimbursement.

Contact Recruitment Office, Student Conservation Association (SCA), New Hampshire, PO Box 550, Charlestown, New Hampshire 03603. Telephone: 603-543-1700. Fax: 603-543-1828. World Wide Web: http://www.sinc.org. Application deadline: continuous.

THE WHALE'S TALE WATER PARK
ROUTE 3 NORTH
LINCOLN, NEW HAMPSHIRE 03251

General Information Water park with more than 10 wet and dry attractions. Established in 1985. 17-acre facility located 100 miles from Boston. Features: 5 water slides; wave pool; children's play area; lazy river; volleyball courts; great mountain views.

Profile of Summer Employees Total number: 80; typical ages: 16–25. 48% men; 52% women; 60% high school students; 10% college students; 30% local applicants.

Employment Information Openings are from June 1 to September 1. Jobs available: ▶ 10–20 *food service staff* (minimum age 16) at $6–$10 per hour ▶ 10–20 *lifeguards* (minimum age 16) with ARC certification at $6–$10 per hour ▶ 5–10 *sales staff* (minimum age 16) with money handling and customer service skills at $6–$8 per hour. Applicants must submit formal organization application. International applicants accepted; must obtain own visa, obtain own working papers, apply through a recognized agency. An in-person interview is required.

Benefits and Preemployment Training Meals at a cost and on-the-job training. Preemployment training is required and includes accident prevention and safety, first aid, interpersonal skills, leadership skills.

Contact Jeb Boyd, General Manager, The Whale's Tale Water Park, PO Box 67, Lincoln, New Hampshire 03251. Telephone: 603-745-8810. Fax: 603-745-6958. World Wide Web: http://www.whitemtn.org/whale.html. Application deadline: continuous.

YOGI BEAR'S JELLYSTONE PARK
ROUTE 132N, RR 1, BOX 396
ASHLAND, NEW HAMPSHIRE 03217

General Information Family fun resort and campground offering day trips, overnights, and weekend vacations in a trailer, log cabin rental, or campsite. Theme park with planned daily activities for all ages. Established in 1978. 40-acre facility located 20 miles from Concord. Features: sandy-bottomed river; pool and hot tub; hayrides; movies; snack bar and mini golf; large general store.

Profile of Summer Employees Total number: 50; typical ages: 14–69. 50% men; 50% women; 10% minorities; 10% high school students; 20% college students; 20% retirees; 20% non-U.S. citizens; 20% local applicants. Nonsmokers preferred.

Employment Information Openings are from April to October. Year-round positions also offered. Jobs available: ▶ 3 *food service staff* (minimum age 18) with salary starting at minimum wage ▶ 10 *general operations and maintenance staff* (minimum age 16) with salary starting at minimum wage ▶ 14 *housekeepers* (minimum age 16) with salary starting at minimum wage ▶ 3–4 *recreation directors* (minimum age 16) with salary starting at minimum wage ▶ 2–3 *reservationists* (minimum age 16) with computer experience preferred; salary starts at minimum wage ▶ 2–3 *store clerks* (minimum age 16) with salary starting at minimum wage. Applicants must submit formal organization application, cover letter, resume, three personal references, two letters of recommendation. International applicants accepted; must obtain own visa, obtain own working papers, apply through a recognized agency. An in-person interview is recommended, but a telephone interview is acceptable.

Benefits and Preemployment Training Free housing, possible full-time employment, and on-the-job training.

Contact Stephanie Crowley, Administrative Assistant, Yogi Bear's Jellystone Park, RR1, Box 396, Ashland, New Hampshire 03217. Fax: 603-968-7349. E-mail: yogi@jellystonenh.com. World Wide Web: http://www.jellystonenh.com. Application deadline: continuous.

NEW JERSEY

ACE COMPUTER CAMP–NEW JERSEY
See ACE Computer Camp–Washington on page 307 for complete description.

APPEL FARM ARTS AND MUSIC CENTER
457 SHIRLEY ROAD
ELMER, NEW JERSEY 08318

General Information Fine and performing arts center concentrating on 3 areas: presenting arts (music, dance, theater) to the local community, providing affordable meeting and work space for artists and art organizations, and offering arts education for children through a summer camp. Established in 1960. 100-acre facility located 35 miles from Philadelphia. Features: 10 air-conditioned studios; 300-seat theater; 2 dance studios; photo labs; extensive art barn; organic vegetable garden.

Profile of Summer Employees Total number: 90; typical age: 21. 40% men; 60% women; 20% minorities; 15% college students; 20% non-U.S. citizens; 10% local applicants. Nonsmokers required.

Employment Information Openings are from June 20 to August 23. Jobs available: ▶ 10 *art instructors* (minimum age 21) with extensive experience in painting, drawing, printmaking, sculpture, weaving, and ceramics at $1200 per season ▶ 1 *community-outreach coordinator* with organizational ability and office work experience at $1100–$1400 per season ▶ 3 *dance instructors* (minimum age 21) with experience and expert knowledge of modern, jazz, and ballet dancing at $1200 per season ▶ 10 *music instructors* (minimum age 21) with extensive experience in woodwinds, piano, strings, percussion, voice, brass, electronic music, and rock at $1200 per season ▶ 5 *photography instructors* (minimum age 21) with experience in the field at $1200 per season ▶ 2 *registered nurses* (minimum age 21) with RN license, NJ certification preferred ▶ 3 *sports staff members* (minimum age 21) with experience in tennis and noncompetitive sports at $1200 per season ▶ 4 *swimming instructors* (minimum age 21) with Red Cross lifeguard training or WSI certification and Bronze Medallion at $1200 per season ▶ 3 *technical theater personnel* (minimum age 21) with experience in stagecraft, set design, costumes, and lighting at $1200 per season ▶ 10 *theater instructors* (minimum age 21) with directing experience at $1200 per season ▶ 3 *video instructors* (minimum age 21) with experience in the field at $1200 per season. Applicants must submit three personal references, performance audio tapes, slides of present work. International applicants accepted; must obtain own visa, apply through a recognized agency. An in-person interview is recommended, but a telephone interview is acceptable.

Benefits and Preemployment Training Free housing, free meals, formal training, and on-the-job training. Preemployment training is required and includes accident prevention and safety, interpersonal skills, leadership skills, counseling skills.

Contact Rena Levitt, Camp Director, Appel Farm Arts and Music Center, PO Box 888, Elmer, New Jersey 08318. Telephone: 609-358-2472. Fax: 609-358-6513. E-mail: appelcamp@aol.com. World Wide Web: http://www.appelfarm.org. Application deadline: continuous.

CAMP LOUEMMA
43 LOUEMMA LANE
SUSSEX, NEW JERSEY 07461

General Information Nonprofit traditional, general interest sleepaway camp for girls and boys ages 7-15. Established in 1941. 152-acre facility located 30 miles from Newark. Features: private lake; pool; hockey rink (roller); beach volleyball; athletic fields; climbing wall.

Profile of Summer Employees Total number: 80; typical ages: 16–50. 20% high school students; 75% college students. Nonsmokers preferred.

Employment Information Openings are from June 24 to August 20. Jobs available: ▶ 4–8 *male counselors* (minimum age 18) must enjoy working with children at $750–$1500 per season ▶ 2 *male supervisors* (minimum age 25) must have supervisory skills and be mature and responsible at $2000–$3000 per season. Applicants must submit formal organization application, two personal references. International applicants accepted; must obtain own visa, apply through a recognized agency. An in-person interview is recommended, but a telephone interview is acceptable.

Benefits and Preemployment Training Free housing, free meals, and on-the-job training. Preemployment training is required and includes accident prevention and safety, interpersonal skills, leadership skills, role play.

Contact Hal Pugach, Director, Camp Louemma, 214-45 42nd Avenue, Bayside, New York 11361. Telephone: 973-316-0362. Fax: 973-316-0980. E-mail: topbrass1@aol.com. Application deadline: continuous.

COLLEGE GIFTED PROGRAMS
DREW UNIVERSITY
MADISON, NEW JERSEY 07940

General Information Residential educational academic summer camp for gifted and talented students in grades 4-11. Program blends in-depth academics with recreational and cultural activities. Established in 1984. 186-acre facility located 20 miles from New York. Features: dormitories; campus classroom facilities; campus recreational facilities include pool, tennis courts, and gym; campus library; beautiful college setting.

Profile of Summer Employees Total number: 65; typical ages: 19–70. 50% men; 50% women; 30% minorities; 50% college students; 10% retirees; 10% non-U.S. citizens; 25% local applicants. Nonsmokers required.

Employment Information Openings are from June 26 to July 17. Jobs available: ▶ 30 *counselors* with two years of college completed and experience working with children at $800 to $1200 per 3-week session ▶ 4 *directors* with at least 5 years teaching/supervisory experience; master's degree required, doctorate preferred at $5000–$8000 ▶ 6 *housemasters/instructors (residential)* with master's degree, teaching and supervisory experience at $2500 to $4500 per 3-week session ▶ 20 *instructors (non-residential)* with master's degree and teaching experience at $600 to $2500 per 3-week session ▶ 2 *nurses* with RN license; school experience preferred at $1300 per week. Applicants must submit formal organization application, resume, academic transcripts, two personal references, two letters of recommendation. International applicants accepted; must apply through a recognized agency. An in-person interview is recommended, but a telephone interview is acceptable.

Benefits and Preemployment Training Free housing and free meals. Preemployment training is required and includes accident prevention and safety, interpersonal skills, leadership skills, instructional strategies for gifted students.

Contact Margaret Solitario or Dr. Albert Dorhout, Executive Directors, College Gifted Programs, 120 Littleton Road, Suite 201, Parsippany, New Jersey 07054-1803. Telephone: 973-334-6991. Fax: 973-334-9756. E-mail: info@cgp-sig.com. World Wide Web: http://www.cgp-sig.com. Application deadline: continuous.

EASTER SEALS CAMP MERRY HEART
21 O'BRIAN ROAD
HACKETTSTOWN, NEW JERSEY 07840

General Information Residential camp for persons with a disability ages 5–60, day camp for nondisabled children ages 5–12, and Travel Recreation Experiences in Camping(TREC) program for persons with a disability, ages 18-35. Established in 1949. 121-acre facility located 50 miles from New York, New York. Features: woodlands; freshwater lake; cabins; pool; tennis court/volleyball court; accessible facility.

Profile of Summer Employees Total number: 55; typical ages: 16–60. 50% men; 50% women; 25% minorities; 10% high school students; 75% college students; 25% non-U.S. citizens; 10% local applicants. Nonsmokers preferred.

Employment Information Openings are from June 9 to August 28. Jobs available: ▶ 1 *boating* *specialist* (minimum age 21) with small craft and first aid certifications and CPR at $1200–$1300 per season ▶ 2 *cooks* (minimum age 21) with knowledge of cooking for groups at $3600–$4800 per season ▶ 20 *counselors (female)* (minimum age 18) should be college students with education backgrounds at $1100–$1200 per season ▶ 20 *counselors (male)* (minimum age 18) should be college students with education backgrounds at $1100–$1200 per season ▶ 1 *nature specialist* (minimum age 21) with ecology background at $1200–$1300 per season ▶ 2 *nurses* with experience and NJ state RN license, first aid, and CPR certification at $3600–$4800 per season ▶ 1 *program specialist* (minimum age 19) with experience in the field at $1600–$2500 per season ▶ 1 *recreation specialist* (minimum age 21) with therapeutic background at $1200–$1300 per season ▶ 1 *swimming instructor* (minimum age 21) with CPR, first aid, lifeguard certification, experience, teaching ability, and WSI at $1200–$1300 per season. Applicants must submit formal organization application, three personal references, three letters of recommendation. International applicants accepted; must apply through a recognized agency. An in-person interview is recommended, but a telephone interview is acceptable.

Benefits and Preemployment Training Free housing, free meals, formal training, and on-the-job training. Preemployment training is required and includes accident prevention and safety, interpersonal skills, leadership skills, how to work with people with disabilities.

Contact Mary Ellen Ross, Director of Camping, Easter Seals Camp Merry Heart, 21 O'Brien Road, Hackettstown, New Jersey 07840. Telephone: 908-852-3896. Fax: 908-852-9263. Application deadline: continuous.

FAIRVIEW LAKE ENVIRONMENTAL TRIP
1035 FAIRVIEW LAKE ROAD
NEWTON, NEW JERSEY 07860

General Information Facility offering discovery and challenge trips to enhance an appreciation of the natural environment while fostering skills in communication, cooperation, and trust through physical challenges. Established in 1992. 600-acre facility located 60 miles from New York City. Features: 110-acre glacial lake; 20 minute walk to the Appalachian Trail; 500 acres of woods; serene setting; rustic housing; many species of endangered wildlife.

Profile of Summer Employees Total number: 10; typical ages: 23–35. 50% men; 50% women; 10% minorities; 50% college students; 10% non-U.S. citizens; 30% local applicants. Nonsmokers preferred.

Employment Information Openings are from June to August 15. Year-round positions also offered. Jobs available: ▶ 3 *trip counselors* (minimum age 21) with lifeguard training, first aid, and CPR certification at $180–$200 per week ▶ 3 *trip leaders* (minimum age 21) with lifeguard training, first aid, and CPR certification at $200–$250 per week. Applicants must submit cover letter, resume, two letters of recommendation. International applicants accepted; must obtain own visa, obtain own working papers, apply through a recognized agency. An in-person interview is recommended, but a telephone interview is acceptable.

Benefits and Preemployment Training Free housing, free meals, possible full-time employment, and on-the-job training.

Contact Christina Henriksen, Director, Fairview Lake Environmental Trip, 1035 Fairview Lake Road, Newton, New Jersey 07860. Fax: 973-383-6386. Application deadline: continuous.

FAIRVIEW LAKE YMCA CAMP
1035 FAIRVIEW LAKE ROAD
NEWTON, NEW JERSEY 07860

General Information Coed residential camp serving 200 campers. Emphasis is on improving self-esteem through creativity and/or physical challenges. Large sports, drama, and communications programs offered. Established in 1915. 600-acre facility located 65 miles from New York City. Features: mile long freshwater lake; Appalachian Trail borders camp; in-line skating rink; 2 waterfronts; modern cabins; large sports facility.

Profile of Summer Employees Total number: 55; typical ages: 18–35. 50% men; 50% women; 25% minorities; 15% high school students; 80% college students; 5% retirees; 25% non-U.S. citizens; 5% local applicants. Nonsmokers preferred.

Employment Information Openings are from June 21 to August 22. Jobs available: ▶ *counselors* with lifeguard certification at $1000–$1300 per season ▶ *junior counselors* at $500 per season ▶ *nurses* with RN and state license at $300–$450 per week ▶ *riding director* with a minimum of 3 years of experience at $1800–$2500 per season ▶ 1–3 *unit leaders* (minimum age 21) at $1800–$2500 per season ▶ *waterfront director* with WSI certification at $1800–$2500 per season. Applicants must submit formal organization application, three personal references. International applicants accepted; must obtain own visa, obtain own working papers, apply through a recognized agency. An in-person interview is recommended, but a telephone interview is acceptable.

Benefits and Preemployment Training Free housing, free meals, and on-the-job training. Preemployment training is required and includes accident prevention and safety, interpersonal skills, leadership skills.

Contact Matt Block, Summer Camp Director, Fairview Lake YMCA Camp, 1035 Fairview Lake Road, Newton, New Jersey 07860. Telephone: 973-383-9282. Fax: 973-383-6386. E-mail: mattblock@worldnet.att.net. Application deadline: continuous.

FELLOWSHIP DEACONRY, INC. (DAY CAMP SUNSHINE AND FELLOWSHIP CONFERENCE CENTER)
3575 VALLEY ROAD
LIBERTY CORNER, NEW JERSEY 07938

General Information Children's day camp and adult conference center that provides a well-balanced program to meet the spiritual and physical needs of all participants by providing the study of God's word, rest, and recreation in a Christian community. Established in 1933. 50-acre facility located 40 miles from New York City. Features: location surrounded by beautiful Watchung Mountains; well-stocked Christian bookstore/gift shop; 2 swimming pools and a pond for canoeing; historic areas with sight-seeing attractions; miniature golf course; tennis courts.

Profile of Summer Employees Total number: 35; typical age: 20. 45% men; 55% women; 10% minorities; 20% high school students; 60% college students; 10% non-U.S. citizens; 25% local applicants. Nonsmokers required.

Employment Information Openings are from June 15 to September 10. Year-round positions also offered. Jobs available: ▶ 10 *counselors* (minimum age 18) at $250–$300 per week ▶ 10 *counselors-in-training* (minimum age 16) at $140–$200 per week ▶ 2 *housekeeping staff* at $140–$270 per week ▶ 2 *kitchen crew* at $140–$200 per week ▶ 5 *lifeguards* with Red Cross advanced lifesaving and CPR/first aid certifications at $160–$300 per week ▶ 1 *pantry person* at $200–$280 per week ▶ 5 *waitresses* at $85–$280 per week.

Benefits and Preemployment Training Free housing, free meals, on-the-job training, and laundry facilities.

Contact Rita Krohn, Directing Deaconess, Fellowship Deaconry, Inc. (Day Camp Sunshine and Fellowship Conference Center), PO Box 204, Liberty Corner, New Jersey 07938. Telephone: 908-647-1777. Fax: 908-647-4117. Application deadline: May 15.

GREEN GLEN
1045 ROUTE 18
EAST BRUNSWICK, NEW JERSEY 08816

General Information Boarding, grooming, training, and breeding dogs and selling supplies. Established in 1962. 2-acre facility located 6 miles from New Brunswick. Features: wooded; computer; super dogs; learning opportunity.

Profile of Summer Employees Nonsmokers required.

Employment Information Openings are from January 1 to December 31. Jobs available: ▶ 1–2 *kennel assistants* must be self-motivated and hard worker; salary is 10% commission. Applicants must submit a formal organization application, resume, three personal references. International applicants accepted; must obtain own visa, obtain own working papers. An in-person interview is recommended, but a telephone interview is acceptable.

Benefits and Preemployment Training Free housing, possible full-time employment, and opportunity to attend seminars/workshops. Preemployment training is required.

Contact Felicia Luburich, Owner, Green Glen. Telephone: 732-257-0175. E-mail: fesrigohl@ hotmail.com. Application deadline: continuous.

L.G. COOK 4-H CAMP
100A STRUBLE ROAD
BRANCHVILLE, NEW JERSEY 07826

General Information Residential camp facility with a weekly capacity of 150 campers ages 7–13. Established in 1914. 100-acre facility located 65 miles from New York, New York. Features: freshwater lake; located in a state forest; cabins; shooting sports areas.

Profile of Summer Employees Total number: 23; typical ages: 16–24. 40% men; 60% women; 10% minorities; 35% high school students; 35% college students; 10% non-U.S. citizens; 10% local applicants. Nonsmokers preferred.

Employment Information Openings are from June 28 to August 14. Jobs available: ▶ 2 *assistant cooks* with food preparation experience at $170–$180 per week ▶ 2 *boating/canoeing instructors* with lifeguard certification and experience in the field at $180–$210 per week ▶ 6 *cabin counselors* (minimum age 18) with experience working with youth at $230–$270 per season ▶ 1 *chef* with kitchen, ordering, and supervisory experience at $230–$260 per week ▶ 1 *cook* with experience in the field at $180–$200 per week ▶ 2 *crafts shop managers* with experience maintaining inventories at $200–$230 per week ▶ 1 *fishing instructor* with experience working with youth at $210–$240 per week ▶ 2 *health directors* with Red Cross advanced first aid and CPR certification (as a minimum) at $270–$370 per week ▶ 1 *hiking/camping instructor* with Red Cross standard first aid and CPR certification at $210–$240 per week ▶ 2 *lifeguards* with certification in field at $180–$210 per week ▶ 2 *nature instructors* with experience working with youth at $210–$240 per week ▶ 1 *waterfront supervisor* with lifeguard certification at $230–$250 per week. Applicants must submit formal organization application, three personal references. International applicants accepted; must apply through a recognized agency. An in-person interview is recommended, but a telephone interview is acceptable.

Benefits and Preemployment Training Free housing, free meals, formal training, health insurance, and on-the-job training. Preemployment training is required and includes accident prevention and safety, first aid, CPR, interpersonal skills, leadership skills, conflict resolution.

Contact Donna J. MacNeir, Assistant Director, 4-H Outdoor Education Center, L.G. Cook 4-H Camp, 100A Struble Road, Branchville, New Jersey 07826. Telephone: 973-948-3550. Fax: 973-948-0735. E-mail: 4hcamp@aesop.rutgers.edu. World Wide Web: http://www.rce.rutgers. edu. Application deadline: continuous.

NEW JERSEY SUMMER ARTS INSTITUTE
MARIE KATZENBACH SCHOOL
EWING, NEW JERSEY 08648

General Information Residential 5-week school of the arts serving 40 artistically talented students entering grades 8 through freshman year in college. Established in 1981. 100-acre facility located 3 miles from Trenton. Features: wooded setting; dormitories; library.

Profile of Summer Employees Total number: 10; typical ages: 20–50. 16% minorities; 50% college students, 90% local applicants. Nonsmokers required.

Employment Information Openings are from July 5 to August 6. Jobs available: ▶ 1 *assistant to the residence director* (minimum age 21) with at least junior year of college completed; experience in the arts preferred at $2000–$2500 per season ▶ 4–8 *residence advisors* (minimum age 20) with at least sophomore year in college completed, preferably in an arts or social sciences major at $800–$2500 per season ▶ 1 *residence director* (minimum age 23) with at least a master's level education, preferably in the arts or social work; supervisory experience preferred at $2000–$2500 per season. Applicants must submit a cover letter, resume, training in at least one art form. International applicants accepted; must obtain own visa, obtain own working papers. An in-person interview is required.

Benefits and Preemployment Training Free housing, free meals, possible full-time employment, and on-the-job training. Preemployment training is required and includes interpersonal skills, leadership skills.

Contact Dr. Rina Shere, Executive Director, New Jersey Summer Arts Institute, 100 Jersey Avenue, Suite B-104, New Brunswick, New Jersey 08901. Telephone: 732-220-1600. Fax: 732-220-1515. E-mail: iahe@bellatlantic.net.

NEW JERSEY YMHA–YWHA CAMP NESHER
FAIRFIELD, NEW JERSEY 07004

General Information Seven Jewish residential camps: Nah-Jee-Wah–coed for 1st–6th grades (350 campers); Cedar Lake–coed for 7th–9th grades (500 campers); Teen-Age Camp–coed for 10th–11th grades (150 campers); Round Lake–coed for children with ADHD or learning disabilities (200 campers); Nesher–coed orthodox for grades 3rd–9th (300 campers); Camp MountainTop-coed for 3rd–7th grades, 1 and 2 week programs (100 campers). Established in 1920. 2,400-acre facility located 120 miles from New York, New York. Features: Olympic-size swimming pool; acres of wooded hiking area; top-quality athletic facility; 30-foot and 70-foot high ropes course with zip line; lake; 6 separate art programs.

Profile of Summer Employees Total number: 700; typical ages: 18–25. 40% men; 60% women; 10% high school students; 75% college students; 2% retirees; 50% non-U.S. citizens; 50% local applicants. Nonsmokers preferred.

Employment Information Openings are from June 20 to August 20. Jobs available: ▶ 40 *athletics staff members (all sports plus archery and gymnastics)* with coaching experience; must be high school graduate at $1100–$1600 per season ▶ 75 *counselors* with camp experience or course study in early childhood education, psychology, sociology, recreation, or special needs; must be high school graduate at $1100–$1600 per season ▶ 25 *division heads* with supervisory experience; must be a college graduate with camp experience at $1900–$2500 per season ▶ 100 *kitchen/dining room staff members* should be at least a high school senior with food preparation/ waiter/waitress experience at $500–$1500 per season ▶ 20 *nurses* with RN license at $3500– $4000 per season ▶ 50 *specialists (radio, computers, art, photo, cooking, nature, and ropes course)* with teaching experience in area of specialization; must be high school graduate at $1100–$1600 per season ▶ 50 *waterfront–boating and pool staff members* with WSI, canoeing, sailing, and lifeguard certification; must be high school graduate at $1200–$1700 per season. Applicants must submit formal organization application, academic transcripts, three personal references, two letters of recommendation. International applicants accepted; must apply through a recognized agency. An in-person interview is recommended, but a telephone interview is acceptable.

Benefits and Preemployment Training Free housing, free meals, formal training, on-the-job training, and travel reimbursement. Preemployment training is required and includes accident prevention and safety, first aid, CPR, leadership skills.

Contact Anne Tursky, Assistant Director, New Jersey YMHA–YWHA Camp Nesher, 21 Plymouth Street, Fairfield, New Jersey 07004. Telephone: 973-575-3333 Ext. 125. Fax: 973-575-4188. E-mail: staff@njycamps.org. World Wide Web: http://www.njycamps.org. Application deadline: continuous.

PALISADES INTERSTATE PARK COMMISSION
PO BOX 155
ALPINE, NEW JERSEY 07620

General Information State park serving the cultural, historical, environmental, and recreational needs of the general public. Established in 1900. 2,500-acre facility located 10 miles from New York, New York. Features: 3 picnic areas; 2 boat basins; 2 historic sites; 30 miles of hiking trails; scenic overlook; cross-country ski trails.

Profile of Summer Employees Total number: 40; typical ages: 18–65. 60% men; 40% women; 20% minorities; 49% high school students; 50% college students; 1% retirees; 100% local applicants. Nonsmokers preferred.

Employment Information Openings are from April 1 to November 1. Year-round positions also offered. Jobs available: ▶ 4 *boat basin stewards* (minimum age 19) with knowledge of the Hudson River; boating experience preferred at $9 per hour ▶ 4–8 *concession stand operators* (minimum age 16) at $6–$7 per hour ▶ 12–20 *fee collectors/parking attendants* (minimum age

16) at $5.50–$6.50 per hour ▶ 2 *historic site assistants* with strong interest in history, research, giving tours, and related activities at $5–$6 per hour ▶ 10–15 *maintenance workers* (minimum age 16) with interest in learning grounds maintenance, recycling, and trail maintenance at $7–$8 per hour ▶ 4–8 *park rangers* (minimum age 19) with environmental knowledge, interpretive experience, and trail clearing skills; should have leadership ability including people/communication skills at $8–$9 per hour ▶ 4–8 *trail crew* (minimum age 16) with trail clearing, hand tools, and general maintenance experience at $7–$8.50 per hour. Applicants must submit a formal organization application, resume, three personal references. An in-person interview is recommended, but a telephone interview is acceptable.

Benefits and Preemployment Training On-the-job training.

Contact Jennifer A. March, Supervisor of Visitor Services, Palisades Interstate Park Commission, PO Box 155, Alpine, New Jersey 07620. Telephone: 201-768-1360. Fax: 201-767-3842. Application deadline: continuous.

SIX FLAGS GREAT ADVENTURE THEME PARK
PO BOX 120, ROUTE 537
JACKSON, NEW JERSEY 08527

General Information Amusement Theme Park and Wild Safari Animal Park in the Jackson Pine Barrens. Established in 1974. Located 15 miles from Trenton. Features: more than 75 rides; dozens of shows; wooded setting; Looney Tune characters; special events for employees; star-studded concerts.

Profile of Summer Employees Total number: 5,500; typical ages: 15–78. 52% men; 48% women; 40% high school students; 30% college students; 11% retirees; 20% local applicants.

Employment Information Openings are from April 1 to October 31. Spring break positions also offered. Jobs available: ▶ 300–400 *food service host/hostess staff* (minimum age 15) at $5.50–$7 per hour ▶ 100–200 *groundskeepers* (minimum age 15) at $5.35–$7.35 per hour ▶ 500–700 *ride operators* (minimum age 16) at $5.35–$6.35 per hour ▶ 50–100 *security officers* (minimum age 18) at $7.50 per hour. Applicants must submit formal organization application. International applicants accepted; must apply through a recognized agency. An in-person interview is required.

Benefits and Preemployment Training Housing at a cost, meals at a cost, formal training, on-the-job training, opportunity to attend seminars/workshops, and free admission to the park. Preemployment training is required and includes leadership skills, customer service training.

Contact Human Resources Employment Center, Six Flags Great Adventure Theme Park, PO Box 120, Route 537, Jackson, New Jersey 08527. Telephone: 732-928-2000. Fax: 732-928-6779. E-mail: smorris@sftp.com. World Wide Web: http://www.sixflags.com. Application deadline: continuous.

SOMERSET COUNTY PARK COMMISSION
ENVIRONMENTAL EDUCATION CENTER
190 LORD STIRLING ROAD
BASKING RIDGE, NEW JERSEY 07920

General Information Environmental education center/park providing leisure and learning opportunities for the public, schools, and scouting groups. Established in 1971. 430-acre facility located 10 miles from Morristown. Features: 8½ miles of walking trails; boardwalk; forest; exhibit hall; fields; ponds and swamps.

Profile of Summer Employees Total number: 27; typical ages: 19–24. 50% men; 50% women; 100% college students; 80% local applicants. Nonsmokers preferred.

Employment Information Openings are from June to August. Jobs available: ▶ 3 *conservation crew members* (minimum age 19) with CPR/first aid preferred; college graduate or upperclassman with outdoor skills, trail and general maintenance skills, and ability to use hand tools at $6.75 per hour ▶ 7 *seasonal naturalists* (minimum age 19) with CPR, first aid, and LGT preferred; college graduate or upperclassman with summer camp, student teaching, or similar volunteer experience at $8.50 per hour. Applicants must submit a formal organization application, cover letter, driver's license.

Benefits and Preemployment Training Possible full-time employment, names of contacts, and on-the-job training.

Contact Supervisor of Environmental Science, Somerset County Park Commission Environmental Education Center, 190 Lord Stirling Road, Basking Ridge, New Jersey 07920. Telephone: 908-766-2489. Fax: 908-766-2687. Application deadline: April 30.

THE SOUTHWESTERN COMPANY, NEW JERSEY
See The Southwestern Company, Tennessee on page 284 for complete description.

STONY BROOK-MILLSTONE WATERSHED ASSOCIATION-ENVIRONMENTAL EDUCATION DAY CAMP
31 TITUS MILL ROAD
PENNINGTON, NEW JERSEY 08534

General Information Environmental education day camp conducting one- and two-week programs. Established in 1949. 785-acre facility located 9 miles from Trenton. Features: nature center; butterfly house; woodlands and rolling fields; 8 miles of trails; freshwater pond.

Profile of Summer Employees Total number: 21; typical ages: 16–36. 40% men; 60% women; 10% minorities; 10% high school students; 50% college students; 100% local applicants.

Employment Information Openings are from June 22 to August 13. Year-round positions also offered. Jobs available: ▶ 2 *camp group leaders* with experience in camp setting, teaching, and ecology at $2500 per season ▶ 4 *camp interns* with experience or interest in camps, teaching, and ecology at $1500 per season ▶ 2 *camp naturalists* with extensive knowledge of local ecology at $2000 per season ▶ 2 *teacher/naturalist* with experience in nature center or environmental education at $2000 per season. Applicants must submit a cover letter, resume, two personal references, letter of recommendation. International applicants accepted. An in-person interview is recommended, but a telephone interview is acceptable.

Benefits and Preemployment Training Formal training and on-the-job training. Preemployment training is required and includes accident prevention and safety, first aid, CPR, interpersonal skills, leadership skills.

Contact Jeff Hoagland, Education Director, Stony Brook-Millstone Watershed Association-Environmental Education Day Camp, 31 Titus Mill Road, Pennington, New Jersey 08534. Telephone: 609-737-7592. Fax: 609-737-3075. E-mail: sbmwa@nj1.aae.com. World Wide Web: http://www.princetonol.com/groups/stonybrook. Application deadline: April 15.

STUDENT CONSERVATION ASSOCIATION (SCA), NEW JERSEY
See Student Conservation Association (SCA), New Hampshire on page 193 for complete description.

TOMAHAWK LAKE WATER PARK
TOMAHAWK TRAIL, PO BOX 109
SPARTA, NEW JERSEY 07871-0109

General Information Swimming and picnicking park with water rides, boating, mini-golf, ball fields, arcade, snackbar, and a beer garden; open to the public between Memorial Day weekend and Labor Day weekend. Established in 1952. 150-acre facility located 50 miles from New York, New York. Features: freshwater lake; large white sand beach; shaded picnic groves; 6 water slides; boat rides; mini golf course.

Profile of Summer Employees Total number: 60–80; typical ages: 16–20. 50% men; 50% women; 2% minorities; 44% high school students; 36% college students; 7% retirees; 9% non-U.S. citizens; 2% local applicants. Nonsmokers preferred.

Employment Information Openings are from May 29 to September 19. Year-round positions also offered. Jobs available: ▶ 2 *arcade/mini golf attendants* (minimum age 24) with first aid/CPR (training available) at $6.50–$7 per hour ▶ 2 *bartenders* (minimum age 18) at $3.00 per hour plus tips ▶ 9–12 *food service staff (snack bars)* (minimum age 16) with food safety and handling certification preferred at $5.15–$6.15 per hour ▶ 3–4 *front office assistants* (minimum age 21) with first aid/CPR (training available) and college degree or fulltime, year-round work experience at $8–$9 per hour ▶ 2–3 *front office attendants* (minimum age 19) with first aid/CPR (training available) at $6 per hour ▶ 8 *lifeguards (shallow water)* (minimum age 15) with national pool and waterpark lifeguard license (training available) at $5.50–$5.75 per hour ▶ 15–25 *lifeguards (special facilities)* (minimum age 16) with national pool and waterpark lifeguard license (training available) at $6.50–$7.50 per hour ▶ 10–20 *parking attendants* (minimum age 16) with first aid/CPR certifications preferred (training available) at $5.15 per hour ▶ 15–17 *ride dispatchers (water rides)* (minimum age 17) with first aid and CPR; national pool and waterpark lifeguard license preferred at $5.25–$5.50 per hour. Applicants must submit formal organization application, working papers if under 18; cover letter and resume from foreign applicants. International applicants accepted; must obtain own visa, obtain own working papers, apply through a recognized agency. An in-person interview is recommended, but a telephone interview is acceptable.

Benefits and Preemployment Training Housing at a cost, meals at a cost, formal training, on-the-job training, and use of facility for staff in good standing; complimentary water and lemonade. Preemployment training is required and includes accident prevention and safety, first aid, CPR, interpersonal skills, leadership skills, lifeguard training.

Contact June Wallace, Staffing Coordinator, Tomahawk Lake Water Park, PO Box 109, Sparta, New Jersey 07871. Telephone: 973-398-7785. Fax: 973-398-5056. World Wide Web: http://www.waterparks.com/members.

TRAIL BLAZER CAMPS
210 DECKERTOWN TURNPIKE
MONTAGUE, NEW JERSEY 07827

General Information Residential camp serving inner-city campers in a primitive setting. Established in 1887. 1,000-acre facility located 70 miles from New York, New York. Features: 55-acre lake; 1000 forested acres; minutes from Appalachian Trail; minutes from the Delaware River.

Profile of Summer Employees Total number: 75; typical ages: 19–75. 40% men; 60% women; 15% minorities; 50% college students; 5% retirees; 35% non-U.S. citizens; 10% local applicants. Nonsmokers preferred.

Employment Information Openings are from June 11 to August 21. Jobs available: ▶ 45 *group leaders* (minimum age 19) with one year of college completed or equal experience at $1200–$1300 per season ▶ 2 *head cooks* (minimum age 19) at $2500–$3000 per season ▶ 2 *infirmary staff members* (minimum age 19) with RN, EMT, or LPN license at $1500–$3500 per season ▶ 8 *kitchen staff members* (minimum age 19) at $1200–$1300 per season ▶ 1 *secretary* (minimum age 19) at $1200–$1300 per season ▶ *waterfront director* (minimum age 21) with WSI and lifeguard certification at $1600–$2000 per season ▶ 6–7 *waterfront staff members* (minimum age 19) with WSI, ALS, and lifeguard certification, lake module at $1200–$1300 per season. Applicants must submit formal organization application, writing sample, three personal references. International applicants accepted; must apply through a recognized agency. A telephone interview is required.

Benefits and Preemployment Training Free housing, free meals, formal training, possible full-time employment, on-the-job training, opportunity to attend seminars/workshops, travel reimbursement, and tuition assistance.

Contact Paige Minear, Staff Recruitment Coordinator, Trail Blazer Camps, 45 East 20th Street, 9th Floor, New York, New York 10003. Telephone: 212-529-5113. Fax: 212-529-2704. E-mail: TBCNY@aol.com. World Wide Web: http://trailblazers.org. Application deadline: June 1.

YMCA CAMPS OCKANICKON AND MATOLLIONEQUAY
1303 STOKES ROAD
MEDFORD, NEW JERSEY 08055

General Information YMCA brother/sister summer resident camp with traditional activities, high ropes, low ropes, climbing wall, and multiple lakes in the scenic pine barrons of New Jersey. Established in 1906. 560-acre facility located 20 miles from Philadelphia. Features:

climbing wall; zip lines; high ropes; low ropes; freshwater lakes; rustic housing.

Profile of Summer Employees Total number: 120; typical ages: 19–29. 50% men; 50% women; 15% minorities; 15% high school students; 75% college students; 10% non-U.S. citizens; 5% local applicants.

Employment Information Openings are from June 20 to August 27. Year-round positions also offered. Jobs available: ▶ 1–10 *activity directors* (minimum age 21) with experience in nature, sports, and arts and crafts at $1400–$1700 per season ▶ 1–60 *cabin counselors* (minimum age 19) with willingness to live in cabin with campers at $1300–$1500 per season ▶ 1–15 *lifeguard counselors* (minimum age 18) with current certifications at $1400–$1700 per season ▶ 1–5 *ropes instructors* (minimum age 19) with experience or training at $1500–$1800 per season. Applicants must submit formal organization application, three personal references. International applicants accepted; must obtain own visa, obtain own working papers, apply through a recognized agency. An in-person interview is recommended, but a telephone interview is acceptable.

Benefits and Preemployment Training Free housing, free meals, and on-the-job training. Preemployment training is required and includes accident prevention and safety, interpersonal skills, leadership skills, asset-based training.

Contact Mr. Tom Rapine, Summer Camp Director, YMCA Camps Ockanickon and Matollionequay. Telephone: 609-654-8225. Fax: 609-654-8895. E-mail: matolly@erols.com. Application deadline: continuous.

NEW MEXICO

ACE COMPUTER CAMP–NEW MEXICO
See ACE Computer Camp–Washington on page 307 for complete description.

BRUSH RANCH CAMPS FOR GIRLS AND BOYS
HC 73, BOX 32
TERERRO, NEW MEXICO 87573

General Information Residential camp serving 80 girls ages 8–15 and 50 boys ages 8–14 with camp programs in a noncompetitive atmosphere. Also, high adventure, family camp, Trailblazers, and Mountaineers programs. Established in 1957. 550-acre facility located 40 miles from Santa Fe. Features: pool; tennis courts; ropes course; soccer field; modern log cabins; 1.5 miles of Pecos River.

Profile of Summer Employees Total number: 60; typical age: 21. 50% men; 50% women; 1% high school students; 90% college students; 1% non-U.S. citizens; 1% local applicants. Nonsmokers preferred.

Employment Information Openings are from May 20 to August 30. Jobs available: ▶ 2 *archery instructors* (minimum age 19) with NAA or NFAA certification or qualification at $130 per week ▶ 3 *art instructors* (minimum age 19) with ceramics experience especially helpful at $130 per week ▶ 2 *backpacking counselors* (minimum age 21) with WFR at $160 per week ▶ 1 *dance instructor* (minimum age 19) at $130 per week ▶ 1 *drama instructor* (minimum age 21) at $130 per week ▶ 2 *fencing instructors* (minimum age 19) at $130 per week ▶ 2 *fishing instructors* (minimum age 19) with fly-fishing experience at $130 per week ▶ 2 *mountain biking instructors* (minimum age 21) with WFR at $160 per week ▶ 1 *music instructor* (minimum age 19) with piano playing experience at $130 per week ▶ 1 *nature instructor* (minimum age 19) at $130 per week ▶ 1 *nurse* (minimum age 21) with RN license at $2500 per season ▶ 5 *riding instructors* (English- and Western-style) (minimum age 19) with CHA or quivalent certification at $130 per week ▶ 3 *ropes challenge-course instructors* (minimum age 21) with a minimum of 40 hours training or 100 hours of leadership on ropes course in last 12 months; should be certified in field at $140 per week ▶ 2 *shooting instructors* (minimum age 19) with NRA or comparable training at $130 per week ▶ 1 *soccer instructor* (minimum age 19) at $130 per week ▶ 3 *swimming instructors* (minimum age 19) with WSI certification and synchronized swimming experience at $130 per week ▶ 2 *tennis instructors* (minimum age 19) at $130 per week. Applicants must submit formal organization application, four personal references. International applicants accepted; must apply through a recognized agency. An in-person interview is recommended, but a telephone interview is acceptable.

Benefits and Preemployment Training Free housing, free meals, on-the-job training, and travel reimbursement. Preemployment training is required and includes accident prevention and safety, first aid, CPR, interpersonal skills, leadership skills, ropes and challenge course, archery, and driver training.

Contact Scott Rice, Director, Brush Ranch Camps for Girls and Boys, PO Box 5759, Santa Fe, New Mexico 87502-5759. Telephone: 800-722-2843. Fax: 505-757-8822. World Wide Web: http://www.brushranchcamps.com. Application deadline: continuous.

FENTON RANCH
26473 HIGHWAY 126
JEMEZ SPRINGS, NEW MEXICO 87025

General Information Residential facility that houses the environmental education program for a private elementary school, Manzano Day School. Established in 1974. 5-acre facility located 80 miles from Alburquerque. Features: small pond; evergreen forests; small stream; nearby hot springs; wildflower meadows; red rock cliffs.

Profile of Summer Employees Total number: 3–5; typical ages: 16–26. 40% men; 60% women; 25% high school students; 50% college students; 25% local applicants. Nonsmokers preferred.

Employment Information Openings are from July 1 to August 5. Year-round positions also offered. Jobs available: ▶ 2 *camp counselors* (minimum age 21) with first aid/CPR certification and experience with children, outdoor recreation, crafts, and games at $850 per season ▶ 2 *junior counselors* (minimum age 15) with experience working with children, outdoor recreation, crafts, and games at $150 per season. International applicants accepted; must obtain own visa, obtain own working papers.

Benefits and Preemployment Training Free housing, free meals, and on-the-job training. Preemployment training is required and includes accident prevention and safety, interpersonal skills, leadership skills, counselor training.

Contact Stephanie Stansbury, Director, Fenton Ranch, 1801 Central Avenue, NW, Albuquerque, New Mexico 87104. E-mail: ss@mds.k12.nm.us. Application deadline: continuous.

GLORIETA BAPTIST CONFERENCE CENTER
EXIT 299, I-25
GLORIETA, NEW MEXICO 87535

General Information Support facilities and services for approximately 28,000 guests attending summer conferences. Established in 1952. 2,271-acre facility located 18 miles from Santa Fe. Features: mountain setting; arid climate.

Profile of Summer Employees Total number: 350; typical ages: 19–25. 40% men; 60% women; 15% minorities; 13% high school students; 78% college students; 5% retirees; 20% local applicants. Nonsmokers preferred.

Employment Information Openings are from May 15 to September 15. Year-round positions also offered. Jobs available: ▶ *chuckwagon workers* ▶ *conference service workers* ▶ *day-camp workers* ▶ *food service workers* ▶ *front desk staff* ▶ *housekeepers* ▶ *maintenance/ grounds workers* ▶ *preschool workers* ▶ 1–2 *residence hall/campus ministry coordinators* ▶ *sound and lighting technicians*. Applicants must submit a formal organization application, three personal references. International applicants accepted; must obtain own visa, obtain own working papers.

Benefits and Preemployment Training Housing at a cost, meals at a cost, on-the-job training, and opportunity to attend seminars/workshops.

Contact Billie L. Koller, Administrative Coordinator, Glorieta Baptist Conference Center, PO

Box 8, Glorieta, New Mexico 87535. Telephone: 505-757-4208. Fax: 505-757-6149. E-mail: bkoller@lifeway.com. Application deadline: continuous.

PHILMONT SCOUT RANCH
ROUTE 1, PO BOX 35
CIMARRON, NEW MEXICO 87714

General Information Camp and family conference center offering mountain backpacking with a wide variety of outdoor and historical experiences. Established in 1938. 137,493-acre facility located 200 miles from Albuquerque. Features: mountain backpacking-12,440 feet; 3 horseback riding camps; 3 rockclimbing camps; over 220 miles of hiking trails; 32 staffed backcountry camps; exceptional wildlife and fishing.

Profile of Summer Employees Total number: 850; typical ages: 18–25. 75% men; 25% women; 5% minorities; 1% high school students; 95% college students; 1% retirees; 3% local applicants.

Employment Information Openings are from May 15 to August 22. Jobs available: ▶ 4 *backcountry manager* (minimum age 21) at $800–$1200 per month ▶ 4 *bookkeeping clerk and clerks/typists* (minimum age 18) at $600 per month ▶ 30–35 *camp directors* (minimum age 21) at $800–$925 per month ▶ *commissary staff members (clerks)* (minimum age 18) at $600 per month ▶ 70–75 *conservation staff members* (minimum age 18) at $600–$900 per month ▶ 10 *crafts lodge manager and staff members* (minimum age 18) at $600–$800 per month ▶ 30–40 *custodial staff members (custodian, housekeeper, and lawn maintenance personnel)* (minimum age 18) at $600 per month ▶ 40 *family programs staff members* (minimum age 18) including manager, assistant manager, nursery leader, and leaders for activities for various age groups at $600–$800 per month ▶ 60 *food services staff members* (minimum age 18) including dining hall manager, backcountry cook, assistant dining hall manager, dining hall staff, and snack bar clerks at $600–$1000 per month ▶ 20 *headquarters activities manager and staff members* (minimum age 18) at $600–$800 per month ▶ 13–15 *headquarters maintenance staff members* (minimum age 18) at $600 per month ▶ 20 *headquarters services manager, assistant manager, and staff members* (minimum age 18) at $600–$900 per month ▶ 30–35 *horse department staff members (supervisors and wranglers)* (minimum age 18) must be an experienced horseman at $700–$900 per month ▶ 20 *logistic services manager, assistant manager, and staff members* (minimum age 18) at $700–$900 per month ▶ 25–30 *medical/health lodge staff members* (minimum age 18) including administrator, medics, medical secretary, nurse, and health lodge drivers at $700–$900 per month ▶ 4 *museum shop clerks and guides* (minimum age 18) at $600 per month ▶ 20 *news and photo service members* (minimum age 18) including manager, assistant manager, photo lab manager, and photographers at $600–$800 per month ▶ 1 *postmaster* (minimum age 21) at $700 per month ▶ 150–200 *program counselors* (minimum age 18) with knowledge of and experience in one or more of the following: adobe construction, archaeology, black powder weapons, blacksmithing, burro packing and racing, challenge events, environmental ecology and nature studies, fishing and fly tying, gold mining and panning, mountain technology at $600–$660 per month ▶ 6 *quartermaster staff members* (minimum age 18) including equipment and tent repair manager, tent repair helper, and warehouse clerk at $600 per month ▶ 160 *rangers* (minimum age 18) including chief ranger, associate chief ranger, Rayado trek coordinator, mountain trek coordinator, and training rangers at $600–$660 per month ▶ 5 *seasonal registrars* (minimum age 18) at $700–$900 per month ▶ 13–15 *security staff members* (minimum age 21) at $700 per month ▶ 5 *support services manager and staff members* (minimum age 18) at $600 per month ▶ 6 *tent city managers and assistant managers* (minimum age 21) at $700–$800 per month ▶ *trading post managers and clerks for headquarters, craft lodge, and backcountry* (minimum age 18) at $600–$800 per month ▶ 5 *training center office staff members* (minimum age 18) at $600 per month ▶ 3 *transportation managers* (minimum age 21) at $700 per month ▶ 5 *truck drivers* (minimum age 21) with experience driving a two-ton truck over dirt roads at $700 per month. Applicants must submit a formal organization application, resume, two personal references.

Benefits and Preemployment Training Free housing, free meals, formal training, health insurance, and on-the-job training. Preemployment training is required and includes accident prevention and safety, first aid, CPR, interpersonal skills, leadership skills.

Contact Richard A. Mahalik, Associate Director of Program, Philmont Scout Ranch. Telephone: 505-376-2281. Fax: 505-376-2236.

THE SOUTHWESTERN COMPANY, NEW MEXICO
See The Southwestern Company, Tennessee on page 284 for complete description.

STUDENT CONSERVATION ASSOCIATION (SCA), NEW MEXICO
See Student Conservation Association (SCA), New Hampshire on page 193 for complete description.

ACE COMPUTER CAMP–NEW YORK
See ACE Computer Camp–Washington on page 307 for complete description.

ADIRONDACK MOUNTAIN CLUB
PO BOX 867
LAKE PLACID, NEW YORK 12946
General Information Nonprofit conservation organization. Established in 1922. 640-acre facility located 7 miles from Lake Placid. Features: lake; campground; information center; lodge; wooded; cabins.

Profile of Summer Employees Total number: 40; typical ages: 18–22. 50% men; 50% women; 5% minorities; 10% high school students; 80% college students; 5% local applicants.

Employment Information Openings are from June to September. Year-round positions also offered. Jobs available: ▶ 4 *HPIC crew* (minimum age 16) at $5.15 per hour ▶ 10 *LOJ crew* (minimum age 16) at $5.15 per hour. Applicants must submit three personal references. International applicants accepted; must obtain own visa, obtain own working papers, apply through a recognized agency. An in-person interview is recommended, but a telephone interview is acceptable.

Benefits and Preemployment Training Housing at a cost, meals at a cost, possible full-time employment, on-the-job training, and opportunity to attend seminars/workshops. Preemployment training is required and includes interpersonal skills, leadership skills.

Contact Adirondack Mountain Club, PO Box 867 Applications, Lake Placid, New York 12946. Telephone: 518-523-3480. Fax: 518-523-3518. World Wide Web: http://www.adk.org. Application deadline: February 15.

ADIRONDACK WOODCRAFT CAMPS
RONDAXE ROAD, PO BOX 219
OLD FORGE, NEW YORK 13420
General Information Residential coeducational camp and environmental education center offering teaching, learning, and outdoor activities. Established in 1925. 400-acre facility located 50 miles from Utica. Features: 2 private wilderness lakes; pristine 400-acre wooded setting; 26-foot climbing wall; archery, riflery, tennis, basketball, volleyball areas; large crafts areas; extensive environment education area.

Profile of Summer Employees Total number: 35–40; typical ages: 18–25. 10% minorities; 10% high school students; 55% college students; 5% retirees; 20% non-U.S. citizens; 15% local applicants. Nonsmokers preferred.

Employment Information Openings are from May 10 to September 7. Jobs available: ▶ 19 *counselors* (minimum age 19) with experience working with children at $900–$1600 per season

▶ 2–5 *kitchen assistants* (minimum age 18) at $110–$180 per week ▶ 2 *kitchen assistants* (minimum age 18) at $800–$1400 per season ▶ 1 *office assistant* (minimum age 19) with typing, computer, and good communication skills at $180–$250 per week ▶ 4 *waterfront staff members* (minimum age 19) with WSI, lifeguard, BLS certification, and experience at $1000–$2000 per season ▶ 2–6 *wilderness trip leaders* (minimum age 19) with experience at $1000–$1700 per season. Applicants must submit formal organization application, resume, three personal references. International applicants accepted; must obtain own visa, apply through a recognized agency. An in-person interview is recommended, but a telephone interview is acceptable.

Benefits and Preemployment Training Free housing, free meals, formal training, on-the-job training, and travel reimbursement. Preemployment training is required and includes accident prevention and safety, first aid, CPR, interpersonal skills, leadership skills.

Contact Chris Clemans, Program Director, Adirondack Woodcraft Camps, PO Box 219, Old Forge, New York 13420. Telephone: 315-369-6031. Fax: 315-369-6032. E-mail: awc1@telenet. net. World Wide Web: http://www.awc1.com. Application deadline: continuous.

AHRC/NYC–CAMP CATSKILL
350 REVONAH HILL ROAD
LIBERTY, NEW YORK 12754

General Information Nonprofit organization serving the comprehensive needs of people with developmental disabilities. Camp Catskill serves children and adults. Established in 1949. 100-acre facility located 100 miles from New York. Features: heated cabins; large pool; country setting; Catskill Mountains; large gazebo; large grass fields.

Profile of Summer Employees Total number: 165; typical ages: 18–25. 45% men; 55% women; 40% minorities; 90% college students; 10% retirees; 50% non-U.S. citizens; 20% local applicants.

Employment Information Openings are from June 15 to August 24. Jobs available: ▶ 2–4 *activity counselors* (minimum age 18) must be willing to work with people with developmental disabilities at $1450–$1900 per season ▶ 15–40 *counselors* (minimum age 18) must be willing to work with people with developmental disabilities at $1250–$1600 per season ▶ 2–3 *lifeguards* (minimum age 20) must be a strong swimmer and available beginning June 1 at $1650–$2200 per season ▶ 2–3 *nurses* (minimum age 21) with RN/LPN license in New York at $6000–$8400 per season. Applicants must submit formal organization application, cover letter, resume, three personal references, three letters of recommendation. International applicants accepted; must apply through a recognized agency. An in-person interview is recommended, but a telephone interview is acceptable.

Benefits and Preemployment Training Free housing, free meals, formal training, possible full-time employment, and on-the-job training. Preemployment training is required and includes accident prevention and safety, first aid, CPR, interpersonal skills, leadership skills.

Contact Ricky Lyons, Director, AHRC/NYC–Camp Catskill, 208 Park Avenue South, New York, New York 10003. Telephone: 212-780-2526. Fax: 212-777-3771. E-mail: campahrc@aol. com. Application deadline: continuous.

AMERICAN CAMPING ASSOCIATION
12 WEST 31ST STREET
NEW YORK, NEW YORK 10001

General Information Employment clearinghouse for camps that offers a free placement service for college students and faculty, teachers, and school administrators who desire a summer job outdoors.

Profile of Summer Employees Total number: 9. 50% men; 50% women; 10% minorities; 90% college students; 2% retirees; 2% local applicants.

Employment Information Openings are from May to September. Jobs available: ▶ *EMT staff members* with experience with children and certification ▶ *drama staff members* with experience with children and certification in field ▶ *general counselors* with experience with children and certification in the field ▶ *individual sports staff members* (minimum age 18) with experience with children and certification in field ▶ *kitchen staff members* with experience with children and certification ▶ *land and water sports staff members* with experience with children and certification in the field ▶ *maintenance staff members* (minimum age 18) with experience with children ▶ *medical doctors* with experience with children and certification ▶ *music staff members* with experience with children and certification in field ▶ *registered nurses* with experience with children and certification ▶ *secretarial staff members* (minimum age 18) with computer skills and experience with children ▶ *swimming instructors* (minimum age 18) with WSI or lifeguard certification and experience with children at $1200 per season ▶ *team sports staff members* with experience with children and certification in field ▶ *visual and performing arts staff members* (minimum age 18) with experience with children and certification in the field. Applicants must submit a formal organization application, resume.

Benefits and Preemployment Training Free housing, free meals, formal training, on-the-job training, and travel reimbursement.

Contact Staff Placement Coordinator, American Camping Association, 12 West 31st Street, 12th Floor, New York, New York 10001. Telephone: 800-777-2267. Fax: 212-594-1684. E-mail: acany@thorn.net. World Wide Web: http://www.aca-ny.org. Application deadline: July 1.

BRANT LAKE CAMP
7586 STATE ROUTE 8
BRANT LAKE, NEW YORK 12815

General Information Eight-week high-tuition private residential camp for boys ages 7–15 with a capacity of 330 campers. Also 2 three-week sessions for 41 teenage girls in dance, arts, and sports–particularly tennis. Established in 1917. 95-acre facility located 70 miles from Albany. Features: 6 mile long freshwater lake; 16 tennis courts; 7 basketball courts; 4 baseball fields.

Profile of Summer Employees Total number: 150; typical ages: 19–40. 85% men; 15% women; 10% minorities; 5% high school students; 70% college students; 2% retirees; 20% non-U.S. citizens; 5% local applicants. Nonsmokers required.

Employment Information Openings are from June 5 to August 20. Jobs available: ▶ 9 *athletics specialists* must be college-age at $1200–$1800 per season ▶ 15 *general staff members* must be college-age at $1200–$1500 per season ▶ 2 *group heads/athletics directors* (minimum age 25) with experience teaching/coaching at $1800–$2500 per season ▶ 2 *swimming instructors* with lifeguard certification at $1200–$1500 per season ▶ 6 *waterfront staff members* with WSI certification/lifeguard training; must be college age at $1100–$1600 per season. Applicants must submit formal organization application, resume, three personal references, three letters of recommendation. International applicants accepted; must apply through a recognized agency. A telephone interview is required.

Benefits and Preemployment Training Free housing, free meals, and on-the-job training. Preemployment training is required and includes accident prevention and safety, first aid, CPR, leadership skills.

Contact Richard Gersten, Director, Brant Lake Camp, 1202 Lexington Avenue, Suite 342, New York, New York 10028. Telephone: 212-734-6216. Fax: 212-288-0937. E-mail: brantlakec@aol. com. World Wide Web: http://www.brantlake.com. Application deadline: continuous.

CAMP BACO FOR BOYS
ROUTE 28 NORTH
MINERVA, NEW YORK 12851

General Information Residential camp serving 190 boys in a traditional eight-week program. 100-acre facility located near New York City.

Profile of Summer Employees Total number: 120. 20% high school students; 80% college students. Nonsmokers required.

Employment Information Openings are from June to August. Jobs available: ▶ *baseball/ softball instructor* at $1400–$2500 per season ▶ *basketball instructor* with experience at $1400–$2500 per season ▶ *canoeing instructors* with LGT, BLS, and American Red Cross small crafts instructor certification at $1400–$2500 per season ▶ *ceramics instructors* at $1400–$2500 per season ▶ *hiking/pioneering instructor* with first aid or CPR certification at $1400–$2500 per season ▶ *music instructors* with ability to accompany on the piano at $1400–$2500 per season ▶ *sailing/windsurfing instructors* with LGT, BLS, and American Red Cross small crafts instructor certification at $1400–$2500 per season ▶ *soccer instructor* at $1400–$2500 per season ▶ *sports instructors* at $1400–$2500 per season ▶ *swimming instructors* with WSI, LGT, and BLS certification at $1200–$2500 per season ▶ *tennis instructors* with college team playing or coaching experience at $1400–$2500 per season. Applicants must submit formal organization application, portfolio, two personal references, security check. International applicants accepted; must apply through a recognized agency. An in-person interview is recommended, but a telephone interview is acceptable.

Benefits and Preemployment Training Free housing, free meals, formal training, and on-the-job training. Preemployment training is required and includes accident prevention and safety, first aid, CPR, interpersonal skills, leadership skills.

Contact Bob Wortman, Director, Camp Baco for Boys, 484 South Wood Road, Rockville Center, New York 11570. Telephone: 516-867-3895. Fax: 516-868-3819. E-mail: campbaco@aol.com. World Wide Web: http://www.campbaco.com. Application deadline: continuous.

CAMP CHE-NA-WAH FOR GIRLS
ROUTE 28 NORTH
MINERVA, NEW YORK 12851

General Information Residential camp serving 160 girls in a traditional eight-week program. 100-acre facility.

Profile of Summer Employees Total number: 120. 20% high school students; 80% college students.

Employment Information Jobs available: ▶ *baseball/softball instructor* at $1400–$2500 per season ▶ *basketball instructor* with experience in the field at $1400–$2500 per season ▶ *canoeing instructors* with LGT, BLS, and American Red Cross small crafts instructor certification at $1400–$2500 per season ▶ *ceramics instructors* at $1400–$2500 per season ▶ 1 *dance instructor* at $1200–$2500 per season ▶ 1 *gymnastics instructor* with college team experience at $1400–$2500 per season ▶ *hiking/pioneering instructor* with first aid or CPR certification at $1400–$2500 per season ▶ *music instructors* with ability to accompany on the piano at $1400–$2500 per season ▶ *sailing/windsurfing instructors* with LGT, BLS, and American Red Cross small crafts instructor certification at $1400–$2500 per season ▶ *soccer instructor* at $1400–$2500 per season ▶ *sports instructors* at $1400–$2500 per season ▶ *swimming instructors* with WSI, LGT, and BLS certification at $1200–$2500 per season ▶ *tennis instructors* with college team playing or coaching experience at $1400–$2500 per season. Applicants must submit a formal organization application, two personal references. An in-person interview is recommended, but a telephone interview is acceptable.

Benefits and Preemployment Training Free housing, free meals, formal training, and on-the-job training. Preemployment training is required and includes accident prevention and safety, first aid, CPR, interpersonal skills, leadership skills.

Contact Mr. Robert Wortman, Director, Camp Che-Na-Wah for Girls, 484 South Wood Road, Rockville Center, New York 11570. Telephone: 516-867-3895. Fax: 516-868-3819. E-mail: campbaco@aol.com. World Wide Web: http://www.campchenawah.com. Application deadline: continuous.

CAMP HILLARD, INC.
26 ELIZABETH STREET
SCARSDALE, NEW YORK 10583

General Information Children's summer day camp. 17-acre facility located 15 miles from New York City. Features: 6 heated pools; 16 buildings; multiple fields and courts; many trees and shade; outdoor amphitheater; unique mini-golf course.

Profile of Summer Employees Total number: 275; typical ages: 18–30. 33% men; 67% women; 25% high school students; 50% college students.

Employment Information Openings are from June 28 to August 20. Jobs available: ▶ *general counselors* ▶ *swim counselors*. Applicants must submit a formal organization application, three personal references. International applicants accepted; must obtain own visa, obtain own working papers. An in-person interview is required.

Benefits and Preemployment Training Preemployment training is required and includes accident prevention and safety, first aid, CPR, interpersonal skills, leadership skills, role of camp counselor, camp's policies and procedures.

Contact Jim Libman, Director, Camp Hillard, Inc., Box 1226, Scarsdale, New York 10583. Telephone: 914-949-8857. E-mail: hillcamp@aol.com. Application deadline: continuous.

CAMP HILLTOP
HC 72, BOX 56
HANCOCK, NEW YORK 13783

General Information Traditional residential coed camp for campers ages 7-15. Established in 1924. 400-acre facility located 40 miles from Binghamton. Features: lake; pool; lighted tennis courts; beautiful wooded setting; 300-foot zip line; well-equipped horsebarn.

Profile of Summer Employees Total number: 80; typical ages: 19–28. 50% men; 50% women; 5% minorities; 60% college students; 30% non-U.S. citizens. Nonsmokers required.

Employment Information Openings are from June 20 to August 20. Jobs available: ▶ 3 *archery staff members* (minimum age 20) with archery certification at $1000–$1500 per season ▶ 5 *arts and crafts staff members* (minimum age 19) at $1000–$1500 per season ▶ 2 *computer staff members* (minimum age 19) at $1000–$1500 per season ▶ 3 *horseback riding staff members* (minimum age 20) at $1000–$2000 per season ▶ *lifeguards* with WSI certification at $1000–$2000 per season ▶ 4 *sports staff members* (minimum age 19) at $1000–$1500 per season ▶ 2 *tennis staff members* (minimum age 19) at $1000–$1500 per season ▶ 7 *waterfront staff members* (minimum age 19) with ARC lifeguard or WSI certification at $1300–$2000 per season. Applicants must submit formal organization application, three personal references, two letters of recommendation. International applicants accepted; must obtain own visa, apply through a recognized agency. An in-person interview is recommended, but a telephone interview is acceptable.

Benefits and Preemployment Training Free housing, free meals, on-the-job training, and travel reimbursement. Preemployment training is required and includes accident prevention and safety, first aid, CPR, interpersonal skills, leadership skills.

Contact William H. Young, Director, Camp Hilltop, HC 72, Box 56, Hancock, New York 13783. Telephone: 607-637-5201. Fax: 607-637-2389. World Wide Web: http://www.camphilltop.com. Application deadline: continuous.

CAMP JEANNE D'ARC
154 GADWAY ROAD
MERRILL, NEW YORK 12955

General Information Residential camp for 120 girls ages 6–17 focusing on individual activities and personal achievement. Established in 1922. 230-acre facility located 30 miles from Plattsburgh. Features: location on 14-mile lake in Adirondack State Park; surrounded by woodlands; Swiss chalet-type cabins with fireplaces and indoor baths; mile-long 28-station fitness trail; 3 tennis courts.

Profile of Summer Employees Total number: 50; typical ages: 19–23. 5% men; 95% women; 10% minorities, 10% high school students, 75% college students, 20% non-U.S. citizens, 15% local applicants. Nonsmokers required.

Employment Information Openings are from June 24 to August 18. Jobs available: ▶ 1 *administrative assistant* (minimum age 19) with computer, organizational, and writing skills at $2000–$2500 per season ▶ 2 *arts and crafts instructors* (minimum age 19) at $1000–$1500 per season ▶ 1 *canoeing instructor* (minimum age 19) with current CPR (preferred) and LGT (training available) at $1000–$1500 per season ▶ 1 *dance instructor* (minimum age 19) at $1000–$1500 per season ▶ 1 *drama instructor* (minimum age 19) at $1000–$1500 per season ▶ 1 *music/guitar instructor* (minimum age 19) at $1000–$1500 per season ▶ 2 *nurses* salary negotiable with RN, EMT, or LPN ▶ 5 *other land sports instructors* (minimum age 19) at $1000–$1500 per season ▶ 5 *other water sports instructors* (minimum age 19) with current CPR (preferred) and LGT (training available) at $1000–$1500 per season ▶ 2 *outdoor camping counselors* (minimum age 19) with current CPR (preferred) and RTE (training available) at

$1000–$1500 per season ▶ 3 *riding instructors* (minimum age 19) with CHA certification and RTE (training available) at $1000–$2000 per season ▶ 1 *riflery instructor* (minimum age 19) with NRA rifle instructor certification at $1000–$1500 per season ▶ 1 *sailing instructor* (minimum age 19) with current CPR (preferred) and LGT (training available) at $1000–$1500 per season ▶ 3 *swimming instructors* (minimum age 19) with WSI and American Red Cross lifeguard certification; current CPR (preferred) at $1000–$1500 per season ▶ 2 *tennis instructors* (minimum age 19) at $1000–$1500 per season ▶ 2 *waterskiing instructors* (minimum age 19) with LGT (training available) and boat driving experience at $1000–$1500 per season. Applicants must submit formal organization application, three personal references, three letters of recommendation. International applicants accepted; must apply through a recognized agency. An in-person interview is recommended, but a telephone interview is acceptable.

Benefits and Preemployment Training Free housing, free meals, on-the-job training, and travel reimbursement. Preemployment training is required and includes accident prevention and safety, first aid, CPR, interpersonal skills, leadership skills, RTE (responding to emergencies).

Contact Jehanne McIntyre Edwards, Associate Director, Camp Jeanne d'Arc, 11 Landings Court, Annapolis, Maryland 21403. Telephone: 410-295-6869. Fax: 410-295-7254. E-mail: funatcjda@aol.com. World Wide Web: http://www.campjeannedarc.com. Application deadline: continuous.

CAMP JENED–A FACILITY OF THE UNITED CEREBRAL PALSY ASSOCIATION OF NEW YORK STATE
ADAMS ROAD
ROCK HILL, NEW YORK 12775

General Information Nonprofit residential vacationing facility for adults who have physical, intellectual and/or behavioral disabilities. Established in 1978. 150-acre facility located 90 miles from New York. Features: located in the Catskill Mountains; wheelchair accessible buildings; freshwater, well stocked lake; wheelchair accessible swimming pool; wheelchair accessible cooking and camping out facilities; 2 hours from New York City.

Profile of Summer Employees Total number: 165; typical age: 21. 35% men; 65% women; 23% minorities; 90% college students; 61% non-U.S. citizens; 1% local applicants.

Employment Information Openings are from June 1 to August 26. Jobs available: ▶ 1 *cook* (minimum age 25) with ability to prepare meals for large groups; salary is negotiable ▶ 20 *counselors* (minimum age 18) at $1400 per season, plus room and board. Applicants must submit formal organization application, two letters of recommendation. International applicants accepted; must apply through a recognized agency. A telephone interview is required.

Benefits and Preemployment Training Free housing, free meals, and partial travel reimbursement. Preemployment training is required and includes accident prevention and safety, interpersonal skills, leadership skills, skills to provide personal care.

Contact Katherine Mace, Camp Director, Camp Jened–A Facility of the United Cerebral Palsy Association of New York State, PO Box 483, Rock Hull, New York 12775. Telephone: 914-434-2220. Fax: 914-434-2253. E-mail: jened@catskill.net. World Wide Web: http://www.campjened.org. Application deadline: continuous.

CAMP LOYALTOWN-AHRC
GLEN AVENUE
HUNTER, NEW YORK 12442-0316

General Information Summer residential recreational vacation camp for mentally retarded and developmentally disabled children and adults of all ages and functional levels. Established in 1947. 240-acre facility located 125 miles from New York City. Features: rolling tree-covered mountain; heated swimming pool; studios for ceramics, arts and crafts, and dance; lighted stage; indoor and outdoor athletic facilities.

Profile of Summer Employees Total number: 160; typical ages: 18–28. 50% men; 50% women; 10% minorities; 3% high school students; 90% college students; 30% non-U.S. citizens.

Employment Information Openings are from June 13 to August 15. Jobs available: ▶ 2 *arts and crafts instructors* (minimum age 19) with experience presenting arts and crafts to the developmentally disabled at $1600–$1800 per season ▶ 1 *athletics instructor* (minimum age 19) with experience in the field at $1600–$1800 per season ▶ 80 *cabin counselors* (minimum age 18) with a major in special education or related field, (physical therapy, occupational therapy, psychology, or similar) at $1400–$1600 per season ▶ 1 *ceramics instructor* (minimum age 19) with experience in the field at $1600–$1800 per season ▶ 1 *cooking instructor* (minimum age 19) with experience in the field at $1600–$1800 per season ▶ 4 *cooks* with experience in quantity food preparation and nutrition ▶ 1 *dance instructor* (minimum age 19) with experience in the field at $1600–$1800 per season ▶ 1 *drama instructor* (minimum age 19) with experience in the field at $1600–$1800 per season ▶ 6 *kitchen assistants* (minimum age 18) at $1400–$1600 per season ▶ 4 *lifeguards* with ALS or WSI certification; experience preferred at $1600–$1800 per season ▶ 1 *music instructor* (minimum age 19) with experience in the field at $1600–$1800 per season ▶ 1 *nature instructor* (minimum age 19) with experience in the field at $1600–$1800 per season ▶ 4 *office staff members* (minimum age 19) with knowledge of office procedures and typing clerical skills; experience with WordPerfect, Word and Paradox database at $1200–$1600 per season ▶ 1 *recreation instructor* (minimum age 19) with experience in the field at $1600–$1800 per season ▶ 1 *sewing/fabric arts instructor* (minimum age 19) with experience in the field at $1600–$1800 per season ▶ 1 *waterfront director* (minimum age 21) with ALS and WSI certification at $2200–$2500 per season ▶ 1 *woodshop instructor* (minimum age 19) with experience in the field at $1600–$1800 per season. Applicants must submit formal organization application, three personal references. International applicants accepted; must apply through a recognized agency. An in-person interview is recommended, but a telephone interview is acceptable.

Benefits and Preemployment Training Free housing, free meals, formal training, and on-the-job training. Preemployment training is required and includes accident prevention and safety, interpersonal skills, leadership skills, education on working with various disability conditions.

Contact Paul H. Cullen, Director of Camping, Camp Loyaltown-AHRC, 115 East Bethpage Road, Plainview, New York 11803. Telephone: 516-263-2016 Ext. 410. Fax: 516-719-8100. E-mail: camp.ahrc@psinet.com. World Wide Web: http://www.ahrc.org. Application deadline: continuous.

CAMP MADISON
201 POWDER MILL BRIDGE ROAD
KINGSTON, NEW YORK 12401

General Information Residential camp for boys and girls who are members of the Madison Square Boys and Girls Club. Established in 1884. 118-acre facility located 100 miles from New York City. Features: swimming pool; wooded area; lake and pond; 21 cabins; 2 tennis courts; theater.

Profile of Summer Employees Total number: 50; typical ages: 18–24. 50% men; 50% women; 60% minorities; 10% high school students; 90% college students; 30% non-U.S. citizens; 10% local applicants. Nonsmokers preferred.

Employment Information Openings are from June 15 to August 30. Year-round positions also offered. Jobs available: ▶ 1–2 *arts and crafts staff members* (minimum age 18) with experience preferred at $1000–$1400 per season ▶ 1 *computer instructor* (minimum age 18) with experience preferred at $1000–$1400 per season ▶ 23 *general camp counselors* (minimum age 18) must be high school graduates attending college at $900–$1100 per season ▶ 3 *lifeguards* (minimum age 21) with lifeguard, BLS, CPR, and first aid certifications at $1000–$1200 per season ▶ 2 *nurses* (minimum age 21) with RN, LPN, EMT, or PA (New York state licensed) at $2500–$4000 per season ▶ 1 *outdoor educator* (minimum age 18) with experience preferred at $1000–$1400 per season. Applicants must submit formal organization application, cover letter, resume, three personal references. International applicants accepted; must apply through a recognized agency. An in-person interview is recommended, but a telephone interview is acceptable.

Benefits and Preemployment Training Free housing, free meals, formal training, and on-the-job training. Preemployment training is required and includes accident prevention and safety, first aid, interpersonal skills, leadership skills.

Contact Jack Thomas, Camp Director, Camp Madison, 301 East 29th Street, New York, New

York 10016. Telephone: 212-532-5751. Fax: 212-213-6502. E-mail: campmad84@aol.com. Application deadline: continuous.

CAMP MICHIKAMAU–YMCA OF GREATER BERGEN COUNTY
BEAR MOUNTAIN, NEW YORK 10911

General Information Coed residential YMCA camp in rustic setting serving 110 campers ages 8–15. Features traditional camping, waterfront activities, arts and crafts, and outdoor activities. Established in 1927. 20-acre facility located 30 miles from New York. Features: freshwater lakes; wooded setting; rustic cabins; miles of hiking trails; basketball courts/low ropes; location in a state park.

Profile of Summer Employees Total number: 35; typical ages: 18–26. 60% men; 40% women; 20% high school students; 80% college students; 10% non-U.S. citizens; 60% local applicants. Nonsmokers preferred.

Employment Information Openings are from June 28 to August 26. Jobs available: ▶ 1 *arts and crafts director* (minimum age 20) at $1000–$1600 per season ▶ 20 *counselors* (minimum age 18) at $900–$1400 per season ▶ 5 *lifeguards/counselors* (minimum age 17) with American Red Cross lifeguard training at $900–$1600 per season ▶ 2 *nurses* (minimum age 20) with LPN, RN, or EMT license at $1600–$2800 per season ▶ 1–2 *waterfront directors* (minimum age 21) with WSI certification/lifeguard training at $1800–$2200 per season. Applicants must submit formal organization application, cover letter, two letters of recommendation. International applicants accepted; must obtain own visa, apply through a recognized agency. An in-person interview is recommended, but a telephone interview is acceptable.

Benefits and Preemployment Training Free housing, free meals, and on-the-job training. Preemployment training is required and includes accident prevention and safety, first aid, CPR, interpersonal skills, leadership skills.

Contact Ken Riscinti, Camping Director, Camp Michikamau–YMCA of Greater Bergen County, 360 Main Street, Hackensack, New Jersey 07601. Telephone: 201-487-6600. Fax: 201-487-4539. Application deadline: continuous.

CAMP MONROE
MONROE, NEW YORK 10950

General Information A well-structured, coed camp meeting the needs and interests of today's youth in a traditional Jewish camp setting. Established in 1941. 192-acre facility located 60 miles from New York City. Features: swimming pool; freshwater lake; horseback riding trails and ring; 5 tennis courts; 2 hockey rinks; 2 indoor gyms.

Profile of Summer Employees Total number: 150; typical ages: 20–24. 50% men; 50% women; 10% high school students; 60% college students; 1% retirees; 30% non-U.S. citizens; 10% local applicants. Nonsmokers required.

Employment Information Openings are from June 24 to August 26. Jobs available: ▶ 1 *arts and crafts instructor* (minimum age 21) with related experience and ability to use pottery wheel at $450–$1200 per season ▶ 6 *general counselors* (minimum age 20) with experience working with children at $450–$1200 per season ▶ 1 *gymnastics/aerobics instructor* (minimum age 21) with related teaching experience at $450–$1200 per season ▶ 1 *hockey instructor* (minimum age 21) with relevant teaching experience at $450–$1200 per season ▶ 1 *softball instructor* (minimum age 21) with related teaching experience at $450–$1200 per season ▶ 2 *swimming instructors* (minimum age 21) with lifeguard/WSI certification at $450–$1200 per season ▶ 1 *volleyball instructor* (minimum age 21) with related teaching experience at $450–$1200 per season. Applicants must submit formal organization application, cover letter, three personal references, three letters of recommendation. International applicants accepted; must apply through a recognized agency. An in-person interview is required.

Benefits and Preemployment Training Free housing, free meals, formal training, and on-the-job training. Preemployment training is required and includes accident prevention and safety, first aid, CPR, interpersonal skills, leadership skills.

Contact Stanley Felsinger, Director, Camp Monroe, PO Box 475, Monroe, New York 10950.

Telephone: 914-782-8695. Fax: 914-782-2247. Application deadline: continuous.

CAMP OF THE WOODS
ROUTE 30
SPECULATOR, NEW YORK 12164

General Information Nondenominational Christian family camp serving over 1000 people each week and Christian girls camp, Tapawingo, serving 72 girls ages 8–16 per week. Established in 1900. 120-acre facility located 80 miles from Albany. Features: 1000-foot beach; 1700-seat auditorium; 16-element challenge course; fantastic chapel speakers; Adirondack Mountains; family-oriented entertainment.

Profile of Summer Employees Total number: 270; typical ages: 17–24. 45% men; 55% women; 10% minorities; 25% high school students; 75% college students; 2% retirees; 1% non-U.S. citizens; 1% local applicants. Nonsmokers required.

Employment Information Openings are from May 15 to September 7. Winter break and year-round positions also offered. Jobs available: ▶ 50 *counselors/teachers* (minimum age 17) with ability to provide leadership and programming for children in preschool through high school at $1000–$1700 per season ▶ 45 *food service personnel* (minimum age 18) at $1000–$2000 per season ▶ 45 *musical performance staff members (instrumental/vocal; double as waitstaff)* (minimum age 17) at $1500–$2500 per season ▶ 3 *nurses* (minimum age 21) with RN, LPN, or EMT license at $1500–$2100 per season ▶ 10 *office/clerical staff members* (minimum age 18) at $1000–$1300 per season ▶ 50 *operational personnel (dishwashers, maintenance staff, and housekeepers)* (minimum age 16) at $500–$1200 per season ▶ 10–15 *recreation leaders* (minimum age 17) with tennis, hiking, rafting, and team sports experience at $1000–$1500 per season ▶ 15 *supervisors (all departments)* (minimum age 21) at $1500–$2100 per season ▶ 10 *waterfront staff members* (minimum age 17) with WSI certification (director), lifeguard training, and CPR training (staff) at $1000–$1500 per season. Applicants must submit formal organization application, three personal references. International applicants accepted; must obtain own visa, obtain own working papers, apply through a recognized agency. A telephone interview is required.

Benefits and Preemployment Training Free housing, free meals, on-the-job training, opportunity to attend seminars/workshops, and tuition assistance. Preemployment training is required and includes first aid, CPR, leadership skills, lifeguarding, RTE.

Contact Scott Sonju, Personnel Director, Camp of the Woods, Route 30, Speculator, New York 12164. Telephone: 518-548-4311. Fax: 518-548-9751. E-mail: personnel@camp-of-the-woods. org. World Wide Web: http://www.camp-of-the-woods.org. Application deadline: continuous.

CAMP POK-O-MACCREADY
100 MOUNTAIN ROAD
WILLSBORO, NEW YORK 12996

General Information Traditional camp in the Adirondacks serving 230 boys and girls. Established in 1905. 450-acre facility located 20 miles from Burlington, Vermont. Features: Adirondack Lake; 3 swimming docks; 15 sailboats; 2 beautiful stables; wilderness setting; working farm.

Profile of Summer Employees Total number: 73; typical ages: 18–68. 51% men; 49% women; 2% high school students, 85% college students, 10% non-U.S. citizens, 2% local applicants. Nonsmokers preferred.

Employment Information Openings are from June 20 to August 19. Year-round positions also offered. Jobs available: ▶ 1 *Indian crafts/Indian lore instructor* (minimum age 18) at $1200–$1600 per season ▶ *kayak instructor* (minimum age 18) with lifeguard training; WSI at $1300–$1800 per season ▶ 1 *lacrosse instructor* (minimum age 18) at $1200–$1600 per season ▶ *rock climbing instructor* (minimum age 18) with 2 years experience at $1200–$1800 per season ▶ 2 *swimming instructors* (minimum age 18) with WSI and lifeguard certification at $1200–$1800 per season ▶ *theater director* at $1200–$1800 per season ▶ 1 *woodworking instructor* (minimum age 18) at $1200–$1600 per season. Applicants must submit formal organization application, resume, personal reference, letter of recommendation. International applicants accepted; must apply through a recognized agency. An in-person interview is recommended, but a telephone interview is acceptable.

Benefits and Preemployment Training Free housing, free meals, possible full-time employment, on-the-job training, opportunity to attend seminars/workshops, and travel reimbursement. Preemployment training is required and includes accident prevention and safety, first aid, CPR, interpersonal skills, leadership skills, lifeguard training.

Contact Jack Swan, Director, Camp Pok-O-MacCready, PO Box 5016, Brookfield, Connecticut 06804. Fax: 203-740-7984. World Wide Web: http://members.aol.com/POKOMAC/. Application deadline: continuous.

CAMP REGIS AND APPLEJACK
PO BOX 245
PAUL SMITHS, NEW YORK 12970

General Information Residential coed children's camp serving 280 campers ages 6–16. Established in 1946. 100-acre facility located 18 miles from Lake Placid. Features: majestic Adirondack lake setting; extensive waterfront (60 boats); 7 tennis courts; large theater, music room, and arts and crafts studio; wilderness trip program originating from our doorstep; chalet-type cabins with fireplaces and bathrooms.

Profile of Summer Employees Total number: 90; typical ages: 18–60. 50% men; 50% women; 20% minorities; 70% college students; 5% non-U.S. citizens; 10% local applicants. Nonsmokers required.

Employment Information Openings are from June 19 to August 23. Jobs available: ▶ 2 *arts and crafts instructors* with teaching experience preferred at $1100–$2400 per season ▶ 3 *athletics instructors* with broad knowledge of numerous sports required at $1200–$2600 per season ▶ 10 *cabin counselors for boys groups* (minimum age 19) with at least one year of college completed at $1100–$1600 per season ▶ 10 *cabin counselors for girls groups* (minimum age 19) with at least one year of college completed at $1100–$1600 per season ▶ 5 *cooks* at $1600–$3600 per season ▶ 1 *dance instructor* with teaching exprience preferred at $1100–$2000 per season ▶ 3 *dishwashers* at $1000–$1300 per season ▶ 2 *dramatics instructors* with teaching and directing experience preferred at $1100–$3000 per season ▶ 1 *gymnastics instructor* with coaching experience required at $1100–$2000 per season ▶ 2 *health care workers* with RN, LPN or EMT required at $1200–$2000 per month ▶ 1 *in-camp nature/ecology instructor* with knowledge of animals and their care at $1100–$2400 per season ▶ 1 *laundry worker* at $1000–$1600 per season ▶ 1 *mountain biking instructor* with Red Cross, CPR, and first aid required at $1100–$2000 per season ▶ 1 *music instructor* whose main instrument is the piano at $1100–$2400 per season ▶ 1 *office manager* with computer/office machines experience preferred at $1100–$2000 per season ▶ 3 *pioneering/trips instructors* with Red Cross, CPR, and first aid required at $1100–$2400 per season ▶ 2 *program directors* with camp experience preferred at $1500–$3500 per season ▶ 2 *sailing and windsurfing instructors* at $1100–$2600 per season ▶ 3 *swimming instructors* with Red Cross, lifeguarding and CPR required at $1100–$3000 per season ▶ 3 *tennis instructors* at $1100–$2400 per season ▶ 4 *unit leaders/head counselors* with camp experience preferred at $1400–$2400 per season ▶ 2 *waterskiing instructors* with boat driving experience required at $1100–$2400 per season. Applicants must submit formal organization application, personal reference. International applicants accepted; must apply through a recognized agency. An in-person interview is recommended, but a telephone interview is acceptable.

Benefits and Preemployment Training Free housing, free meals, formal training, possible full-time employment, on-the-job training, opportunity to attend seminars/workshops, travel reimbursement, and tuition assistance. Preemployment training is required and includes accident prevention and safety, first aid, CPR, interpersonal skills, leadership skills.

Contact Michael P. Humes, Director, Camp Regis and Applejack, 60 Lafayette Road West, Princeton, New Jersey 08540. Telephone: 609-688-0368. Fax: 609-688-0367. E-mail: campregis@ aol.com. World Wide Web: http://www.campregis-applejack.com. Application deadline: continuous.

CAMP SEVEN HILLS
OLEAN ROAD
HOLLAND, NEW YORK 14080

General Information Residential Girl Scout camp serving 150–200 girls ages 6–17 offering one-week, two-week and mini-sessions which include challenge courses, horseback riding, and out-of-camp trips. Established in 1930. 610-acre facility located 42 miles from Buffalo. Features: ropes course; horse stables; pool; sports complex; hiking trails; farm area.

Profile of Summer Employees Total number: 60; typical ages: 18–24. 2% men; 98% women; 5% minorities; 10% high school students; 90% college students; 5% non-U.S. citizens; 95% local applicants. Nonsmokers preferred.

Employment Information Openings are from June 19 to August 15. Jobs available: ▶ 5 *activity counselors/unit assistants* (minimum age 18) with specialization in sports/recreation, nature, arts and crafts, drama, and campcraft and ability to supervise adults and instruct classes at $1500–$1700 per season ▶ 1 *archery director* (minimum age 18) with camping experience, knowledge of Girl Scout Program, certification in archery, and ability to teach adolescents at $1500–$1700 per season ▶ 1 *assistant camp director* (minimum age 20) with camping experience, knowledge of Girl Scout program, and experience supervising and training staff at $2300–$2900 per season ▶ 1 *assistant cook* (minimum age 20) with experience in food preparation for large groups and ability to meet deadlines at $1500–$1800 per season ▶ 1 *assistant waterfront director* (minimum age 18) with current lifeguard training and first aid and CPR certification at $1600–$1800 per season ▶ 1 *boating director* (minimum age 18) with current lifeguard and CPR/BLS certification, certification in the fundamentals of canoeing and/or boating or will provide at $1500–$1900 per season ▶ 1 *business manager* (minimum age 20) with knowledge of bookkeeping and budgeting and ability to manage truck-shop operation; sales/office experience and clean driving record at $1900–$2150 per season ▶ 1 *camp aide* (minimum age 16) with ability to work with limited supervision at $750–$900 per season ▶ 1 *counselor-in-training director* (minimum age 20) with extensive Girl Scout camp experience and experience teaching older adolescents at $1500–$1700 per season ▶ 1–2 *dining hall managers* (minimum age 18) with ability to supervise operation and procedures of dining hall at $1600–$1800 per season ▶ 1 *handyperson* (minimum age 18) with knowledge of basic machinery, and some maintenance skills; position is full- or part-time at $1100–$1300 per season ▶ 1 *health supervisor* (minimum age 21) with RN, LPN, or EMT level 4 physician's assistant at $2300–$3100 per season ▶ 7 *junior counselors* (minimum age 17) with camp experience and successful completion of CIT program preferred at $850–$1000 per season ▶ 3 *kitchen aides* (minimum age 16) with ability to work under supervision and as a team player at $750–$950 per season ▶ 5 *lifeguards/unit assistants* (minimum age 17) with lifeguard certification, first aid, and CPR at $1200–$1700 per season ▶ 1 *program director* (minimum age 20) with Girl Scout and camping background preferred and creativity at $2000–$2300 per season ▶ 1 *riding director* (minimum age 20) with Western and English riding ability, knowledge of horses, simple medications, and proper care, ability to manage horse program, and CHA certification preferred, but will provide at $1600–$2200 per season ▶ 5 *riding instructors/unit assistants* (minimum age 20) with Western and English riding ability and knowledge of simple horse medications at $1400–$1650 per season ▶ 5 *ropes course counselors/unit assistants* (minimum age 18) with Project Adventure/ropes course certification (will provide certification) and group dynamics experience at $1500–$1800 per season ▶ 1 *stable manager* (minimum age 18) with knowledge of barn management and equine care, experience in English and Western riding at $1250–$1400 per season ▶ 4 *trip counselors* (minimum age 18) with experience in backpacking, canoeing, and outdoor living at $1600–$2100 per season ▶ 7 *unit assistants* (minimum age 18) with experience working with children and camping and Girl Scout background preferred at $1125–$1300 per season ▶ 7 *unit leaders* (minimum age 20) with camping and Girl Scout background preferred and experience working with children at $1500–$1700 per season ▶ 1 *waterfront director* (minimum age 21) with WSI and lifeguard certification at $1900–$2200 per season. Applicants must submit formal organization application, three personal references. International applicants accepted; must apply through a recognized agency. An in-person interview is recommended, but a telephone interview is acceptable.

Benefits and Preemployment Training Free housing, free meals, health insurance, and on-the-job training. Preemployment training is required and includes accident prevention and safety, first aid, CPR, interpersonal skills, leadership skills.

Contact Janet M. DePetrillo, Director of Outdoor Program, Camp Seven Hills, 70 Jewett Parkway, Buffalo, New York 14214. Telephone: 716-837-6400. Fax: 716-837-6407. E-mail: jdepetrillo@ bflogirlscouts.org. World Wide Web: http://www.bflogirlscouts.org. Application deadline: July 4.

CAMP TEL YEHUDAH
11 NYS ROUTE 97
BARRYVILLE, NEW YORK 12719

General Information Residential kosher Zionist camp serving teens ages 14–17. Established in 1948. 12,500-acre facility located near Port Jervis.

Employment Information Openings are from June to August. Jobs available: ▶ *arts and crafts specialists* with experience and skill with a variety of crafts at $1050–$1500 per season ▶ *drama specialists* with experience in play directing and education background at $1050–$1500 per season ▶ *drivers* with CDL training and experience with 15-passenger vans at $1200–$1500 per season ▶ *general counselors* with experience working with teens and group leadership skills at $1050–$1500 per season ▶ *hiking and outdoor specialists* with personal and group hiking experience at $1050–$1500 per season ▶ *kitchen workers* at $1050–$1500 per season ▶ *lifeguards* with BLS and WSI certification at $1050–$1500 per season. Applicants must submit formal organization application, three personal references. International applicants accepted; must apply through a recognized agency. An in-person interview is recommended, but a telephone interview is acceptable.

Benefits and Preemployment Training Free housing, free meals, on-the-job training, and travel reimbursement.

Contact Mr. Seth Schwartz, Director, Camp Tel Yehudah, 50 West 58th Street, New York, New York 10019. Telephone: 800-970-CAMP. Fax: 212-303-4572. E-mail: telyehudah@aol.com. Application deadline: continuous.

CAMP WENDY
151 SAINT ELMO ROAD
WALLKILL, NEW YORK 12589

General Information Combination three-week residential camp and three-week day camp. Activities offered cover badge work for the Girl Scouts. Well-rounded program of outdoor activities. Established in 1926. 54-acre facility located 75 miles from New York City. Features: wooded setting; pool; lake.

Profile of Summer Employees Total number: 25; typical ages: 18–45. 2% men; 98% women; 20% minorities; 10% high school students; 35% college students; 10% non-U.S. citizens; 25% local applicants. Nonsmokers preferred.

Employment Information Openings are from June 21 to August 14. Jobs available: ▶ 1 *health director* (minimum age 21) should be RN or EMT with first aid and CPR certification at $1900–$2400 per season ▶ 2 *kitchen helpers* (minimum age 16) with interest in food preparation at $400–$500 per season ▶ 10 *unit counselors* (minimum age 18) with desire to work with children in the out-of-doors at $1000–$1400 per season ▶ 4 *unit directors* (minimum age 21) with desire to work with children in the out-of-doors at $1400–$1800 per season ▶ 1 *waterfront director* (minimum age 21) with ARC lifeguard and/or WSI; pool and supervisory experience at $2000–$2400 per season ▶ 4 *waterfront staff* (minimum age 18) with ARC lifeguard or small craft certification or equivalent at $1200–$1600 per season. Applicants must submit formal organization application, three personal references. International applicants accepted; must apply through a recognized agency. A telephone interview is required.

Benefits and Preemployment Training Free housing, free meals, and on-the-job training. Preemployment training is required and includes accident prevention and safety, first aid, CPR, interpersonal skills, leadership skills.

Contact Ms. Phileshia Dombroski, Camp Director, Camp Wendy, 65 St. James Street, PO Box 3039, Kingston, New York 12402. Telephone: 914-338-5367. Fax: 914-338-6802.

CAROUSEL DAY SCHOOL
9 WEST AVENUE
HICKSVILLE, NEW YORK 11801

General Information Summer day camp for children ages 3–15. Established in 1956. 4-acre facility located near New York City. Features: deck hockey; 2 pools; archery range; beach volleyball.

Profile of Summer Employees Total number: 100; typical ages: 18–55. 95% college students. Nonsmokers preferred.

Employment Information Openings are from June 26 to August 18. Jobs available: ▶ 1 *archery instructor* with knowledge of archery and ability to teach $at $1400-$1500 per season plus tips ▶ 1 *director/instructor for crafts program* with ability to order, supervise, and implement crafts programs at $2500 per season ▶ 30 *general counselors* with ability to relate to children at $950-$1200 per season plus tips ▶ 12 *group leaders* (minimum age 21) at $1400 per season plus tips ▶ 1 *nature instructor* with ability to develop a nature science program at $1200–$1400 per season ▶ 1 *ropes/challenge course instructor* at $1800 per season plus tips ▶ 4 *sports instructors/ counselors* with knowledge of basketball coaching and skills in soccer and baseball at $900–$1300 per season ▶ 4 *swimming instructors and lifeguards* with WSI, Nassau County, and CPR/BLS certification at $2000–$2400 per season. Applicants must submit a formal organization application, resume, five personal references. International applicants accepted. An in-person interview is recommended, but a telephone interview is acceptable.

Benefits and Preemployment Training Formal training and on-the-job training. Preemployment training is required and includes accident prevention and safety, interpersonal skills, leadership skills.

Contact Mike Epstein, Personnel Director, Carousel Day School, 9 West Avenue, Hicksville, New York 11801. Telephone: 516-938-1137. Fax: 516-822-9269. Application deadline: June 15.

CHAUTAUQUA INSTITUTION
CHAUTAUQUA, NEW YORK 14722

General Information Residential summer school focusing on orchestra, piano, drama, and dance/ballet. Established in 1874. 751-acre facility located 90 miles from Buffalo. Features: lake; concert/lecture programs; golf course; tennis courts; library; summer resort.

Profile of Summer Employees Total number: 1,800; typical ages: 20–50. 70% men; 30% women; 20% minorities; 3% high school students; 50% college students; 20% retirees; 1% non-U.S. citizens; 40% local applicants.

Employment Information Openings are from June 27 to August 23. Jobs available: ▶ *carpenter intern* at $1220 per season ▶ *costume designers (theater interns)* at $1220 per season ▶ *lighting designers (theater)* at $3200 per season ▶ *lighting intern* at $1220 per season ▶ *scenic designers (theater)* at $2000 per season ▶ *stage managers (theater)* at $1220 per season ▶ *technical director (theater)* at $2000 per season. Applicants must submit a formal organization application, cover letter, resume. International applicants accepted; must obtain own visa, obtain own working papers.

Benefits and Preemployment Training Formal training and on-the-job training. Preemployment training is required and includes accident prevention and safety, first aid, CPR.

Contact Richard R. Redington, Vice President, Chautauqua Institution, PO Box 1098, Chautauqua, New York 14722. Telephone: 716-357-6232. Fax: 716-357-9014. World Wide Web: http://www. chautauqua-inst.org. Application deadline: February 15.

CHINGACHGOOK YMCA OUTDOOR CENTER
1872 PILOT KNOB ROAD
KATTSKILL BAY, NEW YORK 12844

General Information Outdoor, environmental, and adventure education center in the Adirondacks that teaches school children, college students, families, and adult groups. Established in 1913. 220-acre facility located 8 miles from Lake George. Features: waterfront; beautiful mountain; mountain stream; wetlands; ropes course.

Profile of Summer Employees Total number: 110; typical ages: 17–25. 50% men; 50% women;

5% minorities; 20% high school students; 75% college students; 15% non-U.S. citizens; 30% local applicants. Nonsmokers preferred.

Employment Information Openings are from June 10 to September 5. Spring break, winter break, and year-round positions also offered. Jobs available: ▶ 6 *adventure trip leaders* at $1200–$2000 per season ▶ 35 *counselors* at $1000–$1500 per season ▶ 45 *general camp staff members* (minimum age 16) at $500–$4500 per season. Applicants must submit formal organization application, three personal references. International applicants accepted; must apply through a recognized agency. An in-person interview is recommended, but a telephone interview is acceptable.

Benefits and Preemployment Training Free housing, free meals, formal training, and on-the-job training. Preemployment training is required and includes accident prevention and safety, first aid, CPR, interpersonal skills, leadership skills.

Contact George Binter, Executive Director, Chingachgook YMCA Outdoor Center, Kattskill Bay, New York 12844. Telephone: 518-656-9462. Fax: 518-656-9362. Application deadline: continuous.

COLLEGE GIFTED PROGRAMS
VASSAR COLLEGE
POUGHKEEPSIE, NEW YORK 12601

General Information Residential educational academic summer camp for gifted and talented students in grades 4-11. Program blends in-depth academics with recreational and cultural activities. Established in 1984. 1,000-acre facility located 70 miles from New York. Features: dormitories; campus classroom facilities; campus recreational facilities include pool, tennis courts, and gym; campus library; beautiful college setting.

Profile of Summer Employees Total number: 87; typical ages: 19–70. 50% men; 50% women; 30% minorities; 50% college students; 10% retirees; 10% non-U.S. citizens; 25% local applicants. Nonsmokers required.

Employment Information Openings are from July 3 to July 24. Jobs available: ▶ 45 *counselors* with two years of college completed and experience working with children at $800 to $1200 per 3-week session ▶ 4 *directors* with at least 5 years teaching/supervisory experience; master's degree required, doctorate preferred at $5000–$8000 ▶ 9 *housemasters/instructors (residential)* with master's degree, teaching and supervisory experience at $2500 to $4500 per 3-week session ▶ 20 *instructors (non-residential)* with master's degree and teaching experience at $600 to $2500 per 3-week session ▶ 2 *nurses* with RN license; school experience preferred at $1300 per week. Applicants must submit formal organization application, resume, academic transcripts, two personal references, two letters of recommendation. International applicants accepted; must apply through a recognized agency. An in-person interview is recommended, but a telephone interview is acceptable.

Benefits and Preemployment Training Free housing and free meals. Preemployment training is required and includes accident prevention and safety, interpersonal skills, leadership skills, instructional strategies for gifted students.

Contact Margaret Solitario or Dr. Albert Dorhout, Executive Directors, College Gifted Programs, 120 Littleton Road, Suite 201, Parsippany, New Jersey 07054-1803. Telephone: 973-334-6991. Fax: 973-334-9756. E-mail: info@cgp-sig.com. World Wide Web: http://www.cgp-sig.com. Application deadline: continuous.

EASTERN EXCEL TENNIS
LONG ISLAND UNIVERSITY
BROOKVILLE, NEW YORK 11545

General Information Camp that trains children in playing all aspects of tennis, including competition and match play. Established in 1991. 25 miles from New York City. Features: 37 tennis courts.

Profile of Summer Employees Total number: 25; typical ages: 18–35. 75% men; 25% women; 10% high school students; 60% college students; 5% non-U.S. citizens. Nonsmokers required.

Employment Information Openings are from June 28 to August 27. Jobs available: ▶ 5–15 *tennis instructors* (minimum age 18) with some teaching experience at $150–$300 per week. Applicants must submit a formal organization application, resume, three personal references. International applicants accepted; must obtain own visa. An in-person interview is recommended, but a telephone interview is acceptable.

Benefits and Preemployment Training On-the-job training. Preemployment training is required and includes accident prevention and safety, interpersonal skills.

Contact Lawrence Kleger, Owner, Eastern Excel Tennis, Eastern Excel Tennis, 269-23 Grand Central Parkway, Floral Park, New York 11005. Telephone: 718-224-1596. Fax: 718-224-1736. E-mail: lk10sinc@mindspring.com. Application deadline: June 1.

ENCHANTED FOREST/WATER SAFARI AND OLD FORGE KOA
3183 STATE ROUTE 38
OLD FORGE, NEW YORK 13420

General Information Amusement/theme/water park, KOA Kampground, and family entertainment center. Established in 1956. 200-acre facility located 50 miles from Utica. Features: water rides; amusement park rides; circus shows; KOA campground; kamping kabins; go-carts.

Profile of Summer Employees Total number: 350; typical ages: 14–20. 50% men; 50% women; 5% minorities; 70% high school students; 30% college students; 5% retirees; 1% non-U.S. citizens; 10% local applicants. Nonsmokers preferred.

Employment Information Openings are from May to October. Jobs available: ▶ 10 *admissions staff* (minimum age 16) at $5.15 per hour ▶ 20 *food service personnel* (minimum age 14) at $5.15 per hour ▶ 10 *games attendants* (minimum age 14) at $5.15 per day ▶ 20 *grounds crew/housekeeping staff* (minimum age 16) at $5.15 per hour ▶ 20 *lifeguards* (minimum age 15) with CPR/lifeguard certification at $5.15 per hour ▶ 10 *registration/reservations* (minimum age 16) at $5.15 per hour ▶ 20 *retail personnel* (minimum age 14) at $5.15 per hour ▶ 30–40 *ride operators* (minimum age 18) at $5.15 per hour ▶ 75 *water/amusement ride operators* (minimum age 14) at $5.15 per hour. Applicants must submit a formal organization application, two personal references. International applicants accepted; must obtain own visa, obtain own working papers. An in-person interview is required.

Benefits and Preemployment Training Housing at a cost, meals at a cost, formal training, on-the-job training, and scholarships; parties; discounts. Preemployment training is required and includes interpersonal skills, leadership skills, in-service training for lifeguards, guest relations.

Contact Peter Pepper, Human Resources Manager, Enchanted Forest/Water Safari and Old Forge KOA, 3183 State Route 28, Old Forge, New York 13420. Telephone: 315-369-6145. Fax: 315-369-6400. E-mail: safari@telenet.net. World Wide Web: http://www.watersafari.com. Application deadline: continuous.

FIVE RIVERS CENTER
GAME FARM ROAD
DELMAR, NEW YORK 12054

General Information Environmental education center serving schools and families. Established in 1973. 330-acre facility located 10 miles from Albany. Features: natural setting; many ponds; wooded areas; open meadows; visitor center; picnic area.

Profile of Summer Employees Total number: 6–8; typical ages: 18–65. 50% men; 50% women; 10% minorities; 10% high school students; 30% college students; 30% retirees; 20% local applicants. Nonsmokers required.

Employment Information Openings are from January 1 to December 31. Jobs available: ▶ 2 *naturalist interns* (minimum age 18) at $100 per week with college-level study in natural sciences preferred. Applicants must submit formal organization application, resume, academic transcripts, three personal references. International applicants accepted; must obtain own visa, obtain own working papers. An in-person interview is recommended, but a telephone interview is acceptable.

Benefits and Preemployment Training Free housing, formal training, on-the-job training, and opportunity to attend seminars/workshops.

Contact A. Sanchez, Senior Educator, Five Rivers Center, 56 Game Farm Road, Delmar, New York 12054. Telephone: 518-475-0291. Application deadline: continuous.

FOREST LAKE CAMP
FOREST LAKE ROAD, BOX 67
WARRENSBURG, NEW YORK 12885

General Information Residential brother/sister camp for 100 boys and 85 girls with private lake. Features general program of sports, hobbies, waterfront activities, wilderness trips, and riding. Established in 1926. 400-acre facility located 65 miles from Albany. Features: private lake; 400 acres; vistas; climbing tower; cabins with fireplaces; wooded setting.

Profile of Summer Employees Total number: 80; typical ages: 18–24. 50% men; 50% women; 10% minorities; 5% high school students; 75% college students; 10% non-U.S. citizens; 15% local applicants. Nonsmokers preferred.

Employment Information Openings are from June 24 to August 25. Jobs available: ▶ 1 *archery instructor* with competitive background at $1200–$1600 per season ▶ 1 *baseball coach* with minimum high school varsity playing experience at $1200–$1600 per season ▶ 1 *basketball coach* with minimum high school varsity playing experience at $1200–$1600 per season ▶ 3–8 *general counselors* (minimum age 18) at $1100–$1800 per season ▶ 4 *swimming instructors* with lifeguard, first aid, and CPR training at $1100–$1600 per season ▶ 2 *tennis coaches* with minimum high school varsity playing experience at $1200–$1600 per season ▶ 1–3 *trip leaders* (minimum age 21) with RTE and wilderness expertise at $2000–$4000 per season. Applicants must submit formal organization application, resume, three personal references. International applicants accepted; must apply through a recognized agency. An in-person interview is recommended, but a telephone interview is acceptable.

Benefits and Preemployment Training Free housing, free meals, on-the-job training, travel reimbursement, and tuition assistance. Preemployment training is required and includes accident prevention and safety, first aid, CPR, interpersonal skills, leadership skills, RTE.

Contact Gary Confer, Director, Forest Lake Camp, Box 648, Oldwick, New Jersey 08858. Telephone: 908-534-9809. Fax: 908-534-8474. E-mail: gaconfer@aol.com. Application deadline: continuous.

FORRESTEL FARM CAMP
4536 SOUTH GRAVEL ROAD
MEDINA, NEW YORK 14103

General Information Coed residential camp serving 60 children ages 7–15 for four 2-week sessions. 1,000-acre facility located 40 miles from Buffalo. Features: 800-acre working farm; freshwater pond; 3 miles of oak orchard creek; elaborate stable; tennis court; wooded setting.

Profile of Summer Employees Total number: 20; typical ages: 19–25. 100% college students; 80% non-U.S. citizens; 20% local applicants. Nonsmokers required.

Employment Information Openings are from June 27 to August 20. Jobs available: ▶ 4 *athletics instructors* with Red Cross, CPR, and Basic Life Support training; and coaching and teaching experience in one of the following: soccer, volleyball, basketball, softball, lacrosse, archery, or riflery at $800–$1500 per season ▶ *conservation* ▶ 2 *cooks* with experience in the field ▶ 4 *lifeguards* with Red Cross lifeguard or WSI certification at $800–$1500 per season ▶ 1 *naturalist/conservationist* with experience in the field; pay commensurate with experience ▶ 1 *operations manager* (minimum age 23, 25 preferred) with management skills, strong athletic background, and camp experience; education (or similar) major preferred; starting salary of $3,500 per season increases with experience ▶ 3 *outdoor adventure instructors (canoeing, hiking, mountain biking, and fishing)* with experience in the field at $800–$1500 per season ▶ 8 *riding instructors* with CHA, Red Cross, CPR, Community First Aid and Safety, and Basic Life Support training at $800–$1500 per season ▶ 2 *tennis instructors* with USTA coaching or teaching experience at $800–$1500 per season. Applicants must submit formal organization application, two personal references, two letters of recommendation. International applicants accepted; must apply through a recognized agency. An in-person interview is recommended, but a telephone interview is acceptable.

Benefits and Preemployment Training Free housing, free meals, on-the-job training, and travel reimbursement. Preemployment training is required and includes accident prevention and safety, first aid, CPR, interpersonal skills, leadership skills.

Contact Mary Herbert, Camp Owner/Director, Forrestel Farm Camp, 4536 South Gravel Road, Medina, New York 14103. Telephone: 716-798-0941. Fax: 716-798-2222.

THE FRESH AIR FUND
SHARPE RESERVATION, VAN WYCK LAKE ROAD
FISHKILL, NEW YORK 12524

General Information Five residential camps serving 3,000 inner-city children each summer. Established in 1877. 3,000-acre facility located 65 miles from New York City.

Profile of Summer Employees Total number: 400; typical ages: 18–23. 55% men; 45% women; 35% minorities; 3% high school students; 90% college students; 15% non-U.S. citizens; 30% local applicants. Nonsmokers preferred.

Employment Information Openings are from June 15 to August 24. Jobs available: ▶ 5 *farmers* (minimum age 18) with course work in animal biology or experience working with livestock at $1600–$2000 per season ▶ 200 *general counselors* (minimum age 18) with some college and experience with children at $1600–$2000 per season ▶ 9 *nurses* with RN license and one year of nursing experience required at $4500–$5000 per season ▶ 2 *nutritionists* (minimum age 18) with cooking experience and course work in nutrition at $1600–$2000 per season ▶ 35 *program specialists* (minimum age 18) with ability to teach in one of the following specialties: photography, video, music, sewing, pioneering, nature, or arts and crafts at $1600–$2200 per season ▶ 6 *ropes course facilitators* (minimum age 19) with experience as an instructor or participant on high and/or low ropes course programs; facilitators will be trained and certified during orientation at $1600–$2000 per season ▶ 22 *village leaders* (minimum age 20) with residential camp employment experience required at $2000–$2600 per season ▶ 20 *waterfront assistants* (minimum age 18) with lifeguard training and CPR for the professional rescuer at $1700–$2100 per season ▶ 5 *waterfront directors* (minimum age 21) with lifeguard training and CPR for the professional rescuer; three years of waterfront experience required; WSI preferred at $2300–$3000 per season. Applicants must submit formal organization application. International applicants accepted; must apply through a recognized agency. An in-person interview is recommended, but a telephone interview is acceptable.

Benefits and Preemployment Training Free housing, free meals, formal training, on-the-job training, and travel reimbursement. Preemployment training is required and includes accident prevention and safety, first aid, CPR, leadership skills, lifeguard training.

Contact Thomas S. Karger, Associate Executive Director, The Fresh Air Fund, The Fresh Air Fund, 1040 Avenue of the Americas, New York, New York 10018. Telephone: 800-367-0003. Fax: 212-302-7875. E-mail: freshair@freshair.org. World Wide Web: http://www.freshair.org. Application deadline: continuous.

FROST VALLEY YMCA CAMPS
2000 FROST VALLEY ROAD
CLARYVILLE, NEW YORK 12725

General Information Camp offering traditional activities. Established in 1901. 6,000-acre facility located 100 miles from New York City. Features: 6000 acres of woods and waterfalls; 200 staff from around the world; state-of-the-art programs.

Profile of Summer Employees Total number: 300; typical ages: 17–24. 50% men; 50% women; 15% minorities; 15% high school students; 65% college students; 2% retirees; 15% non-U.S. citizens; 5% local applicants. Nonsmokers preferred.

Employment Information Openings are from June 1 to August 30. Year-round positions also offered. Jobs available: ▶ 3 *art instructors* with experience in the field at $1000–$1500 per season ▶ 40 *counselors* with experience in the field at $900–$1500 per season ▶ 2 *nurses* with license in the field at $2500–$3500 per season ▶ 8 *program area directors* (minimum age 18) with ability to supervise staff and develop programs in various areas, including riding, waterfront, art, sports, and health at $1300–$2200 per season ▶ 5 *riding staff members* with experience teaching Western riding at $1000–$1500 per season ▶ 3 *sports staff members* with experience in the field at $1000–$1300 per season ▶ 10 *trip leaders* (minimum age 21) with experience in canoeing, biking, and hiking at $140–$180 per week ▶ 10 *unit leaders* with experience in the field at $1600–$2000 per season ▶ 5 *waterfront staff members* with lifeguard, CPR, and first aid certification at $1000–$1500 per season. Applicants must submit formal organization application, three personal references. International applicants accepted; must apply through a recognized agency. A telephone interview is required.

Benefits and Preemployment Training Free housing, free meals, possible full-time employment, on-the-job training, and travel reimbursement. Preemployment training is required and includes accident prevention and safety, first aid, CPR, interpersonal skills, leadership skills.

Contact Rob Lehman, Director of Camping, Frost Valley YMCA Camps, 2000 Frost Valley Road, Claryville, New York 12725. Telephone: 914-985-2291. Fax: 914-985-0056. E-mail: camp4me@frostvalley.org. World Wide Web: http://www.frostvalley.org. Application deadline: continuous.

GIRL'S VACATION FUND, INC.
NEW YORK

General Information A charitable organization with the mission to help less privileged girls discover their own self worth and grow through caring, educational camp experience. Established in 1935. 500-acre facility located 30 miles from Albany. Features: lake; wooded Castskill Mountains setting; learning center; gardens; small farm; Adirondack cabins.

Profile of Summer Employees Total number: 50; typical ages: 19–30. 5% men; 95% women; 25% minorities; 5% high school students; 80% college students; 30% non-U.S. citizens; 5% local applicants. Nonsmokers required.

Employment Information Openings are from June 20 to August 25. Jobs available: ▶ 2 *chefs* (minimum age 21) must have institutional cooking experience at $600 per week ▶ 25 *counselors* (minimum age 19) must be able to live in cabins with girls, early education majors preferred at $200–$250 per week ▶ 2 *crafts directors* (minimum age 21) must have teaching or youth group experience at $250 per week ▶ 2 *hiking directors* (minimum age 21) must have RTE certification and be able to take youth groups on hiking trips out of camp at $250–$300 per week ▶ 4 *lifeguards* (minimum age 19) with current WSI, lifeguard training, and CPR certifications at $250–$350 per week ▶ 2 *naturalists* (minimum age 20) must be able to teach environmental concepts to children ages 8-15 at $200–$250 per week ▶ 2 *program directors* (minimum age 21) must have extensive organized camp experience at $300–$400 per week ▶ 3 *registered nurses* (minimum age 21) must be able to legally act as a registered nurse in New York state at $400–$500 per week ▶ 2 *sports directors* (minimum age 21) must have teaching experience with emphasis on non-competitive sports and physical education at $250 per week ▶ 2 *theater directors* (minimum age 21) must have teaching experience at $250 per week. Applicants must submit formal organization application, three personal references. International applicants accepted; must apply through a recognized agency. An in-person interview is recommended, but a telephone interview is acceptable.

Benefits and Preemployment Training Free housing, free meals, possible full-time employment, and on-the-job training. Preemployment training is required and includes accident prevention and safety, first aid, CPR, interpersonal skills, leadership skills.

Contact Ms. Eva Lewandowski, Executive Director, Girl's Vacation Fund, Inc., 370 Lexington Avenue #913, New York, New York 10017. Telephone: 212-532-7050. Fax: 212-532-7061. E-mail: gvfnyc@aol.com. Application deadline: continuous.

GOLDEN ACRES FARM AND RANCH RESORT
COUNTY ROAD 14
GILBOA, NEW YORK 12076

General Information Kosher family farm and ranch resort catering to young professional families with children. Established in 1950. 600-acre facility located 60 miles from Albany. Features: horseback riding stable; indoor and outdoor pools; Catskill Mountain location; tennis, volleyball, and paddleball courts; children's day camp; theater productions.

Profile of Summer Employees Total number: 100; typical age: 22. 40% men; 60% women; 10% minorities; 51% college students; 2% retirees; 30% non-U.S. citizens; 10% local applicants.
Employment Information Openings are from August 1 to September 7. Jobs available: ▶ 1 *baker* with experience at $600–$700 per week ▶ 1 *bartender/barmaid* (minimum age 21) with cash-handling references and experience at $200–$275 per week ▶ 3 *bellhops/maintenance personnel* with mechanical abilities and driver's license at $215–$250 per week ▶ 11 *chamber staff members* (minimum age 19) with clean and neat appearance at $215–$250 per week ▶ 1–2 *chefs* (minimum age 25) with experience in banquet cooking; kosher experience preferred at $500–$600 per week ▶ 13 *counselors* (minimum age 19) with experience at $215–$250 per week ▶ 1–2 *dining room managers* (minimum age 25) with supervisory and serving experience at $300–$350 per week ▶ 20 *food service assistants* (minimum age 19) with experience at $215–$250 per week ▶ 4 *front desk clerks* with computer, cash, and credit card experience at $215–$250 per week ▶ 1 *head housekeeper* (minimum age 20) with supervisory skills at $250–$350 per week ▶ 3 *nursery counselors* with experience at $215–$250 per week ▶ 1 *social director* (minimum age 21) with driver's license and experience in the field at $215–$250 per week ▶ 2 *swimming instructors* with American Red Cross lifesaving certification at $215–$250 per week ▶ 8 *wranglers* with experience at $215–$300 per week. Applicants must submit formal organization application, resume, two letters of recommendation, 2 employment references. International applicants accepted; must obtain own visa, obtain own working papers, apply through a recognized agency.
Benefits and Preemployment Training Free housing, free meals, names of contacts, and on-the-job training. Preemployment training is optional.
Contact Patricia Gauthier, Golden Acres Farm and Ranch Resort, HCR 1, Box 53, Gilboa, New York 12076. Telephone: 607-588-7329. Fax: 607-588-6911. E-mail: farmresort@aol.com. World Wide Web: http://www.upstateguide.com/goldenacres/. Application deadline: continuous.

GORDON KENT'S NEW ENGLAND TENNIS CAMP AT TRINITY-PAWLING SCHOOL
300 ROUTE 22
PAWLING, NEW YORK 12564

General Information Tennis camp located at Trinity-Pawling School in Pawling, New York, for 80 campers ages 9–17. Established in 1965. 150-acre facility located 20 miles from Danbury. Features: 12 tennis courts; school dorms; many athletic fields; beautiful campus; gymnasium.
Profile of Summer Employees Total number: 20; typical ages: 18–25. 60% men; 40% women; 10% minorities; 5% high school students; 90% college students; 20% non-U.S. citizens. Nonsmokers required.
Employment Information Openings are from June 27 to August 20. Jobs available: ▶ 5–10 *counselors/tennis instructors* with experience playing tennis (on school team), outgoing personality, and patience; at least one year of college completed at $1250–$2000 per season. Applicants must submit formal organization application, three personal references, three letters of recommendation. International applicants accepted; must apply through a recognized agency. An in-person interview is recommended, but a telephone interview is acceptable.
Benefits and Preemployment Training Free housing, free meals, on-the-job training, and opportunity to attend seminars/workshops. Preemployment training is required and includes interpersonal skills, leadership skills, tennis teaching skills.
Contact Gordon Kent, Owner/Director, Gordon Kent's New England Tennis Camp at Trinity-Pawling School, PO Box 143, Riverdale, New York 10471. Telephone: 800-528-2752. Fax: 212-932-2462. E-mail: netennis@aol.com. Application deadline: continuous.

GURNEY'S INN RESORT AND SPA
290 OLD MONTAUK HIGHWAY
MONTAUK, NEW YORK 11954

General Information International health and fitness timeshare resort, inn, and spa with oceanfront restaurant. Established in 1926. 5-acre facility located 200 miles from New York City.

Features: ocean; fresh, open-air environment; 2 restaurants; indoor seawater pool; salon on premises; weight room.

Profile of Summer Employees Total number: 270; typical ages: 19–35. 50% men; 50% women; 25% minorities; 5% high school students; 40% college students; 2% retirees; 30% non-U.S. citizens; 10% local applicants. Nonsmokers preferred.

Employment Information Openings are from January to December. Year-round positions also offered. Jobs available: ▶ *beach attendants* (minimum age 14) at $6 per hour ▶ *cafe servers* at $6 per hour ▶ *front desk/spa desk staff* (minimum age 18) with computer literacy at $7–$8 per hour ▶ *lifeguards for pool and ocean* (minimum age 14) with all appropriate certifications at $8–$10 per hour ▶ *valets/bellpersons* (minimum age 18) with clean driver's license and ability to carry heavy bags at $4 per hour ▶ *waitstaff/buspersons* (minimum age 14, 21 for serving alcohol) with ability to carry trays on shoulder, some knowledge of food and wines, and familiarity with restaurant procedure (service, bussing, running, catering) at $3 per hour ▶ *weight room attendants* (minimum age 18) with certification as personal trainer preferred at $6–$8 per hour. Applicants must submit a formal organization application. International applicants accepted; must obtain own visa, obtain own working papers. An in-person interview is required.

Benefits and Preemployment Training Housing at a cost, meals at a cost, possible full-time employment, on-the-job training, and opportunity to attend seminars/workshops. Preemployment training is required.

Contact Sunshine Lemme, Director of Human Resources, Gurney's Inn Resort and Spa, 290 Old Montauk Highway, Montauk, New York 11954. Telephone: 516-668-2345. Fax: 516-668-3576. E-mail: hr@gurneysweb.com. World Wide Web: http://www.gurneysweb.com. Application deadline: continuous.

HILLSIDE OUTDOOR EDUCATION CENTER DAY, TRIPPING, AND HORSE CAMP
GAGE ROAD
BREWSTER, NEW YORK 10509

General Information Coed day, tripping, and residential horse camp serving approximately 150 children ages 5–15. 100-acre facility located 60 miles from New York City. Features: farm; high and low ropes course; climbing tower; natural playground; Croton River for canoeing; rural setting.

Profile of Summer Employees Total number: 40–50; typical ages: 15–35. 30% men; 70% women; 2% minorities; 1% high school students; 80% college students; 25% non-U.S. citizens; 25% local applicants. Nonsmokers required.

Employment Information Openings are from June 20 to August 29. Jobs available: ▶ 2–4 *adventure specialists* (minimum age 21) with experience leading ropes courses, climbing tower, caving, and canoeing at $250 per week ▶ 1 *archery instructor* (minimum age 21) with archery instructor certification at $250 per week ▶ 1 *arts and crafts instructor* (minimum age 20) with experience in the field at $250 per week ▶ 10–20 *general counselors* (minimum age 18) with experience teaching children at $175–$200 per week ▶ 8 *horseback riding instructors* (minimum age 20) with experience teaching riding and children at $175–$250 per week ▶ 2 *swimming instructors* (minimum age 20) with WSI certification and experience as pool director at $500–$650 per month. Applicants must submit formal organization application, cover letter, resume, three letters of recommendation. International applicants accepted; must obtain own visa, apply through a recognized agency. An in-person interview is recommended, but a telephone interview is acceptable.

Benefits and Preemployment Training Free housing, free meals, formal training, possible full-time employment, and on-the-job training. Preemployment training is required and includes accident prevention and safety, first aid, interpersonal skills, leadership skills.

Contact Marty Newell, Director, HOEC, Hillside Outdoor Education Center Day, Tripping, and Horse Camp, Gage Road, Brewster, New York 10509. Telephone: 914-279-2996 Ext. 316. Fax: 914-279-2714. E-mail: marty@pcnet.com.

THE INSTITUTE FOR THE ACADEMIC ADVANCEMENT OF YOUTH/THE JOHNS HOPKINS UNIVERSITY–HAMILTON COLLEGE

See The Institute for the Academic Advancement of Youth/ The Johns Hopkins University on page 135 for complete description.

THE INSTITUTE FOR THE ACADEMIC ADVANCEMENT OF YOUTH/THE JOHNS HOPKINS UNIVERSITY–SKIDMORE COLLEGE

See The Institute for the Academic Advancement of Youth/ The Johns Hopkins University on page 135 for complete description.

INTRODUCTION TO INDEPENDENCE
NEW YORK INSTITUTE OF TECHNOLOGY
CENTRAL ISLIP, NEW YORK 11722

General Information Residential pre-college/independent living experience serving 30–45 moderately to severely learning disabled young adults ages 16–20. 600-acre facility located 40 miles from New York City. Features: golf course; gymnasium; fitness center; bowling alley; university dormitories; library.

Profile of Summer Employees Total number: 25; typical ages: 21–50. 33% men; 67% women; 15% minorities; 15% college students. Nonsmokers preferred.

Employment Information Openings are from June 21 to August 15. Year-round positions also offered. Jobs available: ▶ *resident advisors* with special education, psychology, or social work background (graduate students) at $1000 per season. Applicants must submit a cover letter, resume. An in-person interview is required.

Benefits and Preemployment Training Free housing, free meals, and on-the-job training. Preemployment training is required and includes interpersonal skills, leadership skills, discussion about learning disablities.

Contact Lauri Alpern, Director, Introduction to Independence, PO Box 730, Central Islip, New York 11722. Telephone: 516-348-3354. Fax: 516-348-0437. Application deadline: continuous.

L.I. ADVENTURELAND
2245 ROUTE 110
EAST FARMINGDALE, NEW YORK 11735

General Information Amusement Park with rides, games and restaurant facilities. We cater to a wide age range througout the months between April and October. Established in 1962. 10-acre facility located 35 miles from New York City. Features: roller coaster; ferris wheel; merry go round; restaurant; arcade; miniature golf course.

Profile of Summer Employees Total number: 500; typical ages: 16–24. 40% men; 60% women; 50% minorities; 65% high school students; 35% college students; 5% retirees; 100% local applicants.

Employment Information Openings are from April 1 to October 31. Spring break positions also offered. Jobs available: ▶ 50 *concession stand staff* (minimum age 16) at $5.50 per hour ▶ 150–225 *ride operators* (minimum age 16) at $5.50 per hour. Applicants must submit a formal organization application. International applicants accepted; must obtain own visa. An in-person interview is required.

Contact Paul Gentile, Personnel Manager, L.I. Adventureland, 2245 Route 110, East Farmingdale, New York 11735. Telephone: 516-694-6868. Fax: 516-694-6816. Application deadline: continuous.

MIDWAY PARK, INC.
ROUTE 430, PO BOX E
MAPLE SPRINGS, NEW YORK 14756

General Information Amusement Kiddie Park located on Chautauqua Lake with rides, go-karts, mini-golf, bumper boats, food, and arcade. Established in 1898. 26-acre facility located 12 miles from Jamestown. Features: on Chautauqua Lake; picnic grove; ride area; roller rink.

Profile of Summer Employees Total number: 100; typical ages: 16–25. 50% men; 50% women; 5% minorities; 30% high school students; 60% college students; 10% retirees; 95% local applicants. Nonsmokers preferred.

Employment Information Openings are from May 23 to September 13. Jobs available: ▶ 10 *arcade attendants* (minimum age 16) at $5.15 per hour ▶ 10 *food concession staff* (minimum age 16) at $5.15 per hour ▶ 5 *lifeguards* (minimum age 16) at $5.15 per day ▶ 30 *ride attendants* (minimum age 16) at $5.15 per hour. Applicants must submit a formal organization application, three personal references. An in-person interview is required.

Benefits and Preemployment Training On-the-job training. Preemployment training is required and includes accident prevention and safety.

Contact Robin DeLong, Office Manager, Midway Park, Inc., PO Box E, Maple Springs, New York 14756. Fax: 716-386-4700. Application deadline: continuous.

MOHAWK PATHWAYS GIRL SCOUTS–HIDDEN LAKE CAMP
945 PALMER AVENUE
SCHENECTADY, NEW YORK 12309

General Information Girl Scout summer resident camp. 400-acre facility located 70 miles from Albany. Features: lake; wooded setting; hiking trails; ropes course; near Lake George.

Profile of Summer Employees Total number: 25–30; typical ages: 16–25. 100% women; 5% minorities; 5% high school students; 80% college students; 5% retirees; 25% non-U.S. citizens; 75% local applicants. Nonsmokers preferred.

Employment Information Openings are from June 27 to August 19. Jobs available: ▶ 10–20 *unit counselors* (minimum age 18) with experience working with children preferred at $1250–$1500 per season. Applicants must submit formal organization application, three personal references, three letters of recommendation. International applicants accepted; must obtain own visa, obtain own working papers, apply through a recognized agency. An in-person interview is recommended, but a telephone interview is acceptable.

Benefits and Preemployment Training Free housing, free meals, and on-the-job training. Preemployment training is required and includes accident prevention and safety, first aid, CPR, interpersonal skills, leadership skills.

Contact Jennifer Ulicnik, Camp Co-Director, Mohawk Pathways Girl Scouts–Hidden Lake Camp, 945 Palmer Avenue, Department CW, Schenectady, New York 12309. Telephone: 518-274-4440 Ext. 284. E-mail: julicnik@emma.troy.ny.us. Application deadline: continuous.

MUSIKER TOURS
1326 OLD NORTHERN BOULEVARD
ROSLYN, NEW YORK 11576

General Information Active tours and adventure travel for students ages 13–18. Travel through the United States, Canada, and Europe, staying in campgrounds, dormitories, and hotels. Established in 1967. Features: national parks; university dorms; whitewater rafting; mountain biking.

Profile of Summer Employees Total number: 100; typical ages: 21–34. 50% men; 50% women; 10% minorities; 40% college students. Nonsmokers required.

Employment Information Openings are from June 20 to August 20. Jobs available: ▶ 100–200 *summer counselors* (minimum age 21) with valid driver's license and experience in summer camp and with junior and senior high school students; first aid/CPR certification preferred at $50–$150 per week. Applicants must submit a formal organization application, three personal references. An in-person interview is recommended, but a telephone interview is acceptable.

Benefits and Preemployment Training Free housing, free meals, and travel reimbursement. Preemployment training is required and includes accident prevention and safety, interpersonal skills, leadership skills.

Contact Jen Strauss, Director of Personnel, Musiker Tours, 1326 Old Northern Boulevard, Roslyn, New York 11576. Telephone: 516-621-3939. Fax: 516-625-3438. E-mail: jen@summerfun. com. World Wide Web: http://www.summerfun.com. Application deadline: continuous.

92ND STREET Y CAMPS
1395 LEXINGTON AVENUE
NEW YORK, NEW YORK 10128

General Information Summer camps for children ages 5 to 15 that focus on building self-esteem, exposing children to the outdoors in a safe, comfortable environment where they will make new friends. Established in 1956. 100-acre facility located 20 miles from New York. Features: rope challenge course; athletic fields; art and ceramic centers; nature center; basketball courts; swimming pools.

Profile of Summer Employees Total number: 250; typical ages: 17–25. 50% men; 50% women; 20% minorities; 35% high school students; 50% college students; 5% non-U.S. citizens; 90% local applicants. Nonsmokers preferred.

Employment Information Openings are from June 28 to August 20. Jobs available: ▶ 25 *activity specialists (arts, sports, ropes, nature, music, karate)* (minimum age 19) at $2000–$4000 per season ▶ 100 *camp counselors* (minimum age 17) at $1000–$2000 per season. Applicants must submit a formal organization application, two personal references. An in-person interview is required.

Benefits and Preemployment Training Names of contacts and on-the-job training. Preemployment training is required and includes accident prevention and safety, first aid, CPR, interpersonal skills, leadership skills.

Contact Steve Levin, Program Coordinator, 92nd Street Y Camps. Telephone: 212-415-5600. Fax: 212-415-5637. E-mail: steve@njycamps.org. World Wide Web: http://www.92ndsty.org. Application deadline: June 15.

NORTH SHORE HOLIDAY HOUSE
74 HUNTINGTON ROAD
HUNTINGTON, NEW YORK 11743

General Information Residential camp serving girls from low-income homes. Established in 1914. 5-acre facility located 40 miles from New York City.

Profile of Summer Employees Total number: 20; typical ages: 19–25. 100% women; 50% minorities; 80% college students; 33% non-U.S. citizens; 20% local applicants. Nonsmokers preferred.

Employment Information Openings are from June 25 to August 23. Jobs available: ▶ 1 *arts and crafts staff member* at $1000–$1500 per season ▶ 5 *bunk counselors* at $1000 per season ▶ *computer instructor* at $1000–$1500 per season ▶ 1 *dance staff member* at $1000–$1500 per season ▶ 1 *music staff member* at $1000–$1500 per season ▶ 1 *swimming instructor* with WSI and lifeguard certification at $1500 per season. Applicants must submit formal organization application, three letters of recommendation. International applicants accepted; must apply through a recognized agency. An in-person interview is recommended, but a telephone interview is acceptable.

Benefits and Preemployment Training Free housing, free meals, formal training, and on-the-job training. Preemployment training is required and includes accident prevention and safety, first aid, CPR, interpersonal skills, leadership skills.

Contact Debra Deal, Director, North Shore Holiday House, 74 Huntington Road, Huntington, New York 11743. Telephone: 516-427-7630. Fax: 516-427-1185. Application deadline: continuous.

PECONIC DUNES CAMP
SOUNDVIEW AVENUE
PECONIC, NEW YORK 11958

General Information Residential and day camp emphasizing environmental and recreational activities including canoeing, archery, swimming, fishing, and arts and crafts. Established in 1931. 98-acre facility located 75 miles from New York City. Features: private beach on Long Island Sound; mile-long spring-fed lake; biodiverse habitats.

Profile of Summer Employees Total number: 40; typical age: 20. 50% men; 50% women; 15% minorities; 90% college students; 10% local applicants. Nonsmokers preferred.

Employment Information Openings are from June 21 to August 15. Jobs available: ▶ *assistant* *cook* at $250–$325 per week ▶ 1 *athletics director* at $300–$325 per week ▶ 4 *environmental educators* at $400 per week ▶ 1 *head cook* with mature, responsible personality (pay commensurate with experience) at $400–$475 per week ▶ 3 *kitchen helpers* should be high school student with mature attitude at $125–$150 per week ▶ 2 *maintenance personnel* with maturity and full knowledge of carpentry, plumbing, and electrical wiring at $150–$400 per week ▶ 1 *nurse* with RN license at $600–$630 per week ▶ 1 *outdoor educator* at $400 per week ▶ 12 *senior counselors* should be college senior or graduate with experience at $285–$325 per week ▶ 1 *waterfront director* with WSI certification at $400 per week ▶ 4 *waterfront staff members* with lifesaving or WSI certification at $300–$350 per week.

Benefits and Preemployment Training Free housing, free meals, and laundry facilities. Preemployment training is required and includes accident prevention and safety, first aid, CPR, interpersonal skills, leadership skills.

Contact Employment Office, Peconic Dunes Camp, PO Box 204, Peconic, New York 11958. Telephone: 516-765-5770. Fax: 516-765-0017. Application deadline: continuous.

POINT O'PINES CAMP
7201 STATE ROUTE 8
BRANT LAKE, NEW YORK 12815-2236

General Information Eight-week traditional residential girls camp with professional sports instruction as well as arts, performing arts, and horsemanship for 300 campers; winter restaurant and wedding caterers. Established in 1957. 523-acre facility located 90 miles from Albany. Features: peninsula location; freshwater lake; surrounded by wooded mountains; 12 tennis courts (4 with lights); winterized bunks with full bathrooms; winterized dining room with fireplace.

Profile of Summer Employees Total number: 160; typical ages: 18–55. 10% men; 90% women; 10% minorities; 80% college students; 10% non-U.S. citizens; 5% local applicants. Nonsmokers preferred.

Employment Information Openings are from June 20 to August 20. Year-round positions also offered. Jobs available: ▶ 4 *English horseback riding instructors* with at least two years of teaching experience at $1200–$2500 per season ▶ 6 *arts and crafts staff members* with professional teaching experience and/or a major in art at $1000–$1500 per season ▶ 6 *athletics staff members* with experience as college team player or professional instructor at $1000–$1500 per season ▶ 2 *boating instructors* with experience in the field at $1000–$1500 per season ▶ *cleaning and kitchen help* with references and experience ▶ 1 *drama director* with experience in the field at $2000–$3000 per season ▶ 1 *drama technical person* with at least two years of experience in college or community theater at $1000–$1800 per season ▶ *drama-costume director* must sewing ability at $1000–$1600 per season ▶ *fitness and conditioning instructor* with extensive training, certification, and experience in the field at $1000–$2000 per season ▶ 6 *gymnastics/dance staff members* with experience as college team player or instructor at $1000–$1500 per season ▶ 1 *music director* with experience as piano accompanist for theater (must be able to transpose) at $1400–$2000 per season ▶ 3 *nurses* with RN certification and clinical experience at $2500–$4000 per season ▶ 4 *outdoor adventure staff members* with extensive training in safety and experience in the field at $1200–$1600 per season ▶ 2 *photography staff members* with college or professional experience at $1000–$1500 per season ▶ 3 *sailing instructors* with experience in the field at $1000–$1500 per season ▶ 14 *tennis staff members* with experience as college team player or professional instructor at $1000–$1500 per season ▶ 2 *video/radio instructors* with at least two years of experience in operating equipment at $1500–$2000 per season ▶ 23 *waterfront staff members* with extensive water sports experience at $1100–$1600 per season ▶ 8 *waterskiing instructors* with experience in the field at $1000–$1500 per season ▶ 1 *year-round dining room manager for restaurant* with college degree and experience in business management or hotel and resort management. Applicants must submit formal organization application, resume, three personal references. International applicants accepted; must apply through a recognized agency. An in-person interview is recommended, but a telephone interview is acceptable.

Benefits and Preemployment Training Free housing, free meals, formal training, on-the-job training, travel reimbursement, and free laundry service. Preemployment training is required and includes accident prevention and safety, first aid, CPR, leadership skills.

Contact Sherie Alden, Associate Director, Point O'Pines Camp, 7201 State Route 8, Brant Lake, New York 12815-2236. Telephone: 888-726-9908. Fax: 518-494-3489. E-mail: info@pointopines. com. World Wide Web: http://www.pointopines.com. Application deadline: continuous.

SAIL CARIBBEAN
79 CHURCH STREET
NORTHPORT, NEW YORK 11768

General Information Summer sailing and scuba diving program in the Caribbean for teens. Extensive water sports, island exploration, marine sciences, and cultural activities. Established in 1979. Located 60 miles from San Juan. Features: Caribbean Sea; island exporation; 51' yachts; windsurfers; kayaks; waterskiing; scuba diving; beach sports.

Profile of Summer Employees Total number: 50; typical ages: 20–30. 66% men; 34% women; 60% college students. Nonsmokers required.

Employment Information Openings are from June to August. Jobs available: ▶ 2 *ARC lifeguard instructors* (minimum age 20) with CPR/first aid ▶ 4 *PADI divemasters* (minimum age 20) with CPR/first aid ▶ 6 *PADI scuba instructors* (minimum age 20) with CPR/first aid ▶ 6 *assistant skippers* (minimum age 20) with CPR/first aid ▶ 2 *food supervisors* (minimum age 20) with CPR/first aid ▶ 4 *marine biology teachers* (minimum age 20) with CPR/first aid ▶ 6 *skippers* (minimum age 20) with CPR/first aid; (US Sailing basic keelboat instructor for one position). Applicants must submit a cover letter, resume, 3-5 personal references, an in-person interview is highly recommended. International applicants accepted; must obtain own visa.

Benefits and Preemployment Training Free housing, free meals, possible full-time employment, on-the-job training, and travel reimbursement. Preemployment training is required and includes accident prevention and safety, interpersonal skills, leadership skills.

Contact Michael D. Liese, Founder/Director, Sail Caribbean, 79 Church Street, Northport, New York 11768. Telephone: 800-321-0994. Fax: 516-754-3362. E-mail: info@sailcaribbean.com. World Wide Web: http://www.sailcaribbean.com. Application deadline: continuous.

THE SOUTHWESTERN COMPANY, NEW YORK
See The Southwestern Company, Tennessee on page 284 for complete description.

STAGEDOOR MANOR THEATRE AND DANCE CAMP
KARMEL ROAD
LOCH SHELDRAKE, NEW YORK 12759

General Information Residential coeducational camp serving 240 campers in performing arts. Established in 1974. 25-acre facility located 95 miles from New York City. Features: dormitory style hotel; indoor-outdoor pools; 5 on-campus theatres; rural setting by lake; two and a half hours from New York City; excellent technical facilities.

Profile of Summer Employees Total number: 119; typical ages: 24–35. 40% men; 60% women; 5% minorities; 25% college students; 50% non-U.S. citizens; 20% local applicants. Nonsmokers preferred.

Employment Information Openings are from June 18 to August 23. Jobs available: ▶ 1 *canteen manager* (minimum age 21) with retail experience at $1800 per season ▶ 2 *modeling instructors* (minimum age 21) with runway experience at $2000–$2500 per season ▶ 3 *nurses* (minimum age 21) with RN or LPN license at $2500–$3000 per season ▶ 6 *scenic designers* (minimum age 21) with theater experience at $2000–$2500 per season ▶ 10 *technicians* (minimum age 21) with theater experience at $1800–$2000 per season ▶ 2 *tennis counselors* (minimum age 21) with coaching experience at $1500–$1800 per season. Applicants must submit a cover letter, resume, personal reference. International applicants accepted. A telephone interview is required.

Benefits and Preemployment Training Free housing, free meals, formal training, names of contacts, on-the-job training, and opportunity to attend seminars/workshops. Preemployment training is required and includes accident prevention and safety, first aid, CPR, interpersonal skills, leadership skills.

Contact Konnie Kittrell, Production Director, Stagedoor Manor Theatre and Dance Camp, 651

Skyline Drive, Gatlinburg, Tennessee 37738. Telephone: 423-436-3030. Fax: 423-436-3030. Application deadline: June 15.

STIVERS TEMPORARY PERSONNEL–NEW YORK
See Stivers Temporary Personnel–Illinois on page 103 for complete description.

STUDENT CONSERVATION ASSOCIATION (SCA), NEW YORK
See Student Conservation Association (SCA), New Hampshire on page 193 for complete description.

TIMBER LAKE CAMPS
144 WOODBURY ROAD
WOODBURY, NEW YORK 11797

General Information Coeducational residential camp. Established in 1980. 500-acre facility located 29 miles from Kingston. Features: 2 lakes; indoor and outdoor heated pools; horseback riding; golf; indoor gym; 9 tennis courts.

Profile of Summer Employees Total number: 240; typical ages: 18–23. 50% men; 50% women; 10% high school students; 50% college students; 5% retirees; 20% non-U.S. citizens; 5% local applicants. Nonsmokers preferred.

Employment Information Openings are from June 20 to August 22. Jobs available: ▶ *arts and crafts instructors* (minimum age 18) at $1200–$2000 per season ▶ *field sports instructors* (minimum age 18) at $1200–$2000 per season ▶ *general counselors* (minimum age 18) at $1200–$2000 per season ▶ *outdoor adventure staff (ropes, hiking, overnights)* (minimum age 18) at $1200–$2000 per season ▶ *tennis instructors* (minimum age 18) at $1200–$2000 per season ▶ *waterfront staff* (minimum age 18) at $1200–$2000 per season. Applicants must submit formal organization application, two letters of recommendation. International applicants accepted; must apply through a recognized agency. An in-person interview is recommended, but a telephone interview is acceptable.

Benefits and Preemployment Training Free housing, free meals, possible full-time employment, on-the-job training, and travel reimbursement. Preemployment training is required and includes interpersonal skills.

Contact Janie Schwartz, Head Counselor, Timber Lake Camps, 144 Woodbury Road, Woodbury, New York 11797. Telephone: 516-367-6700. Fax: 516-367-2737. World Wide Web: http://www.camptlc.com. Application deadline: continuous.

TIMBER LAKE WEST
BURNT HILL ROAD
ROSCOE, NEW YORK 12776

General Information Residential camp serving 320 campers in a traditional four-week program. Established in 1988. 320-acre facility located 120 miles from New York City. Features: lake; 2 heated pools; main lodge; 6 tennis courts; movie theater; indoor gym.

Profile of Summer Employees Total number: 180; typical ages: 18–23. 50% men; 50% women; 4% high school students; 75% college students; 15% non-U.S. citizens; 1% local applicants. Nonsmokers preferred.

Employment Information Openings are from June 22 to August 22. Jobs available: ▶ 15 *arts and crafts instructors* (minimum age 18) at $1600 to $2000 plus $200 for travel over 350 miles ▶ 3 *boating instructors* (minimum age 18) with lifeguard certification at $1600 to $2000 plus $200 for travel over 350 miles ▶ 70 *general counselors* (minimum age 18) at $1600 to $2000 per season and $200 for travel over 350 miles ▶ 8 *housekeeping/maintenance staff members* (minimum age 18) at $1750 per season ▶ 14 *kitchen staff members* (minimum age 18) at $1750 per season ▶ 6 *tennis instructors* (minimum age 18) at $1600-$2000 plus $200 for travel over 350 miles ▶ 6 *water safety instructors* (minimum age 18) with WSI, first aid, lifeguard, and CPR certification at $1850-$2250 plus $200 for travel over 350 miles. Applicants must submit formal organization application, two personal references, two letters of recommendation. International applicants accepted; must apply through a recognized agency. An in-person interview is recommended, but a telephone interview is acceptable.

Benefits and Preemployment Training Free housing, free meals, names of contacts, on-the-job training, and travel reimbursement. Preemployment training is required and includes accident prevention and safety, first aid, CPR, interpersonal skills, leadership skills.

Contact Jennifer A. Quinn, Assistant Director, Timber Lake West, 144 Woodbury Road, #36, Woodbury, New York 11797. Telephone: 516-367-6700. Fax: 516-367-2737. E-mail: west@ camptlc.com. World Wide Web: http://www.camptlc.com. Application deadline: continuous.

TIMBERLOCK VOYAGEURS
INDIAN LAKE, NEW YORK 12864

General Information Resident wilderness trip camp for nine boys and nine girls needing highly qualified leadership. 66-acre facility located 150 miles from Albany.

Profile of Summer Employees 50% men; 50% women; 100% college students.

Employment Information Openings are from June 16 to August 28. Jobs available: ▶ *group leader* at $300–$400 per week.

Benefits and Preemployment Training Free housing, free meals, and on-the-job training. Preemployment training is required and includes accident prevention and safety, first aid, CPR, interpersonal skills, leadership skills.

Contact Richard Catlin, Director, Timberlock Voyageurs, RR1, Box 630, Woodstock, Vermont 05091. Telephone: 802-457-1621. Fax: 802-457-1621. Application deadline: continuous.

TRAILMARK OUTDOOR ADVENTURES
16 SCHUYLER ROAD
NYACK, NEW YORK 10960

General Information Travel adventure program in New England, the Northern Rockies, the Pacific Northwest, and Southwest Colorado. Established in 1985.

Profile of Summer Employees Total number: 50; typical ages: 23–26. 50% men; 50% women; 10% college students. Nonsmokers required.

Employment Information Openings are from June 17 to August 17. Jobs available: ▶ 50 *trip leaders* (minimum age 21) with first aid/CPR, lifeguarding preferred; good interpersonal skills and experience working with children at $100–$300 per week. Applicants must submit a formal organization application, cover letter, resume, three personal references. A telephone interview is required.

Benefits and Preemployment Training Free housing, free meals, health insurance, and on-the-job training. Preemployment training is required and includes accident prevention and safety, first aid, CPR, interpersonal skills, leadership skills, lifeguarding.

Contact Rusty Pedersen, Director, Trailmark Outdoor Adventures, 16 Schuyler Road, Nyack, New York 10960. Telephone: 800-229-0262. Fax: 914-348-0437. E-mail: staff@trailmark.com. World Wide Web: http://www.trailmark.com. Application deadline: continuous.

TYLER HILL CAMP
ROUTE 371
TYLER HILL, NEW YORK 18469

General Information Residential coeducational camp for ages 8–16 features full sports program and traditional camp activities. Established in 1955. 220-acre facility located 100 miles from New York, NY. Features: 9-hole golf course; 2 magnificent lakes; 12 tennis courts; modern wood-paneled cabins; indoor roller hockey and basketball; 15 arts and crafts shops.

Profile of Summer Employees Total number: 225; typical age: 18. 50% men; 50% women; 20% minorities; 3% high school students; 95% college students; 30% non-U.S. citizens; 5% local applicants. Nonsmokers preferred.

Employment Information Openings are from June 23 to August 20. Jobs available: ▶ *creative arts staff (aerobics, dance, piano, drama)* at $250–$2000 per season ▶ *general counselors* (minimum age 18) at $250–$2000 per season ▶ 1–3 *nurses* at $4000 per season ▶ *sports staff* (minimum age 18) at $250–$2000 per season ▶ *waterfront staff* with first aid/CPR and WSI at

$250–$2000 per season. Applicants must submit formal organization application, cover letter, resume, three personal references, three letters of recommendation. International applicants accepted; must apply through a recognized agency. An in-person interview is recommended, but a telephone interview is acceptable.

Benefits and Preemployment Training Free housing, free meals, formal training, possible full-time employment, on-the-job training, opportunity to attend seminars/workshops, and travel reimbursement. Preemployment training is required and includes accident prevention and safety, interpersonal skills, leadership skills.

Contact Andy Siegel, Director, Tyler Hill Camp, 144 Woodbury Road, Woodbury, New York 11797. Telephone: 516-367-6700. Fax: 516-367-2737. E-mail: tylerhill@camptlc.com. World Wide Web: http://www.camptlc.com. Application deadline: continuous.

WEISSMAN TEEN TOURS
517 ALMENA AVENUE
ARDSLEY, NEW YORK 10502

General Information Owner-operated and escorted personalized student travel program in the United States, Western Canada, and Europe. Established in 1974.

Profile of Summer Employees Total number: 14; typical ages: 21–29. 50% men; 50% women; 50% local applicants. Nonsmokers required.

Employment Information Openings are from June 29 to August 11. Year-round positions also offered. Jobs available: ▶ 7 *tour leaders-Europe* (minimum age 21) with fluency in French and/or Italian (preferred), experience working with teenagers, CPR, and first aid at $100 per week ▶ 7 *tour leaders-U.S./Western Canada* (minimum age 21) with experience working with teenagers, CPR, and first aid at $100 per week. Applicants must submit a formal organization application, cover letter, resume, three personal references, three letters of recommendation. An in-person interview is required.

Benefits and Preemployment Training Free housing, free meals, formal training, on-the-job training, and first class travel. Preemployment training is required and includes accident prevention and safety, interpersonal skills, leadership skills.

Contact Ronee Weissman, Owner/Director, Weissman Teen Tours, 517 Almena Avenue, Ardsley, New York 10502. Telephone: 914-693-7575. Fax: 914-693-4807. E-mail: wtt@cloud.9.net. World Wide Web: http://www.weissmantours.com. Application deadline: continuous.

WESTCOAST CONNECTION TRAVEL CAMP
154 EAST BOSTON POST ROAD
MAMARONECK, NEW YORK 10543

General Information Exciting travel programs in the United States, western Canada, Europe, and Israel for students ages 13–18, including active teen tours and outdoor adventure trips. Established in 1982.

Profile of Summer Employees Typical ages: 21–35. 50% men; 50% women; 50% college students. Nonsmokers required.

Employment Information Openings are from June 20 to August 25. Jobs available: ▶ *tour staff members/leaders* (minimum age 20) with experience working with teens; driver's license (CDL for some trips); CPR, lifeguard, first aid, WSI, and lifeguard certification preferred at $50–$400 per week. Applicants must submit a formal organization application, three personal references. International applicants accepted; must obtain own visa, obtain own working papers. An in-person interview is required.

Benefits and Preemployment Training Free housing, free meals, formal training, possible full-time employment, on-the-job training, opportunity to attend seminars/workshops, and travel reimbursement. Preemployment training is required and includes accident prevention and safety, first aid, interpersonal skills, leadership skills, organizational skills.

Contact Mark Segal, Director, Westcoast Connection Travel Camp, 154 East Boston Post Road, Mamaroneck, New York 10543. Telephone: 914-835-0699. Fax: 914-835-0798. E-mail: usa@ westcoastconnection.com. World Wide Web: http://www.westcoastconnection.com. Application deadline: continuous.

YMCA/YWCA CAMPING SERVICES–CAMPS GREENKILL/ MCALISTER/TALCOTT
300 BIG POND ROAD
HUGUENOT, NEW YORK 12746

General Information Residential camps serving general population. Camps are split into two age groups: 6–11 and 11–15. Established in 1924. 1,000-acre facility located 90 miles from New York City. Features: 3 freshwater lakes; 7 tennis courts; 5 basketball courts; new environmental education building and auditorium; wooded setting; numerous hiking trails through all types of terrain.

Profile of Summer Employees Total number: 130; typical ages: 18–25. 50% men; 50% women; 30% minorities; 8% high school students; 60% college students; 35% non-U.S. citizens; 10% local applicants.

Employment Information Openings are from June 10 to August 21. Winter break and year-round positions also offered. Jobs available: ▶ 3 *aquatic directors* with WSI, LGT, CPR, Basic Life Support, and first aid certification at $170–$200 per week ▶ 30 *general counselors* at $110–$130 per week ▶ 2 *high ropes instructors* at $110–$130 per week ▶ 10 *kitchen staff members* at $130–$160 per week ▶ *naturalist/counselor (2 weeks only)* at $140–$200 per week ▶ 2 *nurses* with RN or LPN certification at $275–$350 per week ▶ 2 *small craft instructors* with certification in field at $110–$130 per week ▶ 6 *swimming instructors* with WSI certification at $120–$140 per week ▶ 12 *unit directors* with leadership and camp experience at $150–$170 per week. Applicants must submit formal organization application, three personal references, cover letter and resume are not required but recommended. International applicants accepted; must apply through a recognized agency. A telephone interview is required.

Benefits and Preemployment Training Free housing, free meals, formal training, on-the-job training, and possible partial travel reimbursement. Preemployment training is required and includes accident prevention and safety, first aid, CPR, interpersonal skills, leadership skills.

Contact John Nystrom, Director of Camping, YMCA/YWCA Camping Services–Camps GreenKill/McAlister/Talcott, 300 Big Pond Road, Huguenot, New York 12746. Telephone: 914-858-2200. Fax: 914-858-7823. E-mail: nyYcamp5@pikeonline.net. World Wide Web: http://www.ymcanyc.org.

NORTH CAROLINA

ACE COMPUTER CAMP–NORTH CAROLINA
See ACE Computer Camp–Washington on page 307 for complete description.

A CHRISTIAN MINISTRY IN THE NATIONAL PARKS–NORTH CAROLINA
See A Christian Ministry in the National Parks–Massachussetts on page 138 for complete description.

CAMP HIGH ROCKS
PO BOX 210
CEDAR MOUNTAIN, NORTH CAROLINA 28718

General Information Small residential boys camp focusing on development of skills in a non-competitive environment. There is a strong emphasis on outdoor adventure programming with many off-site trips. Established in 1958. 1,100-acre facility located 8 miles from Brevard. Features: freshwater lake; 50-foot climbing tower; 3 tennis courts; 2 activity fields; 29-stall barn facility; wooded mountainous setting.

Profile of Summer Employees Total number: 65; typical ages: 19–26. 67% men; 33% women; 80% college students. Nonsmokers required.

Employment Information Openings are from June 4 to August 12. Jobs available: ▶ 2 *athletics/ tennis instructors* at $180–$240 per week ▶ 6 *backpacking instructors* at $180–$240 per week ▶ 23 *cabin counselor/skill instructors* at $180–$240 per week ▶ 3 *crafts instructors* at $180– $240 per week ▶ 8 *horseback riding instructors* at $180–$240 per week ▶ 4 *mountain biking instructors* at $180–$240 per week ▶ 2 *pottery instructors* at $180–$240 per week ▶ 7 *rock climbing instructors* at $180–$240 per week ▶ 3 *ropes course facilitators* at $180–$240 per week ▶ 3 *swimming instructors* with WSI certification at $180–$240 per week ▶ 7 *white-water canoeing instructors* at $180–$240 per week. Applicants must submit formal organization application, three personal references. International applicants accepted; must apply through a recognized agency. An in-person interview is recommended, but a telephone interview is acceptable.

Benefits and Preemployment Training Free housing, free meals, and opportunity to attend seminars/workshops. Preemployment training is required and includes accident prevention and safety, first aid, interpersonal skills, leadership skills, wilderness first aid, rock rescue, and white-water instructor.

Contact Henry Birdsong, Camp Director, Camp High Rocks, PO Box 127-H, Cedar Mountain, North Carolina 28718. Telephone: 828-885-2153. Fax: 828-884-4612. E-mail: mail@highrocks. com. World Wide Web: http://www.highrocks.com. Application deadline: continuous.

CAMP KANATA
13524 CAMP KANATA ROAD
WAKE FOREST, NORTH CAROLINA 27587

General Information Coeducational residential YMCA camp for children ages 6–15. Established in 1954. 188-acre facility located 10 miles from Raleigh. Features: 2 lakes; 17 cabins; 2 ball fields; high/low ropes course; wooded setting; 7,000-square foot gym.

Profile of Summer Employees Total number: 42; typical ages: 18–21. 50% men; 50% women; 2% minorities; 30% high school students; 70% college students; 4% non-U.S. citizens; 35% local applicants. Nonsmokers preferred.

Employment Information Openings are from June 1 to August 8. Year-round positions also offered. Jobs available: ▶ 1 *arts and crafts director* (minimum age 19) with experience in the field at $1650 per season ▶ 37 *cabin counselors* (minimum age 18) with child work experience at $1550–$1700 per season ▶ 2 *nature instructors* (minimum age 18) at $1500–$1600 per season ▶ 1 *program director* (minimum age 20) with creativity and camp experience at $2100– $2400 per season ▶ 1 *ropes course director* (minimum age 20) with 2-3 years camp experience and ropes course training at $1600–$1700 per season ▶ 1 *staff-trainee director* (minimum age 21) with camp experience at $2200–$2400 per season ▶ 1 *summer assistant director* (minimum age 21) with past camp supervisory experience at $2500–$3000 per season ▶ 1 *waterfront director* (minimum age 20) with lifeguard, lake usage, and camp experience; WSI, lifeguard instructor, or YMCA certification at $2100–$2300 per season. Applicants must submit formal organization application, four personal references, criminal background check. International applicants accepted; must apply through a recognized agency. An in-person interview is recommended, but a telephone interview is acceptable.

Benefits and Preemployment Training Free housing, free meals, and on-the-job training. Preemployment training is required and includes accident prevention and safety, first aid, CPR, interpersonal skills, leadership skills.

Contact Mr. Richard R. Hamilton, Director, Camp Kanata, 13524 Camp Kanata Road, Wake Forest, North Carolina 27587. Telephone: 919-556-2661. Fax: 919-556-9459. E-mail: kanata@ worldnet.att.net. World Wide Web: http://www.campkanata.citysearch.com. Application deadline: continuous.

CAMP MERRIE-WOODE
100 MERRIE-WOODE ROAD
SAPPHIRE, NORTH CAROLINA 28774

General Information A residential girls summer camp dedicated to building self-esteem and confidence through traditional camp and high adventure activities. Established in 1919. 230-acre facility located 60 miles from Asheville. Features: location in mountains of Western North Carolina, 3500-foot elevation; 1-mile-long freshwater lake; indoor riding arena; 3 tennis courts; gym and indoor climbing wall; rustic cabins.

Profile of Summer Employees Total number: 80–90; typical age: 19. 10% men; 90% women; 80% college students. Nonsmokers preferred.

Employment Information Openings are from May 31 to August 15. Jobs available: ▶ *archery staff members* (minimum age 19) salary commensurate with age and experience beginning at $170 per week; all wages paid at the end of the season, but weekly advances may be drawn on request ▶ *arts/crafts staff members* (minimum age 19) salary commensurate with age and experience beginning at $170 per week; all wages paid at the end of the season, but weekly advances may be drawn on request ▶ *canoeing and kayaking staff members* (minimum age 19) with lifeguard/river rescue/first aid certification and experience; salary commensurate with age and experience beginning at $170 per week; all wages paid at the end of the season, but weekly advances may be drawn on request ▶ *jewelry staff members* (minimum age 19) with experience in the field; salary commensurate with age and experience beginning at $170 per week; all wages paid at the end of the season, but weekly advances may be drawn on request ▶ *land sports staff members* (minimum age 19) salary commensurate with age and experience beginning at $170 per week; all wages paid at the end of the season, but weekly advances may be drawn on request ▶ *mountaineering staff members* (minimum age 19) with experience in the field; salary commensurate with age and experience beginning at $170 per week; all wages paid at the end of the season, but weekly advances may be drawn on request ▶ *nature staff members* (minimum age 19) salary commensurate with age and experience beginning at $170 per week; all wages paid at the end of the season, but weekly advances may be drawn on request ▶ *performing arts staff members* (minimum age 19) with experience in the field; salary commensurate with age and experience beginning at $170 per week; all wages paid at the end of the season, but weekly advances may be drawn on request ▶ *photography staff members* (minimum age 19) with experience in the field; salary commensurate with age and experience beginning at $170 per week; all wages paid at the end of the season, but weekly advances may be drawn on request ▶ *riding staff members* (minimum age 19) with strong riding skills and technique; some barn work and grooming required; salary commensurate with age and experience beginning at $170 per week; all wages paid at the end of the season, but weekly advances may be drawn on request ▶ *rock climbing staff members* (minimum age 19) with strong leadership and organizational skills; orienteering, first aid, strong climbing and backpacking skills; college degree preferred for head position salary commensurate with age and experience beginning at $170 per week; all wages paid at the end of the season, but weekly advances may be drawn on request ▶ *sailing staff members* (minimum age 19) with lifeguard certification and experience; salary commensurate with age and experience beginning at $170 per week; all wages paid at the end of the season, but weekly advances may be drawn on request ▶ *swimming staff members* (minimum age 19) with lifeguard and WSI certification; salary commensurate with age and experience beginning at $170 per week; all wages paid at the end of the season, but weekly advances may be drawn on request ▶ *tennis staff members* (minimum age 19) with experience; salary commensurate with age and experience beginning at $170 per week; all wages paid at the end of the season, but weekly advances may be drawn on request ▶ *weaving staff members* (minimum age 19) with experience in the field; salary commensurate with age and experience beginning at $170 per week; all wages paid at the end of the season, but weekly advances may be drawn on request ▶ *woodworking staff members* (minimum age 19) with experience in the field; salary commensurate with age and experience beginning at $170 per week; all wages paid at the end of the season, but weekly advances may be drawn on request. Applicants must submit formal organization application, three writing samples, three personal references. International applicants accepted; must apply through a recognized agency. An in-person interview is recommended, but a telephone interview is acceptable.

Benefits and Preemployment Training Free housing, free meals, opportunity to attend seminars/workshops, and tuition assistance. Preemployment training is required and includes accident prevention and safety, first aid, interpersonal skills, leadership skills.

Contact Ms. Laurie Strayhorn, Director, Camp Merrie-Woode, 100 Merrie Woode Road, Sapphire, North Carolina 28774. Telephone: 828-743-3300. Fax: 828-743-5846. E-mail: laurie@merriewoode.com. Application deadline: continuous.

CAMP MERRI-MAC
MONTREAT ROAD
BLACK MOUNTAIN, NORTH CAROLINA 28711

General Information Residential camp for girls. Established in 1950. 150-acre facility located 15 miles from Asheville. Features: private lake; 3 climbing walls; 3 tennis courts; outstanding facility.

Profile of Summer Employees Total number: 60; typical ages: 19–25. 5% men; 95% women; 5% high school students; 80% college students; 5% non-U.S. citizens; 10% local applicants. Nonsmokers required.

Employment Information Openings are from June 6 to September 10. Jobs available: ▶ 35 *counselors* with strong expertise and requisite certification in activity at $1000–$1500 per season ▶ *skilled activity instructors* with documented experience and certifications at $1000–$1500 per season. Applicants must submit formal organization application, two personal references. International applicants accepted; must apply through a recognized agency. An in-person interview is required.

Benefits and Preemployment Training Free housing, free meals, formal training, on-the-job training, and opportunity to attend seminars/workshops. Preemployment training is required and includes accident prevention and safety, first aid, CPR, interpersonal skills, leadership skills.

Contact Spencer Boyd, Director, Camp Merri-Mac, Black Mountain, North Carolina 28711. Telephone: 828-669-8766. Fax: 828-669-6822. E-mail: sboydjr@aol.com. World Wide Web: http://www.merri-mac.com. Application deadline: continuous.

CAMPS MONDAMIN AND GREEN COVE
TUXEDO, NORTH CAROLINA 28784

General Information Residential camps focusing on noncompetitive, lifetime, and outdoor skills with an emphasis on extended trips. Established in 1922. 800-acre facility located 6 miles from Hendersonville. Features: freshwater lake; location in mountains; 800 acres of trails; near Smoky Mountains; tennis courts and climbing tower; horseback riding facilities.

Profile of Summer Employees Total number: 175; typical ages: 19–30. 50% men; 50% women; 2% minorities; 60% college students; 5% retirees; 2% non-U.S. citizens; 5% local applicants. Nonsmokers required.

Employment Information Openings are from May 30 to August 23. Jobs available: ▶ 2 *crafts and games instructors* (minimum age 18) with archery and riflery experience at $1600–$2000 per season ▶ 4 *horseback riding instructors* (minimum age 18) with hunter-style riding and barn experience at $1600–$2500 per season ▶ 2 *mountain biking instructors* (minimum age 18) with camping experience and mechanical expertise at $1600–$2300 per season ▶ 6 *mountaineering instructors* (hiking, rock climbing) (minimum age 20) at $1600–$2300 per season ▶ 2 *sailing instructors* (minimum age 18) with experience at $1600–$2300 per season ▶ 4 *swimming instructors* (minimum age 18) with ARC lifeguard and WSI at $1600–$2300 per season ▶ 2 *tennis instructors* (minimum age 18) with experience at $1600–$2300 per season. Applicants must submit formal organization application, five personal references. International applicants accepted; must apply through a recognized agency. An in-person interview is recommended, but a telephone interview is acceptable.

Benefits and Preemployment Training Free housing, free meals, on-the-job training, and opportunity to attend seminars/workshops. Preemployment training is required and includes accident prevention and safety, first aid, CPR, interpersonal skills, leadership skills, ARC lifeguard, WSI, WMA wilderness first aid, ARC first aid.

Contact Frank or Nancy Bell, Directors, Camps Mondamin and Green Cove, PO Box 8, Tuxedo, North Carolina 28784. Telephone: 704-693-7446. Fax: 704-696-8895. E-mail: mondamin@ioa.com. Application deadline: continuous.

CAMP TIMBERLAKE
BLACK MOUNTAIN, NORTH CAROLINA 28711

General Information A Christian camp for boys offering a traditional residential program with outstanding staff. Established in 1983. 150-acre facility located 16 miles from Asheville. Features: private lake; 3 tennis courts; 3 climbing walls; outstanding riding facility; ropes course; classic camp atmosphere.

Profile of Summer Employees Total number: 40; typical ages: 17–26. 5% women; 10% high school students; 85% college students; 1% retirees; 1% non-U.S. citizens; 5% local applicants. Nonsmokers required.

Employment Information Openings are from June 5 to August 11. Jobs available: ▶ *activity heads* (minimum age 20) with doumented experience and certification at $1000–$1500 per season ▶ 35 *counselors* with strong expertise and requisite certification in activity at $1000–$1500 per season. Applicants must submit formal organization application, two personal references. International applicants accepted; must apply through a recognized agency. An in-person interview is required.

Benefits and Preemployment Training Free housing, free meals, formal training, on-the-job training, and opportunity to attend seminars/workshops. Preemployment training is required and includes accident prevention and safety, first aid, CPR, interpersonal skills, leadership skills, Christian discipleship.

Contact Adam Boyd, Director, Camp Timberlake, Black Mountain, North Carolina 28711. Telephone: 828-669-8766. Fax: 828-669-6822. E-mail: adboyd@aol.com. World Wide Web: http://www.camptimberlake.com. Application deadline: continuous.

DUKE TENNIS CAMP
DUKE UNIVERSITY WEST CAMPUS COURTS AND EAST CAMPUS COURTS
DURHAM, NORTH CAROLINA 27715

General Information Camp teaching the fundamentals of tennis to residential, day, and half-day campers. Focus is on fun and learning including footwork, racquet work, timing, strokes, strategy, mental toughness, and match play. For the beginner through tournament player. Located 30 miles from Raleigh. Features: 22 tennis courts; indoor aquatic center; air-conditioned dorms; beautiful Duke campus; video review of each player; special dates for tournament players.

Profile of Summer Employees Total number: 15–20; typical ages: 18–40. 40% men; 60% women; 95% college students. Nonsmokers required.

Employment Information Openings are from June 10 to July 10. Jobs available: ▶ 14–16 *tennis instructors/general counselors* (minimum age 18) with experience teaching tennis and working with young people at $200–$300 per week. Applicants must submit a formal organization application, cover letter, resume, three personal references. International applicants accepted; must obtain own working papers. An in-person interview is recommended, but a telephone interview is acceptable.

Benefits and Preemployment Training Free housing, free meals, and on-the-job training.

Contact Stacey Flur, Administrative Director, Duke Tennis Camp, PO Box 2553, Durham, North Carolina 27715-2553. Telephone: 919-479-0854. Fax: 919-471-8268. E-mail: camp@duketennis.com. World Wide Web: http://www.duke-tennis.com. Application deadline: continuous.

DUKE YOUTH PROGRAMS–DUKE UNIVERSITY CONTINUING EDUCATION
203 BISHOP'S HOUSE, BOX 90702
DURHAM, NORTH CAROLINA 27708

General Information Five summer enrichment programs serving 650 middle and high school students. Established in 1982. 20 miles from Raleigh. Features: university campus.

Profile of Summer Employees Total number: 50; typical ages: 19–22. 40% men; 60% women; 50% college students. Nonsmokers preferred.

Employment Information Openings are from June 10 to August 10. Jobs available: ▶ 1–2 *office assistants* (minimum age 19) with driver's license at $6–$10 per hour ▶ 14–16 *residential counselors* (minimum age 19) with driver's license at $1200–$2000 per season. Applicants must submit a formal organization application, cover letter, resume, two personal references, two letters of recommendation. An in-person interview is recommended, but a telephone interview is acceptable.

Benefits and Preemployment Training Free housing, free meals, formal training, and on-the-job training. Preemployment training is required and includes accident prevention and safety, first aid, interpersonal skills, van driving, programming.

Contact Kim Price, Program Director, Duke Youth Programs–Duke University Continuing Education, Box 90702, Durham, North Carolina 27708. Telephone: 919-684-5387. Fax: 919-681-8235. E-mail: kprice@mail.duke.edu. World Wide Web: http://www.learnmore.duke.edu/youth. Application deadline: April 1.

EAGLE'S NEST CAMP
43 HART ROAD
PISGAH FOREST, NORTH CAROLINA 28768

General Information Residential camp serving 185 campers in three 3-week sessions. Experiential education for young people, promoting the natural world and the betterment of human character. Specializes in wilderness adventure and the arts. Established in 1927. 40-acre facility located 30 miles from Asheville. Features: freshwater lakes; tennis courts; open air cabins with hot and cold running water; high ropes course; wooded setting; 12-stall barn and horses.

Profile of Summer Employees Total number: 80; typical ages: 19–26. 50% men; 50% women; 1% minorities; 80% college students; 3% non-U.S. citizens; 1% local applicants. Nonsmokers required.

Employment Information Openings are from May 15 to August 19. Year-round positions also offered. Jobs available: ▶ 5–8 *arts instructors* (minimum age 19) with creativity, teaching experience, CPR, and basic first aid certification at $150–$250 per week ▶ 5–8 *athletics instructors* (minimum age 19) with CPR, first aid, and experience working with children at $150–$250 per week ▶ 6–8 *canoeing instructors* (minimum age 19) with experience or American Canoe Association Instructor, CPR, and basic first aid certification at $150–$250 per week ▶ 4 *horseback instructors* (minimum age 19) with CPR and basic first aid certfication and experience in the field at $150–$250 per week ▶ *kitchen staff* (minimum age 18) with experience in whole foods cooking at $150–$250 per week ▶ *medical staff members* should be RN, NP, PA or MD with CPR certification at $200–$300 per week ▶ 6–10 *rock climbing instructors* (minimum age 19) with CPR and basic first aid (minimum) and experience in the field at $150–$250 per week ▶ 4–6 *swimming instructors* (minimum age 19) with WSI, LGT, CPR, and basic first aid certification; teaching and/or lifeguarding experience at $150–$250 per week ▶ 10 *wilderness instructors* (minimum age 19) with wilderness first aid, CPR, basic first aid certification and experience leading groups in the field at $150–$250 per week. Applicants must submit formal organization application, personal statement (with application). International applicants accepted; must apply through a recognized agency. A telephone interview is required.

Benefits and Preemployment Training Free housing, free meals, formal training, and on-the-job training. Preemployment training is required and includes accident prevention and safety, interpersonal skills, leadership skills.

Contact Ms. Noni Waite-Kucera, Summer Director, Eagle's Nest Camp, 633 Summit Street, Winston-Salem, North Carolina 27101. Telephone: 336-761-1040. Fax: 336-727-0030. E-mail: noni@enf.org. World Wide Web: http://www.enf.org.

FALLING CREEK CAMP FOR BOYS
PO BOX 98
TUXEDO, NORTH CAROLINA 28784

General Information Privately owned camp in the western North Carolina mountains provides boys ages 7–16 with opportunity for growth and fun. Established in 1969. 1,000-acre facility located 12 miles from Hendersonville.

Profile of Summer Employees Total number: 100; typical ages: 19–25. 90% men; 10% women; 90% college students; 10% non-U.S. citizens. Nonsmokers preferred.

Employment Information Openings are from May 30 to August 16. Jobs available: ▶ 2 *Indian lore counselors* (minimum age 19) with knowledge of Indian lore at $1800–$1950 per season ▶ 2 *archery instructors* (minimum age 19) with experience in the field and archery instructor certification (on-site certification avaliable) at $1800–$1950 per season ▶ 3–4 *arts and crafts instructors* (minimum age 19) at $1800–$1950 per season ▶ 4 *camp nurses* (minimum age 21) with RN (North Carolina) at $2500–$3000 per season ▶ 4–5 *canoeing staff members* (minimum age 19) with experience in white water in closed and open boats; American Canoeing Association whitewater instructor certification at $1800–$1950 per season ▶ 2 *horseback riding staff members* (minimum age 19) with experience in English-saddle instruction at $1800–$1950 per season ▶ 4 *land sports counselors* (minimum age 19) with experience in soccer, lacrosse, or basketball at $1800–$1950 per season ▶ 2–4 *mountain biking instructors* (minimum age 20) with mountain biking and bike maintenance experience at $1800–$1950 per season ▶ 4–6 *mountaineering staff members* (minimum age 19) with experience in rock climbing and backpacking trips at $1800–$1950 per season ▶ 2 *nature counselors* (minimum age 19) with background in biology, zoology, or ecology at $1800–$1950 per season ▶ 2 *riflery instructors* (minimum age 19) with experience in the field and riflery instructor certification (on-site certification available) at $1800–$1950 per season ▶ 2–3 *sailing instructors* (minimum age 19) with sailing experience and lifeguard certification at $1800–$1950 per season ▶ 5 *swimming instructors* (minimum age 19) with WSI and lifeguard certification at $1800–$1950 per season ▶ 4–6 *tennis instructors* (minimum age 19) with experience at $1800–$1950 per season ▶ *waterskiing instructor* (minimum age 21) with waterskiing experience and lifeguard certification at $1800–$1950 per season. Applicants must submit formal organization application, three personal references. International applicants accepted; must apply through a recognized agency. An in-person interview is required.

Benefits and Preemployment Training Free housing, free meals, and on-the-job training. Preemployment training is required and includes accident prevention and safety, first aid, CPR, interpersonal skills, leadership skills.

Contact Donnie Bain, Director, Falling Creek Camp for Boys, PO Box 98, Tuxedo, North Carolina 28784. Telephone: 704-692-0262. Fax: 704-696-1616. E-mail: fallingcrk@ioa.com. World Wide Web: http://www.fallingcreek.com. Application deadline: continuous.

GRANDY FARM MARKET
PO BOX 673
GRANDY, NORTH CAROLINA 27939

General Information Retail fresh fruits and vegtables, bakery goods, and frozen yogurt in an open farm market on a farm setting catering to the tourists on their way to the beaches of the outerbanks of North Carolina. Established in 1987. Located 50 miles from Norfolk, Virginia. Features: near the beach; farm setting; frozen yogurt stand.

Profile of Summer Employees Total number: 30; typical ages: 16–24. 25% men; 75% women; 30% high school students; 25% college students; 10% retirees; 35% non-U.S. citizens. Nonsmokers required.

Employment Information Openings are from April 1 to October 31. Jobs available: ▶ 4 *general staff positions* (minimum age 18) with supermarket experience at $5.15–$5.50 per hour. International applicants accepted; must obtain own visa, apply through a recognized agency.

Benefits and Preemployment Training Meals at a cost, free housing, and on-the-job training.

Contact Colon Grandy, Owner, Grandy Farm Market, PO Box 673, Grandy, North Carolina 27939. Telephone: 252-453-2658. Application deadline: continuous.

GWYNN VALLEY
1080 ISLAND FORD ROAD
BREVARD, NORTH CAROLINA 28712

General Information Noncompetitive, creative, residential camp for younger boys and girls ages 5–12. Established in 1935. 350-acre facility located 45 miles from Asheville. Features: turn-of-the-century gristmill; 50-acre family farm; waterfall; spectacular view of Blue Ridge Mountains; spring-fed lake; swimming pool.

Profile of Summer Employees Total number: 120; typical ages: 20–50. 50% men; 50% women; 5% minorities; 5% high school students; 60% college students; 5% retirees; 30% non-U.S. citizens; 5% local applicants. Nonsmokers required.

Employment Information Openings are from June 1 to August 16. Jobs available: ▶ *archery instructor* (minimum age 19) at $110–$200 per week ▶ *cabin counselors* (minimum age 19) at $110–$200 per week ▶ *climbing/low ropes instructor* (minimum age 21) with rock site management; lead climber to 5.8 at $175–$250 per week ▶ *drama specialist* (minimum age 19) at $110–$200 per week ▶ *ecology specialist* (minimum age 19) at $110–$200 per week ▶ *horseback riding (English) instructor* (minimum age 21) at $110–$200 per week ▶ *lifeguards* (minimum age 19) with LGT at $110–$200 per week ▶ *male cabin counselor* (minimum age 19) at $110–$200 per week ▶ *miller* (minimum age 19) at $110–$200 per week ▶ *older programs manager* (minimum age 21) with some outdoor skills, driver, and leadership skills at $175–$275 per week ▶ *on-site farm manager* (minimum age 19) at $110–$200 per week ▶ *potter* (minimum age 19) at $110–$200 per week ▶ *swimming instructors* (minimum age 19) with LGT and WSI at $110–$200 per week ▶ *weaver* (minimum age 19) at $110–$200 per week. Applicants must submit formal organization application, three letters of recommendation. International applicants accepted; must apply through a recognized agency. An in-person interview is required.

Benefits and Preemployment Training Free housing, free meals, formal training, on-the-job training, and opportunity to attend seminars/workshops. Preemployment training is required and includes accident prevention and safety, first aid, CPR, interpersonal skills, leadership skills, lifeguard training and certification.

Contact Heather Gordon, Assistant Director–Staff, Gwynn Valley, 1080 Island Ford Road, Brevard, North Carolina 28712. Telephone: 828-885-2900. Fax: 828-885-2413. E-mail: gwynnvalley@citcom.net. World Wide Web: http://www.gwynnvalley.com. Application deadline: continuous.

KEYSTONE CAMP
CASHIERS VALLEY ROAD
BREVARD, NORTH CAROLINA 28712

General Information A camp for girls (ages 6–16) offering programs in horsemanship, daily horseback riding, tennis, land sports, water sports on two lakes, gymnastics, rock climbing, and hiking in Pisgah National Forest. Established in 1916. 80-acre facility located 30 miles from Asheville. Features: 2 lakes; climbing wall; 4 tennis courts; low ropes course; 3 riding rings; beautiful wooded setting.

Profile of Summer Employees Total number: 35; typical ages: 18–30. 10% men; 90% women; 20% minorities; 100% college students; 20% non-U.S. citizens. Nonsmokers preferred.

Employment Information Openings are from June 1 to August 15. Jobs available: ▶ *adventure program director* (minimum age 21) at $1500–$2000 per season ▶ 1 *aerobics instructor* (minimum age 18) at $1100–$1800 per season ▶ 1 *archery instructor* (minimum age 18) at $1100–$1800 per season ▶ 3 *art instructors* (minimum age 18) at $1100–$1800 per season ▶ 1 *badminton instructor* (minimum age 18) at $1100–$1800 per season ▶ 2 *canoeing instructors* (minimum age 18) with lifeguard certification at $1100–$1800 per season ▶ 1 *dance instructor* (minimum age 18) at $1100–$1800 per season ▶ *dramatics instructor* (minimum age 18) at $1100–$1800 per season ▶ *head counselor* (minimum age 21) at $1500–$2000 per season ▶ 3 *hiking and camping instructors* (minimum age 18) at $1100–$1800 per season ▶ *nature instructor* (minimum age 18) at $1100–$1800 per season ▶ *program director* (minimum age 18) at $1500–$2000 per season ▶ *riding instructor* (minimum age 18) at $1100–$1800 per season ▶ 2 *rock climbing* *instructors* (minimum age 18) at $1100–$1800 per season ▶ *stable helper* (minimum age 18) at $1100–$1800 per season ▶ *swimming instructor* (minimum age 18) with WSI and/or lifeguard certification at $1100–$1800 per season ▶ 2 *trip staff* (minimum age 18) at $1100–$1800 per season ▶ *various sports instructors* (minimum age 18) at $1100–$1800 per season. Applicants must submit formal organization application, two personal references. International applicants accepted; must apply through a recognized agency. An in-person interview is recommended, but a telephone interview is acceptable.

Benefits and Preemployment Training Free housing, free meals, formal training, on-the-job training, and opportunity to attend seminars/workshops. Preemployment training is required and includes accident prevention and safety, first aid, CPR, interpersonal skills, leadership skills.

Contact Ms. Katherine Kaderabek, Associate Director, Keystone Camp, PO Box 829, Brevard, North Carolina 28712. Telephone: 828-884-9125. Fax: 828-883-8234. E-mail: kathkad@aol. com. World Wide Web: http://www.keystonecamp.com. Application deadline: continuous.

NORTH BEACH SAILING/BARRIER ISLAND SAILING CENTER
BOX 8279
DUCK, NORTH CAROLINA 27949

General Information Sailing center specializing in rental and sale of windsurfing, sailing, and jet ski equipment and teaching proper use of this equipment. Offers a line of clothing for enthusiasts. Also offers parasailing and kayak eco-tours. Established in 1984. 75 miles from Virginia Beach, Virginia. Features: ocean beaches; flat water sailing on Currituck Sound.

Profile of Summer Employees Total number: 25–28; typical ages: 20–25. 50% men; 50% women; 5% high school students; 70% college students; 10% non-U.S. citizens; 5% local applicants. Nonsmokers required.

Employment Information Openings are from May 1 to October 1. Jobs available: ▶ 2–3 *kayaking and canoeing instructors* with experience in teaching, renting, and conducting eco-tours at $200–$250 per week ▶ 1–2 *parasailing instructors/captains* with Coast Guard Master license at $550–$650 per week ▶ 8 *rental/desk persons* with knowledge of sailing, windsurfing, and watersports at $200–$250 per week ▶ 3–4 *retail salespersons* with retail experience at $200–$300 per week ▶ 4 *sailing instructors* with experience and ability to relate to students in a positive manner at $250–$350 per week ▶ 8 *windsurfing instructors* with experience and ability to relate to students in a positive manner at $250–$350 per week. Applicants must submit a formal organization application, resume. International applicants accepted; must obtain own visa, obtain own working papers. An in-person interview is recommended, but a telephone interview is acceptable.

Benefits and Preemployment Training Housing at a cost and on-the-job training.

Contact Bill Miles, President, North Beach Sailing/Barrier Island Sailing Center, Box 8279, Duck, North Carolina 27949. Telephone: 252-261-1499. Fax: 252-261-4395. E-mail: nbsail@ interpath.com. World Wide Web: http://www.islandwatersportsinc.com.

PARAMOUNT'S CAROWINDS
14523 CAROWINDS BOULEVARD
CHARLOTTE, NORTH CAROLINA 28273

General Information Theme park entertaining close to 2 million guests each season with thrilling rides, shows, concerts, food, and games. Seasonal operation March through October. Established in 1972. 360-acre facility located 15 miles from Charlotte. Features: new Top Gun Steel roller coaster; division of Viacom International; newly expanded waterpark.

Profile of Summer Employees Total number: 2,000; typical ages: 15–80. 49% men; 51% women; 50% minorities; 35% high school students; 27% college students; 9% retirees; 1% non-U.S. citizens; 28% local applicants.

Employment Information Openings are from March to October. Jobs available: ▶ 100 *entertainers (singers/dancers/performers)* (minimum age 18) with neat appearance, and outgoing personality; separate audition required ▶ 300–500 *food and beverage associates* (minimum age 16) with neat appearance and outgoing personality at $6–$8 per hour ▶ 50 *lifeguards* (minimum age 18) with free Ellis training and certification provided at $7–$9 per hour ▶ 500–600 *merchandise, games, and admissions associates* (minimum age 16) with neat appearance and outgoing personality at $6–$7 per hour ▶ 300–500 *ride operators* (minimum age 18) with neat appearance and outgoing personality at $6–$8 per hour ▶ 300 *team leaders (for food and beverage and merchandise departments)* (minimum age 18) with neat appearance and outgoing personalities at $7–$9 per hour. Applicants must submit formal organization application. International applicants accepted; must apply through a recognized agency. An in-person interview is required.

Benefits and Preemployment Training Housing at a cost, health insurance, on-the-job training, opportunity to attend seminars/workshops, and internships and cooperative education programs available. Preemployment training is required and includes accident prevention and safety, interpersonal skills, leadership skills, guest service, lifeguard training, EMT training, basic supervisory skills training.

Contact Human Resources Department, Paramount's Carowinds, PO Box 410289, Charlotte, North Carolina 28241-0289. Telephone: 704-587-9002. Fax: 704-587-9101. World Wide Web: http://www.carowinds.com. Application deadline: continuous.

ROCKBROOK CAMP
HIGHWAY 276
BREVARD, NORTH CAROLINA 28712

General Information Residential camp serving girls ages 6–16, promoting independence in a non-competitive enviroment. Camp has two-, three-, and four-week sessions. Established in 1921. 185-acre facility located 30 miles from Asheville. Features: 1 freshwater lake; wooded setting; 6 tennis courts; climbing wall; Alpine Tower; on-site pottery studio.

Profile of Summer Employees Total number: 70; typical ages: 20–30. 8% men; 92% women; 8% minorities; 3% high school students; 75% college students; 2% retirees; 8% non-U.S. citizens; 8% local applicants. Nonsmokers required.

Employment Information Openings are from May 27 to August 8. Jobs available: ▶ 50 *cabin counselors* (women only) (minimum age 19) with CPR/first aid certification at $150–$175 per week ▶ 2–4 *raft and canoeing guides* at $150–$200 per week ▶ 6 *registered nurses* (women only) with RN license at $450 per week ▶ 2 *riding instructors* (women only) at $150–$175 per week ▶ 2 *rock climbers* at $150–$200 per week. Applicants must submit formal organization application, three personal references. International applicants accepted; must obtain own visa, obtain own working papers, apply through a recognized agency. An in-person interview is recommended, but a telephone interview is acceptable.

Benefits and Preemployment Training Free housing, free meals, on-the-job training, and laundry. Preemployment training is required and includes accident prevention and safety, interpersonal skills, leadership skills.

Contact Charlotte Page, Associate Director, Rockbrook Camp, PO Box 792, Brevard, North Carolina 28712. Telephone: 828-884-6151. Fax: 828-884-6151. E-mail: rockbrook@citcom.net. World Wide Web: http://www.rockbrookcamp.com. Application deadline: continuous.

RUBIN'S OSCEOLA LAKE INN
PO BOX 2258
HENDERSONVILLE, NORTH CAROLINA 28793

General Information Summer resort hotel with 80 rooms, serving 3 meals daily. Established in 1941. 12-acre facility located 1 mile from Hendersonville. Features: lake; wooded setting; tennis; shuffelboard; putting green; ping-pong.

Profile of Summer Employees Total number: 30; typical ages: 18–50. 50% men; 50% women; 25% minorities; 25% college students; 25% non-U.S. citizens; 25% local applicants. Nonsmokers preferred.

Employment Information Openings are from June to October. Jobs available: ▶ 3 *bellhops* (minimum age 18) ▶ 6 *buspersons* (minimum age 18) ▶ 1 *chauffeur* (minimum age 20) ▶ 4 *desk clerks* (minimum age 18) ▶ 6 *housekeeping personnel* (minimum age 18) ▶ 3 *kitchen aides* (minimum age 18) ▶ 1 *secretary* (minimum age 18) with typing and computer skills ▶ 6 *waiters/waitresses* (minimum age 18). Applicants must submit resume, two personal references, two letters of recommendation. International applicants accepted; must obtain own visa, obtain own working papers, apply through a recognized agency.

Benefits and Preemployment Training Housing at a cost, meals at a cost, possible full-time employment, and on-the-job training.

Contact Stuart Rubin, Owner/Manager, Rubin's Osceola Lake Inn, 5005 Collins Avenue, PH7, Miami Beach, Florida 33140. Telephone: 305-865-6015. Application deadline: continuous.

THE SOUTHWESTERN COMPANY, NORTH CAROLINA
See The Southwestern Company, Tennessee on page 284 for complete description.

STUDENT CONSERVATION ASSOCIATION (SCA), NORTH CAROLINA
See Student Conservation Association (SCA), New Hampshire on page 193 for complete description.

TUITION PAINTERS
511 KEISLER DRIVE, SUITE 101
CARY, NORTH CAROLINA 27511

General Information Hire, train, and support college students who operate their own franchised painting outlets under the name "Tuition Painters." Established in 1996. Located 10 miles from Raleigh. Features: entrepreneurial experience; "real life" management experience; profit potential.

Profile of Summer Employees Total number: 200; typical ages: 18–22. 75% men; 25% women; 10% minorities; 99% college students; 1% local applicants.

Employment Information Openings are from March 1 to September 30. Jobs available: ▶ 50–80 *branch managers* profit is based on business; 1998 average profit was $5000 for the summer ▶ 100–300 *painters* at $6.50–$9.50 per hour. International applicants accepted; must obtain own visa. An in-person interview is required.

Benefits and Preemployment Training Formal training, possible full-time employment, on-the-job training, and opportunity to attend seminars/workshops. Preemployment training is required and includes interpersonal skills, leadership skills.

Contact Barry Lake, President, Tuition Painters, 511 Keisler Drive, Suite 101, Cary, North Carolina 27511. Telephone: 919-468-9925. Fax: 919-468-9902. E-mail: tuipaint@bellsouth.net. World Wide Web: http://www.tuitionpainters.com. Application deadline: March 15.

UNITED METHODIST CAMPS
1307 GLENWOOD AVENUE
RALEIGH, NORTH CAROLINA 27605

General Information Three campsites located in eastern North Carolina providing camping and outdoor experiences in an atmosphere of Christian faith. Established in 1948. 1,000-acre facility.

Profile of Summer Employees Total number: 150; typical ages: 18–25. 40% men; 60% women; 20% minorities, 10% high school students, 90% college students. Nonsmokers required.

Employment Information Openings are from May to August. Jobs available: ▶ *arts and crafts instructors* ▶ *cabin counselors* at $130–$165 per week ▶ *lifeguards* ▶ *naturalists* at $130–$160 per week ▶ *nurses* ▶ *sailing staff members/canoeing instructors*. Applicants must submit formal organization application, three personal references. International applicants accepted; must apply through a recognized agency. An in-person interview is recommended, but a telephone interview is acceptable.

Benefits and Preemployment Training Free housing, free meals, health insurance, and on-the-job training. Preemployment training is required and includes accident prevention and safety, first aid, CPR, interpersonal skills, leadership skills.

Contact Sue Ellen Nicholson, Director, Camping Ministries, United Methodist Camps, PO Box 10955, Raleigh, North Carolina 27605. Telephone: 919-832-9560. Fax: 919-834-7989. Application deadline: March 1.

YMCA CAMP CHEERIO
CAMP CHEERIO ROAD
GLADE VALLEY, NORTH CAROLINA 28627

General Information Residential camp serving 200 campers in one- and two-week sessions. A high-adventure camp serving 50 campers per week is also offered, as well as a program for senior adults in the spring and fall. Established in 1960. 194-acre facility located 60 miles from Winston-Salem. Features: freshwater lake; mountain setting; riding program; climbing towers; 4 tennis courts; swimming pool.

Profile of Summer Employees Total number: 100; typical ages: 17–26. 50% men; 50% women; 10% minorities; 40% high school students; 60% college students; 5% non-U.S. citizens; 10% local applicants. Nonsmokers required.

Employment Information Openings are from June 1 to August 15. Year-round positions also offered. Jobs available: ▶ 1 *aquatic director* with WSI certification at $170–$240 per week ▶ 1 *climbing director* (minimum age 21) at $170–$210 per week ▶ 16–32 *junior cabin counselors* should be at least a high school senior at $120–$135 per week ▶ 1–2 *riding director* (minimum age 20) with CHA certification preferred at $800–$1300 per month ▶ 16–32 *senior cabin counselors* should be at least a college sophomore at $145–$165 per week ▶ 1 *target sports director* (minimum age 21) at $185–$210 per week ▶ 10–14 *wilderness trip leaders* (minimum age 20) at $135–$155 per week. Applicants must submit formal organization application, three personal references. International applicants accepted; must apply through a recognized agency. An in-person interview is recommended, but a telephone interview is acceptable.

Benefits and Preemployment Training Free housing, free meals, health insurance, on-the-job training, and opportunity to attend seminars/workshops. Preemployment training is required and includes accident prevention and safety, first aid, CPR, interpersonal skills, leadership skills.

Contact Teressa Lewis, Program Director, YMCA Camp Cheerio, PO Box 6258, High Point, North Carolina 27262. Telephone: 336-869-0195. Fax: 336-869-0118. E-mail: cheerio123@aol. com. World Wide Web: http://www.campcheerio.org. Application deadline: continuous.

YMCA CAMP HANES
1225 CAMP HANES ROAD
KING, NORTH CAROLINA 27021

General Information Residential camp serving 150 campers weekly. Special programs for the physically disabled and diabetic. 400-acre facility located 17 miles from Winston-Salem.

Profile of Summer Employees 50% men; 50% women; 10% minorities; 2% high school students; 90% college students; 25% non-U.S. citizens; 75% local applicants.

Employment Information Openings are from May to August. Jobs available: ▶ 25 *cabin counselors* (minimum age 16) at $110–$200 per week ▶ *counselor-in-training director* with at least one year of college at $150–$200 per week ▶ *equestrian director* with riding experience at $150–$200 per week ▶ *program director* at $150–$200 per week ▶ *registered nurse* with RN degree at $250–$300 per week ▶ *waterfront director* with WSI certification at $180–$220 per week ▶ *wrangler director* at $150–$200 per week.

Benefits and Preemployment Training Free housing, free meals, and on-the-job training. Preemployment training is required and includes accident prevention and safety, first aid, CPR, interpersonal skills, leadership skills, blood-borne pathogens, lifeguard training.

Contact Patrick Kelly, Executive Director, YMCA Camp Hanes, 1225 Camp Hanes Road, King, North Carolina 27021. Telephone: 336-983-3131. Fax: 336-983-4624. World Wide Web: http://www.camphanes.org. Application deadline: continuous.

NORTH DAKOTA

A CHRISTIAN MINISTRY IN THE NATIONAL PARKS– NORTH DAKOTA
See A Christian Ministry in the National Parks–Massachussetts on page 138 for complete description.

INTERNATIONAL MUSIC CAMP
INTERNATIONAL PEACE GARDEN
DUNSEITH, NORTH DAKOTA 58329

General Information Residential camp serving 500 students per week in 24 different arts programs. Established in 1956. 120-acre facility located 117 miles from Minot. Features: wooded setting in a state park; 2,000-seat concert hall.

Profile of Summer Employees Total number: 225; typical ages: 18–65. 50% men; 50% women; 5% minorities; 35% college students; 5% retirees; 10% non-U.S. citizens; 20% local applicants. Nonsmokers preferred.

Employment Information Openings are from June 1 to July 30. Jobs available: ▶ 11 *concessioners/housekeepers/maintenance persons* (minimum age 18) at $175 per week ▶ 6 *cooks* (minimum age 18) with cooking experience at $200–$250 per week ▶ 20 *deans/ counselors* (minimum age 21) should be college seniors or graduates at $200–$250 per week ▶ 4 *dishwashers* (minimum age 18) at $175 per week ▶ 1 *first aid technicians* (minimum age 21) with CPR, first aid certification; RN or LPN license at $175–$250 per week ▶ 4 *music librarians* (minimum age 18) with instrumental knowledge at $175–$200 per week ▶ 6 *secretaries* (minimum age 18) with ability to type 50 wpm and knowledge of computers at $175–$200 per week. Applicants must submit a formal organization application, cover letter, resume, three letters of recommendation. International applicants accepted; must obtain own visa, obtain own working papers. An in-person interview is recommended, but a telephone interview is acceptable.

Benefits and Preemployment Training Free housing, free meals, opportunity to attend seminars/ workshops, and private music lessons at no cost. Preemployment training is required and includes accident prevention and safety, interpersonal skills, leadership skills.

Contact Joseph T. Alme, Camp Director, International Music Camp, 1725 11th Street SW, Minot, North Dakota 58701. Telephone: 701-838-8472. Fax: 701-838-8472. E-mail: imc@minot. com. World Wide Web: http://musiccamp.minot.com. Application deadline: continuous.

THE SOUTHWESTERN COMPANY, NORTH DAKOTA
See The Southwestern Company, Tennessee on page 284 for complete description.

STUDENT CONSERVATION ASSOCIATION (SCA), NORTH DAKOTA
See Student Conservation Association (SCA), New Hampshire on page 193 for complete description.

OHIO

ACE COMPUTER CAMP–OHIO
See ACE Computer Camp–Washington on page 307 for complete description.

CAMP ECHOING HILLS
36272 COUNTY ROAD 79
WARSAW, OHIO 43844

General Information Camp experience for 650 mentally and physically disabled campers of all ages. Full camping program with highest standards of care for special population campers. Established in 1966. 72-acre facility located 60 miles from Columbus. Features: wooded setting; lake; go-carts; wilderness camping.

Profile of Summer Employees Total number: 40; typical ages: 19–23. 35% men; 65% women; 20% minorities; 20% high school students; 70% college students; 10% non-U.S. citizens. Nonsmokers required.

Employment Information Openings are from June 5 to August 13. Jobs available: ▶ *assistant nurses* (minimum age 21) at $200–$300 per week ▶ 40 *counselors* (minimum age 18) at $175–$250 per week ▶ 20–25 *support staff members* (minimum age 16) at $175–$250 per week. Applicants must submit formal organization application, three personal references, three letters of recommendation. International applicants accepted; must obtain own visa, obtain own working papers, apply through a recognized agency. An in-person interview is recommended, but a telephone interview is acceptable.

Benefits and Preemployment Training Free housing, free meals, possible full-time employment, and on-the-job training. Preemployment training is required and includes accident prevention and safety, first aid, interpersonal skills, leadership skills, caregiving for disabled population.

Contact Shaker Samuel, Camp Administrator, Camp Echoing Hills, 36272 County Road 79, Warsaw, Ohio 43844. Telephone: 740-327-2311. Fax: 740-327-6371. E-mail: campechohl@aol. com. Application deadline: continuous.

CAMP O'BANNON
9688 BUTLER ROAD, NE
NEWARK, OHIO 43055

General Information Residential camp serving children ages 9–14 with the goal of increasing self-esteem. Established in 1922. 169-acre facility located 40 miles from Columbus. Features: main camp; outpost camp; 2 high ropes courses.

Profile of Summer Employees Total number: 22; typical ages: 19–22. 40% men; 60% women; 20% high school students; 80% college students. Nonsmokers preferred.

Employment Information Openings are from June 8 to August 14. Jobs available: ▶ 1 *arts and crafts counselor* with one year of college at $1200–$1400 per season ▶ 1 *assistant cook* at $900–$1400 per season ▶ 8 *cabin counselors* with one year of college at $1200–$1400 per season ▶ *camp director* with college degree (preferred) at $1800 per season ▶ 1 *cook* with ability to cook for 65 or more people at $1500–$1800 per season ▶ 1 *lifeguard* with WSI certification (preferred) at $1200–$1400 per season ▶ 1 *maintenance counselor* at $1000–$1200 per season ▶ 1 *nature counselor* with one year of college at $1200–$1400 per season ▶ 1 *nurse* with RN license at $1400 per season ▶ 3 *outpost counselors* with one year of college at $1200–$1400 per season ▶ 1 *outpost director* with 2 years of college at $1500–$1800 per season ▶ 1 *program director* with 2 years of college at $1500 per season. Applicants must submit a formal organization application, three personal references, three letters of recommendation. International applicants accepted; must obtain own visa, obtain own working papers. An in-person interview is recommended, but a telephone interview is acceptable.

Benefits and Preemployment Training Free housing, free meals, health insurance, names of contacts, and on-the-job training. Preemployment training is required and includes accident prevention and safety, first aid, CPR, interpersonal skills, leadership skills.

Contact Ted Cobb, Camp Director, Camp O'Bannon, 62 West Locust Street, Newark, Ohio 43055. Telephone: 614-349-9646. Fax: 614-349-8618. Application deadline: continuous.

CEDAR POINT
CAUSEWAY DRIVE
SANDUSKY, OHIO 44871

General Information Amusement/theme park with 54 rides, 3 resort hotels, a campground, and a water park. Established in 1870. 365-acre facility located 60 miles from Cleveland. Features: 12 roller coasters; 365-acre water park; 3 resort hotels; mile-long sandy beach.

Profile of Summer Employees Total number: 3,700; typical ages: 18–22. 40% men; 60% women; 20% high school students; 60% college students; 20% retirees.

Employment Information Openings are from May 1 to October 10. Jobs available: ▶ 450–500 *games/arcades staff* (minimum age 18 if housing is required) at $5.25 per hour plus bonus ▶ 450–500 *gift shop cashiers* (minimum age 18 if housing is required) at $5.25 per hour plus bonus ▶ 450–500 *hotel housekeeping staff* (minimum age 18 if housing is required) at $5.50 per hour plus bonus ▶ 1500 *quick service workers, restaurant staff* (minimum age 18 if housing is required) at $5.50 per hour plus bonus ▶ 850–900 *ride operators* (minimum age 18) at $5.25 per hour plus bonus. Applicants must submit formal organization application. International applicants accepted; must obtain own visa, obtain own working papers, apply through a recognized agency. An in-person interview is recommended, but a telephone interview is acceptable.

Benefits and Preemployment Training Housing at a cost, meals at a cost, on-the-job training, and employee activities program.

Contact Amanda Rose, Assistant Director of Human Resources, Cedar Point, PO Box 5006, Sandusky, Ohio 44870. Telephone: 800-668-JOBS. Fax: 419-627-2163. World Wide Web: http://www.cedarpoint.com. Application deadline: August 1.

COLLEGE GIFTED PROGRAMS
DENISON UNIVERSITY
GRANVILLE, OHIO 43023

General Information Residential educational academic summer camp for gifted and talented students in grades 4-11. Program blends in-depth academics with recreational and cultural activities. Established in 1984. 1,200-acre facility located 30 miles from Columbus. Features: dormitories; campus classroom facilities; campus recreational facilities include pool, tennis courts, and gym; campus library; beautiful college setting.

Profile of Summer Employees Total number: 64; typical ages: 19–70. 50% men; 50% women; 30% minorities; 50% college students; 10% retirees; 10% non-U.S. citizens; 25% local applicants. Nonsmokers required.

Employment Information Openings are from July 24 to August 14. Jobs available: ▶ 24 *counselors* with two years of college completed and experience working with children at $800 to $1200 per 3-week session ▶ 4 *directors* with at least 5 years teaching/supervisory experience; master's degree required, doctorate preferred at $5000–$8000 ▶ 6 *housemasters/instructors (residential)* with master's degree, teaching and supervisory experience at $2500 to $4500 per 3-week session ▶ 20 *instructors (nonresidential)* with master's degree and teaching experience at $600 to $2500 per 3-week session ▶ 2 *nurses* with RN license; school experience preferred at $1300 per week. Applicants must submit formal organization application, resume, academic transcripts, two personal references, two letters of recommendation. International applicants accepted; must apply through a recognized agency. An in-person interview is recommended, but a telephone interview is acceptable.

Benefits and Preemployment Training Free housing and free meals. Preemployment training is required and includes accident prevention and safety, interpersonal skills, leadership skills, instructional strategies for gifted students.

Contact Margaret Solitario or Dr. Albert Dorhout, Executive Directors, College Gifted Programs, 120 Littleton Road, Suite 201, Parsippany, New Jersey 07054-1803. Telephone: 973-334-6991. Fax: 973-334-9756. E-mail: info@cgp-sig.com. World Wide Web: http://www.cgp-sig.com. Application deadline: continuous.

FRIENDS MUSIC CAMP
61830 SANDY RIDGE ROAD
BARNESVILLE, OHIO 43713

General Information Residential camp offering musical instruction to 75 10–18 year olds featuring private music lessons, orchestra, band, jazz, chorus, and musical theater. Established in 1980. 30-acre facility located 30 miles from Wheeling, West Virginia. Features: boarding school dormitories; soccer fields; boarding school main building; woods, rolling hills.

Profile of Summer Employees Total number: 20; typical ages: 18–67. 50% men; 50% women; 5% minorities; 50% college students; 10% retirees; 5% non-U.S. citizens. Nonsmokers required.

Employment Information Openings are from July 9 to August 8. Jobs available: ▶ 1–2 *counselors* with leadership skills and experience at $900 per season ▶ 4–10 *musical instructors* (minimum age 18) with experience in the field at $900 per season. Applicants must submit a cover letter, resume, three personal references. An in-person interview is recommended, but a telephone interview is acceptable.

Benefits and Preemployment Training Free housing, free meals, on-the-job training, and travel reimbursement. Preemployment training is required and includes leadership skills.

Contact Peg Champney, Director, Friends Music Camp, PO Box 427, Yellow Springs, Ohio 45387. Telephone: 937-767-1311. Fax: 937-767-2254. Application deadline: continuous.

GIRL SCOUT CAMP MOLLY LOUMAN
LUCASVILLE, OHIO 45648

General Information Girl Scout residential camp that serves campers ages 7-16. General activities include swimming, cookouts, horseback riding, and archery. Specialized activities include adventure travel: backpacking, mountain biking, river rafting, and bicycle touring. Established in 1929. 160-acre facility located 20 miles from Portsmouth. Features: wooded setting; lake accesss; use of surrounding public lands; modern, air-conditioned dining hall; staff lodge (air-conditioned); stables.

Profile of Summer Employees Total number: 40; typical ages: 18–25. 12% men; 88% women; 5% minorities; 2% high school students; 75% college students; 1% retirees; 10% non-U.S. citizens; 5% local applicants. Nonsmokers preferred.

Employment Information Openings are from June 20 to August 15. Jobs available: ▶ 1 *business manager* (minimum age 21) with record keeping, inventory skills, human relations skills, and driver's license at $2000–$2800 per season ▶ 2 *cooks* (minimum age 18) with experience cooking for large groups or willingness to learn at $1600–$2200 per season ▶ 10–21 *general counselors* (minimum age 18) with human relations skills and camping skills at $1400–$2200 per season ▶ 1–2 *horseback riding instructors* (minimum age 18) with western riding skills and camping skills at $1400–$2000 per season ▶ 1 *kitchen manager/head cook* (minimum age 21) with experience cooking for large groups and supervisory experience/skills at $2200–$2800 per season. Applicants must submit formal organization application, three personal references, BCI fingerprint check. International applicants accepted; must apply through a recognized agency. An in-person interview is recommended, but a telephone interview is acceptable.

Benefits and Preemployment Training Free housing, free meals, formal training, health insurance, on-the-job training, and opportunity to attend seminars/workshops. Preemployment training is required and includes accident prevention and safety, first aid, CPR, interpersonal skills, leadership skills.

Contact Becky Foreman, Camp Director, Girl Scout Camp Molly Louman, 1700 Water Mark Drive, Columbus, Ohio 43215. Telephone: 614-487-8101. Fax: 614-878-3499. E-mail: dawnlauman@aol.com. Application deadline: continuous.

PARAMOUNT'S KINGS ISLAND
6300 KINGS ISLAND DRIVE
KINGS ISLAND, OHIO 45034

General Information Family Amusement park that places associates in seasonal summer positions in various departments. Established in 1972. 600-acre facility located 15 miles from Cincinnati. Features: banquet picnic facility; water park; Eiffel Tower; campground; international showplace theater; home of The Beast, Vortex, and Outer Limits: Flight of Fear rollercoasters.

Profile of Summer Employees Total number: 5,000; typical ages: 15–30. 51% men; 49% women; 35% minorities; 60% high school students; 20% college students; 5% retirees; 98% local applicants.

Employment Information Openings are from April 4 to November 1. Spring break, winter break, and year-round positions also offered. Jobs available: ▶ 1700 *food service staff* (minimum age 16) at $6–$6.25 per hour ▶ 400–500 *games and attractions attendants* (minimum age 16) with loud speaking voice at $5.50 per hour ▶ 8–15 *inventory control* (minimum age 18) with computer skills at $6.20 per hour ▶ 500 *merchandise staff* (minimum age 16) at $5.50 per hour ▶ 800–900 *ride operators* (minimum age 16) at $5.50 per hour ▶ 5–10 *warehouse staff* (minimum age 18) must have a valid driver's license at $6.75–$7.75 per hour. Applicants must submit a formal organization application. International applicants accepted; must obtain own working papers. An in-person interview is required.

Benefits and Preemployment Training Meals at a cost, possible full-time employment, health insurance, on-the-job training, and free meals for food service staff. Preemployment training is required and includes accident prevention and safety, interpersonal skills.

Contact Human Resources, Paramount's Kings Island, 6300 Kings Island Drive, PO Box 901, Kings Island, Ohio 45034. Telephone: 513-754-5748. Fax: 513-754-5745. World Wide Web: http://www.pki.com. Application deadline: continuous.

THE SOUTHWESTERN COMPANY, OHIO
See The Southwestern Company, Tennessee on page 284 for complete description.

STOIBER ENTERPRISES
BOX 240, DELAWARE AVENUE
PUT-IN-BAY, OHIO 43456

General Information Restaurants, 2 taverns, and 3 gift shops located on an island in Lake Erie serving customers April-October. Established in 1948. Located 60 miles from Cleveland. Features: freshwater lake; safe dormitory; volleyball; nightlife; cycling; family atmosphere.

Profile of Summer Employees Total number: 85; typical ages: 18–25. 40% men; 60% women; 75% college students; 20% non-U.S. citizens; 5% local applicants.

Employment Information Openings are from April 1 to November 1. Jobs available: ▶ 2–4 *janitorial staff* (minimum age 18) with cleaning experience preferred at $7–$9 per hour ▶ 10–12 *retail clerks* (minimum age 18) at $6–$6.50 per hour ▶ 3–4 *short order cooks* (minimum age 18) with line cooking experience at $6–$6.50 per hour ▶ 18–20 *waitstaff* (minimum age 19) with experience at $3 per hour. Applicants must submit formal organization application. International applicants accepted; must apply through a recognized agency. An in-person interview is recommended, but a telephone interview is acceptable.

Benefits and Preemployment Training Housing at a cost, meals at a cost, and on-the-job training.

Contact June Stoiber, Owner, Stoiber Enterprises, Box 240, Put-In-Bay, Ohio 43456. Telephone: 419-285-4741. Fax: 419-285-2718. E-mail: jobs@frostys.com.

STUDENT CONSERVATION ASSOCIATION (SCA), OHIO
See Student Conservation Association (SCA), New Hampshire on page 193 for complete description.

WYANDOT LAKE, PREMIER PARKS INC.
10101 RIVERSIDE DRIVE
POWELL, OHIO 43065

General Information Amusement park with wet and dry rides, slides, and a water park. Established in 1984. 20-acre facility located 20 miles from Columbus. Features: 10 water slides; 7 covered pavilions; aquatic playground; public eating area; million-gallon wave pool; beautiful 20-acre landscaped facility.

Profile of Summer Employees Total number: 700–800; typical ages: 16–22. 60% men; 40% women; 10% minorities; 45% high school students; 20% college students; 5% non-U.S. citizens; 20% local applicants.

Employment Information Openings are from May 15 to October 31. Spring break positions also offered. Jobs available: ▶ 4 *EMTs* (minimum age 18) with EMT experience required ▶ 30 *admissions staff* (minimum age 15) at $6 per hour ▶ 7 *cash control personnel* (minimum age 16) with some accounting experience required at $6 per hour ▶ 50 *catering department staff* (minimum age 15) at $6 per hour ▶ 100 *food concessions personnel* (minimum age 15) at $6 per hour ▶ 20 *games/arcade attendants* (minimum age 15) at $6 per hour ▶ 10 *gift shop attendants* (minimum age 15) at $6 per hour ▶ 5–10 *interns (all departments)* (minimum age 16) with some leadership experience required, educational background preferred (academic credit available) at $6.50 per hour ▶ 20–30 *leadership positions* (minimum age 17) with management experience required at $7.25–$8.25 per hour ▶ 100 *lifeguards* (minimum age 16) with Ellis and Associates training (provided on-site at a cost of $95 paid by applicant) at $6.90–$7.05 per hour ▶ 20–25 *park services/grounds staff* (minimum age 15) at $6.50–$8 per hour ▶ 5 *photoscopes staff* (minimum age 15) with photgraphy experience preferred (training available) at $6 per hour ▶ 5–10 *raft/locker rental staff* (minimum age 15) at $6 per hour ▶ 4 *receptionists* (minimum age 15) at $6 per hour ▶ 40–50 *ride operators* (minimum age 16) at $6 per hour ▶ 6–10 *security personnel* (minimum age 18) with some security experience and background check required. Applicants must submit a formal organization application, three personal references, cover letter and resume for leadership positions. International applicants accepted; must obtain own visa, obtain own working papers. An in-person interview is required.

Benefits and Preemployment Training Meals at a cost, formal training, possible full-time employment, on-the-job training, and tuition assistance. Preemployment training is required and includes accident prevention and safety, first aid, CPR, interpersonal skills, leadership skills, guest service training, specific department training.

Contact Melissa Clouse, Human Resources Manager, Wyandot Lake, Premier Parks Inc., 10101 Riverside Drive, Powell, Ohio 43065. Telephone: 614-889-9283 Ext. 220. Fax: 614-766-4753. E-mail: wyandothr@aol.com. Application deadline: continuous.

YMCA CAMP TIPPECANOE
81300 YMCA ROAD
TIPPECANOE, OHIO 44699

General Information Residential camp serving 80–120 campers per week, with an emphasis on horsemanship, waterfront activities, and the natural world. Established in 1958. 1,100-acre facility located 55 miles from Canton. Features: 3 barns with riding rings; year-round conference center; wooded setting; foothills; primitive lake; miles of trails to hike and ride.

Profile of Summer Employees Total number: 35; typical ages: 18–42. 15% minorities; 5% high school students; 85% college students; 5% retirees; 15% non-U.S. citizens; 20% local applicants. Nonsmokers preferred.

Employment Information Openings are from May 27 to August 20. Jobs available: ▶ 1 *assistant equestrian director* with riding instructor certification (preferably CHA) at $150–$200 per week ▶ 1 *assistant registrar* (minimum age 18) with customer service and computer skills at $160–$200 per week ▶ 12 *cabin counselors* (minimum age 18) with caring demeanor and sensitivity to needs of campers at $155–$200 per week ▶ 1 *health director* (minimum age 18) with RN or EMT license at $200–$225 per week ▶ 2 *lifeguards/waterfront staff members* (minimum age 18) with WSI or equivalent, boating, and lifeguard certification at $160–$200 per week ▶ 2 *nature/crafts coordinators* (minimum age 18) with knowledge and experience at $160–$200 per week ▶ 1 *program director* (minimum age 21) with ability to plan, lead, and discipline at $210–$250 per week ▶ 2 *ranger counselors* (minimum age 19) with outdoor living skills at $155–$200 per week ▶ 4 *riding instructors* (minimum age 18) with CHA certification or equivalent at $145–$200 per week ▶ 2–4 *teen counselors* (minimum age 19) with ability to relate to and lead teenagers at $155–$200 per week ▶ 2–3 *village coordinators* (minimum age 19) with ability to plan, lead, and discipline at $170–$200 per week. Applicants must submit formal organization application, three personal references, background check, fingerprints. International applicants accepted; must obtain own visa, obtain own working papers, apply through a recognized agency. An in-person interview is recommended, but a telephone interview is acceptable.

Benefits and Preemployment Training Free housing, free meals, formal training, on-the-job training, and opportunity to attend seminars/workshops. Preemployment training is required and includes accident prevention and safety, first aid, CPR, interpersonal skills, leadership skills.

Contact Brian Seagraves, Camp Director, YMCA Camp Tippecanoe, 81300 YMCA Road, Tippecanoe, Ohio 44699. Telephone: 740-922-0679. Fax: 740-922-1152. E-mail: camptippe@ juno.com. Application deadline: continuous.

OKLAHOMA

ACE COMPUTER CAMP–OKLAHOMA
See ACE Computer Camp–Washington on page 307 for complete description.

CAMP RED ROCK
ROUTE 1, BOX 110B
BINGER, OKLAHOMA 73009

General Information Residential camp serving weekly 150 girl scouts ages 6–17. Offers general camping, Western horse riding, swimming, archery, vaulting, crafts, low ropes course, and outdoor skills. Established in 1959. 285-acre facility located 60 miles from Oklahoma City. Features: canyon; wooded settings; swimming pool; sandstone rock outcroppings; dining hall; cabins and tents.

Profile of Summer Employees Total number: 22; typical ages: 18–30. 3% men; 97% women; 10% minorities; 20% high school students; 70% college students; 10% non-U.S. citizens; 90% local applicants.

Employment Information Openings are from June 5 to July 20. Jobs available: ▶ 1 *assistant camp director* (minimum age 21) with management and supervisory experience with outdoor and camp programs at $1100–$1300 per season ▶ 1 *assistant cook* (minimum age 17) should have familiarity with kitchen operation at $900–$1100 per season ▶ 1 *business manager* (minimum age 21) with knowledge of bookkeeping and office procedures; must have current driver's license at $1100–$1300 per season ▶ 1 *camp director* (minimum age 25) with experience hiring, training, and supervising personnel and knowledge of outdoor program at $2500–$3000 per season ▶ 1 *head cook* (minimum age 21) with food service skills for large groups and ability to purchase and plan within a budget at $1200–$1500 per season ▶ 1 *health supervisor* (minimum age 21) with RN, LPN, or EMT license, ability to adapt to camp life, and knowledge of emotional and physical needs of campers at $1200–$1500 per season ▶ 1 *pool director* (minimum age 21) with WSI or equivalent certification, ability to teach, and knowledge of pool maintenance at $1200–$1500 per season ▶ 1 *pool instructor* (minimum age 17) with current ARC lifeguard certification and ability to teach at $900–$1100 per season ▶ 1 *program instructor* (minimum age 17) with ability to plan and implement all camp activities, craft experience, archery and ropes course certification or experience at $800–$1000 per season ▶ 1 *riding director* (minimum age 21) with extensive riding experience and supervisory skills and knowledge of vaulting, and Western riding at $1100–$1300 per season ▶ 2 *riding instructors* (minimum age 17) with teaching skills, experience with horses, knowledge of vaulting, and Western riding at $900–$1100 per season ▶ 7 *unit assistants* (minimum age 17) with experience working with youth, leadership ability, and able to teach activities to campers at $800–$1000 per season ▶ 4 *unit leaders* (minimum age 21) with supervisory and leadership skills, experience working with youth, and outdoor program at $900–$1100 per season. Applicants must submit formal organization application, three personal references. International applicants accepted; must apply through a recognized agency. An in-person interview is recommended, but a telephone interview is acceptable.

Benefits and Preemployment Training Free housing, free meals, health insurance, and on-the-job training.

Contact Eva Ryan, Camp Director, Camp Red Rock, 121 Northeast 50th Street, Oklahoma City, Oklahoma 73105. Telephone: 405-528-3535 Ext. 115. Fax: 405-528-3535. E-mail: evaryan@juno.com. Application deadline: continuous.

THE SOUTHWESTERN COMPANY, OKLAHOMA
See The Southwestern Company, Tennessee on page 284 for complete description.

STUDENT CONSERVATION ASSOCIATION (SCA), OKLAHOMA
See Student Conservation Association (SCA), New Hampshire on page 193 for complete description.

OREGON

ACE COMPUTER CAMP–OREGON
See ACE Computer Camp–Washington on page 307 for complete description.

A CHRISTIAN MINISTRY IN THE NATIONAL PARKS–OREGON
See A Christian Ministry in the National Parks–Massachussetts on page 138 for complete description.

CRATER LAKE COMPANY
CRATER LAKE NATIONAL PARK
CRATER LAKE, OREGON 97604

General Information Operates all concession facilities in Crater Lake National Park. Established in 1941. 75 miles from Medford. Features: deepest lake in USA; 1 of the 7 scenic wonders in the world.

Profile of Summer Employees Total number: 300; typical ages: 20–60. 40% men; 60% women; 10% minorities; 50% college students; 30% retirees; 20% local applicants. Nonsmokers preferred.

Employment Information Openings are from May 3 to October 31. Jobs available: ▶ 3 *bellhops* (minimum age 18) with customer service experience at $6.50 per hour plus gratuities ▶ 7 *boat tour operators* (minimum age 18) with current US Coast Guard Limited Master license or Master license, Red Cross card, and extensive boating experience at $9 per hour ▶ 6 *campground staff members* (minimum age 18) with lodging experience at $216 per week ▶ 12 *convenience store clerks* (minimum age 18) with cashiering and customer service experience at $6.50 per hour ▶ 110 *food service workers (dishwashers/cooks)* (minimum age 18) at $6.50–$10 per hour ▶ 11 *front desk personnel* (minimum age 18) with customer service and cashier experience at $6.50 per hour ▶ 27 *gift shop personnel (retail)* (minimum age 18) with retail/cashiering/customer service experience at $6.50 per hour ▶ 16 *housekeeping staff members* (minimum age 18) with housekeeping experience or willingness to learn and work hard at $6.50 per hour ▶ 7 *laundry staff members* (minimum age 18) with laundry or housekeeping experience at $6.50 per hour ▶ 7 *maintenance/janitorial/registration personnel* (minimum age 18) with valid driver's license and experience at $6.50–$8 per hour ▶ 5 *office workers* (minimum age 18) with accounting skills and experience at $6.50 per hour. Applicants must submit a formal organization application, cover letter, resume, personal reference. International applicants accepted; must obtain own visa, obtain own working papers. An in-person interview is recommended, but a telephone interview is acceptable.

Benefits and Preemployment Training Housing at a cost, meals at a cost, names of contacts, on-the-job training, opportunity to attend seminars/workshops, and employee assistance program; rebate for season completion for housing; employee recognition program. Preemployment training is required and includes accident prevention and safety, interpersonal skills, extra activities program.

Contact Renee Shaw, Employment Manager, Crater Lake Company, 1211 Avenue C, White City, Oregon 97503. Telephone: 541-830-4053. Fax: 541-830-8514. E-mail: jobs@craterlake.com. World Wide Web: http://www.crater-lake.com. Application deadline: continuous.

THE INN OF THE SEVENTH MOUNTAIN
18575 SW CENTURY DRIVE
BEND, OREGON 97702

General Information Full-service destination resort. Established in 1970. 40-acre facility located 7 miles from Bend. Features: 2 pools; white-water rafting; canoeing; tennis courts; ice skating, roller skating, roller blading; wooded setting.

Profile of Summer Employees Total number: 201; typical ages: 16–35. 50% men; 50% women; 5% minorities; 10% high school students; 30% college students; 5% retirees; 90% local applicants. Nonsmokers preferred.

Employment Information Openings are from May 15 to September 6. Spring break and year-round positions also offered. Jobs available: ▶ 4–6 *buspeople* (minimum age 16) at $6.00-6.50 per hour plus tips ▶ 2–3 *dishwashers* (minimum age 16) at $6.50 per hour ▶ 3 *front desk staff* (minimum age 18) with computer literacy at $7.25–$9 per hour ▶ *host/cashier* (minimum age 18) with cashier/restaurant experience at $6.50–$7 per hour ▶ *housekeeper* (minimum age 16) at $6.50–$7.50 per hour ▶ 8 *recreation leaders* (minimum age 18) with first aid/CPR/lifeguard certification at $6.50–$8 per hour ▶ *waitstaff* (minimum age 18) with restaurant experience and food handlers permit at $6.50 per hour. Applicants must submit formal organization application, resume, personal reference, letter of recommendation, video if necessary. International applicants accepted; must obtain own visa, obtain own working papers, apply through a recognized agency. An in-person interview is recommended, but a telephone interview is acceptable.

Benefits and Preemployment Training Possible full-time employment, on-the-job training, and free recreation; free meals provided in some departments.

Contact Carol Garrison, Human Resources Director, The Inn of the Seventh Mountain, 18575 SW Century Drive, Bend, Oregon 97702. Telephone: 541-382-8711. Fax: 541-382-3517. E-mail: executiveoffice@7thmtn.com. World Wide Web: http://www.7thmtn.com. Application deadline: continuous.

ROCK SPRINGS GUEST RANCH
64201 TYLER ROAD
BEND, OREGON 97701

General Information Dude ranch with riding, youth program. Established in 1969. 580-acre facility located 180 miles from Portland. Features: riding stables; pool; trout pond; 2 tennis courts; youth center; rural setting.

Profile of Summer Employees Total number: 45; typical ages: 16–22. 34% men; 66% women; 25% high school students; 70% college students; 5% local applicants.

Employment Information Openings are from June 14 to August 30. Year-round positions also offered. Jobs available: ▶ 9 *wranglers* (minimum age 18) with strong horsemanship and interpersonal skills at $1130 per month plus bonus ▶ 5 *youth counselors* (minimum age 18) with genuine interest in and experience with children at $1130 per month plus bonus. Applicants must submit a formal organization application, three personal references. International applicants accepted; must obtain own visa, obtain own working papers. An in-person interview is recommended, but a telephone interview is acceptable.

Benefits and Preemployment Training Housing at a cost, free meals, possible full-time employment, and on-the-job training. Preemployment training is required and includes accident prevention and safety, interpersonal skills, training specific to our operation.

Contact Rachel Worbes, Guest Services Manager, Rock Springs Guest Ranch, 64201 Tyler Road, Bend, Oregon 97701. Telephone: 541-382-1957. Fax: 541-382-7774. E-mail: rachel@ rocksprings.com. World Wide Web: http://www.rocksprings.com. Application deadline: continuous.

THE SOUTHWESTERN COMPANY, OREGON
See The Southwestern Company, Tennessee on page 284 for complete description.

STUDENT CONSERVATION ASSOCIATION (SCA), OREGON
See Student Conservation Association (SCA), New Hampshire on page 193 for complete description.

YWCA CAMP WESTWIND
7495 NORTH FRASER ROAD
OTIS, OREGON 97368

General Information Coeducational residential camp with traditional activities for children ages 7–18 and adults. Established in 1936. 500-acre facility located 90 miles from Portland. Features: oceanfront; river; 5 ecosystems.

Profile of Summer Employees Total number: 40; typical ages: 18–22. 30% men; 70% women; 4% minorities; 2% high school students; 97% college students; 2% non-U.S. citizens; 40% local applicants. Nonsmokers required.

Employment Information Openings are from June 13 to September 1. Jobs available: ► 2 *kitchen aides* (minimum age 16) with food handlers certification at $1200–$1300 per season ► 1 *nature/marine science specialist* with CPR/first aid certification at $100–$110 per week ► 1 *waterfront director* (minimum age 21) with lifeguarding and CPR/first aid certification, and small craft instructor status at $115–$125 per week. Applicants must submit formal organization application, two personal references, police check form. International applicants accepted; must apply through a recognized agency. An in-person interview is recommended, but a telephone interview is acceptable.

Benefits and Preemployment Training Free housing, free meals, formal training, and on-the-job training. Preemployment training is required and includes accident prevention and safety, interpersonal skills, leadership skills, child management, programming.

Contact Miriam Callaghan, Camp Administrator, YWCA Camp Westwind, 1111 Southwest Tenth Avenue, Portland, Oregon 97205. Telephone: 503-294-7472. Fax: 503-294-7473. E-mail: miriam.callaghan@ywca.fabrik.com. Application deadline: continuous.

PENNSYLVANIA

ACE COMPUTER CAMP–PENNSYLVANIA
See ACE Computer Camp–Washington on page 307 for complete description.

BRYN MAWR CAMP
RR 5, BOX 410
HONESDALE, PENNSYLVANIA 18431

General Information Camp serving 340 girls ages 5–15 for eight weeks. Year-round conference center and mountain retreat. Established in 1921. 135-acre facility located 103 miles from New York, New York. Features: 18 tennis courts; indoor and outdoor climbing; 2 heated pools; 12,000 square-foot gymnastics center; outdoor education center; adventure museum.

Profile of Summer Employees Total number: 140; typical ages: 19–55. 15% men; 85% women;

5% minorities; 2% high school students; 60% college students; 3% retirees; 15% non-U.S. citizens; 5% local applicants. Nonsmokers required.

Employment Information Openings are from June 15 to September 15. Year-round positions also offered. Jobs available: ▶ 5 *English riding instructors* (minimum age 19) at $900–$1900 per season ▶ 4 *arts and crafts instructors* with experience in the field at $1000–$2300 per season ▶ 7 *athletics instructors* (minimum age 19) at $900–$1900 per season ▶ 3 *dance instructors* at $900–$1900 per season ▶ 4 *drama instructors* (minimum age 19) at $900–$1900 per season ▶ 12 *general counselors* (minimum age 19) at $900–$1700 per season ▶ 8 *gymnastics instructors* (minimum age 18) at $1000–$2100 per season ▶ 12 *kitchen assistants* (minimum age 19) at $1100–$1900 per season ▶ 5 *laundry/light housekeeping personnel* (minimum age 18) at $1000–$1500 per season ▶ 2 *nine-month recreation/marketing/sales interns* (minimum age 23) must be college graduate at $775–$1300 per month ▶ 2 *office staff members* (minimum age 19) with word processing and phone skills at $1100–$2100 per season ▶ 3 *piano/technical theater personnel* (minimum age 21) at $1000–$2100 per season ▶ 4 *registered nurses* (minimum age 21) at $1600–$2900 per season ▶ 5 *ropes challenge/outdoors counselors* with facilitator training at $1100–$2100 per season ▶ 2 *small craft instructors* (minimum age 20) with American Red Cross small craft license/certification at $1100–$1700 per season ▶ 16 *swimming instructors* (minimum age 19) with SLS and WSI certification at $1100–$2100 per season ▶ 20 *tennis instructors* (minimum age 19) with USPTA/USPTR certification; experience teaching tennis to beginners and advanced players at $950–$2400 per season ▶ 4 *waterskiing instructors* with experience in the field; boat drivers must be at least 23 years old; at $1100–$2400 per season. Applicants must submit formal organization application, resume, two personal references, two letters of recommendation. International applicants accepted; must apply through a recognized agency. An in-person interview is recommended, but a telephone interview is acceptable.

Benefits and Preemployment Training Free housing, free meals, formal training, possible full-time employment, on-the-job training, opportunity to attend seminars/workshops, travel reimbursement, and uniforms; stipend for accomplishments.

Contact Dan Kagan, Director of Personnel, Bryn Mawr Camp, 81 Falmouth Street, Short Hills, New Jersey 07078. Telephone: 973-467-3518. Fax: 973-467-3750. E-mail: hrynmawrcc@aol. com. Application deadline: continuous.

CAMP AMERICA DAY CAMP
341 LOWER STATE ROAD
CHALFONT, PENNSYLVANIA 18914

General Information Summer day camp for children ages 2¼ to 14 offers 4-, 6-, and 8-week sessions that include transportation, lunch, and the option for extended hours. Established in 1967. 42-acre facility located 20 miles from Philadelphia. Features: challenge course (ropes and wall); 6 tennis courts; 4 swimming pools; pond for boating and fishing; indoor soccer stadium; softplay facility.

Profile of Summer Employees Total number: 85; typical ages: 15–30. 45% men; 55% women; 1% minorities; 20% high school students; 20% college students; 7% non-U.S. citizens; 93% local applicants. Nonsmokers preferred.

Employment Information Openings are from June 20 to August 14. Jobs available: ▶ 2 3 *challenge/ropes course instructors* (minimum age 19) with driver's license and car and ability to run an adventure program ▶ 5–10 *general counselors* (minimum age 19) with driver's license and car ▶ 2 *go-kart instuctors* (minimum age 19) with driver's license and car ▶ 1–2 *nature instructors* (minimum age 19) with driver's license and car and ability to plan and implement nature program ▶ 5 *pool staff* (minimum age 19) with driver's license and car, WSI and lifeguard certification. Applicants must submit formal organization application, personal reference. International applicants accepted; must apply through a recognized agency. An in-person interview is required.

Benefits and Preemployment Training Preemployment training is required and includes accident prevention and safety, interpersonal skills, leadership skills.

Contact Norma Levin, Director, Camp America Day Camp, PO Box 3157, Maple Glen, Pennsylvania 19002. Telephone: 215-822-6313. Fax: 215-822-3444. World Wide Web: http://

www.camp-america.com. Application deadline: continuous.

CAMP ARCHBALD
RR 2, BOX 123
KINGSLEY, PENNSYLVANIA 18826

General Information Camp for girls ages 6–17 with the purpose of providing an opportunity to make friends, develop an appreciation of nature, learn new skills, and develop self-confidence. Established in 1920. 288-acre facility located 35 miles from Scranton. Features: glacier lake; wooded setting; large buildings for rainy day program; platform tents; house boats.

Profile of Summer Employees Total number: 35–42. 2% men; 98% women; 1% minorities; 25% high school students; 75% college students; 3% non-U.S. citizens. Nonsmokers preferred.

Employment Information Openings are from June 5 to August 7. Jobs available: ▶ 1 *arts and crafts/nature director* with knowledge of environmental education activities at $120–$150 per week ▶ 15 *assistant unit leaders* with camp and/or Girl Scout experience at $100–$120 per week ▶ 3 *cooks/kitchen staff members (various positions)* with knowledge of food preparation at $120–$240 per week ▶ 1 *food service manager* with supervisory skills and ability to manage kitchen, food ordering, and purchasing at $220–$275 per week ▶ 1 *health care supervisor* with RN or EMT license and CPR certification at $175–$220 per week ▶ 1 *horseback riding director* with instructor certification or documented experience at $120–$160 per week ▶ 1 *office manager* with etiquette and ability to manage camp store and money at $120–$145 per week ▶ 1 *program director* with ability to supervise and coordinate all phases of camp program at $145–$190 per week ▶ 1 *small craft director* with canoe instructor, first aid, CPR certification, and knowledge of rowing, sailing, and canoeing at $100–$130 per week ▶ 7 *unit leaders* with camp and/or Girl Scout experience at $120–$160 per week ▶ 2 *waterfront assistants* with WSI, lifeguard, first aid, and CPR certification at $100–$130 per week ▶ 1 *waterfront director* with WSI, lifeguard, first aid, and CPR certification at $120–$160 per week. Applicants must submit formal organization application, resume, personal reference, letter of recommendation. International applicants accepted; must apply through a recognized agency. An in-person interview is recommended, but a telephone interview is acceptable.

Benefits and Preemployment Training Free housing, health insurance, and on-the-job training. Preemployment training is required and includes accident prevention and safety, first aid, CPR, interpersonal skills, leadership skills.

Contact Diane E. Bleam, Camp Director, Camp Archbald, Scranton Pocono Girl Scout Council, 333 Madison Avenue, Scranton, Pennsylvania 18510. Telephone: 570-344-1224. Fax: 570-346-7259. E-mail: spgsc@epix.net. Application deadline: continuous.

CAMP BALLIBAY FOR THE FINE AND PERFORMING ARTS
1 BALLIBAY ROAD
CAMPTOWN, PENNSYLVANIA 18815

General Information Coeducational residential camp serving up to 155 children ages 6–16 in two- to nine-week sessions. Established in 1964. 500-acre facility located 45 miles from Scranton.

Profile of Summer Employees Total number: 44; typical ages: 20–22. 40% men; 60% women; 60% college students; 5% retirees; 15% non-U.S. citizens; 5% local applicants.

Employment Information Openings are from June 21 to August 28. Jobs available: ▶ *WSI instructors* ▶ *art instructors* (all areas) ▶ *costume instructors* ▶ *dance instructors* (all phases) ▶ *golf instructors* ▶ *music instructors* (vocal and instrumental) ▶ *office staff members* ▶ *riding instructors* ▶ *supervisory staff members* ▶ *technical instructors* (lighting and sound) ▶ *tennis instructors* ▶ *theater directors* at $750–$2000 per season ▶ *video instructors*. Applicants must submit formal organization application, resume, three personal references. International applicants accepted; must obtain own visa, apply through a recognized agency. An in-person interview is recommended, but a telephone interview is acceptable.

Benefits and Preemployment Training Free housing and free meals. Preemployment training is required and includes accident prevention and safety, first aid, interpersonal skills, leadership skills.

Contact Gerard J. Jannone, Owner/Director, Camp Ballibay for the Fine and Performing Arts,

Box 1, Camptown, Pennsylvania 18815. Fax: 717-746-3691. E-mail: jannone@ballibay.com. World Wide Web: http://www.ballibay.com. Application deadline: continuous.

CAMP CANADENSIS
RR1, BOX 150, LAKE ROAD
CANADENSIS, PENNSYLVANIA 18325

General Information Coeducational residential camp offering all activities in an eight-week program for children ages 7–16. Established in 1941. 1,000-acre facility located 160 miles from New York, New York. Features: 75-acre lake; 2 pools; 16 tennis courts; 13 miles of trails; modern cabins; excellent facilities and equipment.

Profile of Summer Employees Total number: 160; typical ages: 19–24. 50% men; 50% women; 95% college students; 5% non-U.S. citizens. Nonsmokers required.

Employment Information Openings are from June 20 to August 17. Jobs available: ▶ 2 *archery instructors* with experience; instructor certificate preferred at $1400–$1600 per season ▶ 7 *arts and crafts instructors* at $1400–$1600 per season ▶ 30 *athletics instructors* with team experience at $1400–$1600 per season ▶ 2–3 *cooking instructors* at $1400–$1600 per season ▶ 5–6 *drama instructors* with ability to direct shows at $1400–$1600 per season ▶ 50 *general counselors* at $1400–$1600 per season ▶ 4–4 *gymnastics instructors* with experience in the field at $1400–$1600 per season ▶ 3 *maintenance staff members* with grounds work experience at $1400–$1600 per season ▶ 4–5 *motorcycles trail riding staff* with riding experience at $1400–$1600 per season ▶ 2 *nature instructors* at $1400–$1600 per season ▶ 4–5 *nurses* with RN license at $2500–$4000 per season ▶ 4 *photography/newspaper instructors* with experience taking and developing pictures and writing at $1400–$1600 per season ▶ 2 *radio station staff* with radio experience at $1400–$1600 per season ▶ 7 *rafting/kayaking/scuba instructors* with experience in the field; lifeguard certification preferred at $1400–$1600 per season ▶ 3 *riflery instructors* with NRA certification or willing to attend school at $1400–$1600 per season ▶ 8–12 *ropes course/climbing/low ropes instructors* with climbing experience at $1400–$1600 per season ▶ 8–10 *sailing/waterskiing/windsurfing/jetski instructors* with lifeguard certification at $1400–$1600 per season ▶ 7 *swimming instructors* with WSI and lifeguard certification at $1400–$1600 per season ▶ 14 *tennis instructors* with college team/coaching experience at $1400–$2000 per season. Applicants must submit formal organization application, three personal references or three letters of recommendation. International applicants accepted; must apply through a recognized agency. An in-person interview is recommended, but a telephone interview is acceptable.

Benefits and Preemployment Training Free housing, free meals, and travel allowance. Preemployment training is required and includes accident prevention and safety, interpersonal skills, leadership skills, child care, problem solving.

Contact Terri or Steve Saltzman, Directors, Camp Canadensis, Box 182, Wyncote, Pennsylvania 19095. Telephone: 215-572-8222. Fax: 215-572-8298. E-mail: camp4you@canadensis.com. World Wide Web: http://www.canadensis.com. Application deadline: continuous.

CAMP CAYUGA IN THE POCONOS
POCONO MOUNTAINS, RR 1, BOX 1180, DEPARTMENT PETG
HONESDALE, PENNSYLVANIA 18431

General Information Private coed nonsectarian residential summer camp for children ages 5–15 specializing in first-time campers. Traditional noncompetitive program offering instruction in over sixty activities. Established in 1957. 350-acre facility located 110 miles from New York, New York. Features: modern cabins with bathrooms; 3 swimming pools (1 heated); equestrian center with 25 horses; 13 tennis courts; 2 large gymnasiums with stages; separate teen campus for ages 13–15.

Profile of Summer Employees Total number: 135; typical ages: 19–55. 50% men; 50% women; 9% minorities; 98% college students; 2% retirees; 10% non-U.S. citizens; 2% local applicants. Nonsmokers preferred.

Employment Information Openings are from June 19 to August 18. Jobs available: ▶ 4–6 *Honda ATV quad-riding instructors* (minimum age 19) with experience riding ATV's and teaching children; at least one year of college completed at $1400–$1600 per season ▶ 6–10 *academic tutors and ESL instructors* (minimum age 19) with experience tutoring children; at least one year of college completed at $1300–$1500 per season ▶ 15–20 *activity specialists* (minimum age 19) with at least one year of college completed and experience playing and coaching children in one of the following activities: video camera, model rocketry, radio broadcasting, or roller skating/roller blading at $1300–$1600 per season ▶ 6–8 *archery instructors* (minimum age 19) with National Archery Association certification preferred; experience teaching archery to children; at least one year of college completed at $1300–$1600 per season ▶ 2–3 *art directors* (minimum age 25) with state teacher's license preferred; experience teaching art to children; supervisory, organizational, and managerial skills necessary at $2000–$3000 per season ▶ 10–12 *arts and crafts instructors* (minimum age 19) with experience teaching art to children; at least one year of college completed at $1300–$1500 per season ▶ 2 *athletics directors* (minimum age 25) with experience working with children in a sports environment; teachers and coaches preferred at $2000–$3000 per season ▶ 6–8 *basketball instructors* (minimum age 19) with experience playing basketball and coaching children; at least one year of college completed at $1300–$1600 per season ▶ 6–8 *canoeing and boating instructors* (minimum age 19) with American Red Cross lifeguard and American Canoeing Association certification preferred; experience canoeing and ability to instruct; at least one year of college completed at $1400–$1700 per season ▶ 10–12 *ceramics instructors/pottery instructors* (minimum age 19) with kiln and pottery wheel operating experience; experience teaching ceramics to children; at least one year of college completed at $1300–$1500 per season ▶ 4–6 *chorus/singing instructors* (minimum age 19) with experience in chorus and ability to instruct; at least one year of college completed at $1300–$1500 per season ▶ 6–12 *drama instructors* (minimum age 19) with theater experience including directing plays and improvisation; at least one year of college completed at $1300–$1500 per season ▶ 2–3 *evening activity directors* (minimum age 25) with experience in organizing and implementing activities; outgoing, good sense of humor, creative personality required at $2000–$3000 per season ▶ 4–6 *fishing instructors* (minimum age 19) with experience fishing and ability to instruct; at least one year of college completed at $1300–$1500 per season ▶ 10–12 *flying trapeze and circus instructors* (minimum age 19) with experience teaching or coaching children; at least one year of college completed; experience on the flying trapeze and circus skills; strong gymnastic skills helpful at $1400–$1600 per season ▶ 15–18 *food service staff (cooks, dining hall service, food prep)* (minimum age 20) with experience in quantity food production required; at least one year of college completed at $2000–$8000 per season ▶ 6–7 *golf instructors* (minimum age 19) with experience playing golf and coaching children; at least one year of college completed at $1300–$1500 per season ▶ 10–12 *gymnastics instructors* (minimum age 19) with experience on all gymnastics apparatus; teaching gymnastics experience preferred; at least one year of college completed at $1400–$1600 per season ▶ 4–6 *head counselors* (minimum age 30) with supervisory skills and experience working with children and young adults at $2000–$3000 per season ▶ 10–15 *horseback riding instructors* (minimum age 19) with CHA certification preferred; experience riding and caring for horses and stables; experience teaching children; at least one year of college completed at $1400–$1700 per season ▶ 2 *horsemanship directors* (minimum age 25) with CHA certification preferred; experience teaching equestrian skills to children; supervisory, organizational, and managerial skills necessary at $2000–$3000 per season ▶ 2–3 *intercamp tournament directors* (minimum age 25) with teacher's license preferred; experience working with children and young adults; strong organizational and scheduling skills necessary at $2000–$3000 per season ▶ 6–7 *lacrosse instructors* (minimum age 19) with experience playing lacrosse and coaching children; at least one year of college completed at $1300–$1600 per season ▶ 2 *lakefront directors* (minimum age 25) with American Red Cross lifeguard certification or equivalent required; experience instructing canoeing, sailing, and boating; supervisory and managerial skills necessary at $2000–$3000 per season ▶ 6–7 *martial arts instructors* (minimum age 19) with black belt in karate preferred; experience competing and teaching martial arts to children; at least one year of college completed at $1400–$1600 per season ▶ 6–10 *mountain biking instructors* (minimum age 19) with experience in biking and ability to instruct; at least one year of college completed at $1300–$1600 per season ▶ 4–6 *musical instruments instructors (keyboard, guitar, violin, trumpet, flute, etc)* (minimum age 19) with experience playing an instrument and ability to instruct; at least one year of college completed at $1300–$1500 per season ▶ 6 *nurses* (minimum age 25) with RN, LPN or EMT and experience working with children at $2000–$3000 per season ▶ 4–6 *office personnel* (minimum age 19) with experience working in a business office; good organizational skills, excellent telephone manner, and administration skills needed at $1300–$1600 per season ▶ 2–4 *program directors* (minimum age 30) with teaching/coaching license preferred; organizational and supervisory skills needed; experience in scheduling activities and staff at $2500–$3500 per season ▶ 6–7 *riflery instructors* (minimum age 20) with NRA instructor certification or equivalent preferred; experience with 22-caliber rifles; at least one year of college completed at $1400–$1600 per season ▶ 6–8 *ropes course/rock climbing instructors* (minimum age 19) with experience teaching rock climbing and zip line to children; professionally trained individuals; at least one year of college completed at $1300–$1600 per season ▶ 6–7 *sailing instructors* (minimum age 19) with American Red Cross sailing and lifeguard certification preferred; experience teaching sailing to children; at least one year of college completed at $1400–$1700 per season ▶ 12–18 *swimming instructors* (minimum age 19) with American Red Cross WSI and lifeguard certification or equivalent preferred; experience teaching swimming to children; at least one year of college completed at $1600–$1800 per season ▶ 30–40 *team sports instructors (soccer, frisbee, field hockey, softball, baseball)* (minimum age 19) with experience playing the sport and coaching children; at least one year of college completed at $1300–$1600 per season ▶ 12–14 *tennis instructors and certified tennis professional* (minimum age 19) with USTA license required for director position; experience playing and coaching tennis; at least one year of college completed at $1300–$3000 per season ▶ 2–3 *transportation directors* (minimum age 25) with driver's license and mechanical skills required; experience driving 15-passenger vans at $1800–$2500 per season ▶ 6–8 *volleyball instructors* (minimum age 19) with experience playing and coaching volleyball and at least one year of college completed at $1300–$1600 per season ▶ 2–3 *waterfront directors* (minimum age 25) with WSI and American Red Cross lifeguard certification or equivalent; pool management and maintenance skills; experience instructing children and supervisory skills at $2200–$3500 per season ▶ 4–6 *weight-lifting instructors* (minimum age 19) with experience in weight training and ability to instruct; at least one year of college completed at $1400–$1600 per season ▶ 4–6 *windsurfing instructors* (minimum age 19) with American Red Cross lifeguard certification or equivalent preferred; experience teaching windsurfing to children; at least one year of college completed at $1500–$1700 per season ▶ 4–6 *wrestling instructors* (minimum age 19) with experience teaching wrestling to children; at least one year of college completed at $1400–$1600 per season. Applicants must submit formal organization application, three personal references, two letters of recommendation, copies of certifications, if applicable. International applicants accepted; must apply through a recognized agency. An in-person interview is recommended, but a telephone interview is acceptable.

Benefits and Preemployment Training Free housing, free meals, formal training, on-the-job training, opportunity to attend seminars/workshops, and 3-day all expenses-paid winter camp ski reunion; camp tuition is free for children of senior staff members; free weekly laundry service. Preemployment training is required and includes accident prevention and safety, first aid, CPR, interpersonal skills, leadership skills.

Contact Brian B. Buynak, Camp Director, Camp Cayuga in the Poconos, PO Box 151, Department PSJ, Peapack, New Jersey 07977. Telephone: 800-422-9842. Fax: 908-470-1228. E-mail: info@campcayuga.com. World Wide Web: http://www.campcayuga.com. Application deadline: continuous.

CAMP CHEN-A-WANDA
RR 1, BOX 32
THOMPSON, PENNSYLVANIA 18465

General Information Coeducational residential camp serving 350 campers for a 7½-week session. Established in 1939. 183-acre facility located 25 miles from Scranton. Features: heated Olympic-size pool; freshwater lake; indoor fitness center; indoor basketball court; 7 tennis courts; 3 soccer fields.

Profile of Summer Employees Total number: 140; typical ages: 19–24. 54% men; 46% women; 80% college students; 20% non-U.S. citizens. Nonsmokers preferred.

Employment Information Openings are from June 20 to August 20. Jobs available: ▶ 3 *arts and crafts specialists* (minimum age 19) at $600–$1000 per season ▶ 4 *baseball specialists* (minimum age 19) at $600–$1000 per season ▶ 4 *basketball specialists* (minimum age 19) at $600–$1000 per season ▶ 2 *go-cart/all terrain vehicle specialists* (minimum age 19) at $600–$1000 per season ▶ 1 *golf specialist* (minimum age 19) at $600–$1000 per season ▶ 2 *gymnastics specialists* (minimum age 19) at $600–$1000 per season ▶ 2 *lacrosse specialists* (minimum age 19) at $600–$1000 per season ▶ 2 *roller hockey specialists* (minimum age 19) at $600–$1000 per season ▶ 2–4 *ropes/rock climbing/rappelling specialists* (minimum age 19) at $700–$1000 per season ▶ 4 *soccer specialists* (minimum age 19) at $600–$1000 per season ▶ 2 *stage management/scenery staff members* (minimum age 19) at $600–$1000 per season ▶ 3 *tennis specialists* (minimum age 19) at $600–$1000 per season ▶ 2 *volleyball specialists* (minimum age 19) at $600–$1000 per season ▶ 10 *waterfront specialists (swimming, sailing, or waterskiing)* with WSI certification for swimming at $600–$1200 per season. Applicants must submit resume, two personal references, two letters of recommendation. International applicants accepted; must apply through a recognized agency. A telephone interview is required.

Benefits and Preemployment Training Free housing, free meals, and travel reimbursement. Preemployment training is required and includes accident prevention and safety, interpersonal skills, leadership skills.

Contact Morey Baldwin, Director, Camp Chen-A-Wanda, 8 Claverton Court, Dix Hills, New York 11747. Telephone: 516-643-5878. Fax: 516-643-0920. Application deadline: continuous.

CAMP LOHIKAN IN THE POCONO MOUNTAINS
WALLERVILLE ROAD
LAKE COMO, PENNSYLVANIA 18437

General Information Coed summer camp for campers 6 to 15 years old that features more than 60 daily acivities, evening activities, weekly special events, trips, and more. Established in 1957. 1,200-acre facility located 30 miles from Scranton. Features: private lake; swimming pool; 11 tennis courts; 30 horses; 7 sports fields; 14 arts workshops.

Profile of Summer Employees Total number: 200. 5% minorities; 65% college students; 2% retirees; 5% non-U.S. citizens; 5% local applicants. Nonsmokers required.

Employment Information Openings are from June 1 to September 30. Jobs available: ▶ 6 *canoeing instructors* (minimum age 19) at $1300–$2000 per season ▶ 12 *creative arts instructors* (minimum age 19) at $1200–$2000 per season ▶ 7 *gymnastics instructors* (minimum age 19) at $1200–$2000 per season ▶ 10 *horseback riding instructors* at $1400–$2200 per season ▶ 10 *lifeguards* (minimum age 19) at $1400–$2200 per season ▶ 5 *performing arts instructors* (minimum age 19) at $1200–$2000 per season ▶ 4 *pottery instructors* (minimum age 19) at $1200–$2000 per season ▶ 5 *rock climbing instuctors* (minimum age 19) at $1200–$2000 per season ▶ 4 *ropes course instructors* (minimum age 19) at $1200–$2000 per season ▶ 6 *sailing instructors* (minimum age 19) at $1300–$2000 per season ▶ 3 *skateboarding instructors* (minimum age 19) at $1300–$2000 per season ▶ 10 *sports instructors* (minimum age 19) at $1200–$2000 per season ▶ 12 *tennis instructors* (minimum age 19) at $1200–$2000 per season ▶ 3 *woodworking instructors* (minimum age 19) at $1300–$2000 per season. Applicants must submit formal organization application, three personal references, three letters of recommendation. International applicants accepted; must apply through a recognized agency. An in-person interview is recommended, but a telephone interview is acceptable.

Benefits pnd Preemployment Training Free housing, free meals, formal training, possible full-time employment, on-the-job training, and travel reimbursement. Preemployment training is required and includes accident prevention and safety, first aid, CPR, interpersonal skills, leadership skills.

Contact Ian Brassett, Staffing Director, Camp Lohikan in the Pocono Mountains, PO Box 189, Gladstone, New Jersey 07934. Telephone: 908-470-9317. Fax: 908-470-9319. E-mail: mail@lohikan.com. World Wide Web: http://www.lohikan.com. Application deadline: continuous.

CAMP NOCK-A-MIXON
249 TRAUGERS CROSSING ROAD
KINTNERSVILLE, PENNSYLVANIA 18930

General Information All-around residential coeducational camp serving 380 youngsters ages 7–15 during a seven-week session. Established in 1938. 115-acre facility located 45 miles from Philadelphia. Features: 2 heated swimming pools; 4 covered athletic pavilions; 2 spring-fed lakes; 10 tennis courts; 230-yard golf driving range; 7 basketball courts.

Profile of Summer Employees Total number: 150; typical ages: 18–40. 55% men; 45% women; 10% high school students; 80% college students; 10% non-U.S. citizens. Nonsmokers required.

Employment Information Openings are from June 21 to August 15. Jobs available: ▶ *adventure course (ropes and climbing wall) teacher* at $1500–$2200 per season ▶ *athletic directors* at $1400–$3000 per season ▶ 1 *crafts director* at $1500–$2000 per season ▶ *division leaders* (minimum age 22) with college degree at $1800–$3000 per season ▶ 2 *drama directors* at $1200–$1800 per season ▶ 2 *general cleaning and grounds workers* at $1500–$1800 per season ▶ 60 *general counselors* must be high school graduates at $1000–$1500 per season ▶ 6 *kitchen staff members* at $1500–$1800 per season ▶ *nurses* with RN license at $2800–$3200 per season ▶ 30 *specialists and counselors* at $1000–$1500 per season ▶ 10 *swimming instructors* with WSI certification and/or lifeguard training at $1000–$2000 per season ▶ 6 *tennis counselors* at $1000–$1600 per season. Applicants must submit formal organization application, three personal references. International applicants accepted; must obtain own visa, obtain own working papers, apply through a recognized agency. An in-person interview is recommended, but a telephone interview is acceptable.

Benefits and Preemployment Training Free housing, free meals, formal training, on-the-job training, opportunity to attend seminars/workshops, and internship credits through colleges. Preemployment training is required and includes accident prevention and safety, first aid, CPR, interpersonal skills, leadership skills, ropes, climbing wall certification, lifeguard training.

Contact Mark Glaser, Director, Camp Nock-A-Mixon, 16 Gum Tree Lane, Lafayette Hill, Pennsylvania 19444. Telephone: 610-941-0128. Fax: 610-941-1307. E-mail: mglaser851@aol. com.

CAMP SUSQUEHANNOCK FOR GIRLS
FRIENDSVILLE, PENNSYLVANIA 18818

General Information Residential camp for 85 girls ages 7–17. Offers three-, four-, or eight-week sessions. Established in 1986. 750-acre facility located 17 miles from Binghamton, New York. Features: private fresh water lake (natural); wooded setting; 4 tennis courts; 14 saddle horses; large fieldstone lodge; excellent playing fields.

Profile of Summer Employees Total number: 53; typical ages: 17–28. 13% men; 87% women; 15% high school students; 47% college students; 6% retirees; 28% non-U.S. citizens; 43% local applicants. Nonsmokers required.

Employment Information Openings are from June 15 to August 25. Jobs available: ▶ 2 *arts and crafts instructors* at $1000–$1500 per season ▶ 2 *camp craft (outdoor camping skills)/nature/ ecology instructors* at $1000–$2000 per season ▶ 2 *field sports staff members (hockey, lacrosse, and soccer)* with team play experience (high school and above), experience instructing the sport preferred; must be high school graduate at $1000–$2000 per season ▶ 2 *horseback riders* with Horsemanship Association, Pony Club or similar certification preferred; should have experience riding, competing, and handling horses; teaching horsemanship experience preferred at $1000– $2500 per season ▶ 1 *nurse* with RN license; salary negotiable ▶ 2 *swimming instructors* with lifeguard certification at $900–$1500 per season ▶ 2 *tennis instuctors* at $1200–$2000 per season. Applicants must submit formal organization application, cover letter, resume, three personal references. International applicants accepted; must apply through a recognized agency. An in-person interview is recommended, but a telephone interview is acceptable.

Benefits and Preemployment Training Free housing, free meals, formal training, on-the-job training, opportunity to attend seminars/workshops, and travel reimbursement. Preemployment training is required and includes accident prevention and safety, first aid, CPR, interpersonal skills, leadership skills, teaching, coaching, officiating, campcraft.

Contact George C. Shafer, Director, Camp Susquehannock for Girls, 860 Briarwood Road, Newtown Square, Pennsylvania 19073. Telephone: 610-356-3426. Fax: 610-353-1768. E-mail: dds4g@aol.com. World Wide Web: http://www.susquehannock.com. Application deadline: continuous.

CAMP WATONKA
PO BOX 127
HAWLEY, PENNSYLVANIA 18428

General Information Residential science camp for 120 boys offering hands-on experience in all areas of science combined with traditional camp activities. Established in 1963. 250-acre facility located 30 miles from Scranton. Features: lake; fishing stream; sports facilities; biking trails; hiking trails; modern buildings.

Profile of Summer Employees Total number: 60; typical ages: 20–40. 95% men; 5% women; 10% minorities; 5% high school students; 55% college students; 20% non-U.S. citizens; 10% local applicants. Nonsmokers required.

Employment Information Openings are from June 20 to August 20. Jobs available: ▶ *archery instructor* should be college student or graduate at $1100–$2500 per season ▶ 3 *arts and crafts staff members* at $1100–$1400 per season ▶ 15 *cabin counselors* should be college juniors or seniors at $1100–$1400 per season ▶ *magic instructor* should be college student or graduate at $1100–$2500 per season ▶ 3 *minibike riding instructors* with experience in the field at $1100–$1800 per season ▶ *photography instructor* should be college student or graduate at $1100–$2500 per season ▶ 8 *science instructors* should be college student or graduate at $1100–$2500 per season ▶ 8 *science supervisors* with teaching certification at $1500–$3000 per season ▶ 1 *waterfront director* with ARC certification at $1500–$3000 per season ▶ 5 *waterfront/water sports instructors* with ARC certification at $1100–$1500 per season ▶ 2 *woodworking instructors* with teaching certification at $1500–$3000 per season. Applicants must submit formal organization application, cover letter, resume. International applicants accepted; must apply through a recognized agency. An in-person interview is recommended, but a telephone interview is acceptable.

Benefits and Preemployment Training Free housing, free meals, formal training, and on-the-job training. Preemployment training is required and includes accident prevention and safety, first aid, CPR, leadership skills.

Contact Donald P. Wacker, Director, Camp Watonka, PO Box 127, Hawley, Pennsylvania 18428. Telephone: 570-857-1401. World Wide Web: http://www.watonka.com. Application deadline: continuous.

CAMP WESTMONT
ROUTE 370
POYNTELLE, PENNSYLVANIA 18454

General Information Residential camp offering all land and water sports, individual and team athletics, arts and crafts, drama and dance, woodworking and ceramics, and circus and gymnastics to 380 campers ages 6–16 for eight weeks. Established in 1980. 225-acre facility located 100 miles from New York, New York. Features: freshwater lake and olympic size pool; wooded setting; 8 tennis courts; 3 soccer fields and 4 baseball fields; flying and stationary trapeze; 2 hockey rinks.

Profile of Summer Employees Total number: 150; typical ages: 18–45. 50% men; 50% women; 5% minorities; 5% high school students; 85% college students; 2% retirees; 10% non-U.S. citizens; 5% local applicants. Nonsmokers required.

Employment Information Openings are from June 15 to August 21. Jobs available: ▶ 80 *general counselors* (minimum age 18) with camp experience and experience working with children (coaching, Scouts, or similar) at $1200–$1500 per season ▶ 6 *group leaders* (minimum age 25) with camp or teaching experience with children at $1800–$3000 per season ▶ 6 *tennis specialists* (minimum age 18) with experience playing and/or teaching tennis at $1500–$2000 per season ▶ 6 *waterfront specialists* (minimum age 18) with WSI/lifeguard certification and experience as a swimming instructor or lifeguard at $1500–$2000 per season. Applicants must submit formal organization application, cover letter, resume, two personal references, two letters of recommendation, photo and copy of proof of age. International applicants accepted; must obtain own visa, apply through a recognized agency. An in-person interview is recommended, but a telephone interview is acceptable.

Benefits and Preemployment Training Free housing, free meals, on-the-job training, and travel reimbursement. Preemployment training is required and includes accident prevention and safety, interpersonal skills, leadership skills.

Contact Jack Pinsky, Owner/Director, Camp Westmont, 14 Squirrel Drive, East Rockaway, New York 11518. Telephone: 516-599-2963. Fax: 516-599-1979. E-mail: campwestmt@aol.com. World Wide Web: http://www.campwestmont.com. Application deadline: continuous.

COLLEGE GIFTED PROGRAMS
GEORGE SCHOOL
NEWTOWN, PENNSYLVANIA 18940

General Information Residential educational academic summer camp for gifted and talented students in grades 4–11. Program blends in-depth academics with recreational and cultural activities. Established in 1984. 265-acre facility located 20 miles from Philadelphia. Features: dormitories; campus classroom facilities; campus recreational facilities include pool, tennis courts, and gym; campus library; beautiful campus setting.

Profile of Summer Employees Total number: 68; typical ages: 19–70. 50% men; 50% women; 30% minorities; 50% college students; 10% retirees; 10% non-U.S. citizens; 25% local applicants. Nonsmokers required.

Employment Information Openings are from June 26 to July 17. Jobs available: ▶ 30 *counselors* with two years of college completed and experience working with children at $800 to $1200 per 3-week session ▶ 4 *directors* with at least 5 years teaching/supervisory experience; master's degree required, doctorate preferred at $5000–$8000 ▶ 8 *housemasters/instructors (residential)* with master's degree, teaching and supervisory experience at $2500 to $4500 per 3-week session ▶ 20 *instructors (non-residential)* with master's degree and teaching experience at $600 to $2500 per 3-week session ▶ 2 *nurses* with RN license; school experience preferred at $1300 per week. Applicants must submit formal organization application, resume, academic transcripts, two personal references, two letters of recommendation. International applicants accepted; must apply through a recognized agency. An in-person interview is recommended, but a telephone interview is acceptable.

Benefits and Preemployment Training Free housing and free meals. Preemployment training is required and includes accident prevention and safety, interpersonal skills, leadership skills, instructional strategies for gifted students.

Contact Margaret Solitario or Dr. Albert Dorhout, Executive Directors, College Gifted Programs, 120 Littleton Road, Suite 201, Parsippany, New Jersey 07054-1803. Telephone: 973-334-6991. Fax: 973-334-9756. E-mail: info@cgp-sig.com. World Wide Web: http://www.cgp-sig.com. Application deadline: continuous.

COLLEGE GIFTED PROGRAMS
BRYN MAWR COLLEGE
BRYN MAWR, PENNSYLVANIA 19010

General Information Residential educational academic summer camp for gifted and talented students in grades 4-11. Program blends in-depth academics with recreational and cultural activities. Established in 1984. 135-acre facility located 11 miles from Philadelphia. Features: dormitories; campus classroom facilities; campus recreational facilities include pool, tennis courts, and gym; campus library; beautiful college setting.

Profile of Summer Employees Total number: 70; typical ages: 19–70. 50% men; 50% women; 30% minorities; 50% college students; 10% retirees; 10% non-U.S. citizens; 25% local applicants. Nonsmokers required.

Employment Information Openings are from July 24 to August 14. Jobs available: ▶ 35 *counselors* with two years of college completed and experience working with children at $800 to $1200 per 3-week session ▶ 4 *directors* with at least 5 years teaching/supervisory experience;

master's degree required, doctorate preferred at $5000–$8000 ▶ 7 *housemasters/instructors (residential)* with master's degree, teaching and supervisory experience at $2500 to $4500 per 3-week session ▶ 20 *instructors (non-residential)* with master's degree and teaching experience at $600 to $2500 per 3-week session ▶ 2 *nurses* with RN license; school experience preferred at $1300 per week. Applicants must submit formal organization application, resume, academic transcripts, two personal references, two letters of recommendation. International applicants accepted; must apply through a recognized agency. An in-person interview is recommended, but a telephone interview is acceptable.

Benefits and Preemployment Training Free housing and free meals. Preemployment training is required and includes accident prevention and safety, interpersonal skills, leadership skills, instructional strategies for gifted students.

Contact Margaret Solitario or Dr. Albert Dorhout, Executive Directors, College Gifted Programs, 120 Littleton Road, Suite 201, Parsippany, New Jersey 07054-1803. Telephone: 973-334-6991. Fax: 973-334-9756. E-mail: info@cgp-sig.com. World Wide Web: http://www.cgp-sig.com. Application deadline: continuous.

COLLEGE SETTLEMENT OF PHILADELPHIA
600 WITMER ROAD
HORSHAM, PENNSYLVANIA 19044

General Information Residential and day camp serving mostly economically disadvantaged youths ages 7–14 from the Philadelphia metropolitan area. Established in 1922. 235-acre facility located 15 miles from Philadelphia. Features: small lake/pond; low ropes/high ropes course; 2 pools; lighted hard-top for tennis and sports; 6 cabins and large house/dormitory; full-service dining hall.

Profile of Summer Employees Total number: 65; typical ages: 16–30. 50% men; 50% women; 20% minorities; 10% high school students; 80% college students; 20% non-U.S. citizens; 10% local applicants. Nonsmokers preferred.

Employment Information Openings are from June 15 to August 25. Year-round positions also offered. Jobs available: ▶ 12 *cabin counselors* at $1600 per season ▶ 2 *environmentalists* at $1600–$1800 per season ▶ 1 *provisions coordinator* (minimum age 21) at $1600–$1800 per season ▶ 3 *swimming instructors* (minimum age 19) with WSI and LGT certification at $1700–$1900 per season ▶ 3 *trip leaders* with first aid and CPR certification at $1800–$2000 per season ▶ 3 *unit leaders* at $1800 per season. Applicants must submit formal organization application, cover letter, resume, three personal references. International applicants accepted; must apply through a recognized agency. An in-person interview is recommended, but a telephone interview is acceptable.

Benefits and Preemployment Training Free housing, free meals, possible full-time employment, on-the-job training, and possible certification training for archery, boating, lifeguard. Preemployment training is required and includes accident prevention and safety, first aid, CPR, interpersonal skills, leadership skills.

Contact Mr. Wally Grummun, Director of Resident Programs, College Settlement of Philadelphia, 600 Witmer Road, Horsham, Pennsylvania 19044. Telephone: 215-542-7974. Fax: 215-542-7457. E-mail: camps@i-bob.com.

DORNEY PARK AND WILDWATER KINGDOM
3830 DORNEY PARK ROAD
ALLENTOWN, PENNSYLVANIA 18104

General Information Amusement park featuring more than 100 rides and attractions, including 4 world-class roller coasters and a premier waterpark. Established in 1860. 200-acre facility located 50 miles from Philadelphia. Features: 5 designated children's areas; 11 water slides; wave pool; 1921 antique wooden Dentzel carousel; daily live entertainment.

Profile of Summer Employees Total number: 2,500.

Employment Information Openings are from May 1 to October 1. Jobs available: ▶ 350 *food hosts and hostesses* ▶ 100 *game attendants* ▶ 200 *lifeguards* ▶ 180 *merchandise clerks* ▶ 75

performers ▶ 350 *ride operators* ▶ *security staff.* International applicants accepted; must apply through a recognized agency.
Benefits and Preemployment Training On-the-job training and scholarships available.
Contact Eileen Minninger, Personnel Manager, Dorney Park and Wildwater Kingdom, 3830 Dorney Park Road, Allentown, Pennsylvania 18104. Telephone: 610-391-7752. Application deadline: continuous.

FORT NECESSITY NATIONAL BATTLEFIELD
1 WASHINGTON WAY
FARMINGTON, PENNSYLVANIA 15437

General Information George Washington's first command and battlefield commemorating the opening battle of the French and Indian War and westward expansion along the National Road. Established in 1931. 903-acre facility located 70 miles from Pittsburgh. Features: reconstructed fort and battlefield; visitor center; 19th-century tavern; picnic area; grave site of General Braddock; skirmish site, Jumonville Glen.
Profile of Summer Employees Total number: 4; typical ages: 22–65. 75% men; 25% women; 25% minorities; 50% college students; 25% retirees.
Employment Information Openings are from June 1 to August 25. Jobs available: ▶ 3–4 *interpretive park rangers* (minimum age 18) with public speaking experience and interest in history at $9–$10 per hour. Applicants must submit a formal organization application.
Benefits and Preemployment Training Housing at a cost, formal training, and on-the-job training.
Contact Jane S. Clark, Supervisory Park Ranger, Fort Necessity National Battlefield, 1 Washington Parkway, Farmington, Pennsylvania 15437. Telephone: 724-329-5512. Fax: 724-329-8682. E-mail: jane_clark@nps.gov. World Wide Web: http://www.nps.gov/fone. Application deadline: January 15.

HERSHEYPARK
100 WEST HERSHEYPARK DRIVE
HERSHEY, PENNSYLVANIA 17033

General Information Facility producing four residential shows, song and dance revues, and other types of family entertainment. Established in 1907. 100-acre facility located 100 miles from Philadelphia.
Profile of Summer Employees Total number: 5,000. 50% men; 50% women.
Employment Information Openings are from May 13 to September 6. Jobs available: ▶ 10 *seamstresses/dressers* with experience in the field at $300–$400 per week ▶ 60 *singing/dancing performers* with experience in the field at $375–$405 per week ▶ 4 *sound technicians* with experience in the field at $330–$350 per week ▶ 5 *stage managers* with experience in the field at $330–$400 per week. Applicants must submit a formal organization application, cover letter, resume. International applicants accepted.
Benefits and Preemployment Training Housing at a cost. Preemployment training is required.
Contact Cherie Lingle, Assistant Entertainment Manager, Hersheypark, 100 West Hersheypark Drive, Hershey, Pennsylvania 17033. Telephone: 717-534-3349. Fax: 717-534-3336. World Wide Web: http://www.800hershey.com/attractions/hersheypark/hp_homepage.html. Application deadline: continuous.

HIDDEN VALLEY CAMP
PO BOX 98
EQUINUNK, PENNSYLVANIA 18417

General Information Residential camp serving girls ages 7–17. Located on 1200 acres in the Pocono Mountains, surrounded by a picturesque lake. Established in 1971. 1,200-acre facility located 6 miles from Hancock, New York. Features: horseback riding ring and trails; sports field; arts and crafts; nature center; docks for swimming and boating; hiking trails.
Profile of Summer Employees Total number: 30; typical ages: 16–45. 2% men; 98% women; 5% minorities; 5% high school students; 75% college students; 5% non-U.S. citizens. Nonsmokers preferred.

Employment Information Openings are from June 16 to August 18. Jobs available: ▶ 1–2 *assistant cooks* (minimum age 18) with knowledge of a working kitchen ▶ 1 *boating director* (minimum age 21) with WSI and canoe certifications; small craft training preferred; knowledge of canoes, kayaks, and sailboats ▶ 1–2 *business administrators* (minimum age 21) with camp experience required ▶ 1 *food services supervisor* (minimum age 21) with experience in quantity cooking required; (must know budgeting, buying, and price per plate for large groups) ▶ 1–2 *health supervisors/nurses* (minimum age 21) with RN license; possibility of working part-time within a season ▶ 2–4 *kitchen aides* (minimum age 16) ▶ 1–2 *program managers* (minimum age 21) with CPR, first aid and, camp employment experience required ▶ 1 *riding instructor* (minimum age 21) with CHA/AAHS certification or equivalent experience in the field ▶ 10–16 *unit counselors* (minimum age 18) with camp experience required and first aid/CPR certification a plus at $1200 per season ▶ 4–6 *unit leaders* (minimum age 21) with CPR, first aid, WSI (preferred) and 2-3 years camp experience ▶ 1 *waterfront assistant* (minimum age 18) with lifeguard, CPR, and first aid certification ▶ 1 *waterfront director* (minimum age 21) with WSI, CPR, first aid, and lifeguard certification. Applicants must submit formal organization application, resume, three personal references, three letters of recommendation. International applicants accepted; must apply through a recognized agency. An in-person interview is recommended, but a telephone interview is acceptable.

Benefits and Preemployment Training Free housing, free meals, health insurance, on-the-job training, travel reimbursement, and college intern/credit. Preemployment training is required and includes accident prevention and safety, first aid, CPR, interpersonal skills, leadership skills, blood-borne pattogens, and life-saving recertification.

Contact Ms. Lois C. Klimsey, Director of Camps, Hidden Valley Camp, 1171 Highway 28, North Branch, New Jersey 08876. Telephone: 908-725-1226. Fax: 908-725-4933. E-mail: rhgsc@ mail.eclipse.net. Application deadline: continuous.

HILL SCHOOL SUMMER PROGRAM
717 EAST HIGH STREET
POTTSTOWN, PENNSYLVANIA 19464

General Information Residential coed academic enrichment camp serving up to 125 students for a four-week intensive studies program. Established in 1851. 200-acre facility located 35 miles from Philadelphia. Features: 12 tennis courts; new 12 million dollar academic center; 7 million dollar arts center; renovated library; renovated science building.

Profile of Summer Employees Total number: 30; typical ages: 19–25. 50% men; 50% women; 10% minorities; 80% college students; 10% non-U.S. citizens.

Employment Information Openings are from June 25 to July 21. Jobs available: ▶ 18 *interns* must be a junior or senior in college at $1600–$1700 per season. Applicants must submit formal organization application, cover letter, resume, academic transcripts, personal reference, letter of recommendation. International applicants accepted; must obtain own visa, obtain own working papers. A telephone interview is required.

Benefits and Preemployment Training Free housing, free meals, and on-the-job training. Preemployment training is required and includes accident prevention and safety, CPR, interpersonal skills, leadership skills, lifeguard training.

Contact Burt Merriam, Director of Summer Program, Hill School Summer Program, 717 East High Street, Pottstown, Pennsylvania 19464. Telephone: 610-326-1000. Fax: 610-326-3647. E-mail: summer@thehill.org. World Wide Web: http://www.thehill.org/. Application deadline: continuous.

THE INSTITUTE FOR THE ACADEMIC ADVANCEMENT OF YOUTH/THE JOHNS HOPKINS UNIVERSITY–DICKINSON COLLEGE

See The Institute for the Academic Advancement of Youth/ The Johns Hopkins University on page 135 for complete description.

THE INSTITUTE FOR THE ACADEMIC ADVANCEMENT OF YOUTH/THE JOHNS HOPKINS UNIVERSITY–FRANKLIN AND MARSHALL COLLEGE

See The Institute for the Academic Advancement of Youth/ The Johns Hopkins University on page 135 for complete description.

THE INSTITUTE FOR THE ACADEMIC ADVANCEMENT OF YOUTH/THE JOHNS HOPKINS UNIVERSITY–MORAVIAN COLLEGE

See The Institute for the Academic Advancement of Youth/ The Johns Hopkins University on page 135 for complete description.

JULIAN KRINSKY SCHOOL OF TENNIS, GOLF, AND SQUASH CAMP
HAVERFORD COLLEGE
HAVERFORD, PENNSYLVANIA 19041

General Information Overnight camp with concentration in tennis, golf, or squash serving 100–150 overnight and 20–40 day campers per week. Established in 1979. 250-acre facility located 20 miles from Philadelphia. Features: university dormitories; 28 tennis courts; 6 squash courts; use of 9 golf courses; beautiful historic suburban campus; outdoor and indoor athletic facilities.

Profile of Summer Employees Total number: 250; typical ages: 20–30. 50% men; 50% women; 20% minorities; 70% college students; 2% retirees; 15% non-U.S. citizens; 10% local applicants. Nonsmokers required.

Employment Information Openings are from June 11 to August 13. Jobs available: ▶ 2–6 *computer counselors* (minimum age 20) with strong technical skills in HTML and Java Script and teaching experience desirable at $2000–$2500 per season ▶ 2–20 *golf counselors* (minimum age 20) with low handicap and coaching experience required at $225–$325 per week ▶ 15–30 *resident counselors* (minimum age 20) with desire to work with children at $1600–$2000 per season ▶ 2–3 *squash counselors* (minimum age 20) with coaching experience required at $8–$12 per hour ▶ 2–4 *swimming instructors* (minimum age 20) with WSI certification, lifeguard and swimming instructor experience required at $1600–$2000 per season ▶ 2–20 *tennis counselors* (minimum age 20) with coaching experience required at $8–$12 per hour. Applicants must submit formal organization application, cover letter, resume, two letters of recommendation. International applicants accepted; must obtain own visa, apply through a recognized agency. An in-person interview is recommended, but a telephone interview is acceptable.

Benefits and Preemployment Training Free housing, free meals, and on-the-job training. Preemployment training is required and includes accident prevention and safety, interpersonal skills, leadership skills.

Contact Alex Bratty, Program Coordinator, Julian Krinsky School of Tennis, Golf, and Squash Camp, PO Box 333, Haverford, Pennsylvania 19041. Telephone: 610-265-9401. Fax: 610-265-3678. E-mail: alex@jkst.com. World Wide Web: http://www.jkst.com. Application deadline: continuous.

JULIAN KRINSKY SUMMER ENRICHMENT CAMP
HAVERFORD COLLEGE
HAVERFORD, PENNSYLVANIA 19041

General Information Residential enrichment camp serving 125 overnight and 60 day campers in two sessions over an eight-week season. Established in 1989. 250-acre facility located 20 miles from Philadelphia. Features: university dormitories; beautiful historic suburban campus; spectacular learning environment; computer center; wonderful athletic facilities; drama, business, music, and cooking schools.

Profile of Summer Employees Total number: 80; typical ages: 20–30. 50% men; 50% women; 20% minorities; 70% college students; 2% retirees; 15% non-U.S. citizens; 10% local applicants. Nonsmokers required.

Employment Information Openings are from June 11 to August 13. Jobs available: ▶ 5–10 *computer counselors/teachers* (minimum age 20) with strong technical skills in HTML and Java Script and teaching experience required at $25–$30 per hour ▶ 20–30 *part-time teachers* (minimum age 20) with desire to work with children; teaching experience required at $20–$25 per hour ▶ 18–30 *resident counselors* (minimum age 20) with desire to work with children, experience preferred at $1600–$2000 per season. Applicants must submit formal organization application, cover letter, resume, two letters of recommendation. International applicants accepted; must obtain own visa, apply through a recognized agency. An in-person interview is recommended, but a telephone interview is acceptable.

Benefits and Preemployment Training Free housing, free meals, and on-the-job training. Preemployment training is required and includes accident prevention and safety, interpersonal skills, leadership skills.

Contact Alex Bratty, Program Coordinator, Julian Krinsky Summer Enrichment Camp, PO Box 333, Haverford, Pennsylvania 19041. Telephone: 610-265-9401. Fax: 610-265-3678. E-mail: alex@jkst.com. World Wide Web: http://www.jkst.com. Application deadline: continuous.

JUMONVILLE
887 JUMONVILLE ROAD
HOPWOOD, PENNSYLVANIA 15445

General Information Residential Christian camp serving 250–300 persons of all age levels per week. Established in 1941. 281-acre facility located 50 miles from Pittsburgh. Features: 60-foot tall steel cross; high- and low-elements ropes course; adventure center; campuslike setting; mountain location; excellent sports facilities.

Profile of Summer Employees Total number: 45; typical ages: 16–25. 50% men; 50% women; 5% minorities; 10% high school students; 90% college students; 5% non-U.S. citizens; 10% local applicants. Nonsmokers required.

Employment Information Openings are from May 15 to August 25. Jobs available: ▶ 2 *adventure staff members* at $150 per week ▶ 1 *assistant program director and arts and crafts instructor* at $135 per week ▶ 2–3 *audio/visual specialists and intern staff* at $135 per week ▶ 1 *business manager/truck driver* at $135 per week ▶ 1 *cookout staff member* at $135 per week ▶ 5 *counselors* at $150 per week ▶ 2 *dining room staff members* at $135 per week ▶ 4 *dishroom staff members* at $135 per week ▶ 1 *health-care staff member* with paramedic, LPN, or RN license at $135 per week ▶ 1 *kitchen helper* at $135 per week ▶ 2 *lifeguards* with certification at $135 per week ▶ 2 *maintenance/housekeeping helpers* at $135 per week ▶ 1 *multipurpose floater* at $135 per week ▶ 1 *office assistant/business manager* at $135 per week ▶ 1 *ropes course supervisor* at $135 per week ▶ 3 *snack shop workers* at $135 per week. Applicants must submit formal organization application, three personal references. International applicants accepted; must apply through a recognized agency. An in-person interview is required.

Benefits and Preemployment Training Free housing, free meals, and on-the-job training. Preemployment training is required and includes accident prevention and safety, first aid, CPR, interpersonal skills, leadership skills.

Contact Larry Beatty, President, Jumonville, 887 Jumonville Road, Hopwood, Pennsylvania 15445. Telephone: 724-439-4912. Fax: 724-439-1415. E-mail: lrbeatty@aol.com. World Wide Web: http://www.jumonville.org. Application deadline: March 15.

KENNYWOOD PARK
4800 KENNYWOOD BOULEVARD
WEST MIFFLIN, PENNSYLVANIA 15122

General Information Amusement park servicing more than 1 million guests per season. Established in 1898. 40-acre facility located 7 miles from Pittsburgh. Features: roller coasters; cafe; lagoon; dark rides; pavilions; food concessions.

Profile of Summer Employees Total number: 1,500–1,600; typical ages: 16–26. 47% men; 53% women; 18% minorities; 20% high school students; 70% college students; 10% retirees; 100% local applicants.

Employment Information Openings are from April 15 to September 6. Jobs available: ▶ 1500 *team members (rides, games, and refreshments)* (minimum age 15) at $5 per hour. Applicants must submit a formal organization application, personal reference. An in-person interview is required.

Benefits and Preemployment Training Formal training and on-the-job training. Preemployment training is required and includes accident prevention and safety, interpersonal skills.

Contact Joe Barron, Human Resources Director, Kennywood Park, 4800 Kennywood Boulevard, West Mifflin, Pennsylvania 15122. Telephone: 412-461-0500 Ext. 106. Fax: 412-464-0719. Application deadline: continuous.

LONGACRE EXPEDITIONS
RD 3, BOX 106
NEWPORT, PENNSYLVANIA 17074

General Information Adventure travel program in Pennsylvania for teenagers, emphasizing group living skills and physical challenges. Using base camp as a staging area, 2–3 staffers and 10–16 campers participate in novice and intermediate expeditions on which they engage in human-powered sports. Established in 1981. 35-acre facility located 35 miles from Harrisburg. Features: ropes course; climbing wall; wooded setting.

Profile of Summer Employees Total number: 30; typical ages: 21–32. 50% men; 50% women; 10% minorities; 40% college students; 10% local applicants. Nonsmokers required.

Employment Information Openings are from June 15 to August 15. Jobs available: ▶ 24 *assistant trip leaders* (minimum age 21) with good driving record, wilderness first aid, and CPR at $252–$300 per week ▶ 1 *caving instructor* (minimum age 21) with good driving record, wilderness first aid, and CPR at $300–$450 per week ▶ 1 *equipment manager* (minimum age 21) with good driving record, wilderness first aid, and CPR at $180–$240 per week ▶ 2 *rock climbing instructors* (minimum age 21) with wilderness first aid and CPR at $300–$450 per week ▶ 8 *support and logistics staff members* (minimum age 21) with good driving record, wilderness first aid, and CPR at $180–$240 per week. Applicants must submit a formal organization application, three personal references. International applicants accepted; must obtain own visa, obtain own working papers. An in-person interview is recommended, but a telephone interview is acceptable.

Benefits and Preemployment Training Free housing, free meals, on-the-job training, and pro-deal purchase program. Preemployment training is required and includes accident prevention and safety, interpersonal skills, leadership skills.

Contact Meredith Schuler, Director, Longacre Expeditions, RD 3, Box 106, Newport, Pennsylvania 17074. Telephone: 717-567-6790. Fax: 717-567-3955. E-mail: longacre@longacreexpeditions.com. World Wide Web: http://www.longacreexpeditions.com. Application deadline: continuous.

ONEKA
TAFTON, PENNSYLVANIA 18464

General Information Residential girls camp serving 120 campers in 3½- and 7-week sessions. Established in 1908. 7-acre facility located 30 miles from Scranton. Features: freshwater lake; wooded setting; 3 tennis courts.

Profile of Summer Employees Total number: 35; typical ages: 18–55. 5% men; 95% women; 5% high school students; 95% college students; 30% non-U.S. citizens; 15% local applicants. Nonsmokers preferred.

Employment Information Openings are from June 24 to August 25. Jobs available: ▶ 1 *aquatic director* (minimum age 21) with WSI, LGT, CPR and first aid; experience preferred at $1600–$2000 per season ▶ 1 *archery instructor* (minimum age 19) with good personal shooting skills (employee may be sent for further training) at $1000–$1400 per season ▶ 2 *arts and crafts instructors* (minimum age 19) with experience at $1000–$1400 per season ▶ 1 *assistant program director* (minimum age 21) with two years of camp experience at $1500–$2000 per season ▶ 1 *campcraft instructor* (minimum age 19) with experience in the field at $1000–$1400 per season ▶ 3 *canoeing/kayaking/boating/sailing instructors* (minimum age 19) with LT, CPR, first aid, and WSI certification (preferred) and experience in the field at $1000–$1500 per season ▶ 1 *drama instructor* (minimum age 21) with experience in directing and set design at $1400–$1800 per season ▶ 3 *field sports/hockey/soccer/softball instructors* (minimum age 19) with experience in the field at $1000–$1400 per season ▶ 2 *maintenance helpers* (minimum age 16) at $600–$750 per season ▶ 1 *music instructor* (minimum age 19) with piano-playing ability and knowledge of show tunes at $1000–$1400 per season ▶ 1 *nurse* with RN license at $1800–$2500 per season ▶ 1 *program director* (minimum age 25) with three years of camp experience and good management and people skills preferred at $1800–$2500 per season ▶ 5 *swimming instructors/lifeguards* (minimum age 19) with LT, CPR, first aid, WSI certification, and experience at $1000–$1500 per season ▶ 2 *tennis instructors* (minimum age 19) with experience at $1000–$1400 per season ▶ 1 *volleyball instructor* (minimum age 19) with experience at $1000–$1400 per season. Applicants must submit formal organization application, resume, three personal references. International applicants accepted; must apply through a recognized agency. An in-person interview is recommended, but a telephone interview is acceptable.

Benefits and Preemployment Training Free housing, free meals, on-the-job training, and opportunity to attend seminars/workshops. Preemployment training is required and includes accident prevention and safety, interpersonal skills, leadership skills.

Contact Dale H. Dohner, Camp Director, ONEKA, 10 Oakford Road, Wayne, Pennsylvania 19087. Telephone: 610-687-6260. Fax: 610-687-6260. World Wide Web: http://www.oneka.com. Application deadline: continuous.

PENNSYLVANIA DEPARTMENT OF TRANSPORTATION
BUREAU OF PERSONNEL, 555 WALNUT STREET, 9TH FLOOR, FORUM PLACE
HARRISBURG, PENNSYLVANIA 17101-1900

General Information State government agency responsible for the planning, design, construction, and maintenance of Pennsylvania's transportation systems. Established in 1903. Features: walking distance to Capitol; 3 miles to Governor's Mansion; 12 miles to Hersey Park; walking distance to state library; walking distance to Citi Island where basketball games are played and other attractions are held.

Profile of Summer Employees 10% minorities; 85% college students.

Employment Information Openings are from May 1 to September 15. Jobs available: ▶ *engineering/scientific/technical interns* should be currently enrolled as a college student and majoring in engineering, math, science, or architecture at $8.06 per hour ▶ *government service interns* should be currently enrolled as a college student in any major at $8.06 per hour ▶ *highway maintenance workers* at $8.06 per hour ▶ *transportation/construction inspectors* with 2 years of construction inspection experience at $8 per hour. Applicants must submit personal data sheet with resume attached. International applicants accepted; must obtain own visa. An in-person interview is recommended, but a telephone interview is acceptable.

Benefits and Preemployment Training On-the-job training and travel reimbursement.

Contact Diana Hershey, College Relations Coordinator, Pennsylvania Department of Transportation, 555 Walnut Street, 9th Floor/ Forum Place, Harrisburg, Pennsylvania 17101-1900. Telephone: 717-783-2680. World Wide Web: http://www.dot.state.pa.us. Application deadline: April 15.

SALVATION ARMY OF LOWER BUCKS
215 APPLETREE DRIVE
LEVITTOWN, PENNSYLVANIA 19055

General Information Community-based center that offers a full range of service and multi-generational programs. Established in 1865. 8-acre facility located 7 miles from Philadelphia. Features: air-conditioned facility; full-size gym; computer room; craft room; ballfield; church connected to building.

Profile of Summer Employees Total number: 10; typical ages: 18–25. 20% men; 80% women; 10% minorities; 10% high school students; 80% college students; 10% retirees; 90% local applicants. Nonsmokers preferred.

Employment Information Openings are from June 12 to August 30. Jobs available: ▶ 6–8 *day care counselors* (minimum age 17) with experience caring for children (babysitting, day care, or similar) at $6–$7 per hour ▶ 6–10 *summer camp counselors* (minimum age 18) with any type of childcare background and first aid/CPR (training provided) at $6–$7 per hour. Applicants must submit formal organization application, cover letter, resume, academic transcripts, two personal references, two letters of recommendation. International applicants accepted; must apply through a recognized agency. An in-person interview is required.

Benefits and Preemployment Training Free meals. Preemployment training is required and includes accident prevention and safety, first aid, CPR, interpersonal skills, leadership skills.

Contact Maureen C. Carson, Community Programs Coordinator, Salvation Army of Lower Bucks, Appletree Drive and Autumn Lane, Levittown, Pennsylvania 19055. Telephone: 215-945-0718. Fax: 215-945-0607. Application deadline: January 20.

SHAVER'S CREEK ENVIRONMENTAL CENTER, PENNSYLVANIA STATE UNIVERSITY
508A KELLER BUILDING
UNIVERSITY PARK, PENNSYLVANIA 16802

General Information Center providing exemplary day and residential environmental education and outdoor adventure programming. Established in 1976. 7,000-acre facility located 13 miles from State College. Features: 20 birds of prey; team buliding low element course; 25 miles of hiking trails; herb and flower gardens; 72-acre lake; hands-on exhibits.

Profile of Summer Employees Total number: 15; typical ages: 20–30. 50% men; 50% women; 10% minorities; 90% college students; 25% non-U.S. citizens; 5% local applicants. Nonsmokers preferred.

Employment Information Openings are from June 7 to August 27. Year-round positions also offered. Jobs available: ▶ 4–6 *environmental education interns* with first aid and CPR certification (preferred) at $125 per week. Applicants must submit formal organization application, resume, 3 letters of recommendation (international applicants only). International applicants accepted; must apply through a recognized agency. A telephone interview is required.

Benefits and Preemployment Training Free housing, formal training, on-the-job training, and opportunity to attend seminars/workshops.

Contact Doug Wentzel, Intern Coordinator, Shaver's Creek Environmental Center, Pennsylvania State University, 508A Keller Building, University Park, Pennsylvania 16802. Telephone: 814-863-2000. Fax: 814-865-2706. E-mail: shaverscreek@cde.psu.edu. World Wide Web: http://www.outreach.psu.edu/shaverscreek/. Application deadline: March 1.

THE SOUTHWESTERN COMPANY, PENNSYLVANIA
See The Southwestern Company, Tennessee on page 284 for complete description.

SPORTS AND ARTS CENTER AT ISLAND LAKE
ISLAND LAKE ROAD
STARRUCCA, PENNSYLVANIA 18462

General Information Residential camp serving 500 campers ages 7–17, with emphasis on individualized programming and a well-rounded program in all sports and performing and visual arts. 525-acre facility located 150 miles from New York, New York. Features: 2 freshwater lakes; 13 tennis courts; 17,000-square foot gym; 800-seat theater; full athletic facilities; indoor flying trapeze.

Profile of Summer Employees Total number: 250; typical age: 18. 50% men; 50% women; 10% minorities; 85% college students; 1% retirees; 20% non-U.S. citizens; 1% local applicants. Nonsmokers required.

Employment Information Openings are from June 19 to August 18. Jobs available: ▶ *department heads* with experience in the field at $2500–$8000 per season ▶ *doctors* at $700–$1000 per week ▶ 8 *group leaders* (minimum age 23) with strong leadership skills and experience with children at $2500 per season ▶ *head counselors* with experience at $3500–$6000 per season ▶ *nurses* with experience at $200–$500 per week ▶ *specialists (in all areas)* with experience in the field at $1300–$1700 per season ▶ *swimming instructors* with WSI certification at $1300–$1700 per season. Applicants must submit formal organization application, two letters of recommendation. International applicants accepted; must apply through a recognized agency. An in-person interview is recommended, but a telephone interview is acceptable.

Benefits and Preemployment Training Free housing, free meals, formal training, on-the-job training, and travel reimbursement. Preemployment training is required and includes accident prevention and safety, interpersonal skills, leadership skills, child-care skills.

Contact Matt or Mike Stoltz, Directors, Sports and Arts Center at Island Lake, PO Box 800, Pomona, New York 10970. Telephone: 914-354-5517. Fax: 914-362-3039. E-mail: islndlake@aol.com. World Wide Web: http://www.islandlake.com. Application deadline: continuous.

STIVERS TEMPORARY PERSONNEL–PENNSYLVANIA
See Stivers Temporary Personnel–Illinois on page 103 for complete description.

STREAMSIDE CAMP AND CONFERENCE CENTER
RURAL ROUTE 3, BOX 3307
STROUDSBURG, PENNSYLVANIA 18360

General Information Residential Christian camp with a focus on providing a quality camping experience for inner-city children, youth, and families. Established in 1942. 137-acre facility located 90 miles from Philadelphia. Features: 2 ponds; pool; wooded setting; dormitory cabins.

Profile of Summer Employees Total number: 45; typical ages: 15–25. 50% men; 50% women; 15% minorities; 25% high school students; 60% college students; 5% retirees; 10% non-U.S. citizens; 60% local applicants. Nonsmokers required.

Employment Information Openings are from June 14 to August 28. Year-round positions also offered. Jobs available: ▶ 1–2 *program specialists* (minimum age 18) with ability to teach and relate a specific area of expertise to the Christian daily life at $120–$250 per week ▶ 20–26 *cabin counselors* (minimum age 18) at $100–$250 per week ▶ 2–4 *dining room workers* (minimum age 15) at $60–$120 per week ▶ 4–6 *kitchen aides* (minimum age 15) with desire to learn at $60–$120 per week ▶ 1–2 *lifeguards* (minimum age 16) with lifeguard certification at $120–$250 per week ▶ 2–4 *maintenance team workers* (minimum age 15) at $60–$120 per week ▶ 1–2 *water safety instructors* (minimum age 18) with WSI certification at $120–$250 per week. Applicants must submit formal organization application, three personal references. International applicants accepted; must apply through a recognized agency. A telephone interview is required.

Benefits and Preemployment Training Free housing, free meals, formal training, possible full-time employment, health insurance, on-the-job training, opportunity to attend seminars/workshops, travel reimbursement, and tuition assistance. Preemployment training is required and includes accident prevention and safety, first aid, CPR, interpersonal skills, leadership skills, lifeguard training.

Contact Mr. Dale L. Schoenwald, Streamside Program Director, Streamside Camp and Conference Center, RR #3, Box 3307, Stroudsburg, Pennsylvania 18360. Telephone: 570-629-1902. Fax: 570-629-9650. E-mail: streamsidecamp@juno.com. World Wide Web: http://www.streamside.org. Application deadline: continuous.

STUDENT CONSERVATION ASSOCIATION (SCA), PENNSYLVANIA
See Student Conservation Association (SCA), New Hampshire on page 193 for complete description.

SWARTHMORE TENNIS CAMP
500 COLLEGE AVENUE
SWARTHMORE, PENNSYLVANIA 19081

General Information Operates both a junior and adult camp from mid-June to mid-August, resident and day campers. 5 hours daily. Adults 3-day, 5-day, and weekend programs. Juniors 9–18, coed weekly and multiweek sessions. Established in 1981. 325-acre facility located 12 miles from Philadelphia. Features: wooded campus; tennis courts; swimming pool.

Profile of Summer Employees Total number: 12–14; typical ages: 19–40. 80% men; 20% women; 70% college students; 10% non-U.S. citizens. Nonsmokers required.

Employment Information Openings are from June 17 to August 9. Jobs available: ▶ 10 *tennis* *instructors* (minimum age 19) with collegiate tennis experience at $225–$250 per week. Applicants must submit a formal organization application. International applicants accepted; must obtain own visa.

Benefits and Preemployment Training Free housing and free meals. Preemployment training is required and includes interpersonal skills, leadership skills.

Contact Lois Broderick, President, Swarthmore Tennis Camp, 444 East 82nd Street, Suite 31D, New York, New York 10028. Telephone: 212-879-0225. Fax: 212-452-0816. E-mail: greatennis@ aol.com. Application deadline: continuous.

WALDAMEER PARK, INC.
220 PENINSULA DRIVE
ERIE, PENNSYLVANIA 16505

General Information Amusement park and water park with rides, water slides, midway games, arcade, gift shops, refreshment stands, picnic/catering facilities and entertainment. Established in 1896. 42-acre facility located 5 miles from Erie. Features: 17 major rides; 11 major water slides; kiddie rides and slides; midway games; food and gift shops; picnic shelters.

Profile of Summer Employees Total number: 400; typical ages: 14–22. 50% men; 50% women; 7% minorities; 70% high school students; 30% college students; 1% retirees; 1% non-U.S. citizens; 95% local applicants. Nonsmokers preferred.

Employment Information Openings are from May 1 to September 7. Jobs available: ▶ 15 *cashiers* (minimum age 18) ▶ 30 *food service personnel* (minimum age 16) ▶ 30 *games attendants* (minimum age 16) ▶ 30–40 *lifeguards* (minimum age 16) with first aid, CPR, and lifeguard certification ▶ 20 *picnic staff* (minimum age 18) ▶ 30–40 *ride operators* (minimum age 18). Applicants must submit a formal organization application, two personal references. International applicants accepted; must obtain own visa, obtain own working papers. An in-person interview is required.

Benefits and Preemployment Training Meals at a cost, on-the-job training, and use of amusement park facility. Preemployment training is required.

Contact Steve Gorman, General Manager, Waldameer Park, Inc., PO Box 8308, Erie, Pennsylvania 16505. Telephone: 814-838-3591. Fax: 814-835-7435. E-mail: info@waldameer.com. World Wide Web: http://www.waldameer.com. Application deadline: continuous.

YMCA CAMP FITCH
NORTH SPRINGFIELD, PENNSYLVANIA 16430

General Information Traditional residential camp serving 210 campers; special population camp serving 30–70 campers with special needs; specialty camps such as computer, running, and swimming camps serving 30 campers. Established in 1914. 450-acre facility located 15 miles from Erie. Features: location on Lake Erie; 4-acre inland lake; swimming pool; 450 wooded acres and horse trails; soccer and ball fields; many activity areas.

Profile of Summer Employees Total number: 120; typical ages: 17–60. 50% men; 50% women; 15% minorities; 35% high school students; 65% college students; 10% non-U.S. citizens; 60% local applicants. Nonsmokers preferred.

Employment Information Openings are from June 7 to August 31. Jobs available: ▶ *kitchen steward* (minimum age 19) with food service/cleaning experience at $150–$175 per week ▶ *special population counselor* (minimum age 18) with camp counselor experience or experience with special populations at $110–$150 per week ▶ *summer camp counselors* (minimum age 18) at $100–$130 per week. Applicants must submit formal organization application, cover letter, three personal references. International applicants accepted; must obtain own visa, obtain own working papers, apply through a recognized agency. An in-person interview is recommended, but a telephone interview is acceptable.

Benefits and Preemployment Training Free housing, free meals, formal training, on-the-job training, and opportunity to attend seminars/workshops. Preemployment training is required and includes accident prevention and safety, first aid, CPR, interpersonal skills, leadership skills.

Contact Bill Lyder, Executive Camp Director, YMCA Camp Fitch, 17 North Champion Street,

Youngstown, Ohio 44501-1287. Telephone: 330-744-8411. Fax: 330-744-8416. E-mail: campfitch@hotmail.com. Application deadline: continuous.

RHODE ISLAND

THE SOUTHWESTERN COMPANY, RHODE ISLAND
See The Southwestern Company, Tennessee on page 284 for complete description.

STUDENT CONSERVATION ASSOCIATION (SCA), RHODE ISLAND
See Student Conservation Association (SCA), New Hampshire on page 193 for complete description.

UNIVERSITY OF RHODE ISLAND SUMMER PROGRAMS
W. ALTON JONES CAMPUS, 401 VICTORY HIGHWAY
WEST GREENWICH, RHODE ISLAND 02817-2158

General Information Residential facility serving 100 campers in seven 1-week sessions with nature awareness and conservation programs; expedition program for 40 teens in eight 1-week sessions includes backpacking, kayaking, canoeing, and rock-climbing activities. Farm and ecology day camp for ages 5–11 utilizes historic working farm and nature preserve. Established in 1962. 2,300-acre facility located 30 miles from Providence. Features: 75-acre lake; 2,300-acre property; 40,000 acres of state forests; 20 miles of hiking trails; low ropes challenge course.

Profile of Summer Employees Total number: 50; typical ages: 14–29. 50% men; 50% women; 5% minorities; 10% high school students; 90% college students; 15% non-U.S. citizens; 50% local applicants. Nonsmokers preferred.

Employment Information Openings are from June 15 to August 22. Year-round positions also offered. Jobs available: ► 1 *camp EMT or nurse assistant* (minimum age 20) with CPR/first aid certification; EMT preferred at $200–$250 per week ► 10 *day camp teachers* (minimum age 18) with CPR/first aid certification and experience working with children at $190–$220 per week ► 10–12 *field teachers/naturalists* (minimum age 21) with CPR/first aid certification; must be available September through June for the academic year at $175–$200 per week ► 2 *lifeguards* (minimum age 18) with driver's license, first aid, CPR, and lifeguard certification at $6.50–$8 per hour ► 18 *naturalists/counselors* (minimum age 18) with CPR/first aid certification and experience working with children at $150–$180 per week ► 10 *teen expedition leaders* (minimum age 21) with driver's license, CPR, first aid, and lifeguard certification; should have experience working with teens and/or outdoor skills at $185–$200 per week. Applicants must submit a formal organization application, cover letter, resume, three personal references, two letters of recommendation. International applicants accepted; must obtain own visa. A telephone interview is required.

Benefits and Preemployment Training Free housing, free meals, formal training, and on-the-job training. Preemployment training is required and includes accident prevention and safety, first aid, CPR, interpersonal skills, leadership skills.

Contact John Jacques, Manager, Environmental Education Center, University of Rhode Island Summer Programs, 401 Victory Highway, West Greenwich, Rhode Island 02817-2158. Telephone: 401-397-3304 Ext. 6043. Fax: 401-397-3293. E-mail: urieec@etal.uri.edu. World Wide Web: http://www.uri.edu/ajc. Application deadline: continuous.

SOUTH CAROLINA

ACE COMPUTER CAMP–SOUTH CAROLINA
See ACE Computer Camp–Washington on page 307 for complete description.

BROADWAY AT THE BEACH
921 NORTH KINGS HIGHWAY
MYRTLE BEACH, SOUTH CAROLINA 29577
General Information Amusement, retail, shopping, and entertainment complex. Established in 1994. Located 100 miles from Columbia.

Profile of Summer Employees Total number: 75; typical age: 16. 50% men; 50% women; 75% high school students; 25% college students; 90% local applicants.

Employment Information Openings are from April to October. Spring break positions also offered. Jobs available: ▶ *cashiers* (minimum age 16) at $6.40–$6.95 per hour ▶ *paddleboat operators* (minimum age 16) at $6.40–$6.95 per hour ▶ *ride attendants* (minimum age 16) with ability to withstand sun at $6.40–$6.95 per hour. Applicants must submit formal organization application. International applicants accepted; must obtain own visa, obtain own working papers, apply through a recognized agency. An in-person interview is required.

Benefits and Preemployment Training Housing at a cost, meals at a cost, formal training, possible full-time employment, health insurance, on-the-job training, and tuition assistance. Preemployment training is required.

Contact Sandy Wright, Human Resource Associate, Broadway at the Beach. Telephone: 843-626-6623. Fax: 843-626-8461. E-mail: sandy.wright@burroughs-chapin.com. World Wide Web: http://www.broadwayatthebeach.com. Application deadline: continuous.

CAMP CHATUGA
291 CAMP CHATUGA ROAD
MOUNTAIN REST, SOUTH CAROLINA 29664
General Information Residential coeducational camp serving 155 campers in the heart of Sumter National Forest in the Blue Ridge Mountain foothills. Established in 1956. 60-acre facility located near Atlanta, Georgia. Features: private lake; surrounded by national forest; football field; screened wood cabins; recreation hall; lodge.

Profile of Summer Employees Total number: 40–50; typical ages: 19–50. 50% men; 50% women; 10% minorities; 75% college students; 5% retirees; 20% non-U.S. citizens; 40% local applicants. Nonsmokers required.

Employment Information Openings are from June 4 to August 9. Jobs available: ▶ 1 *Western horseback riding director* (minimum age 21) with horse experience at $1000–$1500 per season ▶ 1–4 *camp "moms"* at $150 to $225 per week and tuition discounts for children ▶ 25 *counselors* (minimum age 19) at $1000–$1500 per season ▶ 1 *dining hall supervisor* (minimum age 21) with supervisory skills and interest in food service at $1100–$1500 per season ▶ 1–4 *health supervisors* (minimum age 21) with CPR/first aid certification, RN, BSN, MD, pediatric experience preferred at $200 per week and tuition discounts for children ▶ 1 *nanny* (minimum age 18) at $1000–$1500 per season ▶ 1 *waterfront director* (minimum age 21) with lifeguard certification required, WSI preferred at $875–$1200 per season. Applicants must submit formal organization application, three personal references. International applicants accepted; must obtain own visa, apply through a recognized agency. A telephone interview is required.

Benefits and Preemployment Training Free housing, free meals, formal training, on-the-job training, opportunity to attend seminars/workshops, and transportation to camp from airport/staff training certifications. Preemployment training is required and includes accident prevention and safety, first aid, CPR, interpersonal skills, leadership skills.

Contact Kelly Moxley, Director/Personnel, Camp Chatuga, 291 Camp Chatuga Road, Mountain Rest, South Carolina 29664. Telephone: 864-638-3728. Fax: 864-638-0898. E-mail: mail@ campchatuga.com. World Wide Web: http://www.campchatuga.com. Application deadline: continuous.

MYRTLE BEACH PAVILION
921 NORTH KINGS HIGHWAY
MYRTLE BEACH, SOUTH CAROLINA 29577

General Information Amusement park with more than forty rides and twenty concession stands. 12-acre facility located 100 miles from Columbia/Charleston. Features: oceanfront; 2 roller coasters; 2 large water rides.

Profile of Summer Employees Total number: 650. 50% men; 50% women; 60% minorities; 70% high school students; 25% college students; 5% retirees; 10% non-U.S. citizens; 75% local applicants.

Employment Information Openings are from February to October. Spring break positions also offered. Jobs available: ▶ *Attic staff (doorman and concessions)* (minimum age 16) at $6.40–$6.95 per hour ▶ *admissions staff* (minimum age 16) with good interpersonal skills, computer ability, and cashier experience at $6.40–$6.95 per hour ▶ *arcade attendants* (minimum age 16) with good interpersonal skills at $6.40–$6.95 per hour ▶ *food service staff (cooks and cashiers)* (minimum age 14) with good interpersonal skills at $6.40–$6.95 per hour ▶ *games attendants* (minimum age 14) with good interpersonal skills at $6.40–$6.95 per hour ▶ *general service staff (custodians)* (minimum age 14) at $6.40–$6.95 per hour ▶ *ride operators* (minimum age 16) with good interpersonal skills at $6.40–$6.95 per hour. Applicants must submit formal organization application. International applicants accepted; must obtain own visa, obtain own working papers, apply through a recognized agency. An in-person interview is required.

Benefits and Preemployment Training Housing at a cost, meals at a cost, formal training, possible full-time employment, health insurance, on-the-job training, and tuition assistance. Preemployment training is required.

Contact Carolyn Newell, Human Resources Associate, Myrtle Beach Pavilion, 921 North Kings Highway, Myrtle Beach, South Carolina 29577. Telephone: 843-626-6623. Fax: 843-626-8461. E-mail: carolyn.newell@burroughs-chapin.com. World Wide Web: http://www.mbpavilion.com. Application deadline: continuous.

MYRTLE WAVES WATER PARK
921 NORTH KINGS HIGHWAY
MYRTLE BEACH, SOUTH CAROLINA 29577

General Information Waterpark with 30 rides including children's area. Established in 1984. 20-acre facility located 100 miles from Columbia. Features: resort area.

Profile of Summer Employees Total number: 150; typical age: 14. 50% men; 50% women; 75% high school students; 90% local applicants.

Employment Information Openings are from April to September. Spring break positions also offered. Jobs available: ▶ *cashiers-retail and admissions* at $6.40–$6.95 per hour ▶ *custodial staff* (minimum age 16) at $6.40–$6.95 per hour ▶ *food service-cooks-cashiers* at $6.40–$6.95 per hour ▶ *lifeguards* (minimum age 15) with ability to withstand sun at $6.55–$7.35 per hour ▶ *slide operators* (minimum age 14) with ability to withstand sun at $6.40–$6.95 per hour. Applicants must submit formal organization application. International applicants accepted; must obtain own visa, obtain own working papers, apply through a recognized agency. An in-person interview is required.

Benefits sand Preemployment Training Housing at a cost, meals at a cost, formal training, possible full-time employment, health insurance, on-the-job training, and tuition assistance. Preemployment training is required.

Contact Wanda Housand, Human Resources Associate, Myrtle Waves Water Park, 921 North Kings Highway, Myrtle Beach, South Carolina 29577. Telephone: 843-626-6623. Fax: 843-626-8461. E-mail: wanda.housand@burroughs-chapin.com. World Wide Web: http://www.myrtlewaves.com. Application deadline: continuous.

NASCAR SPEEDPARK
921 NORTH KINGS HIGHWAY
MYRTLE BEACH, SOUTH CAROLINA 29577

General Information Large go-cart amusement park with NASCAR theme. Established in 1997. 26-acre facility located 100 miles from Columbia. Features: resort area.

Profile of Summer Employees Total number: 150; typical age: 16. 50% men; 50% women; 70% high school students; 10% college students; 90% local applicants.

Employment Information Openings are from January to December. Jobs available: ▶ *go-cart track attendants* (minimum age 16) at $6.40–$6.95 per hour ▶ *guest services-customer service* at $6.40–$6.95 per hour ▶ *retail-gift shop, food, mini golf staff* at $6.40–$6.95 per hour. Applicants must submit formal organization application. International applicants accepted; must obtain own visa, obtain own working papers, apply through a recognized agency. An in-person interview is required.

Benefits and Preemployment Training Housing at a cost, meals at a cost, formal training, possible full-time employment, health insurance, on-the-job training, and tuition assistance. Preemployment training is required.

Contact Wanda Housand, Human Resource Associate, NASCAR Speedpark. Telephone: 843-626-6623. Fax: 843-626-8461. E-mail: wanda.housand@burroughs-chapin.com. World Wide Web: http://www.nascarspeedpark.com. Application deadline: continuous.

THE SOUTHWESTERN COMPANY, SOUTH CAROLINA
See The Southwestern Company, Tennessee on page 284 for complete description.

STUDENT CONSERVATION ASSOCIATION (SCA), SOUTH CAROLINA
See Student Conservation Association (SCA), New Hampshire on page 193 for complete description.

WILD DUNES RESORT
5801 PALMETTO DRIVE
ISLE OF PALMS, SOUTH CAROLINA 29451

General Information Resort offering summer recreational programs for all age groups who are guests at the resort. Established in 1976. 1,700-acre facility located 15 miles from Charleston. Features: 2 18-hole golf courses; 17 Har-Tru tennis courts; 20 swimming pools; 3 miles of beach; marina; conference centers.

Profile of Summer Employees Total number: 700; typical ages: 19–24. 30% men; 70% women; 100% college students.

Employment Information Openings are from May 12 to September 10. Year-round positions also offered. Jobs available. ▶ 20–24 *recreation Interns* with CPR certification, driver's license, and at least a Junior in college at $200 per month. Applicants must submit a formal organization application, cover letter, resume, three personal references, three letters of recommendation. International applicants accepted; must obtain own visa, obtain own working papers. A telephone interview is required.

Benefits and Preemployment Training Meals at a cost, free housing, formal training, possible full-time employment, names of contacts, on-the-job training, opportunity to attend seminars/ workshops, and nationally accredited internship program. Preemployment training is required and includes accident prevention and safety, interpersonal skills, leadership skills.

Contact Eric Carlson, Recreation and Internship Director, Wild Dunes Resort, 5801 Palmetto Drive, Isle of Palms, South Carolina 29451. Telephone: 843-886-2171. Fax: 843-886-2195. E-mail: ecarlson@wilddunes.com. World Wide Web: http://www.wilddunes.com. Application deadline: continuous.

SOUTH DAKOTA

A CHRISTIAN MINISTRY IN THE NATIONAL PARKS– SOUTH DAKOTA

See A Christian Ministry in the National Parks–Massachussetts on page 138 for complete description.

AMERICAN PRESIDENTS RESORT
HIGHWAY 16A
CUSTER, SOUTH DAKOTA 57730

General Information Resort consisting of cabins, campground, and motel units rented nightly from mid-May to mid-September. Established in 1950. 12-acre facility located 40 miles from Rapid City.

Profile of Summer Employees 20% men; 80% women; 35% high school students; 35% college students; 10% retirees; 50% local applicants.

Employment Information Openings are from May 15 to September 15. Jobs available: ▶ 10 *desk clerks* at $5–$6 per hour ▶ 5 *laundry workers* at $5–$6 per hour ▶ 20 *maids* at $5–$6 per hour.

Benefits and Preemployment Training On-the-job training. Preemployment training is required.

Contact Ione Fejfar, Manager, American Presidents Resort, PO Box 446, Custer, South Dakota 57730. Telephone: 605-673-3373. Fax: 605-673-3449. Application deadline: May 1.

AMFAC PARKS & RESORTS
PO BOX 178
KEYSTONE, SOUTH DAKOTA 57751

General Information Authorized National Park concessionaire. Established in 1951. 25-acre facility located 25 miles from Rapid City. Features: beautiful Black Hills; camping; fishing; hiking; Custer State Park; Badlands National Park.

Profile of Summer Employees Total number: 160; typical ages: 18–70. 50% men; 50% women; 15% minorities; 2% high school students; 80% college students; 20% retirees; 2% non-U.S. citizens. Nonsmokers preferred.

Employment Information Openings are from April 15 to October 15. Jobs available: ▶ 75 *food attendants* (minimum age 18) at $5.75 per hour ▶ 75 *gift shop attendants* (minimum age 18) at $5.50 per hour. Applicants must submit formal organization application. International applicants accepted; must obtain own visa, obtain own working papers, apply through a recognized agency.

Benefits and Preemployment Training Housing at a cost, meals at a cost, possible full-time employment, and on-the-job training. Preemployment training is required and includes accident prevention and safety, interpersonal skills.

Contact Russ Jobman, Human Resource Manager, AmFac Parks & Resorts, PO Box 178, Keystone, South Dakota 57751. Telephone: 605-574-2515. Fax: 605-574-2495. E-mail: fharvey@ mtrushmoregiftshop.com. World Wide Web: http://www.coolworks.com/showme/rushmore. Application deadline: continuous.

CUSTER STATE PARK RESORT COMPANY
HC 83, BOX 74
CUSTER, SOUTH DAKOTA 57730

General Information Operator of 4 resorts offering services such as lodging, dining, groceries, gas, and souveniers and gifts as well as activities that include trail rides, jeep tours, and cookouts. Established in 1989. 73,000-acre facility located 25 miles from Rapid City. Features: wooded setting; freshwater lakes; hiking trails; buffalo safari jeep tours; guided horseback rides; hayride/chuckwagon cookouts.

Profile of Summer Employees Total number: 300; typical ages: 18–65. 35% men; 65% women; 15% minorities; 10% high school students; 50% college students; 20% retirees; 1% non-U.S. citizens; 20% local applicants. Nonsmokers preferred.

Employment Information Openings are from May 1 to October 15. Jobs available: ▶ 5 *bartenders* (minimum age 21) at $700–$900 per month ▶ 4–6 *bookkeepers* (minimum age 21) at $900–$1200 per month ▶ 15–25 *cook's assistants* (minimum age 18) at $700–$900 per month ▶ 10 *cooks/chefs* with ServSafe certification and experience required at $1000–$2000 per month ▶ 18 *dishwashers/buspersons* (minimum age 16) at $700–$800 per month ▶ 17–20 *front desk/reservations personnel* at $750–$950 per month ▶ 5–8 *hosts/hostesses* (minimum age 16) at $800–$900 per month ▶ 50–60 *housekeeping personnel* at $700–$850 per month ▶ 5–12 *jeep drivers* (minimum age 21) with clean driving record and CPR certification at $750–$900 per month ▶ 8–25 *kitchen/food preparation personnel* (minimum age 18) at $700–$800 per month ▶ 6–8 *maintenance personnel* at $900–$1200 per month ▶ 12 *manager trainees* (minimum age 21) with desire to learn the resort business at $1200–$1400 per month ▶ 35–50 *sales clerks* at $700–$900 per month ▶ 45–50 *waitpersons* at $600–$750 per month ▶ 8–14 *wranglers* (minimum age 18) at $800–$1000 per month. Applicants must submit formal organization application, resume, three personal references, photo. International applicants accepted; must obtain own visa, obtain own working papers, apply through a recognized agency. An in-person interview is recommended, but a telephone interview is acceptable.

Benefits and Preemployment Training Formal training, possible full-time employment, on-the-job training, opportunity to attend seminars/workshops, tuition assistance, and room and board are available as part of total compensation package. Preemployment training is required and includes accident prevention and safety, first aid, CPR, specific job training.

Contact Phil Lampert, President, Custer State Park Resort Company, HC 83, Box 74, Custer, South Dakota 57730. Telephone: 605-255-4772. Fax: 605-255-4706. E-mail: e-mail@custerresorts.com. Application deadline: continuous.

PALMER GULCH RESORT/MT. RUSHMORE KOA
PO BOX 295, 12620 HIGHWAY 244
HILL CITY, SOUTH DAKOTA 57745

General Information Full-service resort located 5 miles west of Mount Rushmore. Established in 1972. 150-acre facility located 30 miles from Rapid City. Features: proximity to Custer State Park; 2 pools and waterslide; campsites and cabins; lodge motel.

Profile of Summer Employees Total number: 85; typical ages: 18–25. 50% men; 50% women; 5% minorities; 20% high school students; 50% college students; 30% retirees; 40% local applicants. Nonsmokers preferred.

Employment Information Openings are from May to September. Jobs available: ▶ 10–15 *campground registration office/store personnel* (minimum age 16) at $5.50 per hour plus bonus ▶ 10–15 *housekeeping staff members* (minimum age 14) at $5.50 per hour plus bonus ▶ 4–6 *lodge front desk and registration staff members* (minimum age 16) at $5.50 per hour plus bonus ▶ 10 *maintenance personnel* (minimum age 16) at $5.50 per hour plus bonus ▶ 3 *reservations staff members* (minimum age 16) at $5.50 per hour plus bonus ▶ 4 *waterslide staff members* (minimum age 16) with lifesaving, CPR, or first aid certification at $5.50 per hour plus bonus. Applicants must submit formal organization application, three personal references. International applicants accepted; must apply through a recognized agency. A telephone interview is required.

Benefits and Preemployment Training Housing at a cost, formal training, and on-the-job training. Preemployment training is optional and includes first aid, CPR.

Contact Sharon Nilson, Assistant Manager, Palmer Gulch Resort/Mt. Rushmore KOA, Box 295, Hill City, South Dakota 57745. Telephone: 605-574-2525. Fax: 605-574-2574. E-mail: palmerkoa@aol.com. Application deadline: continuous.

THE SOUTHWESTERN COMPANY, SOUTH DAKOTA
See The Southwestern Company, Tennessee on page 284 for complete description.

STUDENT CONSERVATION ASSOCIATION (SCA), SOUTH DAKOTA

See Student Conservation Association (SCA), New Hampshire on page 193 for complete description.

TENNESSEE

ACE COMPUTER CAMP–TENNESSEE

See ACE Computer Camp–Washington on page 307 for complete description.

A CHRISTIAN MINISTRY IN THE NATIONAL PARKS–TENNESSEE

See A Christian Ministry in the National Parks–Massachussetts on page 138 for complete description.

CAMP TANNASSIE
ROUTE 4, BOX 4174
TULLAHOMA, TENNESSEE 37388

General Information Residential summer camp where girls enjoy swimming, canoeing, sailing, waterskiing, snorkeling, arts and crafts, and traditional Girl Scout programs. Established in 1912. 37-acre facility located 60 miles from Chattanooga. Features: freshwater lake.

Profile of Summer Employees Total number: 12; typical ages: 18–23. 100% women; 90% college students; 5% non-U.S. citizens; 5% local applicants. Nonsmokers preferred.

Employment Information Openings are from June 13 to July 31. Jobs available: ▶ *administrative staff/camp director* (minimum age 25) at $350–$450 per week ▶ 1 *canoeing instructors* (minimum age 18) with certification; training is available at $135–$150 per week ▶ 3 *lifeguards* (minimum age 19) with certification; training is available at $135–$150 per week ▶ 1 *sailing instructors* (minimum age 18) with certification at $150–$200 per week ▶ 4 *unit counselors* (minimum age 18) at $125–$150 per week ▶ 1 *waterfront director* (minimum age 21) with certification and experience at $150–$200 per week ▶ *waterskiing instructor* (minimum age 18) with experience in the field at $150–$200 per week. Applicants must submit formal organization application, three personal references. International applicants accepted; must apply through a recognized agency. An in-person interview is recommended, but a telephone interview is acceptable.

Benefits and Preemployment Training Free housing, free meals, health insurance, on-the-job training, and accident insurance. Preemployment training is required and includes accident prevention and safety, first aid, CPR, interpersonal skills, leadership skills.

Contact Dawn M. Strunk, Outdoor Program Manager, Camp Tannassie, PO Box 40466, Nashville, Tennessee 37204. Telephone: 800-395-5318 Ext. 252. Fax: 615-383-2288. E-mail: gscouts@edge. net. Application deadline: continuous.

CHEROKEE ADVENTURES WHITEWATER RAFTING
2000 JONESBOROUGH ROAD
ERWIN, TENNESSEE 37650-9524

General Information Guided rafting and mountain-biking trips; also ropes course emphasizing team building and camping. Established in 1979. 50-acre facility located 17 miles from Johnson City. Features: located on a river; wooded setting; volleyball courts.

Profile of Summer Employees Total number: 35–40; typical ages: 21–25. 60% men; 40% women; 40% college students; 2% non-U.S. citizens; 58% local applicants. Nonsmokers preferred.

Employment Information Openings are from May to October. Year-round positions also offered.

Jobs available: ▶ 6 *cooks/cleaning staff members* (minimum age 19) with ability to prepare lunches and perform general cleaning at $5.25–$6.50 per hour ▶ *dishwasher* (minimum age 16) at $5.25–$6.50 per hour ▶ 6 *raft guides* (minimum age 18) with responsible, outgoing personalities and Red Cross first aid/CPR certification (salary begins after training completed) at $400–$600 per month ▶ 3 *reservationists/general office personnel* (minimum age 19) with good phone manner and the ability to type 40 wpm at $5.25–$6.50 per hour ▶ *server/waitstaff* (minimum age 18) at $2.35 per hour plus tips. Applicants must submit a formal organization application, three personal references. International applicants accepted; must obtain own visa, obtain own working papers.

Benefits and Preemployment Training Housing at a cost, meals at a cost, and on-the-job training. Preemployment training is optional and includes first aid, CPR, leadership skills.

Contact Dennis I. Nedelman, President, Cherokee Adventures Whitewater Rafting, 2000 Jonesborough Road, Erwin, Tennessee 37650-9524. Telephone: 423-743-7733. Fax: 423-743-5400. E-mail: ca2raft@usit.net. Application deadline: continuous.

GIRL SCOUT CAMP SYCAMORE HILLS
2020 GIRL SCOUT ROAD
ASHLAND CITY, TENNESSEE 37015

General Information ACA-accredited residential camp serving 175 girls per session with swimming, canoeing, archery, arts and crafts, ropes and rappelling, horseback programs, and trip and travel programs. Established in 1912. 742-acre facility located 35 miles from Nashville. Features: equestrian center; high ropes course; rappel bluffs; pool; creek with canoeing; arts and crafts facility.

Profile of Summer Employees Total number: 62; typical ages: 18–23. 1% men; 99% women; 85% college students; 10% local applicants. Nonsmokers preferred.

Employment Information Openings are from May 30 to July 25. Jobs available: ▶ 2 *arts and crafts staff members* (minimum age 18) with experience in the field preferred at $135–$200 per week ▶ 1 *assistant camp director* (minimum age 21) with Girl Scout residential camp experience at $300–$400 per week ▶ 1 *business manager* (minimum age 21) with accounting training at $200–$300 per week ▶ 1 *canoeing director* (minimum age 21) with certification (training available) at $150–$200 per week ▶ 8 *equestrian counselors* (minimum age 18) with experience in the field and CHA certification (training available) at $135–$175 per week ▶ 1 *health supervisor* (minimum age 21) with RN or paramedic certification in the state of Tennessee at $300–$550 per week ▶ 1 *nature director* (minimum age 21) with background in the field preferred at $150–$200 per week ▶ 1 *program director* (minimum age 21) with Girl Scout residential camp experience at $250–$300 per week ▶ 3 *rappelling and ropes staff members* (minimum age 18) with certification (training available) at $150–$200 per week ▶ 1 *ropes and rappelling director* (minimum age 21) with at least two years experience and certification (training available) at $175–$200 per week ▶ 1 *target sports director* (minimum age 21) with certification at $150–$200 per week ▶ 25 *unit counselors* (minimum age 18) at $125–$150 per week ▶ 1 *unit director* (minimum age 21) with Girl Scout residential camp experience at $250–$300 per week ▶ 9 *unit leaders* (minimum age 21) at $150–$200 per week ▶ 3 *waterfront counselors* (minimum age 18) with lifeguard certification (training available) at $135–$175 per week ▶ 1 *waterfront director* (minimum age 21) with lifeguard and WSI certification (training available) at $175–$200 per week. Applicants must submit formal organization application, three personal references. International applicants accepted; must apply through a recognized agency. An in-person interview is recommended, but a telephone interview is acceptable.

Benefits and Preemployment Training Free housing, free meals, health insurance, on-the-job training, and accident insurance. Preemployment training is required and includes accident prevention and safety, first aid, CPR, interpersonal skills, leadership skills.

Contact Dawn M. Strunk, Outdoor Programs Manager, Girl Scout Camp Sycamore Hills, PO Box 40466, Nashville, Tennessee 37204. Telephone: 800-395-5318 Ext. 252. Fax: 615-383-2288. E-mail: gscouts@edge.net. Application deadline: continuous.

OPRYLAND HOTEL
2802 OPRYLAND DRIVE
NASHVILLE, TENNESSEE 37214

General Information Hotel convention center with golf club and river-cruising showboats. Established in 1977. 100-acre facility. Features: 18 hole PGA golf club; 2 showboats; 9½ acres under glass in hotel with gardens, waterfalls, and laser shows; 30 retail shops; 15 restaurants and lounges; 300 room inn for smaller, family environment.

Profile of Summer Employees Total number: 5,000; typical ages: 20–22. 50% men; 50% women.

Employment Information Openings are from March to September. Year-round positions also offered. Jobs available: ▶ *various positions (front desk, servers, housekeeping, retail, laundry, dishroom attendant, culinary)* (minimum age 18) at $6–$8 per hour. Applicants must submit cover letter, resume, and personal references are preferred depending on position. International applicants accepted; must obtain own visa, obtain own working papers.

Benefits and Preemployment Training Housing at a cost, free meals, formal training, possible full-time employment, on-the-job training, opportunity to attend seminars/workshops, and food allowance. Preemployment training is required and includes accident prevention and safety, customer service.

Contact Employment Manager, Opryland Hotel, Employment Office, 2802 Opryland Drive, Nashville, Tennessee 37214. Telephone: 615-871-6621. Fax: 615-871-7638. World Wide Web: http://www.opryhotel.com. Application deadline: continuous.

THE SOUTHWESTERN COMPANY, TENNESSEE
2451 ATRIUM WAY
NASHVILLE, TENNESSEE 37214

General Information Summer work program for college students selling educational books and software. Established in 1868.

Profile of Summer Employees Total number: 4,000; typical ages: 18–24. 70% men; 30% women; 1% high school students; 99% college students; 20% non-U.S. citizens.

Employment Information Openings are from April 25 to October 1. Jobs available: ▶ 4000 *sales staff* (minimum age 18) with average wage of $6500 first season (12 weeks). International applicants accepted; must obtain own visa, obtain own working papers, apply through a recognized agency. An in-person interview is required.

Benefits and Preemployment Training Formal training, possible full-time employment, on-the-job training, and opportunity to attend seminars/workshops. Preemployment training is required and includes interpersonal skills, leadership skills.

Contact Melanie Yappen, Manger, Interactive Marketing, The Southwestern Company, Tennessee, PO Box 305140, Nashville, Tennessee 37230. Telephone: 615-391-2837. Fax: 615-291-2822. E-mail: sw@southwestern.com. World Wide Web: http://www.southwestern.com. Application deadline: June 15.

STUDENT CONSERVATION ASSOCIATION (SCA), TENNESSEE
See Student Conservation Association (SCA), New Hampshire on page 193 for complete description.

TEXAS

ACE COMPUTER CAMP–TEXAS
See ACE Computer Camp–Washington on page 307 for complete description.

A CHRISTIAN MINISTRY IN THE NATIONAL PARKS–TEXAS
See A Christian Ministry in the National Parks–Massachussetts on page 138 for complete description.

ASTRO-ART AMUSEMENTS
9603 PENNINGTON LANE
MISSOURI CITY, TEXAS 77459
General Information Operates face-painting, hair-wraps, temporary tattoos, painted-parasols, and caricature concessions at major theme parks in Texas. Established in 1982. 200-acre facility. Features: Six Flags Over Texas; Six Flags Houston; Six Flags Fiesta Texas; rides; thrills; fun.

Profile of Summer Employees Total number: 60; typical ages: 16–26. 50% men; 50% women; 50% minorities; 40% high school students; 40% college students; 5% retirees; 2% non-U.S. citizens; 13% local applicants.

Employment Information Openings are from March 6 to January 2. Spring break and winter break positions also offered. Jobs available: ▶ 35–40 *face-painters and caricaturists* (minimum age 16) with artistic skills; 26-30% of sales and profit share/bonus ▶ 15–20 *hair-wraps* (minimum age 16) with skillful and strong fingers; 26-30% of sales and profit share/bonus. Applicants must submit a formal organization application, portfolio, two personal references, proof of age, proof of eligibility to work in the United States. International applicants accepted; must obtain own visa, obtain own working papers. An in-person interview is required.

Benefits and Preemployment Training Meals at a cost, formal training, possible full-time employment, on-the-job training, opportunity to attend seminars/workshops, and Six Flags seasonal employee benefits/tickets. Preemployment training is required and includes accident prevention and safety, interpersonal skills, leadership skills, artistic development and training.

Contact David Jennings, Owner, Astro-Art Amusements, 9001 Kirby Drive, Retail Department, Houston, Texas 77054. E-mail: djennings@entouchonline.net. Application deadline: continuous.

CAMP CABO RIO FOR BOYS
MO RANCH, HC 1, BOX 158
HUNT, TEXAS 78024
General Information Residential camp serving boys ages 10–15 in two 3-week sessions. Established in 1993. 434-acre facility located 80 miles from San Antonio. Features: freshwater river; water slide; dormitory; Christian camp; nature studies; horseback riding.

Profile of Summer Employees Total number: 120; typical ages: 21–28. 99% men; 1% women; 20% minorities; 30% high school students; 70% college students; 1% local applicants. Nonsmokers preferred.

Employment Information Openings are from May 31 to September 6. Jobs available: ▶ 6–12 *counselors/instructors* (minimum age 21) with Christian faith at $1000–$1500 per month ▶ 3–6 *swimming instructors* (minimum age 17) at $6.50–$6.75 per hour. Applicants must submit formal organization application, resume, two personal references. International applicants accepted; must obtain own visa, obtain own working papers, apply through a recognized agency. An in-person interview is recommended, but a telephone interview is acceptable.

Benefits and Preemployment Training Free housing, free meals, possible full-time employment, on-the-job training, and travel reimbursement. Preemployment training is required and includes accident prevention and safety, first aid, CPR, interpersonal skills, leadership skills.

Contact Scott Walker, Director of Human Resources, Camp Cabo Rio for Boys, Route 1, Box 158, Hunt, Texas 78024. Telephone: 800-460-4401. Fax: 830-238-4202. E-mail: human_rsources@moranch.com. World Wide Web: http://www.moranch.com. Application deadline: continuous.

CAMP EL TESORO
2700 MEACHAM BOULEVARD
FORT WORTH, TEXAS 76137
General Information Residential camp for boys and girls ages 6–16. Established in 1934. 228-acre facility located 45 miles from Fort Worth. Features: 2 swimming pools; 20 horses; 2 tennis courts; creek and riverfront; natural wood setting; hiking trails.

Profile of Summer Employees Total number: 50; typical ages: 18–25. 40% men; 60% women; 12% minorities; 8% high school students; 85% college students; 50% local applicants.

Employment Information Openings are from May 20 to August 1. Jobs available: ▶ 1 *arts and crafts director* (minimum age 21) with experience working with children, teaching arts and crafts at $95–$200 per week ▶ 20 *cabin counselors* with one year of college and CPR/first aid certification at $75–$150 per week ▶ 4 *horseback staff members* with CHA certification (preferred) at $80–$180 per week ▶ 4 *kitchen staff members* at $135–$200 per week ▶ 1 *program director* (minimum age 21) with experience in the field at $100–$225 per week ▶ 4 *special needs staff members* (minimum age 18) with one year of college completed and some experience; desire to work with children with special needs at $95–$150 per week ▶ 3 *unit coordinators* (minimum age 21) with supervisory experience at $100–$225 per week ▶ 4 *waterfront staff members* with lifeguard, CPR, and first aid certification at $80–$180 per week. Applicants must submit formal organization application, three personal references, criminal background check. International applicants accepted; must obtain own visa, apply through a recognized agency. An in-person interview is recommended, but a telephone interview is acceptable.

Benefits and Preemployment Training Free housing, free meals, health insurance, on-the-job training, and opportunity to attend seminars/workshops. Preemployment training is required and includes accident prevention and safety, first aid, CPR, interpersonal skills, leadership skills.

Contact Laurie Johnston, Camp Director, Camp El Tesoro, 2700 Meacham Boulevard, Fort Worth, Texas 76137. Telephone: 817-831-2111. Fax: 817-831-5070. E-mail: campfire@netarrant. net. World Wide Web: http://www.startext.net/np/campfire. Application deadline: continuous.

CAMP FERN
1046 CAMP ROAD
MARSHALL, TEXAS 75672-9441

General Information Residential camp providing fun, adventure, learning, self-esteem development, and lasting friendships. Established in 1934. 100-acre facility located 9 miles from Marshall. Features: lake, wooded setting, log cabins; English horseback riding; Red Cross swimming, water skiing; tennis, golf, archery, riflery; trampoline, nature, campcrafts; team sports.

Profile of Summer Employees Total number: 75; typical age: 19. 50% men; 50% women; 100% college students. Nonsmokers required.

Employment Information Openings are from May 23 to August 14. Jobs available: ▶ *English horseback riding staff members* at $125–$150 per week ▶ *crafts staff members* at $125–$150 per week ▶ *riflery staff members* at $125–$150 per week ▶ *ropes course staff members* with certification in field at $125–$150 per week ▶ *tennis staff members* at $125–$150 per week ▶ *waterfront staff members* with WSI, lifeguard, and CPR certification at $125–$150 per week. Applicants must submit a formal organization application, resume. International applicants accepted; must obtain own visa, obtain own working papers. An in-person interview is recommended, but a telephone interview is acceptable.

Benefits and Preemployment Training Free housing, free meals, on-the-job training, and laundry facilities.

Contact Margaret R. Thompson, Director, Camp Fern, 1040 Camp Road, Marshall, Texas 75672-9441. Telephone: 903-935-5420. Fax: 903-935-6372. E-mail: info@campfern.com. World Wide Web: http://www.campfern.com. Application deadline: April 1.

CAMP LA JUNTA
PO BOX 136
HUNT, TEXAS 78024

General Information Private residential camp with a focus on individual lifetime activities serving 200 boys in 2- or 4-week terms. Established in 1928. 150-acre facility located 75 miles from San Antonio. Features: spring-fed river; modern stone cabins; hill country setting.

Profile of Summer Employees Total number: 75; typical ages: 17–25. 90% men; 10% women; 5% minorities; 100% college students; 5% non-U.S. citizens; 25% local applicants. Nonsmokers required.

Employment Information Openings are from June 1 to August 5. Jobs available: ▶ *junior* *counselors* (minimum age 18) at $500–$600 per month ▶ *senior counselors* (minimum age 21) at $600–$700 per month. Applicants must submit formal organization application. International applicants accepted; must apply through a recognized agency. An in-person interview is recommended, but a telephone interview is acceptable.

Benefits and Preemployment Training Free housing, free meals, formal training, on-the-job training, and travel reimbursement. Preemployment training is required and includes accident prevention and safety, first aid, CPR, interpersonal skills, leadership skills.

Contact Blake W. Smith, Director, Camp La Junta, PO Box 136, Hunt, Texas 78024. Telephone: 830-238-4621. Fax: 830-238-4888. E-mail: lajunta@ktc.com. World Wide Web: http://www. lajunta.com. Application deadline: continuous.

CAMP LOMA LINDA FOR GIRLS
MO RANCH, HC 1, BOX 158
HUNT, TEXAS 78024

General Information Residential camp serving girls ages 10-15 in two 3-week sessions. Established in 1977. 434-acre facility located 80 miles from San Antonio. Features: freshwater river; dormitory housing; Christian camp; water slide; horseback riding; nature studies.

Profile of Summer Employees Total number: 120; typical ages: 21–28. 1% men; 5% high school students; 95% college students; 1% local applicants. Nonsmokers preferred.

Employment Information Openings are from May 31 to September 6. Year-round positions also offered. Jobs available: ▶ 6–12 *counselors/instructors* (minimum age 21) with Christian faith at $1000–$1500 per month. Applicants must submit formal organization application, resume, two personal references. International applicants accepted; must obtain own visa, obtain own working papers, apply through a recognized agency. An in-person interview is recommended, but a telephone interview is acceptable.

Benefits and Preemployment Training Free housing, free meals, possible full-time employment, on-the-job training, and travel reimbursement. Preemployment training is required and includes accident prevention and safety, first aid, CPR, interpersonal skills, leadership skills.

Contact Scott Walker, Director of Human Resources, Camp Loma Linda for Girls, Route 1, Box 158, Hunt, Texas 78024. Telephone: 800-460-4401. Fax: 830-238-4202. E-mail: human_resources@ moranch.com. World Wide Web: http://www.moranch.com. Application deadline: continuous.

CAMP RIO VISTA FOR BOYS
HCR 78, BOX 215
INGRAM, TEXAS 78025

General Information Private residential camp providing 100–150 boys, ages 6–16, with a fun-filled learning experience in a safe, wholesome environment. Established in 1921. 120-acre facility located 75 miles from San Antonio. Features: river; tennis courts; full-size gym; 3 softball fields; lighted footfall field; golf course.

Profile of Summer Employees Total number: 45; typical ages: 19–23. 100% men; 5% minorities; 10% high school students; 85% college students; 5% non-U.S. citizens; 2% local applicants. Nonsmokers preferred.

Employment Information Openings are from June 1 to August 2. Jobs available: ▶ 45 *cabin/ activity counselors* (minimum age 19) with ability to be good role models and who enjoy working with children at $148 per week ▶ 10 *counselors/lifeguards* (minimum age 19) with lifeguard certification at $148 per week ▶ 2 *nurses* with RN/LVN/EMT, experience with children, and field experience at $200–$250 per week. Applicants must submit formal organization application, three personal references, three letters of recommendation. International applicants accepted; must obtain own visa, obtain own working papers, apply through a recognized agency. An in-person interview is recommended, but a telephone interview is acceptable.

Benefits and Preemployment Training Free housing, free meals, health insurance, and on-the-job training. Preemployment training is required and includes accident prevention and safety, first aid, CPR, interpersonal skills, leadership skills, child management, liability management.

Contact James Rice, Director, Camp Rio Vista for Boys, HCR 78, Box 215, Ingram, Texas

78025. Telephone: 830-367-5353. Fax: 830-367-4044. E-mail: riovista@ktc.com. World Wide Web: http://www.vistacamps.com. Application deadline: May 10.

CAMP SIERRA VISTA FOR GIRLS
HCR 78, BOX 215
INGRAM, TEXAS 78025

General Information Private residential camp for girls ages 6–16. Provides a safe, wholesome, fun-filled, learning experience to 75–90 girls per term. Established in 1982. 120-acre facility located 75 miles from San Antonio. Features: riverfront; game fields; golf course; tennis courts; rock gymnasium; 30 activities.

Profile of Summer Employees Total number: 24; typical ages: 19–23. 100% women; 5% minorities; 10% high school students; 85% college students; 10% non-U.S. citizens; 5% local applicants. Nonsmokers preferred.

Employment Information Openings are from June 1 to August 2. Jobs available: ▶ 20–24 *cabin/activity counselors* (minimum age 19) with the ability to be good role models and who enjoy working with children at $148 per week ▶ 2 *nurses* with LVN, RN, or EMT certification, experience with children, and field experience at $200–$250 per week ▶ 2 *office staff members* (minimum age 19) with organizational skills and good telephone skills at $148 per week ▶ 2 *swimming instructors* (minimum age 19) with lifeguard certification at $148 per week. Applicants must submit formal organization application, three personal references, three letters of recommendation. International applicants accepted; must obtain own visa, obtain own working papers, apply through a recognized agency. An in-person interview is recommended, but a telephone interview is acceptable.

Benefits and Preemployment Training Free housing, free meals, health insurance, and on-the-job training. Preemployment training is required and includes accident prevention and safety, first aid, CPR, interpersonal skills, leadership skills, child management and liability management.

Contact James Rice, Personnel Director, Camp Sierra Vista for Girls, HCR 78, Box 215, Ingram, Texas 78025. Telephone: 830-367-5353. Fax: 830-367-4044. E-mail: riovista@ktc.com. World Wide Web: http://www.vistacamps.com. Application deadline: May 10.

CAMP VAL VERDE
1007 CAMP ROAD
MCGREGOR, TEXAS 76657

General Information Residential camp serving 75–100 campers, some economically disadvantaged and others from foster homes, for 1-week sessions. Established in 1948. 397-acre facility located 7 miles from Waco.

Profile of Summer Employees Typical ages: 18–23. 34% men; 66% women; 2% minorities; 1% high school students; 97% college students; 20% local applicants.

Employment Information Openings are from May 23 to July 15. Jobs available: ▶ 25 *counselors* at $650–$800 per season ▶ 2 *horseback instructors* at $650–$800 per season ▶ 4 *lifeguards* with certification at $650–$800 per season ▶ 1 *nurse* with nursing degree at $800–$1000 per season. Applicants must submit a formal organization application, personal reference. An in-person interview is recommended, but a telephone interview is acceptable.

Benefits and Preemployment Training Free housing and free meals. Preemployment training is required and includes accident prevention and safety, first aid, CPR, interpersonal skills, leadership skills.

Contact Director, Camp Val Verde, 1826 Morrow Avenue, Waco, Texas 76707. Telephone: 254-752-5515. Fax: 254-752-0088. Application deadline: continuous.

CAMP WALDEMAR
HC 1, BOX 120
HUNT, TEXAS 78024

General Information Private residential girls camp offering sports, arts, and drama activities. Established in 1926. 560-acre facility located 80 miles from San Antonio. Features: beautiful river; trees and hills; 8 tennis courts; 85 horses; buildings/cabins made of rock, tile, and ceder.

Profile of Summer Employees Total number: 200; typical ages: 18–96. 30% men; 70% women; 20% minorities; 10% high school students; 50% college students; 5% retirees; 12% non-U.S. citizens; 3% local applicants. Nonsmokers preferred.

Employment Information Openings are from May 29 to August 20. Jobs available: ▶ 5 *arts and crafts (ceramics, jewelry, and weaving) staff members* (minimum age 18) with ability to teach at $450–$700 per month ▶ 2 *fencing staff members* (minimum age 18) with college team playing experience and ability to teach at $450–$700 per month ▶ 4–5 *gymnastics staff members* (minimum age 18) with team experience at $450–$700 per month ▶ 10 *riding teachers or wranglers* (minimum age 15) with English or Western equitation horsemanship and ability to teach or wrangle at $450–$700 per month ▶ 4–6 *rifle staff members* (minimum age 18) with NRA certification and ability to teach at $450–$700 per month ▶ 16 *swimming/diving instructors* (minimum age 18) with WSI and/or lifesaving certification; teaching or swim/dive team experience at $450–$700 per month ▶ 6–8 *tennis staff members* (minimum age 18) with varsity high school or college experience and ability to teach at $450–$700 per month. Applicants must submit formal organization application, three personal references. International applicants accepted; must apply through a recognized agency. An in-person interview is recommended, but a telephone interview is acceptable.

Benefits and Preemployment Training Free housing, free meals, formal training, possible full-time employment, health insurance, names of contacts, on-the-job training, opportunity to attend seminars/workshops, and travel reimbursement. Preemployment training is required and includes accident prevention and safety, first aid, CPR, interpersonal skills, leadership skills.

Contact Meg Clark, Owner/Directors, Camp Waldemar, HC 1, Box 120, Hunt, Texas 78024. Telephone: 830-238-4821. Fax: 830-238-4051. E-mail: info@waldemar.com. Application deadline: May 30.

LAZY HILLS GUEST RANCH
HENDERSON BRANCH ROAD
INGRAM, TEXAS 78025

General Information Resort ranch catering to families and groups. Established in 1959. 750-acre facility located 80 miles from San Antonio. Features: swimming pool; volleyball; basketball; 2 tennis courts; game room; horseback riding.

Profile of Summer Employees Total number: 12; typical ages: 16–23. 20% men; 80% women; 10% minorities; 25% high school students; 75% college students; 30% local applicants. Nonsmokers preferred.

Employment Information Openings are from May 15 to September 5. Spring break positions also offered. Jobs available: ▶ 1 *activities director* (minimum age 16) with enthusiasm and ability to work well with children and adults at $500-$600 per month plus tips ▶ 1 *office worker* (minimum age 18) with computer experience at $400 per month plus tips ▶ 5 *waiters/waitresses* (minimum age 16) at $400 per month plus tips ▶ 2 *wranglers* (minimum age 18) with Red Cross certification and experience with horses at $400-$600 per month plus tips. Applicants must submit a formal organization application, three personal references. International applicants accepted; must obtain own visa, obtain own working papers. A telephone interview is required.

Benefits and Preemployment Training Free housing, free meals, possible full-time employment, and on-the-job training.

Contact Beth Steinruck, Office Manager, Lazy Hills Guest Ranch, Box G, Ingram, Texas 78025. Telephone: 830-367-5600. Fax: 830-367-5667. E-mail: lhills@ktc.com. World Wide Web: http://www.lazyhills.com. Application deadline: continuous.

MO RANCH
HC1, PO BOX 158
HUNT, TEXAS 78024

General Information Conference center with variety of accommodations for families individuals and groups. Established in 1949. 434-acre facility located 80 miles from San Antonio. Features: swimming pool; ropes course; auditorium; fully equipped meeting facilities; crystal clear river front; canoeing/fishing.

Profile of Summer Employees Total number: 120; typical ages: 16–30. 50% men; 50% women; 40% high school students; 10% college students; 1% retirees; 1% non-U.S. citizens; 90% local applicants. Nonsmokers preferred.

Employment Information Openings are from May 1 to September 1. Year-round positions also offered. Jobs available: ▶ *cooks* with quantity cooking experience at $7.50–$8.50 per hour ▶ *housekeeping staff* at $6.50–$7 per hour ▶ *kitchen staff* at $6.50–$7 per hour ▶ *registration staff* with computer skills preferred at $6.50–$7 per hour ▶ 2–4 *ropes course/field instructors* with preference for certification or experience in facilitating ropes challenge course groups at $6.75–$7.50 per hour. Applicants must submit formal organization application, cover letter, resume, two personal references. International applicants accepted; must obtain own visa, obtain own working papers, apply through a recognized agency. An in-person interview is required.

Benefits and Preemployment Training Meals at a cost, possible full-time employment, and on-the-job training. Preemployment training is required and includes management training.

Contact Scott Walker, Director of Human Resources, Mo Ranch, Route 1, Box 158, Hunt, Texas 78024. Telephone: 800-460-4401. Fax: 830-238-4202. E-mail: human_resources@moranch. com. World Wide Web: http://www.moranch.com. Application deadline: continuous.

THE SOUTHWESTERN COMPANY, TEXAS
See The Southwestern Company, Tennessee on page 284 for complete description.

STUDENT CONSERVATION ASSOCIATION (SCA), TEXAS
See Student Conservation Association (SCA), New Hampshire on page 193 for complete description.

WESTERN PLAYLAND AMUSEMENT PARK
6900 DELTA
EL PASO, TEXAS 79905

General Information Amusement park with more than 30 rides, games, concession stands, and other attractions catering to families, school children, and corporations in the area. Established in 1960. 15-acre facility located 700 miles from Dallas. Features: 2 roller coasters; 2 flume rides; racetrack and go-carts; kiddie area; 2 corporate party pavilions; concert stage.

Profile of Summer Employees Total number: 120–135; typical ages: 16–20. 50% men; 50% women; 98% minorities; 95% high school students; 5% college students; 25% non-U.S. citizens; 100% local applicants. Nonsmokers required.

Employment Information Openings are from March 1 to October 1. Year-round positions also offered. Jobs available: ▶ 100 *seasonal employees* (minimum age 16) at $5.15 per hour (starting wage). Applicants must submit a formal organization application, two personal references. International applicants accepted; must obtain own visa, obtain own working papers. An in-person interview is recommended, but a telephone interview is acceptable.

Benefits and Preemployment Training Formal training and on-the-job training. Preemployment training is required and includes accident prevention and safety, first aid, interpersonal skills, leadership skills.

Contact Rudy Gandarilla, General Manager, Western Playland Amusement Park, 6900 Delta, El Paso, Texas 79905. Telephone: 915-772-3953 Ext. 16. Fax: 915-778-9821. E-mail: gandar7542@ aol.com. World Wide Web: http://www.westernplayland.com. Application deadline: continuous.

UTAH

ACE COMPUTER CAMP–UTAH
See ACE Computer Camp–Washington on page 307 for complete description.

A CHRISTIAN MINISTRY IN THE NATIONAL PARKS–UTAH

See A Christian Ministry in the National Parks–Massachussetts on page 138 for complete description.

FOUR CORNERS SCHOOL OF OUTDOOR EDUCATION
PO BOX 1029
MONTICELLO, UTAH 84535

General Information Program offering educational adventures using the spectacular Colorado Plateau as an outdoor classroom. Three day to 2-week programs are available on natural and human history via raft, backpack, van, or skis. Established in 1984. 7-acre facility located 300 miles from Salt Lake City. Features: easy access to 3 national parks; rustic historic homestead.

Profile of Summer Employees Total number: 70; typical ages: 20–55. 70% men; 30% women; 5% minorities; 5% high school students; 95% college students; 5% local applicants. Nonsmokers preferred.

Employment Information Openings are from March 1 to October 30. Jobs available: ▶ *outdoor education interns* (minimum age 21) with interest in a career in outdoor education and knowledge of the Southwest; First Responder and CPR certification preferred at $75 per week. Applicants must submit a formal organization application, cover letter, resume, personal reference. International applicants accepted; must obtain own visa, obtain own working papers. A telephone interview is required.

Benefits and Preemployment Training Free housing, free meals, and on-the-job training. Preemployment training is required.

Contact Janet Ross, Director, Four Corners School of Outdoor Education, PO Box 1029, Monticello, Utah 84535. Telephone: 435-587-2156. Fax: 435-587-2193. E-mail: fcs@igc.apc. org. World Wide Web: http://www.sw-adventures.org. Application deadline: December 15.

LAGOON AMUSEMENT PARK
375 NORTH LAGOON DRIVE
FARMINGTON, UTAH 84025

General Information Amusement park with rides, resort hotels, camping, a water park and live entertainment. Established in 1886. 110-acre facility located 20 miles from Salt Lake City. Features: 47 thrill rides; water park; kids area; camping; entertaiment; 4 roller coasters.

Profile of Summer Employees Total number: 2,500; typical ages: 16–21. 50% men; 50% women; 5% minorities; 85% high school students; 10% college students; 2% retirees.

Employment Information Openings are from April 1 to October 31. Year-round positions also offered. Jobs available: ▶ 60–75 *entertainers* at $10–$15 per hour ▶ 1000–1500 *front line seasonal hosts/hostesses* (minimum age 16) must be friendly with big smile at $6–$8 per hour. Applicants must submit a formal organization application, three personal references. International applicants accepted; must obtain own visa, obtain own working papers. An in-person interview is required.

Benefits and Preemployment Training Meals at a cost, formal training, possible full-time employment, on-the-job training, and opportunity to attend seminars/workshops. Preemployment training is required and includes accident prevention and safety, first aid, CPR, leadership skills.

Contact John Jachim, Human Resources Manager, Lagoon Amusement Park, 375 North Lagoon Drive, Farmington, Utah 84025. Telephone: 804-451-8035. Fax: 801-451-8011. E-mail: john@ lagoonpark.com. World Wide Web: http://www.lagoonpark.com. Application deadline: continuous.

SNOWBIRD SKI & SUMMER RESORT
7350 WASATCH BOULEVARD
SALT LAKE CITY, UTAH 84121

General Information Year-round ski and summer resort. Established in 1979. 2,500-acre facility located 25 miles from Salt Lake City. Features: cliff lodge; tram; conference center; 3 other hotels; food and beverage restaurants.

Profile of Summer Employees Total number: 1,000; typical ages: 18–35. 60% men; 40% women; 10% minorities; 10% high school students; 30% college students; 50% local applicants.

Employment Information Openings are from January 1 to December 30. Jobs available: ▶ 5 *administrative positions* at $7–$8 per hour or $5.15–$7 per hour plus commission ▶ *banquet staff* at $5.75 per hour plus tips ▶ 15 *food service workers (room servers, buspeople, cooks, waitpeople, and dishwashers)* salaries vary depending on position ▶ *hotel staff (housekeepers, concierge, and desk manager)* at $5.25–$9 per hour ▶ 2 *security officers* at $8–$8.50 per hour. Applicants must submit formal organization application. International applicants accepted; must obtain own visa, obtain own working papers, apply through a recognized agency. An in-person interview is recommended, but a telephone interview is acceptable.

Benefits and Preemployment Training Meals at a cost, possible full-time employment, and ski pass, EAP, transportation (bus). Preemployment training is required.

Contact Kent Boam, Recruiting Manager, Snowbird Ski & Summer Resort. Telephone: 801-947-8240. Fax: 801-947-8244. E-mail: kboam@snowbird.com. World Wide Web: http://www.snowbird. com. Application deadline: continuous.

THE SOUTHWESTERN COMPANY, UTAH
See The Southwestern Company, Tennessee on page 284 for complete description.

STUDENT CONSERVATION ASSOCIATION (SCA), UTAH
See Student Conservation Association (SCA), New Hampshire on page 193 for complete description.

VERMONT

A CHRISTIAN MINISTRY IN THE NATIONAL PARKS–VERMONT
See A Christian Ministry in the National Parks–Massachussetts on page 138 for complete description.

BRIDGES RESORT AND RACQUET CLUB
SUGARBUSH ACCESS ROAD
WARREN, VERMONT 05674

General Information Tennis and condominium facility at major ski area in Vermont's Green Mountains. Established in 1970. 45-acre facility located 48 miles from Burlington. Features: 12 tennis courts; health club; wooded setting; 3 pools.

Profile of Summer Employees Total number: 50; typical ages: 17–25. 60% men; 40% women; 10% minorities; 10% high school students; 20% college students; 10% non-U.S. citizens; 80% local applicants.

Employment Information Openings are from May 31 to September 4. Jobs available: ▶ 4 *cafe servers/cooks* (minimum age 18) at $150–$250 per week ▶ *swimming instructors* (minimum age 17) with WSI and Red Cross certification at $6 per hour ▶ 2 *tennis desk/front desk staff* (minimum age 18) at $6 per hour ▶ 4–7 *tennis staff* (minimum age 18) with USPTA professional tennis instructor certification at $200–$400 per week. Applicants must submit a formal organization application, cover letter, resume. International applicants accepted; must obtain own visa. An in-person interview is recommended, but a telephone interview is acceptable.

Benefits and Preemployment Training Free housing, possible full-time employment, and on-the-job training.

Contact Holly Hodgkins, General Manager, Bridges Resort and Racquet Club, Sugarbush Access Road, Warren, Vermont 05674. Telephone: 802-583-2922. Fax: 802-583-1018. E-mail: bridges@ madriver.com. Application deadline: continuous.

BURKLYN BALLET THEATRE
JOHNSON STATE COLLEGE
JOHNSON, VERMONT 05656

General Information Classical ballet workshop offers weekly performance opportunity to 136 boys and girls ages 12–20 in one 6-week program. Established in 1976. 35 miles from Burlington. Features: mountains; rural village; college campus; dormitories; library; pool.

Profile of Summer Employees Total number: 20; typical ages: 12–23. 50% men; 50% women; 10% minorities; 60% high school students; 25% college students; 5% non-U.S. citizens. Nonsmokers preferred.

Employment Information Openings are from June 19 to August 3. Jobs available: ▶ 14 *counselors* (minimum age 20) with current professional dance contract or college dance major; salary is program tuition, room, and board ▶ 1 *registered nurse* should be experienced RN with Vermont nursing license; salary is child's tuition waiver ▶ 1 *technical director* (minimum age 25) with professional experience or college technical theater major at $100–$200 per week. Applicants must submit resume, in-person/video audition. International applicants accepted; must obtain own visa, obtain own working papers.

Benefits and Preemployment Training Meals at a cost, free housing, formal training, names of contacts, on-the-job training, opportunity to attend seminars/workshops, and tuition assistance. Preemployment training is required and includes interpersonal skills, leadership skills.

Contact Angela Whitehill, Artistic Director, Burklyn Ballet Theatre, PO Box 907, Island Heights, New Jersey 08732. Fax: 732-288-2663. Application deadline: April 15.

BURKLYN BALLET THEATRE II, THE CHILDREN'S PROGRAM
JOHNSON STATE COLLEGE
JOHNSON, VERMONT 05656

General Information Classical ballet workshop for 18 girls ages 8–11 in one 3-week session. Established in 1995. 35 miles from Burlington. Features: college campus; rural village; streams and mountains; library; 4 studios.

Profile of Summer Employees Total number: 6; typical ages: 35–45. 100% women. Nonsmokers required.

Employment Information Jobs available: ▶ *registered nurse* should be experienced RN with Vermont nursing license; salary is child's tuition waiver ▶ 4 *teachers* with certification in the field. Applicants must submit a formal organization application, cover letter, resume, personal reference. International applicants accepted; must obtain own visa, obtain own working papers. An in-person interview is required.

Benefits and Preemployment Training Free housing, free meals, on-the-job training, opportunity to attend seminars/workshops, travel reimbursement, and tuition assistance. Preemployment training is required and includes interpersonal skills.

Contact Angela Whitehill, Artistic Director, Burklyn Ballet Theatre II, The Children's Program, PO Box 907, Island Heights, New Jersey 08732. Telephone: 732-288-2660. Fax: 732-288-2663. Application deadline: March 15.

CAMP FARNSWORTH
ROUTE 113
THETFORD, VERMONT 05074

General Information Residential Girl Scout camp for girls ages 6–16 offering four 2-week sessions. Established in 1959. 300-acre facility located 150 miles from Boston, Massachusetts. Features: private lake; variety of terrain: woods, meadows, hills; 50-foot waterslide into lake; high ropes course.

Profile of Summer Employees Total number: 110; typical ages: 18–40. 1% men; 99% women; 5% minorities; 50% college students; 30% non-U.S. citizens; 20% local applicants. Nonsmokers preferred.

Employment Information Openings are from June 16 to August 25. Jobs available: ▶ 1 *adventure director* with experience instructing ropes course at $1800–$3200 per season ▶ 3 *arts assistants* (minimum age 18) with experience teaching in the field at $1400–$1800 per season ▶ 1 *arts* *director* with supervisory experience at $2400–$3200 per season ▶ 2 *cooks* with quantity cooking experience at $2400–$3200 per season ▶ 1 *counselor-in-training director* (minimum age 21) with camp supervisory experience at $1800–$2400 per season ▶ *driver/shopper* (minimum age 21) with driver's license at $1800–$2300 per season ▶ 1 *ecology director* with experience in the field at $1600–$2700 per season ▶ 1 *food supervisor* (minimum age 21) with experience in menu planning and quantity cooking at $3000–$5000 per season ▶ 2 *health directors* (minimum age 21) with RN, LPN, or EMT license at $2000–$4000 per season ▶ 1 *horseback riding director* (minimum age 21) with experience supervising English riding program, CHA preferred at $2400–$3200 per season ▶ 4 *riding assistants* (minimum age 18) with instructor experience, CHA preferred at $1400–$2400 per season ▶ 15–20 *unit assistants* (minimum age 18) with child supervisory experience and high school diploma at $1400–$1800 per season ▶ 12 *unit leaders* with high school diploma and experience supervising adults and working with groups of children at $1800–$2400 per season ▶ 8 *waterfront assistants* (minimum age 18) with Red Cross or YMCA lifeguard certification (WSI preferred) and experience teaching swimming at $1400–$2400 per season ▶ 1 *waterfront director* (minimum age 21) with WSI and LGT certification, supervisory experience and experience teaching swimming at $2400–$3200 per season. Applicants must submit formal organization application, three personal references. International applicants accepted; must apply through a recognized agency. A telephone interview is required.

Benefits and Preemployment Training Free housing, free meals, formal training, health insurance, and on-the-job training. Preemployment training is required and includes accident prevention and safety, first aid, CPR, interpersonal skills, leadership skills, child development, camp program.

Contact Nancy Frankel, Camp Director, Camp Farnsworth, 88 Harvey Road, #4, Manchester, New Hampshire 03103. Telephone: 603-627-4158. Fax: 603-627-4169. E-mail: camping@ swgirlscouts.org. World Wide Web: http://www.swgirlscouts.org. Application deadline: continuous.

CAMP THOREAU-IN-VERMONT
ONE THOREAU WAY
THETFORD CENTER, VERMONT 05075-9601

General Information Interracial coeducational democratic community living for 140 campers and 64 staff members. Established in 1972. 280-acre facility located 25 miles from White River Junction. Features: rural environment; on-site riding facility; 4 clay tennis courts; campsite on 64-acre lake; hiking in nearby White and Green Mountains; fully equipped darkroom and video studio.

Profile of Summer Employees Total number: 65; typical ages: 17–35. 50% men; 50% women; 15% minorities; 8% high school students; 60% college students; 20% non-U.S. citizens; 10% local applicants. Nonsmokers preferred.

Employment Information Openings are from June 15 to August 22. Jobs available: ▶ 1 *counselor/newspaper person* with experience at $1400–$2200 per season ▶ 3 *counselors/arts and crafts instructors* with CPR/first aid certification and experience at $1200–$2000 per season ▶ 2 *counselors/drama instructors* with experience in the field at $1400–$2200 per season ▶ 2 *counselors/evening programs instructors* with experience and creativity to design activities for the entire camp at $1400–$2200 per season ▶ 2 *counselors/high-ropes instructors* with experience at $1400–$2200 per season ▶ 2 *counselors/hiking and outdoor living instructors* with experience, familiarity with area, CPR/first aid certification, and Wilderness First Responder or Wilderness EMT (preferred) at $1400–$2200 per season ▶ 12 *counselors/lifeguards* with LGT, CPR/FPR, and first aid certification at $1400–$2200 per season ▶ 2 *counselors/low-ropes instructors* with CPR/first aid certification and experience at $1400–$2200 per season ▶ 2 *counselors/ martial arts and fencing instructors* with experience, belt and CPR/first aid certification; at $1400–$2200 per season ▶ 2 *counselors/nature (small animals) instructors* with CPR/first aid certification and experience at $1400–$2200 per season ▶ 2 *counselors/photography instructors* with CPR/first aid certification and experience at $1200–$2000 per season ▶ 4 *counselors/ riding instructors* with CHA and CPR/first aid certification at $1400–$2200 per season ▶ 6 *counselors/small craft instructors* with LGT and canoeing/sailing/kayaking instructor certification at $1400–$2200 per season ▶ 4 *counselors/sports instructors* with CPR/first aid certification and experience at $1400–$2200 per season ▶ 8 *counselors/swimming instructors* with WSI, LGT, first aid, and CPR/FPR certification at $1400–$2200 per season ▶ 2 *counselors/top-rope rock climbing instructors* with experience at $1400–$2200 per season ▶ 2 *counselors/woodshop instructors* with CPR/first aid certification and experience at $1200–$2000 per season ▶ *maintenance staff* with experience at $1400–$2800 per season ▶ *nurses* with RN license, ability to obtain Vermont RN license, and CPR certification at $3300–$3600 per season ▶ *office manager* with filing, simple bookkeeping, and telephone skills at $1300–$2500 per season. Applicants must submit formal organization application, cover letter, personal reference, letter of recommendation. International applicants accepted; must apply through a recognized agency. An in-person interview is recommended, but a telephone interview is acceptable.

Benefits and Preemployment Training Free housing, free meals, health insurance, on-the-job training, travel reimbursement, and laundry facilities; opportunity to work with diverse, multi-cultural staff in several different program areas.

Contact Gregory H. Finger, Director, Camp Thoreau-In-Vermont, 157 Tillson Lake Road, Wallkill, New York 12589-3213. Telephone: 914-895-2974. Fax: 914-895-1281. Application deadline: continuous.

CAMP THORPE, INC.
680 CAPEN HILL RAOD
GOSHEN, VERMONT 05733

General Information Summer residential camp that serves children and adults with special needs. Established in 1927. 200-acre facility located 70 miles from Burlington. Features: large pool; tennis court; pond; small stage; cabins; small farm.

Profile of Summer Employees Total number: 25; typical ages: 18–22. 40% men; 60% women; 10% high school students; 90% college students; 25% non-U.S. citizens; 75% local applicants. Nonsmokers preferred.

Employment Information Openings are from June 22 to August 15. Jobs available: ▶ 1 *camp nurse* with RN, LPN, or EMT license at $2000–$3000 per season ▶ 1 *cook* with previous experience at $2500–$3000 per season ▶ 12 *general counselors* (minimum age 18) with a desire to work with children and adults with special needs at $1100–$1400 per season ▶ 2 *head counselors* (minimum age 18) with two years of college completed at $1500–$2000 per season ▶ 5 *specialists (art, nature, music, pool, and sports)* (minimum age 18) with one year of college completed at $1300–$1500 per season. Applicants must submit formal organization application, three personal references. International applicants accepted; must apply through a recognized agency. An in-person interview is recommended, but a telephone interview is acceptable.

Benefits and Preemployment Training Free housing, free meals, and on-the-job training. Preemployment training is required and includes accident prevention and safety, first aid, CPR, interpersonal skills, leadership skills.

Contact Lyle P. Jepson, Director, Camp Thorpe, Inc., 680 Capen Hill Road, Goshen, Vermont 05733. Telephone: 802-247-6611. E-mail: mjep@sover.net. Application deadline: continuous.

CHALLENGE WILDERNESS CAMP FOR BOYS
ROARING BROOK ROAD
BRADFORD, VERMONT 05033

General Information Residential camp serving 45 boys ages 9–16 with outdoor skills and wilderness trips. Established in 1965. 650-acre facility located 26 miles from Hanover, New Hampshire. Features: 650-acre forest preserve; 15-acre trout-stocked private lake; adirondack shelters; blacksmith shop; playing fields.

Profile of Summer Employees Total number: 10–12; typical ages: 21–30. 100% men; 60% college students; 40% non-U.S. citizens. Nonsmokers required.

Employment Information Openings are from June 18 to August 25. Jobs available: ▶ 1 *blacksmithing instructor* (minimum age 21) with ability to be trained at $1300–$2000 per season ▶ 1 *fishing/fly-tying instructor* (minimum age 21) with trout speciality at $1300–$2000 ▶ 1 *food services director* (minimum age 21) with outdoorsman and cooking skills at $1300–$2000 per season ▶ 1 *kayak instructor* (minimum age 21) with ACA or BCU certification; LGT preferred at $1300–$2000 per season ▶ 1 *kitchen assistant* (minimum age 21) with outdoorsman skills at $1300–$2000 per season ▶ 1 *marksmanship instructor* (minimum age 21) with .22-caliber and military experience at $1300–$2000 per season ▶ 3 *rock climbing instructors* (minimum age 21) with one 5.10 lead plus two 5.9 seconds at $1300–$2000 per season ▶ 1 *waterfront director* with lifeguard training required; WSI preferred at $1300–$2000 per season ▶ 1 *woodworking instructor* (minimum age 21) with background in carpentry, woodwork, and cabinet-making at $1300–$2000 per week. Applicants must submit formal organization application, cover letter, resume, three personal references. International applicants accepted; must apply through a recognized agency. A telephone interview is required.

Benefits and Preemployment Training Free housing, free meals, on-the-job training, and outdoor leadership training. Preemployment training is required and includes accident prevention and safety, first aid, CPR, interpersonal skills, leadership skills, water safety rescue.

Contact Dr. J. Thayer and Candice L. Raines, Directors, Challenge Wilderness Camp for Boys, 300 North Grove Street, #4, Rutland, Vermont 05701. Telephone: 800-832-HAWK. Fax: 802-786-0653. E-mail: rainest@sover.net. World Wide Web: http://www.challengewilderness.com. Application deadline: continuous.

FARM AND WILDERNESS CAMPS
263 FARM AND WILDERNESS ROAD
PLYMOUTH, VERMONT 05056

General Information Five separate individual residential programs for boys/girls ages 9–17 offering diverse outdoor wilderness activities within Quaker-based communities. Also day camp for boys and girls ages 3–10. Established in 1939. 3,000-acre facility located 23 miles from Rutland. Features: freshwater lake; certified organic farm; Green Mountain National Forest; surrounded by 3000 acres of forest; farm animals; 3-sided cabins.

Profile of Summer Employees Total number: 200; typical ages: 19–24. 55% men; 45% women; 10% minorities; 5% high school students; 75% college students; 2% retirees; 2% non-U.S. citizens; 15% local applicants. Nonsmokers required.

Employment Information Openings are from June 15 to August 25. Year-round positions also offered. Jobs available: ▶ 18 *cooks* (minimum age 18) at $1800–$4000 per season ▶ 120–150 *counselors* (minimum age 18) at $1500–$2250 per season ▶ 5 *maintenance staff members* (minimum age 21) with carpentry and plumbing experience at $1350–$2250 per season ▶ 6 *nurses* (minimum age 21) with RN license or graduate nursing student status at $2000–$3500 per season ▶ 15 *swimming instructors* (minimum age 18) with LGT/WSI certification at $1350–$2250 per season. Applicants must submit formal organization application, three personal references. International applicants accepted; must apply through a recognized agency. A telephone interview is required.

Benefits and Preemployment Training Free housing, free meals, formal training, health insurance, and on-the-job training. Preemployment training is required and includes accident prevention and safety, first aid, CPR, interpersonal skills, leadership skills.

Contact Sonny Cloward, Staff Recruiter, Farm and Wilderness Camps. Telephone: 802-422-3761. Fax: 802-422-8660. E-mail: sonny@fandw.org. World Wide Web: http://www.fandw.org. Application deadline: continuous.

KILLOOLEET
ROUTE 100
HANCOCK, VERMONT 05748-0070

General Information Full-season, noncompetitive, coeducational camp serving 100 campers ages 9–14 for 7 or more weeks. Emphasis is on developing techniques in group leadership and individual areas of expertise. Children specialize in a variety of sports and arts activities. Established in 1927. 300-acre facility located 35 miles from Rutland. Features: beautiful valley, streams and woods; flat campus and bicycles; freshwater lake; horses and riding program; all counselors go on hikes and overnight trips.

Profile of Summer Employees Total number: 48; typical ages: 18–30. 50% men; 50% women;

7% minorities; 12% high school students; 65% college students; 20% non-U.S. citizens; 15% local applicants. Nonsmokers preferred.

Employment Information Openings are from June 20 to August 23. Jobs available: ▶ 1 *boating (canoeing, windsurfing) instructor* at $1200–$1800 per season ▶ 1 *drama counselor* with ability to direct a musical as well as teach improvisation/creative dramatics at $1300–$2000 per season ▶ 1 *electronics instructor* at $1300–$2000 per season ▶ 2 *horseback riding (English) instructors* with Pony Club or equivalent group teaching experience at $1400–$2000 per season ▶ *mountain biking/rock climbing/campig skills instructor* with teaching experience and other interests at $1300–$2000 per season ▶ 1–2 *music (folk, rhythm and blues/funk) instructors* with interest in working with camper bands, teaching individual lessons, and running group sings at $1300–$1800 per season ▶ 1 *music counselor* with ability to play piano for the camp musical and help campers with learning their songs (other activity skills desirable, too) at $1300–$1800 per season ▶ 1 *nature instructor* with teaching ideas using pond, fields, stream, and woods at $1300–$1800 per season ▶ 1 *secretary* at $1300–$1800 per season ▶ 1 *shop counselor (woodworking or crafts)* at $1200–$1700 per season ▶ 2 *sports (individual and team) instructors* at $1300–$1800 per season ▶ *swimming instructor* with current WSI and lifeguard certification at $1400–$2100 per season ▶ 1 *video, control room, and editing instructor* at $1400–$2000 per season. Applicants must submit formal organization application, cover letter, three personal references, brief biographical statement. International applicants accepted; must apply through a recognized agency. An in-person interview is recommended, but a telephone interview is acceptable.

Benefits and Preemployment Training Free housing, free meals, formal training, health insurance, on-the-job training, opportunity to attend seminars/workshops, and partial travel reimbursement. Preemployment training is required and includes accident prevention and safety, first aid, CPR, interpersonal skills, leadership skills.

Contact Kate Spencer-Seeger, Director, Killooleet, 70 Trull Street, Somerville, Massachusetts 02145. Telephone: 617-666-1484. Fax: 617-666-0378. E-mail: camp05748@aol.com. World Wide Web: http://www.killooleet.com. Application deadline: continuous.

LOCHEARN CAMP FOR GIRLS
LAKE FAIRLEE
POST MILLS, VERMONT 05058

General Information Private residential camp for girls ages 7–16 offering a comprehensive activity program with special emphasis on positive character development of children. Established in 1916. 51-acre facility located 150 miles from Boston, Massachusetts. Features: freshwater lake; wooded setting; lakeside cabins; gymnastics center; 5 tennis courts; 16- horse stable and riding facilities.

Profile of Summer Employees Total number: 75; typical ages: 18–26. 10% men; 90% women; 10% high school students; 80% college students; 10% retirees; 15% non-U.S. citizens. Nonsmokers required.

Employment Information Openings are from June 10 to August 22. Jobs available: ▶ 2 *English-style riding instructors* (minimum age 18) with experience in the field at $1400–$1600 per season ▶ 2 *canoeing instructors* (minimum age 18) with LGT certification or small crafts safety certification at $1300–$1500 per season ▶ 1 *diving instructor* (minimum age 18) with LGT certification at $1300–$1500 per season ▶ 5 *field sports instructors* (minimum age 18) at $1300–$1600 per season ▶ 3 *gymnastics instructors* (minimum age 18) with floor and full apparatus experience; coaching experience preferred at $1300–$1600 per season ▶ 3 *kitchen assistants* (minimum age 18) at $1600–$1800 per season ▶ 2 *leadership trainers* (minimum age 21) with experience in the field at $1500–$1700 per season ▶ 2 *outdoor adventure staff* (minimum age 21) with WFA/First Responder at $1400–$1600 per season ▶ 2 *performing arts instructors* (minimum age 18) with experience in the field at $1300–$1600 per season ▶ 2 *registered nurses* (minimum age 22) with RN (Vermont temporary license); CPR/first aid certification and pediatric experience at $3500–$4000 per season ▶ 2 *sailing instructors* (minimum age 18) with LGT or small crafts safety certification at $1300–$1600 per season ▶ 4 *studio arts instructors* (minimum age 18) at $1300–$1600 per season ▶ 2 *swimming instructors* (minimum age 18) with LGT/WSI certification at $1300–$1600 per season ▶ 4 *tennis instructors* (minimum age 18) with coaching experience preferred at $1300–$1600 per season ▶ 2 *waterskiing instructors/boat drivers* (minimum age 18) with LGT certification or waterski instructors certification at $1400–$1600 per season. Applicants must submit formal organization application, three personal references. International applicants accepted; must apply through a recognized agency. A telephone interview is required.

Benefits and Preemployment Training Free housing, free meals, formal training, on-the-job training, and travel reimbursement. Preemployment training is required and includes accident prevention and safety, interpersonal skills, leadership skills, character education, curriculum training.

Contact Rich Maxson, Owner/Director, Lochearn Camp for Girls, Camp Lochearn on Lake Fairlee, Post Mills, Vermont 05058. Telephone: 800-235-6659. Fax: 802-333-4856. E-mail: lochearn@aol.com. Application deadline: continuous.

MOUNT SNOW
ROUTE 100
WEST DOVER, VERMONT 05356

General Information Major ski area. Summer operations include mountain biking, lift service for downhill bikers, kids camp, hotels, golf, golf school, hiking, bus tours, lift rides, schools for biking, 2 swimming pools, and lakes. Established in 1954. 1,000-acre facility located 50 miles from Albany. Features: 2 swimming pools; 2 hotels; wooded setting; 3 lifts operational (summer); golf course (18 holes); climbing wall and in-line skate park.

Profile of Summer Employees Total number: 350; typical ages: 18–60. 70% men; 30% women; 10% high school students; 20% college students; 70% local applicants. Nonsmokers preferred.

Employment Information Openings are from May 31 to September. Spring break, winter break, and year-round positions also offered. Jobs available: ▶ *food and beverage staff* ▶ *lift operators* (minimum age 18). Applicants must submit a formal organization application. International applicants accepted; must obtain own visa. An in-person interview is required.

Benefits and Preemployment Training Possible full-time employment, on-the-job training, and free golf/skiing depending on season, discounted bike rentals, use of bike trail network. Preemployment training is required and includes accident prevention and safety, interpersonal skills, leadership skills, guest service cross training.

Contact Charlie Romano, Recruiter-Trainer, Mount Snow, Human Resources, Route 100, West Dover, Vermont 05356. Telephone: 802-464-1100 Ext. 4321. Fax: 802-464-4135. E-mail: cromano@mountsnow.com. World Wide Web: http://www.mountsnow.com. Application deadline: continuous.

POINT COUNTER POINT CHAMBER MUSIC CAMP
LAKE DUNEMORE, VERMONT 05733

General Information Residential camp serving 50 string players and pianists for three-, four-,or seven-week sessions. Established in 1963. 2-acre facility located 50 miles from Burlington. Features: freshwater; mountains; small student body.

Profile of Summer Employees Total number: 22; typical ages: 19–40. 34% men; 66% women; 16% minorities; 33% college students; 16% non-U.S. citizens; 27% local applicants. Nonsmokers preferred.

Employment Information Openings are from June 20 to August 14. Jobs available: ▶ 1 *activities director* (minimum age 21) with interpersonal skills at $2400–$3000 per season ▶ 6 *activity counselors* (minimum age 19) with WSI, first aid, and CPR certification (preferred) at $1500–$1700 per season ▶ *cooks* with experience in the field at $2200–$3500 per season ▶ 8 *music staff members (4 violinists, 1 violist, 2 cellists, and 1 pianist)* with performing and teaching experience at $2500–$2800 per season. Applicants must submit a formal organization application, resume, three personal references, audition tape for music faculty. International applicants accepted; must obtain own visa, obtain own working papers. A telephone interview is required.

Benefits and Preemployment Training Free housing and free meals. Preemployment training is required and includes interpersonal skills, leadership skills.

Contact Paul Roby, Director, Point Counter Point Chamber Music Camp, PO Box 3181, Terre Haute, Indiana 47803. Telephone: 812-877-3745. Fax: 812-877-2174. E-mail: pointcp@aol.com. World Wide Web: http://www.pointcp.com. Application deadline: continuous.

PUTNEY SUMMER PROGRAMS
ELM LEA FARM
PUTNEY, VERMONT 05346

General Information Residential program for 80 students in visual and performing arts, writing, English as a second language, chamber music, farming, and gardening. Established in 1987. 500-acre facility located 10 miles from Brattleboro. Features: superb arts facilities; working farm; residential cottages; state-of-the-art computer lab; miles of biking/running trails; hilltop setting.

Profile of Summer Employees Total number: 45; typical ages: 21–32. 40% men; 60% women; 10% minorities; 30% college students; 10% non-U.S. citizens; 40% local applicants. Nonsmokers required.

Employment Information Openings are from June 22 to August 8. Jobs available: ▶ 12–15 *residential assistants* (minimum age 21) with experience in arts, music, farming, writing, or English as a Second Language preferred; also residential and outdoor experience and first aid training at $1600 per season. Applicants must submit a formal organization application, cover letter, resume, three personal references. International applicants accepted; must obtain own visa, obtain own working papers. An in-person interview is recommended, but a telephone interview is acceptable.

Benefits and Preemployment Training Free housing, free meals, formal training, on-the-job training, and travel reimbursement. Preemployment training is required and includes accident prevention and safety, first aid, CPR, interpersonal skills, leadership skills.

Contact Brian D. Cohen, Director, Summer Programs, Putney Summer Programs, The Putney School, Putney, Vermont 05346. Fax: 802-387-6216. E-mail: summer@pegasus.putney.com.

THE SOUTHWESTERN COMPANY, VERMONT
See The Southwestern Company, Tennessee on page 284 for complete description.

STUDENT CONSERVATION ASSOCIATION (SCA), VERMONT
See Student Conservation Association (SCA), New Hampshire on page 193 for complete description.

SUMMER DISCOVERY AT VERMONT
UNIVERSITY OF VERMONT
BURLINGTON, VERMONT 05401

General Information Precollege enrichment program for high school students at University of Vermont. Established in 1990. Features: sport facilities; beaches; mountains; lakes; major cities nearby; college towns.

Profile of Summer Employees Total number: 20; typical ages: 21–35. 10% minorities; 60% college students. Nonsmokers required.

Employment Information Openings are from June 20 to August 25. Jobs available: ▶ 20 *resident counselors* (minimum age 21) with experience working with high school students/children at $150–$400 per week. Applicants must submit a formal organization application, resume, three personal references. International applicants accepted; must obtain own visa, obtain own working papers. An in-person interview is required.

Benefits and Preemployment Training Free housing, free meals, possible full-time employment, on-the-job training, and travel reimbursement. Preemployment training is required and includes accident prevention and safety, CPR, leadership skills.

Contact Jason Walley, Admissions Director, Summer Discovery at Vermont, 1326 Old Northern Boulevard, Roslyn, New York 11576. Telephone: 516-621-3939. Fax: 516-625-3438. E-mail: staff@summerfun.com. World Wide Web: http://www.summerfun.com. Application deadline: continuous.

WINDRIDGE TENNIS CAMP AT CRAFTSBURY COMMON
PO BOX 27
CRAFTSBURY COMMON, VERMONT 05827

General Information Residential coeducational camp serving 110 campers with an emphasis on tennis along with traditional camp activities. Owned by Windridge Tennis Camp, Inc. Established in 1973. 50-acre facility located 35 miles from Montpelier. Features: 16 tennis courts; private lake; lakeside cabins; sculling facilities; soccer fields; rural wooded setting.

Profile of Summer Employees Total number: 40; typical ages: 18–25. 50% men; 50% women; 10% minorities; 80% college students; 20% non-U.S. citizens; 10% local applicants. Nonsmokers required.

Employment Information Openings are from June 5 to August 24. Jobs available: ▶ 1 *archery instructor* (minimum age 18) with American Archery Association Level-1 certification at $1800–$2500 per season ▶ 1 *arts and crafts instructor* at $1800–$2500 per season ▶ 3 *lifeguards* with LGT at $1800–$2000 per season ▶ 1 *mountain bike instructor* (minimum age 18) with riding and mechanical skills at $1800–$2500 per season ▶ 1 *photography instructor* at $1800–$2000 per season ▶ 1 *registered nurse* at $400–$425 per week ▶ 2 *sailing instructors* with LGT at $1800–$2000 per season ▶ 3 *soccer instructors* at $1800–$2500 per season ▶ 12–16 *tennis instructors* (minimum age 18) with college or high school competitive experience at $1800–$2500 per season ▶ 1 *waterfront director* with LGT at $2000–$3000 per season. Applicants must submit formal organization application, three personal references. International applicants accepted; must apply through a recognized agency. A telephone interview is required.

Benefits and Preemployment Training Free housing, free meals, and on-the-job training. Preemployment training is required and includes accident prevention and safety, first aid, CPR, interpersonal skills, leadership skills.

Contact Charles Witherell, Director, Windridge Tennis Camp at Craftsbury Common, PO Box 4518, Burlington, Vermont 05406. Telephone: 802-586-9646. Fax: 802-658-0288. E-mail: wcampcc@aol.com. Application deadline: continuous.

WINDRIDGE TENNIS CAMP AT TEELA-WOOKET, VERMONT
1215 ROXBURY ROAD
ROXBURY, VERMONT 05669

General Information Residential camp for boys and girls ages 9–15 specializing in tennis, riding, and soccer. Established in 1986. 235-acre facility located 55 miles from Burlington. Features: 21 clay tennis courts; 2 regulation soccer fields; 40-stall horse barn; rustic cabins; swimming pool; in-line hockey facility.

Profile of Summer Employees Total number: 70; typical ages: 18–24. 50% men; 50% women; 5% minorities; 5% high school students; 45% college students; 40% non-U.S. citizens; 10% local applicants. Nonsmokers required.

Employment Information Openings are from June 4 to August 22. Jobs available: ▶ 1–2 *activity specialists* (minimum age 18) with experience in mountain biking, in-line hockey, basketball, and team sports required at $1800–$2000 per season ▶ 1 *archery instructor* (minimum age 18) with experience preferred at $1800–$2000 per season ▶ 1 *childcare worker for staff children* (minimum age 18) with driver's license and ability to swim preferred at $1300–$2000 per season ▶ 1 *lifeguard* (minimum age 18) with Red Cross Lifeguard Training or equivalent at $1800–$2000 per season ▶ 1 *program director* (minimum age 21) with previous camp experience at $4000–$5000 per season ▶ 4–5 *riding instructors* (minimum age 18) with good riding skills and teaching experience at $1800–$2000 per season ▶ 18–23 *tennis instructors* (minimum age 18) with experience required and teaching experience preferred at $1800–$2000 per season. Applicants must submit formal organization application, resume, three personal references, three letters of recommendation. International applicants accepted; must apply through a recognized agency. An in-person interview is recommended, but a telephone interview is acceptable.

Benefits and Preemployment Training Free housing, free meals, on-the-job training, and travel reimbursement. Preemployment training is required and includes accident prevention and safety, first aid, CPR, interpersonal skills, leadership skills.

Contact Cub Momsen, Director, Windridge Tennis Camp at Teela-Wooket, Vermont, PO Box

4518, Burlington, Vermont 05406-4518. Telephone: 802-658-0313. Fax: 802-658-0288. E-mail: wcamps@aol.com. World Wide Web: http://www.windridgetw.com. Application deadline: continuous.

VIRGIN ISLANDS

LONGACRE EXPEDITIONS
VIRGIN ISLANDS

General Information Adventure travel program in the Virgin Islands for teenagers, emphasizing group living skills and physical challenges. Established in 1981. Near St. Thomas.

Profile of Summer Employees Total number: 4; typical ages: 23–30. 50% men; 50% women; 100% college students. Nonsmokers required.

Employment Information Openings are from June 15 to July 30. Jobs available: ▶ 2 *assistant leaders* (minimum age 21) with scuba certification, first aid or WFR, CPR, and lifeguard training at $252–$300 per week. Applicants must submit a formal organization application, three personal references. International applicants accepted; must obtain own visa, obtain own working papers. An in-person interview is recommended, but a telephone interview is acceptable.

Benefits and Preemployment Training Free housing, free meals, on-the-job training, and pro-deal purchase program. Preemployment training is required and includes accident prevention and safety, interpersonal skills, leadership skills.

Contact Meredith Schuler, Director, Longacre Expeditions, RD 3, Box 106, Newport, Pennsylvania 17074. Telephone: 717-567-6790. Fax: 717-567-3955. E-mail: longacre@longacreexpeditions.com. World Wide Web: http://www.longacreexpeditions.com. Application deadline: continuous.

VIRGINIA

ACE COMPUTER CAMP–VIRGINIA
See ACE Computer Camp–Washington on page 307 for complete description.

A CHRISTIAN MINISTRY IN THE NATIONAL PARKS–VIRGINIA
See A Christian Ministry in the National Parks–Massachussetts on page 138 for complete description.

CAMP CARYSBROOK/CAMP CARYSBROOK DAY CAMP
3500 CAMP CARYSBROOK ROAD
RINER, VIRGINIA 24149

General Information Traditional residential camp for girls ages 6–16 in two-, four-, six-, and eight-week sessions; one-week day camp in late August. Established in 1923. 200-acre facility located 30 miles from Roanoke. Features: freshwater lake; mountains; wooded setting; cabins; 2 tennis courts; stables.

Profile of Summer Employees Total number: 30; typical ages: 18–25. 2% men; 98% women; 10% minorities; 90% college students; 10% non-U.S. citizens; 5% local applicants.

Employment Information Openings are from June 12 to August 24. Jobs available: ▶ 1 *archery instructor* (minimum age 18) with experience in the field at $550–$1000 per season ▶ 1 *arts and crafts instructor* (minimum age 18) with experience in the field at $550–$1000 per season ▶ 1 *canoeing instructor* (minimum age 18) with Red Cross canoe and lifesaving certification at $550–$1000 per season ▶ 1 *climbing, rappelling, and caving instructor* (minimum age 21) with experience in the field at $550–$1200 per season ▶ 1 *dance instructor* (minimum age 18) with experience in the field at $550–$1000 per season ▶ 1 *drama instructor* (minimum age 18) with experience in the field at $550–$1000 per season ▶ 1 *ecology instructor* (minimum age 18) with experience in the field at $550–$1000 per season ▶ 1 *fencing instructor* (minimum age 18) with experience in the field at $500–$1000 per season ▶ 1 *outdoor living skills instructor* (minimum age 21) with experience in the field at $550–$1000 per season ▶ 1 *recreational sports staff member* (minimum age 18) with experience in the field at $550–$1000 per season ▶ 2 *riding instructors* (minimum age 18) with CHA certification and experience in the field at $550–$1200 per season ▶ 1 *riflery instructor* (minimum age 18) with experience in the field at $550–$1000 per season ▶ 3 *swimming instructors* (minimum age 18) with WSI or lifesaving certification at $550–$1200 per season ▶ 2 *team sports staff members* (minimum age 18) with experience in the field at $550–$1000 per season ▶ 1 *tennis instructor* (minimum age 18) with experience in the field at $550–$1000 per season. Applicants must submit formal organization application, three personal references. International applicants accepted; must apply through a recognized agency. An in-person interview is recommended, but a telephone interview is acceptable.

Benefits and Preemployment Training Free housing, free meals, names of contacts, on-the-job training, and opportunity to attend seminars/workshops. Preemployment training is required and includes accident prevention and safety, first aid, CPR, interpersonal skills, leadership skills.

Contact Toni M. Baughman, CCD, Director, Camp Carysbrook/Camp Carysbrook Day Camp, 4421 Seminary Road, Alexandria, Virginia 22304. Telephone: 703-836-7548. Fax: 703-751-2974. E-mail: tmoose@aol.com. World Wide Web: http://www.campcarysbrook.com. Application deadline: continuous.

CAMP FRIENDSHIP
PO BOX 145
PALMYRA, VIRGINIA 22963

General Information Residential camp with a traditional program, specialized equestrian program, golf, gymnastics, and tennis camps, and adventure trips for teens in one- and two-week sessions. Established in 1966. 730-acre facility located 25 miles from Charlottesville. Features: lake; junior Olympic-size pool; 2 gymnasiums; 80-stall stable; 60-event ropes course; 4 tennis courts.

Profile of Summer Employees Total number: 140; typical ages: 16–30. 50% men; 50% women; 5% minorities; 5% high school students; 50% college students; 15% non-U.S. citizens; 10% local applicants. Nonsmokers preferred.

Employment Information Openings are from June 8 to September 4. Year-round positions also offered. Jobs available: ▶ 55 *cabin counselors/trip leaders* (minimum age 19) with teaching skills at $1150–$1400 per season ▶ 1 *creative arts director* (minimum age 21) with crafts and drama skills at $1200–$1400 per season ▶ 3 *drivers/maintenance personnel* (minimum age 21) with driver's license at $1200–$1400 per season ▶ 11 *kitchen staff members* at $1000–$2000 per season ▶ 2 *nurses* with RN license at $2000–$4000 per season ▶ 8 *riding counselors/instructors* with experience in the field at $1100–$1500 per season ▶ 1 *ropes course director* (minimum age 21) with experience in the field at $1200–$1800 per season ▶ 1 *tennis instructor* with experience in the field at $1200–$1800 per season ▶ 4 *village directors* with college degree and supervisory experience at $1600–$2000 per season ▶ 1 *waterfront director* (minimum age 21) with WSI and lifeguard instructor certification at $1200–$2000 per season. Applicants must submit formal organization application, three personal references. International applicants accepted; must apply through a recognized agency. An in-person interview is recommended, but a telephone interview is acceptable.

Benefits and Preemployment Training Free housing, free meals, formal training, possible full-time employment, on-the-job training, and opportunity to attend seminars/workshops.

Preemployment training is required and includes accident prevention and safety, first aid, CPR, interpersonal skills, leadership skills, specific activity instructor training.

Contact Linda Grier and Ray Ackenbom, Directors, Camp Friendship, PO Box 145, Palmyra, Virginia 22963. Telephone: 804-589-8950. Fax: 804-589-5880. E-mail: info@campfriendship. com. World Wide Web: http://www.campfriendship.com. Application deadline: continuous.

CAMP HORIZONS
3586 HORIZONS WAY
HARRISONBURG, VIRGINIA 22802

General Information Summer residential camp for children ages 7–16. Corporate training center and retreat center for schools, churches, and universities in the spring and fall. Teen adventure and traditional camp programs. Established in 1983. 240-acre facility located 15 miles from Harrisonburg. Features: mountain setting; lake; pool; tennis courts; ropes course; modern cabins.

Profile of Summer Employees Total number: 100; typical ages: 19–45. 50% men; 50% women; 10% minorities; 90% college students; 50% non-U.S. citizens; 30% local applicants. Nonsmokers required.

Employment Information Openings are from June 1 to August 31. Year-round positions also offered. Jobs available: ▶ 14–20 *adventure counselors/adventure specialists* (minimum age 21) with skills in caving, rock climbing, canoeing, ropes course, and backpacking; CPR/first aid, valid driver's license, and good driving record at $1050–$1600 per season ▶ 6 *custodial/ maintenance staff* (minimum age 19) with CPR/first aid certification at $1500–$1800 per season ▶ 20 *general activities counselors* (minimum age 19) with first aid, CPR certification, and experience in any combination of the following: swimming, French, Spanish, Japanese, ESL, drama, model rocketry, caving, or rock climbing at $1050–$1400 per season ▶ 60 *general counselors* (minimum age 19) with CPR/first aid, valid driver's license, and good driving record at $1050–$1400 per season ▶ 5 *kitchen staff/cooks* (minimum age 19) with CPR/first aid certification at $1500–$1800 per season ▶ 5 *program directors* (minimum age 21) with bachelor's degree, experience and skills in education, administration, international education, and counseling; CPR/first aid, valid driver's license, and good driving record at $1400–$2000 per season ▶ *registered nurse* must reside at camp at $400 per week ▶ 3 *riding counselors* (minimum age 20) with first aid, CPR certification, and knowledge of Western-style horseback riding at $1050– $1400 per season ▶ 4 *village coordinators* must be a college graduate at $1800–$2500 per season ▶ 4 *waterfront counselors* (minimum age 19) with lifeguard, first aid, and CPR certification at $1050–$1400 per season. Applicants must submit formal organization application, three personal references, three letters of recommendation, medical form. International applicants accepted; must apply through a recognized agency. An in-person interview is recommended, but a telephone interview is acceptable.

Benefits and Preemployment Training Free housing, free meals, and on-the-job training. Preemployment training is required and includes accident prevention and safety, first aid, CPR, interpersonal skills, leadership skills, ropes course training.

Contact Dave Nealon, Camp Director, Camp Horizons, 3586 Horizons Way, Harrisonburg, Virginia 22802. Telephone: 540-896-7600. Fax: 540-896-5455. E-mail: camphorizo@aol.com. World Wide Web: http://www.camphorizonsva.com. Application deadline: continuous.

CAT'S CAP–ST. CATHERINE'S CREATIVE ARTS PROGRAM
6001 GROVE AVENUE
RICHMOND, VIRGINIA 23226

General Information Day camp concentrating on exploration of the visual and performing arts, as well as offering sports, horseback riding, computer, creative writing, and river exploration. Established in 1978. 16-acre facility located 100 miles from Washington, DC. Features: small college campus-type setting; 2 libraries; full gymnasium facilities; 6 tennis courts and 3 athletic fields; large dining hall; air-conditioned classrooms.

Profile of Summer Employees Total number: 130; typical ages: 14–50. 50% men; 50% women;

9% minorities; 25% high school students; 15% college students; 1% non-U.S. citizens; 98% local applicants. Nonsmokers preferred.

Employment Information Openings are from June 16 to July 31. Jobs available: ▶ 20–30 *counselors* (minimum age 16) at $5–$5.50 per hour ▶ *instructors* with certification in dance, music, art, theater, physical education, visual or performing arts, art education, or elementary education at $11–$13 per hour ▶ 10–15 *junior counselors* (minimum age 15) at $4.50–$5 per hour ▶ 1 *nurse/clerk* with RN license; camp/school nursing experience preferred at $11–$15 per hour ▶ 10–20 *senior counselors* (minimum age 18) with early childhood or education major and experience working with children at $6–$7.50 per hour ▶ *teaching assistants* with training or degree in education and experience working with children at $7–$10 per hour. Applicants must submit a formal organization application, cover letter, resume, two personal references. International applicants accepted; must obtain own visa, obtain own working papers. An in-person interview is required.

Benefits and Preemployment Training Possible full-time employment, on-the-job training, tuition assistance, and free lunch. Preemployment training is required and includes child development.

Contact Jann Holland, Director, Cat's CAP–St. Catherine's Creative Arts Program, 6001 Grove Avenue, Richmond, Virginia 23226. Fax: 804-285-8169. E-mail: jholland@st.catherines.org.

CHEERIO ADVENTURES
754 FOX KNOB ROAD
MOUTH OF WILSON, VIRGINIA 24363

General Information Program in adventure tripping and wilderness travel serving campers ages 10–17. Established in 1982. 60-acre facility located 125 miles from Charlotte. Features: on New River; mixture of woodlands and fields; mountain setting; close proximity to many natural forests.

Profile of Summer Employees Total number: 20; typical ages: 19–25. 50% men; 50% women; 20% minorities; 90% college students. Nonsmokers required.

Employment Information Openings are from May 26 to August 15. Spring break positions also offered. Jobs available: ▶ 1 *assistant logistics director* (minimum age 21) with driver's license at $140–$200 per week ▶ 8–10 *counselors* (minimum age 18) at $150–$190 per week ▶ 1 *logistics director* (minimum age 21) with driver's license and experience in the field at $175–$230 per week ▶ 1 *program director* (minimum age 21) with experience in the field at $200–$250 per week ▶ 2 *trip leaders* (minimum age 21) at $160–$210 per week. Applicants must submit a formal organization application, four personal references. International applicants accepted; must obtain own visa. An in-person interview is recommended, but a telephone interview is acceptable.

Benefits and Preemployment Training Free housing, free meals, health insurance, and on-the-job training. Preemployment training is required and includes accident prevention and safety, first aid, CPR, interpersonal skills, leadership skills.

Contact Keith Russell, Director, Cheerio Adventures, 1430 Camp Cheerio Road, Glade Valley, North Carolina 28627. Telephone: 336-363-2604. Fax: 336-363-3671. E-mail: advcamp@aol.com. World Wide Web: http://www.campcheerio.org. Application deadline: continuous.

4 STAR ACADEMICS PLUS CAMP AT THE UNIVERSITY OF VIRGINIA
PO BOX 3387
FALLS CHURCH, VIRGINIA 22043

General Information Residential tennis camp that offers golf, outdoor adventure, and academic enrichment courses daily and other sporting events in the evenings. Programs are available for campers ages 9-18. Established in 1975. Located 100 miles from Washington, DC. Features: university facilities; 13 tennis courts; full athletic facilities.

Profile of Summer Employees Total number: 30; typical ages: 20–25. 60% men; 40% women; 10% minorities; 70% college students; 10% local applicants. Nonsmokers required.

Employment Information Openings are from June 20 to August 15. Jobs available: ▶ 2 *dormi-*

tory supervisors (minimum age 19) with good organization and problem-solving skills at $1575–$2025 per season ▶ 1 *evening activities director/recreation director* (minimum age 19) with good organization and planning skills at $1800–$2250 per season ▶ 10 *general counselors* (minimum age 19) with ability to work with young people at $900–$1400 per season ▶ 25 *tennis instructors/golf instructors* (minimum age 19) should be advanced-level tennis players with some competitive experience; must be college students or older at $900–$1400 per season. Applicants must submit a formal organization application, cover letter, resume, two personal references, two letters of recommendation. An in-person interview is recommended, but a telephone interview is acceptable.

Benefits and Preemployment Training Free housing, free meals, and on-the-job training. Preemployment training is required and includes interpersonal skills, leadership skills, teaching tennis training.

Contact Ann Grubbs, Assistant Director, 4 Star Academics Plus Camp at the University of Virginia, PO Box 3387, Falls Church, Virginia 22043. Telephone: 703-573-0890. Fax: 703-573-0297. E-mail: info@4starcamps.com. World Wide Web: http://www.4starcamps.com. Application deadline: continuous.

FREDERICKSBURG AND SPOTSYLVANIA NATIONAL MILITARY PARK
120 CHATHAM LANE
FREDERICKSBURG, VIRGINIA 22405

General Information Historic park preserving and interpreting four Civil War battlefields in the Fredericksburg area. Established in 1927. 6,461-acre facility located 50 miles from Washington, DC. Features: 4 Civil War battlefields; 2 visitor centers; historic structures; park housing; historical trails; book store.

Profile of Summer Employees Total number: 50; typical ages: 21–40. 50% men; 50% women; 20% minorities; 5% high school students; 40% college students; 5% retirees; 30% local applicants.

Employment Information Openings are from May 23 to September 6. Year-round positions also offered. Jobs available: ▶ 1 *seasonal cultural resource assistant* (minimum age 18) at $10.05–$10.99 per hour ▶ 1 *seasonal natural resource assistant* (minimum age 18) at $10.05–$10.99 per hour ▶ 6–10 *seasonal park historians* (minimum age 18) at $8.46–$10.99 per hour.

Benefits and Preemployment Training Housing at a cost, formal training, and on-the-job training. Preemployment training is required and includes interpersonal skills, interpretive skills.

Contact Gregory A. Mertz, Supervisory Historian, Fredericksburg and Spotsylvania National Military Park, 120 Chatham Lane, Fredericksburg, Virginia 22405. Telephone: 540-373-6124. Fax: 540-654-5521. E-mail: greg_mertz@nps.gov. World Wide Web: http://www.nps.gov/frsp or http://www.scp.nps.gov. Application deadline: January 15.

THE INSTITUTE FOR THE ACADEMIC ADVANCEMENT OF YOUTH/THE JOHNS HOPKINS UNIVERSITY–EPISCOPAL HIGH SCHOOL
See The Institute for the Academic Advancement of Youth/ The Johns Hopkins University on page 135 for complete description.

LEGACY INTERNATIONAL'S GLOBAL YOUTH VILLAGE
1020 LEGACY DRIVE
BEDFORD, VIRGINIA 24523

General Information Program that creates opportunities to address controversial issues through cooperation and advances problem-solving through cross-cultural understanding. Established in 1979. 80-acre facility located 30 miles from Lynchburg. Features: wooded, rural setting; swimming pool; sports field; nearby mountains and lakes.

Profile of Summer Employees Total number: 5; typical ages: 22–45. 40% men; 60% women; 15% minorities; 10% college students; 30% non-U.S. citizens; 1% local applicants. Nonsmokers preferred.

Employment Information Openings are from June 13 to August 18. Jobs available: ▶ 1 *English* *as a second language instructor* must be native English speaker with classroom teaching experience at up to $1500 per season or on a volunteer basis ▶ 1 *adventure/outdoor skills instructor* with first aid and CPR certification and rock-climbing teaching experience (preferred) at up to $1500 per season or on a volunteer basis ▶ 3 *art instructors* with experience in the field; one position requires ability to teach pottery using the wheel and kiln at up to $1500 per season or on a volunteer basis ▶ 1 *bookkeeper* with knowledge of Excel and experience in the field at up to $1500 per season or on a volunteer basis ▶ 6–8 *counselors (female)* (minimum age 21) must have demonstrated professional youth work experience; at up to $1500 per season or on a volunteer basis ▶ 4–6 *counselors (male)* (minimum age 21) must have demonstrated professional youth work experience at up to $1500 per season or on a volunteer basis ▶ 1 *environmental educator* with experience in the field; classroom teaching experience helpful at up to $1500 per season or on a volunteer basis ▶ 1 *evening and special program coordinator* with performing arts background (preferred) and very good organizational and motivational skills at up to $1500 per season or on a volunteer basis ▶ 1 *global issues instructor* with background and knowledge in international relations and teaching experience at up to $1500 per season or on a volunteer basis ▶ 1 *housekeeper* (minimum age 21) with valid driver's license and motivational and organizational skills at up to $1500 per season or on a volunteer basis ▶ 7 *kitchen staff members* at up to $1500 per season or on a volunteer basis ▶ 1 *leadership instructor* with ability to teach skills such as event planning, setting priorities, and running meetings; experience in the field at up to $1500 per season or on a volunteer basis ▶ 1 *pool director* (minimum age 21) with first aid, CPR, lifeguarding, and management experience at up to $1500 per season or on a volunteer basis ▶ 1 *ropes course instructor* with certification or documentation of training in high and low ropes and experience at up to $1500 per season or on a volunteer basis ▶ 1 *sports and games coordinator* with ability to lead and guide large groups in various games and sports and familiarity with new games and noncompetitive sports at up to $1500 per season or on a volunteer basis ▶ 1 *summer office manager* with orientation to detail, bookkeeping and organizational skills, and an interest in working with people at up to $1500 per season or on a volunteer basis ▶ 1 *theater arts instructor* with improvisational theater experience and experience teaching youths at up to $1500 per season or on a volunteer basis. Applicants must submit 2-3 professional references with phone/fax numbers. International applicants accepted; must obtain own visa, obtain own working papers, apply through a recognized agency.

Benefits and Preemployment Training Free housing, free meals, formal training, health insurance, names of contacts, and on-the-job training. Preemployment training is required and includes accident prevention and safety, first aid, CPR, interpersonal skills, leadership skills, cross-cultural communication, counselor training.

Contact Paul Harvey, Staff Director, Legacy International's Global Youth Village, 1020 Legacy Drive, Bedford, Virginia 24523. Fax: 540-297-1860. E-mail: staff@legacyintl.org. World Wide Web: http://www.legacyintl.org/gyvhome.htm.

OAKLAND SCHOOL AND CAMP
BOYD TAVERN
KESWICK, VIRGINIA 22947

General Information Coed residential and day camp for 130 students ages 8-14 with learning disabilities or other academic difficulties. Established in 1950. 450-acre facility located 65 miles from Richmond. Features: riding ring and trails; swimming pool; 2 tennis courts; unique classrooms; gym and recreation center; hiking trails and streams.

Profile of Summer Employees Total number: 70; typical ages: 20–25. 10% minorities; 75% college students; 25% local applicants. Nonsmokers preferred.

Employment Information Openings are from June 7 to August 6. Year-round positions also offered. Jobs available: ▶ 10 *camp counselors* (minimum age 19) with experience working with children; residential camp experience preferred at $2200–$2800 per season ▶ 2 *swimming instructors* (minimum age 20) with lifesaving certification at $2200–$2800 per season ▶ 3 *teachers* with Virginia teacher certification, special education preferred at $3300–$3800 per 7 weeks. Applicants must submit a formal organization application, cover letter, resume, two personal references. International applicants accepted; must obtain own visa, obtain own working papers.

An in-person interview is recommended, but a telephone interview is acceptable.

Benefits and Preemployment Training Free housing, free meals, formal training, possible full-time employment, and on-the-job training. Preemployment training is required and includes accident prevention and safety, first aid, CPR, interpersonal skills, recreational activity planning; behavior management.

Contact Judith Edwards, Director, Oakland School, Oakland School and Camp, Boyd Tavern, Keswick, Virginia 22947. Telephone: 804-293-9059. Fax: 804-296-8930. Application deadline: continuous.

THE SOUTHWESTERN COMPANY, VIRGINIA
See The Southwestern Company, Tennessee on page 284 for complete description.

STUDENT CONSERVATION ASSOCIATION (SCA), VIRGINIA
See Student Conservation Association (SCA), New Hampshire on page 193 for complete description.

WOODBERRY FOREST SUMMER SCHOOL
WOODBERRY STATION
WOODBERRY FOREST, VIRGINIA 22989

General Information Coeducational boarding school for approximately 200 students grades 8–12. Established in 1889. 1,000-acre facility located 30 miles from Charlottesville. Features: woodlands and river; 6 tennis courts; 4 athletic fields; computer labs/network; 2 pools.

Profile of Summer Employees Total number: 21; typical age: 21. 60% men; 40% women; 40% college students. Nonsmokers preferred.

Employment Information Openings are from June 17 to August 3. Jobs available: ▶ 21 *interns (math, science, English)* (minimum age 21) with three or four years of college (or recent graduate) at $1300 per season ▶ 30 *teachers (all subjects)* with experience in teaching at $2500 per season. Applicants must submit cover letter, resume, academic transcripts, two letters of recommendation. International applicants accepted; must obtain own visa.

Benefits and Preemployment Training Free housing, free meals, and on-the-job training.

Contact Ben C. Hale, Director, Woodberry Forest Summer School, 354 Woodberry Station, Woodberry Forest, Virginia 22989. Telephone: 540-672-6047. Fax: 540-672-9076. E-mail: wfs_summer@woodberry.org. World Wide Web: http://www.woodberry.org. Application deadline: March 1.

WASHINGTON

ACE COMPUTER CAMP–WASHINGTON
WASHINGTON

General Information Summer camps that teach children to use computers with over 80 locations in the United States, Canada, and England. Established in 1993. Features: university settings; full Internet access; computer language classes; outdoor sports activities; university library; dormitories.

Profile of Summer Employees Typical ages: 16–35. 50% men; 50% women; 50% minorities; 10% high school students; 90% college students; 5% non-U.S. citizens; 95% local applicants. Nonsmokers preferred.

Employment Information Openings are from June to August. Jobs available: ▶ *camp directors* (minimum age 27) must have a Bachelor's degree and prior experience working at a camp at $900 per week ▶ *counselors-in-training* (must have been a former ACE camper) second year counselors-in-training receive a salary of $100 per week ▶ *junior teachers* at $200 per week (must be a least a junior in high school) ▶ *teachers* must be energetic, creative, and patient at $300–$400 per week. Applicants must submit formal organization application, resume, criminal background check. International applicants accepted; must obtain own visa, obtain own working papers, apply through a recognized agency. An in-person interview is recommended, but a telephone interview is acceptable.

Benefits and Preemployment Training Free housing, on-the-job training, opportunity to attend seminars/workshops, and learn computer languages and applications.

Contact Sterling Daniels, Personal Director, ACE Computer Camp–Washington, 540 Northeast Northgate Way, Suite C, Seattle, Washington 98125. Telephone: 206-440-9309. Fax: 206-440-9335. E-mail: jobs@computercamp.com. World Wide Web: http://www.computercamp.com. Application deadline: July 1.

A CHRISTIAN MINISTRY IN THE NATIONAL PARKS–WASHINGTON

See A Christian Ministry in the National Parks–Massachussetts on page 138 for complete description.

CAMP BERACHAH
19830 SOUTHEAST 328TH PLACE
AUBURN, WASHINGTON 98002

General Information Offers eleven day camps (150 campers each), ten horse camps (24 campers each), junior and teen camp (300 campers each), gymnastics camp (200 campers each), and soccer camp (200 campers). Established in 1973. 160-acre facility located 30 miles from Seattle. Features: wooded setting; indoor pool; large gym; mountain bikes; horses; climbing wall/high ropes course.

Profile of Summer Employees Total number: 120; typical ages: 17–28. 40% men; 60% women; 5% minorities; 30% high school students; 70% college students; 8% non-U.S. citizens; 25% local applicants. Nonsmokers required.

Employment Information Openings are from June 10 to September 30. Spring break, winter break, and year-round positions also offered. Jobs available: ▶ *climbing wall facilitator* (minimum age 18) at $110–$135 per week ▶ *counselors* at $110–$135 per week ▶ 1 *crafts director* at $125–$135 per week ▶ 1 *high ropes course facilitator* (minimum age 18) at $110–$135 per week ▶ *horsemanship wrangler/instructor* at $900–$1500 per season ▶ *lifeguard* at $500–$600 per month ▶ *mountain bike leader* at $125–$150 per week ▶ 1 *nurse* at $125–$150 per week ▶ 1 *recreation director* at $125–$135 per week. Applicants must submit a formal organization application, two personal references, two letters of recommendation. International applicants accepted; must obtain own visa, obtain own working papers. A telephone interview is required.

Benefits and Preemployment Training Free housing, free meals, possible full-time employment, and on-the-job training. Preemployment training is required and includes accident prevention and safety, first aid, CPR, interpersonal skills, leadership skills.

Contact James Richey, Program Director, Camp Berachah, 19830 Southeast 328th Place, Auburn, Washington 98092. Telephone: 253-939-0488. Fax: 253-833-7027. E-mail: berachah.program@ juno.com. World Wide Web: http://www.berachah.org. Application deadline: continuous.

COLLEGE GIFTED PROGRAMS
PACIFIC LUTHERAN UNIVERSITY
TACOMA, WASHINGTON 98447

General Information Residential educational academic summer camp for gifted and talented students in grades 4-11. Program blends in-depth academics with recreational and cultural activities. Established in 1984. 160-acre facility located 5 miles from Tacoma. Features: dormitories; campus classroom facilities; campus recreational facilities include pool, tennis courts, and gym; campus library; beautiful college setting.

Profile of Summer Employees Total number: 35; typical ages: 19–70. 50% men; 50% women; 30% minorities; 50% college students; 10% retirees; 10% non-U.S. citizens; 25% local applicants. Nonsmokers required.

Employment Information Openings are from July 24 to August 14. Jobs available: ▶ 20 *counselors* with two years of college completed and experience working with children at $800 to $1200 per 3-week session ▶ 4 *directors* with at least 5 years teaching/supervisory experience; master's degree required, doctorate preferred at $5000–$8000 ▶ 6 *housemasters/instructors (residential)* with master's degree, teaching, and supervisory experience at $2500 to $4500 per 3-week session ▶ 20 *instructors (non-residential)* with master's degree and teaching experience at $600 to $2500 per 3-week session ▶ 2 *nurses* with RN license; school experience preferred at $1300 per week. Applicants must submit formal organization application, resume, academic transcripts, two personal references, two letters of recommendation. International applicants accepted; must apply through a recognized agency. An in-person interview is recommended, but a telephone interview is acceptable.

Benefits and Preemployment Training Free housing and free meals. Preemployment training is required and includes accident prevention and safety, interpersonal skills, leadership skills, instructional strategies for gifted students.

Contact Margaret Solitario or Dr. Albert Dorhout, Executive Directors, College Gifted Programs, 120 Littleton Road, Suite 201, Parsippany, New Jersey 07054-1803. Telephone: 973-334-6991. Fax: 973-334-9756. E-mail: info@cgp-sig.com. World Wide Web: http://www.cgp-sig.com. Application deadline: continuous.

ENCHANTED PARKS, INC.
36201 ENCHANTED PARKWAY SOUTH
FEDERAL WAY, WASHINGTON 98003

General Information Amusement/theme park with rides, food stands, and a water park. Established in 1977. 60-acre facility located 16 miles from Seattle. Features: roller coaster; 9 water slides; wavepool; 22 amusement rides; daily shows.

Profile of Summer Employees Total number: 500–800; typical ages: 16–24. 30% minorities; 60% high school students; 20% college students; 10% retirees; 5% non-U.S. citizens; 85% local applicants.

Employment Information Openings are from April 11 to September 20. Winter break positions also offered. Jobs available: ▶ 100–200 *lifeguards* (minimum age 16) with water park training course at $5.70–$5.85 per hour ▶ 300–500 *park employees* (minimum age 16) at $5.70–$6.05 per hour. Applicants must submit a formal organization application, two personal references. International applicants accepted. An in-person interview is required.

Benefits and Preemployment Training Meals at a cost, on-the-job training, and opportunity to attend seminars/workshops. Preemployment training is required and includes accident prevention and safety.

Contact Kimberly Zier, Human Resources Manager, Enchanted Parks, Inc., 36201 Enchanted Parkway South, Federal Way, Washington 98003. Telephone: 253-661-8027. Fax: 253-661-8065. E-mail: wildwaves@tribnet.com. World Wide Web: http://www.wildwaves.com. Application deadline: continuous.

LONGACRE EXPEDITIONS, WASHINGTON
GLACIER, WASHINGTON

General Information Adventure travel program emphasizing group living skills and physical challenges. Using base camp as a staging area, 2–3 staffers and 10–16 campers participate in expeditions in which they engage in human-powered sports. Established in 1981. Located 15 miles from Bellingham.

Profile of Summer Employees Total number: 30; typical ages: 21–28. 50% men; 50% women; 10% minorities; 40% college students; 30% local applicants. Nonsmokers required.

Employment Information Openings are from June 15 to August 10. Jobs available: ▶ 8 *assistant trip leaders* (minimum age 21) with good driving record, CPR, and WFR preferred or wilderness first aid at $252–$300 per week ▶ 1 *mountaineering instructor* (minimum age 21) with advanced first aid or advanced wilderness first aid and CPR at $300–$400 per week ▶ 1 *rock climbing instructor* (minimum age 21) with good driving record, WFR, and CPR at $300–$400 per week ▶ *sea kayaking instructor* (minimum age 21) with lifeguard training, CPR, WFR preferred or wilderness first aid at $300–$400 per week ▶ 3 *support and logistics staff members* (minimum age 21) with good driving record, WFR, and CPR at $180–$240 per week. Applicants must submit a formal organization application, three personal references. International applicants accepted; must obtain own visa, obtain own working papers. An in-person interview is recommended, but a telephone interview is acceptable.

Benefits and Preemployment Training Free housing, free meals, on-the-job training, and pro-deal purchase program. Preemployment training is required and includes accident prevention and safety, interpersonal skills, leadership skills.

Contact Meredith Schuler, Directors, Longacre Expeditions, Washington, RD 3, Box 106, Newport, Pennsylvania 17074. Telephone: 717-567-6790. Fax: 717-567-3955. E-mail: longacre@ longacreexpeditions.com. World Wide Web: http://www.longacreexpeditions.com. Application deadline: continuous.

MT. RAINIER GUEST SERVICES
PO BOX 108
ASHFORD, WASHINGTON 98304

General Information Operates hotels, food services, and gift shops in Mt. Rainier National Park. 244,000-acre facility located 100 miles from Tacoma. Features: old growth forests; wildlife; mountain meadows; glaciers; canyons; wilderness.

Profile of Summer Employees Total number: 240; typical ages: 18–75. 50% men; 50% women; 10% minorities; 75% college students; 25% retirees; 10% local applicants. Nonsmokers preferred.

Employment Information Openings are from May to October. Jobs available: ▶ 20 *cook's helpers/pantry persons* (minimum age 18) with ability to perform prep work plus make salads and sandwiches at $6.50 per hour ▶ 10 *cooks* (minimum age 21) with fine dining cooking experience and ability to work in casual and fine dining restaurants at $7.50–$10.50 per hour ▶ 10 *desk clerks* (minimum age 18) with ability to register guests and handle cash at $6.25 per hour ▶ 30 *fast food attendants* (minimum age 18) with ability to take/fill orders, bus tables, and operate cash register at $5.90 per hour ▶ 20 *housekeeping staff members* (minimum age 18) with ability to clean guest rooms and hotel at $5.90 per hour ▶ 5 *janitors (night and day)* (minimum age 18) with ability to clean halls, restrooms, windows, and carpets and empty garbage at $5.90–$8 per hour ▶ 5 *kitchen porters (night and day)* (minimum age 18) with ability to clean hoods, ovens, and floors and assist in dishwashing at $6–$7 per hour ▶ 30 *kitchen/utility personnel* (minimum age 18) at $6 per hour ▶ 20 *retail clerks* (minimum age 18) with ability to perform retail sales, stocking, and cleaning duties at $6 per hour. Applicants must submit formal organization application. International applicants accepted; must obtain own visa, obtain own working papers, apply through a recognized agency.

Benefits and Preemployment Training Housing at a cost, meals at a cost, and on-the-job training.

Contact Sandra Miller, Personnel Manager, Mt. Rainier Guest Services, PO Box 108, Ashford, Washington 98304. Telephone: 360-569-2400 Ext. 119. Fax: 360-569-2770. Application deadline: continuous.

THE SOUTHWESTERN COMPANY, WASHINGTON
See The Southwestern Company, Tennessee on page 284 for complete description.

STUDENT CONSERVATION ASSOCIATION (SCA), WASHINGTON
See Student Conservation Association (SCA), New Hampshire on page 193 for complete description.

SUPER 24 FOOD STORE
6402 LAKE WASHINGTON BOULEVARD, NE
KIRKLAND, WASHINGTON 98033

General Information Retail grocery store; small neighborhood store. Established in 1994. Located 3 miles from Bellevue.

Profile of Summer Employees Total number: 5; typical ages: 21–32. 50% men; 50% women; 100% local applicants.

Employment Information Openings are from June 1 to September 30. Spring break, winter break, and year-round positions also offered. Jobs available: ▶ 3 *cashiers* (minimum age 21) at $7–$9 per hour ▶ 1 *stock person* (minimum age 16) at $5.50–$7 per hour. Applicants must submit a formal organization application. International applicants accepted; must obtain own visa, obtain own working papers. An in-person interview is required.

Benefits and Preemployment Training Meals at a cost, possible full-time employment, and on-the-job training.

Contact Navid Veiseh, Director, Super 24 Food Store, PO Box 974, Kirkland, Washington 98083-0974. Telephone: 425-822-5231. Fax: 425-822-5231. E-mail: nveiseh@scn.org. Application deadline: continuous.

WILDERNESS EDUCATION INSTITUTE–TEEN ADVENTURE WASHINGTON
WASHINGTON

General Information Nonprofit environmental education organization that runs camping and backpacking programs for ages 9–13 during the summer. Established in 1996. Located 150 miles from Seattle. Features: freshwater lake; access to national parks; hiking trails; rustic setting.

Profile of Summer Employees Total number: 8; typical ages: 19–30. 50% men; 50% women; 80% college students; 2% non-U.S. citizens; 10% local applicants. Nonsmokers preferred.

Employment Information Openings are from June 20 to August 20. Jobs available: ▶ 8–12 *backpacking instructors* (minimum age 21) with first aid and CPR certifications, backpacking, and teaching experience at $1600 per season ▶ 6–8 *teaching counselors/instructors* (minimum age 19) with first aid and CPR certifications, teaching, and camp experience at $1600 per season. Applicants must submit formal organization application, resume, academic transcripts, three personal references, three letters of recommendation. International applicants accepted; must obtain own visa, obtain own working papers. A telephone interview is required.

Benefits and Preemployment Training Free housing, free meals, formal training, health insurance, names of contacts, and on-the-job training. Preemployment training is required and includes accident prevention and safety, interpersonal skills, leadership skills, backpacking, "leave no trace" camping, and basic mountaineering.

Contact Anne Dubinsky, Co-Director, Wilderness Education Institute–Teen Adventure Washington, PO Box 660652, Sacramento, California 95866. Telephone: 877-628-9692. Fax: 877-628-9692. E-mail: dubinsky@alumni.stanford.org. World Wide Web: http://www.pages.prodigy.net/wilderness/wei. Application deadline: March 15.

YMCA CAMP SEYMOUR
9725 CRAMER ROAD KPN
GIG HARBOR, WASHINGTON 98329

General Information Residential camp serving 140 campers weekly and biweekly. Shorter minicamps of four days are also available. Camp provides adventure travel and teen leadership. Established in 1906. 150-acre facility located 20 miles from Tacoma. Features: wooded setting; located on Southern Puget Sound; saltwater touch tanks; co-op course; outdoor pool; waterfront/dock.

Profile of Summer Employees Total number: 50; typical ages: 17–30. 55% men; 45% women; 10% minorities; 10% high school students; 45% college students; 5% non-U.S. citizens; 40% local applicants. Nonsmokers preferred.

Employment Information Openings are from June 17 to August 28. Spring break and winter break positions also offered. Jobs available: ▶ 1 *arts and crafts director* (minimum age 18) with first aid and CPR certification and relevant experience at $147–$182 per week ▶ 12 *assistant cabin leaders* (minimum age 17) with first aid and CPR certifications, prefer lifeguard certification, and some experience in the field at $98–$112 per week ▶ 12 *cabin leaders* (minimum age 18) with first aid and CPR certifications, experience in the field, and completed one year of college at $112–$133 per week ▶ 1 *camp nurse* with preference for RN/LPN license in Washington state; minimum requirement is entering final year of degree at $210–$239 per week ▶ 1 *pool director* (minimum age 21) with lifeguard certification, first aid, WSI, CPR, and experience in the field at $161–$196 per week ▶ 1 *program director* (minimum age 21) with first aid and CPR certifications, prefer lifeguard certification, and experience with summer camp programming at $196–$238 per week ▶ 4–6 *trip leaders* (minimum age 21) with experience in the field; ability to lead bike, backpacking, canoe, and kayak trips; and wilderness first aid and CPR certifications at $133–$175 per week ▶ 3 *unit directors* (minimum age 20) with CPR and first aid certification, prefer lifeguard certification, and experience in the field is a must at $161–$196 per week ▶ 1 *van driver/outfitter* (minimum age 21) with driver's license, ability to outfit all extended trips and overnights, oversee pre-trip meetings and menu planning, and drive trips to remote locations at $168–$210 per week ▶ 1 *waterfront director* (minimum age 21) with lifeguard certification, first aid, CPR, and experience in the field at $161–$196 per week. Applicants must submit formal organization application, cover letter, resume, three personal references, three professional references. International applicants accepted; must apply through a recognized agency. An in-person interview is recommended, but a telephone interview is acceptable.

Benefits and Preemployment Training Free housing, free meals, formal training, and on-the-job training. Preemployment training is required and includes accident prevention and safety, first aid, CPR, interpersonal skills, leadership skills, working/communicating with children.

Contact Aaron Keating, Camp Director, YMCA Camp Seymour, 9725 Cramer Road KPN, Gig Harbor, Washington 98329. Telephone: 253-884-3392. Fax: 253-884-5654. E-mail: keating@ymcatacoma.org. World Wide Web: http://www.ymcatacoma.org. Application deadline: continuous.

WEST VIRGINIA

CAMP RIM ROCK
BOX 69
YELLOW SPRING, WEST VIRGINIA 26865

General Information Residential camp serving 200 girls offering a strong general program and horseback riding, aquatics, and performing arts programs. Established in 1952. 600-acre facility located 90 miles from Washington, D.C. Features: river runs through the property; mountains frame the camp; spacious modern stables with 55 horses; large amphitheatre; several pavilions; 2 tennis courts.

Profile of Summer Employees Total number: 80–90; typical ages: 18–30. 5% men; 95% women; 10% minorities; 75% college students; 40% non-U.S. citizens. Nonsmokers required.

Employment Information Openings are from June 5 to August 14. Jobs available: ▶ 1 *archery instructor* (minimum age 19) with certification starting at $200 per week ▶ *arts and crafts instructor* (minimum age 19) with skills in this field starting at $200 per week ▶ 2 *canoeing instructors* (minimum age 19) with certification starting at $200 per week ▶ *dance instructors* (minimum age 19) with skills in teaching dance and experience working with children starting at $200 per week ▶ *drama instructors* (minimum age 19) with skills and experience in drama and working with children starting at $200 per week ▶ *drawing instructor* (minimum age 19) with sills in this field starting at $200 per week ▶ 20 *general counselors* with ability to work with children starting at $200 per week ▶ *guitar instructor* with ability to teach basic folk guitar and experience working with children starting at $200 per week ▶ *nature instructor* (minimum age 19) with skills in this field starting at $200 per week ▶ 2–6 *nurses* with RN (full season or partial season position available); salary negotiable ▶ 12 *riding staff members* with teacher certification starting at $200 per week ▶ *soccer instructor* (minimum age 19) with skills in this field starting at $200 per week ▶ *storyteller* with skills in this field and experience working with children starting at $200 per week ▶ 5–8 *swimming counselors* (minimum age 19) with

WSI certification and ability to teach starting at $200 per week ▶ 2 *tennis counselors* with experience in the field and working with children starting at $200 per week ▶ *volleyball instructor* (minimum age 19) with skills in this field starting at $200 per week. Applicants must submit formal organization application, three personal references. International applicants accepted; must apply through a recognized agency. An in-person interview is recommended, but a telephone interview is acceptable.

Benefits and Preemployment Training Free housing, free meals, formal training, on-the-job training, travel reimbursement, and 24 hours off per week. Preemployment training is required and includes accident prevention and safety, first aid, CPR, interpersonal skills, leadership skills.

Contact Jim or Deborah Matheson, Directors, Camp Rim Rock, Box 69, Yellow Spring, West Virginia 26865. Telephone: 800-662-4650. Fax: 304-856-3201. E-mail: office@camprimrock. com. World Wide Web: http://www.camprimrock.com. Application deadline: continuous.

GREENBRIER RIVER OUTDOOR ADVENTURES
PO BOX 160
BARTOW, WEST VIRGINIA 24920

General Information Coed outdoor adventure program with variety of itineraries and focuses, including backpacking, rock climbing, mountain biking, caving, white-water rafting, farming, community service, canoeing, and kayaking. 1-, 2-, and 3-week sessions in West Virginia and New England. Established in 1993. 250-acre facility located 45 miles from Elkins. Features: river; mountainous setting; recreational activities; wooded setting; excellent climbing; mountain bike trails.

Profile of Summer Employees Total number: 28–32; typical ages: 21–35. 50% men; 50% women; 60% college students; 5% non-U.S. citizens; 15% local applicants. Nonsmokers required.

Employment Information Openings are from June 10 to August 20. Jobs available: ▶ *assistant leaders* (minimum age 21) with driver's license, CPR/first aid, and some experience with groups at $28.33 per day ▶ *canoeing/kayaking specialist* (minimum age 21) with driver's license, CPR/first aid; WFR and lifeguard preferred at $33.33–$38.33 per day ▶ *caving specialist* (minimum age 21) with driver's license, CPR/first aid; WFR and lifeguard preferred; and experience leading caving trips at $33.33–$38.33 per day ▶ *climbing specialist* (minimum age 21) with first aid/CPR; WFR and lifeguard preferred; driver's license and general climbing experience at $33.33–$38.33 per day ▶ *group leaders* (minimum age 21) with first aid/CPR/ WFR preferred; driver's license and clean driving record; and experience working with youth at $33.33–$38.33 per day ▶ 1–2 *mountain biking specialists* (minimum age 21) with first aid/CPR/ WFR and lifeguard preferred; driver's license, riding and mechanical skills experience at $33.33– $38.33 per day ▶ *summer interns* (minimum age 19) with CPR/first aid at $75 per week. Applicants must submit a formal organization application, resume, three personal references. International applicants accepted; must obtain own visa, obtain own working papers. A telephone interview is required.

Benefits and Preemployment Training Free housing, free meals, on-the-job training, and equipment pro-deal oportunities. Preemployment training is required and includes accident prevention and safety, first aid, CPR, interpersonal skills, leadership skills, wilderness first responder re-certification.

Contact Nekr and Chris Jenkins, Directors/Owners, Greenbrier River Outdoor Adventures, PO Box 160, Bartow, West Virginia 24920. Telephone: 304-456-5191. Fax: 304-456-3121. E-mail: groa@groa.com. World Wide Web: http://www.groa.com. Application deadline: continuous.

THE SOUTHWESTERN COMPANY, WEST VIRGINIA
See The Southwestern Company, Tennessee on page 284 for complete description.

STUDENT CONSERVATION ASSOCIATION (SCA), WEST VIRGINIA
See Student Conservation Association (SCA), New Hampshire on page 193 for complete description.

ACE COMPUTER CAMP–WISCONSIN
See ACE Computer Camp–Washington on page 307 for complete description.

BIRCH TRAIL CAMP FOR GIRLS
PO BOX 527
MINONG, WISCONSIN 54859
General Information Residential camp serving 185 girls ages 8–15 in two 4-week sessions including extensive wilderness trips. Established in 1959. 310-acre facility located 55 miles from Duluth, Minnesota. Features: freshwater lake; low and high ropes course; tournament water ski slalom course; wooded setting; 3-sided climbing tower; beautiful rustic area.
Profile of Summer Employees Total number: 90; typical ages: 17–40. 5% men; 95% women; 10% minorities; 10% high school students; 80% college students; 15% non-U.S. citizens; 5% local applicants. Nonsmokers preferred.
Employment Information Openings are from June 12 to August 13. Jobs available: ▶ 25–50 *cabin counselors* (minimum age 18) at $1300–$1900 per season ▶ 1–2 *caretaker's assistants* at $1350–$1750 per season ▶ *housekeepers* at $1350–$1750 per season ▶ *kitchen helpers* at $1350–$1750 per season ▶ 1–3 *nurses* (minimum age 21) with RN or LPN at $2150–$3500 per season ▶ 1–3 *swimming instructors* (minimum age 18) with LGT or WSI certification at $1300–$2000 per season ▶ 3–6 *wilderness trip leaders* (minimum age 21) with LGT certification; canoeing, backpacking, and climbing experience preferred at $1700–$2300 per season. Applicants must submit formal organization application. International applicants accepted; must apply through a recognized agency. An in-person interview is recommended, but a telephone interview is acceptable.
Benefits and Preemployment Training Free housing, free meals, formal training, health insurance, on-the-job training, and travel reimbursement. Preemployment training is required and includes accident prevention and safety, first aid, CPR, interpersonal skills, leadership skills, wilderness skills.
Contact Richard Chernov, Owner/Director, Birch Trail Camp for Girls, PO Box 527, Minong, Wisconsin 54859. Fax: 715-466-2217. E-mail: brchtrail@aol.com. World Wide Web: http://www. birchtrail.com. Application deadline: May 1.

BOYD'S MASON LAKE RESORT
PO BOX 57
FIFIELD, WISCONSIN 54524
General Information American-plan family resort that rents 18 cabins, serves 3 meals daily, and performs daily maid service for up to 100 guests. Established in 1895. 2,600-acre facility located 250 miles from Madison. Features: 4 freshwater, spring-fed lakes; 2600 private acres; heavily forested; wooded setting; very secluded; miles of hiking/biking trails; very old resort with modern conveniences.
Profile of Summer Employees Total number: 30; typical ages: 17–60. 30% men; 70% women; 7% high school students; 15% college students; 10% retirees; 75% local applicants. Nonsmokers preferred.
Employment Information Openings are from May 15 to October 15. Jobs available: ▶ 1 *children's recreation supervisor* (minimum age 18) with background in elementary education at $5.75 per hour ▶ 5 *dining room attendants* (minimum age 18) at $270–$290 per week ▶ 1 *dishwasher* (minimum age 18) at $270–$290 per week ▶ 2 *housekeepers* (minimum age 18) at $5.75 per hour ▶ 1 *pots and pans washer* (minimum age 18) at $270–$290 per week ▶ 1 *receptionist* (minimum age 18) at $5.75 per hour ▶ 1 *swing cook* (minimum age 18) at $270–

$290 per week. Applicants must submit formal organization application, resume, two personal references. International applicants accepted; must obtain own visa, obtain own working papers, apply through a recognized agency. An in-person interview is recommended, but a telephone interview is acceptable.

Benefits and Preemployment Training Free housing, free meals, on-the-job training, and outdoor recreational activities (boating, swimming, hiking).

Contact Richard Simon, Manager/Owner, Boyd's Mason Lake Resort, PO Box 57, Fifield, Wisconsin 54524. Telephone: 715-762-3469. Application deadline: continuous.

CAMP BIRCH KNOLL FOR GIRLS
EAGLE RIVER, WISCONSIN 54554

General Information Residential camp with 40 instructed activities for girls ages 8–16. Established in 1945. 400-acre facility located 250 miles from Milwaukee. Features: indoor gynmastics and dance center; 5 new tennis courts; on-site horseback riding arena; excellent art facilities; extensive waterfront equipment.

Profile of Summer Employees Total number: 50; typical ages: 18–22. 20% men; 80% women; 5% high school students; 70% college students; 5% local applicants. Nonsmokers required.

Employment Information Openings are from June 2 to August 13. Jobs available: ▶ *cook* (minimum age 18) with experience in quantity cooking at $200–$400 per week ▶ *counselors/ instructors* (minimum age 17) must be high school graduate at $1700–$2000 per season ▶ *gymnastics director* (minimum age 18) at $2000–$2500 per season ▶ *registered nurse* at $3000–$3500 per season with RN or LPN license ▶ *riding director* (minimum age 18) at $2500–$3500 per season ▶ *swimming director* (minimum age 18) at $1500–$2500 per season ▶ *tennis director* (minimum age 18) at $2000–$2500 per season. Applicants must submit a formal organization application, two personal references, two letters of recommendation. An in-person interview is recommended, but a telephone interview is acceptable.

Benefits and Preemployment Training Free housing, free meals, on-the-job training, and laundry service. Preemployment training is required and includes accident prevention and safety, first aid, CPR, interpersonal skills, leadership skills.

Contact Gary Baier, Director, Camp Birch Knoll for Girls, PO Box 13, Stevens Point, Wisconsin 54481. Telephone: 800-843-2904. Fax: 715-341-4261. E-mail: cbkfun@aol.com. World Wide Web: http://www.campchannel.com/cbkfun. Application deadline: continuous.

CAMP EDWARDS
PO BOX 16
EAST TROY, WISCONSIN 53120

General Information Residential camp serving youth and families with six- and eleven-day sessions. Established in 1929. 132-acre facility located 45 miles from Milwaukee. Features: extensive freshwater lake frontage; 2 low ropes courses; 1/2 mile-elevated marsh boardwalk; 7 distinct ecosystems.

Profile of Summer Employees Total number: 40; typical age: 20. 50% men; 50% women; 2% minorities; 10% high school students; 90% college students; 1% retirees; 1% local applicants. Nonsmokers required.

Employment Information Openings are from June 7 to August 14. Year-round positions also offered. Jobs available: ▶ *aquatic directors* (minimum age 21) with appropriate certifications at $165–$250 per week ▶ *cabin counselors* (minimum age 18) at $125–$135 per week ▶ *nurse* (minimum age 23) with RN license of EMT at $250–$300 per week ▶ *support staff positions* (minimum age 20) at $165–$250 per week. Applicants must submit formal organization application, three personal references, two letters of recommendation. International applicants accepted; must apply through a recognized agency. An in-person interview is recommended, but a telephone interview is acceptable.

Benefits and Preemployment Training Free housing, free meals, on-the-job training, and laundry facilities.

Contact Mr. Kim Harron, Executive Director, Camp Edwards, PO Box 16, East Troy, Wisconsin

53120. Telephone: 414-642-7466. Fax: 414-642-5108. E-mail: camped@wcf.net. Application deadline: continuous.

CAMP MANITO-WISH YMCA
PO BOX 246
BOULDER JUNCTION, WISCONSIN 54512

General Information Facility offering wilderness tripping, canoeing, kayaking, and backpacking for 220 campers ages 11–15 in a 3-week session. Traditional camp programs offer variety when campers are not on the trail. Established in 1919. 300-acre facility located 275 miles from Milwaukee. Features: freshwater lake; north woods setting; wilderness travel; climbing wall; Manito-wish Leadership center.

Profile of Summer Employees Total number: 200; typical ages: 19–23. 50% men; 50% women; 10% high school students; 90% college students; 1% non-U.S. citizens; 1% local applicants. Nonsmokers preferred.

Employment Information Openings are from June 3 to October 31. Jobs available: ▶ 20–40 *cabin counselors* (minimum age 19) with LGT and first aid/CPR certification at $125–$140 per week ▶ 10 *program area staff* (minimum age 19) with first aid/CPR certification at $125 per week ▶ 2–5 *ropes course instructors/logistical assistants* (minimum age 19) with first aid/CPR certification at $500–$550 per month ▶ 1 *ropes course lead instructor* (minimum age 21) with ropes course certified training and experience in the field at $170 per week ▶ 10–24 *tripping assistants* (minimum age 17) with LGT and first aid/CPR certification at $113–$118 per week ▶ 5 *wilderness adventure teachers* (minimum age 19) with Wilderness First Responder certification (training available), CPR, and LGT at $500–$550 per month. Applicants must submit formal organization application, three personal references. International applicants accepted; must apply through a recognized agency. An in-person interview is recommended, but a telephone interview is acceptable.

Benefits and Preemployment Training Free housing, free meals, formal training, health insurance, names of contacts, on-the-job training, and opportunity to attend seminars/workshops. Preemployment training is optional.

Contact Anne Derber, Camp Director, Camp Manito-wish YMCA, N14 W24200 Tower Place, # 205, Waukesha, Wisconsin 53188. Telephone: 414-523-1623. Fax: 414-523-1626. E-mail: expmwish@execpc.com. World Wide Web: http://www.manito-wish.org. Application deadline: continuous.

CAMP NEBAGAMON FOR BOYS
11451 CAMP NEBAGAMON DRIVE
LAKE NEBAGAMON, WISCONSIN 54849

General Information Residential boys camp for 220 campers from forty different communities and several countries. Established in 1929. 70-acre facility located 30 miles from Duluth, Minnesota. Features: 914-acre freshwater lake; nearby state forests; wooded campsite; proximity to Lake Superior and to Brule River.

Profile of Summer Employees Total number: 115; typical ages: 16–55. 80% men; 20% women; 5% minorities; 27% high school students; 40% college students; 10% non-U.S. citizens; 18% local applicants.

Employment Information Openings are from June 14 to August 16. Jobs available: ▶ 2 *cooks* with experience cooking for large groups at $200–$250 per week ▶ 2 *drivers* (minimum age 21) with clean driving record at $1400–$1700 per season ▶ 25 *junior cabin counselors* with skills in water and land sports, tennis, target skills, art, campcraft, and photography; 11th and 12th graders at $900–$975 per season ▶ 1 *nurse* with RN license at $200–$250 per week ▶ 2 *photography specialists* at $1500–$2200 per season ▶ 25 *senior cabin counselors* with skills in water and land sports, tennis, target skills, art, campcraft, and photography; must be college age at $1100–$1250 per season ▶ 2 *swimming instructors* with WSI or lifeguard certification at $800–$1200 per season ▶ 2 *waterfront directors* (minimum age 21) with WSI or Red Cross lifeguard certification at $1400–$2200 per season. Applicants must submit formal organization application, three personal references. International applicants accepted; must obtain own visa, obtain own working papers, apply through a recognized agency. An in-person interview is required.

Benefits and Preemployment Training Free housing, free meals, formal training, health insurance, names of contacts, on-the-job training, opportunity to attend seminars/workshops, and travel reimbursement. Preemployment training is required and includes accident prevention and safety, first aid, CPR, interpersonal skills, leadership skills.

Contact Roger and Judy Wallenstein, Directors, Camp Nebagamon for Boys, 5237 North Lakewood, Chicago, Illinois 60640. Telephone: 773-271-9500. Fax: 773-271-9816. E-mail: cnebagamon@aol.com. World Wide Web: http://www.campnebagamon.com. Application deadline: continuous.

CAMP SHEWAHMEGON FOR BOYS
DRUMMOND, WISCONSIN 54832

General Information Non-competitive residential camp for 80 boys ages 8–14 offering daily choice of activities; emphasizing growth in skills, confidence, and independence. Established in 1934. 45-acre facility located 70 miles from Duluth, Minnesota. Features: clearwater lake; sand beach; surrounded by national forest; laminated beam dining hall; recreation lodge and a boathouse; screened and glass cabins.

Profile of Summer Employees Total number: 25; typical ages: 18–44. 90% men; 10% women; 5% minorities; 20% high school students; 40% college students; 12% non-U.S. citizens; 10% local applicants. Nonsmokers preferred.

Employment Information Openings are from June 12 to August 12. Jobs available: ▶ 1 *arts and crafts instructor* (minimum age 18) with knowledge of a variety of crafts techniques and ability to teach at $1200–$2000 per season ▶ 1–2 *assistant cooks* (minimum age 18) with quantity cooking experience at $2000–$3000 per season ▶ 2 *campout trip leaders* (minimum age 19) with campcraft experience and first aid certification at $1400–$2000 per season ▶ 3 *dishwashers* with a responsible work ethic at $1200–$2000 per season ▶ 8 *general staff members* (minimum age 19) with instructional skill and youth work experience at $1200–$2000 per season ▶ 1 *head (first) cook* (minimum age 19) with experience in quantity cooking and capable of organizing and directing kitchen staff at $2500–$4000 per season ▶ 2 *lifeguards* with ARC certification at $1400–$2000 per season ▶ 1 *riflery instructor* with NRA certification (preferred), knowledge of gun safety, and teaching ability at $1400–$2000 per season ▶ 2 *swimming instructors* with WSI certification at $1400–$2000 per season ▶ 1 *woodshop instructor* (minimum age 19) with woodworking experience and capable of instructing use of hand tools and small power equipment at $1200–$2000 per season. Applicants must submit formal organization application, resume, three personal references. International applicants accepted; must obtain own visa, obtain own working papers, apply through a recognized agency. An in-person interview is recommended, but a telephone interview is acceptable.

Benefits and Preemployment Training Free housing, free meals, on-the-job training, opportunity to attend seminars/workshops, travel reimbursement, and laundry service. Preemployment training is required and includes accident prevention and safety, interpersonal skills, leadership skills, child development seminar.

Contact Bill Will, Director, Camp Shewahmegon for Boys, 1208 East Miner Street, Arlington Heights, Illinois 60004. Telephone: 847-255-9710. E-mail: wwill57321@aol.com. World Wide Web: http://members.aol.com/wwill57321/campwill.html. Application deadline: continuous.

CAMPS WOODLAND AND TOWERING PINES
EAGLE RIVER, WISCONSIN 54521

General Information Residential camps on separate sites having four- or six-week seasons. Established in 1946. 400-acre facility located 22 miles from Rhinelander. Features: north woods and lakes; resort area.

Profile of Summer Employees Total number: 60; typical ages: 18–70. 60% men; 40% women; 5% high school students; 80% college students; 5% retirees; 5% non-U.S. citizens; 5% local applicants. Nonsmokers preferred.

Employment Information Openings are from June 20 to August 10. Year-round positions also offered. Jobs available: ▶ *cooks/assistant cooks* with experience at $200–$300 per week ▶ *crafts/Indian lore staff members* at $150 per week ▶ *dishwashers* at $150–$200 per week ▶ *nurse* with RN license at $250–$350 per week ▶ *riflery/archery staff members* with NRA training at $150–$250 per week ▶ *swimming/small craft staff members* with WSI certification at $200 per week ▶ *tennis/gymnastics staff members* at $150–$250 per week. Applicants must submit formal organization application, four personal references. International applicants accepted; must obtain own visa, apply through a recognized agency. A telephone interview is required.

Benefits and Preemployment Training Free housing, on-the-job training, and travel reimbursement. Preemployment training is required and includes accident prevention and safety, first aid, CPR, interpersonal skills, leadership skills.

Contact John and Anne Jordan, Camps Woodland and Towering Pines, 242 Bristol Street, Northfield, Illinois 60093. Telephone: 847-446-7311. Fax: 847-446-7710. E-mail: towpines@aol. com. Application deadline: continuous.

CAMP TIMBERLANE FOR BOYS
11400 AIRPORT ROAD
WOODRUFF, WISCONSIN 54568

General Information Noncompetitive residential camp offering four- and eight-week sessions serving 150 boys from across the country. Established in 1961. 250-acre facility located 250 miles from Milwaukee. Features: freshwater lake; thickly wooded setting; cabins with bathrooms; climbing wall; horse stables; 4 tennis courts.

Profile of Summer Employees Total number: 80; typical ages: 17–40. 80% men; 20% women; 10% minorities; 25% high school students; 60% college students; 5% non-U.S. citizens; 5% local applicants. Nonsmokers preferred.

Employment Information Openings are from June 4 to August 16. Jobs available: ▶ 1 *assistant cook* (minimum age 21) with experience in the field at $2000–$3000 per season ▶ 1 *counselor/ golf instructor* (minimum age 18) with high school competitive golf or other tournament experience at $1200–$1800 per season ▶ 1 *counselor/guitar instructor* (minimum age 18) with experience teaching chords and progressions at $1200–$1800 per season ▶ 1 *counselor/gymnastics instructor* (minimum age 21) with experience coaching trampoline and tumbling at $1200– $1800 per season ▶ 1 *counselor/photography instructor* (minimum age 18) with experience developing black-and-white film at $1200–$1800 per season ▶ 1 *counselor/pottery instructor* (minimum age 18) with experience in wheel and kiln use at $1200–$1800 per season ▶ 1 *counselor/sailing instructor* (minimum age 21) with sailing experience in small sailboats and some teaching experience at $1200–$1800 per season ▶ 2 *counselors/horseback riding instructors* (minimum age 21) with significant English saddle experience at $1200–$1800 per season ▶ 2 *counselors/rock climbing instructors* (minimum age 21) with rock gym teaching experience at $1200–$1800 per season ▶ 2 *counselors/scuba diving instructors* (minimum age 21) with PADI rescue diver or divemaster certification or equivalent at $1200–$1800 per season ▶ 2 *counselors/swimming instructors* (minimum age 21) with lifeguard or WSI certification at $1200– $1800 per season ▶ 2 *counselors/tennis instructors* (minimum age 18) with high school or college team play and coaching experience at $1200–$1800 per season ▶ 2 *counselors/ waterskiing instructors* (minimum age 18) with teaching and boat driving experience at $1200– $1800 per season ▶ 1 *driver* (minimum age 21) with valid driver's license and good driving record at $1200–$1800 per season ▶ 2 *maintenance persons* (minimum age 18) with carpentry skill at $1000–$2000 per season ▶ 2 *nurses* (minimum age 21) with RN, GN, paramedic, or LPN license at $2500–$3000 per season ▶ 10 *trip leaders* (minimum age 21) with canoeing and/or rock climbing background, lifeguard, and wilderness first responder certification at $1400– $2000 per season. Applicants must submit formal organization application, three personal references, copies of relevant certifications. International applicants accepted; must apply through a recognized agency. An in-person interview is recommended, but a telephone interview is acceptable.

Benefits and Preemployment Training Free housing, free meals, formal training, on-the-job training, opportunity to attend seminars/workshops, and travel reimbursement. Preemployment training is required and includes accident prevention and safety, first aid, CPR, interpersonal skills, leadership skills, lifeguard training, wilderness first responder.

Contact Mike Cohen, Director, Camp Timberlane for Boys, 6202 North Camino Almonte, Tucson, Arizona 85718. Telephone: 520-615-7770. Fax: 520-615-7771. E-mail: mike@ camptimberlane.com. Application deadline: continuous.

CENTRAL WISCONSIN ENVIRONMENTAL STATION/ UNIVERSITY OF WISCONSIN–STEVENS POINT
10186 COUNTY ROAD MM
AMHERST JUNCTION, WISCONSIN 54407

General Information Environmental station that provides a foundation for appreciation and understanding of the environment and develops the skills and attitudes needed to deal with present and future environmental problems. Established in 1975. 400-acre facility located 90 miles from Green Bay. Features: freshwater lake; wooded setting; log cabins; multi-purpose living/teaching building; challenge course.

Profile of Summer Employees Total number: 15; typical age: 18. 50% men; 50% women; 10% minorities; 10% high school students; 90% college students; 10% non-U.S. citizens; 60% local applicants. Nonsmokers preferred.

Employment Information Openings are from June 1 to August 24. Year-round positions also offered. Jobs available: ▶ *assistant summer program director* (minimum age 18) with first aid/CPR, driver's license, experience working with youth, and environmental education or related experience at $150–$180 per week ▶ *counselors/naturalists* (minimum age 18) with first aid/CPR certifications, drivre's license, experience working with youth, and enivironmental education with related experience at $130–$150 per week ▶ *health lodge supervisor* (minimum age 18) with EMT, RN, or advanced first aid training at $140–$170 per week ▶ *summer program director* (minimum age 21) with first aid/CPR, driver's license; experience working with youth and supervising staff; environmental education or related experience at $200–$250 per week ▶ *tripping leaders* (minimum age 18) with first aid/CPR, driver's license, camping, backpacking, and youth leadership experience. at $130–$165 per week ▶ *waterfront director* (minimum age 18) with WSI, lifeguard certification, and driver's license at $135–$160 per week. International applicants accepted; must obtain own visa, obtain own working papers, apply through a recognized agency.

Benefits and Preemployment Training Meals at a cost, free housing, free meals, formal training, and on-the-job training. Preemployment training is required and includes accident prevention and safety, interpersonal skills, leadership skills, teaching skills.

Contact Sterling Strathe, Assistant Director, Central Wisconsin Environmental Station/University of Wisconsin–Stevens Point, 10186 County Road MM, Amherst Junction, Wisconsin 54407. Telephone: 715-824-2428. Fax: 715-824-3201. E-mail: sstrathe@uwsp.edu. World Wide Web: http://www.uwsp.edu/acad/cnr/affil/cwes/index/htm. Application deadline: continuous.

HONEY ROCK CAMP
8660 HONEY ROCK ROAD
THREE LAKES, WISCONSIN 54562

General Information Northwoods campus of Wheaton College providing year-round leadership training and wilderness experiences for college students and young people. Established in 1951. 600-acre facility located 240 miles from Milwaukee. Features: wooded setting; lake; ropes course; computer center for college-aged staff; extensive wilderness program.

Profile of Summer Employees Total number: 200; typical ages: 18–25. 50% men; 50% women; 5% minorities; 20% high school students; 80% college students; 5% non-U.S. citizens; 1% local applicants. Nonsmokers required.

Employment Information Openings are from May 15 to September 1. Year-round positions also offered. Jobs available: ▶ 1–2 *activity area supervisors* (minimum age 21) should be responsible and organized at $110 per week ▶ *barn staff members* (minimum age 18) with experience with horses and ability to teach others at $110–$160 per week ▶ *kitchen staff members* (minimum age 18) at $110–$160 per week ▶ *operational staff members* (minimum age 18) at $110–$160 per week ▶ *waterfront staff members* (minimum age 18) with lifeguarding,

CPR, and emergency water safety at $110–$160 per week. Applicants must submit a formal organization application, two personal references. International applicants accepted; must obtain own visa, obtain own working papers. An in-person interview is recommended, but a telephone interview is acceptable.

Benefits and Preemployment Training Free housing, free meals, and on-the-job training.

Contact Office Manager, Honey Rock Camp, Wheaton College, Wheaton, Illinois 60187. Telephone: 630-752-5124. Fax: 630-752-5148. E-mail: honey.rock@wheaton.edu. World Wide Web: http://www.honeyrockcamp.org. Application deadline: continuous.

LAKE GENEVA CAMPUS, GEORGE WILLIAMS COLLEGE EDUCATION CENTERS
PO BOX 210
WILLIAMS BAY, WISCONSIN 53191

General Information Educational conference center serving families, nonprofit organizations, and groups. Established in 1884. 300-acre facility located 45 miles from Milwaukee. Features: freshwater lake; wooded setting; 2 tennis courts; cabins; 1200 feet of lakefront; 3 piers.

Profile of Summer Employees Total number: 175; typical ages: 14–68. 40% men; 60% women; 60% high school students; 40% college students; 10% non-U.S. citizens. Nonsmokers preferred.

Employment Information Openings are from May 25 to September 9. Jobs available: ▶ 2 *arts and crafts staff members* (minimum age 18) at $6 per hour ▶ 1–2 *conference center set-up crew* (minimum age 18) with driver's license and clean driving record at $6–$6.50 per hour ▶ 20–25 *food service workers* (minimum age 14) at $5.60–$6 per hour ▶ 3–4 *front desk workers* (minimum age 18) at $6–$7 per hour ▶ 5–6 *golf course staff members* (minimum age 18) at $5–$6 per hour ▶ 2–3 *grounds crew* (minimum age 16) at $5–$6 per hour ▶ 6–7 *housekeepers* (minimum age 14) at $5.60–$6 per hour ▶ 4–5 *lifeguards* (minimum age 16) with WSI certification, CPR, and advanced first aid at $6.50–$7 per hour ▶ 2–3 *preschool/day care staff members* (minimum age 18) at $5–$6 per hour ▶ 1 *sailing instructor* (minimum age 18) with Red Cross sailing instructor certification and CPR training at $6–$7 per hour ▶ 3–4 *snack shop clerks* at $5–$6 per hour ▶ 2 *swimming instructors* (minimum age 16) with Red Cross lifesaving, WSI, CPR, and first aid certification at $6.50–$7 per hour. Applicants must submit formal organization application, cover letter. International applicants accepted; must obtain own visa, apply through a recognized agency.

Benefits and Preemployment Training Housing at a cost, meals at a cost, formal training, and on-the-job training. Preemployment training is optional and includes first aid, CPR.

Contact Richard Miller, Director of Personnel, Lake Geneva Campus, George Williams College Education Centers, PO Box 210, Williams Bay, Wisconsin 53191-0210. Telephone: 414-245-5531. Fax: 414-245-5652. E-mail: lkgencam@idcnet.com. Application deadline: May 15.

LAKE LUCERNE CAMP & RETREAT CENTER
W6460 COUNTY YY
NESHKORO, WISCONSIN 54960-9329

General Information Residential camp serving 200 campers weekly; United Methodist affiliated. Established in 1947. 530-acre facility located 40 miles from Oshkosh. Features: private 45-acre lake; wooded setting; Christian environment; 4-season recreational resources; extensive outdoor recreational resources.

Profile of Summer Employees Total number: 30; typical ages: 15–23. 50% men; 50% women; 5% minorities; 5% high school students; 60% college students; 10% non-U.S. citizens; 20% local applicants. Nonsmokers preferred.

Employment Information Openings are from June 1 to August 31. Year-round positions also offered. Jobs available: ▶ 1 *assistant cook* (minimum age 18) at $140–$200 per week ▶ 2–4 *counselors* (minimum age 18) with experience working with children at $140–$170 per week ▶ 3 *dining room hosts* (minimum age 16) at $140–$175 per week ▶ 1–2 *dishwashers* (minimum age 16) at $140–$150 per week ▶ 1 *food service driver* (minimum age 19) with valid driver's license and clean driving record at $140–$185 per week ▶ 1 *health supervisor* (minimum age 18) with first responder, first aid/CPR certification or RN license (preferred) at $160–$200 per week ▶ 1 *maintenance assistant* (minimum age 19) with valid driver's license and clean driving record at $140–$185 per week ▶ 1–2 *program directors* (minimum age 18) with experience in program design and counseling at $140–$175 per week ▶ 1 *waterfront director* (minimum age 21) with lifeguard training and first aid/WSI certification at $140–$200 per week ▶ 2–3 *waterfront personnel* (minimum age 18) with lifeguard training and first aid certification at $140–$175 per week. Applicants must submit formal organization application, three personal references, letter of recommendation. International applicants accepted; must apply through a recognized agency. An in-person interview is recommended, but a telephone interview is acceptable.

Benefits and Preemployment Training Free housing, free meals, formal training, possible full-time employment, names of contacts, on-the-job training, and opportunity to attend seminars/workshops. Preemployment training is required and includes accident prevention and safety, interpersonal skills, leadership skills, legal issues.

Contact Mr. Bob Williams, Site Director, Lake Lucerne Camp & Retreat Center, W6460 County YY, Neshkoro, Wisconsin 54960-9329. Telephone: 920-293-4488. Fax: 920-293-4361. E-mail: lucerne@wirural.net. World Wide Web: http://www.wisconsinumc.org/conference/camps/lucerne. html. Application deadline: continuous.

MENOMINEE FOR BOYS
4985 COUNTRY ROAD D
EAGLE RIVER, WISCONSIN 54521

General Information Residential boys camp serving 160 boys per program from all over the world. Established in 1928. 80-acre facility located 60 miles from Wausau. Features: lake; golf course; wooded setting; 5 tennis courts; modern cabins with water and electricity.

Profile of Summer Employees Total number: 60; typical age: 23. 90% men; 10% women; 5% minorities; 10% high school students; 80% college students; 1% retirees; 10% non-U.S. citizens; 5% local applicants. Nonsmokers required.

Employment Information Openings are from June 15 to August 15. Jobs available: ▶ *golf instructors* ▶ *sailing instructors* ▶ *soccer instructors* ▶ *swimming instructors* ▶ *team sports instructors* at $1200–$1350 per season ▶ *tennis instructors* ▶ *waterskiing instructors/skiboat drivers*. Applicants must submit formal organization application, cover letter. International applicants accepted; must apply through a recognized agency.

Benefits and Preemployment Training Free housing, free meals, formal training, names of contacts, on-the-job training, and travel reimbursement. Preemployment training is required and includes accident prevention and safety, CPR, interpersonal skills, leadership skills.

Contact Steve Kanefsky, Owner/Director, Menominee for Boys, 7421 East McLellan Lane, Scottsdale, Arizona 85250. Telephone: 800-236-2267. Fax: 602-596-6790. E-mail: fun@ campmenominee.com. World Wide Web: http://www.campmenominee.com. Application deadline: continuous.

RED PINE CAMP FOR GIRLS
PO BOX 69
MINOCQUA, WISCONSIN 54548

General Information Private traditional camp providing individual attention for girls ages 6–16, enrolling 115 campers for two-, four-, and eight-week sessions. Established in 1937. 40-acre facility located 60 miles from Wausau. Features: only private property on 1200-acre freshwater lake; tennis courts; cabins; surrounded by state land; shower facilities.

Profile of Summer Employees Total number: 50–55; typical ages: 18–45. 10% men; 90% women; 80% college students; 10% non-U.S. citizens; 8% local applicants.

Employment Information Openings are from June 12 to August 16. Jobs available: ▶ 2–7 *English-style riding instructors or stable managers* (minimum age 18) with skill and love of horses and experience in the field at $1300–$2000 per season ▶ 2–10 *arts and crafts, gymnastics, aerobic jazz, cheerleading, and archery staff members* (minimum age 18) with skill and experience in combination of areas at $1200–$1500 per season ▶ 2–6 *canoeing staff members* with emergency and basic water safety (Red Cross) certification preferred, skill and experience in still waters, and knowledge of campcraft at $1200–$1800 per season ▶ *food service staff members* (minimum age 18) with experience in one or more of the following: cook, assistant to cook, general kitchen and dining room help at $1350–$2000 per season ▶ 2–3 *nurses* (minimum age 21) with RN, LPN, EMT or GN license (Wisconsin) at $1500–$2500 per season ▶ 1–2 *sail boarding staff members* (minimum age 18) with experience in the field; Red Cross certification preferred at $1200–$1800 per season ▶ 2–4 *sailing staff members* (minimum age 18) with swimming, LGT, and small craft certification preferred and skill in sailing Sunfish, Puffers, and Zumas at $1200–$1800 per season ▶ 6–9 *swimming instructors* (minimum age 18) with WSI, LGT, CPR, and first aid certification at $1200–$1800 per season ▶ 2–5 *tennis staff members* with high degree of skill and professional training preferred at $1200–$1800 per season. Applicants must submit formal organization application, three personal references, three letters of recommendation. International applicants accepted; must obtain own visa, obtain own working papers, apply through a recognized agency. An in-person interview is recommended, but a telephone interview is acceptable.

Benefits and Preemployment Training Free housing, free meals, on-the-job training, opportunity to attend seminars/workshops, travel reimbursement, and laundry service. Preemployment training is required and includes accident prevention and safety, first aid, CPR, leadership skills.

Contact A. Irene Boudreaux, Co-Director, Red Pine Camp for Girls, PO Box 69, Minocqua, Wisconsin 54548. Telephone: 715-356-6231. Fax: 715-356-1077. Application deadline: continuous.

SALVATION ARMY WONDERLAND CAMP AND CONFERENCE CENTER
9241 CAMP LAKE ROAD, PO BOX 222
CAMP LAKE, WISCONSIN 53109

General Information Residential Evangelical Christian camping program for Chicago-area Salvation Army, including camps for 120 low-income and at-risk young people for six 8-day sessions. Established in 1924. 140-acre facility located 45 miles from Milwaukee. Features: freshwater lake; upland forest; meadows and prairie; heated outdoor pool and diving tank; gym, tennis and volleyball courts; low ropes course.

Profile of Summer Employees Total number: 90–100; typical ages: 18–26. 50% men; 50% women; 5% minorities; 8% high school students; 90% college students; 2% retirees; 5% non-U.S. citizens; 10% local applicants. Nonsmokers required.

Employment Information Openings are from May to August. Winter break positions also offered. Jobs available: ▶ 1 *aquatics assistant* (minimum age 19) with WSI and LTI certification (preferred); leadership ability and supervisory experience at $180–$185 per week ▶ 1 *aquatics director* (minimum age 22) with WSI and LTI certification (preferred); leadership ability and superivisory experience at $185–$190 per week ▶ 1 *arts and crafts director* (minimum age 20) with two years of college completed and experience working with children at $180–$185 per week ▶ 6 *boys counselors* (minimum age 19) with one year of college completed and experience working with children at $180–$185 per week ▶ 2 *cooks* with experience at $200 per week ▶ 6 *girls counselors* (minimum age 19) with one year of college completed and experience working with children at $180–$185 per week ▶ 1 *health services assistant* (minimum age 20) with student nurse status or experience in nursing; ARC-PFR and first aid; experience working with children at $180–$185 per week ▶ *lifeguard/support counselor* (minimum age 19) with ARC-LGT (on-site training available) at $180–$185 per week ▶ 1 *nature director* (minimum age 20) with two years of college completed at $180–$185 per week ▶ 1 *nurse* (minimum age 22) with BSN or RN license with CPR training (USA certification), PFR, first aid, and experience working with children at $400 per week ▶ 1 *pioneer director* (minimum age 20) with two years of college completed at $180–$185 per week ▶ 4 *program unit directors* (minimum age 20) with two years of college completed, experience working with children; leadership ability and organizational skills at $180–$185 per week ▶ 6 *support counselors* (minimum age 18) with one year of college (preferred) at $165–$175 per week. Applicants must submit formal organization application, resume, three personal references, written interview. International applicants accepted; must apply through a recognized agency. An in-person interview is recommended, but a telephone interview is acceptable.

Benefits and Preemployment Training Free housing, free meals, formal training, on-the-job training, and on-site certifications available. Preemployment training is required and includes accident prevention and safety, first aid, CPR, interpersonal skills, leadership skills, child development.

Contact David Ditzler, Director of Camping Services, Salvation Army Wonderland Camp and Conference Center, 9241 Camp Lake Road, PO Box 222, Camp Lake, Wisconsin 53109-0222. Telephone: 414-889-4305 Ext. 304. Fax: 414-889-4307. E-mail: wonderland@techheadnet.com. World Wide Web: http://www.techheadnet.com/wonderland.

THE SOUTHWESTERN COMPANY, WISCONSIN
See The Southwestern Company, Tennessee on page 284 for complete description.

STIVERS TEMPORARY PERSONNEL–WISCONSIN
See Stivers Temporary Personnel–Illinois on page 103 for complete description.

STUDENT CONSERVATION ASSOCIATION (SCA), WISCONSIN
See Student Conservation Association (SCA), New Hampshire on page 193 for complete description.

WOODSIDE RANCH RESORT
W4015 HIGHWAY 82
MAUSTON, WISCONSIN 53948

General Information Full-service American-plan dude ranch offering log cabins with fireplaces. Established in 1926. 1,200-acre facility located 70 miles from Madison. Features: 5-acre lake with island; buffalo herd; pine plantation; 800 acres of riding and hiking trails; volleyball, tennis, and mini golf; log cabins with fireplace.

Profile of Summer Employees Total number: 70; typical ages: 16–50. 40% men; 60% women; 5% minorities; 25% high school students; 25% college students; 5% non-U.S. citizens; 50% local applicants.

Employment Information Openings are from June 7 to September 7. Winter break positions also offered. Jobs available: ▶ 6 *bartenders/country store clerks* (minimum age 18, 21 preferred) with experience at $200–$220 per week ▶ 6 *food service personnel* (minimum age 18) at $190–$200 per week ▶ 1 *horse-drawn wagon teamster* (minimum age 18) with experience in the field at $200–$250 per week ▶ 6 *horse-trail guides* (minimum age 18) with experience in the field at $190–$200 per week ▶ 2 *housekeepers* at $190–$200 per week ▶ 1 *recreation director* (minimum age 18) with recreation experience at $250 per week ▶ 1 *yard and pool maintenance person* (minimum age 18) at $200–$250 per week. Applicants must submit formal organization application, resume. International applicants accepted; must apply through a recognized agency. An in-person interview is recommended, but a telephone interview is acceptable.

Benefits and Preemployment Training Free housing, free meals, on-the-job training, and use of most resort facilities off-duty.

Contact Rick Feldmann, Woodside Ranch Resort, W4015 Highway 82, Mauston, Wisconsin 53948. Telephone: 608-847-4275. Application deadline: continuous.

YMCA CAMP U-NAH-LI-YA
13654 SOUTH SHORE DRIVE
SURING, WISCONSIN 54174

General Information YMCA camp offering outdoor environmental education and retreats for children grades 5–8 and a summer residential camp with trips. Established in 1937. 140-acre facility located 65 miles from Greenbay. Features: pine forest setting; 2 tennis courts; high and low ropes course; 12 sleeping cabins; modern facilities; 600-acre lake.

Profile of Summer Employees Total number: 45; typical ages: 18–24. 40% men; 60% women; 1% minorities; 70% college students; 1% non-U.S. citizens. Nonsmokers preferred.

Employment Information Openings are from June 6 to August 13. Year-round positions also offered. Jobs available: ▶ 1 *health supervisor* (minimum age 21) with RN/LPN, experience preferred at $165–$225 per week ▶ 6–8 *resident counselors* (minimum age 18) with CPR/first aid and one year of college completed at $130–$140 per week ▶ 4 *tripping counselors* (minimum age 21) with CPR/first aid/lifeguard at $145–$165 ▶ 1 *waterfront director* (minimum age 21) with CPR/first aid, lifeguard, and WSI at $180–$200 per week. Applicants must submit a cover letter, resume, three personal references, personal statement. International applicants accepted; must obtain own visa. An in-person interview is recommended, but a telephone interview is acceptable.

Benefits and Preemployment Training Free housing, free meals, possible full-time employment, names of contacts, on-the-job training, and opportunity to attend seminars/workshops. Preemployment training is required and includes accident prevention and safety, first aid, CPR, interpersonal skills, leadership skills, lifeguard.

Contact Kathleen McKee, Program Director, YMCA Camp U-Nah-Li-Ya, 13654 South Shore Drive, Suring, Wisconsin 54174. Telephone: 715-276-7116. Fax: 715-276-1701. Application deadline: continuous.

WYOMING

ABSAROKA MOUNTAIN LODGE
1231 NORTHFORK HIGHWAY
CODY, WYOMING 82414

General Information Mountain lodge located 12 miles from East Gate of Yellowstone National Park. Offering 16 log cabins; main lodge located along Gunbarrel Creek; lodging, dining, and horseback rides in the Absaroka Wilderness Area. Established in 1910. 10-acre facility located 38 miles from Cody. Features: mountain setting; creek through property; historic lodge and cabins; horseback riding; close to Yellowstone National Park.

Profile of Summer Employees Total number: 14; typical ages: 18–26. 50% men; 50% women; 20% high school students; 70% college students; 10% retirees; 5% non-U.S. citizens; 5% local applicants. Nonsmokers preferred.

Employment Information Openings are from May 1 to September 30. Jobs available: ▶ 1 *cook* (minimum age 18) with cooking experience required at $600–$1200 per month ▶ 4–6 *waiters/ waitresses/cabin cleaners* (minimum age 18) with serving and some cleaning experience at $400–$500 per month ▶ 2–4 *wranglers* (minimum age 18) with horse experience (trail guiding, horse care, etc.) required at $400–$600 per month. Applicants must submit a cover letter, resume, two personal references, two letters of recommendation. International applicants accepted; must obtain own visa. A telephone interview is required.

Benefits and Preemployment Training Free housing, free meals, on-the-job training, and ability to partake in ranch activities and horseback riding.

Contact Bob Kudelski, President/Vice President, Absaroka Mountain Lodge, 1231 Northfork Highway, Cody, Wyoming 82414. Telephone: 307-587-3963. Fax: 307-527-9628. E-mail: aml@ wyoming.com. World Wide Web: http://www.absarokamtlodge.com. Application deadline: continuous.

A CHRISTIAN MINISTRY IN THE NATIONAL PARKS– WYOMING
See A Christian Ministry in the National Parks–Massachussetts on page 138 for complete description.

ALPENHOF LODGE
BOX 288, 3255 WEST MCCOLLISTER AVENUE
TETON VILLAGE, WYOMING 83025

General Information Alpine-style resort lodge with 40 rooms providing clientele with personalized service. Established in 1988. 1-acre facility located 260 miles from Salt Lake City, UT. Features: mountains and rivers.

Profile of Summer Employees Total number: 85; typical ages: 20–25. 50% men; 50% women; 1% high school students; 50% college students; 10% non-U.S. citizens; 39% local applicants. Nonsmokers preferred.

Employment Information Openings are from May 20 to October 12. Year-round positions also offered. Jobs available: ▶ 3 *bellmen* with aptitude for greeting guests in a friendly manner, ability to assist with luggage, run errands, and do light maintenance work at $1040 per month ▶ 8 *dining room staff members* (buspersons and waitstaff) with tableside experience and wine knowledge at $275–$420 per month ▶ 3 *dishwashers* with ability to work quickly at $960–$1040 per month ▶ 8 *food waitstaff members* with interest in working with public and the ability to serve at $370 per month ▶ 5 *housekeeping staff members* with ability to clean rooms and willingness to do hard work at $1040 per month ▶ *prep or line cooks* with ability to cook in line and work quickly at $1120–$1280 per month. Applicants must submit a formal organization application. International applicants accepted; must obtain own visa, obtain own working papers. An in-person interview is required.

Benefits and Preemployment Training Housing at a cost, free meals, formal training, possible full-time employment, and on-the-job training. Preemployment training is required and includes accident prevention and safety, interpersonal skills.

Contact Mark D. Johnson, Assistant General Manager, Alpenhof Lodge, PO Box 288, Teton Village, Wyoming 83025. Telephone: 307-733-3242. Fax: 307-739-1516. E-mail: alpenhof@sisna. com. Application deadline: continuous.

BILL CODY RANCH
2604 YELLOWSTONE HIGHWAY
CODY, WYOMING 82414

General Information Guest ranch catering to families with 14 cabins, cookouts, entertainment, daily horseback rides. Established in 1996. 8-acre facility located 135 miles from Billings, Montana. Features: national forest; 30 minutes from Yellowstone; 70 riding horses; white-water rafting; nightly entertainment; 30 minutes from Cody, Wyoming.

Profile of Summer Employees Total number: 20; typical ages: 18–25. 40% men; 60% women; 1% high school students; 90% college students; 2% local applicants. Nonsmokers preferred.

Employment Information Openings are from May 15 to September 30. Jobs available: ▶ 2 *cooks* with some culinary experience at $500–$1000 per month ▶ 5 *horse wranglers* (minimum age 18) with physical ability to perform required duties, valid driver's license, and a clean driving record at $400–$600 per month ▶ 6 *housekeepers/waitstaff* at $400–$500 per month ▶ 2 *office assistants* at $400–$600 per month ▶ 1 *prep cook* at $400–$600 per month. Applicants must submit formal organization application, resume, two personal references. International applicants accepted; must apply through a recognized agency. A telephone interview is required.

Benefits and Preemployment Training Free housing, free meals, and on-the-job training.

Contact John and Jamie Parsons, Owners, Bill Cody Ranch, 2604 Yellowstone Highway, Cody, Wyoming 82414. Telephone: 307-587-6271. Fax: 307-587-6272. E-mail: billcody@billcodyranch. com. World Wide Web: http://www.billcodyranch.com. Application deadline: continuous.

COWBOY VILLAGE RESORT AT TOGWOTEE
PO BOX 91
MORAN, WYOMING 83013

General Information Mountain lodge serving a varied clientele. 67-acre facility located 48 miles from Jackson Hole.

Profile of Summer Employees Total number: 50–60; typical ages: 18–60. 60% men; 40%

women; 5% high school students; 50% college students; 20% retirees; 5% non-U.S. citizens; 20% local applicants.

Employment Information Openings are from June 1 to October 20. Winter break and year-round positions also offered. Jobs available: ▶ 3 *bartenders* (minimum age 21) with an outgoing personality, desire to perform a thorough job, and experience in the field at $5 to $6 per hour plus gratuities ▶ 2 *convenience store clerks* (minimum age 21) with good math skills and an outgoing personality at $5.50–$6 per hour ▶ 3 *dishwashers* with ability to accomplish tasks neatly and quickly at $5.50–$6 per hour ▶ 8 *experienced saute and broiler line cooks* with neat and efficient work habits at $6–$9 per hour ▶ 6 *front desk/reservations persons* with good math aptitude and an outgoing personality at $6–$6.50 per hour ▶ 2 *general laborers* with efficient work habits at $6–$8 per hour ▶ 9 *housekeepers* with neat appearance and efficient work habits at $5.50–$6 per hour ▶ 1 *night auditor* with good math aptitude (should enjoy working nights) at $6–$6.50 per hour ▶ 1 *resort naturalist* with biology background; experience with large group and children's presentations at $700 per month plus room and board ▶ 7 *waitstaff* (minimum age 18) with an outgoing personality and desire to perform a thorough job at $4.15 per hour plus gratuities. Applicants must submit formal application or resume. A telephone interview is required.

Benefits and Preemployment Training Housing at a cost, meals at a cost, possible full-time employment, on-the-job training, and discounts on horseback riding and other activities.

Contact Personnel Director, Cowboy Village Resort at Togwotee, PO Box 91, Moran, Wyoming 83013. Telephone: 307-543-2847. Fax: 307-543-2391. World Wide Web: http://www.coolworks. com/cowboyvillage/default.htm. Application deadline: continuous.

ELEPHANT HEAD LODGE
1170 YELLOWSTONE HIGHWAY
WAPITI, WYOMING 82405

General Information Guest ranch on eastern edge of Yellowstone National Park with lodging, meals, horseback riding, fishing, cookouts, and other activities. Affiliated with American Automobile Association, Mobil Travel Guide, Cody Chamber of Commerce. Located 100 miles south of Billings, Montana. Established in 1910. 6-acre facility located 40 miles from Cody. Features: historic lodge and 12 log cabins; 25 riding horses; Shoshone river fishing; 80 miles from Grand Teton National Parks and 11 miles from Yellowstone National Park; horseback rides in Shoshone National Forest; abundant wildlife.

Profile of Summer Employees Total number: 10; typical ages: 19–22. 40% men; 60% women; 20% minorities; 10% high school students; 80% college students; 2% retirees; 10% non-U.S. citizens; 8% local applicants. Nonsmokers required.

Employment Information Openings are from May 10 to September 30. Jobs available: ▶ 2 *cooks* (minimum age 18) with ability to plan and cook meals for crew, cook on outdoor grill, experience preferred at $650–$750 per month ▶ 2 *experienced wranglers* (minimum age 19) with valid driver's license and ability to drive a horse trailer at $650–$750 per month ▶ 2 *horse wranglers* (minimum age 19) with outgoing personality and physical ability to perform required duties at $550–$650 per month ▶ 5–7 *housekeepers/waitstaff* (minimum age 16) with interest in working with the public and an outgoing personality at $550–$650 per month. Applicants must submit resume, two personal references, letter of recommendation. International applicants accepted; must obtain own visa, obtain own working papers. A telephone interview is required.

Benefits and Preemployment Training Free housing, free meals, on-the-job training, and laundry facilities; free horseback riding; rodeo pass; river rafting; flyfishing.

Contact Phil and Joan Lamb, Owners, Elephant Head Lodge, 1170 Yellowstone Highway, Wapiti, Wyoming 82450. Telephone: 307-587-3980. Fax: 307-527-7922. E-mail: vacation@ elephantheadlodge.com. World Wide Web: http://ww.elephantheadlodge.com. Application deadline: continuous.

HATCHET MOTEL AND RESTAURANT
PO BOX 316
MORAN, WYOMING 83013

General Information Rustic log motel with 22 units, restaurant, gift shop, and gas station. Established in 1955. 35-acre facility located 30 miles from Jackson. Features: dormitories; mountain surroundings; fishing, hiking, and biking; near Grand Teton and Yellowstone.

Profile of Summer Employees Total number: 17; typical ages: 18–25. 40% men; 60% women; 23% minorities; 15% high school students; 75% college students; 10% local applicants. Nonsmokers preferred.

Employment Information Openings are from May 15 to October 30. Year-round positions also offered. Jobs available: ▶ 4 *cooks* (morning and evening shift) (minimum age 18) at $6–$6.50 per hour ▶ 3 *desk attendants* (morning and evening shift) (minimum age 18) at $5.15–$5.50 per hour ▶ 3 *housekeeping staff members* (minimum age 18) at $5.15–$5.50 per hour ▶ 5 *kitchen helpers* (morning and evening shift) (minimum age 18) at $5.15–$5.50 per hour ▶ 2 *relief position personnel* (minimum age 18) at $5.15–$5.50 per hour ▶ 5 *waiters/waitresses* (morning and evening shift) (minimum age 18) at $3.05–$3.25 per hour ▶ 1 *yard maintenance person* (minimum age 18) at $6–$6.25 per hour. Applicants must submit a formal organization application, three personal references. International applicants accepted; must obtain own visa, obtain own working papers. A telephone interview is required.

Benefits and Preemployment Training Housing at a cost, meals at a cost, formal training, possible full-time employment, and on-the-job training. Preemployment training is required and includes accident prevention and safety, interpersonal skills.

Contact Greg Smith, General Manager, Hatchet Motel and Restaurant. Telephone: 307-543-2413. Fax: 307-543-2034. E-mail: hatchet@rmisp.com. World Wide Web: http://www.hatchetmotel.com. Application deadline: continuous.

SIGNAL MOUNTAIN LODGE
GRAND TETON NATIONAL PARK, PO BOX 50
MORAN, WYOMING 83013

General Information Summer resort providing national park visitors with services such as lodging, food, marinas, gifts, guided fishing, groceries, and gasoline. 30-acre facility located 35 miles from Jackson. Features: employee dormitories; freshwater lake; wooded setting; remote/quiet area; located in Grand Teton National Park.

Profile of Summer Employees Total number: 140. 50% men; 50% women.

Employment Information Openings are from May 1 to October 15. Jobs available: ▶ *accounting personnel (day and night audit)* with experience in the field ▶ *bartenders* with serving or bartending experience required ▶ *buspersons* ▶ *convenience store attendants* with cash register experience preferred ▶ *cooks* with experience planning fine dining and coffee shop menus ▶ *dishwashers* ▶ *employee dining room staff members* ▶ *front desk and reservations persons* with typing and interpersonal skills ▶ *gift store sales clerks* with cash register experience preferred ▶ *hosts/hostesses* ▶ *lodging helpers* with ability to make beds, clean, and do laundry ▶ *management and staff positions* with experience in the field ▶ *marina attendants* with ability to handle boat rentals, shuttle guests to and from boats, and pump gas ▶ *pantry personnel* with ability to prepare salads and desserts ▶ *waitstaff* with serving experience required. Applicants must submit formal organization application. International applicants accepted; must apply through a recognized agency. A telephone interview is required.

Benefits and Preemployment Training Housing at a cost, meals at a cost, on-the-job training, and room and board at $225 per month. Preemployment training is required and includes accident prevention and safety, overall orientation about living and working at Signal Mountain Lodge.

Contact Paulette Phlipot, Personnel Manager, Signal Mountain Lodge, PO Box 50, Moran, Wyoming 83013. Telephone: 307-543-2831. Fax: 307-543-2569. E-mail: signalmountain@compuserve.com. World Wide Web: http://www.coolworks.com/signalmt/. Application deadline: continuous.

THE SOUTHWESTERN COMPANY, WYOMING

See The Southwestern Company, Tennessee on page 284 for complete description.

STUDENT CONSERVATION ASSOCIATION (SCA), WYOMING

See Student Conservation Association (SCA), New Hampshire on page 193 for complete description.

TETON VALLEY RANCH CAMP
JACKSON HOLE, PO BOX 8
KELLY, WYOMING 83011

General Information Residential summer camp serving 125 boys or girls in separate 5-week sessions with Western horseback-riding and backpacking adventures. Features multiday trips into the mountains and exciting in-camp activities. Established in 1939. 1,200-acre facility located 14 miles from Jackson. Features: warm (68 degree) spring-fed pond; log cabin; spectacular mountain setting; working cattle ranch; surrounded by national park and forest.

Profile of Summer Employees Total number: 75; typical ages: 18–30. 50% men; 50% women; 5% minorities; 10% high school students; 70% college students; 10% retirees; 2% non-U.S. citizens; 10% local applicants. Nonsmokers preferred.

Employment Information Openings are from June 3 to August 25. Jobs available: ▶ 16–20 *boys cabin counselors* (minimum age 21) with first aid and CPR certification, outdoor skills, and experience working with children (position is first 5 weeks of summer) at $500–$800 per season ▶ 2 *crafts and nature discovery instructors* (minimum age 21) with CPR/first aid certification, knowledge of appropriate skills, and desire to work with children at $1300–$1400 per season ▶ 3 *dishwashers* (minimum age 18) at $1000–$1200 per season ▶ 16–20 *girls cabin counselors* (minimum age 21) with first aid and CPR certification, outdoor skills, and experience working with children (position is second 5 weeks of summer) at $500–$800 per season ▶ 1–3 *horse wranglers* (minimum age 21) with first aid, CPR, and experience instructing riding and safety; should be confident rider with knowledge of horses at $1200–$1800 per season ▶ 5 *kitchen staff members* (minimum age 18) with cooking and food service experience at $1100–$1500 per season ▶ 1 *lapidary instructor* (minimum age 21) with first aid/CPR certification and lapidary experience at $1300–$1400 per season ▶ 2 *laundry workers* (minimum age 18) at $1300–$1500 per season ▶ *maintenance staff members* (minimum age 18) at $1200–$1800 per season ▶ 4–6 *trip leaders (backpack)* (minimum age 21) with training and background in leadership, environmentally respective camping skills, and wilderness first aid certification at $1000–$1500 per season ▶ 2–3 *trip leaders (pack trip with horses)* (minimum age 21) with knowledge of horse situations, care, and camping leadership with children. Excellent riding and precautionary skills. Wilderness first aid certification at $1000–$1500 per season. Applicants must submit a formal organization application, cover letter, resume, three personal references, three letters of recommendation, drivers record/criminal background check. International applicants accepted; must obtain own visa, obtain own working papers. An in-person interview is recommended, but a telephone interview is acceptable.

Benefits and Preemployment Training Free housing, free meals, on-the-job training, and travel reimbursement. Preemployment training is required and includes accident prevention and safety, interpersonal skills, leadership skills.

Contact Olly Cox, Assistant Director, Teton Valley Ranch Camp, PO Box 3968, Jackson, Wyoming 83001. Telephone: 307-733-2958. Fax: 307-733-2978. Application deadline: continuous.

THE VIRGINIAN LODGE
750 WEST BROADWAY, PO BOX 1052
JACKSON, WYOMING 83001

General Information Resort hotel with 170 rooms. Established in 1965. 15-acre facility located 89 miles from Idaho Falls. Features: mountain town; within 30 minutes of ski areas; south of Yellowstone National Park; public library; Teton Mountains; legendary town square.

Profile of Summer Employees Total number: 40; typical ages: 20–65. 50% men; 50% women;

2% minorities; 1% high school students; 2% college students; 55% retirees; 40% local applicants. Nonsmokers required.

Employment Information Openings are from May 1 to October 1. Year-round positions also offered. Jobs available: ▶ 5 *front desk clerks* (minimum age 18) with computer (Windows 95 applications), switchboard, and reservations experience at $6–$7.50 per hour. Applicants must submit a formal organization application, cover letter, resume. International applicants accepted; must obtain own visa, obtain own working papers. An in-person interview is recommended, but a telephone interview is acceptable.

Benefits and Preemployment Training Possible full-time employment and on-the-job training.

Contact Toby Imus, Assistant Manager, The Virginian Lodge, PO Box 1052, Jackson, Wyoming 83001. Fax: 307-733-4063. E-mail: info@virginianlodge.com. World Wide Web: http://www.jacksonholenet.com/virginian. Application deadline: April 15.

YELLOWSTONE NATIONAL PARK LODGES
PO BOX 165
YELLOWSTONE NATIONAL PARK, WYOMING 82190

General Information Organization offering hospitality services throughout Yellowstone including hotels, restaurants, gift shops, bus/boat/horse tours and campgrounds. Established in 1979. 2,000,000-acre facility located 76 miles from Bozeman, MT. Features: mountains; geysers/thermal features; waterfalls; lakes; employee residences/pubs/recreation halls; wildlife.

Profile of Summer Employees Total number: 3,500; typical ages: 18–80. 45% men; 55% women; 10% minorities; 1% high school students; 40% college students; 20% retirees; 10% non-U.S. citizens; 10% local applicants.

Employment Information Openings are from May 1 to October 22. Jobs available: ▶ 12 *assistant dining room managers* (minimum age 18) with basic supervisory skills and front-of-the-house food and beverage experience at $300 per week ▶ 20 *audit clerks* (minimum age 18) should be familiar with accounting, bookkeeping, basic audit procedures, and cashiering at $5.85 per hour ▶ 200 *cooks* (minimum age 18) with cooking experience including hot/cold, broiler, fryer, fast food, or quantity food at $6.25–$7.50 per hour ▶ 150 *dining room servers* (minimum age 18) with front-of-the-house serving experience at $2.15 per hour plus gratuities (guarantee of minimum wage) ▶ 50 *employee residence coordinators* (minimum age 18) with experience working with people of a variety of ages, organizational skills, and ability to be self-motivated at $6 per hour ▶ 5–10 *food production managers/assistants* (minimum age 18) must supervise BOH operation in a la carte, cafeteria, or employee dining area, have knowledge of food preparation, and supervisory skills at $250–$450 per week ▶ 150 *guest services agents* (minimum age 18) with good interpersonal communication and computer/data entry skills at $5.50–$6.75 per hour ▶ 500 *kitchen help* (minimum age 18) with willingness to learn and work with people at $5.50 per hour with incentives during the busy season-August/September ▶ 50 *laundry personnel* (minimum age 18) with willingness to learn to operate high-volume mechanical laundry, sorting and folding all linen for the park at $6.25 per hour ▶ 7 *painters* (minimum age 19) with a valid driver's license, experience with a brush, roller, airless application, wall preparation and repair at $6.50–$10 per hour ▶ 500 *room attendants* (minimum age 18) with willingness to learn and work with people at $5.50 per hour with incentives during the busy season-August/September. Applicants must submit formal organization application, two letters of recommendation. International applicants accepted; must apply through a recognized agency.

Benefits and Preemployment Training Housing at a cost, meals at a cost, formal training, possible full-time employment, health insurance, on-the-job training, and opportunity to attend seminars/workshops. Preemployment training is required and includes accident prevention and safety.

Contact Human Resources Staff, Yellowstone National Park Lodges. Telephone: 307-344-5324. Fax: 307-344-5441. E-mail: info@ynpjobs.com. World Wide Web: http://www.ynpjobs.com. Application deadline: continuous.

YELLOWSTONE PARK SERVICE STATIONS
YELLOWSTONE NATIONAL PARK
YELLOWSTONE, WYOMING 82190

General Information Automotive service facilities and information service in Yellowstone National Park. Established in 1947. 2,200,000-acre facility located 90 miles from Bozeman, Montana. Features: geysers; lakes; waterfalls; hiking trails; grizzly bears, elk, wolves; mountaineering.

Profile of Summer Employees Total number: 90; typical ages: 18–24. 60% men; 40% women; 5% minorities; 80% college students; 5% retirees; 10% local applicants. Nonsmokers preferred.

Employment Information Openings are from May 12 to October 16. Jobs available: ▶ 3 *accounting clerks* (minimum age 18) with ability to operate 10-key adding machine by touch, plus computer and communication skills at $230 per week ▶ 18 *automobile mechanics* (minimum age 18) with ASE certification or current enrollment in an ASE program at $290–$360 per week ▶ 50 *service station attendants* (minimum age 18) with good interpersonal skills and desire to work outdoors at $230 per week ▶ 1 *warehouse helper* (minimum age 18) with good driving record and communication skills at $230 per week. Applicants must submit formal organization application, cover letter. International applicants accepted; must obtain own visa, obtain own working papers, apply through a recognized agency.

Benefits and Preemployment Training Housing at a cost, meals at a cost, formal training, possible full-time employment, health insurance, names of contacts, on-the-job training, and opportunity to attend seminars/workshops. Preemployment training is required and includes accident prevention and safety, leadership skills.

Contact Hal Broadhead, General Manager, Yellowstone Park Service Stations, PO Box 11–Department WDM, Gardiner, Montana 59030-0011. Telephone: 406-848-7333. Fax: 406-848-7731. E-mail: ypss@ycsi.net. World Wide Web: http://www.coolworks.com/ypss/. Application deadline: June 1.

ALBERTA

CALAWAY PARK
RR #2, SITE 25, BOX 20
CALGARY, ALBERTA T2P 2G5

General Information Amusement/theme park with rides, games, food services, merchandise and entertainment. Established in 1982. 70-acre facility located 6 miles from Calgary. Features: mountain view; roller coaster; campground; country setting; indoor theater; restaurants.

Profile of Summer Employees Total number: 500; typical ages: 14–70. 50% men; 50% women; 25% minorities; 70% high school students; 25% college students; 5% retirees; 100% non-U.S. citizens; 95% local applicants.

Employment Information Openings are from May 1 to October 15. Jobs available: ▶ 50–100 *food service staff and game operators* (minimum age 15) at Can$5.75 to Can$7.00 per hour ▶ 20–25 *merchandise/admissions staff* (minimum age 16) at Can $5.75 to Can $7.00 per hour ▶ 50–100 *ride operators* (minimum age 17) at Can $5.75 to Can $7.00 per hour. Applicants must submit a formal organization application, resume, letter of recommendation. International applicants accepted; must obtain own visa, obtain own working papers. An in-person interview is recommended, but a telephone interview is acceptable.

Benefits and Preemployment Training Formal training, possible full-time employment, on-the-job training, and scholarship program; employee referral program. Preemployment training is required and includes leadership skills, guest service certification, technical training.

Contact Colleen Magee, Human Resource Coordinator, Calaway Park, RR#2, Suite 25, Box 20,

Calgary, Alberta T2P 2G5. Telephone: 403-240-3822 Ext. 145. Fax: 403-242-3885. Application deadline: continuous.

BRITISH COLUMBIA

CAMP ARTABAN
1058 RIDGEWOOD DRIVE
NORTH VANCOUVER, BRITISH COLUMBIA V7R 1H8

General Information Residential camp with Anglican Church affiliation offering traditional program to 100 boys and girls entering grades 3 through 11 in 7-day sessions. Family and specialty weekend adult camps are also offered. Established in 1923. 63-acre facility located 45 miles from Vancouver. Features: waterfront (salt water) on remote island location; swim tank; canoe and row boats; archery range; crafts log hut; outdoor chapel.

Profile of Summer Employees Total number: 18; typical ages: 17–25. 50% men; 50% women; 30% minorities; 20% high school students; 80% college students. Nonsmokers required.

Employment Information Openings are from June 26 to September 4. Jobs available: ▶ 1 *chaplain* (minimum age 25) should be priest or theology student (Anglican/Episcopalian background preferred) able to work with children at Can$2000 per season ▶ 1 *head cook* (minimum age 25) with supervisory experience and quantity cooking experience salary negotiable ▶ 5–6 *kitchen staff members* (minimum age 17) at Can$2000 to Can$6000 per season ▶ 3 *maintenance staff members* (minimum age 17) at Can$2000 to Can$4000 per season ▶ 1 *registrar/ expediter* (minimum age 18) must have a car and insurance; computer skills (Microsoft Word/ Excel) and data entry skills (will train) at Can$2000 to Can$4000 per season ▶ 2 *swimming staff members* (minimum age 18) with WSI and NLS certification at Can$2000 to Can$4000 per season. Applicants must submit a formal organization application, cover letter, resume, personal reference, letter of recommendation. International applicants accepted; must obtain own working papers. An in-person interview is recommended, but a telephone interview is acceptable.

Benefits and Preemployment Training Free housing, free meals, and on-the-job training.

Contact Human Resources/Office Manager, Camp Artaban, 1058 Ridgewood Drive, North Vancouver, British Columbia V7R 1H8. Telephone: 604-980-0391. Fax: 604-980-0395. E-mail: artaban@portal.ca. World Wide Web: http://www2.portal.ca/~artaban/. Application deadline: March 15.

EVANS LAKE FOREST EDUCATION CENTRE
PO BOX 1893
SQUAMISH, BRITISH COLUMBIA V0N 3G0

General Information Residential camp offering environmental education for children 8–11 years old (6-day camp) and 10–14 years old (8-day camp) with a capacity of 80 children. Established in 1997. 604-acre facility located 31 miles from Vancouver. Features: freshwater lake; 604-acre demonstration forest; swimming; boating; 10 kilometers of hiking trails; projects and activities to learn about the forest.

Profile of Summer Employees Total number: 40; typical ages: 17–55. 50% men; 50% women; 10% minorities; 60% high school students; 35% college students; 5% local applicants. Nonsmokers preferred.

Employment Information Openings are from July 1 to August 31. Jobs available: ▶ 16–25 *cabin leaders* (minimum age 16) with counselor training and outdoor experience and experience with children at Can$57.20 per day ▶ *instructor* (minimum age 19) with experience working with children and in outdoor education; occupational First Aid or Wilderness First Aid for Leaders at Can$85 per day ▶ 3–6 *lifeguards* (minimum age 19) with NLS certification and outdoor education experience at Can$85 per day. Applicants must submit a cover letter, resume, three personal references. International applicants accepted; must obtain own visa, obtain own working papers. An in-person interview is required.

Benefits and Preemployment Training Free housing, free meals, and on-the-job training. Preemployment training is required and includes accident prevention and safety, interpersonal skills, leadership skills, child care program.

Contact Matt Thom, Resource Person, Evans Lake Forest Education Centre, 202-304 Columbia Street, New Westminster, British Columbia V3L 1A6. Telephone: 604-520-7600. Fax: 604-520-5450. Application deadline: continuous.

MANITOBA

PEMBINA VALLEY BIBLE CAMP
RR #1
DARLINGFORD, MANITOBA

General Information Christian youth camp serving junior high and senior high youth through resident and wilderness tripping programs. Specializing in horsemanship, theatre, arts, and canoeing. Established in 1994. 245-acre facility located 120 miles from Winnipeg. Features: wooded setting; waterslide; horseback riding; hiking trails; climbing wall.

Profile of Summer Employees Total number: 20; typical ages: 17–22. 30% men; 70% women; 43% high school students; 35% college students; 15% retirees; 85% non-U.S. citizens; 60% local applicants. Nonsmokers required.

Employment Information Openings are from May 1 to August 25. Jobs available: ▶ 1 *head wrangler* (minimum age 21) at Can$2000-Can$3000 per season ▶ 1 *outdoor education instructor* (minimum age 21) at Can$1000-Can$2000 per season ▶ 4 *senior counselors* (minimum age 19) at Can$1000-Can$2000 per season ▶ 1 *summer program director* (minimum age 21) at Can$1000-Can$2000 per season. Applicants must submit a formal organization application, cover letter, resume, three personal references. International applicants accepted; must obtain own visa. A telephone interview is required.

Benefits and Preemployment Training Free housing, free meals, opportunity to attend seminars/workshops, travel reimbursement, and tuition assistance.

Contact Brent Ankrom, Camp Director, Pembina Valley Bible Camp. Telephone: 204-246-2008. Fax: 204-242-2874. E-mail: pvcamp@mb.sympatico.ca. World Wide Web: http://www.mts.net/~npvcamp. Application deadline: June 20.

ONTARIO

CAMP KIAWA GIRL GUIDES
RR#9
DUNNVILLE, ONTARIO N1A 2W8

General Information Residential camp using the Girl Guides of Canada program. 99-acre facility located near Hamilton.

Profile of Summer Employees 100% women; 90% high school students; 10% college students.

Employment Information Openings are from June 27 to August 14. Jobs available: ▶ 2 *craft* *helpers* (minimum age 16) at Can$800 to Can$1300 per season ▶ 1 *program director* at Can$800 to Can$1500 per season ▶ 2 *quartermast assistants* (minimum age 16) at Can$800 to Can$1300 per season ▶ 1 *waterfront director* at Can$1200 to Can$2000 per season ▶ 3 *waterfront staff members* at Can$900 to Can$1500 per season.

Benefits and Preemployment Training Free housing, free meals, and on-the-job training. Preemployment training is required and includes accident prevention and safety, interpersonal skills, leadership skills.

Contact Summer Jobs Director, Camp Kiawa Girl Guides, 918 Main Street East, Hamilton, Ontario L8M 1M5. Telephone: 905-549-2429. Fax: 905-549-3396. E-mail: hamiltongirlguides@sympatico.ca. Application deadline: continuous.

CAMP MANITOU-WABING
MCKELLAR, ONTARIO P0G 1C0

General Information Residential camp for boys and girls ages 8 to 17 offering professional instruction and training in sports, arts, and outdoor adventure. Established in 1959. 200-acre facility located near Parry Sound. Features: freshwater lake and river; wilderness setting; 12 tennis courts; creative arts and dance; golf.

Profile of Summer Employees Total number: 150; typical ages: 19–40. 50% men; 50% women; 50% minorities; 10% high school students; 75% college students; 75% non-U.S. citizens; 50% local applicants.

Employment Information Openings are from June 25 to August 23. Jobs available: ▶ 100–120 *staff members* (minimum age 18) at Can$800 to Can$3000 per season. Applicants must submit a cover letter, resume, two to three personal references. International applicants accepted; must obtain own visa. An in-person interview is recommended, but a telephone interview is acceptable.

Benefits and Preemployment Training Free housing, free meals, formal training, and on-the-job training. Preemployment training is required and includes accident prevention and safety, first aid, CPR, interpersonal skills, leadership skills.

Contact Jeff Wilson, Camp Director, Camp Manitou-wabing, 2660 Yonge Street, 2nd Floor, Toronto, Ontario. Telephone: 416-322-5888. Fax: 416-322-3635. E-mail: camp@manitoucamp.com. World Wide Web: http://www.manitoucamp.com. Application deadline: June 15.

CAMP TRILLIUM
200 MAIN STREET WEST
HAMILTON, ONTARIO L8P 4Y4

General Information Program offering support and recreational activities to children with cancer and their families. Established in 1984. 120-acre facility located 62 miles from Kingston. Features: private lake; island site; brand new facility; tripping program.

Profile of Summer Employees Total number: 60; typical ages: 18–28. 30% men; 70% women; 10% minorities; 10% high school students; 90% college students; 2% local applicants. Nonsmokers required.

Employment Information Openings are from June 1 to August 30. Jobs available: ▶ 1 *adventure program staff member (volunteer)* (minimum age 18) ▶ 3 *arts and crafts/creative writing staff members (volunteer)* (minimum age 18) ▶ 2 *canoe/kayak specialists (volunteer)* (minimum age 18) ▶ 1 *drama instructor (volunteer)* (minimum age 18) ▶ 3 *outtrippers (volunteer)* (minimum age 18) ▶ 3 *sailing instructors (volunteer)* (minimum age 18) with CYA certification ▶ 4 *waterfront/swimming instructors (volunteer)* (minimum age 18) with NLS and Red Cross certifications. Applicants must submit a formal organization application, cover letter, resume, personal reference, two letters of recommendation. International applicants accepted; must obtain own visa. An in-person interview is recommended, but a telephone interview is acceptable.

Benefits and Preemployment Training Free housing, free meals, and on-the-job training. Preemployment training is required and includes accident prevention and safety, first aid, CPR, interpersonal skills, leadership skills, team building.

Contact Marci Shea-Perry, Director of Programs, Camp Trillium, 200 Main Street West, Hamilton,

Ontario L8P 4Y4. Telephone: 905-527-1992. Fax: 905-527-5314. E-mail: marcisp@icom.ca. Application deadline: January 31.

GANADAOWEH
RR#3
AYR, ONTARIO N0B 1E0

General Information Residential, day, and wilderness camping programs offering Christian education to 100 campers weekly. Established in 1982. 174-acre facility located 15 miles from Kitchener. Features: freshwater lake; wooded setting; 1 tennis court; wildlife; high ropes course; pool.

Profile of Summer Employees Total number: 40; typical ages: 17–21. 40% men; 60% women; 10% minorities; 60% high school students; 35% college students; 2% retirees; 5% non-U.S. citizens; 95% local applicants. Nonsmokers required.

Employment Information Openings are from May 1 to August 31. Spring break positions also offered. Jobs available: ▶ 1 *administrative assistant* (minimum age 19) with computer and organizational skills at Can$150 to Can$185 per week ▶ 1 *camp nurse* (minimum age 19) should be student nurse at college or university, RN preferred at Can$175 per week ▶ 4 *cooks* (minimum age 17) with cooking experience (knowledge of nutrition preferred) at $Can150 to Can$175 per week ▶ 15 *counselors* (minimum age 17) with counselor training program completed at Can$150 to Can$175 per week ▶ 1 *head cook* (minimum age 19) with cooking experience and knowledge of nutrition at Can$175 to Can$200 per week ▶ 1 *high ropes/maintenance* (minimum age 18) with assistant high ropes instructor certification (minimum) at Can$150 to Can$175 per week ▶ 2 *lifeguards* (minimum age 17) with NLS or Bronze Cross; leaders and instructors preferred at Can$150 to Can$175 per week ▶ 1 *maintenance staff member* (minimum age 17) with cleaning/groundskeeping experience preferred at Can$150 to Can$175 per week ▶ 2 *program assistants* (minimum age 19) at Can$175 to Can$180 per week ▶ 1 *wilderness assistant director* (minimum age 19) with Bronze Cross, NLS, outtripping and leadership experience at Can$175 per week ▶ 1 *wilderness camp director* (minimum age 19) with NLS or Bronze Cross and leadership and outtripping experience at Can$175 to Can$180 per week. Applicants must submit a formal organization application, three personal references. An in-person interview is recommended, but a telephone interview is acceptable.

Benefits and Preemployment Training Free housing, free meals, formal training, names of contacts, on-the-job training, opportunity to attend seminars/workshops, and limited travel reimbursement. Preemployment training is required and includes accident prevention and safety, first aid, interpersonal skills, leadership skills, Christian program/education development, special needs, child abuse disclosures.

Contact Heather L. Glenister/Kirk Omand, Director/Program Director, Ganadaoweh, RR 3, Ayr, Ontario N0B 1E0. Telephone: 519-632-7559. Fax: 519-632-9607. E-mail: ganadaoweh@on.aibn. com. Application deadline: February 28.

THE HORSE PEOPLE
RR1
WENDOVER, ONTARIO K0A 3K0

General Information Residential equestrian training center serving 60 coed students biweekly. Program emphasizes keen competition and long-term goals. Established in 1976. 200-acre facility located 35 miles from Ottawa. Features: championship site with horse shows; bordered by nature reserve; 3-level cross-country course and steeplechase; 2 dressage rings; permanent hunt course; indoor riding arena.

Profile of Summer Employees Total number: 20; typical ages: 20–24. 25% men; 75% women; 1% minorities; 1% high school students; 95% college students; 1% retirees; 1% non-U.S. citizens; 1% local applicants. Nonsmokers required.

Employment Information Openings are from June 12 to August 20. Jobs available: ▶ 1 *arts and crafts instructor* (minimum age 18) with fine arts major and ability to teach drama and arts and crafts at Can$100 to Can$300 per week ▶ *child counselors* (minimum age 18) with St.

John's Ambulance or Red Cross first aid training or equivalent at Can$100 to Can$200 per week ▶ 6 *riding instructors* (minimum age 19) with NCCP Level I, II, BHSI, BHSAI, and St. John's Ambulance first aid training or equivalent at Can$150 to Can$300 per week ▶ *swimming staff members* (minimum age 18) with Red Cross swimming certification and St. John's Ambulance first aid training or equivalent at Can$150 to Can$200 per week. Applicants must submit a formal organization application, cover letter, resume, two personal references, two letters of recommendation, pertinent certifications. International applicants accepted; must obtain own visa, obtain own working papers. An in-person interview is recommended, but a telephone interview is acceptable.

Benefits and Preemployment Training Free housing, free meals, formal training, on-the-job training, opportunity to attend seminars/workshops, and laundry service; riding lessons. Preemployment training is required and includes accident prevention and safety, leadership skills.

Contact Bev Schinke, The Horse People, RR 1, Wendover, Ontario K0A 3K0. Telephone: 613-673-5905. Fax: 613-673-4787. E-mail: horsefun@fox.nstn.ca. Application deadline: May 15.

HURON CHURCH CAMP
PO BOX 509
BAYFIELD, ONTARIO N0M 1G0

General Information Religious coeducational residential camp serving boys and girls ages 6-14. Owned and operated by the diocese of Huron, Anglican Church of Canada. Established in 1939. 40-acre facility located 60 miles from London, Ontario. Features: frontage on Lake Huron; 2 large sports fields; 3 large program buildings; extensive initiatives course.

Profile of Summer Employees Total number: 40; typical ages: 17–23. 51% men; 49% women; 1% minorities; 51% high school students; 49% college students; 5% retirees; 1% non-U.S. citizens; 1% local applicants.

Employment Information Openings are from June 27 to August 29. Jobs available: ▶ *counselors* (minimum age 17) with first aid, CPR certification, and completion of LIT/CIT program preferred ▶ *kitchen staff* (minimum age 17) with first aid, CPR certification, and completion of LIT/CIT program preferred ▶ *maintenance staff* (minimum age 17) with first aid, CPR certification, and completion of LIT/CIT program preferred ▶ *program supervisors* (minimum age 19) with first aid, CPR certification, and completion of LIT/CIT program preferred; should be university student or graduate. Applicants must submit formal organization application, cover letter, resume, three personal references. International applicants accepted; must obtain own visa, obtain own working papers, apply through a recognized agency. An in-person interview is recommended, but a telephone interview is acceptable.

Benefits and Preemployment Training Free housing, free meals, and on-the-job training. Preemployment training is required.

Contact Ms. Gerry Adam, Director, Huron Church Camp, 397 Springbank Drive, London, Ontario N6J 1G7. Telephone: 519-474-0391. Fax: 519-474-1757. E-mail: gadam@odyssey.on.ca.

KITCHIKEWANA
PO BOX 71
HONEY HARBOUR, ONTARIO P0E 1E0

General Information YMCA Outdoor Education Center serving more than 750 school-age students during spring and fall sessions as well as summer program. Established in 1919. 15-acre facility located 50 miles from Barrie. Features: located on Georgian Bay; sandy beaches; rustic cabins; 30 foot climbing wall; outdoor chapel; low ropes/initiative course.

Profile of Summer Employees Total number: 64; typical ages: 17–22. 40% men; 60% women; 3% minorities; 55% high school students; 35% college students; 7% local applicants. Nonsmokers required.

Employment Information Openings are from March to September. Jobs available: ▶ 3–6 *counselors (male)* (minimum age 16) with NLS (National Lifesaving Award), standard first aid (minimum of Red Cross leaders), level C CPR, and instructor certification at Can$115-Can$130 per week ▶ 1–2 *prep cooks* with Level C CPR and standard first aid certification at Can$200 per week ▶ 1–2 *site staff* (minimum age 17) standard first aid and CPR certifications at $200–$220 per week. Applicants must submit a cover letter, resume, three personal references. An in-person interview is recommended, but a telephone interview is acceptable.

Benefits and Preemployment Training Free housing, free meals, on-the-job training, and opportunity to attend seminars/workshops. Preemployment training is required and includes accident prevention and safety, CPR, leadership skills.

Contact Greg MacQuarrie, Camp Director, Kitchikewana, Little Lake Park, PO Box 488, Midland, Ontario L4R 4L3. Telephone: 705-526-7828. Fax: 705-526-8735. E-mail: kitchi@csolve.net. World Wide Web: http://www.kitchi.com.

NEW FRENDA YOUTH CAMP
SEVENTH-DAY ADVENTIST CHURCH, RR #2
PORT CARLING, ONTARIO P0B 1J0

General Information Residential camp serving more than 100 children ages 8–16. 60-acre facility located 100 miles from Toronto.

Profile of Summer Employees 50% men; 50% women; 20% minorities; 80% college students; 1% retirees.

Employment Information Openings are from June 21 to August 15. Jobs available: ▶ 1 *archery staff member* ▶ 1 *canoeing staff member* ▶ 1 *glass etching staff member* ▶ 4 *horsemanship staff members* ▶ *kitchen staff members* ▶ *maintenance staff members* ▶ *outdoor living skills staff members* ▶ 1 *photography staff member* ▶ 1 *radio broadcasting staff member* ▶ 1 *rappelling staff member* ▶ 1 *sailing staff member* ▶ 1 *silkscreening staff member* ▶ 5 *swimming staff members* ▶ 1 *tumbling staff member* ▶ 4 *waterskiing staff members* ▶ 1 *windsurfing staff member*.

Benefits and Preemployment Training Free housing, free meals, on-the-job training, and tuition assistance.

Contact Milton Perkins, Director, New Frenda Youth Camp, 1110 King Street East, Oshawa, Ontario L1H 1H8. Telephone: 905-571-1022. Fax: 905-571-5995. World Wide Web: http://www. frenda.com. Application deadline: April 30.

NEW STRIDES DAY CAMP
ETOBICOKE CITY HALL, 399 THE WEST MALL
ETOBICOKE, ONTARIO M9C 2Y2

General Information The Adapted-Integrated service section provides resources and transition support to individuals with disabilities; also day camp serving 105 individuals with varying special needs. Established in 1977. 525-acre facility located 12 miles from Toronto. Features: sport fields; mini-golf; tennis courts; indoor swimming pool.

Profile of Summer Employees Total number: 12; typical ages: 18–26. 20% men; 80% women; 30% high school students; 70% college students; 90% local applicants. Nonsmokers preferred.

Employment Information Openings are from July to August. Jobs available: ▶ *LIT and adult life skills programmer* (minimum age 20) with standard first aid/CPR certification (aquatic and CPI preferred) and driver's license; should have program planning and recreation experience with a wide range of age and ability within the special population community at Can$8 per hour ▶ 1 *New Strides director* (minimum age 21) with experience working in camps/recreation and with special needs population; standard first aid/CPR certification; CPI and aquatics helpful at Can$9 per hour ▶ 1 *community integration coordinator* (minimum age 21) with experience in camps/recreation/playgrounds and one-to-one experience with special needs children; standard first aid and CPR; CPI and aquatics helpful at Can$9 to 10 per hour ▶ 4–10 *leader positions* (minimum age 18) with standard first aid and CPR certification; background working with special needs individuals; aquatic skills helpful at Can$7 per hour. Applicants must submit a formal organization application, cover letter, resume, two personal references, possible police checks in the future. An in-person interview is required.

Benefits and Preemployment Training Formal training, names of contacts, on-the-job training, and opportunity to attend seminars/workshops. Preemployment training is required and includes accident prevention and safety, first aid, CPR, interpersonal skills, leadership skills.

Contact Mrs. Lorene A.M. Bodiam, Supervisor, Adapted/Integrated Services, New Strides Day Camp, 399 The West Mall, Etobicoke, Ontario M9C 2Y2. Telephone: 416-394-8533. Fax: 416-394-8935. Application deadline: March 15.

QUEBEC

CAMP NOMININGUE
1889 CHEMIN DES MESANGES
LAC NOMININGUE, QUEBEC J0W 1R0

General Information Residential camp for 220 boys ages 7–15 providing a place to cultivate friendships, self-confidence, and a sense of achievement. Established in 1925. 400-acre facility located 120 miles from Montreal. Features: half mile of sandy beach; freshwater lake; 400 acres of woods and fields; 4 tennis courts.

Profile of Summer Employees Total number: 80; typical ages: 18–25. 99% men; 1% women; 15% minorities; 10% high school students; 70% college students; 1% retirees; 80% local applicants. Nonsmokers preferred.

Employment Information Openings are from June 22 to August 22. Year-round positions also offered. Jobs available: ▶ *TOESL instructors* (minimum age 18) must be current student or graduate in university ESL program at Can$125 to Can$200 per week ▶ *archery instructors* (minimum age 18) with CPR, first aid, and instructors cerifications at Can$125 to Can$200 per week ▶ *athletics instructors* (minimum age 18) with CPR and first aid certifications at Can$125 to Can$200 per week ▶ *campcraft instructors* (minimum age 18) with CPR and first aid certifications at Can$125 to Can$200 per week ▶ *canoeing instructors* (minimum age 18) with CPR and first aid certifications at Can$125 to Can$200 per week ▶ 1–30 *general counselors* (minimum age 18) with CPR and first aid certifications at Can$125 to Can$200 per week ▶ *golf instructors* (minimum age 18) with CPR and first aid certifications at Can$125 to Can$200 per week ▶ 1–3 *kayaking instructors* (minimum age 18) with CPR and first aid certifications at Can$125 to Can$200 per week ▶ 1 *nature awareness instructor* (minimum age 18) with CPR and first aid certifications at Can$200 per week ▶ *orienteering instructors* (minimum age 18) with CPR and first aid certifications at Can$125 to Can$200 per week ▶ *riflery instructors* (minimum age 18) with CPR and first aid certifications at Can$125 to Can$200 per week ▶ 1–3 *sailing instructors* (minimum age 18) with CPR and first aid certifications and can operate motor boat at Can$200 per week ▶ *tennis instructors* (minimum age 18) with CPR and first aid certifications at Can$125 to Can$200 per week ▶ *theater instructors* (minimum age 18) with CPR and first aid certifications at Can$125 to Can$200 per week ▶ 1–3 *windsurfing instructors* (minimum age 18) with CPR and first aid certifications and can operate motor boat at Can$200 per week ▶ 1 *woodworking instructor* (minimum age 18) with CPR and first aid certification and can operate woodworking machinery at Can$200 per week. Applicants must submit a formal organization application, cover letter, resume, three personal references. International applicants accepted; must obtain own visa. An in-person interview is recommended, but a telephone interview is acceptable.

Benefits and Preemployment Training Housing at a cost, meals at a cost, formal training, possible full-time employment, and on-the-job training. Preemployment training is required and includes accident prevention and safety, first aid, interpersonal skills, leadership skills.

Contact Shannon Van Wagner, Executive Director, Camp Nominingue, 897 Chaline Crescent, St. Lazare, Quebec J7T 2A9. Telephone: 450-455-4447. Fax: 450-455-7062. E-mail: camp@axess.

com. World Wide Web: http://www.nominingue.com. Application deadline: continuous.

ACE COMPUTER CAMP–CANADA
See ACE Computer Camp–Washington on page 307 for complete description.

STIVERS TEMPORARY PERSONNEL–CANADA
See Stivers Temporary Personnel–Illinois on page 103 for complete description.

LONGACRE EXPEDITIONS
Recreation Workers

General Information Adventure travel program in Belize for teenagers, emphasizing group living skills and physical challenges. Established in 1981. near Belize City, Belize.

Profile of Summer Employees Total number: 4; typical ages: 21–30. 50% men; 50% women; 1% minorities; 100% college students. Nonsmokers required.

Employment Information Openings are from June 15 to August 15. Jobs available: ▶ 2 *assistant leaders* (minimum age 21) with scuba certification, first aid or WFR, CPR, and lifeguard training at $252–$300 per week. Applicants must submit a formal organization application, three personal references. International applicants accepted; must obtain own visa, obtain own working papers. An in-person interview is recommended, but a telephone interview is acceptable.

Benefits and Preemployment Training Free housing, free meals, on-the-job training, and pro-deal purchase program. Preemployment training is required and includes accident prevention and safety, interpersonal skills, leadership skills.

Contact Meredith Schuler, Director, Longacre Expeditions, RD 3, Box 106, Newport, Pennsylvania 17074. Telephone: 717-567-6790. Fax: 717-567-3955. E-mail: longacre@ longacreexpeditions.com. World Wide Web: http://www.longacreexpeditions.com. Application deadline: continuous.

IT WORX
1 AL-SAADA STREET, ROXI SQUARE, HELIOPLOLIS
CAIRO, EGYPT

General Information IT Worx is a joint venture software development company focusing on the use of leading edge software development tools to create office productivity, client-server, enterprise, Internet, and intranet solutions. Established in 1994. Features: overlooking the Maryland garden; central location.

Profile of Summer Employees Total number: 12; typical ages: 20–23. 50% men; 50% women; 100% college students; 100% local applicants.

Employment Information Openings are from May 20 to September 1. Jobs available: ▶ 8 *software developer trainees* (minimum age 20) must be at least a junior or senior in college; non-Egyptians must have a strong interest in re-locating to Egypt after graduation; must have

computer background at $143 per month ▶ *web designer trainee* (minimum age 20) must be at least a junior or senior in college; non-Egyptians must have a strong interest in re-locating to Egypt after graduation; must have computer background at $143 per month. Applicants must submit resume. An in-person interview is recommended, but a telephone interview is acceptable. **Benefits and Preemployment Training** Formal training, possible full-time employment, and on-the-job training.
Contact Rasha Rashad, Human Resource/Administrative Manager, IT Worx. Fax: 20-2-453-0787. E-mail: rasha.rashad@itworx.com. World Wide Web: http://www.itworx.com.

FRANCE

BOMBARD BALLOON ADVENTURES
CHATEAU DE LABORDE
LABORDE AU CHATEAU, BEAUNE, FRANCE

General Information Bombard Balloon Adventures is a tour operator providing complete luxury travel programs blending daily hot-air ballooning with fine restaurants and hotels and personal visits to an international clientele. Established in 1977.
Profile of Summer Employees Total number: 10–20; typical ages: 18–25. 80% men; 20% women; 80% college students; 99% non-U.S. citizens. Nonsmokers preferred.
Employment Information Openings are from May 1 to November 1. Winter break positions also offered. Jobs available: ▶ 10–20 *hot-air balloon ground crew* (minimum age 18) with driver's license for at least one year; clean driving record; and minimum weight of 150 pounds. Applicants must submit a formal organization application, cover letter, resume, photocopy of driver's license, ID photo, height, weight, and dates of availability. International applicants accepted; must obtain own visa, obtain own working papers. A telephone interview is required.
Benefits and Preemployment Training Free housing and free meals.
Contact Michael Lincicome, Bombard Balloon Adventures. Fax: 33-380-26-69-20. World Wide Web: http://ourworld.compuserve.com/homepages/lincicome. Application deadline: continuous.

UNITED KINGDOM

ACE COMPUTER CAMP–UNITED KINGDOM
See ACE Computer Camp–Washington on page 307 for complete description.

GREENFORCE
11-15 BETTERTON STREET, COVENT GARDEN
LONDON, UNITED KINGDOM

General Information Nonprofit conservation organization that places individuals on environmental projects throughout the world. Also opportunities for long-term staff positions once volunteer phase is over. Established in 1996. Features: Africa; Amazon; Borneo; Fiji; United Kingdom.
Profile of Summer Employees Total number: 50; typical ages: 20–28. 50% men; 50% women; 25% high school students; 75% college students; 90% non-U.S. citizens.
Employment Information Openings are from January 1 to December 31. Jobs available: ▶ 180–200 *research assistants* (minimum age 18). Applicants must submit a formal organization applica-

tion, there is a fee of 2200 British pounds once hired to take part in the program. International applicants accepted. A telephone interview is required.

Benefits and Preemployment Training Free housing, free meals, formal training, possible full-time employment, health insurance, on-the-job training, opportunity to attend seminars/ workshops, and tuition assistance. Preemployment training is optional and includes accident prevention and safety, first aid, CPR, interpersonal skills, leadership skills, kit, map, or dive training subject to location.

Contact M. Watts, Director, Greenforce, Greenforce 11-15 Betterton Street, London WC2H 9BP. Telephone: 171-470-8888. Fax: 171-470-8889. E-mail: greenforce@btinternet.com. World Wide Web: http://www.greenforce.com. Application deadline: continuous.

SUMMER DISCOVERY AT CAMBRIDGE
NEW HALL COLLEGE, CAMBRIDGE UNIVERSITY
CAMBRIDGE, UNITED KINGDOM

General Information Precollege enrichment program for high school students at Cambridge Univeristy in England. Established in 1987. Located 100 miles from London. Features: sport facilities; beaches; mountains; lakes; major cities nearby; college towns.

Profile of Summer Employees Total number: 20; typical ages: 23–35. 10% minorities; 30% college students. Nonsmokers required.

Employment Information Openings are from June 20 to August 25. Jobs available: ▶ 20 *resident counselors* (minimum age 23) with experience working with high school students/children at $150–$400 per week. Applicants must submit a formal organization application, resume, personal reference. International applicants accepted; must obtain own visa, obtain own working papers. An in-person interview is required.

Benefits and Preemployment Training Housing at a cost, free housing, free meals, possible full-time employment, health insurance, on-the-job training, and travel reimbursement. Preemployment training is required and includes accident prevention and safety, CPR, interpersonal skills, leadership skills.

Contact Jason Walley, Admissions Director, Summer Discovery at Cambridge, 1326 Old Northern Boulevard, Roslyn, New York 11576. Telephone: 516-621-3939. Fax: 516-625-3438. E-mail: staff@summerfun.com. World Wide Web: http://www.summerfun.com. Application deadline: continuous.

Religious Organizations

Retail Trade

JOB TYPES INDEX

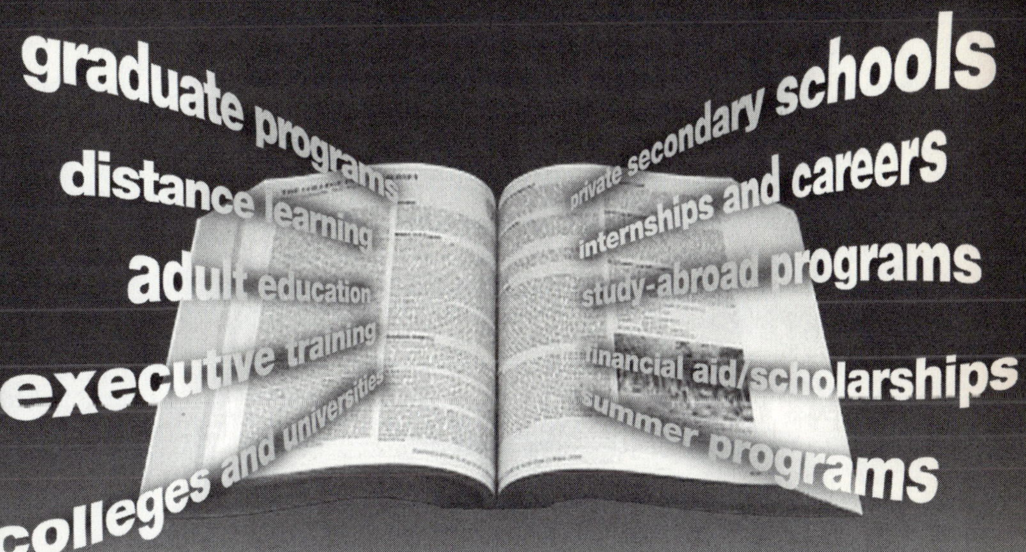

Peterson's
unplugged

graduate programs
distance learning
adult education
executive training
colleges and universities

private secondary schools
internships and careers
study-abroad programs
financial aid/scholarships
summer programs

Peterson's quality on every page!

For more than three decades, we've offered a complete selection of books to guide you in all of your educational endeavors. You can find our vast collection of titles at your local bookstore or online at petersons.com.

High school student headed for college?

Busy professional interested in distance learning?

Parent searching for the perfect private school or summer camp?

Human resource manager looking for executive education programs?

AOL Keyword: Petersons
Phone: 800-338-3282

PETERSON'S
THOMSON LEARNING

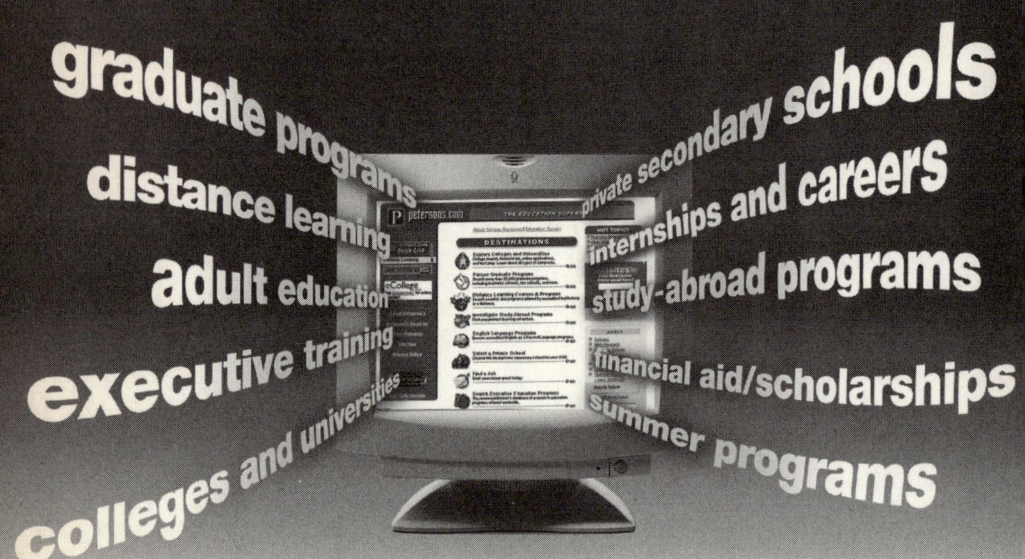

Virtually anything is possible @ petersons.com

Peterson's quality with every click!

Whether you're a high school student headed for college or a busy professional interested in distance learning, you'll find all of the tools you need, literally at your fingertips!

Petersons.com is your ultimate online adviser, connecting you with "virtually any" educational or career need.

Count on us to show you how to

Apply to more than 1,200 colleges online

Finance the education of your dreams

Find a summer camp for your child

Make important career choices

Earn a degree online

Search executive education programs

Visit us today at **petersons.com**
AOL Keyword: Petersons

PETERSON'S ™

THOMSON LEARNING